BELLY UP

THE COLLAPSE OF THE PENN SQUARE BANK

PHILLIP L. ZWEIG

UP

BELLY

THE COLLAPSE OF THE PENN SQUARE BANK

CROWN PUBLISHERS, INC.
· NEW YORK ·

Published by Crown Publishers, Inc.,
One Park Avenue, New York, New York 10016 and simultaneously in Canada by
General Publishing Company Limited
CROWN is a trademark of Crown Publishers, Inc.
Manufactured in the United States of America
Library of Congress Cataloging in Publication Data
Zweig, Phillip L.
Belly up.
Includes index.
1. Penn Square Bank.   2. Bank failures—United States.
I. Title.
HG2613.0354P419   1985   332.1'2'0976638   85-1530
ISBN 0-517-55708-8

10 9 8 7 6 5 4 3 2

FOR MY BROTHER,
STEPHEN (1951–1980),
MY PARENTS,
ARTHUR AND MYRILLYN,
AND MY WIFE, JOSIE

CONTENTS

ACKNOWLEDGMENTS

THIS BOOK IS THE PRODUCT OF THREE YEARS OF RESEARCH, IN-cluding hundreds of interviews conducted by telephone and in person throughout the country. Many of these sources requested anonymity because of the sensitivity of the subject, but nevertheless gave unselfishly of their time so that the full story could be told. To all of them I am deeply grateful.

Others deserve special mention. Foremost among them is my wife, Josie, who gave up a year of her own career at the United Nations to make this book possible. Her well-honed research skills, keen eye for the dangling participle and misplaced metaphor, and comfort during those moments when it seemed the story would never find its way into print were indispensable.

Many thanks go to Sanford Rose, the penetrating columnist for the *American Banker* and student of the American banking industry, whose suggestions were invaluable, and to Manufacturers Hanover Trust's Woody Schafer, one of the top energy lenders in the United States, who brought his many years of experience as a petroleum engineer and banker to his review of the book. Derick Steinmann, the publisher of the *American Banker*, provided considerable assistance. I am grateful too for the generosity and assistance of my journalist colleagues, Judy Fossett of the *Daily Oklahoman*, Gail Donovan, formerly of the *Journal Record*, Michael Parks, editor of the *Marple's Business Newsletter* in Seattle, and *American Banker* librarians, Patricia Bluestein and Louis Leventhal. Dr. Norman Hyne, of the University of Tulsa Division of Continuing Education, taught me most of what I know about petroleum geology. Professor A. O. Holsinger of the Baruch College School of Business also made many suggestions for organizing the material.

Jim Wade, my editor at Crown Publishers, wielded a sharp scalpel in cutting away mounds of underbrush, and both he and his assistant, Jane von Mehren, demonstrated patience beyond the call of duty as I struggled, often unsuccessfully, to meet production deadlines.

ACKNOWLEDGMENTS

And finally, I owe a note of thanks to those who encouraged my early journalistic efforts: Ira Freeman, retired correspondent for the *New York Times,* and his wife, Beatrice; Michael Dobrin, now a public relations consultant of Oakland, California; Bill West of the University of Pennsylvania; and Tom Goff, wherever he may be.

BELLY UP

THE COLLAPSE OF THE PENN SQUARE BANK

PROLOGUE

GOVERNMENT OFFICIALS AREN'T USED TO FLYING ON CHARTERED jets. But on the evening of July 5, 1982, William M. Isaac, the unflappable and strong-willed chairman of the Federal Deposit Insurance Corporation, departed from custom. Before leaving his home in northern Virginia that Monday morning for the office, he told his wife that he probably wouldn't be home for dinner. He didn't know at the time that he'd wind up spending the night at a Hilton hotel in Oklahoma City.

When Comptroller of the Currency C. Todd Conover informed him late that afternoon that he would shortly announce the failure of the Penn Square Bank of Oklahoma City, it was too late for Isaac and his demolition team of bank liquidators to catch the last commercial flight out of Washington National Airport for the Oklahoma capital. Isaac had ordered an aide to charter two private jets and have them on standby. It was to be an excruciating trip for the tanned, square-jawed bank regulator. His lower back problem had flared up again and had tormented him throughout a weekend of nerve-racking, nonstop meetings with Conover and Federal Reserve Board chairman Paul Volcker. In these marathon meetings, the fate of a harmless-looking bank in an Oklahoma City shopping center, and the future of the American financial system, were debated and, to some degree, decided.

Someone said that the slower of the two planes might have to stop and refuel on the way. "I want to get on the one that gets there first," Isaac insisted. So at midnight, a silver and blue Lear 35 carrying the chairman and several of his top aides took off from Washington, followed a few moments later by the second jet with other senior officials aboard.

Intermittently, Isaac tried to catch some sleep on the bench seat in the rear of the plane, but his adrenaline was flowing, and he couldn't lie down, sit, or bend. This was destined to be a working

flight. Isaac and his press aide reviewed some of the questions reporters might ask at the news conference scheduled for the next morning, and the chairman spent the rest of the time scribbling on a
yellow legal pad, honing the opening remarks he would make to the
press.

The passengers and crew would remember the flight for other
reasons. At 12:22 A.M., the earth began to move into a position on a
straight line between the sun and the moon, producing an eclipse of
the moon that was awesome at 35,000 feet. Isaac paused briefly as
the earth's shadow gradually blocked out the moon's reflected light.
The symbolism was appreciated by all of the passengers aboard the
plane. In a few hours Isaac would preside over an earthly event even
rarer than a total lunar eclipse. He would attempt to explain to a
shocked public a bank failure that, in an ironic twist, was to help
trigger, within the next two months, the nation's recovery from the
longest and deepest recession since World War II and, within the
next two years, a chain reaction of bank disasters that would shake
public confidence in the financial system like no other event since
the Great Depression. Indeed, since the 1930s, banks had been
highly regulated institutions that had regained the public's trust
through a nearly unblemished record of prudent management of depositors' money. In the late 1970s and early 1980s, however, intensified competition gave rise to a pattern of reckless lending the likes of
which had not been seen for more than fifty years. Nowhere was that
pattern more evident than at the Penn Square Bank of Oklahoma
City.

The chairman's jet landed at Will Rogers Airport at about 3:00
Tuesday morning, and Isaac and two aides hailed a cab for the 20-
minute ride to the Hilton Northwest Hotel. The hotel was, Isaac
would later learn, owned in part by the head of the bank he would
have to dismantle that morning.

The driver, a burly, unshaven man in his late thirties, immediately launched into a discourse on banks and bankers, obviously inspired by the extensive local media coverage on Penn Square over
the Fourth of July weekend and the Comptroller's announcement
hours earlier.

"Banks can't fail," he said forcefully. "How can banks fail? They
only lend money to people who don't need it. How the hell can
banks fail? Those guys never lose any money. What a racket," he
said, while racing to the hotel at nearly eighty miles an hour. Isaac,
sitting between his two aides, turned to each of them and grinned

broadly. He told the driver, "That sounds like a business you could never go broke in. That's the business I ought to get in, I guess," nodding in agreement with the cabby's analysis. If the driver watched the news on television Tuesday evening, he would have discovered that his fares had come to town because banks can and do fail—and none more spectacularly than the Penn Square Bank of Oklahoma City.

A generation earlier, in 1959, a young Oklahoma geologist boarded a commercial airliner for a flight to New York from the same airport where Isaac's plane would land. The geologist's journey eastward was the beginning of a saga that would reach a climax with Isaac's arrival from Washington on that sultry morning in July 1982. In the intervening years, the worlds of both men—banking and energy—had changed radically. When the geologist left for New York, the cabby's observations about banks and bankers would have been right on the mark. But by 1982 banks were no longer solid gray fortresses, nor were bankers dull, sober fellows in dark pin-striped suits looking for reasons *not* to lend customers money. Banks had become aluminum-and-glass skyscrapers featured in lavish color advertising, and bankers had evolved into hungry, aggressive gunslingers trying to find ways to lend people money whether or not they needed or deserved it.

THE GAS MAN

ROBERT A. HEFNER 3RD TRAVELED TO NEW YORK ONLY WHEN HE had to. It was not that he disliked New York, or minded the flight there from Oklahoma City. It was just that the young geologist's attention was totally concentrated on a huge reserve of high-pressure gas that lay more than three miles beneath the grassy plains of western Oklahoma in an area geologists call the Anadarko Basin. Anadarko is an Indian word that means a "man who eats the honey of the bumble bee." To Hefner that translated into "new energy." That gas, he believed, would someday be worth millions to anyone able to get it out.

Oklahoma City was home to hundreds of wildcatters and small-time gamblers who had gotten rich, gone broke, and gotten rich again exploring for shallow oil. But the world below 15,000 feet gets very expensive. Temperatures soar to 600 degrees and hotter. Drill bits shear off, wells blow out, and holes cave in. Drilling for deep gas would make wildcatting for Oklahoma crude look like a fraternity house poker game. In 1959 the players at the big table were not to be found in Oklahoma City.

Born into a wealthy Oklahoma oil family, Hefner had attended prep school and lived in southern California, where his mother moved the family after her divorce from his father. After declining to attend Yale University, he enrolled at the University of Oklahoma in Norman, where he received a degree in petroleum geology in 1957. It was there he became fascinated with the notion that the earth was not as "hard as a rock," but consisted of massive, constantly shifting continental plates. At the time, this theory, called plate tectonics, was not highly regarded by traditional geologists.

"It all jelled in Professor Chenoweth's stratigraphy course at OU," Hefner said in later years. "I focused on the Anadarko and wrote a paper on semantic problems in geology, and how phrases like 'as hard as a rock' affect thinking."

The geological upheavals that he was studying in his stratigraphy course were no less tumultuous than those in his own life. On New Year's Eve, while a freshman at OU, Hefner married Trudi Ray, his high school sweetheart, a secret he kept from his father and step-mother for nearly three months. By the time he was graduated, Hefner had fathered two children, a third was on the way, and the young couple had filed for a divorce. On at least one occasion while the family was living in a small efficiency apartment in Norman, Trudi attempted suicide. And in the following four years, while for-mulating his theories about the energy potential of the Anadarko Basin, Hefner expended much of his energy fighting for custody of his three children, who were living in California with his emotion-ally distressed former wife. She finally took her own life in late 1962, after the courts ruled in his favor and he remarried. Hefner's second marriage ended in divorce in 1973.

In western Oklahoma's Anadarko Basin, Hefner believed, tectonic movement had thrust layers of sandstone and shale down to depths of nearly eight miles, sandwiching vast quantities of natural gas be-tween geological strata. Hefner also believed that this gas was recov-erable by conventional drilling and well-completion techniques. The skeptics held that even if the gas was there it was not retriev-able—short of exploding an atomic device at those depths. They ar-gued that the high temperatures and pressures would turn sandstone and shale into an impenetrable, bricklike mass.

The perimeter of the basin is a whale-shaped figure running northwest to southeast from the Texas Panhandle to south-central Oklahoma. The basin itself cannot be seen, of course, but modern seismic equipment can transmit sound waves deep beneath the earth. These waves bounce back to the surface to produce a picture of the layers of sandstone, shale, and limestone that *may* contain oil and gas. In southwestern Oklahoma, near the Texas border, the rounded granite ridges of the Wichita Mountain range are the only visible evidence of the fault system that marks the southern edge of the basin. Here, layers of sandstone, shale, and limestone plunge suddenly, reaching down 40,000 feet to the once-molten granite bed-rock. As these rock layers proceed northward beneath the green and brown prairie that was the floor of a shallow sea hundreds of mil-lions of years ago, they rise gently to just a few thousand feet below the wheatfields of northern Oklahoma and southern Kansas.

For the descendants of the pioneers who opened up the Oklahoma Territory for settlement, the Anadarko Basin became a new frontier, one that was, in many ways, more hostile and forbidding than the original. The wildcatters in search of high-pressure gas would find that the earth gave up its riches even more reluctantly than the Indians who once inhabited the Oklahoma plains relinquished their land. Indeed, the search for gas would bring forth individuals whose gambling instincts and opportunistic spirit were bequeathed to them by three generations of Oklahomans who endured Indian raids, dust storms, tornadoes, and oppressive heat. Oklahoma is a state of stark contradictions. Geographically, it is split in the middle, around Oklahoma City, by the Cross Timbers, a band of oaks and elms running north to south that divides the flat prairies to the west from the hillier, more verdant country to the east. Oklahoma is sophisticated Tulsa, with streets named after the prestigious Ivy League colleges of the East. It is also the more boisterous, rough-hewn Oklahoma City, with its broad avenues and unbridled suburban sprawl. Among the most prominent Oklahomans are the descendants of the original Sooners who managed to enter the territory prematurely and stake their claims on the land before it was officially opened for settlement at noon on April 22, 1889. That admiration, even reverence, for the opportunist and the risk-taker and, some would say, the white-collar outlaw, survives to this day, side by side with the rigid moral dictates of Bible Belt fundamentalism.

Hefner's father and grandfather were gamblers, but only to a point. They were veteran oilmen who had grown rich drilling wells no deeper than 6,000 or 7,000 feet, and the gas they found was usually burned off as a waste byproduct. In fact, almost all the gas found through the 1940s and 1950s was "associated" gas, or gas found in drilling for oil, and usually played second, or even third, fiddle to oil. The elder Hefners puzzled over why this member of the third generation of Hefners was not content with relaxing on weekends at the exclusive Oklahoma City Golf and Country Club and helping them drill for sweet, shallow, and easily recoverable Oklahoma crude during the long days of the working week.

Hefner worked briefly for Phillips Petroleum after graduating from OU, then joined the Hefner Company, founded by his grandfather, the venerable Judge Hefner. One of the leading Oklahomans of his day, "The Judge" began his illustrious career as an oil and gas lawyer following the historic, turn-of-the-century oil discoveries at Spindletop in Beaumont, Texas. He later served as a justice of the Oklahoma Supreme Court and mayor of Oklahoma City. In a state that was only fifty years old when Hefner graduated from college, this distinguished lineage qualified the family for membership in Oklahoma's small but well-to-do aristocracy.

"One day, all of a sudden, I realized the ambition was running out of me," Hefner said later. "I knew if I stayed there it would be gone. That afternoon I went in and told my father I couldn't work there anymore. It was kind of a shock but he understood." Hefner figured on doing some consulting work, and his father gave him a microscope for examining rock specimens and loaned him $15,000 to start off, and then another $15,000 later on.

Hefner's mother had been a movie actress in the 1940s and maintained close ties to the film industry. Through her, Hefner was exposed to the real and apparent affluence of Los Angeles and Hollywood. But at twenty-three he recognized that before he could ever run a string of drill pipe into the Deep Anadarko Basin, he would have to make a trip to the center of real wealth. And in 1959, that was not Los Angeles or Tulsa or even Dallas or Houston. The real money was in New York.

Hefner's introduction to Eastern wealth was through his close friend, John Murphy, an instructor in English whom Hefner regarded as something of a genius. Yet more important than Murphy's intellect was the fact that his brother, Donald, was an attorney at the prestigious Wall Street law firm of Milbank, Tweed, Hadley and McCloy.

He had made and rehearsed his pitch many times before. He sensed, however, that this meeting in 1959 with Don Murphy and his client, a wealthy Russian émigré named Vadim Makaroff, and Makaroff's friend Laurence Glover, would be a turning point in his efforts to probe the Anadarko.

Makaroff and Glover arrived at Murphy's office before Hefner. Both were more than twice Hefner's age. Makaroff was remembered by a friend as having the look and demeanor of a "high class Russian naval officer." He was tall and erect and spoke perfect English with only a trace of a Russian accent. Laurence Glover, called Laurie, was tall and mustachioed—a strikingly handsome and elegant man originally from Boston but who spoke with a clipped British accent after having spent much of his life in England.

Hefner himself made an impressive appearance. There was, and still is, a rugged, movie-star quality about him. He had a trim, muscular build, penetrating blue eyes, and an angled nose that seemed to suggest a patrician ancestry. Glover and Makaroff knew each other through the New York Yacht Club and had participated in a number of oil and gas ventures, some of them in Oklahoma. Makaroff, an engineer and inventor of naval instruments, was the son of Admiral S. O. Makaroff, who went down with his ship while commanding Russia's eastern fleet during the war with Japan in 1905, a saga documented in the book *The Fleet That Had to Die.* After the Bolshevik Revolution of 1917, Makaroff unsuccessfully battled the Red forces in Siberia, then fled Russia through China and Hong Kong, and sailed across the Pacific to the United States. Gradually, he made his way eastward, stopping briefly in Wyoming to work as a roughneck in the oil fields, and finally wound up in New York. There he met and married Josephine Hartford, an heiress to the Great Atlantic & Pacific Tea Company fortune.

Glover was a promoter. He was up to date on everything related to the oil and gas business and knowledgeable to the point of being intimidating.

Hefner did not display his nervousness openly. It revealed itself more in what he did not do than in what he did. After talking with Makaroff and Glover for nearly an hour, he realized he was still wearing his heavy camel's-hair overcoat, a holdover of his undergraduate days at the University of Oklahoma.

Glover and Makaroff, it developed, had invested in a well promoted by Hefner's close friend and scientific mentor, Kenneth Ellison, an Oklahoma geologist and wildcatter who was known as the father of the Anadarko Basin. A man of infectious optimism, Ellison was fond of saying, "You never know whether you're a million feet from one dollar or one foot away from a million dollars."

Glover and Makaroff were impressed by Hefner's knowledge of geology, his polished presentation, and his conviction about the potential of the basin that geologists referred to simply as "The Deep." Ironically, at about the same time Hefner was attempting to raise the money to drill for deep gas, he was so financially strapped that he was forced to request a reduction in his child-support payments from $200 to $100 a month.

From 1959 on, the three entrepreneurs would become closely involved in deep gas ventures. They subsequently leased a large tract of land near Elk City, Oklahoma, a small town in the western part of the state, and began drilling the No. 1 Weatherly, their first deep test well in the Anadarko. Usually, oil and gas wells are named for the owners of the property. However, both Makaroff and Glover, as members of the New York Yacht Club, were betting heavily on the success of the United States entrant in the 1962 America's Cup races. They agreed that if the *Weatherly* won the competition and kept the cup in the trophy room at the club, they would name the well after the American 12-meter sloop.

The yacht fared better than the well; *Weatherly* won the cup. The

No. 1 Weatherly was a dry hole. The partners soon discovered that yachts and deep gas wells had a great deal in common. They were both holes, one in the water and the other in the ground, into which their owners poured vast amounts of money. In fact, the Weatherly cost $600,000 to drill to 19,000 feet, a mere fraction of the $5 million to $10 million that would be spent to drill such holes in the Anadarko twenty years later.

Makaroff, in 1963, was also having fits with a more conventional oil and gas investment in Louisiana. The operator had concocted a story that the formation was crumbling into the hole and that the well wasn't likely to be productive. He offered to buy Makaroff out for what he had already invested. On an after-tax basis, the Russian would still manage to turn a small profit.

David O'D. Kennedy, chairman and principal stockholder in the Kentile Corporation, one of the nation's leading floor tile manufacturers, had also invested with the Louisiana oilman and was acquainted with Makaroff through the New York Yacht Club. Makaroff called to suggest that they meet for lunch to figure out how to deal with the Louisiana oilman.

David Kennedy is a Scottish Kennedy who does not like to be confused with a certain Boston-Irish family of the same name. A fourth-generation New Yorker and an alumnus of Princeton, Kennedy took over the family's near-bankrupt flooring business in 1934 after the death of his father, and over the next thirty years turned it into one of the nation's largest and most successful floor tile manufacturers.

Over a champagne lunch at his elegant Fifth Avenue apartment, an excited Makaroff told Kennedy about this bright young Oklahoma geologist named Hefner. Kennedy was intrigued at what he heard. With the housing boom of the 1950s and early 1960s, Kentile had become a cash cow, leaving Kennedy with the problem of how to shelter his substantial income. He had been singularly unsuccessful in most of his earlier oil and gas investments and had become convinced that the successful investors were the ones who actually *owned* the leases. As it turned out, Kennedy had also been buying leases in western Oklahoma and had invested in the No. 1 Weatherly through a tax partnership that later went bankrupt. Kennedy and Makaroff decided to bail out of the Louisiana deal, and Makaroff would introduce Hefner to Kennedy. And so another lunch was arranged at Makaroff's apartment.

Stewart Mark, Hefner's friend and lawyer, was also present at this momentous lunch. He thought the affair was too formal for a midday business meeting. For one thing, he was unsure whether to put the thick white sauce on the salad or the meat. The butler observed Mark's confusion and whispered to him that it went on the meat. Makaroff was not one to celebrate this auspicious gathering of Hefner, Glover, and Kennedy with anything less than one of his elaborate champagne luncheons. Their well had not come in. But a new partner, David O'D. Kennedy, agreed to join the crapshoot for deep gas.

Kennedy is a short, slightly stooped man with a mane of white hair that contrasts vividly with his ruddy complexion. At fifty-six, when he first met Hefner, the kindly industrialist already enjoyed a Gatsbyesque lifestyle. His elegant home, which he modestly describes to a visitor as the "gray barn," overlooks acres of manicured lawn sloping gently down to the shore of Cold Spring Harbor on Long Island's Gold Coast, some thirty miles east of New York City. A major financial backer of the America's Cup races, Kennedy himself was an able racing sailor, having won innumerable trophies in long-distance ocean races at the helm of his own yacht. Kennedy clearly did not need deep gas. But the native New Yorker shared with the young geologist the gambling spirit and frontier grit that seems to be inbred in native or even naturalized Oklahomans.

While Kennedy recalls that Hefner was a "striking-looking fellow with a dynamic personality," it was obvious to him that his new friend from Oklahoma hadn't been around much. From Kennedy's Eastern point of view, Hefner looked "countrified"; he wore, for example, an antique gold watch safely attached to his lapel with a gold chain.

In 1963, Glover, Hefner, Kennedy, and Makaroff formed a partnership and gradually accumulated leases in the area around Elk City. At the time, leases could be purchased for next to nothing: $5 to $15 an acre.

Late that fall, Ellison, the man who had instilled in Hefner the lure and excitement of the basin, collapsed and died of a heart attack while duck hunting on his ranch. He had just gone broke drilling a 17,323-foot, $1 million dry hole. "The basin killed Ken," Hefner said. Standing at the gravesite, Hefner vowed to finish the work his mentor had started.

Makaroff died in January 1964, and Kennedy later bought out the Makaroff interests for under $100,000, something less than Makaroff had put into it. Glover, Hefner, and Kennedy then formed the GHK Companies, taking some license in backdating the establishment of the company to 1959, when Hefner, Glover, and Makaroff had first met in New York.

The partners recognized it would take big banks to finance deep wells. Kennedy was a known quantity whose credit was good at the First National City Bank, Manufacturers Hanover, and the Bank of New York, among others, and he used his considerable financial clout to arrange for Hefner to spread his geological maps before some of the nation's top energy lenders.

A few Oklahoma bankers were willing to lend Hefner money, but they were counting primarily on the creditworthiness of his father, the head of the Hefner Company, whose lead bank was the First National Bank of Oklahoma City, the largest bank in the state at the time. Hefner preferred not to borrow on his father's signature, or to hint that if they did not lend to him, his father would move his business away from First National.

The first banker to lend to Hefner on his own merits was Grady Harris, the young and affable president of the Fidelity Bank of Oklahoma City. When Sen. Robert Kerr and Dean McGee, the founders of Kerr-McGee Oil Corporation, acquired control of Fidelity in 1957, they recruited Harris from another large Oklahoma City bank, where he had been their account officer. Hefner regarded Harris as an innovative banker who understood the oil and gas industry. In the early 1960s, Hefner drilled an oil well but didn't have the money to buy the pipe to produce it.

The meeting with Harris, however, was encouraging. "Give me a week," Harris told him. "I want to check on you as an individual." Hefner returned at the appointed time and got his answer. "I'll do it," Harris said, initiating a relationship with Hefner that would span more than a decade.

Hefner and Kennedy never expected to get their primary financing from Fidelity, or any other Oklahoma bank, regardless of Hefner's relationship with the chief executive officer. Oklahoma, despite its vast petroleum resources, has always been a capital-poor state, and its larger business organizations had to do their banking in Chicago, Dallas, or Houston.

This was due in no small part to Oklahoma's archaic unit banking structure. In contrast with states like California and New York, which permit statewide branching, Oklahoma restricted its banks to a single office until 1983. This limitation gave rise to the establishment of hundreds of small banks and kept all of them from becoming very large.

That, of course, was exactly what the framers of the statutes had in mind. It was a throwback to Oklahoma's Populist tradition and a latent fear of monopoly and bigness. Oklahoma achieved statehood in 1907, in the midst of the trust-busting era, and the fear of size that shaped the antitrust laws was also mirrored in Oklahoma's prohibitions against branch banking. Underlying all of this was the Populist and farmers' distrust of big railroads and big banks.

Moreover, Kennedy and Hefner, though a generation apart, shared a similar business philosophy that made it inevitable that they would have to rely on big banks to finance their exploration program. Like the Hefner family oil and gas interests, Kennedy's Kentile Corporation began and remained a privately held company. Hefner respected those who could build a successful operation without selling stock or public drilling funds. Developing the Anadarko would call for a long-term commitment, and neither he nor Kennedy wanted to be obligated to stockholders who would demand earnings growth, dividends, and capital gains over the short term. Instead, they would use their own money—which for the most part meant Kennedy's and Glover's money—bring in other oil and gas companies as partners, and attempt to find banks willing to lend them money.

That, however, represented a departure from the Hefner family's style of doing business.

"Father and grandfather were of a different era, and wisely so," Hefner said. "My grandfather never borrowed a cent in his life, and my father followed in his footsteps." Like other conservative oil and gas operators, they financed exploration with revenues from existing wells.

Oil and gas bankers, most of whom had been petroleum geologists or engineers at major oil companies, were impressed with Hefner's credentials and conviction. But they disagreed with his geology and his economics. Even if there were large volumes of gas at those depths in the Anadarko, the cost of getting it out would likely exceed revenues because the outdated natural gas regulatory system in existence at that time kept the price of gas at artificially low levels.

Oil and gas are found not in underground pools but in the spaces, or pores, between grains of sandstone and other sedimentary rocks. Porosity, then, is a measure of the oil-bearing capacity of rock, and permeability reflects the ease with which oil and gas travel from pore to pore through a formation. In the 1960s, most geologists believed that the pressures below 15,000 feet would reduce porosity and permeability almost to zero. Said one oilman, "Everyone else thought there would be brick down there."

Hefner's presentations to the bankers were thinly veiled pitches for venture capital. At the time, no prudent bank in the country lent money for pure exploration on unproven acreage.

"We talked about the fact that the basin was one great big gas field," Hefner said, "but in those early days we didn't have a lot of production, so we pitched them on value of leases." Hefner and Kennedy told the bankers that leases were a real commodity and that they ought to be able to lend on them, just as they did on stock, particularly since lease prices kept going up.

"They never bought that," Hefner said, "and I suspect they were right."

They were indeed right. Traditionally, oil and gas lenders have regarded the lease as being of dubious value in securing a loan. In leasing oil and gas property, the purchaser pays the mineral owner a bonus up front, and agrees to a royalty on any production. In the 1960s, when Hefner began approaching banks for credit, lease terms ran anywhere from five to ten years. But if oil and gas are not found, or if the lease expires before drilling begins, the value of the lease evaporates.

Nor were banks anxious to lend on the basis of preliminary studies of the amount of oil and gas that might be contained in a given field. Known as volumetric estimates, these projections typically are made by drilling a test well and gathering data on porosity, permeability, and formation thickness, all of which are plugged into a complex volumetric formula. While volumetric estimates are useful in pointing to how much oil and gas *might* be recovered and how fast, only after a well or group of wells has produced for a period of time can reliable forecasts be made. As one veteran lender put it, "You don't know oil and gas are there until you drill."

In the 1960s and early 1970s, there were only about twenty-five banks in the entire United States that were considered serious energy lenders, and their criteria were rigid. A well would have to show at least a year's production before an oilman could take it to the bank as collateral for a loan. From a well's performance in the first year, a petroleum engineer can calculate a decline curve, a graph that plots the drop in production over the life of a well, and make some projection about future production. Oil and gas wells almost always produce better in their early lives than they do later, but some wells peter out faster than others. How rapidly a well tapers off determines the timing and revenues the operator is likely to receive from it, and consequently his ability to pay off his bank on any outstanding loans backed by the production from the well. Indeed, it is dangerous to lend on the first year of production; a well, for example, could yield 300 barrels a day at first, and quickly level off to 15.

"Forecasting cash flows is more difficult for an oil operator than for a manufacturer, because you can't see or physically get at the product," said Rob Gilbert, president of the First City Bank of Dallas. "There is a mystique about oil and gas lending because the product is in the ground and not in a warehouse."

Moreover, these banks generally tried to spread their risk by insisting that their borrowers diversify their oil and gas properties geographically and geologically. "Loans for just one well were a no-no," recalled one gray haired lender. And if the lender had to look to a borrower's personal financial statement or other assets as security, the loan was not considered an oil and gas loan.

Only the First National City Bank, now Citibank, was willing to lend to GHK in a major way, and that $5 million credit was obtained only with the personal guarantee of Kennedy the tileman, not Kennedy the wildcatter. Using Kennedy's assets as collateral, the partnership borrowed its first $300,000 in December 1963 from the First National to buy more leases, and by 1966 had borrowed nearly $5 million, according to Kennedy. It was then, he said, that "we started to go broke."

Despite the disappointments, Kennedy's relationship with Hefner became very close, almost like that of a father to a son. "There was," said a friend, "much love moving both ways."

"Kennedy is the finest partner I've ever heard of. He put his money in with Hefner and at times it looked bad, but he never complained, and remained a staunch supporter," the friend added.

Hefner recalls that Kennedy liked to say, "You do all the work and I do all the worrying."

"I let Hefner carry the ball. I was in New York, and he was down there. We never had disagreements about anything. I'm a great believer in letting the fellow running the business have a free hand," Kennedy said later. Indeed, there are those who attribute Hefner's closeness to Kennedy and his commitment to the highly risky exploitation of the Anadarko Basin to his strained relationship with his own father.

Hefner was not only financially strapped but also the target of some sharp criticism from oilmen and fellow geologists. Besides Kennedy, one of his leading defenders was Henry "Boots" Taliaferro (pronounced Tolliver), an Oklahoma City lawyer and onetime congressional candidate who met Hefner when they were students at OU, Taliaferro as a law student and Hefner as an undergraduate.

Taliaferro recalls attending many cocktail parties in Oklahoma City, where, inevitably, he would encounter one or more of these critics. " 'Oh, that crazy Robert Hefner,' they'd say. 'Up there in New York taking all those mullets' money for a crazy idea that he's going to find gas at fifteen thousand feet in the Anadarko Basin.' And I'd say to them, 'Now wait a minute. He may be crazy because he's wrong, and I don't think he is, but one thing he's never done is take anybody's money. He never raised a dime from the public for any purpose. He and his partners drilled everything straight up.' "

Of the three partners, Glover was the eternal optimist, but unlike the more volatile Hefner, a voice of calmness and restraint. "Sometimes we'd get close to a deal, and it wouldn't quite jell," Kennedy said, "but he'd keep at it."

One deal that did jell was the No. 1 Green well, GHK's first producer. Because it confirmed that gas *was* there in large quantities, it emerged as a turning point in GHK's search for deep gas and in later legislative efforts to make that search profitable.

The No. 1 Green was made possible, according to David Kennedy, through multimillion-dollar deals negotiated in 1967 with Amerada Hess and Sun Oil. By the end of the year, the partners had drilled down to 8,700 feet, and were once again running short of money. This time a loan from Northern Illinois Gas (now NICOR) a large gas distributor in the Midwest, kept the drill bit turning. Glover was on the phone to Hefner every day, and Kennedy kept up with the progress of the well over lunch with Glover at the New York Yacht Club.

Kennedy recalls that at one point he got a call from Hefner telling him that the well was making gas, then another, frantic one informing him that No. 1 Green had blown up. There was, however, a bright side to the near-disaster. "It proved that gas was there," said Kennedy, "but I didn't think we'd ever straighten that well out." The pressures in the well bore were the highest Hefner had ever contended with, and possibly the highest pressures ever encountered in drilling for oil or gas.

As Hefner recalls the incident: "The five-inch pipe we were using was unable to hold the pressure. We knew we had developed a tubing leak, and I was on the phone to the engineer on site from Oklahoma City." He instructed the engineer to pump enough drilling mud, a fluid used to remove "cuttings" such as rock and dirt from the well bore and to keep the pressures in balance, into the well to "kill it," but not so much as to plug up the formation. That led to an altercation with Sun and Amerada, who were in favor of pumping mud into the surrounding formation. "We got out of operations," Hefner said. "We said we wouldn't do it and told them if you're going to do it and ruin the damn well, then you take over operations." The well was out of control for six weeks, and in just one day the partners spent $65,000 for drilling mud alone.

They later discovered the source of the problem: the lengths of drill pipe were not screwed on tight enough. At the time, said Hefner, there were no specifications on just how tight the joints should be; deep gas technology was still in its infancy.

"We had pipe especially designed," Hefner said. "It was typical of the German engineer that he kept his hand on the pipe as each joint was made up to feel the makeup, not that it makes any difference, or that he could even feel the difference. That process takes about twenty-four hours, and we felt enormously relieved when we got that done successfully."

Some would say Hefner was at least as temperamental as his wildcat well. While he was struggling to tame the No. 1 Green, he was embroiled in a long and embarrassing court battle with an Oklahoma City restaurant owner who accused Hefner and several friends of beating him with dinner plates and inflicting multiple skull and facial fractures. Hefner and another defendant ultimately settled for $10.

Hefner vividly recalls the first day the No. 1 Green actually started producing gas, not so much because it was a landmark event in his efforts to tap the Anadarko, but because for years he had decided he didn't like to smoke and tried to quit, having burned numerous holes in his clothes and geological maps, his most prized material possessions. "I promised myself that if the well produced fifteen million cubic feet a day, I would not smoke another cigarette. In fact, the well produced over nineteen million cubic feet a day, and I never smoked again."

By the time the No. 1 Green was completed in 1969, the tab was $6.5 million, including $2 million for leases, geological, and geophysical work. The cost of the wellhead alone, a Rube Goldberg-like arrangement of pipes and valves that controls gas flow from the well, was $125,000, more than the total cost of an average gas well drilled in the area in the 1960s. The No. 1 Green also earned a place in the annals of oil and gas drilling as the world's second-deepest, and highest-pressure, well at that time.

For all his trouble, Hefner's reward was a 20-year contract, signed in January 1970, to sell the gas in interstate commerce for a mere 21¢ per thousand cubic feet (MCF), with a 1¢ per MCF increase every five years.

The No. 1 Green was an unqualified geological success. But

thanks to an outdated regulatory system that kept the price of 1,000 cubic feet of natural gas below that of an equivalent volume of oil, it was an unmitigated commercial disaster.

This paradox stemmed from the so-called Phillips decision, a 1954 ruling by the United States Supreme Court that brought prices of gas sold by producers to interstate pipelines under the regulation of the Federal Power Commission. The FPC itself had decided earlier that it did not have jurisdiction under the landmark Natural Gas Act of 1938 over prices charged pipelines by gas gatherers and producers.

Technically, the 5–3 Supreme Court ruling addressed the question of whether Phillips Petroleum was a natural gas company as such companies were defined in the act. The FPC contended it was not, and the Court disagreed. In a dissenting opinion that would be quoted for years by opponents of federal regulation of natural gas prices at the wellhead, Justice William O. Douglas wrote that this was a "question the Court has never decided" and "involves considerations of which we know little and with which we are not competent to deal." He contended that the FPC's original decision was "made by men intimately familiar with the background and history" of the Natural Gas Act, and should have been sustained.

Two years later, following revelations that gas industry lobbyists had offered a $2,500 bribe to Sen. Francis Case of South Dakota, President Dwight D. Eisenhower vetoed a bill that for all practical purposes would have reversed the 1954 Supreme Court decision by exempting natural gas producers from federal price regulations. Sen. Case had been in favor of the measure but voted against it after the bribe attempt.

The veto message was unusual in that the President agreed with the bill's objectives, but said he could not sign it without raising concern about what he termed "the integrity of governmental processes." In the message he stated that "legislation conforming to the basic objectives of H.R. 6645 is needed. It is needed because the type of regulation of producers of natural gas which is required under present law will discourage individual initiative and incentive to explore for and develop new sources of supply."

The $2,500 bribe, according to newspaper reports, was to have come from the "personal funds" of the president of the Superior Oil Company of California, which was one of the earlier explorers for deep gas in the Anadarko. The incident prompted a Senate inquiry on the lobbying activities of the natural gas bloc and resulted in fines for the lobbyists and Superior Oil.

"There were twenty-five to thirty years of regulation of the basic energy commodity that kept its price below the marginal cost of finding it," Hefner said. This arrangement disrupted the "whole energy infrastructure of the country."

A shortage was created, most notably in the interstate markets, because producers couldn't afford to drill for gas at the regulated wellhead price, and, indeed, 1967 was the last year in which there was a net addition to gas reserves, according to the American Gas Association. Because of the dual system of regulation, two markets were created: an unregulated market for gas used in the same state in which it was produced, and a tightly regulated interstate market.

As Hefner saw it, there was little pressure to raise gas prices to a level commensurate with that of oil because gas was found primarily by oil companies searching for oil. Some gas is always generated in producing oil, but the reverse is not necessarily true. Since World War I, the gas industry, Hefner said, had been driven by economic analyses based on the price of oil, not gas. "If you happened to hit some gas, that was fine. In 1959, when I was with Phillips, we didn't even use gas in our economic analysis of prospects; it was just a plus factor.

"When you're producing at below the marginal cost of finding, you're subsidizing somebody," Hefner asserted. For example, he said, the United States wound up subsidizing Algeria by using cheap natural gas to convert bauxite to aluminum and exporting that aluminum to Algeria. Under these circumstances, the fortunes of GHK and its partners were at a very low ebb in the early 1970s, despite their success with the No. 1 Green.

Glover, to whom both Kennedy and Hefner had grown very close, died of cancer in late 1969, and the recession that began in early 1970 depressed the market for Kentile's principal product, floor tile. To borrow some $10 million to invest in GHK, Kennedy had pledged all of his personal assets, including his Kentile stock. "It looked as if we'd both be wiped out," Kennedy said later.

"Many times," he recalled, "I regretted getting involved. I was having a tough time and didn't think I'd come out of it, but you get in so far, and you have to keep going. If I hadn't kept putting money in, it would definitely have failed." (One of the few "benefits" Kennedy derived from his association with GHK was the dubious honor of being led to a ramshackle house in Elk City and inducted into the "Old Farts Club," a ritual that required the prospective member to tell a dirty story and toss cow manure chips into a barrel.)

Failure would not have been unusual for the oil and gas business.

Indeed, most people who succeed in finding oil and gas have gone broke at least once. As Lloyd Unsell, executive vice-president of the Independent Petroleum Association of America (IPAA), put it, "To get into the oil business, you almost have to believe in the tooth fairy. If you want a safe niche in life you don't go out drilling wildcat wells. People who get into the business get infected with the 'I can't lose' disease."

In 1973, Hefner himself came close to abandoning the cause. "There was a forty-eight-hour period when I thought perhaps everyone else was right, and I had just taken everybody's money and wasted it," he recalled.

GHK had completed a well called the Gregory, which produced at a half-million cubic feet a day. It was far from being a superwell by Hefner's standards. In an attempt to boost production, they decided to "frac" it, a process that calls for the injection of silica beads and sand into the formation to literally prop it open and allow the gas to flow. At the time, it was the deepest frac job ever, according to Hefner. But the effort backfired, and the gas flow dwindled to almost nothing. Hefner, who was delivering a paper at a gas conference in Nice, France, when the disaster occurred, said later that "we couldn't even project how we would pay the interest on the debt because the price of the gas was too low.

"I just decided everyone else was right and I was wrong. At the time I wanted to give up, and didn't believe we could solve the problem. I went over to Madrid to see a close friend but he wasn't there. I walked into the night, searching myself to determine whether I should go on, trying to decide whether to go home and tell them they were right," he said.

"But then I got another million from a friend, which basically saved GHK and kept us going."

Kennedy remembers that struggle as a constant effort to get a loan here and do a deal there. At one point, however, Hefner negotiated the sale of acreage to the El Paso Gas Company, also one of the early explorers for gas in the Anadarko, which enabled GHK to pay off the $5 million loan to the First National City Bank.

The experience with the No. 1 Green, however, was enough to convince Hefner and his associates that relief required legislation. At the time, there were few in Washington who understood the role played by the federal regulation of natural gas in the nation's economic system. Hefner turned to his old friend, Boots Taliaferro, who by then was practicing natural resources law in Washington, to help him map a strategy for driving home to the Federal Power Commission the economic distinctions between oil and gas and the need to provide incentives for gas exploration.

After losing a congressional race in Oklahoma in the mid-sixties, Taliaferro, with his persuasive manner and a gift for oratory, was appointed by President Lyndon B. Johnson in 1967 to the staff of the Kerner Commission, the panel set up to investigate the root causes of the riots plaguing the nation's cities at the time. Taliaferro later served on the Johnson transition team and then remained in Washington to establish the Washington office of the influential Wall Street law firm of Casey, Lane and Mittendorf.

According to Taliaferro, who, as well as other lawyer friends of Hefner, was representing him without any idea as to how he would get paid, Hefner first addressed the issue in rate hearings before the FPC. "Here we drill this well," Hefner recalls telling the commissioner, "and it's one heck of a well, but it's noncommercial." Taliaferro then persuaded the Senate Commerce Committee, which at the time had jurisdiction over natural gas policy, to schedule Hefner to testify at hearings on gas policy.

"Because of his charismatic appearance," Taliaferro recalled, "it became quite easy to schedule him as a witness. Hefner became the first industry voice to distinguish in pricing policy between old and new gas and pointed up the economic differences between gas found in association with oil and gas that was not.

"His role," Taliaferro added, "as an unconventional spokesman and businessman in an unconventional activity established him as a player to be reckoned with."

A FRIEND AT
THE BANK

GRADY HARRIS, PRESIDENT OF THE FIDELITY BANK OF OKLAHOMA City, and his boss, Chairman Jack Conn, enjoyed a congenial relationship that called for them to meet frequently for lunch at the prestigious Whitehall Club, a watering hole of the city's business elite located on the fifteenth and sixteenth floors of the Fidelity Plaza Building. It was an elegant setting, with crystal chandeliers and a winding staircase connecting the two floors, and a commanding view in all directions of Oklahoma City and the flat expanses beyond it. Managed by a German hotelier, the Whitehall Club had a reputation for serving some of the finest cuisine in the city.

But on this hot day in August 1974 Harris didn't have much of an appetite. Already frail from a year-long battle with cancer, he was to leave the next morning for another round of chemotherapy at the M. D. Anderson Clinic in Houston, and was only able to nibble on a few pieces of fresh fruit.

"Jackson," Harris said to Conn, "this damn stuff has gone to my kidneys, but they can take care of that in Houston. I'll be back in two or three weeks, and you and I can work on the problems we've been talking about."

Harris never made it back.

Bill P. "Beep" Jennings, the usually ebullient executive vice-president of Fidelity, was devastated at Harris's death. He had lost one of his closest friends and a staunch ally through a wrenching period in his career. And Hefner had lost his personal banker, the first one ever to lend him money on his own signature.

Bobby Hefner and Billy Paul Jennings had known each other casually. Harris's death would dramatically change that relationship. Ten years earlier, when Harris brought in his old friend and law school classmate as an executive vice-president, it was assumed that the affable, cigar-smoking Jennings would succeed Harris as president when Harris moved up to the chairmanship. Jennings, a tall man with a round face and thinning white hair, had previously been president of the Penn Square Bank, a small retail institution located in a three-story, whitewashed building wedged between a tobacco store and Shelley's Tall Girls' Shop in the Penn Square shopping mall. Operating out of this undistinguished building, shaped like a child's toy block, Penn Square did business in those early years just like thousands of other similar institutions around the country. It made auto and installment loans, home mortgages, and served the banking needs of the small shops and other businesses in the mall and the surrounding area.

Penn Square Bank was organized in 1960 by Ben Wileman, the shopping center's developer, with help from his friends, Dean A. McGee, chairman of Kerr-McGee Corporation, and Sen. Robert S. Kerr. At that time, Wileman recalled later, it took political pull to obtain a bank charter, and ties to a U.S. senator with friends on the banking committee didn't hurt. Business was fleeing downtown Oklahoma City for the northern suburbs, and the Penn Square mall seemed like an ideal spot for a retail bank.

On a friend's recommendation, Wileman hired Jennings as executive vice-president, and in his four years at Penn Square, Jennings earned what one local banker called "a pretty good reputation."

Harris and Jennings were kindred spirits. Both were popular in the Oklahoma City business community for their willingness to make loans other banks wouldn't. And both came from small-town Oklahoma banking families. Harris was an able and aggressive banker, but he did not always choose the best people or manage them effectively. In 1964 Fidelity sustained heavy losses in its commercial loan portfolio, prompting national bank examiner Frank Brown, a man who was a legend among Southwestern bankers for his toughness, to order the Fidelity board to curtail the bank's risky lending practices, straighten up its shoddy documentation, and bring in a more conservative banker to ride herd over Harris.

A former officer of Fidelity remembered, "Grady was trying to do everything, including civic activities. He just didn't have good people under him."

"Grady was a man's man," said another friend, "but he was almost too nice."

Oilman Dean McGee, the dominant figure on the Fidelity board of directors, tapped Conn for the chairmanship. Formerly the outside counsel for Kerr-McGee, Conn was in the awkward position of having lost his job as chairman of the Oklahoma State Bank in Ada because of a change in ownership at the same time he was nominated as president-elect of the American Bankers Association, the leading industry trade group. The professorial, gravel-voiced Conn had become a banker statesman, but a banker without a bank.

Conn was not a party to any understanding between Jennings and the late Grady Harris. Within hours after receiving word of Harris's death, Conn phoned his friend Quinton Thompson, the respected regional director of the Federal Deposit Insurance Corporation in Dallas. "We lost Grady," Conn told Thompson. "I'd like your help in finding a new president."

Three days later Thompson called back with the name of Wilfred Clarke, the head of the Springer Corporation, a large industrial conglomerate in Albuquerque and the former president of the Bank of New Mexico. Clarke had the big bank experience the board was looking for. He was what bankers call a numbers man, and he did not like surprises. Fidelity had already had enough surprises.

Jennings's name never even surfaced. He had never been suggested or considered. It was bad enough, insiders thought, that Conn didn't look within the bank's executive ranks for Harris's replacement, but he didn't even look in Oklahoma.

According to Conn, Jennings never indicated that he expected to get the top job, nor did he express any disappointment when he didn't get it, but Jennings's friends and former colleagues disagree. "Jennings was disappointed at Fidelity," said one contemporary. "He always assumed when he came down from Penn Square Bank to be an executive vice-president at Fidelity that he'd move up."

Jennings was known at Fidelity Bank as a "marketing wunderkind," a man with an effusive, almost bubbly disposition who, as Jack Conn put it, "could sell sand in the Sahara. The guy just has a tremendous personality." Another former colleague said flatly, "He was just the best damn salesman the bank ever had." According to Conn, Jennings started out at Fidelity doing an awful lot of loans, but as the bank grew larger and was divided into several lending divisions, Jennings wound up concentrating on what bankers call "business development." In addition, as executive vice-president and assistant to the chairman, Jennings ably represented the bank in the United Fund drive and other civic projects.

But Jennings really excelled at bringing in new business. He brought in doctors and apartment house projects. And he brought in the Four Seasons Nursing Home Centers of America, Inc., one of the high-flying glamor stocks on the American Stock Exchange in the late sixties. Four Seasons's appeal was due largely to the widespread interest in medical care for the aged and the popularity of franchising. In 1970, however, Four Seasons's true condition came to light and it filed for protection from its creditors under Chapter 10 of the bankruptcy laws.

Two years later, in what was reported in newspaper accounts as one of the largest securities fraud cases in history, the Securities and Exchange Commission charged eight officers and former officers of the defunct company, its investment banker, and its accounting firm with cheating investors out of an estimated $200 million. According to the SEC, they accomplished this by conspiring to inflate the company's earnings to boost the company's stock price.

Jennings, a director of Four Seasons Equity, which prosecutors alleged bought unprofitable nursing homes from its parent company, Four Seasons Nursing Home Centers, to inflate the parent's profits, squeaked by as an unindicted co-conspirator. Four Seasons chairman Jack Clark pleaded guilty and was sentenced to one year in prison.

According to government prosecutors, Four Seasons set up and controlled Four Seasons Equity, while publicly asserting that it was an independent entity. To show fictitious profits from the construction of nursing homes, Four Seasons directed Four Seasons Equity to buy interests in the unprofitable homes.

The federal indictments charged that the defendants defrauded investors by misrepresenting and falsifying Four Seasons's financial statements to the point where it appeared the company was unusually successful, when in fact it was encountering severe financial difficulties. According to an SEC report, the past accounting practices of Four Seasons and Four Seasons Equity were characterized by a "high degree of informality in handling intercompany transactions."

Such words would be even more fitting in describing the great banking adventure that was to come.

An embarrassed Fidelity Bank took extraordinary steps to keep itself and Jennings out of the fray. Jack Conn flew to New York to plead Jennings's case before the SEC's special prosecutor, and the bank retained the powerful Washington law firm headed by veteran presidential adviser, the ubiquitous Clark Clifford. "Fidelity didn't lose a nickel on Four Seasons," Conn said. "Everything was secured with certificates of deposit." According to Conn, a major reason for the demise of Four Seasons was the "drastic increase in interest rates.

"A lot of money was spent on legal fees," Conn said, "which came out of Jennings's pocket. He lost a lot of money. He didn't sell a share of Four Seasons stock, and didn't do anything wrong." Others saw Jennings's involvement differently. As one former employee of Four Seasons put it, "I knew Bill to be a real player." And a former bank examiner familiar with the episode asserted, "He came out smelling like a rose while others got stuck. He was in a conflict of interest situation, and they should have identified it as such."

Former Fidelity officers say that while the bank did not take Jennings to task over Four Seasons, the incident clearly did not boost his stock at the bank. Jennings was admired for his charm and congeniality but his aggressiveness irritated many of his colleagues. In their opinion, he was a sloppy, scatterbrained manager and a poor lending officer.

"If he had a forte in lending," said a former Fidelity officer, "it was real estate. Everybody considered Beep his friend. He'd really bend to accommodate any request." Jennings was considered better at collecting on bad loans than he was at making good ones. "People were loyal to him and when a deal went sour they'd try to figure out a way to pay him when they wouldn't pay other people," the former Fidelity officer said. However, one customer recalls, "I was always uncomfortable with Beep, because he was always too busy to listen. He gave me whatever I wanted for investments."

A correspondent banking officer for a large money center bank remembers calling on Jennings in the early 1970s and finding him "sitting at his desk puffing on a cigar. He was taking phone calls while people were coming in and asking him to sign checks. Out of a forty-five minute meeting, there was maybe ten minutes of conversation." In his opinion, Jennings seemed disorganized.

In Jennings's early years at Fidelity, former officers recall, he had the authority to lend up to the legal limit of the bank. At the time, bank regulations generally prohibited banks from lending more than 10% of their capital to any single borrower. Eventually, however, the bank set up a loan committee system headed by senior vice-president Forrest Jones. Even though Jennings outranked Jones in title, Jones held sway when it came to approving loan requests. At the same time, "more and more emphasis was put on analyzing financial statements," one former officer said. Analysis of financial statements was not one of Jennings's strong points. "He didn't understand them, or if he did he didn't pay much attention to them," he said. By the time Harris died, Jennings was left with virtually no lending authority and the only person reporting to him was his secretary.

"It came down to where he wasn't doing a whole hell of a lot," an ex-officer recalled. "He had friends he'd tend to call or they'd call and talk to him. He loved to talk on the telephone, so it wasn't as if he wasn't doing anything all day. But whether he was accomplishing anything or not I don't know."

The announcement in early October of 1974 of Wilfred Clarke's election as president was greeted with little more than casual interest by most observers, with the exception of Oklahoma City bankers and businessmen who were privy to Jennings's desire to become the chief executive officer of a major bank. Nearly eight years would pass before the American banking industry would feel the full, though indirect, impact of Clarke's appointment.

There was certainly more important banking news to be concerned about at the time. On October 8, Franklin National Bank of New York was declared insolvent by the Comptroller of the Currency, becoming the biggest bank failure in American history. The problems at Franklin had been well-known in the financial community for months, so when the bank was finally merged with the European American Bank, a consortium of European institutions, there were no expressions of shock or surprise. It was a smooth transition—one day the bank was known as Franklin National, the next day it opened as European American. The three major bank regulatory agencies—the Federal Reserve Board, the Comptroller of the Currency, and the Federal Deposit Insurance Corporation—had been working toward this end for months, fashioning a deal in which no one, except stockholders, would get hurt. This arrangement sent a clear signal to depositors and investors around the country and throughout the world: the United States government would always come to the rescue of *uninsured* depositors.

Beep Jennings possessed a resilience from having lived through boom and bust in the oil fields in and around his hometown of Healdton, in southern Oklahoma. As a child, he had seen his family survive the Depression in Oklahoma, when oil dropped to 10¢ a barrel and dust storms ravaged the flat landscape. Now, in his hour of disappointment, Jennings could look forward to returning to Penn Square Bank, N.A., and with some wealthy friends, buying it. In the opinion of his colleagues, Jennings aimed to show Wilfred Clarke and Jack Conn that he was a better banker than they were.

Jennings dropped into Conn's office to give him the news.

According to Conn, Jennings said, "Jackson, I'm going back home. I've got these partners, we're going to buy Penn Square, and I'm going to run it."

"He always wanted to run his own show," Conn said years later, "and I wished him the best of luck."

The transaction was made possible because Dean McGee offered to sell to Jennings and his partners his own stock as well as that belonging to the Kerr family.

Conn and Wilfred Clarke also helped Jennings exit gracefully from Fidelity: they approved a $2.5 million loan to be used by Jennings's First Penn Corporation, a bank holding company, to purchase the Penn Square Bank stock. Despite Jennings's mixed record, Conn explained later, "No one questioned his ability to run the bank. He had with him investors who were as stout as a mule. He had done a good job out there before, and we saw no reason to worry about it.

"When you lose a person who's been with you a number of years, and he wants to go out and buy his own bank, you want to finance it, if you think it's a good bank and feel the fellow can run it," said Conn. "That way you can keep the correspondent accounts." Moreover, he explained, there is much less incidence of loss on bank stock loans than on almost any other kind of loan.

A bank holding company allows a bank to engage in a baker's dozen list of activities usually forbidden to banks themselves. Holding companies can form real estate or venture capital subsidiaries, and they enjoy more flexibility in raising capital in the money markets than a bank itself. For example, a holding company can sell commercial paper, and then "downstream" the proceeds to the bank. Supervision of such activity by bank holding companies is exercised by the Federal Reserve.

Bobby Hefner also cut his ties to Fidelity Bank. "Hefner had come to feel that Fidelity Bank was shortsighted in its dealings with him," an officer said, "and he told us so."

Fidelity, of course, was not prepared to back Hefner's efforts to find deep gas, even if it had been big enough to do so. The bank, however, did lend him lots of money, according to a former officer, though most of that credit was based on and secured by the financial strength of Kennedy and his Kentile Corporation.

Despite the objections of then Comptroller of the Currency James Smith, the Federal Reserve Board gave its blessing to the acquisition of Penn Square Bank. There was, however, a lone dissenter among the Fed officials in the person of vice-chairman George Mitchell. As the first of many regulators who would criticize Penn Square's excesses, Mitchell declared:

> The debt to be assumed by Applicant in connection with
> its acquisition of Bank is high in relation to Applicant's eq-
> uity. Moreover, the high level of dividend payout required of

Bank for Applicant to service such debt could inhibit growth in Bank's capital at a rate compatible with its projected asset growth and could place an undue strain on the financial condition of Bank, thereby impeding Bank's ability to provide adequate banking services to the community. For these reasons, I do not regard the proposal as being in the public interest, and I would deny the application.

The Fed official was trying to say that Jennings was overleveraged. He hadn't seen anything yet.

On December 23, 1975, Jennings received a welcome Christmas gift. He was notified by the Federal Reserve Board that they had approved his takeover of Penn Square by permitting First Penn to become a "one-bank" holding company with majority control of Penn Square Bank. When Jennings left Fidelity, he did not articulate his intention to remake Penn Square into an oil and gas bank, according to Jack Conn. But it was almost inevitable that Jennings, having grown up in the midst of one of the state's original, turn-of-the-century oil fields, would emphasize oil and gas. "I've seen boom and bust," Jennings said later. "I have a great attraction and feeling for the oil and gas business." And he added, "When we acquired this bank in 1975, it was evident that there was a good likelihood that oil had been underpriced for a number of years, and would probably be moving upward."

Jennings liked to boast that he began his banking career at the age of twelve, when his father hired him to sweep out the lobby of the family-owned Bank of Healdton. Healdton was not much different from hundreds of other small Oklahoma towns, although it earned a place in the state's oil and gas history for the shallow but prolific wells that started to come in around 1914, and for the famous Healdton fire, one of Oklahoma's great oil-field disasters. In the cow pastures surrounding Healdton, cattle still graze around the ubiquitous pitch-black oil pumps, or "grasshoppers," as they are known in the oil patch, which lift crude oil from wells that, in some instances, have been producing for as long as sixty years.

Jennings, an only child (in the opinion of some, a spoiled only child), shared his father's flamboyance and joviality but not his tightfisted approach to banking. Al Jennings, a longtime acquaintance recalled, "never made a loan he didn't expect to be repaid." And another friend, a storekeeper in Healdton, said, "If Al liked you he'd loan you. If he didn't like you he wouldn't lend you a damn thing. He had a pretty good idea he'd get his money back." Beep's mother, Mary, was a home economics teacher who assumed responsibility for running the Bank of Healdton after her husband died. She was known as a feisty, emotionally strong woman who had a lot of influence on other women in the community. As a banker, she was cast in the mold of her husband, local merchants said. "Mary was the tightest thing you ever saw. She made sure she didn't give you anything that wasn't coming to you," one said.

Kenneth Eck, proprietor of Eck's Drugstore, across the main street from the bank, was considerably older than Beep, but often played miniature golf with him as a youth. He remembers Al Jennings as a community spokesman and leader who was "always at the forefront. I often thought, what would happen to the community if something happened to Al?" As for the Bank of Healdton, Eck remembers it as a "real solid institution that helped a lot of companies."

"Billy Paul was just like his dad. He was a leader, a mixer. People rallied around him, we enjoyed having him in the community." And Gib Blevins, of Massad's department store, remembers Billy Paul as a "real talker. Anybody who wanted a speech made would call on him. Everybody liked Billy Paul."

After serving as a pilot in World War II, ferrying bombers between the United States and Europe, Jennings earned degrees in business and law at the University of Oklahoma, where, according to the 1947 yearbook's write-up on Sigma Chi, rush chairman Billy Paul Jennings "had the girls in a dither." That would have included his future wife, Jerry Bass, whom Jennings met at OU. The daughter of wealthy Enid real estate developer Heinie Bass, Jerry was described by a classmate as "the prettiest girl on campus." That union produced five daughters but no sons, which some say was a major disappointment in Jennings's life.

Inevitably, Beep Jennings became president of the Bank of Healdton by the time he was in his mid-thirties. "People thought Healdton was a jumping-off place to hell," a local merchant said, "but there's something about the old town that grows on you." For Jennings, Healdton was somewhere between the two extremes. He was a man in a hurry, and it was clear that his boundless ambition would never be satisfied in his hometown of some 3,000 people. That ambition started to find fulfillment on January 19, 1976, when Jennings, as chairman of Penn Square, announced at the annual meeting of shareholders that the bank's deposits had grown by some 40% in 1975, while those of other Oklahoma City banks had risen, on the average, by a meager 4%. "Management has made a special effort," he noted, "to direct the bank toward a greater penetration of the energy market, more specifically oil and gas and coal production and the service industries associated therewith."

·THREE·

THE PROMOTER
DELUXE

B ILL LAKEY, A NEWLY HIRED COMMERCIAL LOAN OFFICER AT PENN
Square Bank, was not an early riser, and he loathed morning
staff meetings. In 1976, Jennings held them every day. Lakey recalled one of them vividly, the one where Jennings came in and announced that he'd like to start an oil and gas department. "There
wasn't much comment," Lakey recalled years later. "No one there
knew anything about it."

After the meeting he approached Jennings and said, "If you'd like
to start an oil and gas department, I'd like to be the one who does it.
I don't know anything about it, but I can sure learn."

Jennings was not inclined to agonize at length over a decision.
"All right," he said. "You do the deal." And that, Lakey said, "was
the way the oil department got started at Penn Square Bank."

Lakey was a tall, slim man in his mid-thirties when he joined
Penn Square Bank in early 1976. He is a reflective and introspective
person, not one inclined to cover up his foibles or moods, or to disguise his feelings.

After working several years as a national bank examiner scrutinizing troubled Oklahoma banks, Lakey joined a small Oklahoma
City bank, became bored with that, then enrolled in a graduate
program in clinical psychology, but quit without getting a degree.
"My family was Southern Baptist, religious people," he said, "and
they didn't support those kinds of endeavors." At a point when
many of his contemporaries were firmly settled into a career, Lakey
was still searching for a mission that was, as he put it, "different, ex-
citing, and important."

The Dallas regional office of the Comptroller of the Currency is a
training ground for banking talent in the Southwest. As noted earlier, because of the unit banking structure in Texas and Oklahoma,
there are some 2,000 banks in those two states alone, which is more

than 13% of the national total, and their appetite for examiners to fill their middle and senior ranks seems unquenchable.

Lakey was a desirable property. He wasn't sure whether he really wanted to return to the banking business, but shortly after he filed an application with Frank Murphy, Penn Square's president at the time, he got a call from chairman Jennings.

"Well, how about if we try you for a year, and we'll just make a gentleman's agreement that if you don't like it after a year, then I'll understand that," Jennings proposed. "And if we don't like *you* after a year then you'll understand that."

One of the things Lakey felt when he and Penn Square started making energy loans was a sense of pride—pride at being unconventional. At the time, there were only a few banks in Oklahoma daring enough to lend on oil and gas properties.

"It was a statement to the world that we're going to be different," Lakey asserted. "We're going to do things nobody else has the guts to do. I wanted to be a part of it."

Lakey never received any formal training in making oil and gas loans, save for a day spent with officers at the Republic Bank of Dallas, which virtually invented the business. "They said they hardly lost anything on energy loans," Lakey said. "They had a smaller percentage of losses in oil and gas than anywhere else in the bank."

Jennings was, as Lakey put it, a "promoter deluxe" who hated to say no. Thus, according to Lakey, Jennings committed to 90% of the oil loans himself. "He'd send in the guy and say, 'Make this guy a loan for $400,000.' " At the time, the bank's legal lending limit was in the vicinity of $400,000.

"So I'd ask Jennings, 'What's the collateral?' "

"Oil and gas production" was the inevitable answer.

"I'd explain to Jennings that I'd have to get the oil and gas mortgages together, and he'd say, 'Well, you can do that later. He's got to have the money today.'

"So we'd book the $400,000, then try to get the mortgages."

In one deal, a $500,000 loan to a Norman, Oklahoma, oilman, Lakey spent six months trying to coax the customer into supplying mortgages and other documentation.

A proper oil and gas loan is, by definition, a secured loan. If it is not tied to some kind of collateral, like oil and gas production or mortgages, it is little more than a personal line of credit. It is not difficult to file a mortgage. "But if you're going to take the trouble to secure a mortgage," Lakey said, "you have to do it carefully." More time and more information are needed to make an oil and gas loan properly than for a loan on, say, property or equipment. In the case of equipment, the lender can look at an IRS schedule and figure out what it is worth. The value of an oil and gas property, however, is nothing more than a petroleum engineer's best guess. In lending on oil and gas properties or production, however, it is not always clear what the borrower's ownership interest is, or even if he owns anything at all. When done properly, documenting an energy loan requires that an oil and gas attorney prepare a title opinion confirming ownership—a difficult and time-consuming process, particularly if the records of the company buying oil and gas production are incomplete, as they frequently are.

Although the bank can file a blanket mortgage on an oil well, in doing so it runs the risk of tying up other interests. Traditional oil and gas banks demand that the borrower assign the proceeds of production directly to the bank, giving the lender some assurance that he will be paid back directly out of the revenue from the well.

Lakey refused to lend more than $75,000 to one would-be oilman. This time, the promoter was looking to buy an old oil field in southwestern Oklahoma.

"He would do whatever it took to get in the door. He'd sit in front of you, act sincere, and tell the damnedest lie you ever heard," Lakey said. "He went right upstairs to see Jennings and when he came back down he was half in shock."

"I can't believe it," the customer said, shaking his head with a look that suggested a combination of bewilderment and ecstasy. "Jennings committed to $300,000." Lakey couldn't believe it either. He had been willing to lend on the production because that was what he figured it was worth. Jennings, however, went the whole distance, giving him $300,000 for the production and all the equipment in the field. "I told him he'd have to get an appraisal on the equipment," Lakey recalled, "and he came back with one for $200,-000 from a guy I knew was a flake. I told him he'd have to get one from a reputable company and he did come back with an appraisal close to the first one.

"I didn't realize at the time that people in the industry were getting bought off. I now have no doubt that he found a way to buy that appraisal," Lakey said. "These consultants and others who would determine what service companies got used on a well had their closets full of expensive cowboy boots and fifths of Crown Royal." According to Lakey, less than a year later the loan went sour, prompting a former director, one of Jennings's partners in Penn Square, to become uneasy over Jennings's lending practices.

"Bill," the director said, "the easiest man for a con artist to con is another con artist."

(In 1979, this director put his money where his confidence was: he obtained approval to open another Oklahoma City bank and quietly sold out his interests and resigned as a director of Penn Square Bank.)

Lakey began to feel that he was expendable. "I got the word that it would be a good idea if I put Jennings's initials on the loan print-out to show whose loans they really were. Because if Jennings committed on one, and I handled the deal, my initials would go on it, and then he wouldn't know anything about it if something went wrong."

One of the worst ones was the $300,000 loan to the would-be oil-man. "Just looking at the file, there was no way you could tell it was a good loan or a bad loan. There are a lot of intangibles you don't see on paper. You need street knowledge. I could have the best engineer's report and the best properties in the state of Oklahoma, but if the operator isn't worth anything and ruins the well, that engineer's report won't be worth half of the stated value." That happened at Penn Square, Lakey said. "An operator overproduced a well and it went to water.

"Or you could make a loan for drill pipe, but if that pipe is in Houston, how do you control the stuff? You spend a lot of time monitoring; you've got to be a paranoid person."

Nevertheless, there are some telltale signs of a prospective borrower's weaknesses that are not so esoteric, and should be apparent even to the novice lender. Over the next several years, these signs would be missed, or ignored, by Penn Square Bank. One rule of thumb in the energy lending business calls for a customer's borrowings to be limited to 50% or, at most, 60%, of the company's discounted present worth. Traditional bankers generally insist on this "2 to 1" coverage to allow for such possibilities as a drop in oil and gas prices, an increase in interest rates (which would diminish the present value of the properties), and the failure of the wells to produce according to expectations.

"When an applicant comes in with a balance sheet," said one battle-scarred veteran of many years of oil-patch lending, "you look at his cash, receivables, and who those receivables are from. You look at their estimates of their assets, and their present worth. If they're worth two million and their debt is three million, you know they can't pay off their debt from their revenue stream."

When Lakey arrived at Penn Square, there was one energy loan already on the books to a pipe dealer from Oklahoma City, apparently made by Bill Jennings himself.

"He had documentation and assignments. He thought he owned the property, but legally he didn't have a mortgage on anything. I took a notary to Duncan, Oklahoma, and bullshitted some guys into signing an assignment back to us by giving them an overriding royalty interest in it," he recalled. "They could have ended up with the whole thing if they had known they could have. I made sure my notary was with me so there wouldn't be any question."

Although Lakey, as a former national bank examiner, questioned the freewheeling style of the new Penn Square Bank and the people who seemed to be attracted to it, there was another side to him that was fascinated with the oil business and the high-rolling men who were part of it. It was a fascination also shared by Beep Jennings.

"I found the conservative part of myself was always in conflict with the uninhibited side," Lakey recalled. "The directors of the bank would have felt that too. Penn Square was starting to get noticed." In Lakey's view, the conflict he felt about oil and gas lending reflected the contradictory behavioral expectations that are part of growing up and living in Oklahoma, a state whose residents are imbued with the often unrealistic moral demands of fundamentalist Protestantism.

"In Oklahoma," Lakey observed, "there are an awful lot of expectations that you act a certain way, as a Baptist deacon's son should or as a banker's son should. You're not supposed to make any waves, and sometimes you've got to blow off. That's still inside of me. I fight against it sometimes, one of the ways by being unconventional."

The oil business, Lakey said, afforded ample opportunity for the quest for individual expression. "Where else in our society can you picture this robust, off-the-wall, devil-may-care oilman, who, if he doesn't like someone, can tell him to screw it? I'm convinced that Jennings had a streak of ultraconservatism. Anybody who goes to one extreme has the other extreme in him too." Curiously, it was, according to Lakey, hard to sell Jennings on a deal for somebody he didn't know. "But he wasn't afraid to take on a guy another bank wouldn't. A lot of what he did was a rebellion against convention." Jennings, in Lakey's opinion, was the guy who kicked the snowball down the hill.

Beep Jennings had lived all his life in Oklahoma, attending the Oklahoma Military Academy, where he was the school bugler, and the University of Oklahoma for college and law school. By the time he bought Penn Square, he had spent all of his working life as an officer at three Oklahoma banking institutions and had served as a member or officer of dozens of civic and community organizations. In 1975, thousands of bank customers, classmates, politicians, businessmen, University of Oklahoma football players, and even childhood friends became prospective customers of the Penn Square Bank of Oklahoma City, and most of them eagerly responded to Jennings's siren song of easy money.

One of the first to come his way was a wildcatter named Carl Swan, a huge, cigar-smoking teddy bear of a man who knew Bill Jennings from his days at the Fidelity Bank. Swan, who was born in Missouri, played football at the University of New Mexico and was graduated in 1951 with a degree in physical education. He began his career in the oil fields selling drilling mud, then in 1964 joined up with Chet Armbruster, a college football teammate, and Jack Hewitt, an oil-field rig hand, to organize Basin Drilling.

In recounting his story years later in a newspaper interview, Swan said, "Chet borrowed money on his life insurance, and I hocked my house." Hewitt, he said, was a tool pusher who "came with the rig," which cost them $45,000. While Armbruster remained on the job at the mud company where Swan had also worked, Swan scoured the oil patch for clients.

Basin Drilling became a contractor that took a one-eighth interest in every well it drilled. It later merged with another oil company, becoming Basin Petroleum, and the new entity was bought by Reserve Oil and Gas, which subsequently was taken over by Getty Oil. Hewitt remained as a drilling superintendent while Armbruster took his $3 million share and continued to drill for oil on his own. In early 1976, Swan accepted Jennings's invitation to become a member of the Penn Square Bank board of directors.

With five daughters and no son, Beep Jennings was naturally inclined to take young Oklahoma oilmen under his wing, pairing them up with more experienced operators and getting them off to a fast start. Beep was the *shadchen,* or matchmaker, of the oil patch. He was the glue that was to cement hundreds of limited and unlimited partnerships, drilling deals, and conglomerates, as well as friendships, as he booked and sold billions in oil and gas loans like "cotton candy at a carnival," as one observer later described it.

One of Jennings's discoveries was Jerry Dale Allen, or J.D., as he was known to his friends, then a young oil promoter who acknowledges with some pride that he lived out of the back seat of his mud-encrusted Cadillac while trying to make it in the oil business.

A robust man with a thin black mustache, J.D. broke into the oil business through the barn door, so to speak, as a sixteen-year-old high school student and Future Farmer of America in Ringling, Oklahoma, about ten miles or so west of Healdton. "I decided to get into the oil business when I found roughnecking paid $1.50 an hour and hauling hay paid 75¢," J.D. recalled. By the time he was graduated from high school, he had drilled his first wells, made more money than his parents, then lost it all to a couple of clever promoters. After acquiring degrees in petroleum land management and finance from the University of Oklahoma, Allen worked for Mobil for four years, first in the land department, then in exploration and production.

"J.D.," said Bill Malloy, a former business associate, "was the entrepreneur's entrepreneur." While his classmates at OU were reading business case studies, Allen was running a variety of campus-based enterprises, including a "party pix" service that took pictures at fraternity parties, and a dry cleaning delivery service. J.D. even enlisted the aid of a chemistry professor to devise a formula for stripping floor wax that he sold to fraternity houses. "He was the king of the A and B deals," Malloy said. "He'd just buy from A and sell to B."

Bill Lakey, who made Penn Square's first loan to J.D., also recalls lending him $150,000 for some properties in south Texas that got him into financial difficulty. J.D. couldn't pay it, and Carl Swan wound up as guarantor, according to Lakey, in a deal arranged by Beep Jennings, which led to Swan and Allen becoming partners. Their first joint venture was Longhorn Oil and Gas, a company that raised drilling funds through tax-sheltered limited partnership arrangements that were sold largely to East Coast and West Coast investors.

"This is one of the comers, kids," Beep Jennings told his youthful staff as he escorted J.D., who was wearing a quail blue leisure suit and flowered shirt, around the bank for the first time.

Before he met J.D., Swan was apparently planning to retire early on the windfall from the sale of Basin Petroleum to Reserve Oil and Gas, according to acquaintances, and looked forward to raising thoroughbred race horses and serving on the boards of local companies. "J.D. got Carl into Longhorn, and he had to get active," said a friend.

Bobby Hefner was always broke. Beep Jennings loved to lend money. Both were dreamers. It was inevitable that Hefner would call on Jennings, or that Jennings would call on Hefner. The only question was who would call first. Hefner recalls that he did, some-time in 1977 or 1978, probably in Jennings's third-floor office in the Penn Square Bank building.

Though the relationship between the two men had never been close, Hefner and Jennings had quite a bit in common. Hefner's father had begun his career as an oilman almost in Jennings's back-yard. Healdton was known as the "poor man's oil field" because of the low cost of drilling for its shallow reserves; it was where many of Oklahoma's most successful independents got their start. College and fraternal ties also run deep in Oklahoma, perhaps even deeper than the old school ties among alumni of the top Eastern univer-sities, because so many graduates of the University of Oklahoma continue to live and work in the state. Hefner and Jennings had both attended OU, and both pledged at Sigma Chi, Hefner shortly after Jennings graduated from law school.

After sixteen years of trying to peddle deep gas to the nation's banks, Hefner was convinced that big banks were the captives of big oil—companies like Exxon, Mobil, and Gulf—that had too large a stake in the exploration, development, and marketing of oil to invest heavily in natural gas. Yet he believed that just as coal had replaced wood and oil had replaced coal, gas would ultimately replace oil.

Hefner became passionate when he talked about methane gas. "Beep," he said to Jennings, leaning forward in his chair, "methane will be the dominant fuel in the twenty-first century."

Just as a giant industry had grown up around oil in the late nine-teenth century, Hefner predicted that a global multibillion-dollar industry would emerge to develop natural gas. He went on to say that billions would be spent, primarily by independent operators, in the search for gas, and that the only way they could grow would be by mortgaging their reserves.

That was a novel concept at the time.

In contrast, production lending based on cash flow was a time-tested financing device that was elegant in its simplicity, and vir-tually risk free. "It was," as a former energy lender at Chase Man-hattan Bank put it, "like shooting fish in a barrel. You could hardly lose."

Hefner told Jennings that there were no banks with expertise in financing deep natural gas. "You can be the world expert," he said, "because no one else has focused on it." Penn Square, Hefner sug-gested, could develop a local lending facility that could sell those loans to the international money center banks. Such loan participa-tions—shares in a loan sold by one bank to another—are a corner-stone of the American banking system. Through the correspondent bank network, a small bank is able to lend to a local business whose borrowing requirements may be too large for the small bank to handle alone because of regulatory limits on how much a bank can lend to a single borrower. For example, a country bank with a limit of, say, $3 million might have a customer who needs $4 million. The banker could book the loan and sell the balance as an "overline" or participation to his "upstream" correspondent. Likewise, big banks regularly sell participations as accommodations to "downstream" correspondents in areas where loan demand is weak. Few American banks, if any, had ever made and sold more participations than they had loans on their own books. None, that is, until Penn Square.

At the time, Hefner considered himself a rank novice when it came to the workings of banking institutions. What little he knew he had picked up in being turned down for credit at literally dozens of banks around the country. But Hefner was intimately familiar and quite comfortable with the oil and gas industry's version of a participation—the so-called farm-out agreement. Lacking the funds to drill all the superwells he might have wanted, Hefner's GHK companies frequently purchased leases and assigned interests in them to other operators who did the drilling. That enabled GHK to develop production at minimum risk and cost. Oklahoma's antiquated unit banking structure was also a powerful argument in support of Hefner's proposal.

Jennings was intrigued with Hefner's suggestion. It fitted in all too well with Jennings's goal of making Penn Square the largest bank in Oklahoma City. Deep wells required very big bucks and very big banks. As Hefner said later, "It was my idea, but I'm certain he was ready for it too." Before long, the Continental Illinois National Bank and Trust Company would be ready for it as well.

The borrowing relationship between Beep Jennings and Bobby Hefner began, as legend has it, when Jennings helped Hefner over a payroll crunch. "I was always going through a payroll crunch," Hefner admitted later, "so that may have been the case." According to Bill Lakey, the first $60,000 loan extended to Hefner was for his own salary for a year. At the time Hefner was in the hole for some $12 million.

"Jennings knew I was always on the brink, always highly leveraged," Hefner said. "I suspect he thought he was taking a chance. I remember at some point they decided to give me some money; it was about the time intrastate gas prices were beginning to move up and people could drill wells based on the commodity value of gas versus oil."

Indeed, some Penn Square officers expressed misgivings about financing Hefner. In 1977, however, Hefner negotiated a farm-out deal with the Apache Corporation, a major oil and gas producer, whereby Apache put up some $35 million for drilling expenses in return for GHK's leases, with both companies splitting the revenue from production after Apache recovered its expenses. It was the Apache deal, said GHK partner David Kennedy, "that really got us set up in business." It also was the starting gun for one of the biggest oil and gas plays in American history. "That got the north Elk City drilling deal kicked off," said Bill Lakey. "That's what got people excited."

The deal clearly excited Beep Jennings.

According to Lakey, Jennings's name (as an investor) also appeared on division orders—assignments of revenues from production—connected with the Apache deal. The former officer said to himself at the time, "That looks like something I shouldn't be seeing." Jennings, Lakey asserted, "did partnerships and joint ventures with people he loaned money to." Allegations of such cozy dealing with borrowers would form a part of a lengthy and mournful court record in later, less optimistic times.

A WINTER OF DISCONTENT

F EW EVENTS EMBODY THE RIVALRY—SOME SAY HOSTILITY—BE-tween Texas and Oklahoma like the Oklahoma Sooners-Texas Longhorns football game, played every fall at the Cotton Bowl in Dallas, before what is almost invariably a capacity crowd of 75,587 fans, most of them Texans clanking cowbells.

On October 9, 1976, Gov. David Boren of Oklahoma and Gov. Dolph Briscoe of Texas sat together in the governor's box on the 50-yard line during the Texas–Oklahoma game, and at halftime met with National Democratic chairman Bob Strauss, who had been watching from the Texas side. But there was little partisan discussion among them about the relative strengths of either team. Most of the talk, in fact, focused on two issues of vital concern to each of the men: Jimmy Carter's prospects of defeating President Gerald Ford in the November election, and the deregulation of natural gas. Ironically, Ford himself attended the game, which ended in a 6–6 tie. Gov. Boren had been advising Gov. Carter on energy issues, and the three Democrats agreed that it was crucial that Carter come out strongly for deregulation.

Boren, a former Rhodes scholar, decided to make it easy for Carter to take this position. He returned to his office and drafted a letter for Carter's signature advocating deregulation. Boren, in concert with Briscoe, and Gov. Edwin Edwards of Louisiana, the chief executives of the nation's top three gas-producing states, would then release it to the press. Boren sent the letter to Jimmy Carter at his home in Plains, Georgia, with a covering memo suggesting that such a statement would be helpful politically to him in the Southwest if he felt he could take that position.

In the final letter, dated October 19, Carter, or more accurately Boren, proposed three measures to boost domestic energy production. At the top of the list was the deregulation of new natural gas.

"The decontrol of producers' prices for new natural gas would provide an incentive for new exploration," he wrote, "and would help our nation's oil and gas operators attract needed capital. Deregulation of new gas would encourage sales in the interstate market and help lessen the prospect of shortages in the nonproducing states which rely on interstate supplies. While encouraging new production, this proposal will protect the consumer against sudden sharp increases in the average price of natural gas."

Hefner had also hopped aboard the Carter bandwagon, making the rounds at meetings of oil and gas producers, urging support for the peanut farmer from Georgia. The reception he received was usually chilly.

According to Bill Anderson, a top official with the Independent Petroleum Association of America, whose membership consists primarily of smaller independent oil and gas producers, Hefner stood up at a gas committee meeting at the group's annual convention in New Orleans shortly before the November election and "admonished us to get on the Carter bandwagon." Before the convention was over, IPAA officials had received a copy of a telegram from Carter to Gov. Edwards promising to deregulate natural gas; then aides to Gov. Boren distributed copies to the participants.

"Hefner went around asking to speak in support of Carter, and the audience wouldn't let him," recalled Dorsey Buttram, an Oklahoma City independent whose father was one of the pioneers of oil and gas drilling in the state. Nevertheless, Carter went on to win Texas, Oklahoma, and Louisiana in a close election, in no small part, some political pundits say, because of his stand on natural gas.

"By the mid-seventies," Bill Anderson said, "Bobby had become a zealot in his belief in deep Anadarko. When other people were looking at dual distortions of intrastate and controlled interstate, he'd be around a gathering of gas men and say, 'Yeah, but the future's in deep.' " The consensus in his peer group, Anderson said, was, "Yes, there's something there but there's plenty of less expensive stuff."

Hefner was a pragmatist, political and otherwise. "I got involved with Carter because I thought he was going to win," he acknowledged later. "Nixon had made the statement, 'We're all Keynesians now,' and started wage and price controls, which was nonfree enterprise. Ford came along and pulled a cheap political trick," Hefner said, by agreeing to sign an oil price control bill to enhance his chances in an upcoming presidential primary in New Hampshire. "Those were things that really bothered me about the principles of Republicans."

Hefner expected a liberal majority to be elected to Congress, and felt that with a Democrat in the White House there would not be a standoff on deregulation of natural gas. "The Democrats would be responsible for their own actions," he said, "and as it turned out that's exactly what happened."

David O'D. Kennedy, a lifelong Republican, claims to have been in agreement with Hefner on nearly everything except his support of Carter. On political matters, Hefner did not entirely ignore the advice of his elders. Both Kennedy and Taliaferro advised him against a campaign for the U.S. Senate. But if Hefner had run and won, Kennedy said later, "The people who would have run GHK would have been much more conservative."

While Hefner, Boren, and other Democrats from gas-producing states were attempting to muster the political forces necessary to ensure a victory for Carter and, they hoped, gas decontrol, there were other natural forces at work that would, after more than twenty years of congressional indecision, bring the deregulation issue to a head.

Dr. Donald Gilman is a mop-haired, slightly disheveled earth scientist who could easily pass for half of his fifty-three years. A graduate of Harvard and the Massachusetts Institute of Technology, he is the chief of the long-range forecast group of the National Weather Service, a unit of the National Oceanic and Atmospheric Administration (NOAA). The title, unlike some in the federal government, accurately describes what Dr. Gilman actually does: every couple of weeks he and a small group of colleagues issue bulletins on the U.S. weather outlook for the next 30 days and every four weeks for the next 90 days. They occupy a small cluster of offices in a cube-shaped steel-and-glass office building, distinguishable from others of that kind only because of the jungle of antennas and other telecommunications apparatus sprouting from its flat roof. It is on the perimeter of Washington, not far from an entrance ramp to the Beltway and about ten miles from the White House, perhaps some indication of the peripheral importance the federal bureaucracy ascribes to this function of government.

On the average, Dr. Gilman is right only about three times out of five, probably as good a batting average as anyone else in Washington, but unlike many other scientist-bureaucrats Dr. Gilman is expected to be right only slightly more often than he is wrong, which could explain why he has aged rather more slowly than many other government workers of his age who have achieved his status.

However, in mid-October 1976, about the time the oil and gas producers were arguing over Jimmy Carter at their annual convention, Dr. Gilman and two of his associates were approaching a conclusion, rare for its unanimity, on the outlook for the winter of 1976–77. By early November, they agreed that it was going to be bone-chillingly cold.

The primary tool of Dr. Gilman's profession is a set of maps of the Northern Hemisphere, on which he has superimposed a series of wavy, cobweblike contour lines centered on the North Pole. They describe the movement of air masses at 700 millibars of pressure, the air pressure at roughly 10,000 feet above the surface of the earth.

Drawn by computer from data gathered by weather balloons sent aloft around the globe, the contours are normally wavy, flowing gracefully around the pole, and depicting wind flows from west to east. But by mid-October, they looked as though they had been created by a spider that had lost its balance; one line, which normally might be expected to run from British Columbia out over the Great Lakes and continue eastward over northern New England, dipped sharply southward through the Midwest into the central Atlantic states, showing a ridge of high pressure in Canada and a trough of low pressure on the Eastern Seaboard.

The contour lines, drawn from measurements at 10,000 feet, are a rough model of what is taking place in three-fourths of the atmosphere. These readings are relatively unaffected by temperature or gound-level disturbances, and thereby show large-scale weather patterns that can be expected to remain in place for a week or more. However, what was happening on the ground was clearly bearing out what Gilman was observing aloft: temperatures east of the Rockies were abnormally cold for late September and early October. The mean October temperatures in El Paso, New Orleans, Tallahassee, and Pittsburgh were the lowest for any October on record. Toledo and Dayton were suffering their coldest October since 1925.

In his career as meteorologist, Gilman had rarely seen a winter weather system so well defined, so stable, and, more important, so stationary this early in the fall. It was a fairly easy call.

Dr. Gilman anticipates, but resists, questions about what forces cause these patterns to shape up the way they do, saying, without embarrassment, "It is very deep; one can only say that they are the sum total of all the components of the weather at any time." But some weathermen, including Dr. Gilman, believe such extreme weather patterns are somehow related to an abnormal shift in the wind direction over the coastal waters of Peru that causes a significant rise in the water temperature there and, ultimately, the destruction of millions of tons of anchovies, one of Peru's largest exports. This phenomenon is called El Niño, Spanish for the "Christ Child" or "Little One," because on those infrequent occasions when it does occur it is first noticeable around Christmastime.

According to Dr. Henry E. Warren, an economist with the NOAA, the average residential heating customer consumes 1.36 million British thermal units of natural gas for every 1,000 heating degree days. Suffice it to say, however, that there is a straight-line relationship between temperature and natural gas consumption: the colder it gets, the more gas is consumed.

A year earlier, the Senate had passed the Pearson–Bentsen Bill, which would have removed price controls from all new, onshore gas. But the full House did not deal with the issue in 1975, because by mid-December the gas shortages that had been predicted did not come to pass due to relatively mild weather around the country.

On November 2, 1976, a day of sunny skies and cool temperatures in most of the states, Jimmy Carter was elected President of the United States on a platform that promised energy independence for the nation. The timing was uncanny; the first winter of his presidency was the worst on record, depleting natural gas supplies available to the interstate market to their lowest levels ever and resulting in drastic curtailments to industrial users in the Northeast and Midwest. For the most part, supplies were plentiful in the producing states, a situation that led to the venting not of gas but of some latent hostilities of Southwesterners toward Easterners, as embodied in such popular slogans and bumper stickers as "Freeze a Yankee" and "Let the bastards freeze to death in the dark."

Conditions were most severe in the East and Midwest, where schools were closed and businesses shut down, putting millions out of work. Fuel oil barges on the Mississippi and major rivers were blocked by eight-inch-thick layers of ice. Things were so bad, in fact, that Gov. James A. Rhodes of Ohio personally traveled to Oklahoma in 1977 to look for gas for his constituents. Utilities filed suits against the pipelines—suits involving claims that sometimes exceeded the value of the companies—for failure to deliver gas, and some pipelines had to go into the open market to buy gas at prices higher than they were contractually obligated to sell it for.

A pipeline has to maintain a minimum gas pressure in any city; if it drops below a certain threshold, pilot lights go off in stoves and other gas-powered appliances, and there is a risk of explosions in relighting them. Operating out of futuristic gas-dispatching centers, pipelines played what one company official called a "monstrous domino game" of allocating gas through their systems to compensate for shortages and maintain pressures. Superbowl Sunday, January 9, 1977, was another day of subzero temperatures from Missouri to the East Coast. While millions of Americans huddled around their fireplaces and watched the Oakland Raiders crush the Minnesota Vikings 32–14 at the Rose Bowl in Pasadena, California, pressures in pipelines systems around the country approached dangerously low levels. Later that evening, engineers in the Kansas City, Missouri, dispatching center of the Panhandle Eastern Pipeline Co. got a frantic phone call from the Gas Service Company, the supplier to residential customers in Kansas City, requesting an emergency delivery into its system. A Panhandle dispatcher turned to a colleague in the control room and remarked breathlessly, "They almost lost Kansas City." During that relentless winter, Panhandle Eastern was able to deliver only 70% of its contracted supplies, according to an official of the company.

The deliverability problem at Houston-based Transcontinental Gas Pipeline Company, which transmits gas from the Gulf Coast to Eastern markets from Atlanta to New York, was even worse—54%, meaning that 46% of deliveries were curtailed. Like the other interstate pipelines, Transco was prohibited by the Federal Power Commission from paying more than $0.52 per MCF for gas in 1975 and 1976, a period when gas that was sold in the same states where it was produced commanded three and even four times the top interstate price. Thanks to federal regulation, average gas prices lagged far behind the fourfold rise in oil prices that followed the Arab oil embargo of 1973, and consequently production for sale out-of-state did not keep pace with demand. The ensuing shortages prompted utilities and industrial plants to install equipment that would allow them to switch to competing fuels, namely residual fuel oil, with not much more effort than the press of a button.

Amid these shortages, the forecasts by the experts were gloomy, even apocalyptic. Dr. John J. McKetta, a professor of chemical engineering at the University of Texas and a former chairman of the advisory committee on energy to the Secretary of the Interior predicted that by 1985 clothes dryers would be permanently disconnected, Saturday and Sunday driving would be limited to emergencies, air conditioners in cars would be banned, elevators would be restricted in use, and office and apartment building escalators would be shut down altogether.

Exxon's energy outlook for 1977 through 1990 was less cataclysmic in tone, but the general thrust was the same. It assumed that energy prices would increase somewhat faster than the U.S. inflation rate through the 1970s, then rise in tandem with inflation through the 1980s.

"The pipelines were terrified," recalled one administration official. "It doesn't take very severe weather and that big a drop in committed reserves to get yourself into trouble at the margin and send a panic through the whole market."

Although the Federal Power Commission, under the authority granted to it by the Natural Gas Act of 1938, was able to permit emergency sale of gas to interstate pipelines at prices exceeding the regulated levels, these sales were allowed for no more than 60 days. Immediately after taking office, President Carter told Congress, "Our people are in trouble," and asked it for temporary authority to allocate gas, at whatever the price, to areas of shortage.

Just two weeks after his inauguration, President Carter signed the Emergency Natural Gas Act of 1977, giving him authority to declare a natural gas emergency and permitting, through July 31, 1977, emergency puchases by interstate buyers from intrastate markets at unregulated prices.

"We were convinced," a Carter administration official said, "that the pressure could get low enough in the lines to cause explosions and freeze people that winter. There was a genuine fear in the beginning that real physical shortages were upon us and nothing short of a moonshot effort was required."

Unfortunately, there were few in the Carter administration who recognized that the problem was not one of physical supply but of price regulation and distribution.

According to one official of what was to become the Department of Energy under Carter's wide-ranging energy plan, the U.S. Geological Survey had shown that there was plenty of gas. Nevertheless, the official added, "I was hauled into the office of the Deputy Secretary of Energy and was told there wasn't anything left."

John O'Leary, who became Deputy Secretary of Energy when the Energy Department was created later in 1977, was viewed by many energy producers as the "Chicken Little" of the administration. "He was a man who shouldn't have been in the position he was in," Bill Anderson of the IPAA said.

Soon after James Schlesinger was given the task of drafting a national energy plan, Hefner, Bill Dutcher, a baldish, soft-spoken former Oklahoma newspaperman, and Henry Taliaferro arrived on Capitol Hill with a novel concept. Not only was there no physical shortage of natural gas, but they *knew* where the gas could be found and were prepared to go in and get it. All they needed was a little help from Congress and the administration in the form of a special incentive price for deep gas.

Hefner argued that the shortage psychology arose out of estimates by the major oil companies that were based on gas associated with oil. For example, Mobil, according to Hefner, had published statistics pointing to 60 trillion cubic feet of gas left to be found for the entire United States, while Hefner figured that amount was contained in the Anadarko alone. Referring to the major oil companies, Hefner said, "Theirs is a perception through the window of oil."

On Schlesinger's recommendation, Hefner met with geologists at the U.S. Geological Survey. According to Taliaferro, the chief geologist said after the presentation, "Well, Mr. Hefner, this has been fascinating. Your material has been presented based on estimating technologies that are standard. We can't argue with your methods. The thing I'm curious about is why you don't ever talk to the people at Exxon and Shell."

"It's very simple," Hefner replied. "They're in the oil business and we're in the gas business." The government, Taliaferro added, perceived the hydrocarbons business to be "one big monolith."

In an early proposal, Carter would have allowed the Federal Energy Regulatory Commission, an agency within the new Department of Energy, to set an incentive price for certain high-cost gas, including gas deeper than 15,000 feet. Hefner had attempted to get such a provision from the Federal Power Commission but, according to Dutcher, "He'd been caught in a Catch-22, because the FPC would come back and say, 'Yes, we agree it's high cost and higher risk but we don't have enough data to set an incentive price.' Hefner would say, 'Well, people aren't going to drill for data. Until they get an incentive price they're not going to drill.' "

Dutcher recalls a meeting in the spring of 1977 with Hefner and Schlesinger, in which the GHK officials once again advanced their arguments for deregulating deep gas. Schlesinger, Dutcher said, was in favor of deregulating deep gas administratively. He took a puff on his ever-present pipe and told them, "The trouble with you independents is you won't take yes for an answer."

Hefner never lacked for audacity. He responded by saying, "The fact that you won't put it in the legislation makes us question your intent."

"I fully expected to get thrown out of his office," Dutcher chuckled, "because Schlesinger had a reputation of being a hard man to deal with. But he let that comment pass."

In mid-April 1977, a week before President Carter was scheduled to appear on national television to present his energy program, Sam Hammons, an energy adviser to Gov. Boren, got a call from a friend in Washington who told him what the President was really planning to propose. It was a far cry from what he had promised in his letter to the Democratic governors. Hammons was astounded that a President would back out on a promise that everyone involved had regarded as absolutely firm, and he immediately rushed into the governor's office to give him the news.

"Here's what he's going to do," Hammons said, and proceeded to relate the conversation with his Washington contact.

"Nah, you're kidding," Boren replied.

On April 18, before a national television audience, President Carter declared "the moral equivalent of war" to combat the energy crisis and warned that the country was confronted with a possible "national catastrophe" unless it began conserving fuels and accepting higher energy prices. Two days later, the President unveiled the details of his plan in a nationally televised speech before a joint session of Congress. Instead of coming out for the complete decontrol of all new natural gas, as he had indicated he would do in his letter to the three governors, Carter proposed that the ceiling for new gas be set, beginning in 1978, at the energy equivalent value of domestic crude oil. In effect, by establishing a limit of $1.75 on new gas, regardless of whether it was sold inside or outside the state where it was produced, the President imposed controls for the first time on the price of intrastate gas. Interstate gas (i.e., gas produced in one state and sold in another) had of course been regulated for years. At the same time, the plan proposed higher price levels for certain categories of high-cost gas.

The natural gas pricing proposals were just one piece of a master plan encompassing such measures as tax incentives and penalties to spur conservation, encouraging the conversion from gas and oil, deemed to be in short supply, to coal, which was abundant, as well as the development of nonconventional sources of energy like geothermal and solar.

But the natural gas pricing plan would emerge as the most contentious piece of the Carter plan by far. Over the next eighteen months, scores of lobbyists for consumer groups, producers, pipelines, and other vested interests roamed the corridors on Capitol Hill asserting their positions on deregulation. Sen. Henry Jackson, whose influence as chairman of the new Senate Energy Committee was crucial, called it the "thirty-year-war." There was standing room only in the House and Senate hearing rooms during the debate on the gas provisions, and the proceedings were routinely page one news in the *Washington Post* and the *Wall Street Journal.* As one Senate Energy Committee staffer put it, "Energy legislation was the hottest item in town."

As for natural gas pricing, Mike Hathaway, now staff director of the Senate Energy Committee, said, "I thought Carter did a flip-flop. There was no equivocation in the letter he signed. I interpreted it to mean government control of natural gas was going to end, but that was not the position the administration came up with." Hathaway said that the change in position was "all done quietly among a small group of players in the Carter administration. They held it very close, even their friends on the Hill didn't know about it. People in the administration didn't know about it. Then it was sprung as the national energy plan."

And IPAA lobbyist Anderson called it a "godawful scheme." This summed up the feeling of the majority of the gas producers.

Back in early 1977, the Energy Research and Development Administration (ERDA), which was later folded into the new Department of Energy, had initiated a Market Oriented Program Planning Study (MOPPS) that sought to determine if prices for conventional gas higher than the $1.75 Carter was contemplating would encourage the production of more gas. They determined, in fact, that a price of $3.25 would likely double known reserves. If a driller could get more money for gas he would have the incentive to drill for it, even in areas where gas production would be uneconomical under lower prices. But just two weeks before President Carter was to announce his energy plan, ERDA came out with a revised MOPPS study, dubbed MOPPS II, that arrived at precisely the opposite conclusion: higher prices in a deregulated market would not significantly increase gas supplies. The later estimates, said Oklahoma City oilman Buttram, "showed what Carter wanted, that there was a shortage of gas." Price increases, as the Carter administration maintained, would not alone end the critical shortage of gas. It just wasn't to be found—at any price.

The battle lines were drawn early in the debate. Consumer groups and politicians from gas-consuming states generally recognized that somewhat higher prices were needed, but opposed deregulation, while producers and pipelines advocated deregulation of new gas to encourage exploration for it. By the fall, the House and Senate had passed opposing bills. The House measure essentially preserved most of the President's pricing proposals, whereas the Senate bill, spon-

sored by James B. Pearson and Lloyd Bentsen, called for deregulation of new gas. Consequently, the House–Senate Conference Committee was faced with the task of trying to thrash out a compromise
from two diametrically opposed bills.

Hefner, representing his Independent Gas Producers Committee,
originally pushed for what he termed an "independents' exemption," which would have exempted all but the twenty largest producers from regulation of new gas. "That lost by just one or two
votes in the Senate," Hefner recalled. "Our fall-back position was to
get one thing deregulated." Hefner's people then turned their full
attention to that "one thing": getting an exemption for deep gas
(under 15,000 feet) included in the legislation.

When Hefner flew to Washington to deliver testimony and to
meet with legislators, he did not stalk the halls of Congress making
points for deep gas on a day-to-day basis. That job belonged to
GHK aide Bill Dutcher, who camped out at the Washington home
of Boots Taliaferro while carrying on the campaign. "We were more
of a guerrilla operation. There was no one else in Washington representing explorers of new natural gas."

Normally, lobbying groups will line up some senator as their
point man. "The unusual thing about this lobbying effort," Dutcher
said, "was that we didn't have anyone on either side who was our
sponsor."

Hefner was indefatigable and totally committed. "He seemed to
be everywhere," recalled one administration observer, "whether you
were on the House or Senate side, or at the White House. He was a
likable fellow, who seemed to be interested in this one particular
subject. He was pretty effective; he came across as a pretty competent guy."

Hefner used his superwell, the No. 1 Green, as an example to sell
his position to Congress. By this time, there were about thirty wells
in existence, according to Taliaferro, that could be classified as superwells. "We showed that the production by eight of those wells in
one year was greater than the energy output of the Tennessee Valley
Authority." But Hefner and his band of lobbyists didn't limit themselves to successes to drive home their point.

"We used successes, we used failures. Anything that would add to
what was a skimpy set of numbers," Taliaferro said.

By the end of 1977, the House and Senate conferees had failed to
agree on a compromise bill. Just days before Christmas, one senator
came up with a proposal, nicknamed the Christmas Turkey, which
was soundly defeated, and once again Congress adjourned without

passing an energy measure. "There was a question then," recalled Dutcher, "whether there would be any natural gas legislation at all."

All things considered, with the confusing mass of issues raised by the Carter energy plan, the notion of deregulating deep gas was not a particularly controversial or high priority item. A lobbyist for the state of Louisiana recalls a meeting at the White House in the spring of 1977 when he told administration officials that 85% of the potentially productive geological strata had never been tested because they were too deep. "I kept them there until five," he said, "and we went through a series of private meetings."

"How deep should it be?" a Carter aide asked.

The lobbyist pointed to a horizontal crack in the plaster at the base of the office wall and said, "If I were to put a figure on it, I'd say fifteen thousand feet."

"You mean, that's what it takes?" the lobbyist quoted the Carter aide as saying.

"Yeah," the lobbyist replied. "That's what it takes."

THE MAGICAL, MYSTICAL ENERGY LOANS MAN

NATIONAL BANK EXAMINER BILL CHAMBERS IS A LANKY, BEARDED man with a quick smile and a reputation for injecting his wry sense of humor into otherwise dull examination reports. Chambers had worked on Bill Lakey's team in the early 1970s. In the spring of 1977, only two years after Jennings gained control of Penn Square, Chambers arrived in Oklahoma City to conduct his first exam at the bank where his former boss now worked.

Chambers was unschooled in the nuances of energy lending, and Lakey, his friend and former colleague, steered him to the bad loans and showed him how to write them up. Energy loans are a nebulous thing. "There's a mystique, a romance about it," Lakey said. "If the guy making energy loans wanted to pull the wool over the bank examiner's eyes, he could do it."

Bankers in the oil patch enjoy trading tales of examiner incompetence. In oil and gas jargon, a fishing company is an outfit that "fishes" broken drill bits and other paraphernalia from a well. An Elk City banker tells of one examiner who pored over the loan file of such a firm, only to conclude that he was reviewing the financial data on a bait and tackle shop. After nearly a year and a half at Penn Square, Lakey had become very concerned about covering himself on loans Jennings instructed him to make. Ultimately, he prefaced his loan write-ups with the statement: "Customer was introduced to the bank through Chairman Jennings."

At the time of the May 1977 exam, the recent $300,000 loan to the astonished "would-be oilman" had emerged as one of the bank's worst specimens. In Lakey's opinion, the customer was using the money for something other than the intended purpose of the loan, but, said Lakey, "His attitude was that he wasn't doing anything wrong, and he told Jennings that." Lakey made an appointment with Jennings and the customer to review the matter. In discussing the credit, the customer, according to Lakey, acknowledged that he had used some of the money to buy a duplex apartment and furniture instead of oil and gas properties. Jennings fell back in his chair in what Lakey felt was feigned dismay and said, "Oh, my God!"

In extricating Penn Square from the deal, Jennings used a technique that in later years would become a Penn Square trademark. He called on a new customer, the Aggie Oil Company of Hennessey, Oklahoma. Hennessey is a dusty oil, wheat, and cattle town in north-central Oklahoma that took its name from Pat Hennessey, a pioneer wagon train leader who was captured by the Indians and shot full of arrows. Aggie was a small oil and gas concern founded, as the name might suggest, by the owners of a feed company. Penn Square made a loan to Aggie so it could take over the bad loan to the would-be oilman. "We reworked the properties, sold them, and made a nice profit," recalled Tom Eckroat, an Aggie Oil Company officer. "All God's children were happy." Aggie later was asked to take over other deals gone sour from Penn Square. "It got to the point," Eckroat said, "where they'd lend us whatever we needed."

While Chambers's examination indicated that Penn Square was in basically sound condition, it did point up shortcomings that would be magnified by the astounding growth that was to come. Chambers cited the need to avoid concentrations of loans to oil and gas companies, and noted that document exceptions—missing, incomplete, or faulty documentation such as financial statements, mortgages, and the like—were numerous, occurring in 14% of all credits. Chambers also found that earnings were down sharply from 1976, and that the attendance record of bank directors was poor.

Chambers represented part of a massive regulatory system, one designed to ensure the stability of banks and the entire banking system. As a national bank, Penn Square was subject to the supervision of the Comptroller of the Currency, an agency that came into being with the passage of the National Currency Act of 1863. This historic legislation brought the federal government into the bank regulatory business for the first time, and gave rise to what was to be called the dual banking system. The act granted the power to charter national banks to the federal government, through the Comptroller of the Currency, but it did not eliminate that authority for state governments. With the creation of the Federal Reserve Board in 1913, and the Federal Deposit Insurance Corporation twenty years later, some form of federal supervision was extended to nearly all U.S. banks. What evolved was a complex patchwork of overlapping responsibility and authority shared by the federal and state agencies. While the Comptroller has primary responsibility for national banks, the Fed, in a secondary role, is charged with supervising bank holding companies, corporate shells that many banks have created to allow them to conduct various financial activities that are off limits to banks themselves. Finally, the FDIC, as the deposit insuring agency, has the power to withdraw insurance from errant banks and also acts as receiver for banks declared insolvent by the primary regulatory agency. On the average, national banks are larger than state-chartered institutions. Fewer than a third of the nation's approximately 15,000 commercial banks are nationally chartered, but at the end of 1982 they comprised nearly 58% of all commercial bank assets in the country.

Of the state-chartered banks, nearly all are insured by the FDIC, but a relatively small number are members of the Federal Reserve System. The so-called state nonmember banks, nearly 9,000 of them, are supervised jointly by the state banking departments and the FDIC. The 1,040 state member banks, on the other hand, are regulated primarily by the state agency and the Federal Reserve, with the FDIC functioning in a secondary capacity. Then there are the handful of state banks that are members of neither the Fed nor the FDIC.

Regardless of whom the primary regulator happens to be, the goal of bank supervision is the same: to assure the safety and soundness of the American banking system and, to a lesser degree, to monitor compliance with consumer protection laws enacted in recent years. Regulators attempt to accomplish this using two basic tools: reports and examinations.

The *Comptroller's Handbook for National Bank Examiners* sets out the basic purposes of bank examinations:

> (1) to provide an objective evaluation of a bank's soundness; (2) to permit the OCC to appraise the quality of management and directors; and (3) to identify those areas where corrective action is required to strengthen the bank, to improve the quality of its performance, and to enable it to comply with applicable laws, rulings and regulations.

The exam schedule varies from agency to agency according to bank size and condition. A full exam generally encompasses a review of the bank's internal controls; the adequacy of its capital, which provides a safety cushion against losses; and liquidity, a measure of the bank's ability to meet its cash obligations. One of the most important duties of the examiner, however, is to assess loan quality. This task is accomplished by scrutinizing individual loans using statistical sampling techniques and, if necessary, classifying or criticizing those where some question exists about the borrower's ability to repay. Criticized loans fall into four categories, ranging from OAEM, or "other assets especially mentioned," which includes loans currently sound but potentially weak, to substandard, doubtful, and, finally, loss. While loans considered outright losses are "charged off" in their entirety against the bank's earnings or, if there are no earnings, against the bank's capital, other classified loans (which include all of the criticized categories except OAEM) may be written off to a lesser extent depending on how much of the loan is expected to be repaid.

The examination report on even the best managed banks will include some recommendations for improvement. But bankers complain that those reports are all too often a laundry list of technical violations of banking laws and regulations that are cited with no indication as to which ones the regulators consider most, or least, important.

In those rare instances where a bank fails to respond to the regulator's recommendations, and the condition of the bank continues to deteriorate, a senior examiner or agency official will attempt to "jawbone" the bank's management and directors into compliance. Often, this is accompanied, in increasing order of severity, by such measures as the "memo of understanding," "letter agreement," cease and desist order, and, in extreme cases, the closing of the bank.

Accounting firms are also in the business of reviewing the condition of banks, but their objectives are somewhat different. Whereas the regulator aims to protect depositors and investors, the auditor seeks to determine the fairness of bank financial statements and whether they are prepared in accordance with generally accepted accounting principles.

The bank examination process underwent a major overhaul in the mid-1970s, in the aftermath of a study by a Big Eight accounting firm commissioned by Comptroller James Smith. Chambers's review of Penn Square in 1977 was the first exam of that bank under the new rules, which did not sit well with many old-line, rank-and-file examiners. As one former examiner put it, "They broke the morale of everyone on the force."

Under the old procedures, the examiners determined the quality of assets and the solvency of a bank by reviewing loans. "If loans were bad," said a former examiner, "you asked for more capital and removed management. Under the new system, you looked at every aspect of the bank, everything. It took a redwood tree for all the paper that was required," he said. "If a teller had a personal problem we would know it. A $50 million bank would take six weeks. You didn't know whether to rent an apartment or buy a house."

Under the new procedures, field examiners complained, too much time was spent on the soundest institutions, and not enough on those that were poorly managed. According to a former examiner, "We didn't have the manpower to do it."

Most industry observers, however, generally applauded the new approach, pointing out correctly that there is more to evaluating a bank's condition than simply looking at loans.

The changeover to the expanded examination approach seemed to be accompanied by a shift in authority from the regional offices of the Comptroller, which would have included the Dallas regional office that supervised Penn Square, to agency headquarters in Washington. In addition, the revised procedures compounded what was already a severe staffing problem in the Office of the Comptroller of the Currency, an agency that has been plagued by high turnover for years.

The problem is particularly acute in the Southwest because of the large number of banks in the region and their seemingly insatiable thirst for lending talent. Joe Selby, now a senior deputy Comptroller of the Currency in Washington, started out as an examiner in Texas and acknowledges that "turnover in the Dallas region is the worst. We compete well up to five years on the job," he said, "then we lose them. But I don't think we should have to pay an examiner $5,000 more to work in Texas."

Nowhere is the examiners' lack of experience more evident than in their attempts to evaluate those mystical energy loans. "Examiners are used to seeing things in black and white," said Bill Lakey. "They're not flexible enough. They get into an area like oil and gas where there is that mystique, and they can be lied to awfully easily. There's a lot of room for bullshitting.

"When you've got oil and gas leases in Beckham County selling up to $200 an acre, and two years later up to $2,000 an acre, who's to say that a $5 million lease line, which is a bad deal to do in the first place, is not good? You're seeing the son of a bitch grow," Lakey added. "You're seeing the guy pay $1,000 an acre and a week later sell it for $2,000 an acre. That's pretty hard to argue with. Who could go in and classify a loan like that? They could bullshit a lot, but they had some good empirical data to bullshit with."

As one former examiner explained, "You look at the engineering reports and just take what they say."

The Comptroller's office, added a former examiner, did little to help people like himself overcome their deficiencies in understanding oil and gas loans. Most of the training, in fact, was on the job. "We learned about oil and gas by going into a clean bank and finding out how they did it," he said. "The Comptroller's office didn't send you to seminars on oil and gas."

Moreover, these youthful examiners, veterans say, were often intimidated by the wealthy oil-patch bankers and their customers, whose transactions the regulators were charged with scrutinizing. "A guy working for the government, making a car payment, just doesn't have the sophistication to analyze a credit on a guy with two Lear jets," Lakey observed.

"Examiners are young guys," another former examiner observed. "They review a bank, go out and have a good time, get up the next morning, and go back to the bank.

"We're used to going into a bank, hustling the women, and drinking beer. When bank examiners get together they talk about women they screwed at banks—not problem banks."

If the Feds had any misgivings about the banking style of Beep Jennings, those misgivings were to be heightened soon after the arrival in October 1977 of Bill G. Patterson.

Patterson, twenty-eight, had spent the last four years at the First National Bank of Oklahoma, most recently as a junior level marketing officer in the business development department, a job he had gotten through the efforts of his father-in-law, Gene Edwards, the respected chairman of the First National Bank of Amarillo, Texas. The trim, boyish-looking man with the winsome grin was in need of some counsel and advice from a seasoned banker. Despite his family connections, his career at the First was not going well. Eldon Beller, the senior officer with responsibility for Patterson's department, had repeatedly refused to grant him any lending authority, a fairly strong indication that his future at the bank was not particularly bright. One officer at the First thought Patterson "was not highly respected. I can't imagine he would have been given any loan authority." According to Dale Mitchell, then a senior officer at the bank, "He wanted to move faster than older guys were ready to let him move."

Patterson, the oldest of three children, was raised in Bartlesville, Oklahoma, a company town dominated by Phillips Petroleum, in a family of modest means. His father, George Patterson, designed and served as the curator of the nearby Woolaroc Museum (a combination of woods, lakes, and rock), a legacy of Phillips Petroleum founder Frank Phillips. An accomplished painter of Western landscapes and portraits, the elder Patterson, who is part Apache, signs his work with his Indian name, "Kemoha." Kemoha succeeded in passing his own artistic sensibilities, if not his creative talent, on to his oldest son. While Bill Patterson earned the nickname "Monkey Brain" for his fun-loving disposition and childlike antics as an undergraduate at the University of Oklahoma in the early 1970s, he was also admired by his classmates for his taste in paintings and other works of art.

At OU Bill had the good fortune of meeting, on a blind date, the former Eve Edwards of Amarillo, Texas. Eve's mother was a Johnson, a socially prominent Texas family that, as one observer put it, "owned the whole damn panhandle of Texas." Patterson, in contrast, had to work his way through college delivering pizza and cleaning a sorority house, and consequently took five years to complete the four-year program. Gene Edwards, in the opinion of family acquaintances, was not keen on the marriage, and never fully accepted Patterson into the family. But then again Gene Edwards never felt that there was any man in America good enough for his daughter. Patterson's predicament at the First National Bank would have been frustrating for any recent college graduate starting out in a career, but that frustration was aggravated by what friends say was his need to prove himself to his wife's family, including his brothers-in-law, Eddie and Carl Edwards, both of whom had distinguished themselves as campus leaders at OU and later as bankers and businessmen in Oklahoma City.

Despite the intense rivalries between Texas and Oklahoma, the ties of residents of the panhandle and west Texas are typically closer to Oklahoma City than they are to Dallas, Fort Worth, and Houston.

Gene Edwards, for example, was an alumnus of the University of Oklahoma and a zealous booster and fund raiser for the school. Jennings and Edwards met at OU through Jennings's future wife, Jerry Bass, and initiated what was to become a lifelong friendship. So it was natural that Patterson should call on his father-in-law's friend, Bill Jennings, as he contemplated a career change. Patterson, according to Penn Square president Frank Murphy, had planned on taking a job with a savings and loan association, and Jennings asked Murphy to consult with Patterson about the move. Jennings, Patterson said later, "wasn't interested." But Murphy was impressed. "I thought he'd make a good commercial loan officer, and I hired him about a week later. It was my decision."

When Jennings and his partners took over Penn Square, it was understood that Murphy, a conservative and well-regarded banker who had been with Penn Square since its inception, would be in charge of lending, and Jennings would serve chiefly as a promoter. But with the growth of the energy portfolio, and the ascendancy of Bill Patterson, Murphy eventually was relegated to a figurehead role. A thin, bespectacled man with a mane of wavy graying hair swept back from his forehead, Murphy clearly was more comfortable extending loans for the purchase of automobiles than for the production of the fuel that powers them. "Frank never did like anything that was going on," said a colleague. "He just washed his hands of the whole thing."

The Edwards family was not the only bond that linked Bill Patterson and Beep Jennings. Both men had been members of Sigma Chi at the university, and Jennings, as an alumnus, had become a sort of patron saint of the fraternity. Patterson, acquaintances said, soon became the son Jennings never had and, in turn, Jennings became a surrogate father to Bill Patterson. "If I could be like anyone else in the country, I'd want to be like Bill," Patterson told friends. As Patterson's own father put it, "He thought the sun and moon rose and set on Bill Jennings." According to former officers at the bank, Patterson wasted no time in trying to impress his new boss, to the point of working most weekends and walking by Beep's office to make sure the Penn Square chairman knew he was around.

Bill Lakey was assigned to train Patterson, but not long after Patterson arrived, Lakey handed in his resignation. "I left because of the pressure," Lakey said later. "By the time I quit, I was handling 30 to 35 percent of the bank's loans, which were oil-related things." Lakey was deeply troubled about his personal vulnerability on loans where Jennings had ordered the money handed out before the paperwork and documentation was completed. "I liked to have it firmed up, I hated to worry about the loose ends and the exposure you have. I was getting to the point where I couldn't cover all the bases. We were lending $400,000 here, half a million there, and putting it together later," he said. "I felt like I had a guy upstairs who was committing to all these off-the-wall deals and then backing off in the shadows and not taking any responsibility for them in board of directors' meetings." On the advice of another officer, Lakey, just before resigning, wrote up a summary of every loan he had handled. "If something happens," his colleague cautioned, "you might need to have your ass covered." Even back then, said Lakey, there was a "feeling of paranoia."

Jennings's parting words to Lakey were, "It's probably just as well that you're leaving. You ought to be a schoolteacher or something. You're just not aggressive enough."

"That bothered me," Lakey said. "I felt like a wet blanket. I would like to have been more aggressive, but I have an awful strong conservative part of me that doesn't like to be that vulnerable." He went on, asserting that he was scrutinizing loan requests in a way "that would have kept that goddamned bank from going down the shitter. I knew, when Patterson took it, that was it. He was as bad as Jennings about that kind of stuff. Put those two together and there wasn't anything to slow it down. I couldn't believe it when I turned in my resignation and was told that Patterson would take my place."

Lakey's reservations were echoed by other employees of the bank. As one recalled, "Patterson came down and slapped a debit and a credit on my desk and said, 'What do I do with this? One's black and one's red.' Even back then, those who knew anything were too busy to train new people."

Patterson, like Jennings, soon began developing his own clientele network built around his ties to the University of Oklahoma, Sigma Chi, and the First National Bank.

One of his first customers was Hal Clifford, a prematurely bald man with the build of a pro football player who had been an officer at the First's correspondent department during Patterson's tenure there. A founder of Mountain Smoke, a popular Oklahoma City bluegrass ensemble, Clifford, with heavy financial support from Penn Square, ultimately assembled a miniconglomerate that did everything from selling drilling funds to making wallets and even a full-length motion picture. In return, Clifford was to serve a critical role for Patterson. He would, perhaps without even knowing it, become a key player in a game of revolving loans, a game invented by Jennings and refined by Patterson, which enabled Patterson to transform grotesquely bad deals into deals that looked good on the surface.

Lakey's words of foreboding about Penn Square were echoed by Arthur Young and Company, the bank's external auditors, just weeks before Lakey quit. On December 19, 1977, the auditors presented Penn Square with its first qualified opinion. "Due to the lack of evidential data relating to certain real estate and commercial loans," they wrote, "we were unable to satisfy ourselves as to the adequacy of the reserve for loan losses."

PILOT LIGHT FOR
A BOOM

CONGRESS HAD WANTED TO BE ABLE TO PROCLAIM ON APRIL 20, 1978—the first anniversary of the announcement of the Carter energy plan—that it had reached a compromise on the energy program. To accomplish that, however, the conferees would have to alter radically their earlier positions. Representatives of producing states, for example, were confronted for the first time with the distasteful prospect of having to accept price controls on gas produced and consumed *within* their own states. Among the most controversial issues were the definition of new gas, the schedule for increases in the ceiling prices of gas, and the timetable for lifting of price controls for various categories of gas.

"They came out of the late-night sessions looking like they had been in a battle," Dutcher recalls. Senators and congressmen slept in their offices, leaving instructions to aides to wake them up for floor votes. "I'll never forget Barry Goldwater coming out in his pajamas," Hefner said. "No one who didn't live day and night through that experience knows what a battle it was. It was one of the most tedious, difficult political battles in American history."

Although they announced a compromise on April 21, it was so complicated that it took until August for the staff to draft legislation that would reflect the deals that were struck in those late-night sessions. The Hefner forces, however, had gotten what they wanted all along: a provision deregulating new gas found below 15,000 feet. According to one influential Senate staffer, Scoop Jackson was behind the move to incorporate the decontrol of deep gas into the legislation.

From that point on, Dutcher set into motion what he called his "H&R Block method of lobbying" (a reference to TV ads in which Henry Block, the head of the tax preparation service, cited in each commercial one of seventeen reasons for using H&R Block), where each day he would give staff members one of his seventeen reasons for deregulating deep gas. "I'd make sure not to give them more than one or two pieces of paper at a time, with maybe one or two ideas on it. That provided a good excuse to visit them."

On one of Hefner's visits to Washington, a House staffer pulled out a file drawer and showed the Oklahoma gas producer that he had accumulated more position papers and memos from Hefner than from the American Gas Association, one of the largest and most active energy lobbying groups in the capital. "We were prolific, we were persistent, and we were there," Dutcher said later.

Hefner's group used different sets of statistics to press their cause with the liberals and conservatives in Congress. In discussions with such liberal opponents of deregulation as Sen. Edward Kennedy and Sen. Howard Metzenbaum, Dutcher emphasized that deep gas represented only 1% of the drilling, but with the conservatives he pointed out that it represented at least half of the potential remaining undiscovered natural gas reserves in the onshore lower forty-eight states. "We never really got Kennedy and Metzenbaum to agree with us, but we sort of neutralized them on that issue," Dutcher said. The decontrol of prices for deep gas "was really more deregulation than met the eye. That's what the public relations business is all about, selecting those facts that support your argument." As some observers saw it, there was strong opposition when the natural gas battle started the decontrol of deep gas prices, but the issue became lost in the legislative thicket as the debate wore on.

Mike Hathaway said, "At the time deep gas was thought to be a good thing. Congress was opposed to decontrol, and our concern was to get something deregulated. Deep gas was one thing people pretty well agreed to." And Les Goldman, the principal author of the President's energy plan, recalled that deep gas was not a "heavily considered policy item. It was a side issue that got tacked on to build a critical mass, a consensus. It was just an add-on, a throwaway last-minute incentive thing."

The attitude was, he explained, "There can't be that much of that stuff, and it really costs a fortune to go get it, so, yeah, let's encourage these guys to go get it."

Apparently, there was little, if any, analysis of what accountants would call the "risk-adjusted rate of return" of drilling for deep gas as opposed to shallow gas.

Former Deputy Secretary of Energy O'Leary, the object of considerable oil industry criticism, acknowledged later, "Like a hundred other decisions we made, it was not done very scientifically. Did we do a fine analysis? The answer is no."

The geologists, he recalled, said the hope for strategic reserves was deep gas, but there was very little activity at the 15,000-foot level at the time. "We wanted to provide a strong incentive for what wasn't being done but didn't want to reward people for what they were already doing.

"The view of the bureaucratic world was that a relatively modest increase in price would unleash enough highly productive drilling that would then unleash abundant supplies." By that time, natural gas economics had been so completely distorted through years of regulation that "any window was appreciated," O'Leary said, "and the window then was gas below fifteen thousand feet." But with the benefit of hindsight, he acknowledged, "You can't find a more perverse economics than to go after the most expensive resource first. So what else is new?"

IPAA official Bill Anderson called the lobbying effort for deep gas "one of the great snake oil sales we've seen in modern times." The IPAA was one of Hefner's harshest detractors. It is an industry trade group made up, as the name suggests, of independent oil and gas operators, most of them cast in the same mold as Hefner's father and grandfather. In fact, Ray Hefner, the head of an Oklahoma City oil company and a cousin of Robert's, was chairman of the IPAA's gas committee at the time, and took a position 180 degrees from that of his distant relative. As another oilman observed, "Bobby Hefner was not the Oklahoma independent speaking."

"The IPAA fought the whole bill," said Anderson. "We didn't ever fight section 107 [the deep gas provision]. We didn't lock horns with Hefner." The independent producers were torn between their traditional, philosophical leaning toward decontrol, on the one hand, and their belief as oilmen that there was plenty of shallow gas left. "Nobody on the Hill really understood what was being done on deep gas," said Harold "Bud" Scoggins Jr., the general counsel of the IPAA. "We didn't oppose it because our philosophy has always been whatever you can get under government control you should get out from under government control. We didn't oppose it but we should have."

Those who took issue with favored treatment of gas below 15,000 feet argued that "gas is gas," and that it made no sense to encourage drilling for the most expensive stuff first. The notion of spending $5 million or $10 million to sink a drill bit to 20,000 feet while bypassing shallower gas-producing zones was compared to using a helicopter to pick apples from the top of a tree instead of using a ladder to gather them from the lower limbs.

Scoggins said of Hefner, "He knows how to put facts and figures together and sound convincing. He could sell snowballs to Eskimos." Hefner's critics admit, however, that he established that there was a lot of gas in the Deep Anadarko. "But then," Scoggins said, "when he started trying to convince everybody that that was the only gas left in the world, and that we should ignore all our other reserves and skew both our regulatory systems and our market system to encourage the development of that gas at the exclusion of all other gas, that made no sense whatever."

Scoggins and his colleagues also criticized the Washington press for what they felt was its unquestioning acceptance of Hefner as the oracle of the natural gas industry. "He'd host lavish press briefings, with champagne and caviar, and have them eating out of his hand. People would publish statements Hefner made as if they were absolute gospel truth about energy without ever attempting to verify any of his facts. If anybody made the least effort to verify some of his data," Scoggins added, "they could have been shown immediately that what he was defending was totally false. His basic facts were correct but the conclusions he drew from the facts were not.

"Hefner had a knack for taking raw information about one of his wells and publicizing it in a way that really catches people's imagination," Scoggins said.

IPAA's Lloyd Unsell asserted, "Bobby Hefner was going around the country talking about superwells. He hyped the whole thing up." Nevertheless, Unsell awards Hefner high marks for forthrightness. "One thing I particularly respect him for is every time I've ever heard him talk he says, 'I'm speaking for purely selfish interests.' He admits that right up front."

Hefner, however, dismissed the group as "not a major factor. They weren't an effective spokesman for anything."

On October 15, 1978, the Natural Gas Policy Act (NGPA), along with four other bills that made up the energy package, passed in the House by a vote of 231–168, after having been approved earlier in the Senate. (The natural gas bill, however, narrowly avoided defeat two days before when opponents attempted to split it off from the rest of the package and vote on it separately. By a margin of 207–206 the House opted to keep the package intact.)

The final bill, as signed into law by President Carter on November 9, 1978, contained all the ingredients for both the boom and the bust that were to follow. Although the decontrol of deep gas prices led to an immediate surge in prices as gas-starved pipeline companies sought to tie up reserves, that measure, along with the remaining parts of the energy package, would in the long run actually suppress the demand for gas.

For example, the so-called incremental pricing provisions of the Natural Gas Policy Act would set the stage for a shift from gas to oil by forcing industrial natural gas users to accept a disproportionate share of the burden of price increases.

Similarly, the Powerplant and Industrial Fuels Use Act required any new electric power plants to burn coal instead of gas, which was perceived to be in short supply. It also barred existing plants that did not use gas as their primary fuel from converting to it. One wildly perverse result of this bill is that all newly built electric generating plants in Oklahoma, one of the nation's leading gas-producing states, are forced to use coal imported from Wyoming. Overall, the conservation bill would have the intended effect of dampening, in some measure, the nation's demand for and consumption of oil and gas.

Apart from Hefner, who regarded the bill as being close to economic, if not political, perfection, there were few who were especially enthusiastic about the Natural Gas Policy Act. The attitude of the bill's opponents was perhaps best summed up by Unsell. "It was so bad," he asserted, "I don't think there's a politician in Washington willing to take credit for it."

And Les Goldman later observed, "Congress, in its wisdom, substantially changed the intent of what Carter sent up there. It was like seventy-five thousand people trying to put together an elephant. Throughout the process, it was a question of whether this was better than nothing." By the time it passed, Goldman said, there was no longer the same urgency about physical shortages of gas. But he and his colleagues felt it was "nutty" to have absurdly cheap gas, so, he said, "We figured we ought to go through with what we started."

CONTINENTAL ILLINOIS AND PENN SQUARE: MARRIAGE FOR FUN AND PROFIT

THEY CALLED HIM "GENERAL BULL MOOSE." BOB LAMMERTS, A RE-tired marine colonel and the chairman of Lammerts Oil Company, had a reputation in Oklahoma City as a stubborn but successful oilman who was more accustomed to barking out orders than taking them. Even as he approached sixty, Lammerts still looked the part of the marine officer, with athletic build, square jaw, bushy eyebrows, and blond hair.

R.P., as he is known to friends, never liked bankers asking him a lot of questions about his financial affairs, or telling him how much debt he was capable of handling. He was confident that his success in finding oil and gas was related directly to the amount of money available to him. And so he was becoming disenchanted with the fastidiousness of the stodgy First National Bank of Oklahoma City.

Even though he was originally from Buffalo, New York, and the product of a preppy Eastern establishment men's college, Lammerts had acquired a taste for some of the trappings of the Oklahoma oilies. He owned a Lear jet and wore alligator-hide cowboy boots. Moreover, he was comfortable with the informal style of banking being practiced at Penn Square by his old friend Bill Jennings; so comfortable, in fact, that he would wind up becoming one of the major stockholders of the bank.

Early in 1978 Lammerts was seeking to borrow another $1.5 million, but at the time Penn Square's legal lending limit to any one customer was $400,000 and it needed another bank to take the remainder. The much larger Liberty National Bank of Oklahoma City was prepared to do the entire deal, and Patterson and Jennings feared that if they couldn't "participate out" the remaining $1.1 million, they would miss out on the Lammerts business entirely.

Dennis Winget was the officer at the Continental Illinois National Bank and Trust Company responsible for the big Chicago bank's correspondent relationships in Oklahoma. Winget, who was originally from Kansas, was a robust six-footer who began his career as an oil company geologist, an occupation that had taken him to such far-flung outposts as Libya, Venezuela, and French West Africa, where he spent eighteen months in the desert working on a Mobil Oil Company geological reconnaissance survey. Now, as Continental's man in Oklahoma, he had just been handed a new set of marching orders that would take him to Oklahoma City.

His employer had embarked on a radical new business strategy by making a conscious decision to become dramatically more aggressive in putting new business on the books.

Just two years earlier, Continental chairman Roger Anderson had ballyhooed its new aggressiveness to a gathering of reporters at its LaSalle Street headquarters, a monolithic, Corinthian-style edifice located in the heart of Chicago's financial district. The massive Greek columns that make up the building's façade and define the vast banking floor convey the feeling of strength and permanence one senses on a visit to the buildings housing the Treasury Department and the Federal Reserve Board.

Roger Anderson was a serious and unemotional man whose large frame and stern, Nordic features conveyed much the same impression as the building he occupied. But he was in an upbeat mood as he told reporters that the nation's eighth-largest bank, whose motto was "We'll find a way," had found a way to become one of the top three U.S. banks in commercial and industrial loans, and would achieve that ranking by 1981. Anderson and his colleagues may have fantasized about surpassing giant Citibank and Bank of America in overall size, but that goal would have been totally out of reach. Becoming one of the top three corporate lenders in the country was not. And before too long, Continental would set its sights on being Number One.

This new aggressiveness seemed rather 'out of keeping with Anderson's old-fashioned, reserved style. "People assumed he slept in his suit," one former Continental officer said. Anderson's temperament was in sharp contrast with that of John Perkins, the lanky, arrogant, and often abrasive banker whom the Continental board chose as president at the same time Anderson was elected chairman. Despite their differences the two men were likened to the Bobbsey Twins. They had both attended Northwestern University, where Perkins was elected to Phi Beta Kappa. Both joined the navy upon graduation, and later both entered the Continental Illinois management training program the same year, when they met for the first time. The careers of the two men diverged in 1949 when Anderson was assigned to the international division and Perkins to the bond department, a traditional training ground for Continental top management.

Their differences in style showed up clearly soon after their election to the bank's top posts when the board ordered them, according to a former senior Continental officer, to stop driving their cars and use the bank's limousines. Perkins, the officer recalled, fell into the routine easily, while Anderson, even though he had recently broken his ankle, "bitched about the ostentatiousness of it all."

Anderson and Perkins apparently felt there was ample justification for pursuing this new strategy of aggressive lending. In 1976 the nation was just beginning to work its way out of the deep recession that began with the 1973 Arab oil embargo and the subsequent quadrupling of oil prices by the OPEC nations. The demand for credit, however, is a lagging indicator of the economy, and in 1975 and 1976 loan demand took one of its sharpest nosedives since World War II. Part of the reason was that large corporations were able to issue commercial paper at more favorable rates than they would pay for bank loans, and thus were relying more heavily on this device for their short-term financing.

Banks like Continental were also feeling the effects of intensified competition from the so-called "nonbanks" as well as from foreign banks operating in the United States under a regulatory system that actually favored the foreign institutions. According to Federal Reserve statistics, foreign-owned bank assets in the United States skyrocketed from $24 billion in November 1972 to $98 billion in May 1978, a fourfold increase. Put another way, foreign bank assets rose 30% a year in that period, compared with the 10% annual expansion of domestic assets of U.S. commercial banks. In roughly the same period, foreign banks almost doubled their share of the profitable commercial and industrial loan market, from 7% to 13.5%.

"Nonbank" financial institutions, such as investment banking houses, insurance companies, and commercial finance companies, which are not required to operate under the same stringent regulations as banks, also represented a strong challenge to banks for large corporate business. Taken together, these developments prompted institutions like Continental Illinois to look more closely at the smaller, fledgling companies in the "corporate middle market," which included businesses with annual revenues between $5 and $100 million. Although the profits to be earned from lending to such companies are potentially greater than in lending to the Fortune 500, the risks are greater as well. Continental, however, was prepared to accept those risks.

Later, in March 1980, Congress would set the stage for even more intense competition in the financial services arena by passing the landmark Depository Institutions Deregulation and Monetary Control Act, considered among the most significant pieces of banking legislation ever enacted. The law ordered the phasing out, over six years, of interest rate ceilings on passbook savings accounts, expanded the powers of thrifts institutions, and authorized interest-bearing checking accounts throughout the United States, among other key provisions.

But Continental had taken the aggressive route before, and on the first occasion the strategy had ended in disaster. During the 1920s, Continental lent money so liberally that it was dubbed the "promoters' bank." The bank failed and had to be bailed out with a $50 million capital infusion from the Reconstruction Finance Corporation. The RFC assumed control of the bank and in 1934 appointed a new chairman, Walter J. Cummings, who had just finished setting up the Federal Deposit Insurance Corporation and serving as its first chairman.

Continental's logo is a tree with roots in the Midwest and branches reaching out to the world. One of the banks it had reached out to was the Utica National Bank of Tulsa, whose executive vice-president was W. Scott Martin, the son of the chairman of Phillips Petroleum. Martin was a boyhood friend of Patterson's, and the two maintained close ties at the University of Oklahoma, where Martin was a star basketball player. Martin suggested to Winget that if Continental was serious about putting more loans on the books, he should pay a visit to his friend from Bartlesville. But before Winget could contact Patterson at Penn Square, Patterson himself called Continental in 1978 to see if the Chicago bank was interested in taking a piece of the loan to Robert Lammerts. It was indeed interested, and that transaction was the start of Continental's relationship with Penn Square and Penn Square's experiment with selling loan participations.

Continental may not have been aware of it then, but on May 30, 1978, around the time Continental bought the participation in the Lammerts loan, Arthur Young and Company issued a management letter to the Penn Square board criticizing them for, among other things, failure to obtain engineering reports on energy loans, inadequacy of loan documentation, and lack of guidelines for approving oil and gas loans.

Despite the vast difference in their size—at the end of 1977 Continental could boast of having more than $16 billion in deposits, compared with Penn Square's $00 million—Penn Square and Continental had quite a bit in common, having been shaped by similar historical and regulatory forces. Illinois, like Oklahoma, is a unit banking state. For decades, the state's community banks had opposed branching and multibank holding companies, which would have allowed ownership by one holding company of more than one institution. In 1978, banks in Illinois were permitted only two full-service "facilities," one within 1,500 feet of the main office and the other within 3,500 yards, neither of which could book loans.

Moreover, the state had a usury ceiling that limited interest charges on personal loans to a level 1% above the discount rate for commercial paper, although there was no restriction on the rates for business loans. From the standpoint of a banker seeking growth, the laws were among the most repressive in the nation. Thanks to the unit banking statutes, and its own self-imposed preference for the corporate market, Continental was severely constrained in retail banking in Illinois. Unlike, say, a Chase Manhattan, Continental was not permitted to have branches that could funnel in customer deposits to finance the bank's growth ambitions, so Continental was forced to purchase the bulk of its funds in the money markets at increasingly high rates of interest.

In effect, Continental had become a creature of purchased money, which had its origins in a financial instrument called the negotiable certificate of deposit. Invented in the early 1960s by First National City Bank of New York (Citibank), the negotiable CD revolutionized American banking like no other money market instrument before it. At the time, the demand for loans at large U.S. banks was outstripping the availability of deposits, in part because corporate treasurers were becoming more skillful in managing and investing their cash. The CD was born out of the recognition by the money center banks that unless they found a way to bolster their lending capacity, they would be unable to fulfill the borrowing requirements of their customers in a robust economy.

Ordinary time deposits were unappealing to investors for two reasons. First, they lacked liquidity, or the ability to be converted quickly into cash. Second, the rate banks could pay was limited by regulation. Banks can pay whatever rate they choose on deposits over $100,000 with maturities of at least thirty days. Usually, however, negotiable CDs are bought and sold in $1 millon units.

Continental Illinois, however, was by no means depending entirely on the CD. Short-term borrowings in the Federal funds and "repo" markets became an increasingly important source of funding, reaching the point where Continental eventually rolled over more than $8 billion every night. In relying so heavily on this volatile, overnight money, Continental committed one of banking's unpardonable—and deadly—sins: borrowing short and lending long.

At the time Continental teamed up with Penn Square, most major banks were looking for local banks to churn out participations for them. But the pressures on Continental, while mostly self-imposed, were greater than on most large banks. Continental was aggressively scouring the country for business. Penn Square Bank had to look to Continental for money. It seemed like a perfect match of people and institutions.

The engagement between Continental and Penn Square also marked the beginning of the demise of a decades-old correspondent relationship between Continental and the venerable, if ultraconservative, First National Bank of Oklahoma City.

Among the most important customers of a large, money center bank like Continental are other banks like First National, which used Continental to perform a variety of operations services, such as check clearing. It also "upstreamed" loans to Continental that exceeded its own legal lending limit. So for these and other reasons first National would be less than pleased to see Penn Square supplant it as a correspondent bank.

Bill Patterson, who by this time was emerging as Bill Jennings's protégé (the two had fallen in love with each other, as one Penn Square employee put it) flew to Chicago to close on the Lammerts deal. At Continental's offices on LaSalle Street Winget introduced him to his boss, John R. Lytle, a slim, forty-three-year-old vice-president with nearly twenty years of banking experience behind him. Lytle and Patterson were closely matched in style and temperament. Like Patterson, Lytle was arrogant, funny, gregarious. It was to be the start of an alliance that would combine business with friendship, but one where it would become impossible to tell where friendship ended and business began.

Unlike Winget, Lytle had virtually no background in the oil and gas business. According to his biography on file at Continental, he had not worked for a major oil company and had no training in petroleum engineering, save for a course in reservoir estimation for nontechnical personnel. In the aftermath of a corporate-wide reorganization in 1976–77, Lytle moved from a position in Continental's small business unit, where he supervised a portfolio of about $20 million, to the oil and gas division, where he suddenly was responsible for upward of $600 million—a move from a not overly demanding job to a very demanding one.

Following the Lammerts deal, Continental and Penn Square agreed that Penn Square would give Continental the first shot at all energy participations, and Continental agreed not to steal away Penn Square's customers. Bank chairman Jennings also benefited personally from the new relationship with Continental. Over the next several years, Continental lent Jennings about $2.5 million, as well as millions more to various companies in which he had a substantial ownership interest.

Since the 1973 Arab oil embargo, the unit at Continental responsible for oil and gas lending had raked in a quarter of the bank's earnings, becoming perhaps the most prestigious lending area in the entire bank. As one officer observed, "Oil and gas was to lending officers what a SWAT team is to a cop." Oil and gas lending was not only profitable, it was also patriotic. An energy lender at Continental could proudly claim that his efforts were contributing in some way to American self-sufficiency in energy and helping to nudge the nation away from its dangerous reliance on OPEC oil.

Since 1954, Continental had earned a reputation among banks and oil and gas producers as one of the premier energy lenders in the nation. There were few institutions outside the oil patch that were accepted by the Texas and Oklahoma energy lending banks as equals. Continental was. Its officers seemed to understand the industry; they were as comfortable on an oil rig as they were in the home office. Continental, the Texas bankers felt, shared their entrepreneurial spirit and temperament.

Continental, in fact, is widely credited with inventing the so-called evergreen revolver, the financing method used, and later abused, by Continental and Penn Square in making its reserve-based oil and gas loans. The method calls for the bank to establish a "borrowing base" for a customer that was usually about half of the discounted current value of the customer's reserves. The note requires only the payment of interest, with the idea that by the time it matures the reserves can be "reengineered" and a new loan extended to pay back the previous one. In effect, it worked this way: a customer borrows $100,000 at 20%, so by the end of a year he owes $120,000. Then he borrows another $150,000 to pay back the $120,-000, leaving him with $30,000 to play with.

Originally called Group U, for utilities, Continental's energy unit was created by a former Continental chairman who had an interest in developing the coal business in Illinois. In the 1950s, Continental, recognizing that the major oil companies like Mobil, Gulf, and Texaco were largely the province of the New York banks, zeroed in on the independent oil companies. By the mid-1970s, Continental was hitting its legal lending limit on nearly all of its loans to major oil companies, while loan volume was sagging in almost every other area of the bank. According to former officers, it was decided at that point to make a concerted effort to surpass the New York banks in oil and gas lending. The Texas bankers' admiration for Continental began to wane after the bank adopted its new strategy.

Not long after he moved to oil and gas, Lytle began to grate on the nerves of Texas bankers by using tactics aimed at monopolizing and controlling credits and luring business away from them. In the opinion of one former Texas energy lending officer who negotiated with Lytle on joint credits, "Continental was subversive in its dealings with the other banks." In trying to gain control of a credit, the Texas banker said, "Continental fought the efforts of other banks to demand tougher covenants and improve the credit. They'd never feel their way along, they were always ready to do whatever the company wanted."

In one large deal, the Texas bank didn't feel the borrower was prepared for the kind of growth it wanted. "Lytle told us, 'If you want to limit expansion, we'll take you out.'

"Continental made life difficult for us," he said. "They didn't seem to understand the ups and downs of the industry."

More than any other type of lending, oil and gas massages the egos of credit officers. In their contacts with most large corporations, bankers usually call on the chief financial officer, but in oil lending they deal with the "top guy," as one officer put it. "They fly you to the Superbowl in their jets," he said, "but all they really want from you is money.

"There is a tendency," he added, "for you to believe you are as big as the institution, that you are an extension of the institution. You start to feel you can do no wrong."

Continental's drive to boost earnings 15% annually was to be accomplished through an internal reorganization orchestrated by the high-powered management consulting firm of McKinsey and Company. Since the early 1970s, McKinsey had peddled a concept that became known in the industry as "decentralization by market segment."

This is fancy business school jargon that refers to the reorganization of the bank into business units intended to serve various specialized markets, a plan that recognizes that the banking needs of a $5 million company are different from those of an individual depositor with a $2,500 checking account.

Implicit in this approach is that officers in a particular unit should be empowered to do whatever it takes to make their customers happy. Most important, decentralization meant that junior officers would be able to lend much more money and lend it faster than they ever had before, and with far less scrutiny by experienced senior lenders. Even before the McKinsey-inspired reshuffling, Continental had been more decentralized than most banks. For example, it used an "increasing signature" system in approving loans whereby two officers could sign off on a loan up to the lending authority of the more senior lender. In contrast, banks where authority is centralized often require approval by a credit committee before granting a loan request. Continental had what was derisively referred to as the "hindsight" committee that reviewed loans after they had already been committed. Decentralization à la McKinsey short-circuited the credit approval process a step further, giving officers like John Lytle broad discretion in booking loans.

The banker in the field has a lot of flexibility in writing up a specific deal, and decentralization gave Continental's officers even more. Of course, decentralization has its hazards. Allowing junior officers more authority in dispensing the bank's money demands more controls, more checks and balances, than are needed when a loan committee of senior, experienced bankers passes on everything from a $100,000 home mortgage to a $100 million oil and gas production loan. Continental would eventually find that out the hard way.

McKinsey's modus operandi was to implement a new program at great expense to one bank, then sell the proven formula to others. In adopting the McKinsey strategy, Continental followed the lead of Citibank, which already bore the McKinsey stamp. Banks, like individuals, are susceptible to fads. They tend to follow the biggies into whatever form of organization or lending is fashionable at the moment. And at this moment in the life of Continental Illinois, decentralization was one means by which the big Chicago bank would become one of the Big Three in corporate banking.

Suddenly, said one former officer, "You didn't care about the whole bank, you just identified with your department." Continental took decentralization to such an extreme that some employees literally didn't know where the chairman's office was. This was in contrast to the arrangement at archrival First National Bank of Chicago, where, as one FNB officer expressed it, "The ninth floor was the center of power and had a life of its own." It was where the real power was and everyone in the bank knew it.

Also on McKinsey's recommendation, Continental created a new multinational unit that reflected the fact that large domestic corporations had truly become global in their sweep. By the mid-1970s, many large companies were as comfortable doing business in Abu Dhabi as they were in Albuquerque, and the multinational group was designed to coordinate the delivery of banking services that had once been supplied by the domestic group in the United States and the international division overseas.

Continental lagged behind the First National Bank of Chicago and most of its big bank competitors in lending to foreign countries and corporations, so there was already more enthusiasm for domestic than international lending, and it made sense to focus on what the bank was already doing better.

For many international division officers and employees, the new emphasis on domestic lending and the creation of the multinational unit did not go over well. Said one officer, who just returned from an assignment in Teheran when the reorganization was getting underway, "It looked like a plague had swept through international banking. Then they formed multinational and took away a lot of interesting business." Another officer saw it differently, saying, "McKinsey helped us break away from the two-bank mentality."

One of the most vigorous proponents (and later the principal beneficiary) of the reorganization was George Baker, a short, cigar-smoking executive who had a nervous habit of clearing his throat after every sentence. With his appointment as head of Continental's new general banking services group in late 1976, the engaging but often abrasive Baker became the czar of the bank's entire commercial loan portfolio (except real estate), which by the end of 1976 approached $20 billion.

Baker's general banking services initially comprised four line divisions: commercial banking services, multinational, international, and a financial services division. Within the commercial banking unit headed by executive vice-president Eugene Holland, a special industries group was created to oversee Continental's energy lending activities. In charge of special industries was Baker's friend and tennis partner, Gerald K. Bergman, described by associates as a laissez-faire manager but inspired deal maker who, as one colleague put it, "should have been an investment banker instead of a commercial banker."

"He was an ambitious guy," said a friend, "who liked complex deals but didn't care much for details." Jerry Bergman's name hardly ever came up without some reference to his heavy smoking habit. He was a three-pack-a-day smoker who apparently enjoyed the proverbial political smoke filled room as well, having served as treasurer of Illinois Gov. Jim Thompson's Citizens for Thompson Committee.

John Redding, also a senior vice-president, was a cautious, conservative banker who did not share Bergman's political instincts, which perhaps is why Bergman, who joined the bank several years after Redding, wound up supervising him. Redding, said a former colleague, "didn't play the game. He just wasn't very aggressive, and Bergman jumped all over him." Despite Lytle's lack of experience in energy lending, Redding and Bergman could take comfort in the fact that vice-president Jerry Pearson, a veteran petroleum engineer who was widely regarded as one of the best energy lenders in the nation, was backstopping Lytle's every move.

While Baker relished his new role, he was probably less enthusiastic about another duty that came with the territory. He was assigned responsibility for an area of the bank that bankers call the back office, also know as "the trenches." The dull but essential business of loan operations is paperwork. After a lending department approves a loan, it transmits the documents to loan operations, which then advances the funds to the borrower. It then posts payments of principal and interest as the note is repaid.

Top management apparently concluded that bank customers would be more effectively served by merging operations and lending, and there was some merit to that view. However, in taking loan operations away from the bank's able operations chief, Gail Melick, Roger Anderson weakened an important system of checks and balances. By maintaining a separate, autonomous loan operations division, a bank makes its lending people careful, and this tends to prevent overly aggressive officers from taking short cuts. For example, loan operations can serve as a check on lending by refusing to advance funds to a customer before the proper paperwork and documentation has been provided.

A former Continental officer described the process as it worked in the old days:

"The lender," he said, "took an initialed note to the cage, and if the collateral was not in order, they'd [operations] have no obligation to take it. Document exceptions would be reported to the officer's superiors. There was conflict between operations and adminstration, but," he added, "there's nothing wrong with abrasion. That's what makes rough things smooth."

Loan operations has traditionally been the sore spot of banking. The variety of transactions is endless, and the staff assigned to perform them has generally been poorly educated and even more poorly paid. Because of the vast array of transactions, loan operations has defied automation and remains a largely clerical, labor-intensive exercise. Said one former Continental officer bluntly, "Loan operations has been screwed up for as long as I can remember. It was an antiquated system." In fact, although Continental later boasted about its being in the forefront of such technological frills as electronic mail, its core computer systems were reputed to be among the worst of the major U.S. banks.

Because of loan operations' role as a check on lending, it helps to have someone in charge who is not afraid of standing up to a powerful senior lending officer. If anyone could have preserved the autonomy of loan operations, it was Melick, a colorful, capable operations man known for his irreverence toward authority, and for his personal idiosyncrasies, such as his reputed concern that cockroaches were going to take over the bank.

Melick displayed both idiosyncrasies when, according to a story that went around the bank, he found a top bank executive eating a Hostess Twinkie at his desk, in violation of building rules. "You know you're not supposed to eat at your desk," Melick is said to have told his boss. "There'll be cockroaches all over the place." The official ignored Melick's scolding. But after he left for the day, Melick retaliated by ordering a custodian to place a dead roach in his desk drawer, or so the story goes.

Melick got away with such antics because he was responsible for whatever little capability Continental enjoyed in this difficult-to-manage area.

Joe Coriaci, the man assigned to head loan operations after the reorganization, was reportedly not as forceful as Melick and was viewed as resistant to systems improvements through automation.

There are no magic formulas for success in banking, and there is no easy way to make money. Banks make money from their markets, not from reorganizations. "You only move ahead," one senior officer at a large New York bank observed, "by someone else's screw-ups."

To be sure, Continental's biggest competitor, First National Bank of Chicago, was screwing up, and screwing up royally.

In 1976, Robert Abboud had emerged victorious in a four-way horse race for the chairmanship set up by his predecessor, Gaylord Freeman. Two of the four contenders quit the bank, taking some of the First's top talent with them. At one time, First National had been the dominant force in the Chicago banking market, a position it had held for a hundred years. It was, said one analyst, "the most establishment-oriented of banks."

When Abboud took charge, the First, like many other large U.S. banks, was reeling from an ill-conceived love affair gone sour. Real estate investment trusts (REITs), the banking craze of the early 1970s, were going belly up at an astounding rate. First Chicago was particularly hard hit.

Abboud's approach to recovering from the REIT's debacle was to tighten up on lending procedures. While he was making progress in reducing the level of nonperforming loans, he also ordered strict lending controls that made the loan approval process more unwieldy and time-consuming for customers. Additionally, he curtailed the college recruitment program, the major source of homegrown lending talent. From 1976 through 1980, when he was fired in one of the most highly publicized corporate sackings ever, First Chicago lost some 200 officers and such key customers as Deere, Inland Steel, and the Pritzker family holdings, which took their business down the street to Continental Illinois. Continental took full advantage of its rival's weakened condition. According to one New York bank stock analyst, "They said, 'Let's go out and take business away from them,' and lending at Continental soon moved into a feverish pitch." The First's losses were Continental's gain.

Continental had also thrown money in REITs, but through a series of imaginative "asset swaps" arranged by the bank's real estate czar, James Harper, it managed to escape a major bruising. And when the crash came, it proved itself more adept at pulling out of bad deals than First Chicago. Because of his amazing ability to turn around sour real estate loans, Harper earned the nickname "Jimmy the Magician." Said one former officer, "People would tell him, 'Why, you can't do that.' And Harper would smile and say, 'I just did it.'"

Continental, as a former officer at First Chicago put it, "just started to do things better."

By the time Dennis Winget met Bill Patterson, Continental was showing impressive growth in earnings, profitability, and loan volume. It had become the darling of Wall Street and the financial press. In the first half of 1978, Continental's return on stockholder equity of 15.4% placed it among the most profitable large U.S. banks. Following an increase of 18% of its loan portfolio in 1978, *Barron's* wrote: "Penetration of the commercial and industrial loan market by Continental seems all the more impressive considering the lag in bank borrowing by many large corporations. . . . Much of Continental's success can be traced to its solid record as a lender to energy-related businesses—petroleum, natural gas, coal mining and public utilities."

Moreover, the bank was achieving this growth while apparently maintaining one of the lowest ratios of loan losses and nonperforming loans of the major U.S. banks. While demonstrating an aggressive approach to booking new business, it showed its conservative side by beefing up its reserve for loan losses, giving itself what looked like a solid cushion against any future problems. *Dun's Review* rewarded Continental's success by naming it one of the nation's five best-managed companies, along with such corporate stars as Caterpillar, General Electric, Schlumberger, and Boeing.

In 1978, the bank came into its own. That year, Continental's president, John Perkins, was elected president of the American Bankers Association, the national industry trade group, advancing the lanky executive into the ranks of the world's banker statesmen. It looked as though the Continental Illinois National Bank and Trust Company of Chicago could do no wrong.

LIQUID
LEVERAGE

IT WAS A NEW TWIST ON AN OLD THEME: HOW TO MAKE A LITTLE cash go a long way. No one knows for sure who invented the standby letter of credit, but one of its first uses in enticing investors into a drilling program was the Longhorn 1978-II. It was the first spin of the wheel in what was to become a 3½-year-long letter of credit roulette game played out on the third floor of the Penn Square Bank.

The players would be, of course, the Continental Illinois National Bank and Trust, soon to be joined by the likes of Seattle First National Bank and Chase Manhattan. Then there would be the brokerage houses, small ones like Casey Foss of San Francisco, and Ewing, Creath and Brown of Newport Beach, and most of the big wire houses, like Merrill Lynch, Smith Barney, E. F. Hutton, and Paine Webber. And finally, the investors. Thousands of them. There would be wealthy real estate and high-tech entrepreneurs from Newport Beach, and Silicon Valley, California, retired executives from Tampa, St. Petersburg, Florida, wealthy folks of all descriptions from New York, and doctors and lawyers from across the United States. In the locker rooms of yacht and country clubs from New York to San Francisco, everybody would soon be talking about drilling programs backed by standby letters of credit. Everybody would get in on it.

Longhorn 1978-II worked this way. Out of the total subscription of $3 million, investors put up 25%, or $750,000 in cash, and then obtained letters of credit from their own banks in favor of Penn Square for the difference. Then, using those letters of credit as collateral, Penn Square lent the partnership $2.25 million at Penn Square prime plus the "origination fee" of ½% to 1% that Penn Square customarily charged all its customers and which became a major source of its earnings.* Continental, in turn, would purchase a $1.95 million participation in the loan, leaving Penn Square with just $300,-000 on its own books. By the end of a 21-month period, the term loan would become a production loan when, it was hoped, income from oil and gas production would pay off the term loan and the letters of credit would not have to be called. Investors would be able to write off up to 70% of their investment in the program for the same year that Longhorn incurred the drilling costs. Someone in the 50% tax bracket making the minimum $150,000 investment would be able to write off $75,000 by putting up only 25%, or $37,500, in cash. That's a saving of $37,500 on his tax bill, and possibly more if the investor had to borrow to pay his taxes. People recognized that even if they had to fund on the letters of credit, they would be able to take the deductions immediately and pay later in inflated dollars, allowing them in many cases to finance their tax bills with no cash out of pocket.

Since Penn Square's prime rate was at least half a percentage point over Continental's, the big Chicago bank was actually making prime plus two and a half. This was at a time of intensifying competition in the U.S. banking industry, when loan spreads, or the difference between a bank's cost of funds and the rate it charges on a loan, were becoming razor-thin.

A money center bank like Continental was delighted to get a point over prime, so Longhorn Oil and Gas looked like a bonanza. But in other respects, the deal was a giveaway: it was what bankers call a 100% balloon note, meaning that the principal would not be due until maturity. Nor would compensating balances be required; bankers often ask a borrower to maintain deposits of from 10% to 20% of the outstanding balance of a loan.

At the time, the financial statement of Longhorn Oil and Gas, the flagship company of what would become the Swan-Allen corporate empire, hardly seemed to justify all the attention, and the money, Swan and Allen were getting from the Continental Illinois. Longhorn was to become the flagship entity in the Swan-Allen empire of service, rig, exploration, and drilling companies, as well as a number of shell or straw corporations. It was also Continental Illinois's showpiece in Oklahoma, the cornerstone of the burgeoning relationship between Continental and Penn Square. But it was a source of some of the early squabbles between officers of the two institutions,

---

*At one time, the prime rate was the rate at which a bank lent to its best customers. That's changed in recent years with increased competition, and now the best customers are often able to borrow below prime.

---

which occurred when it appeared to Jennings and Patterson that Continental was trying to bypass Penn Square to book the Swan business directly. While Jennings saw Continental as the means of earning a lot of fee income, he was not entirely comfortable with the relationship, and officers of the Chicago bank had to stroke him often, particularly when it came to any business involving Carl Swan.

According to Longhorn's income statement and balance sheet for the fiscal year ending November 30, 1978, Longhorn lost $201,000 on total revenues of $1.050 million. Current liabilities—obligations due within one year—exceeded current assets by more than 5 to 1. Normally, a banker looks for a current ratio, the ratio of current assets to current liabilities, of at least 1.5 to 1. In contrast, Longhorn's was a sickly 1 to 5.

Small independent oil companies defied the traditional credit analysis practiced by conservative lenders for years. There were no typical companies, and the ratios, rules of thumb, and lending guidelines comparable to the ones bankers used to size up a machine shop, clothing manufacturer, or food wholesaler for credit were never invented for the oil patch. One reason for this was that an oil company's primary asset—reserves in the ground—was not listed on the balance sheet.

But creative financing would not alone make Longhorn Oil and Gas a going operation. It took a dash of imaginative promotion as well, a couple of Lear jets and Bell helicopters, dinner at a local country-western nightclub, some "good ole boy" charm, and a well-orchestrated "dog and pony show" that included testimonials by Bill P. Jennings or Bill G. Patterson on the prowess of Carl Swan and J.D. Allen at finding oil and gas. Charlotte Day, who began as J.D. Allen's administrative assistant and later became Longhorn's investor contact, recalled that the meetings were "very informal, comfortable; we'd meet the people, there would be an introduction, and J.D. would talk about how Longhorn was formed, and how J.D. and Carl became partners in this particular venture."

J.D. was more of a storyteller, Ms. Day said in a later deposition; he would talk about the beginnings, how " 'me and Carl drilled my first well at age fourteen, and then good old Pete introduced me to Carl, and ever since then' . . . You know, that kind of thing. And Mr. Jennings, if he was there, would say that he had introduced J.D. to Carl and that 'the credit line of Longhorn was forever'—and when I say forever, it was very substantial, and they were all in good standing."

Patterson would respond to questions about the likelihood of those letters of credit being called. According to Ms. Day, "It was usually in a very boastful way that he would be very emphatic about their belief in Longhorn, that they were oil and gas finders—that, not to be concerned; very positive in his approach, boastful. It was all to the effect that they wouldn't have to be concerned about the letters of credit being drawn" (i.e., called for payment by investors). Patterson and others associated with Longhorn later denied ever making any such claims.

Those who participated, Ms. Day recalled, had the feeling that bills were paid on time—unusual in the oil patch because people usually leave one another hanging for a period of time, and "none of that was a problem.

"They perceived that everything was in place, the banking and credit line. They saw a very energetic J.D., who appeared to have business sense, and Carl, the patriarch of the oil patch, who had friends and wonderful contacts. You know it was headed in a very positive way," she said. "In those meetings you had a feeling of that. It was really very positive."

Patterson later testified that Jennings, Swan, and Allen requested his attendance at the investors' meetings. Asked by a lawyer in a later civil suit brought by investors what Swan said to him, Patterson replied, "Come to the meeting."

"What did Mr. Allen say to you?" the lawyer asked.

"Come to the meeting," Patterson replied. Patterson said that he went on the trips reluctantly, only because Jennings ordered him to go. "It was boring, a waste of time," he said. When he balked, Jennings told him, "Get your ass out the door."

"I was told to go and the reason I was given is they wanted to show that there was a bank involved . . . and then I would give them the name of people at Continental Bank if they wanted to verify beyond that." According to Patterson's later deposition, Lytle told him on one occasion, "Some guy from Colorado called me up to see if you were real." Lytle assured the prospective investor that yes, Patterson indeed was real.

According to Patterson, he, Swan, Allen, and other Longhorn staff would fly from city to city in a private jet, greeting investors at the airports. "The people would meet us out there," Patterson said. "I would shake their hands. We would get back in the plane and go home."

On at least one occasion, Patterson and his associates left the airport. "We did go to see the Mormon Temple in Salt Lake City," he said. "They tried to convert us." He added, "We stayed at a place called Little America, went to a couple of bars, which are hard to find in Salt Lake City." Asked what was discussed on the plane between stops, Patterson said, "Oh, just the same old 'hope that we'd raise the money.' We didn't talk about business too much on the plane. We were busy playing cards."

The Longhorn dog and pony show apparently impressed many brokers and investors. One of them, a former insurance agent turned tax-shelter maven, had previously dabbled in shelters involving pistachio nut trees, which yield nuts for a hundred years, and the breeding of exotic cattle. But in the spring of 1979, the talk at the cocktail parties in the fashionable Bay Area suburbs was oil and gas. The West Coast tax shelter specialist didn't know much about the energy business personally, but a business associate from Salt Lake City suggested he take a look at what the Longhorn Oil and Gas Company was up to in Oklahoma.

He made his first trip to Oklahoma that spring, joining a group of brokers from around the country who wanted to know more about the Longhorn 1979-I and Longhorn 1979-II private drilling programs. After a luncheon at a restaurant near Penn Square, the group met in the bank conference room, where they were introduced to Bill Jennings. Several in the room asked Jennings his opinion of the funds, a question akin to asking the chairman of General Motors what he thinks of the new line of Oldsmobiles. Jennings, patting Swan on the back, said, "We wouldn't lend if we didn't know that Carl was on board." Brokers and investment advisers earned a commission of 8% on all drilling fund units sold, and investors themselves could make a commission if they sold the deal to other investors.

The offices of Carl Swan and J. D. Allen were about the largest and most lavish the West Coast tax adviser had ever seen. Allen's offices were filled with Chinese vases and other Oriental art objects, and on Allen's desk were pictures of him with Ronald Reagan and Nancy, as well as a signed photo of Gerald R. Ford. The two men, J.D. and Carl, looked solid to him. He was impressed with their matching gold nugget watches, their cars, the people they seemed to know. After all, how could one go wrong with the friend of a former President, and a future one?

Continental bank was one of the first institutions to issue standby letters of credit on oil and gas drilling programs. The use of the letter of credit for such investments resulted from provisions of the Tax Reform Act of 1976 that instituted "at risk" rules for tax-sheltered investments. Up until 1976 an investor could put up $10,000 in a drilling program, the operator could take out a loan for another $10,000, spending a total of $20,000. The investor could deduct the entire $20,000 for income tax purposes even though he was "at risk" for only $10,000. In those programs, it was never anticipated that the investor would be responsible for the $10,000 loan. The whole point of leveraging with a letter of credit was to be able to claim the deduction for the money actually spent whether it was put up in cash or borrowed.

According to a former Continental officer, the oil and gas unit researched the letter of credit issue thoroughly and convinced Jerry Pearson, Continental's energy lending guru, that there were no hitches. Pearson said, "I don't like it, but I'll okay it." Continental's Chicago law firm, Mayer, Brown and Platt, drafted the language used in the letter of credit deals, and Continental approved the issuing banks. The Chicago giant regarded Penn Square's loan documents as being from the Stone Age, according to Patterson, and tapped its law firm to help overhaul them.

One reason Pearson approved the arrangement was the usury statute in Illinois, which limited the rate on a personal loan to one point over the discount rate for commercial paper. In effect, Penn Square "fronted" letter-of-credit-backed loans made by Continental to the investors, enabling the big Chicago bank to do an end run around the state's usury ceiling, and in return, Penn Square received an origination fee.

Letter of credit financing was attractive to Continental and Penn Square for other reasons. The "L/C" resides in a gray area of banking; for all practical purposes, it is a loan, but it is not treated as such on a bank's financial statements. It is what accountants call a contingent liability. Since it was not booked as a loan or bank asset, regulators didn't consider letters of credit when specifying how much capital the bank must maintain as a cushion for loan losses or the level of reserves the bank must keep at the Fed. Consequently, L/Cs enabled banks to earn more money with the same amount of equity.

Nevertheless, Continental soon found that being an agent bank or issuing letters of credit themselves was a paperwork nightmare. It meant that the bank had to keep lists of investors and make sure they met the minimum net worth requirements of the program. Penn Square, however, was more than willing to do this legwork.

Ultimately, the letter of credit was bastardized when some prospective investors claimed that their banks didn't understand L/Cs and Penn Square obliged by issuing them to the investors in favor of itself, a shaky transaction that would ultimately put Penn Square in the position of having to pay itself upon the default of the borrower. Commented one letter of credit expert, "That sounds like corporate masturbation to me."

The interest in letter of credit financing was reflected in the attendance at week-long seminars conducted by Lewis Mossburg, a leading oil and gas attorney based in Oklahoma City. Mossburg's programs on "Obtaining Oil Venture Capital from Investors" and "Financing Oil and Gas Deals" were so popular that he conducted them eighteen times a year and could have done more but that was all the time he had available.

According to Mossburg, 95% of the participants were real estate operators who had no previous experience in oil and gas. Bill Patterson was a frequent speaker and on at least one occasion donned a hat with a flashing red light to drive home a point.

By 1980, said one oil promoter, "Everybody who wanted to could sell drilling funds. If you didn't want to find investors they would find you." Brokers, many of whom had no knowledge of the oil and gas business, seized on the letter of credit as a marketing tool and pushed the drilling funds on wealthy but unsophisticated investors. Although the brokerage houses hired oil and gas experts to prepare "due diligence" reports on drilling programs they were selling, a few were not above "burying" a negative report, according to industry observers. On the other hand, it is said that they leaked positive due diligence reports to their salesmen or registered representatives, even though this material was designated "for broker use only." Before long, said one observer, "They were handing out letters of credit like discount coupons at Safeway."

Oil and gas deals generally are among the most complex and bewildering investments one can make, and without doubt the most subject to abuses by unscrupulous operators. And Oklahoma, as a leading oil- and gas-producing state, has had at least its fair share of oil scams. In the mid-1970s, Oklahoma became a haven for fly-by-night salesmen who set up batteries of telephone operators and sold what were represented as "fractional interests" in oil and gas wells to unsuspecting investors throughout the country. Later, the Oklahoma Supreme Court expanded the definition of a security and brought these operations under the jurisdiction of the Oklahoma Securities Commission.

Oklahoma, observed George "Kemoha" Patterson wryly, is a new state, "home to the bullshitter and the wildcatter. You've always had the gambling spirit in Oklahoma."

According to former securities commissioner David Newsome, bad oil deals fall into four categories:

• Take the money and run, where the operator makes no effort at all to drill the lease.

• Punching hole cases, where there is no attempt to evaluate the geologic merits of the prospect, and the operator makes his money from drilling a hole in the ground.

• Abuse of the private offering, where the deal is exempt from registration with the Securities and Exchange Commission or state securities commission, and where the operator uses the proceeds of one program to pay off the previous program.

• And finally, legitimate deals where there is no way the investor can ever make money because of the structure of the programs.*

These deals were packaged in the form of large private offerings to wealthy investors, or as public drilling funds sold in $5,000 to $10,000 units. Almost all of the public funds, and most of the private ones, were marketed as blind pools, where the investor had no idea where the actual wells were. To be sure, the small investor would not have the wherewithal to evaluate a geologic prospect anyway. In most cases, the prospectuses prepared by these operators were far too complex for any layman to understand. As James D. Lair, an oil and

---

* Generally, when an oil and gas operator sells a deal to industry partners and other investors, he does so using a "standard industry promote," which is also known as the "third for a quarter." In this arrangement, the buyer pays a third of the costs until the casing point, when a decision has to be made on whether the well is likely to be productive and worth completing. If tests show that it is, the operator shares the completion costs equally with the investor, who is then entitled to one fourth of the revenues. Expressed another way, if investors pay 100% of the expenses, they will receive 75% of the profits, before royalties and overriding royalties are taken into account. The key figure, however, is the net revenue interest. This is the percentage of the profits the investor *actually* receives. Assuming that the mineral owner gets a royalty interest of one-eighth and the promoter receives an overriding royalty interest of one-eighth, then the total revenue interest will be 75%. The net revenue interest would be 75% × 75%, or 56.25%. Thus, an investor who has paid 10% of the costs through the casing point and 7½% of the subsequent costs would be left with a net revenue interest of 5.625%. As the oil and gas boom heated up, however, the deals became increasingly one-sided. Landowners demanded excess royalties as high as 25% and sometimes more. Geologists took ever larger overriding royalty interests. Promoters stretched the standard promote so that they were "carried" not just to the casing point but to the tanks. And deals passed through so many promoters—each of whom took an overriding interest—that even if the wells paid out there would be no way the investor could make money.

gas accountant in Southfield, Michigan, said, "The economics are so hidden on the drilling fund deals that you can't figure out what you're going to get on payout. The only thing you can do is check the track record of the company."

That, too, is extremely difficult. An operator may present figures showing an impressive "success rate," but he also may make a practice of drilling in "sure thing" fields where production drops off to a trickle after a couple of months.

·NINE·

BRING US MORE GAS

THE INK WAS BARELY DRY ON THE NATURAL GAS POLICY ACT OF 1978 when reserve-starved pipeline companies, the bone-chilling winter of 1976–77 deeply etched in their collective consciousness, rushed into Oklahoma, Texas, and Louisiana to lock up supplies of deep—and soon to be very expensive—natural gas. As an official of Panhandle Eastern put it, "We told the producers, bring us more gas."

NGPA critic Bill Anderson of the Independent Petroleum Association saw things from a different perspective. "The pipelines got caught up in a frenzy and suckered in a lot of bankers and everyone else." Indeed, by the time the gas madness peaked in 1981, pipelines were paying as much as $10.10 per thousand cubic feet (MCF) for deep gas. That is equivalent to paying nearly $60 for a barrel of crude oil at a time when oil itself was commanding about $40 a barrel on the international spot market.

The explanation for this phenomenon is rooted not only in the ill-conceived natural gas regulatory apparatus that evolved from 1938 to 1978, but also in a system of contracts that has few parallels in American industry. With a little help from Iran's Ayatollah Khomeini, the NGPA, and the contracts that followed, it laid the groundwork for a boom-and-bust cycle that would make the South Sea Bubble of 1720 and the California Gold Rush of 1849 look like the line for tickets at a second-run Grade B movie.

Historically, most gas purchase contracts have included a clause called the "take or pay" provision, under which the pipeline promises to take a specified percentage of what the producer is capable of delivering, but if it doesn't need the gas it is obligated to pay for it anyway. Moreover, the pipeline gives the producer a long-term contract, often for as much as twenty years, that guarantees him a reliable cash flow. And it also assures the pipeline a steady stream of natural gas.

According to a spokesman for the American Gas Association, contracts negotiated prior to the passage of the NGPA typically called for 60% "takes," meaning that the pipeline would have to accept 60% of the producers' "deliverability" or pay for it anyway for future delivery. In the aftermath of NGPA, however, the bidding went to 75% and later to 90%, even up to 100%, of the producers' proved reserves.

Deregulation of deep gas did not take effect until November 1, 1979. But the pipelines were already building into their contracts an overwhelming incentive for producers to bring as many wells onstream as fast as they could. The faster the producer could deliver, the better his cash flow. The producer, in fact, had complete control over deliverability. He alone decided on the flow rate of gas out of his wells. So with the dramatic rise in deep gas prices, he drilled more wells to boost deliverability. By establishing greater gas reserves, producers could demand more money from the pipelines.

In turn, there were plenty of incentives for the pipelines to agree to pay for expensive gas whether they used it or not. Under the rules of public utility commissions that regulate gas and electric rates, they could immediately average the cost of the more expensive gas in with the older, cheaper gas and pass the higher average cost on to the consumer as rate increases. Since interstate pipelines had a cheap, albeit inadequate, base supply of gas acquired before the NGPA, they could bid higher for the decontrolled gas. "The pipelines," said Gov. Boren's gas expert Sam Hammons, "get their rate of return just for showing up in the morning."

As the prices of deep gas were pushed into the stratosphere, the pipelines cut their "takes" of cheap, old gas and boosted those of the new expensive stuff. Since rate hearings frequently take fifteen months or more, the consumer would have to pay the higher cost before the utility commission would intervene to force the utility to reimburse the consumer for expensive gas that was not actually used. According to Dr. William Talley, an Oklahoma City oil and gas consultant, El Paso Pipeline Company, a major conduit of gas from Oklahoma to California and one of the largest pipeline companies in the nation, was among the first to sign deep gas contracts following the passage of the NGPA. As a producer, El Paso had itself been one of the early players in exploring for deep gas in the Anadarko Basin. "They were," said Talley, "aware of the costs and aware of the potential."

In the seller's market, El Paso offered producers another deal they found impossible to refuse. It was called the "area rate" or most favored nation clause. This was one of several types of so-called indefinite price escalator clauses that appeared in almost all gas purchase contracts after 1977. Intended to provide price protection for the producer and guaranteed supplies for the pipeline, area rate clauses required the pipelines to pay the producer the prevailing rate in a three-county area surrounding the well.

"It means," said Talley, "that whatever the price at which I, the producer, sell to you, the pipeline, if somebody else in the area wants to pay more for it, you're going to have to match his price, or at least the average of the prices paid to three producers in the area." The result was a chain reaction in prices as interstate pipelines came in and bid up the cost of intrastate gas. Other escalator clauses entitled the producer to renegotiate prices to competitive levels or provided for some other upward adjustment in prices during the life of the contract.

Another phenomenon that contributed to the escalation in price was what Charles Hughes of the Oklahoma Natural Gas Company called "category creep," a reference to the twenty-six pricing categories of natural gas in the Natural Gas Policy Act. According to Hughes, many producers had "tracking clauses" in their contracts that allowed them to get new gas prices on wells drilled in the same field as an existing well that was producing gas at the old gas price. "You could go to the Corporation Commission," he said, "and tell them you were not draining adequately and that you needed another well." After NGPA, a new well on an old field might produce at $2 per MCF, even if an old well commanded only 30¢. That, he said, pushed prices up even more than the deregulation of deep gas.

When deep gas was deregulated, recalled Bob Hefner, GHK had one of the first contracts. "But they were afraid to put a price on it. I said, 'Just give us a price.' And they said, 'We'll pay anything anybody else would.'" Finally, Panhandle Eastern agreed to pay the BTU equivalent price for home heating oil, also called number 2 fuel oil.

Right after that deal was struck, Hefner recalled, "The Shah of Iran fell and we had the second oil shock. That scared the hell out of the Panhandle and they eventually agreed to meet any higher price they gave any other producer.

"It was always easy to get something like that," Hefner recalled. "But what I really wanted was a price, and the pipelines wouldn't pay the price. They wanted to tie it to something. I would have had probably $3.50 per MCF just before the Shah fell and we had the last shocks."

After months of political unrest and bloody reprisals against Shah Mohammed Riza Pahlavi, the Iranian ruler was forced out of the country on January 16, 1979. In protest against his regime, oil workers struck refining and production facilities and by the end of 1978 petroleum exports from Iran had come to a halt. Even after the Shah was replaced by the Moslem fundamentalist regime of the Ayatollah Ruhollah Khomeini, technical difficulties and political turbulence prevented production from reaching its prerevolution level.

Although the shortfall from the cessation of Iranian exports constituted only 4% of the oil supplies of the non-Communist world, the scare led to panic buying and a surge in the OPEC price to as much as $23.50 by midyear. By September, gasoline prices shot up to more than a dollar, from about 70¢ per gallon in 1978. According to a banker who was present at a dinner in early 1979 with Sheik Ahmed Zaki Yamani, the Saudi oil minister, OPEC would have been satisfied with a price of $20 to $22 per barrel at that time, which would have allowed the cartel to recover what it lost in the inflation following the embargo of 1973. A major contributor to the run-up in price, he said, was the frenzied effort by the Japanese, who produce no oil of their own, to buy and stock crude oil.

Once again in 1979, as in 1973, the shortage psychology took hold and motorists queued up at gas stations to top off their tanks. In California, Gov. Jerry Brown authorized counties to implement odd–even gas purchasing programs, whereby motorists with odd-numbered plates could buy gas only on odd-numbered days, and those with even-numbered plates could buy on even-numbered days.

On April 5, President Carter went on national television and declared that Americans would have to consume less oil and spend more for it. In an effort to encourage additional production, the President announced a phased oil price decontrol program that would eliminate controls by September 30, 1981. To prevent producers from realizing a bonanza from the withdrawal of price controls, he proposed that Congress enact a 50% "windfall profits" tax on the new revenues. In this climate, it was hard to imagine that oil and gas prices would go anywhere but up.

While the bankers and oilmen were dining with Sheik Yamani, Penn Square Bank chairman Bill Jennings was reiterating his intention in a meeting with his officers to make Penn Square the biggest bank in Oklahoma City. To accomplish that, he ordered all bank officers, according to a former officer, to make at least two customer calls a week.

And about the time Carter was announcing these new measures, Bill Patterson was placing a long-distance telephone call to the letter of credit department at the Seattle First National Bank.

GAS FUMES

B ILL PATTERSON, RECALLED ONE OF HIS FORMER COLLEAGUES, had an uncanny way of ferreting out the big volume guys at the Northern banks. John Boyd, a towering, wide-girthed vice-president at the Seattle First National Bank, was one of the big volume guys. In April 1979 Patterson encountered the fast-talking thirty-six-year-old Boyd by chance in the course of the phone call he made to Seattle First to resolve the letter of credit problem.

Seattle First had issued a letter of credit to a customer in favor of Penn Square Bank, and a technical problem had arisen about some of the language in the document. Patterson straightened out the matter with an officer in the Seattle bank's letter of credit department, concluding the conversation by asking him if Seafirst had an oil and gas group. Patterson was switched over to Boyd, who in April 1979 had started to carve out a small fiefdom at Seafirst by establishing relationships with the entire spectrum of players in the oil and gas business, from producers to refiners.

Patterson explained, as Boyd recalls, "We're a national bank, a small Oklahoma bank specializing in lending for oil and gas. We have a number of correspondent relationships with major institutions and we'd like to meet with you if you're interested."

Boyd was intrigued with Patterson's concept and was pleased when Patterson offered to fly to Seattle to fill him in on more of the details. In April the two bankers had breakfast at the Rainier Club. Curiously, Patterson struck Boyd as awfully formal, for an Oklahoman. They talked about Oklahoma and its economy, and about the prospects for oil and gas exploration in the state. Patterson outlined Penn Square's loan brokerage operation, and offered the name of Continental Illinois as a reference.

Boyd returned the visit less than a month later, when Jennings told Boyd that he hoped Penn Square and Seattle First would enjoy a long-term relationship, emphasizing that the success of the merchant banking* concept was dependent on the bank's skill in documenting and screening credits it originated. The objective, Jennings and Patterson assured Boyd, was to see that no correspondent lost a nickel on a Penn Square Bank loan. Boyd was impressed with what he thought to be the bank's well thought out and articulated strategy. "I checked out Penn Square and asked about Jennings, and got no negatives," Boyd said later. At the time, Boyd recalled, "A gas glut was inconceivable; we were worrying about Mexico cutting us off, and gas seemed safer than oil to the extent that you had regulated pricing."

After two years with the Boeing Corporation, Boyd joined Seafirst in 1970 as a trainee in the trust department, the area of a bank that manages the funds of corporations, unions, and wealthy individuals. He became a financial analyst, and by 1975 he had risen to vice-president and manager of the bank's pension and profit-sharing units.

Trust departments are not for the ambitious. They are not regarded as a stepping-stone to executive management of a large bank, and no one realized this more than Boyd. In 1975 his boss suggested that he consider moving over to the bank's national division, and Boyd was subsequently assigned to Harry Strong, the wiry, bald, senior vice-president who headed up the bank's East Coast calling program.

Boyd and Strong liked each other personally, but the two men were as different in style and temperament as they were in physical appearance. Strong eventually suggested to his energetic subordinate that he might be happier in another area of the bank.

In November 1976 Boyd transferred to the Southwest region, a move he viewed as a demotion. "He thought he was being sent to hell," said one acquaintance. Boyd asked John Nelson, then the head of Seattle First's corporate banking division, "I've done a good job in the city; why am I being sent to the country?" Nelson replied, "You're not doing your arithmetic; that's where the growth is."

Seafirst was not particularly strong in the Southwest. It had no experience in lending to independent oil and gas operators, but Seattle was becoming a kind of way station for Texas oilmen and industry suppliers working on the Alaska pipeline. Seafirst, as one of the largest correspondent banks in Alaska, and the dominant institution in the Pacific Northwest, was asked frequently by oil and gas producers

---

*Traditional banks earn money from the interest on loans they keep on their books, whereas merchant banks make money from transaction fees.

---

to supply credit references on companies doing business in Alaska. Like many other large U.S. banks, Seafirst had extended credit lines to major oil companies such as Arco, Shell, and Exxon. It takes no special skill to put on a line of credit to a major oil company. A bank officer might develop such a relationship by calling on the corporate treasurer, who will agree to a multimillion-dollar credit line without ever intending to use it. But having such risk-free credits in place was enough to convince Seafirst that it was a big-time player in the high stakes game of energy lending. Although some Seafirst officers later contended that the bank wouldn't have gotten into energy if it had not been for the Alaska connection, others described Alaska as a red herring and asserted that the move into energy stemmed more from Boyd's activities in the Southwest than anything else. Said one senior officer, "There wasn't much sex appeal in doing commercial paper back-up lines for General Motors. We were banking a concept, that oil's going to go up. Energy was an easy sell."

It seemed natural, then, to extend Seafirst's reach into Texas and Oklahoma. And Boyd approached this assignment with his characteristic missionary zeal, calling on accountants, lawyers, and other oil and gas industry professionals.

Seafirst had a strong tradition of equipment lending, financing fishing boats and airplanes. Boyd felt comfortable making loans secured by something tangible, something with apparent resale value, and something mobile. Things like drilling rigs. Seattle First was an experienced collateral lender, and took comfort in the belief that the bank would be protected by security agreements on rig or oil and gas reserve loans.

About the time Boyd was prospecting in the Southwest territory, the consulting firm of McKinsey and Company was working at Seafirst on the same strategic plan that it had put in place at Continental and a number of other large banks since the early 1970s.

McKinsey's Robert Waterman, who would later co-author a bestselling book, *In Search of Excellence*, also reportedly felt Seafirst should look outside its traditional geographical market for new lending opportunities to assure continued growth for the bank. Waterman had met Boyd and was impressed with his eagerness to identify prospects in Texas. He recommended to vice-chairman Joe Curtis that an energy department be created and reportedly urged that Boyd, who doubled as Curtis's personal financial adviser, be appointed to run it. According to former bank officers, McKinsey also recommended that Seafirst consider lending to Mexico and Latin America, another area that was fashionable at the time. And both international lending and energy were to be dumped into a newly created world banking group to be headed by executive vice-president John Nelson, who had earned a reputation as "Mr. Corporate Banker" by making, and collecting, loans to the lumber, fishing, and aircraft industries, the mainstays of the Pacific Northwest economy.

All this meshed well with the goals of William Jenkins, Seafirst's tall, patrician chairman, a flamboyant, often sarcastic banker who had committed himself and his institution to a 15% annual growth rate. "Jenkins felt that every year had to be better than the previous one, and if you didn't show an improvement in your return on assets you were on his shit list," said one officer. And another pointed out that with nationwide banking on the horizon, Jenkins was determined to be "the absorber, not the absorbee."

"Bill always made it clear he wanted to keep things moving. To achieve the kind of growth Jenkins wanted," a former executive said, "you just had to do more difficult kinds of business."

Jenkins was not shy about proclaiming his philosophy to the world at large. He once told *Forbes* that "the history of Seafirst is an ongoing conscious decision to be large for largeness' sake."

Jenkins, whose strong resemblance to the actor had earned him the nickname the "Poor Man's Gregory Peck," rose to the top position at the Northwest's largest bank as a result of an understanding reached in the early 1950s between his father, then the president of First National Bank of Everett, Washington, and Lawrence Arnold, the chairman of Seattle First when the Jenkins bank was merged with Seafirst in 1961. After taking over the helm at Seafirst in 1963, Jenkins brought in a psychologist to determine the compatibility of his officers with his own goals for the bank, according to former Seafirst officers.

By all outward appearances, Jenkins seemed to be the embodiment of the conservative statesmanlike banker. In fact, colleagues said, he was a convivial bachelor and partygoer whose temperament was more akin to that of an Oklahoma oilie than a traditional banker. Yet, as one leading industry analyst remarked, "Seafirst never abandoned its solid, conservative view of itself."

The Seafirst chairman also remained above the humdrum day-to-day running of a large bank, and once told a local business publication that at one time he "could balance the bank's books. Now I couldn't possibly. I don't even know what room they're in." Under his direction, in the late 1970s, Seafirst was in a constant organizational turmoil, with sweeping changes occurring every six to nine months. As part of the McKinsey decentralization drive, Jenkins

disbanded the bank's respected senior loan committee and dramatically raised lending authorities for bank officers.

Senior officers recalled that in this period they never had a clear
understanding on who was second in command in the bank—vice-
chairman Curtis or the bank's well-respected president and head of
the branch network, C.M. "Mike" Berry, described as a warm and
lovable man who took early retirement in 1981. Jenkins's management style was to dangle the carrot in front of his top officers and let
them go for it. Berry, former colleagues said, was a "people guy"
who could deal with Jenkins on his own level and was not smitten
with McKinsey and Company.

Executive vice-president John Nelson, the man assigned to lead
the charge onto foreign soil and into the oil patch, was an unassuming and outgoing "seat of the pants" banker whose new assignment
represented a dramatic change in lifestyle. Described by colleagues
as an avid outdoorsman who was in his element fishing for salmon in
Alaska and lending to lumber companies, Nelson became the proverbial fish out of water in dealing with borrowers in Japan and
Latin America. "Nelson was good when he was in the branch system," a friend said, "but when he had a Rolls-Royce waiting for him
on his trips to Switzerland, it became intoxicating." Added another
colleague, "He was a great one-on-one banker, a great salesman."

Eventually, Boyd began to get Nelson's ear and the two men became close personal friends, or so it appeared to their associates. He
and Nelson traveled on business and went bird hunting in Mexico
and Texas together, and fell into a routine of ending the day with
three or four martinis.

Nelson, a better lending officer than a manager, believed in delegating responsibility entirely to his own subordinates. That was fine
with Boyd, who once told a superior, "Don't harness a race horse."
Boyd, according to former associates, tended to lose sight of objectives. "He'd get very excited about a project but just wouldn't know
when to stop," said a colleague.

Boyd, like Jennings and Patterson at Penn Square, and Lytle at
Continental, was an extraordinary salesman and a poor detail man.
It is rare that a bank can find someone strong in both areas. Though
not a good manager himself, Boyd was a devotee of management
guru Peter Drucker, and read everything written by the professor
several times.

Indeed, Boyd was a pack rat who seemed personally as disorganized as the fledgling energy department itself. He stuffed his pockets
with notes to himself and squirreled away files helter-skelter in cab-

inets and drawers. "The joke at Seafirst was—if your desk was a mess—'Who does your decorating, John Boyd?' "

The department, like the bank, was in a state of disarray. At any given time, the lending officers, operations, the credit files, and the note cage were all on separate floors. "It was difficult to grab everything on a single customer," complained a former officer. World banking's loan operations department, like its opposite number at Continental, was what one former Seafirst officer called a holy mess.

Boyd's charisma and sense of humor enabled him to counter objections raised by members of the world banking loan committee to the energy department's loans. "He had a talent for mimicry," said a friend. "He could imitate Okies, Swedes, Arabs, Germans. His sense of humor helped him in relationships with customers and inside the bank."

In the opinion of those who worked with him, Boyd wanted to make his box on the Seafirst organization chart bigger than anyone else's, and he had plenty of support in that effort from a chairman who wanted his flag flying at the top of the corporate mast. In fact, former Seafirst officers say, Jenkins was known to have overridden the world banking loan committee after the committee turned down energy and international loans.

Seafirst had a history, some of it not so happy, of moving out of its area of expertise, geographically and otherwise. In 1974, German banking authorities shut down Bankhaus I.D. Herstatt, one of the country's leading private banks, because of huge losses from foreign exchange trading. Some of the largest and most prominent money center banks in the United States took their hits, including Manufacturers Hanover Trust, giant Bank of America, and Citibank, and even blue-chip Morgan Guaranty. But Seafirst, trying to play with the big boys, racked up one of the biggest claims—$22 million—although $19.5 million was eventually recovered.

Seafirst did manage to avoid the real estate investment trust debacle that entrapped First of Chicago, Chase Manhattan, and to a much lesser extent, Continental Illinois, because it recognized it didn't understand the business and put a firm cap on REIT lending.

To be sure, there were some strong incentives for the feisty Bill Jenkins to turn his gaze away from Washington State. Seafirst dominated its home market like few other banks in the country. In fact, its 60% market share in Washington was said to be the highest of any bank in the nation, and it was clear even in the early 1970s the bank wasn't going to achieve growth in the Pacific Northwest. Seafirst's branch banking network also had provided it with a base of

stable, or core, deposits. Nonetheless, Jenkins decided in the mid-
1970s to pursue what some associates derisively called a "hot
money" strategy: buying short-term funds in the money markets at
the going rate to finance his extraterritorial ambitions.

Additionally, Seafirst, like all banks in Washington State, labored
under a 12% interest rate ceiling on consumer loans under $50,000,
at a time when Seafirst's marginal cost of funds was hovering
around 12.2%. Besides being a major lender to the Pacific Northwest
lumber, fishing, and aircraft industries, Seafirst was also an important retail bank. It therefore took the lead in what proved to be an
unsuccessful legislative battle to raise the usury ceiling to 18%, but
later managed to circumvent the ceiling through a federal law that
permitted consumer loans to be made at one percentage point above
the Federal Reserve discount rate.

On the labor front, Jenkins was embroiled in an ongoing feud
with the bellicose Retail Clerks International Union. Representatives railed at Jenkins at Seafirst's annual meetings, to the point
where chairs had to be bolted to the floor for fear that union activists
might throw them at bank officers. Seafirst, the nation's only union-
ized bank holding company, had refused to recognize the union as
the bargaining agent for its nonsupervisory employees, and the
union retaliated by launching a boycott of the bank and urging customers to pull out their money. Jenkins once told the Seattle *Business
Journal* that "the more rabble-rousing the goddamned union does,
the more disenchanted our employees become."

Meanwhile, the National Labor Relations Board (NLRB) found
that Seafirst was guilty of unfair labor practices and certified the
Retail Clerks International Union as the legitimate bargaining
agent, confirming a 1978 ruling by an NLRB administrative law
judge.

The competitive relationship between Seafirst and smaller archrival Rainier was not the gentlemanly competition of the sort found,
say, in New York, among the Morgan Guarantys, Chase Manhattans, Manny Hannys, and even Citibanks. Rainier chairman Robert
Truex and Jenkins sniped at each other with the same vengeance
that Jenkins and the union activists brought to their battle. That
spirit was seen even in the advertising campaigns of the two banks.
In television commercials touting its automated tellers, Seafirst, a
recognized leader in electronic banking, used an actor dressed in
turn-of-the-century clothing who depicted bank founder Dexter
Horton pointing to the modern bank's achievements. Rainier
dressed up another actor, with a strong resemblance to the Dexter

Horton in the Seafirst ad, and depicted him confronted by a young man who "proved" to him that Rainier's bank machines were better than "cash machines," the trade name for Seafirst ATMs.

While regarded by its Pacific Northwest stockholders (many of whom were elderly couples and other middle-class investors) as the Ma Bell of the Pacific Northwest, the bank always seemed to be in the thick of controversy, largely because of chairman Jenkins's scrappy disposition. Seafirst had earlier been charged by the Internal Revenue Service with illegally deducting $46,000 in payments to a lawyer who allegedly passed the funds on to the majority leader of the Washington State Senate, Democrat August Mardesich, from Jenkins's hometown, Everett. In 1975 these allegations gave rise to what was labeled by the media as the "Mardesich affair" and prompted charges of influence peddling by Seattle First. In May 1979 Seafirst settled with the IRS for $225,000.

Despite these annoyances, Seafirst was looking good where it counted most to Bill Jenkins, his stockholders, and the financial community. The company had just come off a year where its earnings rose nearly 30%, to $53.8 million. Loan volume had grown by 26%, and return on assets rose from 0.91% to 1.00%, making it one of the most profitable banks of its size in the United States. Like Continental, Seafirst had become a favorite among the bank analysts. In early 1978, the San Francisco securities firm of Robertson, Colman called it "one of the highest quality" bank stocks available . Despite the union difficulties, the firm said the affiliation "does not pose any fundamental negatives" to the company's positive assessment of Seafirst stock.

In the fall of 1979, Penn Square sent two deals to Seattle. They totaled about $10 million, and to the Seafirst officers both deals looked good and complete. About the time Seafirst was wiring the proceeds to Oklahoma, two officers from the Northern Trust Company of Chicago decided to drop in to see Bill Patterson.

Norman "Bud" Staub, the new chairman of the Northern Trust Company—known in Chicago as the "Gray Lady of LaSalle Street"—just wanted to dust off his bank's stodgy image and put a few loans on the books.

Late one afternoon in the fall of 1979, Mike Tighe, a convivial, hardworking son of an Irish immigrant, and his colleague, petroleum engineer Frank Creamer, took a giant step in that direction.

Tighe and Creamer, officers in Northern's newly formed energy department, were well aware that Penn Square was emerging as a major player in lending to independent oil and gas companies in

Oklahoma. They had completed several customer calls in Oklahoma City that day, and decided to drop in and introduce themselves to Penn Square's management. They discovered that the man responsible for Penn Square's aggressive reputation was Bill Patterson, a fraternity brother of Creamer's in the University of Oklahoma chapter of Sigma Chi. Bill hadn't changed much since college. He was a name dropper, sprinkling his conversation with the names of Continental Illinois and the First of Dallas, two of the preeminent names in the energy lending business. By this time, the Continental relationship with Penn Square was well established, and Patterson did not fail to remind the visitors of that. But, he offered magnanimously, "There's no reason Continental has to have everything in Chicago. We'll give you a shot at some deals."

To be sure, the Northern Trust officers felt a great deal of comfort knowing two highly respected institutions like Continental and First of Dallas were already doing business with Penn Square. In deciding whether to buy a participation or join a loan syndication, banks look closely at who else is in the deal. "If Morgan's in a credit, you'd better believe you'd take it," one banker said. Morgan Guaranty was not in Penn Square, but Continental was. And when it came to energy, that was an equally impressive recommendation.

The top management of Northern had little understanding of the intricacies of oil patch lending. Executive vice-president Jim Armstrong for example, was taken aback when he heard one of his energy lenders talk about a frac job, the propping open of a petroleum-bearing formation with chemical agents to accelerate the flow of oil and gas. Armstrong thought a frac job was something dirty, according to Mike Tighe.

Northern Trust's foray into energy began in 1977, when the bank initiated a study to identify some new markets that would enable it to break out of its ultraconservative mold. At the time, the chairman of the bank was Edward Byron Smith, the third generation of the Smith banking family to run Northern Trust. Under the Smith family rule, Northern had remained a highly conservative institution that specialized in managing the estates and portfolios of corporations and wealthy individuals. A top priority item at Northern was not energy but the pursuit of rich customers in Florida and Arizona. It was, after all, the gentleman's bank.

Northern Trust was known for avoiding the banking fads that had lured other institutions into disaster—fads such as the real estate investment trusts, which dealt a body blow to its neighbor First Chicago, as well as tanker loans and loans to Third World countries. In fact, bank analysts and competitors noted sarcastically that

Northern shunned loans altogether. Referring to the ninety-year-old Gray Lady, one analyst commented, "You've got to be willing to take some risks if you want to call yourself a bank." In 1978 Northern wrote off a mere $301,000 in bad loans, just 0.02% of its total portfolio, less than some Penn Square oilmen would lose at the gambling tables in Las Vegas in one night. In late 1979, however, Northern took its licks along with other major U.S. banks when it boosted its loan loss provision fifteenfold in anticipation of possible losses from the troubled Chrysler Corporation and Itel Corporation.

While the loan portfolio, what there was of it, was squeaky clean, Northern's growth and earnings performance from 1974 through 1978 had been lackluster. During that period, its annual compound growth rate was 7%, nothing to cry about, as one executive told a reporter at the time, but not the kind of growth that impresses potential investors and bank securities analysts. The upshot of the 1977 study was the creation of a natural resources unit.

Mike Tighe's superiors at Northern were aware of his fascination with energy. The short, ruddy-complexioned vice-president had spent most of his career at the bank as a correspondent bank officer, calling on other institutions on the West Coast and Hawaii. But he had written his master's thesis at Southern Methodist University's Graduate School of Banking on the "use of evaluation of petroleum appraisal reports for the nontechnical banker" and believed that a good credit officer without petroleum industry experience could successfully lend to oil and gas operators, provided he had help from a trained petroleum engineer. Tighe recommended that Northern hire an engineer, and after a lengthy search, the bank recruited Frank Creamer from Amoco. Jay Rudd, a bank officer who had been making international loans out of an office in New York, returned to Chicago to join the group. To kick off the new venture, Northern pulled $75 million in loans and commitments out of other bank departments and turned them over to the fledgling energy department. Northern felt that it would have a leg up on other energy lenders by accelerating the "turnaround time" on oil and gas loans, and that with an experienced petroleum engineer on the staff it could do so safely. And the bank felt by sticking to a policy of financing only those operations with controlling interests in oil and gas wells it could hedge its risk even further.

In early 1979, after waiting twenty-six years for the opportunity to run the bank, sixty-three-year-old Bud Staub was elected chairman, leaving him with just two years to put his personal stamp on the institution. Staub and Northern could not have been oblivious to the inroads made by foreign banks in their territory, and by an increasingly voracious Continental Illinois. With the Smith family no longer exercising day-to-day control, Staub set out to impress Wall Street with his determination to take some risk. Ever sensitive to Northern's reputation for timidity, the newly elected chairman told a financial reporter, "Now with $1.8 billion, you can't say we're not lending money."

At the time, Northern's return on assets, the key measure of profitability, was 0.63, a hairbreadth above the average of 0.61 for the top thirty-five United States banks. Return on equity, an indicator of what the stockholder is getting back on his investment dollar, was an anemic 11.5%, significantly below the average of 14.2% recorded for the thirty-five institutions. This reflected Northern's reluctance to leverage its capital by making more loans. Worse still, Northern was being outperformed by another Chicago bank, the Harris Bank and Trust, which it considered its major rival.

According to former officers, one reason for the bank's lackluster performance was its slowness in granting promotions, and as a result it lost much of its lending talent in the 1970s. "The bank," said a former officer, "became a fertile ground for headhunters."

Like Continental, Northern Trust under Staub moved to give lending units more authority by decentralizing the loan approval process. For a time, said a bank officer, the "energy people at Northern could do no wrong. Everybody else was getting fifty basis points [half a percentage point] over prime, energy would get 1.5 to 2.0%." But there was no guarantee that energy loans would not lead to very nasty surprises. Although Rudd and Tighe knew enough about the energy business not to make glaring errors, they nevertheless would find themselves in some deals that looked surprisingly weak to other Oklahoma City bankers. "When we were dealing with them they were tough, just like you'd expect them to be," said one Oklahoma City banker of the duo from Chicago. "But they must have trusted Patterson more than us because they seemed to buy some pretty shaky deals from Patterson that were out of character for them." Many of the business transactions between Northern Trust and Penn Square would wind up being conducted not in the Chicago bank's paneled offices but at Butch McGuire's, a popular bar noted for its collection of rare Tiffany lamps and located in the heart of Chicago's singles district. Northern's officers had a reputation for being conservative in their lending practices, but quite flamboyant in their personal behavior. Tighe, for one, was a jolly, hail-fellow-well-met Irishman often found standing at the door of Butch McGuire's holding a mug of beer in one hand and greeting guests with the other.

THE SATURDAY NIGHT SPECIAL

B ANKING NEWS IS RARELY MADE ON A SATURDAY NIGHT. BUT ON October 6, 1979, Paul Volcker, the six-foot-seven cigar-smoking chairman of the Federal Reserve Board, had a Saturday night special lined up for the thousands of American bankers streaming into New Orleans for the annual convention of the American Bankers Association. In the previous weeks, trading in the international gold, commodity, and foreign exchange markets had been speculative and chaotic, reflecting worldwide concern about high inflation, growing signs of a recession, and the declining value of the U.S. dollar. Volcker's surprise package, announced that evening to allow the financial markets time to absorb the shock before they reopened on Monday, was a landmark event in American financial history. The newly appointed Fed chairman outlined three moves that would shape the economic climate in the U.S. for the next several years. First, the Federal Reserve announced a 180-degree turnabout in its conduct of monetary policy. For years, the Fed attempted to manage the money supply by focusing on the Fed funds rate—the interest banks charge each other for overnight money. The new policy meant that the Fed would attempt to exert more control over the money supply, and pay less attention to short-term fluctuations in the Fed funds rate.

Additionally, the U.S. central bank raised the discount rate—the rate at which banks can borrow from the Fed itself—from 11% to a record 12% and announced an 8% reserve requirement on large, short-term certificates of deposit, Eurodollar borrowing, and other bank liabilities. All of this meant that money would be much more expensive for banks—and borrowers.

Taken together, these actions would soon have the intended effect of reducing the amount of money available for lending. Although they were welcomed by business leaders and economists as necessary inflation-fighting measures, they heralded what would soon be dubbed the "Volcker recession" and an era of tight money—tight for individuals and businesses of all kinds throughout the country, tight for everyone except the Oklahoma oilies. On October 9 the Dow Jones Average posted the worst decline in six years, and interest rates quickly began their inexorable ascent into the stratosphere.

Ironically, Volcker's timing was just a few weeks short of the fiftieth anniversary of the stock market crash of October 29, 1929. It is often said that if all the economists were stretched end to end, they would not reach a conclusion. But a sizable majority, if asked to name the month and year of the onset of the deepest recession since World War II, would cite November 1979.

Few areas of the country would be hurt worse by the slump in the housing industry that was to follow than the Pacific Northwest, where the forest products industry contributes 20% of the region's jobs and personal income. Likewise, the aerospace industry, of which Boeing was the mainstay, would be hit hard by the drop in airline travel. But these adverse economic developments would convince Bill Jenkins and his associates at the Seattle First National Bank that their strategy of extraterritorial expansion was the correct and prudent one.

Curiously, as Seattle First was seeking to get in on the action in the oil patch, it was forcefully implementing energy conservation measures in its downtown Seattle headquarters building. Such conservation efforts throughout America in the late 1970s would ultimately contribute to the collapse of oil prices.

On November 1, 1979, with little fanfare, deregulation of gas below 15,000 feet took effect as provided for in the Natural Gas Policy Act passed a year earlier. Coincidently, on November 3, an angry horde of Iranian revolutionaries seized the U.S. Embassy in Teheran, Iran, and took fifty-two Americans hostage, and shortly thereafter the Carter administration ordered a halt to imports of Iranian oil, which had already slowed to a trickle. It was yet another reminder that the availability and price of gasoline, home heating oil, and other petroleum products were inextricably bound up with the whims of religious tyrants ruling medieval fiefdoms thousands of miles from America's shores.

The storming of the embassy also made a deep impression on those who earned their living by forecasting the price of oil and gas. It reinforced the conviction that originated with the Arab oil embargo of 1973, that Mideast turmoil would be the rule rather than the exception. That prospect, they were convinced, would continue to exert upward pressure on the price of oil and gas.

In this climate, panic buying sent the price of oil on the spot markets, where oil not on long-term contract is bought and sold, to $42 a barrel by late 1979, even though the official OPEC price was considerably less than that. Japan, for example, with no oil and gas reserves of its own, bought twenty tankers in which to store surplus crude.

The "shortage," however, would prove to be more psychological than real. Some analysts estimated that the excess of production over consumption by this time was more than one million barrels of oil a day. Besides the worldwide slowdown in economic activity, conservation measures prompted by the oil shocks of the early 1970s were quietly eroding demand. These included the use of more fuel-efficient automobiles and improvements in home insulation. Nevertheless, by late 1979 and early 1980 the "experts," with a few notable exceptions, were predicting that oil prices would rise to $70 per barrel or higher within a few years.

The Oklahoma oilies and their Northern bankers would make at least one crucial error. It was, to be sure, a misjudgment that received a lot of intellectual support from some so-called oil and gas experts. They assumed that the oil and gas industry was recession proof; that the price of oil and gas somehow defied the truisms of economics that applied to apples, automobiles, copper, and most other commodities with the possible exception of salt. They concluded that demand for petroleum products was inelastic and would not be affected by the sharp fly-up in price that had occurred since the fall of the Shah of Iran. In fact, in 1979 and into 1980, while many forecasters were predicting $100 per barrel oil within ten years, the recession and conservation measures had not only slowed down but actually reversed what was once thought to be the inexorable rise in the consumption of energy.

Oil and gas are virtually interchangeable in a variety of applications, and the energy equivalent prices of the two fuels generally parallel each other closely. Many large industrial plants can switch from oil to gas or gas to oil in less than twenty-four hours if shortages develop in either fuel or one becomes more cost efficient than the other. In 1979, when the price of a barrel of fuel oil doubled, the price of a thousand cubic feet of deep gas doubled along with it.

"The pipelines," said a former official of Hefner's GHK, "realized deep gas was the last opportunity to tie up large reserves onshore of gas. El Paso, Michigan, Wisconsin, and Panhandle Eastern were the most aggressive." Even pipelines that didn't have pipelines in the area started bidding, in anticipation of building a pipeline later, he said. The bidding soon looked more like a horse sale at the OK Corral than once-staid gas contract negotiations. And gas prices headed for the roof.

Despite their jubilation that deep gas was now economical to produce, and then some, Hefner and his aides feared a consumer backlash over higher gas prices and questioned whether they should book the contracts at those high rates, according to Boots Taliaferro, then the executive vice president of GHK.

Hefner, his victory in lobbying Congress for his deep gas provision notwithstanding, was having very little success in 1979 persuading bankers to finance the stuff. Continental's Jerry Pearson, for one, thought that the reserve estimates Hefner had given him on various wells in the Anadarko were overly optimistic, and that the wells would likely peter out long before Hefner figured they would. They certainly would not provide enough collateral to support the $15 million in loans he was requesting. The concern over high-priced gas contracts and the difficulty in getting bank loans would both prove to be short-lived.

For Penn Square and its upstream banks, the price forecasts put out by oil and gas experts justified escalating the value of their customers' oil and gas reserves by a like amount. These were reserve figures that, in many instances, were already bloated by overly optimistic volumetric estimates cranked out on Apple computers by engineering consultants who gladly plugged their own price assumptions or whatever assumptions their clients specified, into the formula. In this euphoric atmosphere, the crucial distinctions between proved producing reserves—oil and gas likely to be recovered from existing wells—and other categories of reserves, such as "behind the pipe," probable, and possible, whose recovery was much less certain, became unconscionably fuzzy in the minds of some bankers and engineers.

Petroleum engineers are the prima donnas of the oil patch. During the late 1970s and early 1980s, they were in such short supply that there was little banks and oil companies wouldn't do to hire and retain them. And when the boom was on the engineers did pretty much as they pleased. Reserve estimation and valuation became little more than a phony numbers game that, when combined with standby letters of credit, evergreen revolvers, balloon payments, and other "creative financing" devices, justified multimillion-dollar credit lines to customers most banks wouldn't consider for an auto loan.

Toward the end of 1979, in the atmosphere of high oil prices, rising interest rates, and deep gas deregulation, Penn Square first began to grate on other local bankers, as their own customers started to complain to them that they could get a better deal at the shopping center bank. One banker recalled a customer he was straining to lend a quarter of a million dollars to, who said, "I'll just go out to Penn Square."

"He went out there and borrowed three times the amount we were trying to get collateral together to secure," the banker said. "It got to where you were hearing it so much it was an irritant. I didn't like people to say Penn Square to me. It was kind of a rubbing it in type thing. You'd see customers walk out the door because Penn Square was giving them stuff we wouldn't even dream of doing.

"They'd go in real low," the banker said, adding that Patterson and Jennings didn't hesitate to make fixed rate loans at four points below the prevailing rate to snare new customers. Oklahoma City bankers figured Penn Square was betting on a drop in rates, and that these deals would be good over the long haul. If the customer deserves the money in the first place, and is in a position to take his business to another bank, that assumption would not be true, because the customer could ask to renegotiate the rate.

The Oklahoma gold rush was on.

·T W E L V E·

NEW OILIES AND OLD OILIES

"THERE WAS AN ELECTRICITY IN THE AIR," OKLAHOMA CITY AT-torney M. C. Kratz said wistfully, recalling a brief but exhilarating period in Oklahoma history. It was the electricity generated by a lot of people making a lot of money or, more accurately, by a lot of money changing hands very quickly.

By early 1980 it was clear to even the dullest observer that Oklahoma was in the throes of a classic oil and gas boom. One Oklahoma City lawyer knew something had changed when he didn't see his lawyer friends in the courthouse anymore. "I saw them on the street in blue jeans and cowboy boots and asked, 'Are you a cowboy or a truckdriver?'

"They'd say, 'I'm doing some oil deals.' "

And he knew something was wrong when he visited an appliance store to buy a new electric garage door opener. Somehow, the proprietor sensed that he was a lawyer, and he confirmed that in fact he was.

"Are you in any oil deals?" the owner asked.

"No, I'm not."

"Well," the proprietor said, "I've got a little drilling company on the side. Here's a prospectus."

"You could see it on Interstate 40," said Murray Cohen, a short and stocky transplanted New Yorker who found his way to Oklahoma in the 1940s, studied law at the university, and now specializes in rescuing troubled companies. "I'd drive out to Elk City at sixty-two mph and would almost be run over by trucks running pipe out to the oil fields." And then there were the bumper stickers that said, "Oilfield Trash and Proud of It," and "Please Don't Tell My Mother I'm Working in the Oil Patch. She thinks I'm a Piano Player in a Whorehouse."

A veteran landman who represents a major oil company in lease hearings at the Oklahoma Corporation Commission noticed the overnight appearance of literally hundreds of new companies, nearly all of them incorporating the buzz words "resources," "energy," or "exploration" in their names in place of the more traditional XYZ Oil Company, and most of them operated by people with no previous experience in the oil and gas business. There was, for example, Alpha Energy, headed by Terry Felts, a former Oklahoma City policeman, and Hal Clifford's Clifford Resources. And, incredibly, there were companies and partnerships with names like False Hopes Oil Ventures, Shallow Gushers, Last Chance Partnerships, and Phantom Associates. Wyman Fraley, one of the most successful Mercedes-Benz salesmen in the history of Bolen Imports, quit the dealership in 1980 and went into the oil business as Fraley Oil and Gas. Fraley was the proverbial new oilie. He reportedly acquired most of the items in what one observer called the "Oily Kit": lizard cowboy boots, gold chains, gold nugget diamond rings, saucer-sized belt buckle, Rolex watch, Mercedes, and Lear jet.

"The oil business," said Tom Kenan, once the legislative assistant to former Speaker of the House Carl Albert of Oklahoma, "is wide open. Anybody can get into it. You should be smart, but you really just need some money and some luck."

Entrepreneurs with virtually no capital could break into the business by becoming "lease hounds." They bought leases in a "hot" area and sold them as a package to bigger operators, retaining royalty interests in the prospects for themselves. In turn, the larger operators sold the deals to individual investors, again taking a cut in any revenues for themselves. Many deals were what oilmen call "double promotes" or even "triple promotes." That left very little for the investor who was footing the bill.

Penn Square, however, was not the only source of easy credit for people trying to get into the business. Large well-servicing companies set up people in businesses such as welding with little in the way of credit references. "You could get a $5,000 credit line with nothing more than an oil company credit card," said an Oklahoma City attorney.

One observer of the madness said, "Guys were getting into the business by mortgaging everything, their wives, daughters, and the '59 Ford."

A number of new oilmen made the mistake of trying to create their own mini-Mobils or Exxons. These were well operators who set up drilling companies, or drilling contractors who expanded into the operating side of the business. "Typically," said one veteran energy lender, "you find people in one business or another, either finding it or drilling for it. A lot of small companies do a half-assed job of drilling and operating."

One company that decided to do it all—and later regretted it—was little Aggie Oil, one of Bill Jennings's first customers at Penn Square, and one that had bailed him out of some tight spots by taking on a couple of floundering oil deals. "We had a nice income then, we were rolling right along. We thought we'd look around for a rig," said Aggie's Tom Eckroat, "and Patterson and Jennings thought that would be a good idea. When we got to the borrowing stage, things started to be done on a handshake. The documentation was more sloppy." Eckroat and his associates bid on a 6,000-7,000-foot rig, offering $20,000 more than the next highest bidder. At the time, there was a two-month waiting list for rigs. They couldn't build them fast enough. "The other bidder called back and offered us $50,000 more than we'd paid." Penn Square lent Aggie close to $2 million—the full amount of the rig—to complete the deal. "They'd lend us whatever we needed," Eckroat said. Chase, Michigan National, Seafirst, and Continental ultimately took pieces of Aggie Oil deals, although Eckroat says he didn't know who had them until July 1982.

In 1980 there was a frenzy over penny oil stocks, a market based in Denver. "We figured we could take this little sucker public," Eckroat recalled. "We wanted to build a mini-integrated oil company." All the signs pointed toward the feasibility of that effort.

"The United States was buying underground storage caverns," Eckroat said. "And the most conservative economists were saying the boom would last seven years, and some said it would last ten. We decided to be more conservative, and to figure on only three years. We decided to go public and buy two more rigs. Then it hit the fan. We had to hire twenty more employees, and get a computer. It was all downhill from there."

Despite the insatiable demand for rigs and the constant escalation in their price, most prudent banks either avoided rig loans altogether or required that they be backed by oil and gas production. One banker recalled that after the last big oil patch bust in the mid-1950s a rig was worth only what a scrap dealer would pay for it. Adding to the frenzy was the feeling, as one participant put it, that "if I don't get in on this deal, I'm going to miss out." It reminded him of the story of the cowboy on his way to play poker in a local saloon:

"You know they cheat you there," he was advised.

"Yeah," he said, "but it's the only game in town."

With the hordes of newcomers in the business, the cost of drilling began to rise dramatically, shifting from footage rates to the less efficient day rates, where the contractor was paid regardless of his progress in "making hole." Oilmen like Dorsey Buttram, whose father, Frank, was one of the state's early wildcatters and a candidate for governor of Oklahoma, had seen booms and busts before and decided to sit this one out. Dorsey, now in his seventies, was old enough to remember the Great Depression in Oklahoma, when oil sold for 10¢ per barrel. "The history of gas in Oklahoma is more of a surplus than a scarcity," he observed.

Buttram's father was a close friend of Robert Hefner, Jr., but Dorsey strongly opposed the efforts of Robert Hefner 3rd to deregulate deep gas. He drilled only shallow wells, wells in the 8,000- to 10,000-foot range, and believed it was foolish to drill the far more costly deep wells when there was still shallow gas left in the ground. He was opposed to the distinctions between different types of gas made by Congress in the Natural Gas Policy Act, saying "it all burns the same in your home."

Randy Buttram, Dorsey's son, remembers a brief exchange between two friends, both oilmen, when they passed each other in the corridor of a downtown office building. One asked, "What kind of deals are you doing?"

The other, like Buttram a veteran in the business, replied, "Not much. It's too expensive for me. I'll let the shoe salesmen do their thing."

By 1980 there was a mounting resentment of the newcomers among those Oklahoma City oilmen who "earned their stripes doing what they said they would do," as one more experienced oilman put it. Another said of the new oilies, "They didn't know 'come here' from 'sick 'em'."

The Iranian revolution and the long lines at the gas pumps in 1979 sparked such investor interest in oil and gas that it reached the point where anyone who wanted to sell drilling funds could find an outlet for them. Dewey Dobson, who promoted letter-of-credit-backed drilling funds for Copeland Energy, said, "There was a psychological anticipation of increases in oil and gas prices."

In contrast with the new wave of oil finders, who relied heavily on highly leveraged drilling funds and bank debt to finance their operations, established oilmen traditionally have drilled new wells with the profits from existing wells. To make matters worse, the new oilies were totally unprepared for the complex problems of managing lease positions, interests in wells, and inventories of drill pipe, equipment, and supplies. Nor were they capable of properly allocating expenses among the wells.

Oilmen traditionally loathe paperwork. As the pace of activity picked up, few companies saw to it that the pipe taken from a yard was charged to the same well it was used for. In many cases, unscrupulous oilmen actually used these accounting and paperwork problems to their advantage, balancing expenses among wells so that the poor performers would not seem quite so poor to the investors. In addition, the Natural Gas Policy Act, which had established twenty six different gas pricing categories, also created an accounting nightmare for gas companies with production from a variety of sources. "The revenue systems were never set up to deal with it," one operator said. "Whenever there's a change in regulations, the legal department doesn't tell accounting how to put things on the books."

Oklahoma's so-called force pooling and spacing statutes, originally intended to encourage oil production in the state, actually caused leaseholders to commit themselves to participating in many more wells than they were financially or managerially capable of handling. Under these statutes, an operator who wanted to drill a well but who didn't own all the acreage in the area of the prospect could apply to the Corporation Commission for a force pooling order, whereby leaseholders are required to participate as working interest owners or accept a reasonable lease bonus for their holdings.

Nor were the new oilies prepared for the headache of dealing with hundreds of investors and keeping track of the revenues due each of them. A small oil company might have started out with five investors, and almost overnight found himself with 500. "That's one heck of an investor relations problem" said one seasoned oilman.

One of those investors was Byron Tarnutzer, a multimillionaire Newport Beach, California, real estate developer. On February 28, 1980, his stockbroker, Kae Ewing, advised him about an investment opportunity that seemed too good to be true: the 1980 Deep Program of the Copeland Energy Corporation.

Kae Ewing is a massive man, well over six-feet tall and more than 200 pounds, from an old Newport Beach family—a rarity in California, where only a small number of people can trace their roots back more than two generations. Ewing's family goes back five. If there was an aristocracy in southern California, Ewing was a part of it.

Ewing lives in a sprawling contemporary home overlooking the ocean on the Newport Beach peninsula, owned a 40-foot ocean racing yacht, and belonged to Newport Beach's most exclusive yacht and country clubs. His lifestyle enabled him to move easily among the newly rich high-tech entrepreneurs and real estate developers who had cashed in on southern California's real estate boom. With interest rates and oil prices spiraling upward almost in tandem, oil wells were looking considerably more attractive than shopping centers.

In the late 1970s, Ewing quit his job as a broker with Shearson Loeb and formed the brokerage house of Ewing, Creath and Brown with two former tax shelter specialists from San Francisco's Sutro, Inc. Creath and Brown were associates at Sutro of John Casey and Joe Foss, who had earned something of a reputation for being able to find good oil deals. Casey and Foss teamed up to establish their own firm, Casey Foss of San Francisco.

Foss reportedly worked the lawyers and accountants. According to a former associate, he made upward of fifty calls a day to these and other Bay Area professionals who handled the personal financial affairs of prominent Californians. In this way, Foss sold the Copeland program to such luminaries as cartoonist Charles Schultz, the author of Peanuts, winemaker Robert Mondavi, and William R. Hearst, Jr., the newspaper publisher.

Investors in the early programs had to fill out an offering circular showing that they were worth a minimum of $1 million, but the net worth requirement was raised to $3 million in the later programs, according to Ewing.

"Patterson would sit at a desk in San Francisco," Ewing said, "flipping through piles of applications stacked in front of him, and say, 'This guy's out, this one's in,' like a rush chairman choosing new pledges for a college fraternity house."

Craig Copeland, the youthful head of Copeland Energy and a protégé of Penn Square Bank director Carl Swan, enjoyed putting oil and gas prospects together but disliked selling, preferring to remain home in Oklahoma City and play polo. He left the marketing to Dewey Dobson, a handsome, articulate lawyer in his mid-thirties, whom one investor described as a combination of sophisticated lawyer and slick salesman.

Dobson was funny. He had a knack for rattling off down-home one-liners like no one Ewing had ever met. On one occasion, Ewing was wearing a Western shirt with chrome tips on the collar, prompting Dobson to quip in his melodic Oklahoma drawl, "Boy, you've got more chrome on you than a '59 Mercury." The Californians felt comfortable around the oilmen: the Oklahomans' sense of humor and easy manner greased the relationship and made them feel they were doing business with good friends.

But in 1980 it did not take the golden tongue of a Dewey Dobson to sell drilling funds to rich Californians. One drilling fund merchant said that twenty-five out of every hundred prospects contacted went for the bait.

The arrangement between Ewing and Casey Foss called for the Ewing firm to share the 8% commission on every Copeland drilling fund unit they sold with Casey Foss.

Sutro, Casey Foss, Ewing, and brokerages like it throughout the country were to investment capital what Penn Square was to bank debt, steering hundreds of millions of investors' dollars into 25,000-foot holes—many of them dry—in the Anadarko Basin.

Casey and Ewing flew out to Oklahoma City for the first time in February, where they and the Copeland people dined at Michael's Plum, a restaurant that featured lunch-hour lingerie fashion shows and which was one of the in spots of the Oklahoma new oilies. "Patterson," Ewing recalled, "came by for about fifteen minutes to shake hands. He appeared to be trying to help Copeland get started."

When Tarnutzer, Ewing, and Dobson met on February 28, Ewing and Dobson told him that because of the "special relationship" that existed between Copeland and Penn Square, and because of his own extraordinarily strong financial condition, the bank would finance 100% of his investment. Craig Copeland, they explained, was a former employee of Carl Swan, a successful oil finder who a few years before had made a fortune on the sale of his Basin Petroleum. Swan himself had demonstrated his continued faith in his former employee by purchasing 25% of Copeland stock. The Penn Square note was a sure giveaway. It matured in five years, when it would be renewable for another five years. Tarnutzer wouldn't even have to pay interest out of his own pocket. For the first two years, it would be covered by production profits, and then out of partnership funds for the remaining three.

Tarnutzer signed a $150,000 note due March 1, 1985, at 1% above Chase Manhattan Bank's floating prime. Subsequent programs were backed by letters of credit on which Penn Square would charge a fee of 1–2 points. California real estate had enjoyed a boom, which made investors like Tarnutzer wealthy in the first place. But with the Federal Reserve's move toward tighter credit, interest rates were creeping upward. At the same time, oil and gas prices were rising rapidly.

So in 1980, Tarnutzer would have had a variety of good reasons to invest in a tax shelter drilling program. One of them would have been what tax experts call "bracket creep." Rising inflation and commensurate higher incomes in the late 1970s made more and more U.S. taxpayers subject to higher tax brackets. In 1975, for example, 756,000 taxpayers, representing 1.1% of all tax returns, paid taxes at a marginal tax rate of 50% or more. By 1980 more than 1.25 million taxpayers, or 1.4% of all returns, fell into that category, a 65% increase in just five years in the number of taxpayers who could benefit from tax shelters. Moreover, tax experts point to a growing sense during that period that the tax system was unfair, with the result being more cheating. There was, one Washington, D.C., tax authority said, a decline in taxpayer compliance and a heightened search for legal ways to avoid taxes and illegal ways to evade them.

As the pace of oil and gas drilling picked up, which Penn Square in turn helped to fuel, Jennings and Patterson found new and imaginative short cuts to enable them to lend more money and lend it faster. They gave new meaning to the familiar marketing slogan, "convenience banking." Two of those short-cut devices were the blank note and the dummy note. Amid the frenzy to drill wells and buy leases, Patterson decided that it was a gross imposition on a busy oilman to ask him to come into the bank personally to sign a note, whether it was for $50,000, $500,000, or $5 million. "Sign all these, let me keep them in my desk. If you need any money just call me up and I'll fill in the amount. We'll take care of it," he told borrowers. So he'd ask a customer to sign a stack of blank notes, which would be filed in a drawer and completed when the customer called to say he needed money.

"You could walk in the door," said a former officer, "without a financial statement or any formal written proposal, and if what you outlined verbally sounded feasible you could sit down and sign your name to a note and maybe some oil and gas mortgages all prepared in blank." According to one former officer, most of the documents that were signed at Penn Square were signed in blank.

Blank notes, as well as guarantees signed in blank, also gave Patterson enormous flexibility in moving loans around within Penn Square and substituting the credit of one customer for that of another whose loans were on the verge of going bad. It became the most elaborate shell game in American financial history. Because the customer got his money before he supplied any documentation, such as mortgages or assignments on his collateral, there was little incentive to provide it later. This held true not only for oil and gas loans—or what were supposed to be oil and gas loans—but installment and real estate loans as well.

One former officer contends that because loans were made on that blank note basis, "documentation slipped through the cracks. Things were moving so fast that if the borrower never returned the documents you'd never know it. At one point, there were only three loan officers and some support people managing a $1 billion portfolio," he said. "There were so many demands on your time, there was just no easy way to follow up."

One customer recalls being told by a Penn Square officer, " 'You're on the road so much, why don't you just sign a bunch of notes in blank for us and when you're ready to invest in a program, just call and we'll fill them in ' So I signed fourteen notes in blank. A month later, the officer's secretary calls and says, 'We don't know how to tell you this, but we've lost all fourteen of those notes,' " he recalled. "Three weeks later they phoned and said, 'We found them! We found them!' The next day I took all my money out."

Dummy notes were like slugs in a soda machine. They looked like notes and felt like notes, but in fact they were a means of fooling the system so that funds could be advanced to a borrower before he came in, or without his having to come in to sign bona fide loan documents. This device was also used to advance money to borrowers whose loans had been approved but who couldn't wait for documentation to be completed to get their money. Such practices expose a bank to potentially grave problems.

Another "convenience" for borrowers was Penn Square's laxity on overdrafts. "I never truly understood how someone could be writing checks before they cleared their loan," said one director. Overdrafts were a persistent subject at board meetings. Patterson would explain that certain overdrafts were cleared up—a line would be drawn through items on the list—but others would appear to take their place, the director said. An overdraft is essentially a loan, and in fact Patterson made overdrafts disappear from the list by making loans to customers to replace the overdraft.

There were two distinct types of sloppiness at Penn Square Bank. Some of it, like the blank and dummy notes, was intentional. Some of it was unintentional. One appalling example is that of a nineteen-year-old secretary who was responsible for preparing oil and gas mortgages, which required her to figure out working interest ownerships of wells to several decimal places. Unfortunately, she didn't know the difference between a decimal and a percent. On a document that was intended to secure the bank's interest in an oil and gas property, she might, for example, type out .0057%, instead of .0057. Occasionally, someone would catch a mistake on an oil and gas mortgage and change it with correction fluid on the copies on file at Penn Square or on those sent to an upstream bank, but not on the one that mattered: the copy of record filed in the county courthouse. Apparently no one at the upstream banks ever questioned why there were frequently spaces where the percent sign had been. Said one lawyer who later had to reconcile some of these discrepancies, "They must have had one helluva budget for white-out."

Besides using blank and dummy notes, Patterson introduced an instrument to banking that could have been called the "negotiable cocktail napkin." One of the recipients of this document was twenty-six-year-old Sam Villyard, a golden-haired OU dropout and former wrestling star who would have looked quite at home riding a surfboard on to a southern California beach. Villyard had been playing flag football with Patterson on a team captained by a Zane Fleming, a close friend of the Penn Square officer. At the time Villyard was looking for money to take over his father's polyethylene pipe business. Insta-Pipe, Inc., supplied drilling contractors with tubing used to transport water to mix with drilling mud. Villyard asked Fleming if he knew of any "aggressive bankers with stroke" who might help him do the deal. "Dummy, you've been playing football with one of the most aggressive guys in the business," Villyard recalled Fleming as saying.

"My daddy called me the tooth fairy," Villyard said, when the young entrepreneur got a loan from Patterson for well over half a million dollars, even after the company had posted losses of about $50,000. Shortly thereafter, Villyard was back in the bank for more money. "Oh, damn, what for?" Patterson asked. Insta-Pipe was overdrawn by $50,000. Patterson scribbled $50,000 and his signature on a napkin and told him to "take this to Wilson," another bank officer, who subsequently advanced the funds. Although Villyard was the nemesis of many a Penn Square loan officer, he endeared himself to the secretaries by sending them thousands of dollars worth of long-stem roses; the cards accompanying them were signed "The Polyethylene King."

Bill Patterson would no more turn down an athlete, particularly a football player, and especially a University of Oklahoma football player, for a loan than he would his best friend. In fact, Patterson often cited a prospective borrower's athletic prowess in his loan write-ups, when there were any, and Penn Square's growing stable of borrowers included many former OU football players who had since turned pro.

Oklahoma's enthusiasm for OU football can be more properly described as an obsession. At any home game, the bleachers at Oklahoma Memorial Stadium in Norman will be filled with 75,008 cheering fans, most of them wearing the red- and- white sweatshirts and field jackets of the Big Red. Coach Barry Switzer is a compact, square-jawed man who savors his celebrity status as the coach of one of the top college teams in the nation, and the fringe benefits that go along with it. One of those benefits was easy credit at Penn Square Bank. Switzer would later contend that Patterson had assured him that the maturity dates on his notes were a mere formality, and that under no circumstances would the notes be called for five to seven years, when the revenues from his oil and gas investments would be enough, it was hoped, to repay interest and principal.

Despite his success on the gridiron, coach Switzer's extracurricular activities, including involvement in a chain pyramid scheme, often proved an embarrassment to officials of the University of Oklahoma, a school of such modest academic standing that a top official once remarked that he wanted to build a university "that our football team could be proud of."

In early 1980, national bank examiner Bill Chambers returned to Penn Square Bank to discover that it was operating on "the ragged edge of acceptability." The problems he uncovered—excessive "substandard" loans, inexperienced staff, inadequate capital, and low liquidity, among others—qualified Penn Square for membership in a small, select club run by the Comptroller of the Currency. Penn Square had earned a 3 on the Comptroller's rating scale of 1 to 5, and thereby made it onto an exclusive "watch list" of the most poorly managed banks in the United States. Penn Square was euphemistically designated a "special project." Beep Jennings took strong exception to the criticisms, calling them unjustified and unfair, according to officials of the Comptroller of the Currency.

By this time, the Dallas regional office of the Comptroller of the Currency was aware that Penn Square's participations were heavily oil- and gas-related, and it was worried about how heavily dependent the bank's liquidity was on the sale of these participations. Part of the problem may have been that Patterson loved to sell $100,000 certificates of deposit almost as much as he enjoyed selling loan participations. A candy store would go broke if it sold bars of chocolate the way Patterson peddled CDs. According to bank officers, Patterson sometimes sold CDs at more than six points above the market rate, apparently believing that the bank could survive by selling cheap and buying dear. "He was criticized for this," an officer recalled, but his explanation was, " 'This ole boy is going to be doing a lot of borrowing from us.' There was always an answer."

The bank exam was completed in April with little help from Patterson, who had just been promoted to senior vice-president and always seemed to be flying somewhere. The exam report noted that 1979 earnings were excellent but that liquidity was strained, capital was eroding, growth was excessive, and the loan portfolio was deteriorating. The regulators were also concerned about the uncomplimentary street talk about Penn Square. Said one former examiner, "Other bankers would say, 'Who the hell is examining Penn Square Bank? They stole a loan from us that wasn't worth shit.'"

One examiner's version of a meeting with Patterson to review the loan portfolio was undoubtedly one of the most bizarre encounters between a banker and his regulator since the United States government began supervising banks in the 1800s. Behind Patterson's desk were shelves lined with a colorful array of caps bearing the logos of Penn Square customers. The examiner asked Patterson, "Well, what about E-Z Lay Pipe?" Patterson reached back and pulled E-Z Lay's cap from the shelf, put it on his head, and turned to the examiner, "Well, what about it?"

"Okay," the examiner said, "tell me about Trigg Drilling."

Patterson removed the E-Z Lay cap, placed it back on the shelf, and put on Trigg Drilling.

The examiner named a company that Patterson had no hat for. Instead, he pulled his wild card, a Mickey Mouse cap with strings dangling down from the ears. Patterson once again turned to the national bank examiner, jiggled the strings to make the ears flap, smiled, and said, "Well, what about it?"

Banks that make it to the problem bank list suddenly gain recognition by the Comptroller's Washington bureaucracy. Just for the fun of it, one Washington official took a pencil to Penn Square's balance sheet and figured that if the bank kept growing at the current rate, it would be the third largest bank in the country by the end of the century. Awestruck by Penn Square's phenomenal growth, a senior official of the Comptroller of the Currency in Washington remarked to a colleague, "There's something in Oklahoma City that's growing. It's weird. It's just weird."

THE GOLD CHAIN BOYS

PATTERSON'S LOVE OF FOOTBALL WAS MATCHED ONLY BY THOMAS Sidney Orr's fondness for the Oklahoma quarter horse, a breed peculiar to the West, named for its ability to run one-quarter of a mile faster than any strain of *Equus caballus*. By the spring of 1980, banker-horseman Orr, along with a motley band of horse traders and promoters wearing chrome-studded cowboy shirts and gold chains, had turned Orr's second-floor Penn Square Bank office into their Oklahoma City tack room. It served also as the headquarters of a multimillion-dollar quarter-horse loan and brokerage scheme masterminded by Orr and fueled by the deep gas boom in the Anadarko Basin. Even more damaging to Penn Square Bank than the millions in worthless horse loans Orr ultimately made on his own were the swindlers and deadbeats who continued to milk the bank dry long after Orr was put out to pasture.

Oklahoma is to quarter horses what Kentucky is to thoroughbreds. The state has adequate grass and water, and, most important, a sense of tradition arising out of the horse's vital role in taming the American West. Because of these qualities, breeding farms cluster around Oklahoma City, an arrangement that enables horse buyers from around the country to fly in, rent a car, and inspect a large number of animals in one day. "It's based on the shopping mall concept," says one trader. As the oil and gas boom escalated, horses emerged as one of the status symbols of wealthy oilmen, who were able to write off purchase costs, upkeep, and farm maintenance expenses.

It was for these reasons that in the mid-1970s Orr, a stocky man known for a rather rough-hewn manner, decided to quit his job at the Bank of America in California and move to Oklahoma. Orr told an acquaintance that the crime problem in California had gotten out of hand and someone had willed him some property in Oklahoma.

"Orr was a horse nut," a friend recalled. "All he knew was horses. You'd ask him who he'd think would win the Democratic nomination, and he'd say, 'E-Z Jet or Seattle Slew.' "

In 1976 Orr landed at the First National Bank of Enid, an oil and gas center and a wheat-farming city of 50,000 in the rolling plains of north-central Oklahoma. Orr wasted little time in making it known around the tiny bank that he intended to become its president, despite the fact that lending chief Bill Harris was next in line for the post. According to one director, "Orr was terrible on paperwork. He knew he wasn't going to be president of the bank, and was told he wouldn't." Sources close to the Enid bank say that loan documentation was always a big problem with Orr. "He would say something was being handled when it wasn't," one observer said. "He'd give different stories to different people. He was a salesman, a go-getter, but the bank didn't have confidence in him."

While he was capable of doing the kind of financial analysis that is supposed to precede the granting of a loan, Orr was bored by the tedious details of prudent banking. Moreover, his associates had become suspicious of some of his dealings, and there was a general feeling of relief when he resigned to accept a position at Penn Square.

Ironically, Orr was hired in response to criticism from the national bank examiners that the bank lacked experienced lending personnel. Jennings reportedly emphasized to Orr, as he had to other Penn Square officers, his goal of making Penn Square Bank the largest bank in Oklahoma City, and Jennings trumpeted him as the seasoned lender who would help make that happen. Only a small fraction of his income, however, came from his $44,000 salary. Orr literally made money coming and going. He arranged loans for the buyers of his own horses, which he sold at prices that were grossly inflated because of the easy availability of credit provided by Orr through the bank.

Operating as a broker, Orr exacted a 10% fee for arranging the sale of horses for others, often taking the fee in the form of points on Penn Square loans. "He had an inner circle and an outer circle," said one observer. "In the inner circle the buyers didn't know the sellers. But they all knew the extra cost was for points on loans."

To disguise his wheeling and dealing from other Penn Square officers, Orr wired the loan proceeds to the borrower's account at an out-of-state bank, and in turn the borrower paid Orr his fee through an account at the First National Bank of Chandler, a small town northeast of Oklahoma City. While taking special care to hide his transactions from the bank, he boasted openly to customers about earning $50,000 on horse deals over a single weekend, and how he expected to make more than $400,000 in one year. Orr's easy lending practices attracted horsemen from around the country. As one member of the Oklahoma horsey set told a local reporter, "It took longer to pick out the color of your checks than to get a loan from Tom Orr."

In a one-year period, Penn Square Bank became one of the largest horse lenders in the country. "It didn't take long for people in the business in the United States to find out Orr was a significant horse lender," said U.S. attorney Bill Price. At the time, according to one prominent Oklahoma horseman, there weren't any other banks in the country that were putting money on quarter horses in a significant way, although a few in New York had carved out a niche by making loans on thoroughbreds. According to a veteran of the horse business, "Typically, the guy who gets a horse loan is a flashy promoter type. They lend to a guy who impresses them the most. Not to the guy who brings a financial statement on the back of an envelope, who is probably the honest one."

During the Penn Square-generated horse boom, horsemen were paying upward of $1 million each for quarter horses. "No quarter horse is worth a million, but people got to believe they were," a local dealer said. In his opinion, "Penn Square controlled, and wrecked, the quarter-horse industry. It had a greater effect on pumping up the horse boom than the oil boom."

According to former Penn Square officers, Orr camouflaged his activities by splitting the loans, which were almost always unsecured, into pieces and by noting that they were intended for "oil and gas investment" or "working capital" on the worksheets.

"He used the same modus operandi for all his customers," according to a former Penn Square employee. "Orr sent his sidekick, Clark Long, a former national bank examiner, out to the airport to pick up a customer. They came in, spent an hour in Orr's office, and opened an account. He'd start out by making a loan of $50,000 or $60,000, always for working capital. One guy's financial statement went from $300,000 to $5 million in six weeks."

When Orr and Long weren't trading quarter horses at Penn Square Bank, they were entertaining customers at the Boardroom, a private club tucked away in a small back room at nearby Raffles, a restaurant owned by a horseman and Penn Square customer. The

Boardroom was equipped with a bar, one-way mirror, and side door so members could make a quick escape if they spotted someone coming in they wanted to avoid.

In the spring of 1980, much of the talk at the Boardroom centered on the $30 million syndication of the breeding rights for E-Z Jet, the all-time biggest money-maker in the history of quarter-horse racing. E-Z Jet was ultimately ruined as a stud horse through overbreeding, according to one trader, but in the meantime Thomas Orr earned huge profits buying, selling, and financing shares in the famous stallion.

No one was more smitten with E-Z Jet than Ken "Truck" Tureaud, a flamboyant and high-living real estate and oil and gas promoter whom Orr met at a horse sale while still at the First National Bank of Enid. In the late 1970s, Tureaud suffered adverse publicity in Michigan because of a Securities and Exchange Commission investigation into the activities of his Professional Oil Management operations. In a 1977 complaint the SEC charged Tureaud with misrepresenting facts in the sale of interests in oil and gas leases and stock of POM and diverting $1 million from a POM stock sale to purposes other than drilling. SEC documents state that he paid secret fees and commissions and filed misleading registration statements inflating his oil and gas properties by $1.6 million. According to the securities regulatory agency's charges, Tureaud's financial statements claimed to show earnings when there were actually losses.

Tureaud, a former first-string University of Michigan halfback and onetime eighth-round draft pick for the Dallas Cowboys, sold stock in one of his companies, Racing Stables of America, on the pretense that he would acquire a National Football League expansion franchise and that a former NFL head coach would coach the new team. The SEC enjoined Tureaud from committing further violations of antifraud statutes.

That was not an isolated incident in Tureaud's checkered career. Originally from Ann Arbor, he moved to California in the 1960s, started a swimming pool business, which was cited for securities violations, and later founded Acry-Dent, a false teeth franchise, tapping his football player friends for investments in these deals. Tureaud's other enterprises, according to a report in the *Tulsa Tribune,* included a wild animal refuge, Jingle Jangle Partnerships, and Ding Dong, Inc. In fifteen years of relieving people of their money, Tureaud became well known to the FBI, which filled a small room with files on his shenanigans. In more recent years, Tureaud's once-muscular six-foot frame deteriorated, his hairline receded, and a prominent beer belly gave him the appearance of an overweight former football player.

But if Ken Tureaud was less than impressive in person, he possessed one attribute—a dynamic telephone presence that enabled him to bilk unsuspecting investors out of millions of dollars. Said one acquaintance, "He was a master at using the phone. I was convinced he had some kind of device hooked up to the phone to make him seem more masculine, because he sounded entirely different in person." Tureaud, said another acquaintance, "had an ability to charm people beyond what was healthy for them."

Orr began lending to Tureaud while he was still at the Enid bank, and when he left for Penn Square he brought along Tureaud and a coterie of customers who shared his interest in quarter horses. One of the first loans Orr made to Tureaud at Penn Square was small by Penn Square standards: an $84,400 loan ostensibly for a condominium in Tulsa, where Tureaud had established a company, Saket Petroleum, that would become the foundation for his activities in Oklahoma. In fact, according to a complaint filed later by the U.S. attorney in Oklahoma City, the loan, like many others Orr made to Tureaud and other horse fanciers, was merely a front for a horse deal, since Tureaud had bought the condo a week earlier and paid for it out of other funds. The proceeds of the loan were deposited in Saket's account and out of that amount Orr ordered $70,000 paid through his Chandler bank account to two cronies in the horse business. In turn, Tureaud often paid off Orr by drawing checks on his account at a bank in Riviera Beach, Florida, payable to one of Orr's horse agent associates, which Orr then deposited in his account at the First National Bank of Chandler.

Sometimes Orr himself got cheated, as in the case of a $150,000 loan made to Ken Tureaud on July 15, 1980, supposedly for working capital for Saket Petroleum. This time the money was used for a partial payment on a horse named Miss Jelly Roll. Orr was to get a $20,000 brokerage fee but never received it from the seller. And months later, Orr advanced another $650,000 to Tureaud for working capital, $90,000 of which went for a payment on Miss Jelly Roll and the remainder for real estate, personal expenditures, and other horses. Tureaud's stable included eight of the ten best mares in the country, according to a former associate.

Tureaud lived opulently, indulging a passion for Picassos, Mercedes-Benz automobiles, and white mink bedspreads, as well as horses. Orr, as the financier of Tureaud's lifestyle, also loaned him the money in 1980 to buy a $425,000 Jet Commander through LaCava Management of Encino, California, a firm co-owned by a Paul LaCava, a mutual friend of the two men. Although Tureaud took delivery of the jet, the seller never got his money and later sued LaCava for $10 million. As for LaCava, he was, according to newspaper reports, sentenced to six months in prison on a marijuana smuggling charge for having used his company as a front for the operation.

The foundation for Tureaud's dealings in Oklahoma was the Morris Field in Okmulgee County, just south of Tulsa. Phillips Petroleum had skimmed the cream off the field in the 1930s, but it contained enough reserves so that an operator could boast of a high success rate, even though production declined rapidly after the first few months. It was a field tailor-made for a Ken Tureaud type of oil field scam. "You could call your investors and say we made a well," said one observer familiar with the field. "And when production drops off you can always say we've got some problems and have to spend more money to rework the well." An investor who bought into a Ken Tureaud deal would have the opportunity to get into future deals. Tureaud would typically bill the investor for his share and if he didn't remit the funds he'd lose the chance to invest again later. "Next month we've got a couple of wells going on line that'll blow your socks off," Tureaud would say. "It was the usual high-pressure stuff to keep you going," said a source well acquainted with Tureaud's methods.

An essential element in Tureaud's strategy for recruiting investors was his practice of surrounding himself with a few people with impressive credentials. One such individual was former Sinclair Oil Company executive Hugh Binford, whom Tureaud hired as president of Saket in late 1979. Originally from Wyoming, Binford moved to Tulsa after losing a 1978 Republican primary race for the U.S. Senate in his home state. Tureaud brought in Binford over George Pretsch, a strapping young German national who had worked for him for several years as a personal chef, gofer, and babysitter for his three children at the family's 14-bedroom mansion in Palm Beach, Florida.

Tureaud owned all the perks needed to persuade prospective investors in his Florida real estate or Oklahoma oil and gas deals they were dealing with a big-time operator.

"When a guy has his and hers Jet Commanders, limousines in Florida and Tulsa, and a mansion in Palm Beach, you don't ask too many questions," an acquaintance observed. "People just don't think to check." At the same time, Walter Heller and Company, a large commercial finance company, was propping up Tureaud with millions in loans on his Florida real estate ventures, adding to an investor's sense of security. But a former Penn Square officer said later, "He wasn't the kind of guy you'd want to shoot pool with, let alone lend money to."

One former bank officer recalls that Tureaud, driven in a black stretch limousine by Preacher Smith, a burly black piano player at Raffles who occasionally chauffeured Penn Square customers to and from the airport, made a habit of breezing into the bank early on Friday afternoons and announcing, "Okay, it's time to party." Preacher, wearing red cowboy boots and hat, followed Tureaud into the bank carrying a large ice bucket filled with bottles of champagne.

One of the biggest investors in Saket Petroleum was Denver commodities wizard Thomas D. Chilcott, who had been introduced to Tureaud by an ex-partner. A studious-looking and soft-spoken man then in his early thirties, Chilcott ran a commodities investment scheme out of a "war room" filled with computer screens and dealt in all kinds of commodities from silver to pork bellies. He operated out of a converted garage in Fort Collins, Colorado, where he assembled a sophisticated computer system capable of charting gold and silver trading back to the early 1970s. Recalled one former investor, "It was set up so that when the London exchanges opened in the middle of the night, he'd get all the trades. He used generators so that if the electricity failed he wouldn't go down."

Sometime in 1980 Tureaud introduced Chilcott and his wife to the Penn Square fraternity, where he impressed loan officers as a "very conservative-looking" man who looked more like a choir boy than a commodities trader. They were dressed in black, like Mormons, one former officer recalls, adding that Chilcott could easily have passed for an accountant at a Big Eight firm. Chilcott clearly did not fit the mold of the big-time promoter. He was family-oriented, wore no jewelry, and owned a home that was described as nice, but not extravagant. According to one acquaintance, his only luxury was a used Lear jet that he had rebuilt. "Chilcott and Tureaud were like day and night," the acquaintance observed.

In fact, Chilcott Commodities and Chilcott Portfolio Management and Chilcott Futures Fund were nothing more than variations on the classic Ponzi scheme that survived only because Chilcott was able to persuade hundreds of profit-seeking investors that he never had a losing month. According to James P. Johnson, trustee for the

129

now-defunct Chilcott Commodities, Tureaud blew into Denver and showed Chilcott his $12 million financial statement, and Chilcott showed Tureaud his $20 million statement. Tureaud wound up investing $2 million with Chilcott, and Chilcott borrowed from Penn Square to invest in Acry-Dent and Saket, although Tureaud is said to have misapplied $1 million of Chilcott's money.

One of the largest investors in the Chilcott Fund was the Collins family of Longmont and Denver. Kim Collins, in his early thirties, was a builder of single family homes in the Rocky Mountain states. Ned, his father, had sold his successful canteen business in the late sixties and retired, and brother Wayne "Doc" Collins had made millions selling hot dogs and Crackerjacks in stadiums and concessions around the country. Kim and his father tiptoed into the Chilcott deal in mid-1977 with token investments of $20,000 apiece, and received a return of up to 5% per month. "Occasionally he'd call," said Collins, "and say, 'Do you have an extra $50,000? Gold's going to go crazy.' In those special situations, we told him we had to have our money back in forty-five days. We got our money and a nice return."

Then, in September 1979, the Collins family took the big plunge. Chilcott phoned to say his broker had made a big mistake in his favor on a silver contract, and he needed $1.25 million to meet a margin requirement. "We went ahead and did it, we gave him half a million. Silver went through the ceiling, and then we gave him a total of $1.6 million. After that we just poured money into it." No such error had been made, and only through his duplicity did he avoid going broke, according to later charges by the U.S. attorney in Denver. This is one example of how Chilcott took one customer's money, à la Ponzi, and used it to pay off others.

Chilcott once staged a commodities seminar at a Denver hotel that played to a packed house of several hundred eager investors. "They were excited and happy. Everybody in Fort Collins thought he walked on water," Collins said, adding that Chilcott "liked gold, silver, soybeans, and cotton, the big trade items. He stayed away from potatoes, eggs, the small stuff.

"He was a genius as far as numbers were concerned. He would tell you something and three months later he'd have total recall," Collins said. "But it was all false."

Just as Chilcott and Tureaud invested with each other, they shared each other's investors. It was through Chilcott that the Collins brothers became acquainted with Tureaud. "You've got to meet this man Tureaud," Chilcott told Collins. As Collins recalls it, Orr and Tureaud flew into Fort Collins on one of his jets, the one previously owned by the late actor John Wayne. They arrived late, and Chilcott had to call the airport to have the runway lights turned on. In July 1980 Collins and his father bought Chilcott's interest in Tureaud's Saket Petroleum for $2.5 million. Later, after obtaining credit lines totaling $500,000 from Penn Square Bank, and flying to the Morris Field by chartered jet for Tureaud's dog and pony show, they kicked in another $2.2 million. "The only reason we went with Tureaud was Chilcott," said Collins later.

Ultimately, Tureaud and Chilcott concluded they had bilked each other, Tureaud having overbilled Chilcott for his share of the expenses on the Morris Field, and Chilcott having ripped off Tureaud on the commodities scheme. Said one observer of the two-way con game, "They were scratching each other's back and screwing each other at the same time."

Tom Orr, while genuinely crooked, was a mere sideshow to the main event, Bill G. Patterson, but former officers say Orr may have had a hand in motivating Patterson, and vice versa. Having joined the bank with a higher title than Patterson (Orr was an executive vice-president while Patterson was a senior vice-president), Orr apparently expected to be Patterson's boss, and the two men did not get along at all. "They got into a horse race for the presidency of the bank," recalled one officer. "They were in a contest to see who could book the most loans."

Patterson, however, was emerging as the middleman between the new oilmen of Oklahoma and the money men of Chicago. And his zany style was becoming well established. One of his trademarks was a habit of keeping a lot of people waiting. As the boom in Oklahoma heated up, the reception area outside his second-floor office on a typical business day was invariably packed with customers and would-be customers, and the crowd even spilled over into the corridors, coffee rooms, and staircases of the tiny, three-story shopping center bank. Office space was at such a premium that millions in oil and gas deals were signed and booked over the sink in the second-floor janitor's closet.

One customer recalls visiting Penn Square Bank on a typically chaotic day. "Girls were typing furiously and there were papers all over," he said. Dozens of people were waiting in the reception area. Patterson stood on the coffee table, grinned and said, 'Let me have your attention. We're out of money. You'll have to come back tomorrow.'"

Patterson, however, was democratic in his treatment of customers.

Everybody had to wait. One new customer, who had borrowed more than $30 million from Penn Square after shifting his account from another bank, thought that he would be ushered in to see Patterson on a moment's notice, and was astounded to discover he would have to stand on line like everyone else.

"I asked one of Patterson's junior officers if J.D. Allen had to wait. She said yes."

"What about Swan?" he asked "Him too."

"How about Hefner?" "Even Bobby Hefner," she said.

Hefner and Patterson had become close friends, but the two played a game of one-upmanship in seeing who could make the other wait the longest.

"He had the real recognition that he was the one providing the service," a former officer said. "And all of these people absolutely needed the service. If they didn't want what Patterson had to sell, they could go somewhere else. But at the same time, he knew there wasn't anybody in the industry making loans as aggressively as he was, so he sort of had them exactly in a position where he could make them cool their heels in the stairwell and get away with it."

A new officer recalls asking a colleague shortly after his arrival how Patterson could meet all these people and know all these borrowers. The other officer replied, "Have you ever seen a dog in heat? It will attract dogs from miles around." They cooled their heels not just on the stairwell, but frequently sitting in private jets idling on airport runways at major money centers throughout the United States. Patterson, said a former associate, "was the classic example of a guy who always had to make one more phone call." On one occasion, he flew to Chicago with a customer and a couple of junior officers in the company's Lear jet to negotiate a loan with Continental. "Everybody got to Midway and was about to board the plane to return to Oklahoma," the officer recalled, and Patterson said, 'Just a second, I've got to make a phone call. I'll meet you at the plane.' Half an hour later the plane was still sitting on the tarmac, and customers were fuming. They hadn't gotten everything they wanted at Continental, and he held them up from leaving when they needed to leave, so those oilies were very unhappy."

On the other hand, Patterson became known for committing to multimillion-dollar deals on a cocktail napkin or desk pad at a bar or country club. Patterson's approach to one local oilman was fairly typical. Patterson asked him where he did his banking, and the oilman replied, "First National." He then inquired what his credit line was. The answer was something under a million. Patterson whipped a memo pad out of his pocket, scribbled a message on it, and told the man he could negotiate it for $3 million that afternoon. The oilie later framed the memo and hung it in his office.

For the most part the service was provided by a friendly and attractive, if young and inexperienced, staff. Until late in the game, Penn Square didn't have asset-liability or credit policy committees, but it did have what was only half jokingly called the "entertainment committee," consisting of young women who were encouraged to wine and dine important customers.

Patterson surrounded himself with a loyal following of young women, many of them recent divorcees, who were hired as secretaries and quickly promoted by Patterson to lending officers. Janelle Cates, for example, was a 1968 high school graduate who was hired in 1978 as a secretary to the president of the bank. She had worked for several years managing a doctor's office and selling pegboard accounting systems. By early 1982, Ms. Cates was a $47,000 a year vice-president supervising Penn Square's Oklahoma division and participating in $50 million loan transactions.

TRANSITIONS

WHEN CLIFTON POOLE, THE LANKY, RUSTY-HAIRED REGIONAL administrator for the Comptroller of the Currency in Memphis, was reassigned in June 1979 to head up the Dallas region, bankers in Tennessee and Arkansas raised their glasses in a gleeful toast to his departure, even though the career bank regulator had been stationed in Memphis for little more than one year. "He was tough," said one Arkansas bank president. "We were sure glad to get rid of him."

In Dallas, Poole would need all the toughness he could muster in doing battle with the one institution, Penn Square, that would give him his biggest headache for the next three years.

By June 1980 Penn Square had become a one-of-a-kind bank, having originated and sold more loans than it carried on its own books. The policy and procedure manuals that Poole had committed to memory since he joined the examining force in 1956 were not written for the go-go shopping center bank in Oklahoma City.

Penn Square's designation as a "special project bank" set into motion a flurry of meetings, letters, and memos to the "file" by bureaucrats in Dallas and Washington. The Comptroller's office informed its counterparts at the Federal Deposit Insurance Corporation and the Federal Reserve Board that Penn Square had been accepted into that exclusive fraternity and that the bank was being considered for what is politely known as a "formal administrative action." Cliff Poole was to take the Penn Square board to the woodshed.

The job of regional administrator calls for a certain skill in showmanship and playacting, and Poole was more adept at it than most. Bank regulators have various means of humbling a board of directors, the most drastic, of course, being the power to shut the institution down. There are, however, less draconian measures that when used judiciously normally make the point. One of them is to haul the entire board to the regional administrator's offices for a stern lecture on prudent banking. Traditionally, the regional administrator of the Comptroller of the Currency was given virtually unlimited discretion in handling the banks under his supervision. But after the failure of the Hamilton National Bank of Chattanooga, Tennessee, in 1976, authority ever so subtly shifted to Washington, according to longtime observers of the bank regulatory process. During this period, the once-independent Comptroller's office also became increasingly subservient to the Treasury Department, its parent agency.

On June 9, 1980, Poole sent a letter to each member of Penn Square's board of directors demanding that they appear before him and his staff in Dallas. The letter enumerated a number of serious problems identified in the spring exam; it was a laundry list of most of the things that can be done wrong in running a bank. In Dallas, they were asked to sign the agreement, in which they pledged to halt such practices as making loans without adequate credit information, lending to borrowers whose loans had already been criticized, and exceeding the legal lending limit of the bank. The agreement also called for the bank to maintain a capital-to-asset ratio of at least 7.5%.

For most bank officers and directors, such a request, coming from a bank regulatory agency, is a humiliating event. Most banks live in fear of being investigated or criticized by the examiners. The Penn Square board, said a former examiner present at the meeting, "came down to Dallas ready for bear." Jennings, he said, was combative coming into the meeting, jotting down notes on a pad in preparation for a rebuttal as the regulators stated their position. Poole would later recall before a congressional committee that Mr. Jennings was "resistive, openly resistive to our efforts. He was concerned that our efforts and the use of an administrative agreement would thwart the bank's progress."

No two men could have been more different than Beep Jennings and Cliff Poole. Poole, whose father was also a career bank examiner, was the quintessential self-effacing, by-the-book regulator, whereas Jennings operated out of his back pocket without any book at all. "They detested each other," said Mike Mahoney, Penn Square's operations officer and "Man Friday."

"Afterward," the examiner said, "we felt good about the meeting. We felt we'd won them over." And he added, "If you can get the board to agree with you your battle's half finished. We can tell them what to do but they've got to be the ones to do it." Later, however, the chairman of the House Committee on Banking, Finance and

Urban Affairs, Rep. Fernand St Germain, would speak of this letter agreement as having all the "sting of a flogging with a wet noodle."

The Penn Square board capitulated to the regulators' request and presented a new capital plan that included an equity offering of $4.3 million. A bank's capital, which includes shareholders' equity, is its cushion against losses. Losses suffered through bad investments or loans are charged against earnings and capital, and if those losses exceed capital the bank is a candidate for closing.

Bankers are accustomed to playing a number of games with their regulators. One of them is the letter game, and it is often played over the issue of capital adequacy, the primary bone of contention between bankers and their supervisors. Banks resist requests for more capital in part because earnings per share are diluted by spreading earnings over a larger number of shares. The game goes this way:

The regulator sends a letter demanding that more capital be injected into the bank. The banker, in turn, spends a couple of months drafting a reply to the regulators, pointing out why there is enough capital, and protesting their demands for more. The bank's response takes several months to make its way through a series of in and out boxes before a reply is forthcoming. Penn Square played this game and several variations of it.

Poole may have wished that Penn Square was under the control of more conservative management than Jennings and Patterson, but the notion of removing them would have been inconsistent with the "3" rating they had assigned to the bank in the first place. If the regulators viewed the bank as so bad that management should be forced out, then they should have given them a rating of "4" or "5".

Most removals are done by jawboning. The regulator appears before the board and says, "Your management is bad, what are you going to do about it? And they will normally agree that management is bad and get rid of them," one examiner said. Paradoxically, while the regulators have the power to close an institution, their track record in trying to oust recalcitrant chief executives through court action has been notoriously poor. In the late 1960s, the Comptroller of the Currency initiated an action against a Louisiana banker that lasted eight years, at which point the banker finally gave up and resigned voluntarily.

In 1978, however, as a result of charges of insider dealings at the Georgia bank controlled by Bert Lance, President Carter's close friend and onetime budget director, Congress enacted legislation that eased the removal criteria.

"The hardest job we have," said one former regulator, "is convincing the board they have a problem." But regulators try to avoid being high-handed.

"A twenty-five-year-old boy can't go in there and tell a fifty-year-old man, 'That last cattle loan you made went bad: you're fired,'" observed a former examiner. Bankers are inclined to argue that "there are personal good ole boy relationships that you guys don't understand." Normally, he said, "We hit them over the head and see improvement."

A bank board is charged with running a "safe and sound" institution, and each member takes an oath promising to do so. Their principal task is to determine if the people running the bank are competent, and they basically have just one weapon: the power to fire management.

At the Dallas meeting, it was clear to the regulators that the Penn Square board was a one-man show, a fact conceded by the directors themselves. "There was frustration," one director recalled later, "that things were moving too fast. We weren't permitted to take folders home, so there wasn't much time to absorb and study the details of problems facing the bank.

"There was a set agenda and no time allowed for bullshit," he said. "Votes weren't taken on individual items, such as loan charge-offs, or loans to individual officers, before the board. Everything discussed at the meetings was approved in mass by approving the minutes of the meeting." The board's loan review committee, one member complained, looked at loans after the fact. "We were looking at history," he said, "and the only value was to alter future policy. We saw only the borrower's name, dollar value, and the nature of the collateral, never coverage ratios and cash flows."

There were, however, ample rewards to compensate for the frustrations. Beside the prestige of being on a bank board, members saw their equity investments surge, at least on paper, with the phenomenal growth of the bank. One director who bought bank stock at $40 a share in 1979 said that its market value was more than $100 a share by the end of 1981. Instead of paying dividends to its wealthy shareholders, the bank plowed earnings back into the bank as capital.

In many ways, the directors of Penn Square were typical of the successful men and women who serve on the boards of many American banks. Ford dealer Dub Richardson, one of the original stockholders in the bank, asked Jennings to appoint his son, Jerry, to the board to "give him some banking experience." As the younger Richardson remarked later, "That's how I got on the board, and I got the

137

experience." Jennings had been trying for years to lure Gen. James Randolph, former commander of Tinker Air Force Base and president of Kerr-McGee Coal Company into the fold. The general, however, was already on the board of a savings and loan association, and it wasn't until 1979 that he capitulated to Jennings's persistence. Then there were Dr. Marvin Margo, a prominent orthopedic surgeon, Gene Smelser, a wealthy Oklahoma City restaurateur, Ron Burks, an enterprising young real estate developer, among other well-known individuals who were regarded as some of the most accomplished business and professional people in Oklahoma City. Yet for all their money and accomplishments, the board rarely challenged chairman Jennings. As Rep. Stan Parris (R-Va.) expressed it later, "They wanted to play in the big league and they were bush league."

In 1863, Comptroller of the Currency Hugh McCulloch might have been referring to Penn Square when he sent a letter to all national banks, which had just been organized under the new National Banking Act.

> Let no loans be made that are not secured beyond a reasonable contingency. Do nothing to foster and encourage speculation. Give facilities only to legitimate and prudent transactions. . . . Distribute your loans rather than concentrate them in a few hands. Large loans to a single individual or firm, although sometimes proper and necessary, are generally injudicious, and frequently unsafe. Large borrowers are apt to control the bank, and when this is the relation between a bank and its customers, it is not difficult to decide which in the end will suffer. . . . If you doubt the propriety of discounting an offering, give the bank the benefit of the doubt and decline it, never make a discount if you doubt the propriety of doing it. If you have reason to distrust the integrity of a customer, close his account. Never deal with a rascal under the impression that you can prevent him from cheating you. The risk in such cases is greater than the profits.

One person who was helping to fuel the staggering growth of Penn Square was not mentioned in the letter agreement. His name was John Lytle, and about the time Clifton Poole was demanding the board's presence in Dallas, Lytle's relationship with Bill G. Patterson was taking an all-too-friendly turn.

Although there was an age difference of fourteen years between the two men, Lytle and Patterson were becoming inseparable friends. During baseball season, Lytle, an irrepressible Chicago Cubs fan, took Patterson to games at Wrigley Field, and on many of his trips to Chicago, Patterson brought his wife and children to stay at Lytle's home, as Lytle would do on his visits to Oklahoma City. While unusually cozy, the relationship appeared above board until July 1980, when Patterson lent Lytle $20,000, the first installment in a series of loans that would amount to nearly $600,000 over the next eighteen months. Lytle would later testify before a congressional committee that the loans were for an addition to his house. Federal prosecutors didn't see it that way, however, and indicted him on charges of taking kickbacks from Patterson in return for buying Penn Square participations. Eventually, Lytle and Patterson formed a drilling partnership to invest in wells being drilled by Jennings's crony O. L. Scott. Named SPEKKL, an acronym derived from their children's initials, the partnership was intended as a college trust fund, but it yielded only dry holes, according to Patterson.

Meanwhile, the one person who might have been able to keep this relationship in check was bidding farewell to colleagues at the Continental Illinois National Bank in Chicago and preparing to assume a new position as vice-chairman of the Nucorp Energy Corporation in San Diego, California.

For years, R.L. Burns, Nucorp's silver-haired, silver-tongued chairman, had been trying to lure A.J. Pearson, Continental's energy lending guru, away from Chicago to the West Coast. Pearson was one of the most respected energy lenders in the United States, a man whose presence brought instant credibility to a high-rolling entrepreneur known for taking a long shot on some risky ventures. Indeed, Continental, and Pearson, had already taken a long shot on Burns, having lent most of the $125 million owed by his R.L. Burns Co., an oil and coal company that nearly failed in 1978. Although Continental eventually recovered its money on the deal, Burns resigned from the company. Mysteriously, Pearson liked Burns despite the vast difference in their temperaments and business instincts. Whereas Pearson was a quiet, intensively private man, Burns was aggressive and gregarious.

"A.J. put a blessing on Burns's activities," said one admirer. "He brought to Nucorp an image of honor." He also brought plenty of money. Despite the near-disastrous earlier experience with Burns, Continental ultimately lent Nucorp $173 million—largely because it felt comfortable with Pearson there—before the company went belly up in July 1982.

By August 1980 Pearson, then in his mid-fifties, had been with Continental for twenty years. In the opinion of close friends and associates, he had grown impatient with the Continental bureaucracy, and the constant battles over what kind of couch he could have in his office. Despite his top ranking in the close-knit energy lending fraternity, Pearson, a vice-president, had to fly coach when traveling companions with loftier titles were seated in the first class section. Colleagues say that he felt he had gone as far as he could at Continental, where his salary, his reputation and experience notwithstanding, was a relatively piddling $70,000, and he finally succumbed to a compensation package that soon included a $200,-000 salary plus stock options. At Nucorp, which had embarked on a strategy of buying up small, seemingly profitable oil- and gas-related companies, Pearson ran the exploration program and handled various corporate acquisitions. He could look forward to becoming a millionaire within five years.

At Continental, Pearson was a traditionalist who was uneasy with any energy loan that was not based on well-engineered, proved reserves. He was death on rig and lease line loans, recognizing that their collateral value in a downturn could easily be reduced to almost nothing. That is not to say these loans did not get booked during the so-called Pearson era. But, sources say, they would generally have been backed up with other collateral. Now, with his move to Nucorp, Pearson would help make relations between Continental and Nucorp even tighter and would clear the way for the rise of John Lytle.

Continental solved the problem of choosing a successor for Pearson from among three would-be contenders by splitting Pearson's group into three units. On September 1, the day after Pearson left, John Lytle was assigned to head up a newly created mid-continent division, and two other officers were put in charge of the new Texas and Western divisions. The promotion almost instantaneously boosted the authority and autonomy of John R. Lytle, who, former officers say, was always comparing his loan totals with those of his rival, Jim Cordell, head of the Texas division. When the mid-continent division, profit center 1089, reached the $1 billion mark over the next year, Lytle celebrated by throwing a barbecue for his staff at his comfortable tree-shaded home in the fashionable Chicago suburb of Northfield.

The decision to put Lytle in charge did not sit well with everyone in the energy group. Petroleum engineer Gary Brednich, for one, was furious that Pearson was not replaced with someone with a technical background, namely himself. When Pearson left, the younger engineers also lost their mentor, and the one individual they knew they could go to for professional support. Curiously, however, Pearson himself was "high on Lytle," according to a former colleague of both men.

Pearson's departure gave rise to the era of the lease line and the rig loan. Some of this, according to Dennis Winget (the Continental vice-president, who later joined Penn Square), occurred because "the market heated up." But in turn, the market heated up because of Continental's willingness to make lease line and rig loans. According to Winget, the percentage of rig and lease line loans was the same when Pearson was there, but the dollar volume rose dramatically after he left. Meanwhile, the bank was adding new MBAs to the bank's payroll to put additional loans on the books, while cutting back on the operations staff needed to process and monitor them.

Dale Mitchell, who was with the First National Bank of Oklahoma City at the time, recalls hearing of Pearson's departure. "I remember our energy people talking about Continental losing the wrong guys," he recalled later.

With Pearson gone, Continental lost its first line of defense against reckless lending. Lytle would now report directly to Jack Redding, who, while well respected in the industry as a cautious lender, was a grandfatherly sort who eschewed confrontation. And Redding's boss, Gerald Bergman, who aspired to the presidency of the bank, was little involved in the day-to-day affairs of mid-continent. As one former officer put it, "He had his eyes on the stars."

While Pearson was preparing to leave for the West Coast, Hefner persuaded the First National Bank of Dallas to grant him the $15 million production loan Pearson refused to make. The Dallas institution is one of the nation's original energy lenders. It had a reputation for prudent lending to established firms but also a willingness to take a chance on some high flyers. That willingness had paid off in the past.

In fact, exactly fifty years before Hefner approached them with his proposal, an Arkansas poker player named H.L. Hunt, who then had $19 to his name, audaciously offered a Texas wildcatter $1.5 million for oil leases on some north Texas cotton farms. With the agreement in hand, he approached the First National Bank of Dallas for $30,000 to drill the first of many spectacularly successful wells. Charlie Joiner, who sold him the leases, went on to drill a string of dry holes and died penniless.

* * *

David O'D. Kennedy, Hefner's partner of more than seventeen years, was now seventy-three. He would say later that he felt he was doing well enough himself and that any success should go to Hefner in the future. "I didn't particularly care about making any more money," Kennedy said. That fall he converted his full partnership into a limited partnership, thereby ridding himself of any personal liability for GHK. "It turns out," he recalled later, "that I did a good thing for myself too." A friend once told Kennedy, "They could throw you off the Empire State Building and you'd land on your feet."

Kennedy did have serious misgivings about the prices being offered for deep gas in the post-NGPA era, and he expressed them to Hefner and his associates. "When Bob told me he was being offered $9 MCF, I said, 'That's bad. Gas shouldn't cost that much. It's going to be very destructive.'" Kennedy felt the take-or-pay contracts were pricing gas out of the market, thereby reaffirming an economic principle that holds for gas as well as floor tile. At the time, many observers were expecting oil would rise to $60 per barrel; at that price, it might have made sense, Kennedy thought. But, on balance, he concluded that it was unhealthy, though he discounts his concern about pricing as a factor in the decision to reduce his role at GHK.

The tight relationship between Bill Patterson and John Lytle, and between Penn Square and Continental, was painfully apparent to Seafirst's John Boyd. By the summer of 1980, Volcker's Saturday night special of October 1979 had begun to take its toll on lumber and aviation, the core industries of the Pacific Northwest, just as the boom in Oklahoma began to come into its own. Boyd was keenly interested in becoming part of Penn Square's inner circle, something he felt Lytle and Continental were seeking to discourage. If Lytle was treated like the rich uncle of the oil patch, Boyd was a poor and distant cousin. On one occasion Boyd and a contingent of other bankers were shuttled by vans for a well christening at a site some distance from Oklahoma City. The trip, he recalls, was long and hot, and when they arrived, guests were separated into two groups, with company VIPs and representatives of the major financing banks seated in what he called the "adult" section and minor players in the "children's section." Suddenly, he said, "You heard the sound of a helicopter. It landed on the site and out stepped the owner with John Lytle, who walked around and shook hands like he was a presidential candidate making a campaign stop." And unlike Continental bankers, Seafirst officers had to wait three to four days to get their phone calls returned.

Nevertheless, Boyd, like Lytle, found a kindred spirit in Patterson. While Patterson would become a legend for drinking Amaretto out of Gucci loafers, the gregarious banker from Seattle appeared bare-chested at parties, sporting a cigar in one hand and a cocktail in the other, and before long earned the nickname the "Bill Patterson of the West."

The fragility of the relationship between Penn Square and Seafirst, as Boyd perceived it, was seen in his early efforts to hammer out a master participation agreement with Penn Square. Seafirst wanted Penn Square to put all the documents in its format, as Seafirst customarily requested in dealing with its many other correspondent banks. As Boyd recalled, Jennings said, "No, Penn Square does things its way."

"We were competing for business," Boyd said, "and we wanted to be delicate about it, but at the same time we wanted it done properly." Once signed, however, the master participation agreement gave Boyd a sense of security about his dealings with the Oklahoma bank that would ultimately prove to be unfounded.

As early as the summer of 1980, there were those at Seafirst who felt a sense of uneasiness about energy and international loans. One was Henry Dahl, the demanding and fastidious head of the bank's loan review and policy committee, who took early retirement that year after a rival was promoted over him. Dahl and John Nelson had scrapped with each other over lending policy for ten years, and the move into energy and international lending exacerbated that conflict. Dahl, according to the former associate, referred to Boyd as a "Pied Piper," and Boyd complained that "Dahl is always on my back. He doesn't know anything about energy loans." Nelson, however, was defensive about energy and his fast-moving protégé, and commented some time after Dahl's retirement, "If Henry were here, we'd still have a $100 million cap on energy."

On September 15, 1980, two weeks after Pearson left Continental, Penn Square vice-president Ken Wilson, acting for Bill Patterson, notified John Lang, vice-president of Carl Swan's Longhorn Oil and Gas, that Penn Square would release the letters of credit backing the company's 1978-II drilling program. That normally would be good news. In this case, however, the reserves alone were not sufficient to justify a production loan. So the debt had to be shifted, as in a multimillion dollar shell game, to the parent company. Obscured in the arcane language of high finance was a tacit acknowledgment that one of the earliest drilling programs of Longhorn, the flagship entity of the legendary Carl Swan and the cornerstone of the Continental–Penn Square relationship, was a disaster. Pearson, if he had known about it, would probably not have been happy.

> Dear John:
>
> This is a letter of commitment whereby Penn Square Bank, N.A., will release the letters of credit on the above program and convert to a production loan under the corporate entity, Longhorn Oil and Gas Corp. This transaction will be approximately $1.7mm and will release each participant's letter of credit which will be returned to them so that they in turn can return the letters to the respective banks.

Longhorn's brokers must have been pleased. On the face of it, the first big letter of credit deal with Longhorn Oil and Gas worked according to plan. They would have good news for their clients, news that they could translate into additional commissions on future Longhorn Drilling programs.

Meanwhile, Continental officers were engaged in other financial machinations that would make a debt junkie out of Longhorn Oil and Gas. Penn Square extended a $7 million "secured revolver" to Longhorn (of which $6.95 million was sold to Continental Illinois) that was intended to replace, and increase, two earlier notes totaling $4.5 million. Kurt Wegleitner, a junior lending officer at Continental, noted in his write-up that "although the cushion represented above is below standard, the loan will be further supported by an assignment of leases and the unlimited guarantees of Carl Swan and J.D. Allen." Effectively, he said, "We are looking to the unlimited guarantees and the assignment of lease inventory with a cost of $8 million to support the $1 million short fall in reserves. Due to the assignment of leases and the substantial support provided by Swan's and Allen's guarantees as shown by their statements, we feel comfortably secured." The statements, of course, were unaudited, but claimed a net worth of more than $19 million for each of the two oilmen.

Later, disgruntled investors would allege in lawsuits that they were unaware of the need for personal guarantees, and if they had been, they wouldn't have poured more money into subsequent programs. Longhorn, Continental, Jennings, and Patterson knew that if they demanded payment from the investors on the letters of credit, and if they did not roll the term loan on the 1978-II into the production loan, investor confidence in Longhorn would evaporate, brokers would not be able to sell new programs, and the game would be over just as it was getting started.

Longhorn's J.D. Allen was not much for details. He thought of himself as a big picture guy, a conceptualizer who should spend his time germinating business ideas and letting technical types carry them to fruition. J.D. felt that his time and talents could be better spent dabbling in politics. Presidential politics. So while his bankers and financial managers were assembling secured revolvers for drilling programs, Allen was in Detroit partying with high-ranking Republican dignitaries. The man who, by most accounts, had come out of nowhere, who three years before had slept in the back seat of his mud-splattered Cadillac while peddling leases in southern Oklahoma, also happened to be an early supporter of President Ronald Reagan. Before long, he would be rewarded with invitations to join the President aboard Air Force One. Investors who visited J.D. in his spacious offices at the Oil Center Building could not fail to notice an autographed photo of J.D. with Ron and Nancy Reagan on J.D.'s well-polished mahogany desk. For a man of such eminence, Longhorn 1981-II would be an easy sell.

Despite the fact that the Carter administration had succeeded in passing a natural gas bill that at least partially decontrolled the price of natural gas, something no President in twenty years had been able to do, the new oilies never forgave the President for his anti-oil rhetoric, the windfall profits tax, and his apparent flip-flop on decontrol in 1977. They thanked Carter by using a portion of their bonanza from deep gas and Penn Square Bank to become members of the Republican Eagles, a privilege that accrues to anyone who can afford to donate a minimum of $10,000 a year to the Republican cause.

That summer, the Republican faithful threw a gala fund raiser at the home of oilman Carl Anderson, Jr., who had pitched a tent that one guest described as "big enough to house the Barnum and Bailey Circus." Former President Gerald Ford appeared as guest of honor, and the contributors filled their plates from a buffet table laden with crab claws on ice and oysters flown in from Chesapeake Bay. In one evening, the Oklahomans recruited more than fifty new Eagles and raised more than $500,000 for the Reagan campaign. Whether out of political ideology, perceived self-interest, or simply a desire to be on the winning side, the Oklahoma oilies, as a group, were among the largest financial backers of Ronald Reagan.

According to Federal Election Commission documents, the list of the largest Oklahoma donors to the Reagan campaign read like a page out of Penn Square's dossier of top borrowers. They included Hefner, who, after supporting Carter in 1976, switched to Reagan; horseman Ken Tureaud; socialite Robert Hoover; former bandleader Hal Clifford; and, of course, J.D. Allen. Curiously, Carl Swan made a nominal contribution to the Carter–Mondale Presidential Committee in late 1979, and a substantial donation to the Republican National Committee on the same day. The occasion for some of the $10,000 contributions was the Prelude to Victory celebration prior to the November election. Because the Oklahoma oilies had been so generous in the past, Oklahoma was designated as one of just three locations in the United States to have a closed-circuit television hook-up of the celebration. The dinner at Oklahoma's Skirvan Hotel was a sumptuous affair, but even in Oklahoma there were not enough donors for all the available tables. So the pilots of a few of the oilmen were outfitted in tuxedos and handed tickets to the gala event.

To Bill Patterson, Beep Jennings was a godlike figure. Patterson mimicked Jennings's behavior even to the point of holding and chomping on his long cigars with the same cavalier and self-assured flair as his mentor. That tendency to imitate Jennings apparently extended even into politics. Jennings, though a lifelong Democrat, contributed $1,000 in December 1979 to the presidential primary campaign of John Connally, and likewise, Bill Patterson donated $250.

With a seemingly limitless supply of investor and borrowed money, it was easy, one maven recalls, to get contributions for just about any social or charitable cause. For example, it took just a phone call to find twenty-five people willing to contribute $3,000 each for an anniversary party for University of Oklahoma president Bill Banowsky and his wife. The problem, in fact, was how to pare the guest list. As one socialite recalls, guests came from Tulsa, Houston, and Midland. Art Linkletter delivered the introduction, Oral Roberts gave the invocation, and singer Pat Boone provided the entertainment.

A lot of the money generated by the oil and gas boom and the Penn Square–Continental lending spree went for causes that were not so worthy, and a lot of the parties were not nearly as refined.

An investor who poured several hundred thousand dollars into the deep gas projects of an Oklahoma wildcatter recalls one trip to Acapulco arranged by the oilman. "It was a high-class whorehouse," the investor said. "He rented the entire place. By the time I got there, there were twenty naked women and ten naked men, and one guy with a big bottle of Johnson's baby oil. I was the only guy with clothes on." On another occasion, an Oklahoma oilie stood at the door to a suite at a Las Vegas hotel, greeting the guests, and the hookers, as they paraded in. "According to the investor, the oilman asked the women, 'How much are your clothes worth? I'd like to buy your clothes.' " As the oilman peeled off crisp $100 bills from a wad he held in his hand, the women removed their clothes and tossed them into a pile at the door.

Oklahoma psychic and songwriter Nita Lee expressed the mood in a country-western ballad entitled, "Who Said the South Wouldn't Rise Again!":

> Now we drilled in almost every state,
> We had money from nineteen banks,
> We had visions of wells just a-gushin'
> The whiskey was a-flowin'
> And the girls was a-hustlin'
> Mercy! Who Said the South Wouldn't Rise Again!

A PIECE OF THE ACTION

B ANKERS DON'T GO TO BANKERS' CONVENTIONS JUST TO ATTEND
the formal programs, and the 1980 annual convention of the
American Bankers Association in Chicago was no exception. Paul
Souder, vice-chairman of the Michigan National Bank of Lansing,
went there, as usual, to meet friends and catch up on developments
in the industry. Uppermost in his mind, however, was a large and
excessive portfolio of fixed-rate loans that had begun to strangle the
bank's earnings as interest rates surged to double-digit levels. Souder
needed to infiltrate that portfolio with some credits that would float
with the prime rate.

Michigan National Corporation was in the tail end of a year that
would show a 17.8% decline in its return on average shareholders'
equity and a 51.3% increase in its provision for possible loan losses.
In its 1980 annual report, the bank attributed these dismal returns
to declining automobile sales and rising unemployment in Michigan, pointing out that the corporation was largely a lender to consumers. With loan demand in a trough, Michigan National had
plenty of cash on hand, and figured that buying loan participations
from major banks would be one way to put those surplus funds to
work. One Michigan Bank officer summed the bank's predicament
up this way: "We felt we had to get out of Michigan."

So when Souder ran into a top Continental executive at an ABA
cocktail reception, the two men talked about how Continental could
help Michigan National into some floating rate deals. The Continental executive mentioned that his bank was booking a large number of energy loans and agreed to arrange a meeting between
Michigan National and officers of Continental's oil and gas department.

In mid-November, Michigan National officers Herb Peterson and

Arnie Middeldorf met with John Lytle in Chicago and were shown an assortment of short-term, fixed-rate credits, not the kind that got their adrenaline going. The conversation turned to Oklahoma City and Penn Square Bank. As it happened, Bill Patterson and several of his staff were also in the bank that day. Middeldorf and Peterson were shown some of the deals Continental was considering, and the Michigan relationship with Penn Square was kicked off about a month later when Michigan took its first $12 million in Penn Square participations.

According to Perry Driggs, president of Michigan National's Lansing unit, Continental assured its colleagues that Penn Square Bank was a source of high-quality, secured floating rate loans. "We were pleased to have been accepted initially, as well as later, into what we perceived was a fraternity of reliable energy lenders, including Continental, Chase Manhattan, Seattle First, and Northern Trust," he said. As another Michigan officer put it later, "It was characterized as a privilege to be allowed to invest in these fine loans."

Continental and Michigan viewed the relationship as mutually beneficial, since Continental had no use for loans under a million, and Michigan was looking for secured loans of a million or less. But as Fernand St Germain would say later, "For Continental to introduce Michigan National to Penn Square Bank was like taking one of your children and walking them [sic] into quicksand."

Indeed, Michigan National had done little in the way of oil and gas lending, despite the fact that Michigan is a leading gas-producing state and that U.E. Patrick, the president of Patrick Petroleum, served on the board of Michigan National's flagship unit in Lansing. Having lent money to Patrick Petroleum, and with Patrick himself on the board, Michigan National officers felt some comfort in buying oil and gas loans from Penn Square. Arnie Middeldorf, a short, stocky, bald man who felt he could lead the charge into energy.

The Michigan bank, which made no pretense of its need to rely almost entirely on Continental's energy expertise, would fill an important role for its friends in Chicago. Continental came to regard Michigan as a "spillover" bank; loans that Continental was unable to take because of the heavy volume that was pumped by Penn Square into the mid-continent division would flow across wind-whipped Lake Michigan into the hands of Middeldorf at Battle Creek. As things turned out, Michigan would also become the dumping ground for Chase, Northern Trust, and sometimes even Seafirst, and the last stop on Bill Patterson's whirlwind sales trips around the United States. In the Penn Square shell game of tainted loan participations, the buck would almost inevitably stop in Battle Creek. Michigan National came to embody one of banking's basic precepts: the bigger fool theory of lending, which holds that there will always be a bank more foolish than the next one. Michigan National, like Seafirst, would invariably take what the other "cobanks" flatly turned down.

Michigan National clearly felt comfortable knowing it had Continental and John Lytle to fall back on. Not long after the kick-off meeting, Lytle wrote to Patterson acknowledging his willingness to take back whatever Michigan didn't like:

January 28, 1981

Mr. William Patterson
Executive Vice President
Penn Square Bank
1919 Penn Square
Oklahoma City, Oklahoma 73126

Dear Bill:

Just want to let you know that Caroline Janda and her crew had a meeting with Arnold Middeldorf and his people at Michigan National and determined that they are pleased with the package of credits that we put together last November. I feel they are grateful both to you and to us for the help. It looks like they are growing both in confidence and understanding of oil related lending, but as we did previously, I reassured them that we would take the credits out at maturity or whenever they felt unconfident.

Thanks again for your help. I think that this is a service that working together, we can provide to others.

Sincerely,

John

If at first the relationship with Penn Square was low-key and congenial, it later took on a more strident tone. Michigan's credit approval procedures, unlike those at Continental and Seattle First, were intentionally cumbersome and credits over $3 million had to pass through a gauntlet of lending officers, advisory committees, and even the board of directors. According to Michigan National officers, "Patterson would say to our people, 'If you can't get this credit approved through your procedures, we'll give the whole thing to Continental. You'll have to make your credit decisions faster.'

" 'Look,' Patterson said, 'we've got Seafirst, Continental, Chase. They've expressed a desire to get as much as we can ship them. You'll have to change your way of dealing with credits. If you can tell us in seven days, you can get the credit.' "

Despite their geographical separation, Michigan National and Penn Square had a lot in common. Like Penn Square, Michigan had for a long time been a thorn in the side of the national bank examiners. According to numerous banking industry sources, Michigan National historically was slow to acknowledge and disclose bad loans and bad news. Regulators had been forced to shove their losses down their throat," as one former regulator put it.

Michigan National had also been singled out by the Securities and Exchange Commission for allegedly questionable banking transactions and practices, including millions in insider loans. This reportedly reflected the tight personal grip that Michigan National chairman Stanford Stoddard, who controlled nearly 7% of the company's stock, had over his institution. Said one industry observer, "Stoddard ran Michigan National out of his back pocket."

Stoddard, a man with a diverse range of interests, had a fascination for the Far East, and spent considerable time traveling abroad, particularly in Japan. Described as a big-time Mormon, Stoddard devoted much of his energy to the Religious Heritage Foundation, to which his associate and first cousin, Perry Driggs, also belonged. He was also interested in oil and gas, and along with the director of one of Michigan National Corporation's affiliate banks, invested in a limited partnership drilling program sold by Longhorn Oil and Gas.

In February 1978 the SEC launched an investigation into possible violations of federal securities laws and the failure by Michigan National Corporation to disclose to shareholders its true financial condition and the interests of management in various transactions. Officers and directors purchased bank property and leased it back to the bank at fees amounting to several million dollars. The SEC concluded its investigation in 1981 after the company agreed to certain "undertakings," including the creation of a review committee to scrutinize insider dealings. As one local banker put it in an interview with the *Detroit News*, "There is a certain unpleasant aura about Michigan National."

It is a commonly held myth that banks in economically distressed areas of the country are necessarily mediocre earners. While there were few star performers in the industrial states of Ohio, Indiana, and Michigan at the time Michigan National had its rendezvous with Continental and Penn Square, these institutions as a group appeared to be holding their own. Very often banks in areas of the country prone to economic downturns become more adept, out of necessity, at managing the institutions than their high-flying counterparts in such fast-growth areas as Texas, California, and Florida.

Michigan National may have had a friend at Continental, but the company and its chairman seemed to have few friends in Michigan banking circles or among the regulators in Washington. Stoddard was not a member of the old boy network. On the contrary. Michigan National and Stoddard rankled fellow bankers in the state with their daring attempts to circumvent branch banking restrictions and transform the bank into a statewide institution. In that effort, Stoddard followed the precedent set by his late father, Howard, the bank's founder.

For example, the bank attempted to use automated teller machines to enable customers to deposit or withdraw funds at any location, a move that was disallowed by federal regulators. Back in 1973, the company deployed its own armored cars to pick up deposits of large customers, but regulators determined that the cars were themselves branches and the bank agreed to terminate the program. The same year, the bank introduced "money marts," or loan production offices, where routine banking transactions could be conducted. The Michigan Bankers Association later sued the bank over the practice, and in 1978 a federal judge ruled it a violation of state banking laws. In an interview given to the *Detroit News* in 1978, one banker expressed the opinion, "Most bankers will consult their general counsel about a new idea and if he demurs will drop it. But Stoddard consults his general counsel, then says, 'Let's do it and let the bastards sue us.' "

Under Howard Stoddard's leadership, Michigan National did earn something of a reputation for innovative banking, claiming credit, for example, for introducing the nation's first drive-in teller window in the early 1940s. Michigan National also got itself into the national headlines occasionally by bucking the trends. At a time when the prime lending rate was 12%, Michigan National announced it was lowering its rate to 11%, in an effort to support the Ford administration's anti-inflation drive.

Stoddard's bank was also known for its penny-pinching ways. While its competitors owned imposing-looking offices with marble columns and cavernous banking floors, Michigan National bought up abandoned gasoline stations and affixed on them neon signs of the sort used to advertise the brand of beer dispensed in neighborhood taverns. Michigan National would see a like-minded institution in Penn Square. Both were mavericks in their home states. Both were looking for new ways to challenge the existing banking structure and regulation. And perhaps more important, Michigan National, like Penn Square, featured itself an aggressive and able secured lender, even though Michigan's presumed competence was in making automobile and home appliance loans to blue collar workers and Penn Square's was in making reserve-based loans to the new oilion. Indeed, Michigan National did fairly well as a Mom and Pop bank, lending to virtually everyone and anyone, including people unable to get credit elsewhere. They did well, that is, until they encountered the difficulties that prompted them to move out of Michigan—a move that would lead them into more difficulties than they could ever imagine.

Michigan National was a "family man" kind of bank, as a former Penn Square officer described it. So in his contacts with Michigan officers, Patterson apparently attempted to project that kind of image. Perry Driggs, the chairman of Michigan National–Lansing, later recalled, "Patterson seemed like such a wholesome guy. He'd bring along his wife and kids to meet us. I guess," he shrugged, "that was all part of the act."

When he traveled to Chicago, however, Patterson was less subdued. On one occasion, officers of Penn Square and Northern Trust gathered at a long table in the private dining room of an exclusive Chicago restaurant for a love feast of food, drink, and merriment. At one end of the table, a guest recalled, Jennings and a senior officer of Northern Trust conversed congenially over dinner, while at the other end Patterson pitched tomato slices around the dining room.

Larry Brandt, chairman of Invoil, a drilling fund promoter that borrowed money from Continental Illinois, recalls a dinner at the Palm Restaurant attended by a large contingent of Penn Square customers, when suddenly a hunk of crabmeat landed on the lapel of his blue pinstriped suit. "I got up and returned to my hotel," Brandt said later.

Patterson was known to be even more boisterous, and indeed, destructive. He is reported to have been banned forever from a Chicago hotel for throwing a television set out the window of his suite. And on one midnight cab ride through Chicago's financial district, he reportedly got out of the taxi, dropped his pants to his knees, and flashed a moon at the Continental Illinois National Bank and Trust Company of Chicago.

THE MADNESS
OF CROWDS

IF THE PASSAGE OF THE NATURAL GAS POLICY ACT WAS THE KICK off for the era of deep gas in the Anadarko Basin, then the big Mobil Oil Company farm-out of December 1980 was Bob Hefner's first touchdown. In the oil and gas patch, big deals and successful wells tend to beget bigger deals and more wells. And so it was that at the end of 1980 and into 1981 a few spectacular wells and some eight- and nine-figure deals spawned a feeding frenzy of lease acquisitions in the Anadarko Basin that left some of the old oilies speechless.

Under the agreement with Mobil, the giant multinational oil company contracted to pay Hefner a $32 million downpayment on a $200 million commitment to drill more than a hundred Anadarko Basin wells. Mobil, in return, got half of GHK's acreage in the Elk City area, and Hefner received a carried interest in the wells. It was, according to a former GHK executive, the biggest onshore domestic farm-out ever.

Apart from its size, the deal was a benchmark for other reasons. It was one thing for a visionary like Hefner to promote the basin. It was quite another for one of the majors, an astute, no-nonsense Fortune 500 corporation, to give its blessing to what had been all along an independent's play. The big fish had gone for the worm.

"At that point, things really began looking bullish," said a former GHK official. "We had been looking for a big partner with deep pockets to help drill up this acreage for a long time," adding that Hefner, through his many industry connections, managed to turn on the exploration people at Mobil.

"The Mobil deal," said John Boyd, "made the whole scene in the Anadarko come full circle. You had a continuing stream of cash from the gas wells; they couldn't put them on fast enough to meet the demand. You had all the things I thought were important to what looked like a five- to fifteen-year play."

After the Mobil deal was signed, even the stuffy bankers at the blue chip Wall Street banking house of Morgan Guaranty Trust deigned to talk with Hefner. However, according to the deep gas driller, Morgan's reserve estimates for the Anadarko were only 25% of "what the real amount of production was. They could give good reserve figures for Indonesia or Saudi Arabia," he said, "but when it came to the basin they were sadly lacking."

Hefner said that GHK was close to wrapping up a deal with Morgan as lead bank, when the First National Bank in Dallas (now Interfirst), which earlier had given GHK a production loan, launched a bidding war and took the business away from Morgan, assuring Hefner that they considered his reserve numbers on the mark. As another observer to the transaction saw it, "Hefner played one bank off against another."

Wildcatters like Hefner were nonchalant about interest rates, even though the prime by this time had reached its all-time high of 21.5%. What really mattered was the amount of money they could get. As Hefner put it later, "Everybody was sensitive to opportunity cost. We felt if we could just get the money we could put it to better use. It didn't really matter to us whether it was one over prime or two over prime. Independents," he added, "generally were so gung ho to seize these opportunities before the majors came in and took over everything that they weren't going to argue over rates." That, of course, was a refreshing change for bankers from Chicago and New York accustomed to quibbling at length with a garment manufacturer over whether his $250,000 term loan should be priced at one point or one and a quarter points over the prime.

With Pearson at Nucorp and Hefner in solid with Mobil, GHK and lease line deals apparently began to look more appealing to Continental's Jack Redding and John Lytle. First of Dallas, which had given GHK a production line back in August, recoiled at lease acquisitions. According to the former GHK executive, Continental started out with a $15 million lease line to Hefner personally, because that was not prevented by the restrictions in the First of Dallas loan agreement. Continental, in effect, got their foot in the door by making lines of credit available to Hefner to buy leases outside the Elk City area, where Mobil was paying for the drilling and the First of Dallas had loaned against the production.

Over a period of months, Continental gradually extended more lease lines to Hefner and GHK. And in order to induce the Chicago bank to open the spigot even further, Hefner agreed to move his more conventional production loan from Dallas to Chicago. By August, Continental was firmly in control of the GHK account, providing a significant addition to John Lytle's loan figures. Shrugged Hefner years later, "I was the one who borrowed the money but they were the ones who were pushing it out the door."

Although GHK dealt directly with Continental Illinois on major transactions, Patterson sat in on nearly all the discussions on the account. Lytle seemed intelligent, said a former GHK official, "but was incongruously laid back and relaxed for someone in his position."

Continental, after Pearson, was willing to do lease lines because they were never able to attract the top tier independents that for years had been cozy with Texas banks like the First of Dallas and Texas Commerce. In the past, Continental usually had been compelled to settle for shared control of credits with their competitors in Texas. Penn Square and lease line deals were the cornerstone of Continental's strategy for getting in on the basement level with the Oklahoma independents. Said one observer, "They figured if they're not financing the guy who's doing leases, they'd miss out on a lot of other stuff after the ball got rolling." But it was lines of credit secured by leases that would eventually kill Continental Illinois.

Most traditional energy lenders avoided lease deals because their value can evaporate so quickly under adverse conditions. For example, if someone drills a dry hole on an adjoining lease, all the properties in the area suddenly are condemned. They are only legitimate, said one senior banker, if there is another "take out," or source of repayment.

Not only did Penn Square lend for lease acquisitions, it lent 100% of the purchase price, something a prudent bank wouldn't even do on a new car loan to a creditworthy customer. Ultimately, about 30% of the bank's loans were in leases. Only as long as you can sell a lease for more than you bought it can you stay ahead of financial disaster.

L.R. "Bobby" French, a reclusive wildcatter from Midland-Odessa, Texas, was to the Cyril Basin, or Fletcher Field, what Bobby Hefner was to the Anadarko proper. Named for a small, dusty cattle town in south-central Oklahoma, the Fletcher Field is in an area of gently rolling farmland just north of the Wichita Mountain range. Actually an outcropping of the southeastern flank of the Anadarko, the Fletcher is separated from the main basin by a geologic fault system, and unlike the Anadarko itself, is notable for the complexity and inconsistency of its gas-containing sands. Eons ago, cataclysmic forces caused the folding and faulting of rock layers, literally tearing up what might have been smooth, predictable strata and creating a hotbed of high-pressure gas pockets for the deep gas explorers of the early 1980s. Blowouts and cave-ins go hand in hand with deep gas drilling, but the dips and bends in the Fletcher sands made it difficult just to sink a straight hole. French's Comanche No. 1, drilled in 1980, looked like a prolific producer at first, but twelve hours after it was tested, the well blew out and the hole was lost. French was apparently discouraged by the monumental mechanical problems he found in the Fletcher Field and was troubled with the huge financial risks that his heavy exposure there represented.

But to Bill Saxon, the charismatic chairman of the Saxon Oil Company of Dallas, the blowout sent another kind of signal. It proved to his satisfaction that there were immense reserves in the Fletcher. In January 1981 Saxon, whose experience at drilling for deep gas was negligible at best, bought French's interests in the Fletcher for $40 million. Saxon thought he had found the brass ring.

Court records show that about the time Saxon was sealing his deal with French, two leasehounds on assignment for Texaco were making a no-lose proposition to mineral owners who had sold leases to Kerr-McGee years earlier. Texaco negotiated a lease with the mineral owners, paying them 25% immediately with the balance forthcoming if the Kerr-McGee leases expired. Even if Kerr-McGee chose to drill on or renew the original leases, the lessor would be entitled to keep Texaco's advance payment. This practice is called top leasing, which was an infrequently used tactic in the oil patch up until about 1978. Its use causes panic in the operator holding the original leases because it typically forces a decision before the operator (in this case, Kerr-McGee) is prepared to make one. Angela Mary Doebel, for example, had signed a five-year lease with Kerr-McGee on February 10, 1977. On February 5, 1981, she granted Texaco a three-year lease upon the expiration of Kerr-McGee's. In addition, she received a royalty of three-sixteenths, up from the one-eighth she had gotten from Kerr-McGee four years before. The lease broker, however, waited four months before filing the papers in the Comanche County Courthouse, a move industry observers interpreted as a tactic to keep the competition in the dark for as long as possible. When Kerr-McGee finally woke up to what rival Texaco was doing, its response would touch off one of the hottest gas plays, and contribute to one of the most flamboyant lending sprees, in American history.

According to Dr. William Talley, "It was, up to 1978, a no-no to go in and top-lease guys. Only the bad guys did it. The Anadarko was an independent play, and to get in you had to do joint ventures or top lease." Adding to the euphoria were the optimistic oil and gas price predictions made by consultants like Dr. Talley. In a speech in late 1980 to the Oklahoma Society of Certified Public Accountants, Talley asserted that the U.S. "can count on oil supplies being interrupted in the near future," and predicted that crude oil prices would approach the $100 mark by 1990.

With all this hype, the oil and gas lease became a kind of currency, and leasehounds and promoters financed by Penn Square Bank were making fortunes churning leases. In 1978, the average bonus in the Anadarko was $250 per acre for a five-year lease and a one-eighth royalty; by 1980 that had doubled to $500 for a three-year lease and a three-sixteenths royalty. In 1981, the average bonus soared to $800 and up, and in particularly hot areas some mineral owners received as much as $10,000 per acre.

Nowhere was the frenzy more evident than in the county courthouses, where landmen stood four deep at the counters poring over the heavy, poster-sized books in which titles, deeds, and mineral rights are recorded. Fistfights broke out between landmen over the books, and landmen were reportedly barred from one courthouse for a week because of the altercations. Recalled one promoter, "You'd wait in line for hours for the books; people would even take them to the bathroom." Used car salesmen turned in their order pads to become petroleum landmen, and lawyers just out of school made $100,000 a year rendering title opinions. So many people were getting into the business, in fact, that office equipment stores sold out of the small portable typewriters lease brokers carried around to fill out the legal forms. Promoters even made money on the float by placing their investors' funds in money market accounts for a couple of weeks or so before actually purchasing the leases.

This activity gave rise to what one promoter called the "dirty deals," whereby a company employee would tell a friend where his firm was buying leases, the friend would buy the lease, sell it to the company, and both parties would turn a hefty if malodorous profit. "Everybody was increasing their lease positions," recalled Invoil's Larry Brandt. "We felt the train was leaving the station, and we'd got to get in on it. We thought if we don't get in at $100, prices will soon be $500."

Also promoting the escalation in prices was an informal network among mineral owners in the Anadarko, a network that quickly became organized. "When someone got $500 an acre, his neighbors knew about it the same day," said one oilman, who observed that Penn Square was largely responsible for the fly-up in prices. "Too much money," he said, "was chasing a finite number of leases."

Being a promoter means never having to spend any of your own money. And with lease prices rising almost daily in some areas, a speculator could trade leases and turn a profit without having to spend a nickel out of his own pocket.

As the terms of leases became more favorable to the mineral owner, and as the leases passed through several hands with each promoter taking a piece of the action, the odds of the investor making any money were reduced to nil. The customary, time-honored one-eighth royalty given to mineral owners became a major trading point, frequently increasing to as much as one-quarter. And cash bonuses amounting to thousands of dollars were often thrown in to sweeten the deals. The cavalier granting of overriding royalty interests to geologists skewed the odds against investors even further, since inscrutable geologists with interests in the production frequently recommended completion of wells where the payout potential was next to nothing. Drilling deals were promoted so heavily that the operator made money, if only in the short term, even on dry holes. Other pressures pushed operators into hasty and ill-conceived drilling decisions. These included IRS requirements that operators incur or prepay drilling expenses before year-end in order for investors to be able to write off the expenses in the current tax year. Then, too, operators had to begin "making hole" within six months after filing their "intent to drill" applications with the state. Moreover, Oklahoma's force pooling statutes often prompted inexperienced and overleveraged oil and gas companies to commit themselves to participation in all too many dubious deals.

With landowners, geologists, promoters, and even oil company secretaries getting a piece of the lease action, the dentist from Tampa who might have put up 10% of the cost of the well might be entitled to a mere 3% of the revenue. That would have been fine under ideal conditions. For example, if the working interest owners pay 100% of the $6 million cost of a deep gas well and get 30% of the revenue of $100 million, or $30 million, that's a five to one return. But as lease broker Steve Knox observed, "Few of the wells turned out that way." And another Oklahoma City oilman noted wryly, "It's not in the bank until it's in the tanks."

For mineral owners, many of whom were wheat and cattle farmers whose Oklahoma roots went back to the land run of 1889 and who barely survived the dust storms of the 1930s, six- and seven-figure lease bonus checks were a welcome relief from depressed farm prices. Although there were those whose lifestyles changed radically, others were apparently unaffected by their new wealth. For example, octogenarian Joe Lutonsky, an agile, quick-witted man whose weathered hands reflect more than half a century of working the reddish-brown soil of southern Oklahoma, still wears denim overalls and a straw hat while repairing fences around his Elgin, Oklahoma, farm. Lutonsky said he used most of his $870,000 bonus check to buy another 500 acres of land, and invested the rest in certificates of deposit. Asked by a visitor about the new house on his property, Lutonsky hesitated, and then replied in his deep Oklahoma drawl, "Son, I've been building that house for fifty years."

Elgin cattle rancher and mineral trader Jim Glover carries two calling cards, a flimsy, inexpensive paper one for his cattle trade, and a firm plastic one with blood-red lettering for his oil and gas deals. There were landowners, said Glover, who were greedy, and eventually suffered the consequences. "I offered one guy $1 million for a hundred acres in mineral rights," he said. "He wouldn't sell, he said he could make a million a month from participating in wells." At the other extreme, there were those who, as an official of the Oklahoma Corporation Commission put it, "you could put a recipe for chicken gravy in front of them and they'd sign it."

Among the other beneficiaries of the Anadarko lease play were Oklahoma Indians, one of whom was a sixty-year-old man who bought a new car immediately after receiving his lease check, even though he'd never obtained a driver's license. Later, after stopping off for a beer at a local tavern, the man was picked up by the highway patrol and escorted to the station house. "They found he wasn't drunk," Jim Glover said, "but he left the car at the station and walked to the dealership to buy another one." When he returned home, his children asked him what happened to the first one. "Oh," he replied, "the police took it away." And Glover swears by another story about an Indian woman who tried to cash a check for $825,000 at a 24-hour convenience store.

With the money flowing like gas from a blown-out well, million-dollar oil and gas deals were sealed with a handshake. "Nothing was documented," said one oil and gas attorney. "You'd make deals and agree to write them up later." And so it was at Penn Square Bank. Firmly entrenched in its bad habits on documentation, Penn Square frequently used collateral previously pledged on one loan to secure a new loan to the same borrower. When the second note was sold to another bank, as often happened, the title of the first bank to the collateral became clouded. Penn Square loan officers, in preparing the documents, often confused or neglected to distinguish between the types of ownership of a well, and in many instances the borrower himself did not know what kind of interest he owned. Additionally, bank officers accepted mortgages as collateral that later turned out to be pledged to other banks.

Penn Square, and one or two officers in particular, also had a fondness for an instrument called the negative pledge. "It's the kind of agreement a lawyer can't stand. It's nothing but a written handshake," said one oil and gas attorney. Simply stated, a negative pledge is a one- or two-page form in which the borrower agrees not to sell or otherwise encumber his collateral, but it creates no mortgage lien on a property. So in reality, Penn Square was often making nothing more than unsecured personal loans. One young woman officer was reportedly so enamored of this questionable device that she was nicknamed the "Queen of the Negative Pledges."

Yet on December 31, 1980, while his staff was wallowing in sloppy and uncompleted paperwork, Beep Jennings could boast that in one year the assets of his bank had doubled to nearly $290 million. And he had begun to see his role in cosmic terms. In a letter to the regional office of the Comptroller of the Currency, Frank Murphy wrote:

> Penn Square Bank has committed itself to ending America's dependence on foreign energy and through a very satisfactory relationship with the Nation's top leaders in energy financing, Penn Square Bank has been devoting a lot of its resources to the energy field by participating Energy loans to some of the major upstream banks.

The chaos that reigned inside the whitewashed façade of Penn Square Bank was mirrored in the sleek black high-rise tower, dubbed Black Beauty, which served as the downtown Seattle headquarters of the Seattle First National Bank. Boyd, like Lytle, was high on lease lines, probably more so. In fact, on combination lease line and production deals with certain borrowers, Continental took the wheat—the production loan—while Seafirst took the chaff—the lease line. Energy was becoming the elite spot at Seafirst, as it was at Continental, and a source of resentment for employees on the branch side of the bank. "You'd work your fanny off in the branch system," said a former Seafirst officer, "but international, national, and energy would get all the recognition and perks." More rigorous standards were applied to loans made in the branches. For example, the branches were discouraged from making fixed-rate term loans at all, whereas Nelson's world banking division was "going out" seven to ten years, with interest only for the first three. Drillers with one-year contracts were given five years to pay. And companies that were flat broke got prime rate loans.

Boyd's standing instruction to his youthful staff was, "Your limit is my limit." Like his counterpart in Oklahoma City, Boyd believed in rapid response to loan requests and encouraged anyone who answered a phone call to get on a plane and "do the deal," and twenty-seven-year-old junior officers with two years' experience found themselves signing off on $10 million credits. Moreover, multimillion-dollar disbursements were advanced on the strength of a phone call from the energy department without the documentation and paperwork to back them up.

Unlike Continental and Northern Trust, Seafirst didn't hire an in-house petroleum engineer until February 1982. To do so, according to former Seafirst officers, would have thrown the compensation structure out of kilter, since an experienced petroleum engineer would have commanded a salary of at least $75,000 a year, more than Boyd himself was earning at the time. Meanwhile, Seafirst's management stewed over the loan concentration policy for energy. At Boyd's urging, according to former officers, the energy department's ceiling was constantly being bumped up, and soon skyrocketed from 1% to 15% of total loans.

It took about a year for the senior management of Seattle First National Bank to figure out that John Boyd, the super-salesman, was not a manager. Or, at least, it took them that long to do something about it. In late 1980, Paul Bergevin, a deliberate, soft-spoken manager of the bank's Yakima branch, was recruited by Seafirst's senior management to be the number two man in energy and charged with straightening out the number one guy they were unable to control themselves.

Early on, there were a number of officers, including Bergevin, who had misgivings about energy, Penn Square, and John Boyd. While Boyd's imitations of Oklahomans, Germans, and Arabs sent some of his colleagues into convulsions, they didn't amuse Bob Johnson, who occupied an adjoining office. "John would get boisterous at times," a colleague recalled. "He'd be on the phone to some German customer imitating a Nazi while Johnson was trying to carry on a conversation with the treasurer of Boeing."

"You guys are more trouble than you're worth. You belong on

Skid Row," Johnson is reported to have told Boyd on one occasion.

"No one ever asked aloud, 'Who *is* Penn Square Bank? Are they someone we want to do business with?'" observed one former officer. But several mumbled it to themselves when they saw Penn Square petroleum engineer Jeff Callard, a muscular, bearded former OU wrestling champion who moonlighted as a referee of women's mud wrestling contests, parade into Seafirst wearing dirty blue jeans and a T-shirt, looking like he just left the arena.

According to former Penn Square officers and later court testimony, Callard was not averse to signing off on reserve reports that would justify the loans Patterson and Jennings wanted to extend to certain borrowers in the first place. Later, according to court testimony, Patterson rewarded Callard's loyalty by presenting him with a $20,000 sailboat, a bonus Patterson said was approved by Jennings himself.

Along with the hundreds of millions of dollars that poured into Oklahoma from Seattle, Detroit, and Chicago, thousands of unemployed factory workers from those same cities streamed into Oklahoma City, Elk City, Woodward, and other small Oklahoma towns. It was, as one observer put it later, "a reverse *Grapes of Wrath.*" Entire families slept in tents, trailers, and pickup trucks, paying local farmers up to $300 a month for a place to park or set up camp, preferably near a pond where they could wash up. Motel rooms charged their guests not by the day but for an eight-hour shift and many of the new arrivals had to find a spare table in the laundry room to sleep on. Hundreds of small oil-field service companies and drilling contractors were formed to capitalize on the deep gas boom. One man is said to have become a millionaire selling rags to rigs. He bought assorted scrap cloth, shipped it to Mexico, where it was sorted, bundled, and returned by rail to Oklahoma. Tank truck drivers made $100 or more per job carting off the drilling fluid left in mud pits after wells were completed, and then selling it for $10 per barrel. Businesses were established to supply barbecue to drilling crews, and many entrepreneurs opened hot-shot services—the Federal Expresses of the oil patch—picking up and delivering urgently needed equipment and supplies to rig sites. According to cattleman-mineral trader Jim Glover, one man earned $65 an hour just to keep the steam heating at a rig site trailer house in working order. With backing from Penn Square Bank, the owners of these companies often became millionaires virtually overnight. Western Oklahoma had become the last American frontier.

It was an exuberant, optimistic time. That spirit was expressed in a poem signed by J.D. Allen and sent to his friends encased in plastic for Christmas 1980.

THE WILDCAT

Running high and looking good
Just like wildcats do and should
Fifty feet and sometimes higher
It fills the owner's soul with fire

Although there's stretch in every line,
It's running high and looking fine.
The driller often slips a string
But that is just a trifling thing

They cut a sand line, make a splice,
But only do it once or twice.
They use a steel line in a pinch—
The driller's never off an inch.

Geologists now come take the dope
And with a shining microscope
They study sand and shale and lime.
To think this out takes lots of time.

With their colossal brains they ponder
Mouth-opened farmers stand and wonder
Lease brokers stand in line and wait.
He speaks. "She's running high, looking great."

A thrill that shakes the very ground—
They're gone before you look around.
Royalties and leases sell,
She's running high and looking swell.

Three months have passed—another scene.
The rig is gone, the grass is green.
The gaping slush pit, cracked and dried,
An optimist, here, fought and died.

So thus it is with wildcat wells,
They're spudded in with clanging bells.
When plugged and shouts of joy have died.
You wonder who in hell has lied.

Have a prosperous year.
J.D. Allen.

FOLLOWING
THE PIED PIPER

B ANKING FADS TEND TO RUN IN FIVE-YEAR CYCLES, AND DAVID
Rockefeller's Chase Manhattan Bank was never an institution
to be left out of the latest one. In early 1981 Chase's image and earnings had just begun to recover from its calamitous affair with
REITs. The giant international bank was looking for ways to show
the Wall Street community that it was a reinvigorated institution
equipped to lead the charge into nationwide expansion as well as
nonbank activities like securities dealings, and to challenge the regulatory constraints that prevented banks from competing with the
money market mutual funds.

The business press had applauded the recovery of the Chase
Manhattan Bank from the REIT disaster. Just a year before, *Fortune*
magazine published an article entitled, "It's a Stronger Bank that
David Rockefeller Is Passing to His Successor." Rockefeller, who
was slated for retirement in April 1981, wanted to clear his name
before he left. Although Rockefeller was perceived by the public almost as a kind of head of state, the chairman of the board of the
Eastern establishment, he was viewed by his own colleagues as a nice
guy who was aloof, insecure, and ineffective as a manager. "David
was vulnerable to whoever got to him just before he left on one of his
overseas trips," said one former senior officer.

Chase had displayed a knack for showing up in all of the highly
publicized banking debacles. Rockefeller himself was blamed for
urging President Carter to admit his friend, the Shah of Iran, to the
United States for medical treatment, an event that triggered the
takeover of the U.S. Embassy in Teheran in 1979. Chase had more
than enough Iranian deposits to offset against loans, but the bank's
image was not enhanced by the episode.

Chase under Rockefeller was known for making big international loans and embarking on international projects of cosmic dimensions, such as dispatching a delegation to Peking to help finance China's modernization program. This commitment to international lending was reflected in the appointment of former Secretary of State and presidential adviser Henry Kissinger as chairman of the bank's international advisory committee. In 1980 nearly half of the bank's earnings came from its international activities. While maintaining its stature as a leading international lender during the 1970s, the bank had fallen behind archrival Citibank in almost every measure of financial performance.

Rockefeller's bank entered the 1970s just a smidgen smaller than Citicorp—Chase Manhattan had assets of $22.2 billion compared with $23.1 billion at Citicorp—but over the next ten years Citicorp seemed to make all the right moves, while Chase blundered at every opportunity. In banking, one mistake is often the prologue for the next one, and in trying to make up for the last one banks often stumble headlong into another.

By the end of 1980 the gap between Citi and Chase, in both size and profitability, had widened tremendously. In fact, thanks largely to the REIT episode, Chase's loan losses as a percentage of total loans—a hefty 1%, compared with an average of 0.69% for the top thirty-five banks, according to a Salomon Brothers study—were among the worst in the industry. Instead of profits, Chase earned a reputation as one of the more poorly managed large banks in the United States. By the late 1970s Chase had given up hope of ever catching up with Citibank, and had lowered its goals to simply maintaining its position as one of the top U.S. institutions. Nevertheless, Chase seemed to be on the mend. Loan losses had been scaled down to compare favorably with its peers. And return on assets, that key measure of profitability, was up to 0.53%, more than double the 0.24% to which it had plummeted in 1976.

Yet there were a number of observers within Chase and in the investment community who questioned whether Chase could possibly be stronger with Willard Butcher, David's handpicked successor, in command. He had come up through the branch system, and there were many insiders in the bank who felt he should have remained there.

Thomas S. Labrecque, a tall, gangly man who had worked closely with David Rockefeller during the New York City bond crisis in the mid-1970s, was literally "plucked up from the bowels of the bank" and thrown into a top management spot, as a senior officer put it later. Labrecque, described by one reporter as handsome in the same "ascetic way" as former California governor Jerry Brown, was known as a tough "hands-on" banker cast more in the mold of a "mean and aggressive" Citibanker than the congenial sort who in the past had found his way to 1 Chase Plaza.

Some say the era of congeniality ended in 1975 with the arrival of Alan F. Lafley as Chase's head of personnel, one of a number of new officers recruited from companies known for their enlightened management. Lafley had spent twenty years with General Electric, considered one of the best-managed companies in the United States. Described by fellow officers as the quintessential corporate intriguer, Lafley was credited with, or blamed for, establishing incentive systems that critics said ended up pitting one area of the bank against another. Said one longtime Chase hand, "Lafley came in and said, 'We're going to do away with the old boy network.' So he created a new boy network."

Like Continental and Seattle First, Chase embarked on a program of decentralization, again orchestrated by McKinsey and Company, that segmented its markets and pushed lending authority down to the lowest possible levels in the organization. Another milestone in this evolution came in late 1979, when newly appointed chief executive officer Butcher announced the disbanding of the bank's management committee, while asserting that the move was "not a convulsive or significant change" for the bank. These changes gave rise to a new generation of what one Chase insider called "corporate gunslingers": young, aggressive, and hungry bank officers who engaged in turf fights over who would get credit for the earnings on a loan on the one hand, and who would take the risk on the other. With this kind of organization, observed one Chase insider, "If you don't have controls, some people are going to get greedy."

As part of the reorganization, Chase decided to focus more attention on the domestic market. Chase's correspondent banking unit—the area that provides services to other banks—was split off from corporate banking and quickly staffed with what one insider called a lot of "young, emotionally immature kids." Traditionally, correspondent banking departments have been a haven for pleasant, sales-oriented officers who spend a good deal of their time traveling and entertaining customers. They are not considered the lending heavyweights. The credit decisions they make on U.S. banks are not especially difficult because much of the number crunching and analysis is done by outside consulting firms. While making a separate line of business out of correspondent services, Chase placed new emphasis on buying "downstream" loan participations and attempted to fortify the credit skills of an area where such skills were in short supply. It is considerably riskier, however, for a bank to buy down-stream participations than to make the same loans itself.

All this, said a former Chase officer, occurred in the late 1970s and early 1980s at a time of very thin spreads between what the bank was paying for funds and what it earned on them. "Butcher was pretty aggressive in what he expected," a former officer of the bank said. "You started looking for deals that would bump up your return on assets."

Meg Sipperly, an attractive Chase second vice-president in her late twenties who was responsible for the bank's correspondent bank business in Oklahoma, thought she had found a way to make her contribution to this effort. Penn Square had had what bankers call a "depository relationship" with Chase for years. As a former officer in Penn Square's correspondent unit remembers it, Sipperly made a cold call on the Oklahoma bank in late 1980. "We turned them off when we said we'd like them to look at small credits," said a former Penn Square officer. "We said we dealt with independents, and Chase said, 'Oh, yes, we handle [oil and gas] independents.' "

There was one hitch: oil and gas loans at Chase had historically been the province of its oil and gas division, for years one of the most highly regarded lending units at the nation's third largest bank. Chase, of course, had a long tradition in energy lending, a tradition that grew in part out of the Rockefeller ties to big oil. Big oil served on the Chase board, in the persons of John Swearingen of Standard Oil of Indiana and Howard Kauffmann of Exxon, two corporate legacies of the busting up of the old Rockefeller family oil monopoly.

Chase's elite energy group, which at one time was dominated by technically trained alumni of the major oil companies, was accustomed to assembling $400 million syndications and $200 million offshore oil projects in the North Sea for their ex-employers, and the unit had established a minimum threshold, below which it would not lend at all. In the old days, said a former senior energy lending officer, Chase never lent money on "raw" acreage, or on rigs unless there were contracts on them. As for production loans, the former officer said of the new generation of lenders, "They just looked at the bottom right-hand corner of the reserve reports and said, 'That's the number.' " According to former Chase officers, Sipperly and her boss, Dick Pinney, brought Bill Patterson and four relatively small deals to the petroleum department in early 1981.

But energy had little interest in $1 million loans to independents in Oklahoma that it had barely heard of and scoffed at the four deals, Bill Patterson, and the attempts of the domestic institutions unit to play at energy lending. Growled one petroleum department officer later, "Two of the borrowers were crooks, and the other two were just bad deals."

Nevertheless, the domestic institutions unit was convinced of the merits of the four credits and of the potential of the Penn Square relationship. After all, they figured, Continental, whose reputation in energy lending was equal to or superior to Chase's was fully behind Penn Square. Continental was Chase's big Chicago correspondent, and the New York bank developed a healthy respect for its Midwest colleague and competitor. So not long after the confrontation with the petroleum group, top executives of the domestic institutions division approved the Penn Square loans, which reportedly included lease lines and 100% debt on rigs, a no-no among traditional energy lenders. In doing so, they reversed the long-standing policy restricting to the oil and gas department the making of energy loans, a decision that was followed by an exchange of many heated memos, and much bad blood, between the two divisions. In one of those memos, according to a Chase officer, oil and gas later asked to take a look at some of the Penn Square loans but was told, in so many words, "Mind your own business."And at least one Chase officer, executive vice-president Bill Hinchman, was warned by one Oklahoma City banker about dealing with Penn Square. Dale Mitchell, then president of the First National Bank of Oklahoma City, thought he was doing a favor for a close correspondent when he told Hinchman, " 'You guys are crazy to get involved with them.' He just gave me a blank stare," Mitchell recalled later.

There was plenty of intellectual support for the correspondent division's move into lending to the Oklahoma independents. Around the time Sipperly made contact with Penn Square, Chase's prestigious energy economics department was projecting that oil prices would rise to $104 a barrel by 1990, according to the April 1981 issue of its newsletter, *The Petroleum Situation.*

Actually, many of the participations Chase bought from Penn Square were not energy loans at all, but lifestyle loans, including, for example, a $3.5 million credit to finance Hefner's new Westwind jet. Some weren't even in Oklahoma, or the oil patch. One of the first transactions Chase Manhattan completed with Penn Square was a deal on a Florida marina "dockominium" that the big New York bank foisted on its new partner in Oklahoma City. It was a deal that would eventually spell the beginning of the end of the brief love affair between the two banks.

Allan Senall, a Florida real estate promoter and business associate of Ken Tureaud, planned to convert a 600-slip marina, Maximo Moorings, in St. Petersburg, from a rental arrangement to a kind of marina condominium, a concept one Florida newspaper described as having a track record about as successful as selling "autographed copies of Adolf Hitler's *Mein Kampf* in downtown Tel Aviv." Sipperly, former officers say, proposed the deal to Tom Orr. Penn Square Bank president Frank Murphy turned the deal down. But as an accommodation to a new upstream correspondent, Penn Square later agreed to make the $3.5 million loan and sell the bulk of it to Chase. The coincidental fact that Brooke Grant, the brother-in-law of Chase vice-president Dick Pinney, was an officer of Senall's Semantha Petroleum may or may not have had some bearing on the transaction. Senall gave a mortgage of $2.4 million to the original owners and assured the bank that he owned all of Maximo Moorings stock, when in fact Orr's sidekick Clark Long, the Penn Square officer who handled the negotiations, had been cut in as part owner.

Unfortunately, most of the boat owners balked at the plan and moved their yachts elsewhere, leaving Senall high and dry. For more than a year, however, Penn Square disguised the fact that Maximo Moorings was a flop by advancing interest to Chase without receiving it from Senall. But according to sworn testimony by a former Penn Square officer, Chase, like Continental, was well aware of the practice of advancing interest to upstream banks before, or without, receiving it from the borrower.

A small-framed man with graying hair, Senall was involved with Tureaud in his River Ridge real estate project in Florida, and Tureaud is said to have introduced Senall to Tom Orr at Penn Square Bank. Jennings also had a hand in cementing the Senall ties to Penn Square. At some point, California loan- and money-broker David Robinson contacted Jennings on behalf of Senall and agreed to place $2.5 million in certificates of deposit at Penn Square in return for loans to himself and his client. Jennings, it is alleged by federal investigators, instructed Orr to open a million-dollar line of credit for Senall, and over the next year Orr made a million in loans to him, taking a house brokerage fee in the process. Senall, Penn Square officers said, was a guarantor on many of Orr's deals, and many prospective customers came in and said Senall or Tureaud had recommended them.

Chase was willing, at least in the early days of the relationship, to take small deals and all the administrative headaches that go with them. But Chase had an understanding with its downstream correspondent that was to give the big New York bank some comfort: Penn Square promised to buy back loans from Chase whenever Chase became uneasy with them.

·E I G H T E E N·

THE "A" TEAM

IN JANUARY 1981 REGIONAL ADMINISTRATOR CLIFTON POOLE SENT in his "A" Team. Examiner-in-charge George E. Clifton, Jr., was one of the heavyweights, a numbers man known for his ability to look at a set of figures on a bank and quickly assess its condition. According to one former examiner, there was some debate on whom to send in, because after the bruising Penn Square took the year before, the bank, like an acutely ill patient facing major surgery, reportedly asked for a second opinion. But if the diagnosis Bill Chambers came up with in 1980 could be considered benign, then Clifton concluded that the condition in 1981 was malignant. Mindful of the low esteem Southwestern bankers had for the Comptroller's ability to review energy loans, Dallas dispatched a couple of their top energy loan experts from Houston and Austin to Penn Square.

"They looked in every nook and cranny," said a former Penn Square officer. "They laid it on the line with Jennings." According to former officers, Penn Square's internal auditor asked Clifton, "Is there some way we can take the keys away from Jennings and Patterson?" Clifton reportedly felt that would be difficult because of the large stake Jennings owned in the bank and the control he exercised over the board. This time around, the examiners found "further deterioration in the bank's overall condition," and recognized, at long last, that they were no longer dealing with a mere $300 million bank. Consequently, they wound up spending as much time on Penn Square as they would have on an institution six times as large.

Clifton's examiners discovered a letter from Continental Illinois that revealed the "buyback arrangement" that existed between Penn Square and the Chicago giant, a major concern because it meant that any time Continental got antsy about Penn Square loans, it could ship them back to Oklahoma and put Beep Jennings and Bill Patterson out of business. That was unlikely, of course, because of the close personal and financial links that had developed between John Lytle and Bill Patterson.

Moreover, Clifton found that Penn Square had unloaded $15.4 million in bad loans to its correspondents but, incredibly, Dallas neglected to pass the word to the other regions because it considered the amounts insignificant. Yet it was clear to Clifton that Penn Square hadn't taken the Treaty of Dallas too seriously. Borrowers with bad loans continued to get more loans, and Penn Square persisted in violating lending limits. In a final meeting with Penn Square, he told them that a cease and desist order, one of the regulator's most powerful weapons, was justified and should be considered.

On March 10, Clifton wrote:

> [C]ompliance with all the requirements of the Agreement must be closely monitored if it is to prove effective in this bank. The bank must be maintained on an accelerated exam schedule as an examiner's presence in the bank can be a motivating force to encourage compliance with the terms of the Agreement.

It was at this time that Dallas decided that despite the rat's nest Clifton had turned up, the next exam would be limited in scope, and designed only to monitor compliance with the formal agreement. Dallas likely figured that Clifton had uncovered all the problems he could possibly turn up; in any event, the office had always made a practice of alternating comprehensive exams with limited exams in dealing with 3-rated banks.

This decision went contrary to Clifton's own recommendations. Clifton had found that things had gotten so far out of control that only another general exam could assess Penn Square's compliance. (Later, an audit of the Office of the Comptroller's performance in the Penn Square episode would be critical of the response of the agency to the problems at the bank.) Nonetheless, Poole stuck to the book and scheduled the limited exam. Meanwhile, Penn Square had stopped sending monthly reports to Dallas on its progress in correcting criticized assets and law violations, as well as a required report on its hot money: the $100,000 certificates of deposit report. The Dallas region apparently did not even know these documents were missing, and took no action to obtain them. Penn Square continued to book its evergreen revolvers, rolling over debt to its oilmen customers just as if they were loans to sovereign states like Mexico or Poland.

Arthur Young and Company, the Big Eight accounting firm, was also troubled by what it found. After the accountants completed their audit of the 1980 results, they wrote the kind of letter to Bill P. Jennings no bank chief executive officer likes to receive. The letter, dated March 13, 1981, read: "We were unable to satisfy ourselves as to the adequacy of the reserve for possible loan losses at December 31[1980] due to the lack of supporting documentation of collateral on loans." The Arthur Young team didn't have to look at many files to see that Penn Square's practice of basing loans on some bloated reserve values rather than cash flow was fundamentally flawed.

Penn Square had received another qualified opinion. Indeed, it was a scope qualification, accompanied by a "material adverse letter," one of the worst possible opinions an auditing firm can give a client. Harold Russell, the partner for Arthur Young who signed off on the opinion letter, was a husky, self-effacing professional who, as chairman of a committee on bank audits, had literally written the book on the subject. A little over a year later, he would be elevated by a congressional committee to the status of hero for his opinion on Penn Square, but for Russell it was not a matter of heroics. He would later tell a friend that there was no conflict or extraordinary courage involved at all. He simply called it as he saw it. He did his job.

The senior management of Penn Square knew that, if the Arthur Young opinion became known, it would unquestionably shake public and investor confidence to the point where the house of cards would probably tumble. Fortunately for them, but unfortunately for the banks that would continue to buy hundreds of millions in loans, and the credit unions, thrift institutions, and individuals who would later buy Penn Square's certificates of deposit and commercial paper, Russell was an intensely private man. Just as he would never make a call that he did not believe in, he would never breathe a word about a client's condition to anyone—even to his wife; most of all his wife.

Ironically, George Clifton and Harold Russell arrived at their negative conclusions at a time when Penn Square's reported 1980 earnings—$4.3 million on average assets for the year of $229 million—placed it at the top of its peer group. Clifton and Russell called into question the underlying quality of those earnings, which were derived largely from booking and selling loans, not holding them.

While the examiners were poring over Penn Square's books, the borrowers were taking off in a fleet of Penn Square–financed private jets for the inauguration of President Ronald Reagan in Washington. J.D. Allen and the Eagles had done their jobs well. Oklahoma boasted one of the largest contingents of Republican Eagles of any state, and the delegation from the Sooner state helped set the tone for the four-day affair. As GHK's Bill Dutcher recalls, "The mood was one where people weren't apologetic about being rich. It was a movable feast," he said, and limousines, diamonds, and furs were very much in evidence.

Reagan no sooner took office than he made good on his promise to accelerate the decontrol of domestic oil prices. It was, as Dutcher put it later, a case of "be careful what you want. You might get it." Oilmen expected that decontrol would lead to higher prices, and indeed, for about a month, that is precisely what happened. In April 1981, however, oil prices began their inexorable downward slide.

Bob Hefner's constant critic, IPAA's Bill Anderson, recalled that "we had a new President, and Bobby became a born-again Republican." Having achieved special status for gas below 15,000 feet, Hefner turned his attention to making sure Congress left the Natural Gas Policy Act alone. He had won; now he had to defend the fruits of his victory.

THE TOMCAT

THEY CALLED THEM THE "DRY HOLE DRILLERS." CLARK ELLISON and his partner, Buddy Appleby, had long been convinced of the vast potential of the Anadarko Basin, more specifically a formation on its eastern shelf, some three miles below a peanut farm near Eakly, Oklahoma, seventy-five miles west of Oklahoma City. Ellison had inherited his belief in the Anadarko from his father, Robert Hefner's mentor, who had died of a heart attack in 1963. Living out of cheap motel rooms that doubled as their office, the two men scoured the country for investors and exhausted the patience of countless Oklahoma drilling contractors, who wore out countless drill bits probing for that elusive gas. Finally, they managed to borrow $100,000 and work out a deal with the Washington Gas and Light Company, which distributes gas in the Washington, D.C., area. And in 1980 they put in a call to Cliff Culpepper, a crusty Oklahoma wildcatter who began his career in the oil patch driving a frac truck for Halliburton, the giant oil-field service company.

Known for his irascible disposition as well as a knack for finding oil and gas almost in spite of himself, Culpepper, the head of Ports of Call Oil, had become something of a legend in his own time in Oklahoma. Ellison and Appleby persuaded Culpepper to drill the No.1 Tomcat by offering him an 18% interest, and in June 1980 work began on a well that within the year would focus national attention on the awesome wealth that could be generated from high-pressure deep gas.

Culpepper is a big-boned, broad-shouldered man, who sweeps his graying hair straight back on the sides. He is, said an acquaintance, "A man in his late fifties who likes to pretend he's in his twenties." Unlike the majority of Oklahoma oilmen, Culpepper was not the "cowboy type." In those days, he didn't wear blue jeans and cowboy boots, preferring slacks and penny loafers (he bought ten pairs at a time), and silk short-sleeve sports shirts, which he wore year-round, regardless of the weather. Among other things, Culpepper was known for his unorthodox well-completion techniques and lopsided oil deals designed to make money for Cliff Culpepper whether oil and gas were found or not.

Normally, when an oilman reaches his target depth, he seals off the zone by placing "packers" in the well. Then, using a device called a perforating gun which blasts holes in the well casing, he tests the formation for oil and gas. Culpepper, however, typically perforated the entire well, a practice frowned upon in the oil patch because it permits salt water to intermingle with gas and oil from producing formations. Said Jerry Tilley, his former drilling superintendent, "He'd just perforate the whole thing and hope for the best. He always had to do something a little bit different."

Even if he didn't drill a dry hole, the reserves were sometimes so small in his prospects that the investors never saw a return, according to local oilmen. "People just didn't understand that you could hit a well and still not make money," said one veteran energy banker. But more than his well-completion techniques, Culpepper was notorious for his free spending and heavy gambling. "He'd go into a club and if he really liked the waitress or a particular girl, he'd go over and lay out a lot of bills," said Tilley. "I saw one instance where he laid down $5,000 for one girl just to run around with him. But he'd make such a deal about it, where everybody in the club would hear about it, that the girl became embarrassed and wouldn't go.

"If you wanted to be in good with Cliff you'd go to the bars," Tilley said. "People who went to the bars made more money usually, and got big raises. If you just picked up the $100 bills he dropped behind, that's a pretty good salary by itself." When Culpepper wanted to go to Las Vegas, he'd just call for the Lear jet and take off. "But the most I've seen him lose in Vegas is $200,000," Tilley recalled.

Culpepper would like to have owned the oil field, and everybody in it. "C.W. never has a company unless he owns 51 percent," said Tilley. He paid his employees well, sometimes three or four times what they could make elsewhere; it was not unusual, in fact, for a secretary to start at $2,000 a month, or for a landman who might earn $2,000 at another company to make as such as $6,000 a month working for Culpepper, plus unlimited expenses, a Visa card, and a company car. The theory was that if he paid his employees three times more than they could earn elsewhere, they wouldn't cheat him. "Cliff thought everybody was going to steal off of him sooner or later," Tilley said.

The catch was that "when you work for C.W. he owns you, you had no days off," recalled Tilley, who claimed to have labored thirty-one days a month, and to have been on call seven days a week, twenty-four hours a day, for four years without missing a day.

C.W., his former associates say, seemed to thrive on being the center of attention. On at least one occasion, Culpepper created an uproar by landing his helicopter on the side of the practice field before a home game at the University of Oklahoma, according to Tilley, who noted that Culpepper claimed the distinction of being the first person ever to install a bar in a helicopter. Whether traveling by car or helicopter, Culpepper often arrived at drill sites with a bottle of vodka in one hand. "He didn't drive very well when he drank," Tilley recalled. "One year was all he could get out of a Lincoln. It was a disaster after that."

Compared with some of the other Oklahoma oilies, C.W. was not much of a raconteur. He had about ten or twelve stories that he tended to tell over and over again, most of them somehow related to his prowess as an oilman, and how he succeeded in bringing in a well using methods everyone else frowned upon. As Tilley remembers it, C.W. would boast, " 'Well, I did this job that was twice as big as what they recommended and this well is a good well, or I pumped so much of this or so much of that.' He can't seem to remember that he already told the same story." Cliff was a loner, mused Mr. Tilley, whose best friend was himself.

Despite his idiosyncrasies and questionable business practices, Culpepper had a small circle of investors who gravitated to the flamboyant oilman. Bill Gammie of Yakima, Washington, is a towering figure, a man as solid as a redwood tree from a Pacific Northwest forest. Gammie, a fruit grower nicknamed the "Apple King" of Washington State, first met Culpepper at Big Bay, a bucolic fishing and camping spot north of Vancouver, British Columbia. Gammie had just disembarked from his yacht, the *Golden Delicious,* with a load of salmon he had caught earlier in the day. Culpepper, who was standing on the dock, asked how and where he caught all the fish.

"Who are you to ask the best fisherman in the Pacific Northwest how to catch fish?" Gammie replied in mock disgust.

"I just wanted to know." Culpepper shrugged.

"You'll have to pay for that information," said Gammie.

Culpepper invited Gammie aboard for a rum and tonic. He turned abruptly to the deckhand on his own 85-foot motor yacht and shouted, "Get the man a rum and tonic." The upshot of the encounter was that Gammie invested with Cliff Culpepper, and was introduced to what he remembered wistfully as the social whirl and carnival atmosphere of boom-town Oklahoma City. "Your hotel room was always waiting. Bell jet helicopters picked you up to take you to the rigs. Everyone was going to become a millionaire," said Gammie. Culpepper was not a high-pressure salesman, observed one investor. As C.W. always said, "I don't owe you nothin', you don't owe me nothin'."

Early on, Bill Jennings found little to recommend Cliff Culpepper. According to one former officer, Jennings used to say, "That son-of-a-bitch Culpepper, he'll never get a loan from my bank." But Culpepper eventually got millions in loans from Bill Jennings's bank. For all his foibles, Culpepper, who had only a grade school education, was a shrewd negotiator who waved his arms around like a traffic cop in business meetings as he became increasingly agitated. But one gas well excited him like nothing else in his career as an oilman.

The Tomcat well came in with a vengeance, heralded by a deafening roar that sounded like two Boeing 747 jetliners revving their engines at full throttle before charging down adjoining runways. Ellison and Appleby got a call on the morning of January 28, 1981, and learned that they had become millionaires the night before. Their deep gas well had hit a high-pressure reservoir at 15,300 feet, spewing forth natural gas at a rate of more than 115 million cubic feet a day.

The blowout sucked loose sandstone and shale into the hole, and while doing so boosted the stock price of Washington Gas and Light Company from $21.75 to as much as $37.25 per share on the New York Stock Exchange. Carter Hines, Culpepper's stepson-in-law, and an official of Ports of Call, recalls that when the Tomcat No. 1 came in, the ground literally trembled beneath his feet, and the gas whistled up through the well bore under pressures of 14,000 pounds per square foot. "You could be in a car a hundred yards away and couldn't hear someone right next to you," he said, adding, "You've never seen so many big people run so fast in your life." The pressures were so enormous that they blew up the "watermelon," a massive steel device used to channel gas production out to the flow lines. The blowout created a cloud of invisible gas that hovered over the town of Eakly for a week, forcing its evacuation, and the brilliant, 100-foot-high flare from the well could be seen by passing motorists on Interstate 40 fourteen miles to the north.

The Tomcat tested out at 115 million cubic feet per day, but for years state conservation rules have restricted production to no more than 50% of capacity. And, in practice, most prudent petroleum engineers would limit production to levels considerably less than that. But when unsophisticated investors and reporters took a pencil to the numbers, multiplying 115 million cubic feet times $8 per thousand cubic feet—then the going rate for deep gas—the results were staggering. On the face of it, the well appeared to yield $9,200 a day to an investor with a 1% interest. The Tomcat attracted national media attention, including a lengthy article in the august *Wall Street Journal*.

Within days, investors lined up outside Ports of Call's Oklahoma City offices begging the flamboyant oilman for a piece of the Tomcat. Culpepper told them they'd have to pay 2% for a 1% interest, a double promote. "Sure, sign me up," they said. He flew prospective investors out to the rig in helicopters. "Send me a check before the thirty-first and you'll never have to pay taxes again," he told them expansively.

"Ports of Call didn't have to find investors," said Tilley. "Investors found Ports of Call. They kept coming out there . We had them in from all over, Canada, California, Florida, Arkansas. Everybody was interested in the Tomcat." Said another former employee, "Canadian money was coming in by the truckloads." Apple King Bill Gammie phoned Culpepper from Yakima after hearing about the Tomcat and quipped, "Well, did you get my check?"

In the aftermath of the Tomcat, recalled Hines, ten deep rigs were drilling within a 10-square-mile area of the Tomcat. Once the well blew out, he said, leases in the area went for up to $10,000 an acre. "Gas purchasers," he said, "were salivating to get tied into the wells. We could have sold our acreage for millions.

"You're talking about a well that would make a poor man a millionaire," said Hines. At one point an investor who put up 1%, or $40,000, of the drilling cost incurred up until the first blowout could realistically have anticipated a monthly income of $50,000 for the 15-year life of the well. And of that $40,000, the investor might have spent only $10,000 out of his own pocket, having borrowed the rest.

Ironically, while the blowout pointed up the presence of large gas reserves, it happened in the first place largely because Culpepper and his crew lacked the aptitude or experience in drilling for deep high-pressure gas. Nevertheless, the Tomcat blowout, occurring at a time when the real estate and stock markets were on their ears, fueled investor interest in the Anadarko like few other events before it, exacerbating the already severe shortages of rigs and tubular goods, and sending even more money on a futile chase after a dwindling number of solid prospects.

"In the long run, the Tomcat probably hurt the gas business more than any other single event," according to Sam Hammons, former Gov. Boren's energy adviser. "There was so much money coming in, you found operators drilling for the more marginal targets. They could justify $7 or $8 per MCF, but not a weighted average price of $3, a more realistic economics. Government regulation is the reason there was a shortage, and government legislation is the reason prices went as high as they did." Thanks to Culpepper and others like him, drilling expenditures in Oklahoma would soar to more than $4.6 billion in 1981, up nearly a third over 1980. And all but $800 million of that amount would be spent in the Anadarko alone.

Not long after the Tomcat blew, the prestigious Wall Street investment firm of Lehman Brothers Kuhn Loeb put out a benchmark endorsement of the Anadarko that asserted, "The Anadarko Basin is one of the best areas in the United States to explore for deep gas. There are numerous potential reservoir rocks in a vast undrilled area, and the economics of exploration and development is favorable." While the Lehman Brothers report was one of many issued in 1981, it is said to have been particularly influential in spurring new interest in the basin.

This was not the first blowout of the Tomcat, nor would it be the last. The first time around, late in 1980, Culpepper got into a "mud fight" with Jim Fulton, his drilling superintendent, a man with more than thirty years' experience in the oil patch. Culpepper won the battle but nearly lost the well. There is a delicate balance between mud weight and formation pressure, and Culpepper always insisted on the lightest mud available. Light mud is cheaper, and drilling proceeds faster through it, but the driller also runs the risk that it won't be able to contain the pressures. Fulton had argued for a heavier mud and was countermanded by Culpepper. As Fulton expected, it could not stabilize the pressures, and the well blew out shale, sticking the drill pipe down in the hole. Sometime after the first blowout, Culpepper fired Fulton. Said Tilley later, "It wasn't his fault. It was Culpepper's 100%," adding, "When you work for C.W. you work strictly for him and he calls all the shots." In the short term, however, Culpepper would make money regardless of how poorly drilling went on the well.

Culpepper used a variety of gimmicks to impress naive investors.

One of his favorites was opening up the well to make the flow lines shake. "You'd think there was a lot more gas there when he opened up the well and let more gas flow down the line," said Tilley. The problem was, in doing that to a high-pressure gas well, he ran the risk of causing the well bore to cave in, and that is in fact what happened.

Ports of Call was never able to complete the Tomcat. But before investors removed Culpepper as operator of the well and replaced him with Robinson Brothers, owned by J.D. Hodges, the brother of Culpepper rival Jack Hodges, more than $20 million had disappeared down the hole. According to an audit of the well commissioned later by investors, a substantial portion of that money was allegedly misused by Culpepper.

Culpepper, who has been cited by the Oklahoma Securities Commission for alleged securities law violations, had set up an empire of oil-field service companies and other entities that allegedly submitted inflated charges to Ports of Call, costs that were passed on to investors. Cliff's son Mike owned Mike's Dozer's, which did the excavation work on the drill sites. And a son-in-law owned a tank truck company. Culpepper's aviation company, TravelLear, which owned his fleet of Lear jets, allegedly billed the Tomcat for the costs of flying investors out to the well. "Everybody was making a profit except the investors, except the guys paying the bills," said a former employee.

One of the most flagrant abuses was Tomcat Supply, which bought drill pipe from manufacturers and then sold it to Ports of Call at prices substantially above the market, according to former employees. In fact, the company was apparently little more than a file box for invoices. Bills would come in for supplies, and a clerk would book them and tack on a large mark-up for Ports of Call, explained a source familiar with the operation.

One observer grinned, "I met Tomcat Supply. Her name was Sheila."

Culpepper's employees actually were relieved when the boss took off for one of his vacation retreats, because that would occasionally allow them time to solve a problem without his interference. Often, however, C.W. called up and barked orders to his men over the phone. "We'd look at the situation," said Tilley, "and fix the problem. Then Cliff would call up from somewhere and make a split-second decision, without thinking about it. He'd call up and mess up in a few minutes what it had taken two months to straighten out."

But as long as the investor money continued to flow, the Tomcat and other Culpepper wells financed an opulent lifestyle for everyone connected with them. In addition to a villa in Cancun, Culpepper owned a $3 million mansion overlooking the harbor in Santa Barbara, California, the 85-foot motor yacht, and a large, if somewhat garish, home in Oklahoma City with a suit of medieval armor in the foyer. Likewise, Mike Culpepper bought a palatial vacation home on Grand Lake, a favorite retreat of Oklahoma's new oilmen. Chisled into a cliff below his home were cages housing a lion, a black panther, monkeys, and other wild animals.

"When you've got all that to keep up," observed Jerry Tilley, "you've got to keep the money rolling in."

Ultimately, however, even the most naïve investors became disillusioned with the Tomcat and refused to pay their proportionate share of the costs, called the joint interest billings.

Perhaps more than any other well, the Tomcat embodied, and symbolized, the excesses and the deficiencies of the gas boom era, all of which combined to drive up costs, increase bank borrowings, and turn off investors. Possibly the most serious of the deficiencies was the acute shortage of experienced drilling crews, a problem that became readily apparent as the rig count in Oklahoma soared to more than 800. Where once an engineer with thirty years of experience might have supervised the completion job on a deep gas rig, observed Dr. Talley, one with six months' experience was suddenly in charge of a $3 million hole. In fact, it was not unusual for an engineer in his mid- to late twenties to earn more than $100,000 a year. Similarly, roustabouts, the entry-level position on a drilling crew, often became drillers after only six months on the rig. Crews came in from economically depressed Northern states like Ohio and Michigan, worked for a week, and returned home. Heretofore, a man might work for years as a roustabout before a contractor entrusted the operation of a $10 million drilling rig to him. And young accountants making $30,000 a year working for Big Eight firms suddenly found themselves confronted with offers to work as chief financial officers for oil companies at six-figure salaries, plus bonuses, and overriding royalty interests. Turnover was high in the field as well as the office. "You'd train them and they'd leave after six months," recalled one oilman. Oklahoma's unemployment rate was consistently among the lowest in the nation, and the virtually limitless job opportunities led to a cavalier work ethic. "Rig crews ignored maintenance," said a rig salesman. "They forgot to put oil in the crankcase. If they were criticized for it, they'd just leave and get another job elsewhere."

"People in their twenties and thirties were real spoiled," admitted one young landman. "We thought we were worth more than we were."

Dr. Talley attributes the shortage of qualified help in part to the cheap gas prices of the 1960s, when the average cost of finding gas was higher than the revenue from the production. "If you got out of school in 1964 with a 4.0 average and a master's degree in petroleum engineering you'd be lucky to get $500 a month. So we had old oilies and new oilies," he observed, "but we didn't have people in between."

Shortages of materials, like shortages of men, drove prices into the stratosphere and forced operators to use equipment ill suited for the task at hand. Tight supplies gave rise to hoarding of items such as tubular goods—namely drill pipe—and what one pipe broker called a "daisy chain" in the trading of pipe. "Pipe brokers sold pipe they didn't have," explained one manufacturer's representative, "alluding to the fact that they had it, and in turn bought it from someone else who didn't have it but said he did." Each of them, of course, took a profit on pipe neither of them actually owned when they sold it. Oil companies themselves made fortunes speculating on pipe and other goods, buying at one price and charging it out at another. Similarly, one supplier with the foresight to have bought junk rig components at bargain basement prices in the 1960s sold them at fifty times their cost in the early 1980s. "There was no wholesale," recalled one Oklahoma City oil and gas lawyer. "If you paid cash up front you got suggested retail."

The shortages were so severe that operators even lost their leases because they couldn't find a rig, and if they found a rig, they couldn't drill the hole because they couldn't obtain the tubular goods. The economics of drilling became so perverted that operators put the rig before the hole, so to speak, drilling a well just because they happened to have a rig available, not because they had a good prospect. Wells that were budgeted for $100 a foot on the operator's "authorization for expenditure" forms actually came in at $200 a foot. And drilling reports show that deep gas men sometimes spent as much time fishing broken bits and other lost equipment out of a 23,000-foot hole as they did drilling it. Then when the general partner couldn't pay the bills, he reached into the funds allocated for the next year's drilling program to pay off this year's expenses in yet another variation on the age-old Ponzi scheme. All in all, the 1980 and 1981 programs just didn't find enough gas to make it all worthwhile.

The deeper the well, the more likely it was to exceed its budget, and it was not unusual for the cost of deep well to go over budget by as much as a third or more. According to one loan workout specialist, the last 3,000 feet in a 15,000-foot hole can cost as much as the first 12,000 feet. This occurred largely because of the mechanical failures that resulted from the intense heat and pressures, and the inexperience of the rig crews in dealing with these conditions. Months can be spent, for example, in fishing out a piece of drill pipe that breaks off at 16,000 feet.

Moreover, there was considerable evidence that many operators bypassed shallower producing formations to get down to the deep unregulated gas commanding prices five times that of the shallow stuff. Yet in the frenzy to complete wells, there were few, including investors, who complained about costs. In fact, hardly anyone was conscientiously keeping track of them. Geologists and engineers are the prima donnas of the oil patch, and they don't have a great appreciation for paperwork. Engineers take the attitude that if it weren't for them, accountants wouldn't be there. But for the authorization for expenditures—the budget for a well—to work, the field employees have to supply the office with adequate information. For example, independent operators are not known for their efficient inventory control and typically neglect to keep track of equipment like pipe and sucker rod. In practice, explained the head of a company that sells accounting systems to oil companies, "If you're out in the field and need something, you just go back and get it without doing the paperwork. Most independents," he added, "started out as oil-field hands. Not many bookkeepers rise to the top." The attitude was, said one oil and gas auditor, "there's an unlimited source of funds, so why bother?"

As a result, operators frequently had no idea what they'd spent on a particular well, or whether they had actually made any money. Even worse, the informality that characterized oil company accounting and management practices left plenty of room for some deft maneuvers. For example, operators often "smoothed out" the expenses of their wells, charging pipe and other equipment to a profitable well while using it on a poor one. These loose practices also left room for graft and corruption, oil-patch style. Indeed, the Oklahoma gas boom gave rise to an entirely new code of ethics and morality.

Along with an unlimited expense account and a company car, one of the fringe benefits of an oil rig driller was the right to sell used bits on the side. While most companies kept track of $18,000 diamond bits, which at one time had a salvage value of about $6,000, inventory control on the cheaper models was sometimes lax. After a well was completed or abandoned, bits were often left over, and they had a way of showing up in someone else's well. "It was considered okay to sell a used bit," said one oil-field hand, "but it wasn't okay to sell a new bit."

No one kept good records of mud, or drilling fluid. One oil and gas auditor cited an instance of a drilling superintendent who specified an "asphalt blend" mud, which he ordered at $63 a barrel from a company owned by his two sons. Not only could the mud have been bought for $43 a barrel, but his sons were using sludge from oil tank bottoms to mix with the fluid. There was enough slack in a well costing $10 million to hide $100,000 easily, and usually much more.

The kickbacks paid to the engineers and tool pushers by the rig and service companies took many forms. Some were "innocent," like $500 cowboy boots and salmon fishing trips to Big Bay and Alaska. Some were not. More than one landman received a tin of pralines with a quarter-ounce of cocaine buried at the bottom. Cocaine and drug use, in fact, reached near-epidemic proportions during the boom, rising almost in tandem with the Hughes rig count. At least one major Penn Square borrower was a known trafficker in the white powder, and a not insignificant amount of the money borrowed from the bank went up the nose instead of down the hole. Then there were the women. According to a newspaper account of a trial in Oklahoma City federal court, Danny Merz, a co-owner of the Elk City-based White Stripe Pipe Inspection Company acknowledged that company checks designated "secretarial services" and "supplies" were in fact used to pay for the services of prostitutes. Merz admitted that he would toss $300 to $400 on a table at a night spot and tell the tool pushers who contracted for his company's services to "have a good time" if he couldn't join them. Not surprisingly, Oklahoma's divorce rate, and the number of reported instances of venereal disease, reached record levels during the height of the oil and gas boom.

·T W E N T Y·

THE IRON MEN

IT WAS WEDNESDAY NIGHT—SPORTSMEN'S NIGHT—AT THE COW boys, an Oklahoma City country-western dance hall where drugstore cowboys and cowgirls wearing designer jeans, cowboy hats, and boots danced the "Two Step" and "Cotton-Eyed Joe." Cowboys had become one of Bill Patterson's favorite places to entertain out-of-town bankers, a number of whom happened to be in town this Wednesday. Calls went out to some of Penn Square's preferred customers, like Jack Hodges and Carl Swan, whose borrowings with the bank were well into the eight-figure range. And, as usual, Patterson invited everyone and anyone who happened to be within shouting distance of his second-floor office to join the festivities.

It was an auspicious group for what started out as an impromptu gathering of bankers and about fifteen independent oilmen. They dined on roast quail, the specialty of the house prepared by stuffing the tiny birds with a small purple onion, wrapping them in bacon, and then charcoal-broiling them over a mesquite wood fire. The Cowboys' roast quail and steaks were so popular with the new oilies that they would occasionally order in advance and fly in by jet helicopter from oil centers like Enid and Elk City, land in an adjoining lot, pick up dinner, and take off again.

Patterson arrived late and ordered roast quail and Amaretto and soda, his favorite drink. He then entertained his guests by sipping the Amaretto and soda out of his Gucci loafers. As for the quail, one guest said, "He had one of them, when he wasn't chewing on it, stuffed in his hip pocket, and another one, when he wasn't eating it, stuffed in his shirt pocket. He'd walk along drinking Amaretto out of his shoe and would reach in his pocket and pull out this quail, chew on it a bit, and put it back in his pocket. Just for the general amusement of everyone. Those guys from Manny Hanny were astounded.

"Patterson was a hail-fellow-well-met," the guest said. "People who liked him tended to like him a lot. When he was calmed down, he was a real easy guy to talk to."

Mike Tighe of Northern Trust had attended Dartmouth College

(the setting for the movie *Animal House*) in the late 1950s, and he knew Bluto and Flounder and Otter. So Tighe, having grown accustomed to Patterson's antics, thought his performance that night was pretty funny. Conrad Albert, a quiet, almost shy, senior vice-president of Manufacturers Hanover happened to be in town visiting a customer. His presence at the Cowboys that evening was itself somewhat out of character, and he was not amused. Shaking his head in amazement, he whispered to another guest, "There's just no way we're going to do business with that guy."

Cowboys was one of a number of Oklahoma City nightclubs and restaurants that flourished as the oil and gas boom picked up momentum. The proprietor, Bob Hall, opened the club in September 1979, after hearing that a major motion picture, *Urban Cowboy,* was in production, and anticipating that nightclubs with a cowboy-western theme would take off once it was released. Not only was that expectation realized, but his club soon became the favorite dining and entertainment spot of such high rollers as Carl Swan and Cliff Culpepper. It was not unusual for a waitress to earn up to $200 a night in tips, and single tips of $100 and more were not uncommon. Hall recalls one occasion where a free-spending oilman became enamored of a particular waitress, and gave her a $100 bill each time she brought him a drink.

Even the door attendant who collected the $2 cover charge would frequently be handed a $20 or $50 bill and be told to keep the change. "You always had your high rollers," says Hall, "but you also had a lot who hung around just to sponge off the others."

Two of the Cowboys regulars, Culpepper and trucking mogul Jack Hodges, a man as tall and wide as a doorway, had become legendary in Oklahoma for their free-spending ways, and for the efforts of the one to outdo the other in acquiring expensive cars, rigs, vacation homes, jets, and the other status symbols of the era. According to acquaintances of the two men, they seemed to try to compete with each other on the number of jets in their respective fleets, and on the speed, size, and cruising range of the planes. And when one bought a vacation retreat in Cancun, the other responded with one next door that was said to be just slightly bigger.

Hodges also built a mobile helicopter pad on railroad tracks at his corporate headquarters that enabled passengers to enter the building without leaving the helicopter. "You'd land on the mobile pad," one visitor recalled, "and the second story opened up and the mobile pad carrying the helicopter rolled into the building." Once inside, passengers were just a few steps away from four rooms. "The first door," the visitor said, "opened up to a gym. Behind the second door was a shower and Jacuzzi. The third door opened up to a bedroom and the fourth door led to Hodges's office and a sunken bar."

As for Patterson, no matter how colorful his antics at Cowboys, he generally behaved himself around Hefner, the charismatic gas man said later. "But if he was drinking beer out of his boot, I would have joined him. I don't think there was anything wrong with that. Throughout history," Hefner reflected, "there have always been eccentrics; you just don't find them in the banking business. But there may be more than you think. Patterson just may have brought some of them out of the closet."

Hefner, while more restrained in his behavior, found in Patterson a friend and confidant. "He believed in something," Hefner said later. "He wanted to be the largest owner of the bank someday. And he shared my own beliefs in the amount of wealth in the basin and the necessity for the banking system to help the independent sector get it out."

Byron Tarnutzer was one of the thousands of investors from around the country who were excited by the blowouts in Oklahoma. He had already invested more than $300,000 in the Copeland programs and was contemplating a fourth, this time in the 1981 Deep. Toward the end of January 1981, Kae Ewing and Tarnutzer flew to Oklahoma City to discuss that possibility further. At dinner, Patterson told Tarnutzer that the value of his investments had grown to somewhere between $2 million and $3 million. "Carl and I have invested with Copeland ourselves," Patterson assured the wealthy real estate developer.

Patterson was high on Copeland. He offered to finance 100% of Tarnutzer's participation in the 1981 Copeland program, which would include a good geographical mix and an assortment of deep and shallow wells to spread the risk. Patterson emphasized that by varying the depth and location of the wells, the likelihood of losing any money on the investment would be nil. The next day Tarnutzer and Ewing were taken on a VIP tour of the oil fields with an engineer from Copeland Energy.

A couple of weeks later, it was Ewing's turn to entertain the Oklahomans. Patterson and Dobson went to Newport Beach to promote the 1981 program and were treated to a bay cruise and dinner at the prestigious Newport Harbor Yacht Club. Thus the scene was set for one of the most popular techniques of securities salesmen—convincing investors that the train is about to leave the station, and that they had better hop aboard before it does.

"I'm afraid you'll only have one chance to invest in Copeland Energy in 1981," Patterson and Dobson said. "Unfortunately, you'll have to let us know in two weeks if you're going to participate."

Tarnutzer, of course, wanted to know how his previous deals were doing. Patterson was always ready with an answer. "I'd say they're worth anywhere from $2.7 million to $3.6 million." That represented a return of as much as eight to one, if only on paper, and an increase over the figures Patterson had tossed out when they met in Oklahoma City.

"Byron," Patterson said, "the risk of loss on Copeland is very remote."

At the same time, Patterson advised Tarnutzer that he couldn't go wrong investing in Hadson Oil, the operator of the famous Livingston wells, which helped kindle the gas play in the Fletcher Field. A couple of weeks later, Tarntuzer traveled to Oklahoma City to try to arrive at a decision on the 1981 Deep. "Anyone who has invested as much money as you have deserves to be a full partner," Copeland told Tarnutzer at a meeting in Copeland's Oklahoma City offices. But Tarnutzer was seeking more assurances on the value of his 1980 investment before committing himself to the 1981 deal.

Copeland, unlike Patterson, refused to discuss the multiple values of his investments, but in the car on the way to dinner the youthful oilman told Tarnutzer that all the programs were doing well. According to Tarnutzer, Patterson also told him that Penn Square's engineering staff had reviewed the programs and found that all of them were performing well, noting that he was planning to invest $500,000 himself. Patterson agreed to provide Tarnutzer with copies of the Penn Square engineering studies but never did, Tarnutzer charged later.

Later, Bill Jennings himself reiterated Patterson's assurances about the quality of the Copeland funds.

Tarnutzer hadn't seen a dime from his earlier investments. But he was so impressed with the confidence Jennings and Patterson had expressed in Copeland that he soon arranged for $1.25 million to be invested in the new program. He set up partnerships and trusts for himself, his secretary, accountant, brother, and his children. He even persuaded his father-in-law to kick in $150,000.

Tarnutzer financed $875,000 of his investment with a letter of credit from Utica National Bank, whose president, Scott Martin, was Patterson's friend from Bartlesville and OU. Utica National issued letters of credit to investors in several Penn Square deals and was a kind of "holding pen" for loans that Penn Square could not unload immediately on an upstream correspondent. "Utica National," said one former Penn Square officer, "was a place to lay off loans temporarily. Sometimes Continental couldn't move as fast as they wanted, and Utica would take them." But according to sources close to Utica, Patterson would assure the Tulsa bank that he had a commitment from a correspondent to buy a loan and that the delay was due to paperwork problems, when in fact no commitment had been made at all.

Utica National and Penn Square were sister institutions. Both were located in shopping centers in a fashionable part of town. Utica, like Penn Square, was also getting into the energy loan participation game, though in a more limited way. And Utica, in the person of chairman V.M. Thompson, a longtime friend of another high roller named Beep Jennings, speculated heavily on silver prices, literally betting the bank on the notion that the price of the commodity would go nowhere but up. But when prices collapsed on "Silver Thursday" following revelations that the Hunt brothers of Texas had overextended themselves in their silver trading, Utica was ordered by the Comptroller of the Currency to take its licks and mark its silver investments down to market value. That year, Utica posted a $1.1 million loss.

Some investors couldn't get letters of credit at their own banks or even Utica National. "They'd tell Patterson that their banks didn't understand letters of credit," one officer recalled. So Patterson said, "Okay, we'll do it." Whether Patterson understood it or not, he was agreeing to put up the collateral for his own loan, meaning that if that loan went bad the bank, in effect, would have to pay itself.

Dewey Dobson, who promoted the Copeland programs, recalled that there was a "feeling we were on a ten-year roll, and that there was no end to the escalation of prices. Investors searched you out, and the bankers came knocking.

"I never thought I'd be in deals with so many damn zeros on them," Dobson recalled. "Everything was a big deal; New York, Chicago, Seattle opened up to you. It was intoxicating. Whatever you were doing, you did it four times as hard. I was working twelve to sixteen hours a day, and thought, this is how Carnegie must have made it."

The euphoria was obviously shared by the bankers. Said an upstream officer who helped buy more than $100 million in loans from Penn Square Bank, "It was a kick to book loans, to see the totals go up. It was a lot of fun at the time."

Fueling this euphoria, of course, was the expectation that consumption, and therefore prices, would continue to escalate. In 1980, however, consumption of energy products declined for the first time in five years. Although the average domestic wellhead price of crude oil rose dramatically immediately after President Reagan's accelerated decontrol order in January, prices in April 1981 began to reflect the excess of supply over demand. After reaching a peak of $34.70 in March, domestic prices dropped to $34.05 in April, although the trend line would not be obvious for several more months.

Swan was one of the iron men. He believed in trucks, rigs, and drill pipe. As one friend put it, "That's the way Carl counts his ponies."

So no one in the oil or banking fraternity was surprised when Swan's Continental Drilling Company announced that it had placed an order for some drilling rigs. After all, a rig that was bought in 1972 for $1.8 million could have been sold in 1981 for more than $7 million, and oil-field equipment was rising in value at the rate of 1.5% a month. Moreover, components for rigs were so scarce that there were often ten people bidding on a single piece of equipment such as draw works, blowout preventers, and mud pumps. "When you're putting a rig together in a period of scarcity," explained one energy lender, "you might not get all the correct components. The rig and derrick might be oversized and the blowout preventer undersized. The mud pump may be inadequate for the depth. The rig engines might not be synchronized, one at 1,200 rpm, and the other at 900, and both leaking crankcase oil. The end result is an underbalanced rig."

Still, to many bankers in 1981, it looked impossible to make a bad rig loan. It was only the size of the Continental deal that flabbergasted bankers and veteran oilmen in this town where big oil deals are not uncommon. In what was billed as the biggest rig deal in history, Continental Drilling announced that it had contracted with Dresser Industries to purchase forty-two new rigs at a total cost of $263 million. Continental, Chase, and Seafirst were to be the principal banks. Seafirst, in fact, was emerging as the world's biggest rig lender. In less than two years it would be the world's biggest rig owner.

According to company insiders, Continental Drilling announced the purchase before they had any idea of where they would get the financing. The understanding with Continental Illinois, a former bank officer explained later, was that the rigs were to be financed in small packages. "Here we were their lead bank, and they announced it and we didn't even know about it. We wondered what had happened." Nevertheless, Lytle backed the move completely. According to one Texas banker, "he took the same approach to the industry as a whole."

This agreement, trumpeted Continental Drilling, would establish the company as a major force in the oil and gas industry. The boldness of the move, and the optimism it expressed, would be discussed for months thereafter at the Petroleum Club at the Liberty Bank building in Oklahoma City.

In normal times, a rig can be delivered to its owners in less than 120 days. This order, however, would take more than a year to fill. Swan and Allen were betting that the boom would last forever. On one occasion, they were in Chicago talking with bank officers about their plans. One officer told Allen, "You know, we're going to be overbuilt," and asked, "How many rigs do you think the country can support?" Allen was always ready with an answer, and responded with an exact figure.

There is an aura in the industry that surrounds companies that own rigs, even though most companies that operate wells don't buy rigs. But in 1980 and 1981, some operators said that they wanted to own a few rigs to assure availability. One Oklahoma City lawyer said "To get a hole drilled during the boom, you could either pay a kicker or go to Bill Patterson and buy a rig yourself."

In fact, between 1963 and 1983 there was only one year—1981—when there wasn't an immediate availability of rigs, according to Rob Gilbert, a former energy lender with First National Bank of Oklahoma City. A rig, Gilbert said, is worth nothing more than its scrap value, what it will sell for, or the cash flow it will generate. Another lender from Midland, Texas, insists that a rig should be valued at no more than $75 a ton. Nevertheless, the financing of the 1981 rig deals violated all principles of prudent banking. Five-year loans were made to build rigs on which there were one-year contracts, or no contracts at all.

One lender who was not impressed with the Continental Drilling deal was Bud Ham, then a senior vice-president at the Fidelity Bank. While Carl Swan and his aides at Continental were congratulating themselves on their bold stroke, Ham was delivering a speech to the Oklahoma Bankers Association that some members of the audience found irritating, almost flippant. He reminded the bankers that in the past many institutions had taken substantial losses on rig loans, particularly prior to 1974, and asserted that most banks would not make a rig loan where they were expected to look to the rig for most of the collateral.

"Why take such a conservative view with an asset that is in such high demand and has the potential of generating excellent profits?" Ham asked rhetorically. The drilling business, he said, is highly specialized, requiring specialized supervision and single purpose equipment.

"To my knowledge, no one has come up with an alternate use for a drilling rig. It has been suggested that some components might be suitable for anchoring boats," he said, eliciting a chuckle or two from some members of his audience, "but I doubt this market is significant. I have personal knowledge, however, that the city of Cleveland, Oklahoma, supports its street lights on used drill pipe." Mr. Ham neglected to mention one other popular use: as fencing on stud farms.

Paul Bergevin, who had been with Seafirst's energy department for only a few months, did not need Ham's years of energy lending experience to feel uneasy about all the hoopla over rig loans. A friend recalls asking Bergevin about his new assignment when the two men met for lunch in February 1981.

"It's different," Bergevin replied.

"How do we get paid?"

"The hot energy market," Bergevin said.

"Well, what's our secondary source of repayment?" the friend asked.

"The hot energy market."

Seafirst, meanwhile, had confounded its competitors by coming off its twentieth straight year of increased earnings, despite the dismal state of the Pacific Northwest economy, Mount St. Helens, and nagging union problems. Seafirst smugly titled its 1980 annual report, *The Future Belongs to Those Who Anticipate and Plan.*

As one observer put it, Seafirst's performance in the face of a weak economy looked like "another masterful Jenkins stroke." Earnings from energy credits had contributed significantly to the 1980 results, and John Boyd was looking to some like a banking wunderkind.

Kathy Kenefick of the Continental Illinois National Bank never met Paul Bergevin of Seattle First. But, like Bergevin, Kenefick, a recent arrival in Lytle's mid-continent division quickly figured out that there was something very wrong with the relationship in Oklahoma. She had worked through some numbers on Longhorn Oil and Gas, the parent of Continental Drilling, and determined, as others would more than a year later, that Longhorn was not quite the Cadillac of the drilling funds that it claimed to be.

Kenefick, in a handwritten July 1981 memo to Continental vice-president Dennis Winget that was notable for its almost casual tone, stripped away the façade from Allen and Swan's flagship entity, the Longhorn Oil and Gas Company, and suggested that it was little more than a debt pyramid scheme in disguise.

Re: Longhorn

Have done some rough "number crunching" on Longhorn and some questions arise regarding their debt capacity: the company prepared cash budget shows a desire to increase their debt $8mm over current levels by September. They may have difficulty servicing just the interest on that higher amount and may have some difficulty servicing the current levels of debt if they don't sell some leases or close another drilling program.

I think the way they handle their current operations/cash, they don't ever repay principal in the normal course of operations; first quarter 1981 they generated positive internal cash flow for the first time due to a sale of property. I think the way they handle their "cash" is that when they close a drilling program, they get prepayments on turnkey drilling contracts and then use those funds to repay debt temporarily and [unintelligible] some of the funds to cover current interest expenses as needed. However, they need those funds later when they actually start drilling (reported costs in drilling revenues run between 85–90%); they then either reborrow to pay drilling costs or hope to close another drilling program. Anyway, it seems the rapid growth is all debt financed with no slowing in sight and cash flow growth potentially very slow—possibly negative—could be problem.

"My understanding," she concluded, "of what happens and some of the implications may be totally off base—would like to discuss."

Kenefick was not off base. By recalling a basic question young lenders are taught in credit training— how are we going to be repaid?—Kenefick unmasked the Longhorn version of the classic Ponzi scheme. In cahoots with Penn Square and Continental, Longhorn was simply using new loans and funds from new drilling programs to pay off the debt of previous programs. It was a scheme that could last only as long as rich Californians kept investing in the Longhorn programs and Continental kept funding. Kenefick, the bearer of bad tidings, was regarded by other Continental officers as abrasive, and Patterson himself lobbied energetically to try to get her moved out of Continental's energy department.

By mid-1981, according to Continental's own internal loan worksheets, Longhorn and its affiliated companies had borrowed a staggering $114 million from the bank. That included at least one $10 million credit to the aptly named Continental Drilling Company, on paper a subsidiary of Longhorn but more realistically a subsidiary of the Continental Illinois Bank itself. And that loan was guaranteed by Longhorn Oil and Gas, which couldn't even repay its own outstanding debt without new advances from Penn Square and Continental Illinois.

Once again, Longhorn got off the hook on its 1979-I program when, on April 10, 1981, Bill Patterson himself signed his squiggle to a letter committing Penn Square to convert the letters of credit to a $2,032,750 production loan. Swan and Allen were guaranteeing Longhorn debt, but as one insider put it, "If Swan ever had to cough up on his personal guarantees, he'd be bankrupt three times over." Continental, however, was prepared to buy everything Carl Swan put his signature on. At one point, a curious Penn Square officer reportedly started to look into the Carl Swan relationship but was told not to investigate bank directors.

By 1981, the Swan and Allen empire had grown to a dizzying array of drilling companies, limited partnerships, service companies, and shell entities. Some were owned outright by each partner, some were jointly owned, and others were in partnership with dozens of other individuals. By setting up dozens of companies—even if those companies had little or no assets—Swan and Allen were able to borrow considerably more from Penn Square than they would have been able to individually. Each entity was separately managed, and there was little if any oversight at the top.

Allen, according to a former associate, hoped eventually to take the whole empire public and "become richer than God." And he added, "They felt the problems would be covered up by the strength of the business cycle."

THE CHANGING OF THE GUARD

ELDON BELLER, AN EXECUTIVE VICE-PRESIDENT OF THE FIRST NA-
tional Bank of Oklahoma City, only knew Beep Jennings casually. By the spring of 1981 Beller, like everyone else at the First, was
well aware of Penn Square's high-rolling reputation, and of Bill
Patterson's fondness for cutting $40 million oil and gas deals on
cocktail napkins in less time than it took him to chug a shoeful of
Amaretto and soda.

He was a bit surprised, however, when Jennings phoned him and
said he had "something to talk with me about. I thought," said
Beller later, "that he wanted to talk about loans shared by Penn
Square and First National." In fact, Jennings, after reportedly being
turned down by another First National Bank officer, was calling to
offer Beller the presidency of the Penn Square Bank: the proverbial
offer Beller found impossible to refuse. As part of the arrangement,
an ailing Frank Murphy was kicked upstairs, and out of the way, to
the vice-chairmanship of the bank to await his retirement in October 1982. The examiners had come down hard on Beep Jennings,
telling him, in effect, that he'd better hire a competent and experienced management team or else.

Beller is a tall man with a lumbering gait; he is prim in manner
and appearance, and blunt in speech. "He's not eloquent," said a
friend, "but you always know where you stand with him."

Aware of Penn Square's concentration in oil and gas, Beller told
Jennings matter-of-factly that he was not an energy lender. "He said
he was an energy expert and could deal with it," Beller recalled.
Moreover, Beller told Jennings he had known Patterson at the First
and was not impressed with the ability Patterson displayed there. "I
was not aware Bill had any expertise in energy lending," Beller told
Jennings.

"He's been with me a number of years and I taught him the business," Jennings replied. "He's an expert in energy lending." Jennings told Beller he had turned people like Carl Swan and J.D. Allen over to Patterson, adding that he would supervise and be responsible for his youthful protégé, according to Beller.

Only much later did Beller reveal his job description as president of the bank, something that he managed to keep secret from even his closest associates. The first paragraph read, Beller claimed: "Under overall direction of the chief executive officer, manages all of the bank's activities except the energy division." In conversations with upstream bank officers as well as officers of Penn Square, however, Beller represented that Patterson answered to him. And a bank organizational chart shows Patterson reporting up to Beller, who in turn was responsible to Jennings.

House Banking Committee chairman Fernand St Germain, a salty, irreverent Rhode Island Democrat, later stated his opinion of the arrangement offered to "poor Mr. Beller" by saying, "There was a song, poor Mr. Chisholm, strummed on his mandolin; our impression was he spent a lot of time strumming his mandolin, not that he is not a wonderful gentleman, he is, but Mr. Jennings and Mr. Patterson used him. . . to placate the Comptroller."

"They brought you in," St Germain later told Beller, "because the Comptroller's office had swooped down and said, 'Hey, unless you make changes you've got bad days ahead.' So they brought you in but they tied one and a half arms behind your back and put you in a wheelchair."

In any case, the Penn Square compensation package was irresistible: a 50% increase in annual salary over the $80,000 he was earning at First National, plus a guarantee of $250,000 annually within five years.

Dale Mitchell, Beller's boss at the First National Bank, remembers the day Beller came in to give him notice. "He showed me his employment contract and said, 'I just don't see how I can't accept.' I agreed with him," Mitchell said later, "and if the bank had been successful it would have been a real money-maker for Eldon."

When Beller arrived at Penn Square, he found conditions there chaotic, as he described them later. The credit department had a staff of three, when the bank's size and growth called for at least fifteen. There were no committees set up to review loans and no committee for managing the funding of the bank. Beller thought it would take three years to straighten things out. "Frank Murphy used to kid me about it," Beller recalled later. "He said it would take five years. A few months later Murphy said, 'Do you still think it will take three?'

"How about four?" Beller replied.

Beller also found that his new boss was in many respects an absentee chairman, spending much of his time tending to his personal investments, many of which involved business relationships with Penn Square directors and major borrowers. He owned Trans-Central Airlines with Bob "General Bull Moose" Lammerts and Joe Dan Trigg, hotel and other real estate properties with Lammerts and director Ron Burks, and a partnership, TSJ (Trigg, Swan, Jennings), formed to invest $20 million in one of Hefner's drilling projects. In fact, one of Bill Patterson's duties was to raise capital for his mentor's personal investments and business ventures. The jowly Mr. Trigg, who was involved in virtually every one of Jennings's personal deals, was an old oilie on the outside and a new oilie on the inside. His family had been in the oil business since 1919, but in his spending habits Trigg was as flamboyant as some of the real estate brokers who'd just bought their first rig. Trigg speculated in gold and silver and was a regular at the gambling tables in Las Vegas, according to Patterson's defense attorney in the subsequent criminal trial.

Another close friend and business associate was Western actor Dale Robertson, whom Jennings met as a cadet at the Oklahoma Military Academy in the early 1940s and who later starred in such films as the *City of Bad Men* and *Gambler from Natchez*. Jennings bankrolled Robertson's oil-field service company, Ram Leasing and his stud farm, Haymaker Farms, in which Carl Swan held an 11% interest.

Beller immediately began raiding his former employer of some of its top talent, and Mitchell recalled, "I think that caused a lot of people from the First to get a little disgusted. The guys at the top, particularly, took some of it pretty hard. We lost some good people out there. We were scrambling for people just as hard as anybody else," he said. Penn Square actually had been recruiting at the First for some time before Eldon left for Penn Square. In the five-year period from 1977 through 1982 Penn Square hired as many as sixty officers from the downtown bank, according to Mitchell. Beller's relationship with his former employer quickly deteriorated as he continued to lure the First's top talent out to the shopping center bank.

It was easy to understand why they left. Assistant vice-presidents at Penn Square were making $5,000 more than they could elsewhere, and were handling portfolios of $100 million or more. Additionally, officers at the assistant vice-president level and above were entitled to bank cars, usually late model Oldsmobiles and Buicks. Penn Square's fleet of forty-seven automobiles would likely rank it with some of the biggest banks in the nation in that dubious category of achievement. Secretaries in their early twenties earned $20,000 a year and up, and could even look forward to the prospect of becoming officers, a door that is usually closed to secretaries at more conventional banking organizations. And according to a lawsuit later filed by the Federal Deposit Insurance Corporation, many of those Beller hired soon received excessive personal and home loans at preferential rates in violation of banking statutes on insider lending. As one junior officer put it, "When the bank began to skyrocket, people hitched onto it."

"A lot of guys who went out there were awfully competitive toward the First," Mitchell said. "The First is just one of those organizations, particularly during that era, that are so dominant in the marketplace that it fostered that institutionally. There was a pretty strong competitive bent by the people who went out there. The pressure Penn Square put on other banks was dramatic."

Patterson used to boast, "First National hates me because I get all their good people," and he referred to his downtown rivals as the "slum banks."

Beller's arrival represented a changing of the guard of sorts at Penn Square. At the same board of directors meeting in April 1981 at which Beller's hiring was approved, Patterson was elected a director of the bank and the resignation of horse-trader Tom Orr was accepted, with relief. Later, a goodly portion of Beller's time would be spent cleaning up the mess Orr had left, much of it in the last days of his tenure. According to former officers, bank examiner George Clifton and internal auditor Norma Babb became suspicious about a transaction Orr was handling and notified Murphy, who confronted Orr. Penn Square even reported Orr's dealings to the FBI, but the agency didn't pursue that case until much later. Right up until his departure, Orr continued to lend heavily to Ken Tureaud, under the pretext of oil and gas investments or working capital for Saket Petroleum Company, which Penn Square officers impolitely dubbed the "Sack of Shit" Petroleum Company. All in all, Orr's career at Penn Square Bank had been brief but immensely profitable. In 1980, Orr made $548,582.56—over a half-million more than his $44,000 Penn Square salary. To borrow a phrase used by Congressman Doug Barnard of the House Banking, Finance and

Urban Affairs Committee, getting rid of Orr was like "locking the door after the horse's loan has gone."

Almost immediately, Beller and his new recruits found themselves in a sparring contest with Patterson and his jet-setting oil and gas lenders over everything from loan documentation to expense accounts. Patterson set up an adversarial relationship between his staff and the lower level officers who came in with Beller, viewing them as a threat to his own autonomy, and referring to them as "mongoloids." Said one new recruit, "He created a lot of dissension between us and the oil and gas people. His people hated us because we were making it tough on them." Beller's efforts to improve loan documentation, for example, occasionally resulted in oil and gas officers having to work late to complete missing paperwork. Patterson would tell them, the officer said, "That's why you're here tonight doing the paperwork—that's Dunn [a newly hired executive vice-president] getting Beller to make you do this." Likewise, employees elsewhere in the bank resented the oil and gas staff, because they were being paid so much more. A secretary in the oil and gas division, for example, could expect to earn as much as $200 a month more than her opposite number in commercial lending. "It was a good place to work but frustrating because things weren't done right," said one young woman.

Yet for all Patterson's abruptness with Beller's staff as well as his own, he often displayed a tender side that endeared him to his people, particularly the women. "He treated everyone alike and treated secretaries well," said one young divorcée. "He was a good motivator and always made a point to pick out people who had done a good job." According to one employee's calculations, 75% of the women in Patterson's oil and gas department were divorced. Patterson, she said, seemed to have a special compassion for divorced women with children, and is said to have been particularly generous in granting home loans to his female employees. A devoted father, Patterson frequently shut himself up in his office for hours to sit on the floor with his children and draw with them in their coloring books, while customers waited impatiently in the lounges and stairwells. "Orr was a crook," snapped a friend of Patterson's. "At least Patterson was trying to build something."

"We went in with the assumption that the bank needed more staffing to correct criticism in a previous exam," said one member of the fix-it team. "We thought the problem was too much growth without staff, and felt in six months we'd not only be on the road to recovery but prospering. There was optimism from day one."

At the time, the Orr mess was perceived to be the biggest credit quality problem. "Anything Orr touched was suspect," the officer said, and by the fall a full Orr review was in motion. "We smelled the problems in the Orr portfolio and felt if we could ride that through we'd be home free."

Those officers who joined Penn Square with Beller viewed excessive growth, lack of staff, and the concentration of credit in a single industry as the principal issues, and didn't consider credit quality in the energy portfolio to be a major source of concern. "In the first couple of weeks, I came away impressed," said one new senior officer. "I didn't see that much that concerned me with the major relationships."

The new arrivals were also faced with a back-office paperwork mare's nest caused by the almost total lack of procedures for keeping track of customers' notes and the billions of dollars in disbursements on loans and interest and principal payments. One employee summed up the problem this way: "I just couldn't tell what to do with the money."

There were many variations on the theme. Advances on a note were deposited in the wrong account. Interest was posted to the wrong note. "There were situations where an officer wouldn't tell you that money was due in, and when it came in you wouldn't know where to put it," a former employee said. According to one employee, Penn Square hired a woman who couldn't spell to work in the note cage. She put customer numbers on notes, but the notes were out of order on the bank's trial balance, leading to further errors in debiting and crediting payments and advances.

Penn Square's stone age system of booking loans, renewals, and extensions made it next to impossible for anyone to follow what accountants call an audit trail. Whenever a loan was renewed—and that was more the rule than the exception, since Penn Square was little more than a revolving credit scheme in which the principal never had to be paid back—the number on the note changed. As one officer explained, "It took a lot of digging to find out who the principals were; you could never find out from the trial balances who was borrowing what."

Compounding the basic flaws in the system and inadequate staffing was the bad blood that existed between the oil and gas division and the note cage. So it was not surprising that by July 1982 Penn Square's books would be more than $30 million out of balance, according to federal regulators. "Operations was a consuming issue, an abrasive problem," recalled one former senior officer.

The new recruits also arrived to find the funding side of the bank in disarray. They discovered, for example, that Patterson was, in effect, acting as the chief financial officer, bidding against other officers in the bank for money. In at least one instance, Patterson paid a depositor 30% interest on his funds, according to a former senior bank officer.

Although Patterson and Beller were not openly antagonistic, Patterson's animosity expressed itself in other ways. At one point, Beller wanted to pull the letter of credit department out from under Patterson, until the king of the L/Cs threatened to form his own department and duplicate what Beller was doing. "Patterson took on the appearance of being a monarch. He'd throw temper tantrums, banging his fist on the table when he didn't get his way," the officer said.

Yet it was clear to some who was really calling the shots. Tom Swineford, one of the old hands at Penn Square, had quit around the time Orr joined the bank and came back after the horseman left the barn. Jennings told him on his return, "You'll have to change your ways. We make $10 million loans to people with negative net worth. Patterson will teach you how to make oil and gas loans." Swineford figured maybe there was something about Bill he hadn't seen the first time around. Taking their cues from Jennings, Penn Square loan salesmen peddled deals to correspondents by telling them not to mind the financial statements, and emphasizing that the customer had "hidden net worth."

The newcomers from the first National Bank also must have been shocked to find that Penn Square was in reality a University of Oklahoma fraternity house disguised as a bank. After 5:00 P.M., and sometimes before, "we'd break out the champagne," said a former officer. Nor was it uncommon for employees to leave for Las Vegas after banking hours, gamble most of the night, and be back in the office the next morning.

Working at Penn Square, said a former oil and gas officer, was "like being with your best friends every day. We worked such long hours it became our social life." The bank was so much a part of the life of Patterson's oil and gas staff that he found it easy to recruit a score of them to work on a weekend, and many people hired as temporary office workers eagerly returned to work or visit over Christmas. All told, "nothing really changed when new people came in," said one former officer. "There were just new people on the roster. The only thing that could have been done was to fire the chief executive officer."

As Fernand St Germain warned later, "Always be cautious of the one-man show, the one-man band. The last thing Mr. Jennings wanted was someone to come in strong enough to take over" the operation.

The First National Bank of Oklahoma City was distressed not only because of the loss of valued personnel but because of the loss of customers and the relationship with Continental Illinois. Continental had abandoned the First for a new bride. Rob Gilbert, then a senior officer at the First, "talked to Bergman extensively about it," according to Mitchell, "but to no avail. Bergman just didn't have satisfactory answers. The competitive jealousy issue was always there.

"When you support one bank and take business away from another that you've had a long-time relationship with, you better not be wrong when you change horses," Mitchell said.

First National, as well as many other large banks in the Southwest, was nudged into being a lot more aggressive because of the go-go lending practices of Penn Square and its upstream correspondents. Mitchell recalls people saying on the cocktail party circuit, "You mean you're going to let that Penn Square Bank catch you? I don't understand why they can do these deals and the biggest bank in Oklahoma City can't." Local bankers felt the pressure from their own directors. One Fidelity director reportedly told a top bank officer, "You can't go wrong on an energy credit. We're missing the chance of a lifetime."

Cocktail parties were not the only source of intelligence about the go-go activities at Penn Square. For example, one officer's secretary was married to the First National's chief pilot, and as Mitchell said later, "Occasionally we'd get some stories."

The competitive pressure prompted a number of discussions among local bankers on ways they could "discipline" Penn Square. At some point, Liberty Bank reportedly stopped accepting letters of credit issued by Penn Square, and according to Mitchell, the First forced the shopping center bank to secure its Fed funds lines. "I talked to Gordon Greer [then president of Liberty National Bank] on many occasions about what we could do as presidents of the two biggest banks to get some of this stuff slowed down, and we just never could figure out anything," Mitchell said.

One of the low points in the relationship between Penn Square and the First occurred in mid-1981 when Amarex, then considered a prime company, shifted a large chunk of its business out to Penn Square. Amarex, a high-rolling oil and gas operator heavily committed to deep gas, wanted an eight-figure lease line, and Penn Square priced it to the company at a rate First National couldn't match. "We wondered if there was something wrong with us," Mitchell recalled.

Former employees of Amarex, which was founded in Amarillo, Texas, as Amarillo Exploration, disagree over whether chief financial officer Leroy Belcher was the instigator of leveraging the company to the maximum—and beyond—or whether president John Mason himself pushed mounting quantities of debt on to the Amarex balance sheet. One former employee saw the corporate philosophy this way: borrow everything you can to put money back in the ground. That was certainly a philosophy shared by Bill P. Jennings who, curiously enough, was one of the original directors of the company.

Until April 1980, Mason had been revered by his staff for his prowess as a geologist, if not as a manager. He was, said a former employee, a cultured person, with good credentials, and usually available for impromptu meetings. "You could go to him with an idea, and if it was logically presented and if he trusted you," one employee recalls, "he'd say, 'Run with it.' "

That seemed to end in 1980. Mason became isolated from middle management and what one employee called the "guts of the company." He began spending less time in the office and more time in the air, often on fund-raising trips to Europe. In fact, according to former employees, Amarex employed more pilots than geologists, and its fleet of Mitsubishi prop-jets and a Lear jet, with stylized orange oil derricks emblazoned on their fuselages, became known in the industry as the Amarex Air Force. Amarex, said a former employee of the now defunct company, "always wanted to break into the big time, to become a big player. They liked airplanes, glamour, publicity, and the big plays." Most of all, they liked to borrow. And it was ultimately their craving for borrowed money that got them into trouble.

But there were other problems. "There were an ungodly number of consultants, and ungodly fees," said a former employee. In the opinion of those present at the time, people were hired without any idea of what to do with them, and in many instances they didn't know whom they reported to . Although the company didn't pay as well as some others, the perks were there, including the use of the company planes for jaunts to New Orleans and Jackson Hole. Similarly, the company reportedly drilled gas wells in some areas before it figured out how it was going to hook them up to pipelines.

And Amarex later claimed that it was the victim of malfeasance by at least one employee who allegedly accepted kickbacks from service companies with which it did business, according to former employees and documents on file in Oklahoma County Court. The employee allegedly created a dummy corporation, Marex, that he used to collect "gratuities" from vendors.

Like the lenders at the upstream banks, the gas men at Amarex became cocky, said one observer, and began to feel they were invincible. But just as the bankers in Chicago were taking a lot of bad loans, Amarex began buying more and more risky prospects. Indeed, the financial structure of its drilling programs tended to encourage wildcat drilling. Meanwhile, the California money raisers selling the programs, and the stockbrokers promoting the stock, neither of whom knew much about the oil and gas business, were making fortunes from their 8% commissions. But the basic shortcoming, said a former employee, was that John Mason "bet the company on $9 gas."

Besides Penn Square, another prime cocktail party topic in Oklahoma oil and banking circles was Seafirst. "They had every doggy deal down here. They had the deals other banks wouldn't take," Mitchell said. Back in Seattle, auditors had turned up document exceptions in the energy portfolio, but these problems were downplayed because the cash flows seemed adequate.

As president of one of the nation's larger banks, Mitchell qualified for membership in the prestigious Association of Reserve City Bankers, which usually gathers in Florida for its annual meeting. The youthful bank president from Oklahoma recalls sitting down next to Seafirst chairman Bill Jenkins at a hotel bar during a pause in one of those meetings and wondering whether he should inform Jenkins about the chatter circulating about Seafirst in the Oklahoma banking community. By the early 1980s, Jenkins, as the chairman of one of the Pacific Northwest's leading banks, was considered one of the deans of the U.S. banking industry. Somewhat intimidated by Jenkins's reputation, Mitchell decided not to raise the issue, saying to himself, "Who am I to tell him how to run his bank?"

Seafirst was a frequent victim, but by no means the only victim, of a game Patterson played with his "co-banks"—that of tantalizing them with the prospect of getting them into a glamour credit like Amarex or GHK, which the bankers perceived to be prime deals, if they would only buy a loan that wasn't so good or hold on to one they had become uncomfortable with.

As one former officer recalled the pitch, "He'd say, 'Listen, Seafirst, I'll do you a deal. I'll give you a part of a GHK credit if you'll take dog duty oil company.' And they said, 'Let's look at dog duty oil and see how bad a deal it is.' And after some analysis they would say, 'The earnings on this deal will offset our loss on the other one.' Or he would in fact buy Seafirst out of a bad deal, paying the Seattle bank off with Michigan National money, and sell a loan to Seattle that he had bought back from Chase." As part of the privilege of doing business with Penn Square, added a West Coast banker who looked but declined to buy, "you had to be prepared to take the bad with the good."

Patterson also played on the confusion of Northern bank officers about oil and gas lending. "Confusion," observed a former colleague of the supersalesman, "was opportunity." Patterson would give someone a production loan when it was in fact some other kind of loan. The banker might think he's looking at a lease line, and Patterson would tell him it was a production loan. "He'd play on their embarrassment of being confused," the former Penn Square officer said.

Actually, many of the young and inexperienced bankers who bought loans from Bill Patterson barely knew the difference between an oil rig and a pump jack, much less the difference between a production loan and a lease line, according to former borrowers. One of the pitfalls of being new to oil and gas is that the novice thinks he knows the business when he becomes fluent in the jargon.

Patterson's definition of a good loan was a loan he could sell. But as the account officer for one of Penn Square's upstream banks sheepishly admitted later, "We were beating down the doors to buy those loans."

"We shipped those loan files to Continental in cardboard boxes. They didn't even bother to look at them. They just said, 'Leave them here. We'll wire you the money,' " said one of Patterson's colleagues. "It was a big shell game," another officer said, "and nobody ever knew where the pea was."

One correspondent officer with a large California bank that missed out on the action recalls scheduling an appointment with Patterson several hours before he was due to catch a plane to San Francisco. The officer waited nearly an hour outside Patterson's office, and got to see Patterson only after he handed the energy czar's secretary a business card and told her he had to catch a flight to the West Coast.

According to the officer, who was with the San Francisco-based Wells Fargo Bank, the secretary said, "Bill will see you now," and escorted him into her boss's office. The calling officer expected to find a much older man, but instead saw "a young guy sitting on a couch and drinking a Coke with his arm around a young woman, who was gently massaging his neck as he was talking with another woman seated on a chair in front of him.

"So you want to be in the oil business?" Patterson asked haughtily. "Well, here's a deal for you." He handed the officer a file containing some figures on J.D. Hodges.

The young Californian was taken aback by Patterson's casual approach to doing business. "Well, I don't know," he said hesitantly.

"Okay, if you don't want it, we'll give it to Continental Illinois."

The banker told Patterson he had to catch a plane.

"When you want to be in the energy business, let us know," Patterson called after him as he walked briskly out the door.

MIXED SIGNALS

IN MAY 1981 JOHN R. BOYD LEFT SEATTLE ON HIS ANNUAL TREK TO the Middle East to gather petrodollar deposits for Seattle First National Bank. On this trip, however, the five minutes he would spend with a senior official of the government of Abu Dhabi might have been of far greater value to him and his institution than the jumbo CDs he would bring back to the Pacific Northwest, if he had chosen to use the information. As Boyd recalls it, the official, referring to the role of OPEC in controlling oil prices, told him, "We're kidding ourselves. We're losing our grip. I don't want to be overly pessimistic, but demand figures appear to be declining." Boyd pressed him for more specifics, but the official declined to elaborate.

On his return to the bank, Boyd startled Seafirst's world banking loan committee, not by announcing that it was time to retrench in energy lending but by breezing into a credit meeting dressed in the flowing brown and white robes and headgear of an Arab sheik. In his drive to satisfy the growth objectives of chairman Bill Jenkins, the conversation with the OPEC official became a faded memory.

Later that year, in a talk arranged by Seafirst director Robert Schultz, Boyd drew chuckles from members of the Yakima Rotary Club when he told a luncheon meeting, "There's been talk that oil could go to $30 a barrel. If it does, I'll have my résumé all over the street." Schultz said later, "They were rolling in the aisles."

The sense of foreboding expressed by the Abu Dhabi official seemed to fly in the face of all the outward signs that the boom would indeed last forever. Lease prices, for example, continued to skyrocket, and during the summer of 1981 a Dallas oilman landed by helicopter on the lawn of the county courthouse in Anadarko, Oklahoma, and bid up to $10,000 per acre for three-year leases on Indian lands. By mid-1981, there were more than 500 deep gas projects at work in the Anadarko Basin.

And at a meeting sponsored by Amarex, Inc., in Oregon, oil and gas consultant Dr. William Talley told the gathering, which included a number of the company's bankers, "No matter what happens we'll be looking at $12 gas by 1990," as one participant recalled.

Mindful of these kinds of predictions, banks continued to assume that the price of oil and gas would rise at the rate of inflation, despite the signs of a slowdown in demand and consumption, and engineering consultants persisted in using these premises in figuring future revenue. It was axiomatic that oil prices would rise at 8% to 10% per year from $41 per barrel to $70 to $80 per barrel in ten years. Some banks, however, claim that in 1981 they concluded $9 per MCF gas and $42 per barrel oil would not hold, and stopped escalating prices. Looking back, former Continental vice-president Pat Goy observed, "Nobody was asking, 'what if?' "

Had someone been asking that question, he might have noted that on June 22, 1981, the Senate Finance Committee approved a measure by the Reagan administration, which the new oilies helped put into office, that would cut from 70% to 50% the maximum tax rate on individual income. The President signed the new tax law into effect two months later. According to Dr. Talley, "That made the investors quit doing dumb deals. They asked, 'What am I going to get for my money?' " The new bill also provided for accelerated recovery on real estate investments, so that when the investor looked at the economics of real estate as opposed to oil, many eventually opted for shopping centers and apartment houses. Said one observer, "The oilies never realized they were better off with the inflation and deficit spending usually associated with Democratic administrations."

One Oklahoma oilman claims to have felt some uneasiness about the weakening in demand and price, and raised the point with Continental executive vice-president Jerry Bergman. Bergman, according to the oilman, replied that the bank would not continue to lend heavily to oil and gas companies if it did not believe prices would continue to rise. Although most economists missed the mark in their predictions about oil prices, Continental, despite its prodigious exposure in energy, did not employ an energy economist to monitor the oil and gas marketplace. According to Goy, executive vice-president and lending chief George Baker once told him that "economists were only good for making speeches." Continental, in fact, seemed to use its economists, none of whom specialized in energy, more for marketing than planning. The big Chicago bank held annual "economic briefings" in Tulsa and Oklahoma City that provided an opportunity for senior bank officers like Bergman and Baker to woo important borrowers.

One of the few economists of that era who accurately predicted a long-term decline in demand and price was S. Fred Singer of the Energy Policy Studies Center of the University of Virginia. In the January 11, 1980, issue of the *Wall Street Journal,* Singer wrote prophetically of the growing pressure for a drop in prices, asserting, "The more obvious price decline to be expected over a period of several years would simply reflect an adjustment from short-run to long-run conditions of demand and of supply."

For most players, the outward signs of the boom masked any underlying weakness of the oil and gas economy. Oklahoma Gov. George Nigh confronted the enviable problem of how to spend the state's huge budget surplus, much of which resulted from taxes on oil and gas revenues. The active rig count by June 1981 was at an all-time high of 667 units and still climbing. Rolls-Royce and Mercedes-Benz dealers broke records for sales of the luxury automobiles. Oil companies spent millions for executive gymnasiums, hot tubs, and helicopter pads.

A group of oilmen would find themselves sitting around one of the many discothèques or nightclubs that sprang up during the boom, and as Bill Lakey remembers it, "They'd say 'Let's go to Vegas,' " and pick up the phone and call the pilot. It was like "Fantasy Island."

"Oklahoma City was a good place to be," Lakey reflected. "People were happy, new buildings were going up. Studies showed that Oklahoma was one of the best places to live. I don't think there were many other places where this could have happened. The boom was also going on in Texas, Louisiana, but the same mentality wasn't present.

"Texans," he opined, "have more of a sense of pride in being Texans. But Oklahomans have a reason to feel apologetic," a feeling, he says, that traces itself back to the "Joad mentality" left by Steinbeck's classic novel, *The Grapes of Wrath.*

"This was," said Lakey, "the reverse of *Grapes of Wrath.* I went down to Lubbock, Texas, and the talk was the lease prices being paid in western Oklahoma. It was kind of fun, there was a sense of pride. We were being talked about. People were moving to Oklahoma from all over. It gave us a good, valid, up-front moral reason to go out and have a good time.

"The only time I can remember my dad being happy was when it was raining," Lakey said. "This gave everybody an opportunity to get on the roller coaster. We were ripe for it." And he added, "If it hadn't been for Penn Square Bank things would have been more realistic, more conservative."

There were a few, however, who sensed change and acted on their instincts. Some saw in the obvious excesses and inefficiencies a sign that a downturn was inevitable. A banker once compiled a list of "non-ratio indicators of financial condition," or telltale signs that a company was in trouble, or would soon be in trouble. The banker should be wary, he says, when the borrower rips out the floor tile and installs thick pile carpet. And an Oklahoma oil and gas lawyer adds that there's a rule of thumb in the oil business: "If he's got leather couches, don't do business with him." Yet nearly every major Penn Square borrower owned at least one jet, which cost about $28,000 a month just to keep in the hangar. Assuming a 50% tax rate, a company needed $56,000 per month in revenue to meet the fixed costs alone.

Steve Knox, a young lease broker in Edmond, Oklahoma, recalls a conversation in July 1981 with Dick Schmaltz, then director of research at Morgan Stanley, during a visit by the investment banker to Oklahoma. Schmaltz remarked that when land secretaries start getting overrides and every oilman owns a Lear jet "the thing's going to crater. Steve," he asked, "what are you going to do when this whole thing collapses?"

About the time Schmaltz was in Oklahoma, Tom Kenan, a short, garrulous Oklahoma City lawyer-oilman, had just formed a new company, Monjeb Minerals, Inc., and had begun to sell stock to some private investors with the ultimate intention of taking the firm public. Several partners of Goldman, Sachs in New York had already bought in at 33¢ a share, and by the end of May 1981 the prospects for a public offering were looking good. Oil company prospectuses were popular on Wall Street, and nearly all such offerings were quickly snapped up by zealous investors who were convinced there was no end to the big oil play. Kenan and an associate, Oklahoma City lawyer Jerry Tubb, flew to New York and Philadelphia to meet with prospective investors and investment bankers, but Tubb and Kenan wound up flying back to Oklahoma separately.

On Tubb's flight from Philadelphia, the curly-haired lawyer sat in the first class section next to a man who turned out to be a New York investment banker on his way to Oklahoma to check out some oil and gas deals. It was an ideal match. Bill Forster of the New York investment banking firm of Lehman Brothers was looking to buy. And Tubb had something to sell. Tubb explained the deal to For-

Penn Square Bank: "Something's growing out in Oklahoma City. It's just weird!"

Robert A. Hefner III—The man who believed in deep gas (*GHK Companies*).

CREDIT: *All photographs, unless otherwise noted, are reproduced by permission of the* Oklahoma City Journal Record.

Bill P. Jennings (*left*) and Eldon Beller (*Phillip L. Zweig*).

Bill Patterson in a reflective moment.

Carl Swan.

Roger E. Anderson, chairman of the board and chief executive officer of Continental.

John H. Perkins, president of Continental (*Photographs courtesy of Continental Illinois National Bank and Trust Company of Chicago*).

J.D. Allen.

Harold Clifford.

Thomas S. Orr. Jack Hodges.

The executive dining room at Hodges's headquarters.

James Hudson (*left*), the liquidator, and William Isaac, chairman of the Federal Deposit Insurance Corporation.

The "Over $100,000" lineup outside Penn Square, after the failure.

Depositors waiting to get their money out of the motor bank building of Penn Square.

Directors of Penn Square Bank at the Congressional hearings.

Painting over the sign at the unfinished Penn Square "PennBank Tower."

ster, and the banker was enthusiastic. He encouraged Tubb to have Kenan phone him as soon as he could.

A week later, Kenan called Forster in New York, reminding him of the meeting with Tubb on the plane. "Jerry tells me you might be interested in our company," Kenan said.

"Tom," he said, "I'm going to take a pass."

"Okay." Kenan shrugged. "That's all right. I was just following up on your conversation with Jerry."

"Tom," Forster said quietly, "I would have bought a week ago. But let me tell you, it's turned. It's now time to sell, not to buy."

In one week, Wall Street had started to turn sour on sweet crude.

In June 1981, when banks figured it was virtually impossible to lose money on a rig loan, and when the going price for a rig was escalating at about 1.5% a month, Thorne Stallings decided to get his Tri-State Fabricators Company out of the rig-building business.

A former airline pilot and business consultant who joined Tri-State in September 1980 after being decisively defeated in the Republican U.S. Senate primary race, Stallings found a company that was growing at 300% annually but was unable to turn a profit.

"I saw a panic to get into the business," Stallings recalled, "and a total disregard for costs. There were a lot of amateurs in the business. At the same time, there was a stabilization of prices at the gas pump." He began to feel that the industry was running on inertia, that the income to draw investor capital out of the marketplace had begun to dry up. This, Stallings believed, would lead companies to increase their leverage and the use of what he calls the "Fort Worth contract." "That's where you sell something for $1.00 and book it for $1.10," he explained. "I was the laughingstock of the industry because I'd gotten out during the boom."

By the summer of 1981, it was no secret that Penn Square was the keeper of the brass ring. For months some local oilmen and bankers had a vague feeling that Penn Square would ultimately be forced to face a reckoning for such easy lending practices. But at least one prominent Oklahoma City oil and gas producer was convinced it would end when he learned J. Lynn Thornburgh was borrowing heavily at the bank.

Thornburgh blew into Oklahoma City in the late 1970s following his release from the federal penitentiary in El Reno, Oklahoma, where he had served eighteen months on a mail theft and forgery conviction. A strapping, six-footer, Thornburgh had a reputation for becoming boisterous after a few drinks.

"Lynn was a chameleon," said an acquaintance. "He had a way of changing his speech, mannerisms, and clothes to fit the situation." Sometime after his release from prison, Thornburgh bought some oil properties and eventually got into the lease brokerage game. "He'd put on a thick Texas accent when he was around oilies, and talked like a TV newscaster when he did business in town," the acquaintance said. Buying leases demands that the broker develop a rapport with farmers who, despite the prospect of receiving large lease bonuses, distrust oilmen and fear pollution of their land by mud pits and salt water. "Thornburgh," the source said, "put on his coveralls and went out to talk to them about the wheat crop, the weather, and the new model of John Deere tractor," then pitched them on giving him leases on their property.

"He was slick," the source said, "and he liked to live high on the hog." He had come to the right place.

Also that summer the heads of some of America's largest corporations concluded within days of each other that they had to own Conoco, a decision that erupted into a multibillion-dollar bidding frenzy that climaxed in the takeover of the huge oil company by Du Pont. Inferential Focus, a New York-based intelligence gathering service for large corporations, predicted in the August 1981 issue of its client newsletter that Conoco would not turn out to be the "bargain" people claimed it was. "Since it has taken eight years for the oil merger feeding frenzy to begin, it is quite likely that we are witnessing a phenomenon seen so often before—where confidence was at its highest point just before a fundamental change."

EASY COME,
EASY GO

FOR JOHN BALDWIN, A THIRTY-ONE-YEAR-OLD VICE-PRESIDENT AT a Nashville bank, Tennessee was home, but Oklahoma was roots. He had been languishing in his job for some years with little chance of moving up in the foreseeable future, since his boss was not much older than he was. So when newly hired executive vice-president Rick Dunn called to offer him a chance to return to his boyhood home at a substantial boost in salary, he felt he had to investigate the opportunity further.

Baldwin took the job, arriving at Penn Square in late July 1981, and almost immediately embarked on a single mission: to write a loan policy for Penn Square Bank. The existing one was unconscionably brief, essentially nonexistent. A loan policy is a bank's most important document. Some banks may disregard their lending policies, but few operate without one. Baldwin established lending authorities, criteria for making commercial and real estate loans, and charge-off policies. He also wrote a chapter on oil and gas lending.

Baldwin handed a rough draft of the policy to Bill Patterson and asked him for his comments.

"Bill was not at all interested in participating in writing a policy for his department, and told me so," Baldwin said later. "As far as Patterson was concerned, he was lending on reserves in the ground and didn't believe any policy could cover that."

Patterson didn't return the draft until Baldwin went to Eldon Beller, and Beller asked Patterson to review the document. Finally, Patterson made some comments and the chapter was included in it, according to Baldwin. Baldwin recommended, for example, that the bank lend no more than 50% of the proved producing reserves, a figure Patterson and Jennings raised to 80% in theory, and 100% or more in practice. The policy also called for a borrower's financial statements on loans over a certain amount, but the loans continued to get booked with no statements.

"I don't need a financial statement if I have a reserve report showing that the reserves are in the ground and if my mortgage is properly perfected," Patterson told Baldwin. "What do I need a policy for? It's collateral lending."

Baldwin knew little about oil and gas. But he understood a lot about sound lending principles.

"It was my understanding that those engineering reports are just the best estimates of the reserves in the ground. The engineers could be wrong and the reserves could be depleted," he told Patterson. "At that point," he said, "it would be nice to have some financial statement so you'd know if the borrower had the financial strength to repay the loan without the reserves."

"That's not the way things work," Patterson said defiantly, abruptly terminating the conversation.

Baldwin attempted to take the issue higher, but was told once again that oil and gas lending was collateral lending, and that financial statements wouldn't help much anyway. In theory, Patterson was right. But in practice the loans more often than not exceeded the value of the reserves. Baldwin and his staff were not comfortable with oil and gas lending, and in view of the resistance they were getting from the man some employees in the bank referred to as "god," they concluded they should try out their new procedures on the much smaller commercial loan portfolio. Nine months would pass, however, before the policy was applied to oil and gas, where 80% of the bank's loans were concentrated.

Patterson made some substantive changes in the document, but it proved to be an academic exercise. Even though the policy had been approved by the board of directors, it became apparent to Baldwin after the policy had been distributed that the largest area of the bank, oil and gas, had no intention whatever of following the new guidelines.

Loans were supposed to be passed through a loan approval committee before they could be funded. But in actuality Patterson committed the bank to a loan and directed one of his underlings to put the package together and escort it through the committee. The loan officer would say, "Well, we've already committed to making this loan, and we've already got 95 percent of it sold," according to a former Penn Square lender.

Patterson's loans were rarely, if ever, turned down. Although Beller did, on occasion, tell the loan officer that the loan could not be booked until it was sold, loans were never rejected on the creditworthiness of the customer after Patterson had pledged the bank to the deal. And in fact Beller put his initials on most of the loans made by Patterson prior to their being funded, although he would contend later that he was not approving them, just acknowledging that he had seen them.

Patterson attended few of the scheduled meetings of the committee. On several occasions, Patterson would call Dunn or Baldwin on the phone and chew them out for not booking a deal he had committed on. Baldwin's reply would be, "You get it approved and I'll book it."

Baldwin recalled vividly the first loan committee meeting he attended. Patterson burst through the door of the third-floor conference room, puffing a big cigar, and wearing an expensive suit. He pulled a chair from a corner of the room and threw it up against the table, and as he was sitting down looked to the end of the table past several other officers and began screaming at John Preston, the bank's general counsel. Preston had sent a Patterson customer a demand letter on a defaulted note.

"This is a good customer, why are you doing this to me?" he shouted at the lawyer.

Jennings, who was sitting at the end of the table, as he always did, said, "Bill, settle down, just calm down."

"I'm not going to settle down until I find out what's going on here," Patterson retorted.

Preston, meanwhile, tried to explain why he had done it, but was cut off by Patterson.

Jennings edged up closer to the table. "Sit down and calm down."

Patterson continued his tirade against Preston, and finally Jennings said, "Shut up, Bill. When this meeting is over, I want you to come down to my office." It was, said Baldwin, a "principal-student type of thing."

Jennings often gave Beller and the new officers he had brought in the impression that he was concerned about Patterson's lending excesses and tirades. He had a knack for delaying things, for defusing the issue of Bill Patterson by saying, as one former officer put it, "You're right, we've got to sit down with Bill on this."

Jennings was Patterson's biggest defender. "Jennings gave him the ball and he ran with it," said a member of the Beller team. He ran the bank by telephone from Chicago. "Patterson was a crazy guy, a laugh a minute," recalled the former officer. "We realized we were dealing with the guy who was the bank's greatest asset in an unorthodox way."

Patterson didn't always attend committee meetings well scrubbed and wearing expensive suits. Sometimes he wore thongs and cut-off jeans. On one occasion, Patterson had just returned from a four-day jaunt around the country selling loans, and drove directly to the bank after his private chartered jet touched down at Wiley Post Airport. According to Baldwin, Patterson sat down between two other officers. It was apparent he hadn't shaved in days, and he reeked of body odor. His three-piece suit was ruffled and his shoes were scuffed-up. He looked and smelled horrible.

"Bill, where've you been?" one officer said.

"Well, while you all have been sitting here at the bank administrating and loan-reviewing I've been out on the road trying to hustle up business. I've been wearing these clothes for four days. I haven't had a bath in four days. I haven't shaved in four days. I haven't brushed my teeth in four days. I've got the same underwear on I had four days ago. I've never even had my shoes off."

Wyman Fraley was not one of Patterson's good customers. But three days before the marriage of Prince Charles and Lady Diana in July 1981, the former used-car salesman turned oil promoter called the Associated Press and local newspapers and television stations to announce that he had sent a wedding gift, an interest in an oil well, to the royal couple. Wearing anteater Western boots, a huge gold ring encrusted with diamonds, and a belt buckle almost as big as a salad plate, the Anglophile told a local newspaper that the revenue from the well would represent a "comfortable" income for the newlyweds for the "rest of their lives." Other oilmen familiar with the oil field where the well was drilled were less optimistic, predicting that the well was unlikely to produce more than five barrels a day, if at all. According to a former Patterson aide, Patterson was furious. Fraley was just months away from bankruptcy and was eventually suspended by the Oklahoma franchise tax bureau for failure to pay his taxes. Using $1 million from Penn Square Bank and at least another million fraudulently obtained from other banks and unsophisticated investors, Fraley lived opulently, buying expensive furs and jewelry, and taking trips to Europe. The likable, persuasive used-car salesman claimed to have been in the oil business all of his life, when in fact he had never succeeded in drilling a producing well, and most of those he said were planned were never drilled. When investors became suspicious and demanded an accounting, his records disappeared in a series of mysterious fires, according to allegations by a U.S. attorney.

Despite the presence of questionable credits like Wyman Fraley in

Bill Patterson's so-called oil and gas portfolio, Patterson wasn't initially perceived by the Beller faction to be the source of the bank's credit quality problems. That distinction was reserved for departed horse trader Thomas Orr. For months, the mess that Orr left, and the effort to clean it up, diverted time and attention from the life-threatening problems in the energy portfolio.

It took more than three months after George Clifton completed his exam for his report to be forwarded to the Penn Square board, and for a meeting to be scheduled for Clifton Poole. Consequently, the limited visit scheduled for July was moved back to September. That delay, combined with the fact that the Dallas region based the intervals between exams on their *actual* beginning and ending dates rather than the "as of," or effective dates, bumped the next comprehensive exam back from December 31, 1981, to March 31, 1982, allowing the monster to feed another three months before it would once again be subject to careful scrutiny.

About the time Patterson was giving a dog and pony show to the board on the bank's ten best and two worst rig loans, the Comptroller's office in Washington was putting the finishing touches on an analysis of Penn Square for its Dallas region It concluded:

> [G]iven the volume of off balance sheet participations ($600 million), the high average amount of unfunded commitments, high loans/deposits ratio and relatively small staff, this bank has the potential for serious liquidity problems. This bank can probably continue its high-rolling stance provided investor confidence remains and the market is favorable for the sale of loan participations. However, the sheer volume of commitments and participations funded by $100m certificate of deposits requires close monitoring by management with the bank aware of its position and outstandings at all times.

On July 1, the Dallas region reported to the board on its spring exam, noting that the "overall deterioration in the loan portfolio is of significant concern to this examination due to this institution's overall cash management and liquidity problems." The regulators asserted that the directors and senior management had failed to supervise prudently the bank's activities, and once again demanded that the board appear in Dallas on July 29 for yet another trip to the woodshed.

After receiving the bad report card from Dallas, Penn Square's

219

management, including Jennings, Beller, and Rick Dunn, snowed Poole with a flood of apologetic letters and documentation attesting to their good intentions. These assurances led Poole merely to threaten the bank with a cease and desist order, which would have been the most severe action he could have taken short of closing the bank down.

Meanwhile, the Comptroller's Chicago region had uncovered some disturbing Penn Square participations in a review of Michigan National Bank-Lansing that noted that bank's lack of expertise in oil and gas. The examiners there asked Poole's people for some background on Penn Square's condition but, incredibly, Dallas told Chicago that Penn Square oil and gas loans were "generally good," if "somewhat risky." Regional administrators are said to be as protective of their turf in dealing with other regions as one bank agency is in dealing with another. Had the examiners in Dallas pursued the discussions with its sister regions further, they would have found that loans that appeared to be sold to Continental were actually laid off on Michigan.

In Chicago examiners from the Comptroller's multinational unit, while noting the sharp growth of Bergman's special industries division, found nothing to be concerned about. They stated in their report that "CINB is adequately staffed with both sound lending officers and scientific [engineers and geologists] personnel to handle current relationships and meet continued strong growth anticipations . . . . No significant problems are evident as noted by the fact that only two O&G credits were classified herein."

Staffing in the oil and gas division was in fact one of the unit's biggest problems. But Continental Illinois would never permit lack of staff to stand in the way of booking new business. Continental, said a former officer, was "capital-driven" meaning that the only constraint on its growth was the capital-to-asset ratio required of the bank by the regulators. In the superheated and growth-oriented corporate culture that chairman Anderson had established, senior officers felt their careers would have been damaged irreparably if they protested that they could not take on additional business because of a shortage of lending officers.

Likewise, in Seattle, the national bank examiners wrapped up a cursory exam at Seafirst without detecting that anything was amiss. Reflecting on that exam, a former Seafirst officer observed that "a good lending officer is far tougher on any credit than a bank examiner."

At the July 29 meeting in Dallas, Clifton Poole startled the Penn

Square board by telling them that they were "flirting with disaster" and headed in the wrong direction with the Comptroller of the Currency because they had failed to comply with nine out of ten of the items in the "administrative agreement" signed the year before. Poole told the Oklahomans that he had decided "by a very small margin" not to issue a cease and desist order, which he said, would do "terrible damage" to the association if word of such an order hit the street. One thing that clearly influenced the decision not to issue the C&D was the hiring of Eldon Beller, and Beller's representations to the regulators that he was in charge and was approving Penn Square loans, according to Jerry Lanier, then an examiner with the agency.

One popular jawboning technique is the "good guy–bad guy game," and Poole did not neglect to use it. He stressed that he had "gone to bat" with the Washington office to block the cease and desist order. That was indeed surprising, since Poole "loved" cease and desist orders, according to former colleagues, and counted scalps by the number he issued.

Having passed up the opportunity to slap Penn Square with a dreaded C&D, as it is known among bankers, Poole would not have considered removal of Penn Square management as a viable option at this point, even though he might have made a case that Jennings was jeopardizing the "safety and soundness" of the institution. "If Jennings had contested removal in court," opined one former bank examiner, "we probably would have lost. The last thing we want to do is test one of our dictates on something as wishy-washy as excessive growth. We could have gone to the board," he mused, "but they wouldn't have voted him out."

As Rep. Fernand St Germain remarked later, "They conned the Comptroller of the Currency's office—the past Comptroller, the acting Comptroller, and the new Comptroller."

"That parking lot at the little Penn Square shopping center," St Germain said wryly, "became a veritable traffic jam of money brokers and bankers grabbing on to the financial merry-go-round, trying to get the brass ring, while the OCC continued to search its manual for the chapter on go-go banking."

While the real sore was festering in Oklahoma, Bill Martin, the deputy comptroller of the Currency responsible for monitoring problem banks like Penn Square, was holed up in Wheeling, West Virginia, for more than a month defending the honor of his office against suits filed by the owner of four candy store banks—ranging in size from $6 million to $20 million in assets—accused by the examiners of shuffling bad loans among the banks to avoid detection.

In the spring of 1981, the examiners slapped the owner of the banks, Patrick Crakes, and the boards of the three national banks, with a notice of charges, the step preceding the issuance of a C&D. Under agency procedure, the banks had a choice of consenting to the order or litigating it. Not only did they choose to litigate, they also filed a civil lawsuit against the Comptroller and the individual examiners. That was a move OCC officials viewed as striking at the heart of the supervisory process. If individual examiners could be sued, "we were out of business," said a former regulator. Others, however, saw the deployment of a hefty portion of the Comptroller's enforcement staff on a problem involving such small banks as a gross misuse of the agency's resources, asserting that bank regulators, at the Washington level, seem incapable of properly ordering their priorities.

From April 1981 until June 1982, the senior staff of the Comptroller of the Currency and most of its legal staff were preoccupied nearly full-time with the two-bit loan participation shell game going on in West Virginia, while in Oklahoma City Patterson and Jennings were shuffling billions around the nation's largest banks with reckless abandon. Bureaucrats are deathly afraid of getting sued. And West Virginia might have been on Cliff Poole's mind when he decided by that narrow margin not to issue the much-feared cease and desist. Clearly, the comptroller didn't have enough warm bodies to cope with two landmark lawsuits at one time. Even within the agency, there were protests against throwing all the troops at the skirmish in West Virginia. Some officials asked, "What are we doing fooling around with three institutions in West Virginia?" Robert Serino, the comptroller's director of enforcement, acknowledged later, "It was a major undertaking of our office. We couldn't just back away and turn our backs on those banks." All this was going on at a time when the OCC was being run by a caretaker comptroller. John Heimann, a strong and popular comptroller—who, incidentally, had been a friend of Robert Hefner's for more than twenty years—resigned that spring and was replaced temporarily by Acting Comptroller Charles Lord.

On another level, bankers criticize what they contend is the failure of examiners to properly "prioritize" the violations of law and regulation they find in their reviews, charging that the regulators tend to give the violations equal weight, diminishing a bank's ability to respond to the most critical problems. The regional office of the Comptroller of the Currency, former examiners say, was overly concerned about Penn Square's liquidity, or funding, and skirted the real issue: credit quality.

Actually, these sources point out, Penn Square was quite imaginative in gathering money. By offering one-half to one point or more above the market rate on $100,000 certificates of deposit, Penn Square drew jumbo CDs from around the country like a female dog in heat attracts male dogs from miles around.

Almost to the day that the regional administrator was admonishing Penn Square's directors, a Los Angeles money broker named Professional Asset Management was sending out a letter to its investor clients announcing that it was adding "two fine institutions to our list of well-capitalized banks and savings associations." One of them was Penn Square. The letter pointed to Penn Square's "outstanding growth" and stated that the bank had "become the leading bank in the Southwest servicing the oil and gas industry." Energy-related activities such as exploration, production, and servicing, the letter went on, "have been proceeding at record-breaking rates. It is anticipated that these activities will continue at high levels for the foreseeable future."

Bill Goldsmith, one of the founders of PAM, established the company just three months before to fill what he felt was a vacuum left by big brokerage firms in buying and selling money. "Nobody," he said, "was selling certificates of deposit for institutions below the top tier." A former broker with Merrill Lynch in California, Goldsmith had written an investment guide for credit unions. Now he tapped a loyal following of these institutions he had developed while at Merrill and went into the business of placing their members' funds with other financial institutions in need of deposits, stroking his clientele with chatty letters and luncheon speaker programs. The idea was for Goldsmith to do the credit analysis on the recipients of those deposits, and PAM would collect a 25 basis point fee from the recipient of those funds. Operating out of a small office in Los Angeles equipped with a battery of phones and computer terminals, PAM and a few other peddlers of hot money supplied the lifeblood that would prop up an increasingly shaky Penn Square Bank for nearly a year. Later, the House Banking Committee chairman wondered how "so many small financial institutions wound up delegating their judgments and responsibilities to brokers who peddled Penn Square's get-rich-quick interest rates like cotton candy at a carnival." And his colleague, Rep. Jim Leach of Iowa, observed, "Penn Square was the queen of spades in the house of cards that extended the length and breadth of American banking."

223

According to official sources, Penn Square circumvented banking rules against paying interest on noninterest bearing demand deposit accounts by instructing certain customers to send invoices to Penn Square for services that in fact were never performed. Instead of paying interest on the accounts, Penn Square allegedly remitted the balance due shown on the invoice. Another promotion scheme nearly sent the examiners into cardiac arrest. Penn Square at one time gave away Rolls-Royces in lieu of interest on million-dollar CDs, and even broke through the wall of the bank to move one of the luxury automobiles into the lobby.

Some clever, if questionable, accounting sleights of hand helped too. First Penn Corporation, Penn Square's holding company, transformed itself into a kind of upstream correspondent, buying loans for 5 to 30 days at a time with the proceeds of the holding company's commercial paper sales to get them off the bank's books and bring down the loan-to-deposits ratio. Bank employees would actually take a stack of blank participation certificates to officers of the holding company to be filled out, and reverse the transactions later after the liquidity crisis had passed.

Ed Miller of Founders Bank was not aware Penn Square was buying "hot money," but he knew they must be tapping the national markets when the competition with Penn Square for local deposits began easing, even though Penn Square continued to make loans to the new oilies like there was no tomorrow. Bankers are reluctant to criticize a competitor, even indirectly. So when Miller's customers or prospective customers told him they had been offered one-half to one point higher than the market rate on a $100,000 certificate of deposit, Miller could only bite his lip and reply that "Penn Square was doing pretty aggressive lending and were bidding aggressively for funds." He left it up to the customer to make the connection between aggressive lending, higher rates on funds, and risk.

By this time, however, Penn Square's growth had become a great source of frustration to the board of Founders Bank, as well as other banks in Oklahoma City. It was becoming difficult for these institutions to interpret their own efforts to boost market share—measured in deposits, loans, and total assets—because Penn Square had so distorted the numbers. Boards of directors may not know much about their institutions' internal operations, but they watch market share figures closely out of a combination of envy and pride. Aware that Penn Square was growing rapidly by extending huge lines of credit to inexperienced oil and gas finders, Founders Bank directors concluded that Penn Square's business simply wasn't the kind of business they wanted anyway. So Penn Square's nearest banking neighbor simply backed the maverick bank out of its marketing statistics, treating Penn Square, in evaluating its own progress, as the banking aberration it had become.

The devices Beep Jennings and Bill Patterson used to acquire more capital were equally as imaginative as those it employed to gather more deposits. They had what a former colleague called a "godfather mentality." Bill Patterson and Penn Square expected something in return from its customers for all the evergreen revolvers, renewals, lease lines, and rollovers. The quid pro quo was that good customers should invest in the bank when the regulators demanded new capital. Kevin Leonard of LPCX Corporation was one such customer. Leonard, and his partners, Palm and Cook (Leonard, Palm Cook Exploration) had borrowed millions from Penn Square by mid-1981 not only for its oil and gas activities but to finance an increasingly lavish lifestyle. On June 23, Leonard later alleged, Patterson phoned to suggest that they meet to talk about subscribing in the holding company's new stock offering. The next day Patterson told Leonard that the stock was a great deal which he was offering only to a few "select customers" of the bank. "I'm doing this as a special favor, Kevin," he said. The best part of it, Patterson said, was that the stock purchase would cost Leonard nothing out of pocket, because he would arrange a fixed rate loan (10%) "substantially below Penn Square's then current prime rate." The loan would be larger than the purchase price of the stock. According to the court documents, Patterson handed him an offering circular and Leonard signed a blank note for $175,000, covering the purchase of 1,120 shares of stock at $135 per share with some left over. Although the note was supposed to be secured only by Penn Square stock, it showed as the collateral oil and gas properties already pledged by Leonard on other loans.

Later, Penn Square loaned Leonard's aircraft holding company, U.S. Executive Aircraft, nearly $1.4 million for a Grumman Gulfstream turboprop, operating expenses, salaries for the bookkeeper, pilots, repairs, and even the interest on the loan—all collateralized with little more than an airplane in need of repair and Leonard's guarantee.

Gary Gray, a husky Oklahoma Indian who rose quickly through the hierarchy at the First National Bank and later started his own oil and gas company, also found himself the reluctant owner of First Penn stock. A friend of Patterson from the First National Bank and a heavy borrower at Penn Square, Gray was on a trip to London in May 1981 when he received a wire from his secretary asking him which line of credit he wanted to use to buy Penn Square stock. Gray telexed back, he said later, that he didn't want to buy any. But on returning to Oklahoma City, he learned that an officer of his company had executed a note on his behalf for about $160,000 to buy the stock, having been told by Patterson that Gray wanted to make the investment. According to Gray, Patterson told him afterward, "Oh, I thought you wanted some of that stock," and said that he didn't want to reverse the transaction. Patterson, Gray contended, said he'd make the note for approximately $160,000 to mature in a year, and assured him that in the meantime he, Patterson, would sell the stock to someone else.

The ties between Gray and his Gibraltar Exploration and Penn Square were indeed close ones. Jennings had invested in one of the company's drilling programs, and former astronaut Thomas P. Stafford, the commander of Apollo X, which, in 1969, became the first space capsule to orbit the moon, was a director of Gibraltar and a substantial borrower at the Penn Square Bank.

·T W E N T Y - F O U R·

MORE BAD DEALS

R EAL ESTATE DEVELOPER KIM COLLINS NEVER HAD REASON TO
doubt the word of Tom Chilcott, the Fort Collins commodities
wizard with the look and demeanor of a choirboy. That is, not until
the spring of 1981, when he got a phone call from Chilcott asking if,
by chance, the FBI had called about a Florida stockbroker named
Dennis Elliot Greenman.

On April 1, 1981, federal agents shut down the Barclay Financial
Corporation, a Miami discount brokerage firm that sold a stock options scheme, the Greenman Short Term Trading program, to
wealthy investors. Greenman, who had been a successful broker with
the Miami office of Paine Webber, Jackson and Curtis before establishing Barclay Financial, promised fantastic profits to investors by
arbitraging stocks in the world capital markets. In fact, Greenman
Short Term Trading was, like Chilcott Commodities, just another
twist on the Ponzi scheme. A Securities and Exchange Commission
complaint charged that Greenman intercepted genuine trading account statements before they could reach investors and created
bogus ones that made it appear to the investors that they were reap-
ing huge profits.

According to a report in the *Tulsa Tribune,* one of Greenman's clients was a wealthy Florida real estate promoter named Allan Wolfson, then on probation for a 1978 bank fraud conviction, whose
movements were being closely watched by federal authorities. Wolfson teamed up with another Greenman investor to borrow $3.5
million from the Metropolitan Bank of Tampa to invest with
Greenman.

FBI agents reportedly tipped off bank examiners on Wolfson's ties
to Metropolitan Bank, where they found that bad loans to Wolfson
and his friends amounted to about one-fourth of the bank's $160
million loan portfolio. The discovery that Wolfson had invested
more than $500,000 in Chilcott Commodities sent federal agents

scurrying to Fort Collins, Colorado, to take a second look at Chilcott, who a year earlier had smooth talked his way out of an investigation by federal authorities. Greenman, it turned out, had sunk about $500,000 into the Chilcott scheme. Allen Senall got off easy—he stood to lose only about $150,000, according to the *Tulsa Tribune*.

On June 15, just two and half months after busting Greenman, the FBI closed down Chilcott Commodities, freezing the millions that Tureaud had invested in the deal. Government investigators discovered that Chilcott had poured more than $27 million of the funds he had bilked from his own clients into investments in some twenty-five companies, used $3 million to pay off personal loans, and diverted other funds from the commodities pool to his personal trading and partnership accounts. Chilcott's financial statement claimed more than $7 million in fictitious assets based solely on false and inflated commodity profits, according to a federal plea agreement with Chilcott.

The collapse of Chilcott was a body blow for Ken Tureaud. Tureaud, of course, had diverted funds from Saket to invest with Chilcott. Chilcott, likewise, had pilfered monies from his commodity pool to invest in Saket, funds which in turn Tureaud squandered elsewhere. Tureaud had overbilled Chilcott on his drilling funds, but when Chilcott was shut down, a major source of Tureaud's cash flow evaporated overnight. One of the biggest losers was the Collins family, who had entrusted more than $18 million to Chilcott, and now had nearly $5 million at risk with Ken Tureaud. Tureaud had promised to take the Collins family out of Saket for $7.5 million, but like so many of his other promises, that one never came to pass.

John R. Lytle was alarmed by the developments in Colorado. Penn Square had originated a $1 million note to Chilcott, $850,000 of which it had upstreamed to Continental Illinois. Lytle was fearful, former Continental officers say, that with all the notoriety surrounding the Chilcott affair the $850,000 loan would eventually turn up in the press and focus attention on the lending practices of profit center 1089. The solution was Ken Tureaud, who graciously agreed to take over the $1 million note. "Lytle," said a source acquainted with the transaction, "was grateful that it saved embarrassment for the bank. It saved us a lot of press." John Lytle could not thank Tureaud enough.

The Continental lending officer handling the Tureaud account had long been uncomfortable with the relationship. In checking into the collateral behind the loans on the Morris Field project, the officer had found that Chilcott had claimed interests in the field that, when combined with the interests claimed by Tureaud and others, somehow added up to more than 100%. Sources familiar with the project say that Tureaud never had legal title to the Morris Field leases in the first place. Nevertheless, Continental Illinois rolled over Tureaud's notes whenever they came due.

At the same time, engineers at Continental and Penn Square concluded that the field was not worth anywhere near the amount of money Penn Square was prepared to lend on it. After an outside engineering report severely downvalued the Morris Field reserves, Tureaud complained that the consulting engineers only looked at a couple of geologic zones. Penn Square loan officers reportedly told Patterson that the leases on the Morris Field may have been taken illegally. They told him, "The lawyers say there's no way to know how much he's got." Patterson took a puff on his cigar and replied, "Fuck the lawyers. Hire new ones."

At Penn Square, newly rehired officer Tom Swineford was one of those who harbored serious doubts about the relationship of Tureaud with Penn Square. According to one former employee, Swineford would plop a file down and say, "It's a wormy deal. The guy's a crook." Patterson would then assign it to Dewayne Horton, another bank officer. He, too, would bring it back and say, "I'm not going to do it." Patterson would yell and scream and order a secretary to give it to a junior officer. And, eventually, someone would be found who was willing to sign off Ken Tureaud. Tureaud got to the point where he'd call and announce that he needed a million or so by a certain date, and was taken aback when told by a secretary, "You can't always get your money overnight."

Tureaud, former employees said, was always nervous when he came to see Patterson, "following him around through the bank like a puppy" in seeking more money for his deals. When Tureaud needed money, he exhibited the physical symptoms of an alcoholic or drug addict going cold turkey. "His forehead got sweaty and his hands started to shake," a former Penn Square secretary recalled.

There was at least one Continental energy lender who was becoming concerned to the point of anger over the Penn Square relationship. Kathy Kenefick didn't care for Lytle, and couldn't stand Patterson. Patterson, in turn, felt Kenefick asked too many questions and urged Lytle to get her out of his way. Other officers became demoralized when Penn Square customers "ragged on Kathy and John didn't come to her defense."

Coincidently, on July 29, the same day Clifton Poole was chastising Penn Square's board of directors in Dallas, Kenefick dashed off a fiery memo to her superiors calling into question the Penn Square relationship and the procedures being used by the mid-continent division. Kenefick asserted that the "status of the Oklahoma accounts (particularly Penn Square Bank) is a cause for concern and corrective action should be instigated quickly. . . ." She advised that "potential credit problems could be going unnoticed" because initial credit write-ups were not done correctly, or at all, and "other necessary documentation often was incomplete." Moreover, she pointed up the "lack of control of Penn Square Bank." Later, after no action was taken, an angry and frustrated Kenefick quit Continental for a job at a commercial finance company.

Kenefick, however, was not the only officer in the mid-continent division to express concern over Penn Square. She was, however, the only one to express it in writing, and thereby put her job on the line. A younger, less experienced colleague who shared Kenefick's anxieties, though not to the point of writing a memo about them, recalled, "We saw what she had done, and she got blown away. So we figured, what would happen to someone with five months of banking experience attempting to challenge someone with twenty years?"

At least one officer was worried that no one was checking the condition of the banks issuing the letters of credit for limited partnership drilling funds. "The attitude was," said one young banker, "there's enough of them. We can spread our risk."

Some of the other problems were more prosaic. "We were so incredibly understaffed," said one officer. "How could anyone handle thirty-five loans at once?" Meanwhile, the national bank examiners found little to complain about in the special industries division, the mid-continent division, or Continental Illinois.

By the fall of 1981, Lytle was going through the exception list, instructing his staff to "get this one off, get that one off." Officers were further confused by their fondness for Lytle personally and their recognition, as one put it, that "he was a disaster as a manager. He was a pleasant guy, and good to his people. He'd tell me I was a pain in the ass, but was always supportive. From a personal view he was great." Lytle, former officers said, continued to see himself as a loan officer rather than as a manager, and spent much of his time traveling. Some of those trips were all-expense-paid junkets underwritten by Swan and Allen's Longhorn Oil and Gas Company to Mazatlán, a fashionable resort on the Pacific coast of Mexico, according to court documents. And in June 1981 Longhorn flew Jennings and Lytle, among others, to Hong Kong for what was represented to be an oil and gas seminar.

As Lytle's friendship, and business relationship, with Patterson developed, he tended to side with Patterson on the creditworthiness of borrowers rather than with his own staff. Responding to subordinates who took issue with some Penn Square–originated loans, Lytle asked quizzically, "You mean you're doubting the word of Patterson?" Moreover, it appeared, at least on paper, that profit center 1089 was making gobs of money for the bank.

Baker obtained a copy of the Kenefick memo and informed Bergman of her criticisms of Lytle and the operations of the mid-continent division, a problem Bergman shrugged off as a "personality conflict" between the two officers. The Kenefick memorandum, as it came to be known, remained on Baker's desk until May 1982, when Baker, thinking the problem had been remedied, tossed it in the trash.

Senior vice-president Jack Redding, like John Nelson, his counterpart in Seattle, was a likable, almost grandfatherly figure. Redding, unlike Nelson, possessed a vast knowledge of the petroleum industry, but that knowledge would be rendered useless by one significant weakness. Redding eschewed confrontation, and consequently backed off from unpleasant encounters with Lytle or anyone else, despite the concerns expressed to him by Lytle's own staff.

One officer remembers asking Redding how much of the total bank portfolio should be in oil and gas. "He said he hadn't thought about it. That was the problem. No one was thinking. Everyone was gleeful about all the money being made."

What Kenefick knew to be a credit quality problem, Bergman, Lytle, and others on the lending side insisted were operational or paperwork problems. Gail Melick, the feisty operations man with the obsession about Continental's cockroaches, had long been replaced by Joe Coriaci, who, insiders said, had a reputation of choosing weak subordinates and was considered ill-suited to the job himself. According to a special report later issued by Continental, Penn Square credits that were past due or were deficient in documentation continued to pop out on exception reports produced by Continental's loan operations staff. Lytle, contending that the reports were full of mistakes, refused to discuss them with Coriaci until the alleged errors were cleared up. The exception report problem, as Lytle saw it, was accentuated because Penn Square and Continental used different prime rates. A change in the prime by either one of the banks would cause new items to appear on the list, he said. Operations has traditionally been the whipping boy of banking, and lending officers are known for their tendency to pull rank on their counterparts in the back offices. Bergman and Coriaci often debated the exception issue; Coriaci claimed that lending was shirking the problem, while Bergman charged that the reports were inaccurate. Nevertheless, Bergman was sufficiently concerned in August 1981 to order Redding to send auditors to Oklahoma to review the relationship. "Six weeks to two months later," said Bergman, "I asked him about it and learned that he had not done it, and so I did it myself."

According to Continental insiders, Anderson persisted in hiring more business graduates, and putting them to work booking more loans, while periodically cutting back on operations, the area of a bank where the knife comes down first, and comes down hardest. Continental's paperwork problems weren't limited to the exception report. The bank had no systematic way of knowing at any given time how much it had bought from Penn Square. When that figure was $519 million, estimates cited by Bergman and Redding were more than $250 million off the mark. Accurate and timely information is the foundation on which top management makes decisions and assesses the strengths and weaknesses of internal controls. Not only was Penn Square out of control, as Kenefick stated in her memo, so was giant Continental Illinois National Bank and Trust Company of Chicago.

Continental continued to boast about its prowess in commercial and industrial lending, while enraging regional banks by luring away customers with subprime fixed-rate loans. It was a case of, as one former officer put it, "You get good, you get cocky." Meanwhile, the business press persisted in reinforcing that notion of invincibility, even as the underpinnings of the bank began to unravel. A September 28 article on the front page of the *New York Times* business section cited the remarkable growth and profitability taking place behind Continental's "quiet façade," and lauded what it described as the "conservative" and "subdued" style of the bank and its top management. Despite his stern appearance and reserved demeanor, Roger Anderson and his bank were anything but conservative.

Unlike Kathy Kenefick, Seafirst's Yuan Chi Chao was too fond of his boss to take his concerns to a higher level. In 1979 Chao was a twenty-seven-year-old credit analyst in the bank's international division when John Boyd was poring through the files of bank trainees looking for staff for his fledgling energy department. Chao, a native of Taiwan, had graduated from the University of Michigan and received a master's degree in business administration from New York University. Because he lacked polish in communicating in English, however, his future as a customer contact man at Seafirst didn't look especially bright. Chao felt a strong sense of loyalty to Boyd for plucking him out of the bowels of the international division and giving him his first real opportunity for advancement at the bank. "John," he once told his boss, "you're the only white person I know who doesn't see color." It was a loyalty, however, tempered by a recognition of Boyd's frailties, and his zest for doing deals that lacked merit on their face. "Y.C. thought John was nuts but loved him just the same," said one observer close to both men. Chao, Boyd acknowledged later, warned him often about the Penn Square relationship, pointing out, among other things, that Seafirst didn't really know its borrowers.

Chao, however, was an inveterate pessimist, who Boyd said was "terrified" of the macho, frontier manner of Oklahomans and Texans. Whenever a problem would arise on one of the energy loans, Chao, Boyd said, would throw up his hands and scream, "This is it! It's over! It's over!" Boyd quipped later, "If Y.C. had his way, the energy division would have had $75 in outstandings." As for international lending, Chao remarked on occasion that it was "insanity" to lend to Mexico and other Latin American nations. "We should lend only to Taiwan and Canada," Chao cautioned in his heavily accented English.

Chao was an intellectually brilliant man who lacked patience with stupid people in high positions and identified closely with bright people in lowly positions. Patterson, he felt, fell into the first category. Though he shared the same disdain for Patterson and Penn Square Bank as Kathy Kenefick, it would have gone against Chao's grain to take the matter to a higher authority. John Nelson could have picked up on Chao's uneasiness with the Oklahoma relationship only if he had taken seriously the muted jokes Chao made about the Penn Square borrowers. But Chao wasn't the only person flashing warning signals.

In August 1981 Clinton Manges, the powerful and controversial Texas oil and land baron to whom Boyd eventually lent nearly $20 million, told Boyd, "The Oklahoma gas play is done. Those guys are overplaying this thing." His concerns about the industry were not limited to Oklahoma. "People are starting to slow pay me," Manges told Boyd. "The drilling thing is done. I've seen it before. In the 1950s rigs were stacked on the side of the road." Boyd admired Manges because he had come up from nothing, rising from a young man pumping gasoline at a service station to a major oil and gas producer pumping thousands of barrels of oil from the ground. But Boyd downplayed Manges's advice because the Texas oilman lacked the formal education Boyd regarded as a prerequisite to wisdom. "I figured," Boyd said later, "what does he know about Oklahoma?"

In the meantime, Paul Bergevin, the stalwart branch manager who had been recruited to bring some controls to the energy division, took his concerns to Dick Jaehning, who had just become president-elect of Seattle First as a result of yet another sweeping reorganization. Jaehning, sources say, paid no attention to the warnings, and Bergevin left the bank to return to his hops farm in Yakima. As part of the restructuring Jaehning assumed responsibility for the lending side of the bank and Curtis took on the staff functions, leaving Curtis, as one senior officer put it, "to plan strategically for 1995.

By this time, Boyd was not only comfortable with the Penn Square relationship, he was deathly afraid that the borrowing requirements would be so big, and that the requests would come so fast, that he would be undercut by the likes of Chase and other participating banks. Patterson shrewdly played on that insecurity. In mid-1981 Patterson visited Boyd in Seattle, at a time when, Boyd said, Seafirst wasn't moving as quickly as Patterson would have liked on some credits. As Boyd recalls the conversation, Patterson told him, "My people can't wait. I know you're busy, but if you're going to move this slow, I'll just go to Chicago."

To other observers, it did not look like Boyd was moving all that slowly. As one source put it, "Boyd sat at his desk doing multimillion-dollar deals over the phone like a New York money trader."

Chase Manhattan also had sufficient early warning. Dale Mitchell, the former president of the First National Bank of Oklahoma City, says he cautioned Chase vice-president Dick Pinney about dealing with Penn Square in the summer of 1981, but Pinney, Mitchell said, "thought it was competitive jealousy."

Chase Manhattan officers made a practice of buying a shopping basket full of small loans, figuring they would be protected by diversification, and their buyback arrangement with Penn Square. "They bought $10 million at a shot," said a former Penn Square officer. "They'd give them to a junior analyst, and might find a couple they couldn't stomach, but if there was enough meat on the bones they would take them. They had the big New York bank syndrome. They figured, 'We can handle it.'"

One loan that was not of the market basket variety was to Mahan Rowsey, Inc. It was a borrowing relationship even giant Chase Manhattan eventually found too hot to handle. And it was a company that perhaps more than any other would bring the U.S. banking system to its knees.

The merger of Rowsey Petroleum and Mahan Energy was one of the most unlikely combinations of assets and liabilities of the oil boom era. It began in the summer of 1979 on Grand Lake, the favorite weekend spot of Oklahoma's new oilies, where both Billy and Frankie owned vacation retreats. Grand Lake is, as socialite Robert Hoover remarked later in a deposition, "the kind of place where, if you hadn't been there, you haven't lived."

Frankie, a slender man of medium height known for his short temper, stopped by the marina where Rowsey berthed "The Hawk," a 28-foot black-hulled high-performance racing boat valued at more than $60,000. Someone was working on it at the time, and Frankie persuaded the man to take him out for a quick spin.

Shortly thereafter, Mahan met Rowsey through a woman Rowsey was dating, and the two men soon wound up back at the marina. "Do you want to go for a ride on my boat?" Rowsey asked. "I've already been," Mahan replied. That was the beginning of one of the most notorious joyrides in American banking history. Later that year, Mahan and Rowsey agreed to share offices in Oklahoma City, and then formed their partnership. The ties between the two men became so close that they even ended up marrying sisters.

Mahan, the son of a Oklahoma state legislator, had started out in the oil business in the early 1970s selling mud to drilling contractors. He later bought his own rig and established Delta Oil and Gas, enjoying a moderate degree of success. He soon became more ambitious and subsequently sold the rig and formed a new company, Mahan Energy, to engage in oil and gas exploration and production.

Frank admired Billy's mind and Billy's money. A law graduate of the University of Oklahoma and a member of an oil family said to be worth more than $40 million, Rowsey seemed to possess the savvy and understanding of the legal aspects of the oil business Mahan knew he lacked. Coincidently, Rowsey grew up in Muskogee, Oklahoma, next door to the Rooneys, a major shareholder in Penn Square Bank. According to Stanley Lee, who, together with L.F. Rooney and Jennings, took over Penn Square Bank, he, Rooney, Jennings, and the elder Rowsey were college chums at the University of Oklahoma in the late 1940s.

As Mahan Rowsey, Inc., Billy screened geological prospects, despite a lack of training in engineering and geology, while Mahan oversaw the technical and operations side of the business. Early on, Mahan Rowsey, Inc., relied heavily on investor capital for their drilling program, and quite by accident hit a gusher south of Oklahoma City that was said to have produced some 1,000 barrels per day of sweet crude. At some point, they decided that instead of sharing their bounty with investors, they would share it with a bank. Their subsequent wells, however, turned out to be dry holes.

According to Patterson, Bill Jennings, who knew Mahan from his days at Fidelity, introduced Mahan and Rowsey to the bank, and instructed him to fix them up with a line of credit. Scribbling the figures on a paper napkin, Patterson started Mahan Rowsey off in the spring of 1981 with $4 million for leases and production. In the fall Patterson and several of his associates flew to New York to meet with Mahan and Rowsey, Chase Manhattan vice-president Meg Sipperly, and other Chase officials on a $15 million credit that would put Mahan Rowsey into the drilling business.

After gathering at the Plaza Hotel for drinks, the party adjourned for dinner to the "21" Club on West Fifty-second Street, where Frank began "pawing" at Meg, as one observer put it, and then launched into a litany of off-color jokes.

"Don't you realize who you're sitting with?" Meg said, laughing off his behavior to her superiors as typical of those "wild Oklahoma oilmen."

Chase senior vice-president Wayne Hansen, a patrician-looking Ivy League graduate, wasn't amused, according to others present. "That's enough," he said firmly. "There are ladies here." Patterson himself seemed embarrassed by their behavior, even though he had earlier entertained his clients at the Plaza by drinking liquor out of his shoe, according to a member of the entourage. Suddenly, Mahan and Rowsey got up from the table, as if they were going to the men's room. But they left the restaurant and never returned. Nonetheless, Chase extended the company a $15 million rig loan, which was soon enlarged to $27 million.

Frank enjoyed New York and its restaurants, and made a point of dining in the finest ones when he visited the city. After signing the loan papers, he had lunch at the posh La Cote Basque restaurant on East 55th Street, then ducked into Nat Sherman's tobacco store on Fifth Avenue to pick up a box of his favorite cigars. H. Upmann was a $2 cigar that for years had been manufactured in the Canary Islands. This time, however, Sherman informed him that his purchase was part of a final, $1200 shipment from the Canary Island plant, which was being permanently closed. Taking a puff on an H. Upmann, Mahan said expansively, "Send 'em all to Oklahoma!" Frank and Billy then left for Grand Lake, managing to spend a goodly portion of the loan proceeds on the whirlwind trip home.

The rig loan was supposed to be for the interim construction of seven rigs. But any oilman with seven rigs had to have a jet, and Mahan and Rowsey persuaded Patterson to tack an extra million onto the principal sum to enable them to buy Carl Swan's Aero Commander. The plane was named, appropriately, Rig #8. They had barely taken possession of the aircraft when they got into a food fight at 35,000 feet and did tens of thousands of dollars' worth of damage to the cabin.

It was all play as well in the offices of Mahan Rowsey, Inc. The workday lasted from 9:30 to 12:00 noon, Tuesday through Thursday. At noon, said an observer, they'd say, "It's martini time," and bring out a big jug of Stoley's vodka.

Mahan Rowsey hired a local engineer named Bill Burleson to crank out reserve figures for the company. Armed with an Apple computer, Burleson, using a process one observer derisively termed "imagineering," determined the discounted future value of Mahan Rowsey's reserves to be upward of $150 million, which translated into a borrowing base at Penn Square of between $70 and $100 million. In fact, Mike Gilbert, a respected in-house engineer, calculated in October 1981 that their reserves pointed to a loan value of no more than $5 million in October 1981.

The buyers of the loans at the upstream banks rarely talked to the engineers. "Whatever was going on," said one observer, "was based on the chemistry between the salesmen and the buyers. The standard answer was that there was more to a loan deal than engineering. Patterson always said that the reserve value was only part of what went into a loan."

Engineers were rarely, if ever, permitted to sit in on the deal-making. On at least one occasion, Patterson told an assistant, "We're going to Chase Manhattan for a dog and pony show. Rent a jet and take a couple of girls to take notes and carry files." When the delegation arrived in New York, Patterson told the girls to go out shopping, and instructed the engineer, "Take a walk, I'll see you at the airplane in three hours." The engineer sat in an office while Penn Square loan officers and Chase's Meg Sipperly and Dick Pinney left to cut the deals.

"Meg was always breezing through," said one young bank officer. "She didn't have time for engineers."

Like the national bank examiners, who asked only if the engineering reports were in the file, the upstream bank officers didn't seem to care how the figures were determined. They'd simply turn to the page that showed the reserve estimates and cash flow projections, and do the deal.

Nor did the bank examiners seem to know enough to ask the right questions. While they should have been demanding engineers' evaluations, they asked only for the reports. "They only asked if the evaluations were there," said one former Penn Square officer. "But they weren't interested in what they contained." Moreover, he said, they were unfamiliar with oil and gas terminology, and asked general questions like, "What do you think of this loan?"

With standing orders from the Comptroller and Eldon Beller to keep the loan-to-deposits ratio down to an acceptable level, Patterson's pace typically quickened in the waning days of each quarter. That key ratio told him how many more loans he had to sell, and according to his former colleagues, Penn Square's supersalesman tracked it on an almost daily basis, much as a stockbroker monitors the Dow Jones Industrial Average. When told it was within the guidelines, he'd say, "Oh, good," then go out and book more loans. Ostensibly a measure of bank liquidity, the ratio is actually very misleading, since it does not of itself indicate the source of those deposits. A bank with a large portion of its funds in stable noninterest-bearing accounts can get by with a higher loan-to-deposit ratio than a bank that relies primarily on hot money, as Penn Square did.

Patterson's constant travel created severe problems for his staff. "Bill was out so much you couldn't get hold of him. We wouldn't do anything without his approval," said one officer. His pace amazed his staff, as did his ability seemingly to be in several places at once. John Baldwin was accustomed to getting up early, and soon after arriving at the office one morning he got a call from Patterson, who was in New York. He needed some information, and said he'd call back later to get it. Around noon, Patterson called back. He was in Chicago and needed additional information, and would call back once again. Late that afternoon, Baldwin got another call from Patterson. This time the call was from Seattle. The following week, Baldwin found a message on his desk from one of Patterson's secretaries. Baldwin phoned her and learned the peripatetic loan salesman was calling from Caracas. "What the hell is he doing in Caracas?" Baldwin inquired. "That's none of your business," the secretary replied curtly. Patterson's expenses for entertainment and chartered jets were so large that the bookkeepers didn't bother to compile them until they reached at least $50,000.

But not all of Patterson's end-of-quarter trips were for business. When Patterson announced "Let's rodeo," that usually meant heavy gambling, fast women, and nonstop revelry. The rodeos were frequently held in Las Vegas. On September 16, 1981, welterweight boxing champion Tommy Hearns was scheduled to fight Sugar Ray Leonard in a 15-round bout at Caesars Palace, the kind of event that appealed to the new oilies and their bankers. On some of his trips to the correspondent banks, Bill Patterson took along his wife, Eve, and their children. He apparently wanted to leave the impression that he was a devoted family man. But when he and dozens of other Penn Square officers, customers, and directors took off from Oklahoma City in a small air force of private jets and headed west for Vegas, Eve and the children were not with him. They remained at the family's ranch-style home in northwest Oklahoma City. This trip was strictly for the boys.

Trucking magnate Jack Hodges had bought tickets to the fight for his friends and special customers, and had reserved an entire floor at the Sands Hotel, in one of the several two-story, detached buildings arranged in a horseshoe behind the main facility. There was a spacious reception area surrounded by suites of rooms, where early arrivals could relax while waiting for all the limousines to come in from the airport. When Patterson emerged from his suite he was wearing a yellow cap with wings resembling those of a Greek god. Strings dangled down from the wings to his waist. Patterson grinned broadly and jiggled the strings to make the wings flap. Most of the guests were convulsed with laughter. Others feigned mild amusement. A few turned their heads in disgust. The banker who by that time had sold some $1 billion in oil and gas loans was stark naked.

·T W E N T Y - F I V E·

SWIMMING UPSTREAM

B Y THE FALL OF 1981, DEAN MCGEE AND HIS EXPLORATION DE-partment at the Kerr-McGee Corporation in Oklahoma City had awakened to the fact that they'd been top-leased in the Fletcher Field by rival Texaco. McGee faced two choices. He could either let the leases expire and watch as Texaco moved in, or he could drill. McGee opted to drill. While most of the secrets of the deep basin to the northwest had been revealed by then, the Fletcher Field, geologically and technologically, remained largely a mystery. If oil and gas drilling can be compared with space exploration, the iron men of Oklahoma were just getting ready for their first moon shot.

In the Fletcher Field in September the company launched an invasion force of rigs, men and equipment probably unmatched in the history of oil and gas exploration in the United States. Like a corporate Pied Piper, giant Kerr-McGee led hundreds of smaller fry into one of the most expensive and disastrous oil and gas boondoggles in recent times.

At about the same time Kerr-McGee was preparing to probe the Fletcher Field, Bill Patterson and Bill Jennings embarked on a lending binge unequaled in American banking history. The two events were closely related. In the nine months from October 1981 through June 1982, Patterson and Jennings booked and sold an awesome $1.3 billion in energy loans, and much of this money followed Kerr-McGee into the Fletcher play.

The timing of Kerr-McGee's move into the Fletcher Field and the onset of Penn Square's lending spree couldn't have been worse. From October 1981 on, nearly every leading indicator pointed toward a weakening of the oil and gas economy, although few appreciated just how weak it would become. Seismic testing, for example, is one of the first steps in exploring a new field, and precedes the

240

drilling of a test well by several months or more. In October the number of seismic crews at work in the United States peaked at 741. Drilling activity, as reflected in the more closely watched Hughes Tool rig count, is in fact a lagging indicator of oil and gas activity, and may attain its high point just before a sharp downturn.

Another phenomenon was at work that did not bode well for the natural gas industry. The cost of industrial fuel oil, priced on a "BTU equivalent" basis, was rapidly descending to the BTU equivalent marginal cost of natural gas. With residual fuel prices on the decline, many plant managers were about to press the "oil" button.

Investor interest in oil and gas was also weakening. Larry Brandt, the chairman of Invoil, Inc., a drilling fund promoter and a customer of Penn Square, was encountering mounting investor resistance in his attempts to sell his drilling funds. In earlier years, drilling programs were frequently oversubscribed and the company even had to return checks to disappointed investors.

Bill Bell, a sales executive with Maverick Tube Company, a major tubular goods manufacturer, recalled that in October 1981 the discount off the list price of 2⅜-inch drill pipe—the most commonly used size—was 6% to a distributor; in the next twelve months, the discount would jump to as much as 15%. The same tubing that sold for $3 per foot in the fall of 1981 dropped to $1.35 a foot by the spring of 1983, in part because the high price of domestic pipe had caused an influx of top quality foreign pipe into the market.

By all outward appearances, however, the Oklahoma oilies were "a-blowin' and a-goin'" in the words of one survivor and it was still next to impossible to find a motel room in Elk City. Nevertheless, there were more than a few oilmen and bankers, like one director of a suburban bank near Penn Square, saying, "This is crazy. It just can't last."

The massive buildup in the Penn Square loans occurred despite the efforts of president Eldon Beller to corral Bill Patterson and his energy loan portfolio. He failed at both. Beller returned from a hospital stay at the end of September to find the bank's liquidity severely strained. On September 24, he distributed a strongly worded memo suspending the individual lending authority of all loan officers. "No new funding in excess of $50,000 will be made on any loan without the approval of Eldon Beller or Bill Jennings," he wrote. "Any officer knowingly violating this directive will be subject to immediate termination."

Beller also demanded to be informed daily about any loans over $50,000 that were not already sold to an upstream bank. After the

Beller edict, it became more difficult for officers to get unsold loans through the loan committee, but the memo had no impact on the one individual at whom it was primarily directed: Bill Patterson. In private conversations with other senior bank officers, Beller sighed, "Every time I think I have him trapped, he comes at me from another angle."

One officer said Patterson's loans "didn't appear to go through that committee. They seemed to go through some other approval process." The credit committee was really little more than a rubber stamp for Patterson's loans. Apparently, the only loans seriously questioned by the committee were those to John Lytle, when Beller demanded that Patterson produce a letter from Lytle's superiors saying they were aware of them.

In another September 24 memo, Beller chastised Patterson for his dismal attendance record at the credit policy committee meetings. One person who was skeptical of Beller's ability to discipline Patterson was vice-chairman Murphy, who had seen it all before. "Mr. Murphy," Beller recalled, "wished me a lot of luck." Murphy told Beller that Jennings countermanded his order to curtail Patterson's lending authority the last time he tried it. Jennings was in Europe at the time, Murphy told Beller, and "they burned the phone wires down for several days" talking about it. This time, Beller said, Jennings also reversed his $50,000 restriction "insofar as Bill Patterson's ability to do what he wanted to do." Jennings "came in and said Bill Patterson could not operate without the type of authority he had," said Beller. "I agreed. I thought it was a moot point in that I felt Patterson would not quit what he was doing anyway."

Sam "The Polyethylene King" Villyard was an eyewitness to Patterson's response to the new curb on lending authority. Shortly after the Beller directive came down, Patterson instructed one of his subordinates to make a loan for $200,000. The officer said, "We can't do that. Beller said we can't do that."

"Damn it," Patterson snapped impatiently, "just split it up into four $50,000 notes."

Beller at least recognized the problem. The Dallas regional office of Comptroller of the Currency missed the point altogether.

Jerry Lanier, who had conducted the first examination of Penn Square shortly after Jennings took over the bank, was now, in the fall of 1981, instructed to perform what is termed, in Comptroller's bureaucratese, a "special visitation," or "limited scope" exam. That meant he was to keep it short and simple. He was told to look only at the loans that had been classified in the previous exam early in the year, even though more than $600 million in new loans had been originated and sold since then.

At the time, regional administrator Clifton Poole was comfortably ahead of schedule in his reviews of the top-rated banks in his district. But he was far behind in his examinations of the "Type A's," the problem banks, a category that included his biggest headache, Penn Square Bank of Oklahoma City. Regional administrators themselves are evaluated by their superiors in Washington on their ability to meet certain performance objectives. Poole was apparently determined to meet his, even if that meant Penn Square's review would be "quick and dirty."

Lanier was supposed to have visited Penn Square in August 1981, six months after the general exam conducted earlier in the year. But, as noted earlier, because of long and unexplained delays in forwarding the results of that exam to Penn Square's board of directors, Lanier's exam was rescheduled for October and the next comprehensive exam for April. Between those exams, the regional office of the Comptroller had requested mounds of information and documentation from Penn Square, information that a later audit by the Treasury Department's Inspector General found the office never even used.

Lanier identified most of the same old Penn Square problems—the lending limit violations, loans to previously criticized borrowers, uncontrolled growth of contingent liabilities, among others—but concluded that the bank had shown "modest improvement." On the basis of that limited review, Dallas now held out the hope that the bank could be released from its "letter agreement" by the next exam.

"All the documents we were getting from our regional office until December show they were about ready to recommend that the agreement be lifted, that everything was going along according to plan," said a former official of the Comptroller's office. "We thought by the next exam they would pass all the tests and be out of the problems. It looked like progress was being made."

Said one Penn Square officer, "Jerry Lanier came in and said, 'You've done a fantastic job.' Finally we felt we'd done something right."

Lanier later defended his work at Penn Square, saying that his task was made more difficult because of the way the exam was defined. He said that he had suggested that the office delay the visitation and conduct a full-blown exam instead, but that Preston Morrow, Clifton Poole's deputy, responded that agency policy called for a visitation on a "three-rated" bank. Commenting on the uselessness of that fall "visitation," another former examiner said, "we might as well have sent them a postcard."

According to former bank officers, Lanier was a witness to a financial sleight-of-hand device used frequently by Bill Patterson that may have made things look better than they were. Patterson believed that with enough money, any bad deal could be turned into a good deal. Put another way, his answer to a bad loan was an even bigger loan. One of the worst ones belonged to Sam Villyard, proprietor of Insta-Pipe, the company that laid plastic pipe to supply water for drilling mud. "The Polyethylene King" had difficulty estimating the cost of completing a job, and often charged customers less than the work actually cost him.

The Villyard relationship started out small, but gradually mushroomed into a seven-figure credit. Villyard himself once acknowledged, "I don't know any other bank in the country that would lend me this kind of money. If I were a bank I sure wouldn't lend me this kind of money."

His loans were renewed repeatedly until Insta-Pipe became so visible to bank examiners and the board of directors that a more creative solution had to be devised. That solution was former bandleader Hal Clifford, Patterson's friend from his days at the First National Bank and one of his first customers at Penn Square. Clifford himself was a self-proclaimed "debt junkie" who created a mini-conglomerate with virtually unlimited credit from Penn Square Bank.

Besides Clifford Resources, his flagship entity, Clifford's holdings included a company that leased frac tank trucks, a manufacturer of baseball caps, nylon wallets, and beverage container insulators, and a software marketing company. One of his most recent ventures, financed by a $2.5 million loan from Penn Square Bank, was the production of the film *Savannah Smiles* in partnership with singer Andy Williams, Williams's brother Don, and producer Mark Miller, according to confidential bank documents.

It was only fair, of course, that Hal Clifford help Bill Patterson out of a jam when the need arose. "Patterson dumped a lot on Clifford," said a former officer, "but Hal didn't seem to complain too much."

This time Patterson made a $6 million loan to Clifford to enable him to buy out Villyard's Insta-Pipe, which was merged into one of Clifford's companies. With the flick of a pen, Patterson made a bad loan disappear into thin air.

According to an observer, Patterson looked Jerry Lanier right in the eye and told him, "I've got another customer who is going to buy this company, and assume this debt. He's a creditworthy borrower whose debt you have not yet classified. This borrower is going to take out these loans of Mr. Villyard's."

Lanier appeared stunned by Patterson's audacity. "Well, that's fine," Lanier is said to have told Patterson. "I just want to see a copy of the payout checks just to see that you really do that." As the examiners were preparing to leave, Patterson showed Lanier a copy of the checks.

"That's an unacceptable way to minimize classifications," Lanier is said to have told Patterson. He expressed the same sentiments to Baldwin and Beller and indicated that he would mention it in his write-up.

At the same time Jerry Lanier was preparing to visit Penn Square, one of his colleagues from the Chicago region was meeting at Continental's LaSalle Street offices with Anderson, Perkins, Baker, and the bank's senior management team to review a draft of the 1981 examination report. Honing in on some $2.4 billion in "stale-rated loans," the examiner pointed up the problem of these loans escaping the scrutiny of the bank's loan review mechanism. Anderson replied, "We'll work on it."

The loan review procedures, to be sure, needed plenty of work. One of the cornerstones of the bank's early warning system for bad loans was the "watch list," which was supposed to include loans identified as problems by the account officers themselves. Moreover, Continental, unlike most large banks, had no independent loan workout unit, and the lenders who made the loans in the first place were also supposed to collect on them.

Continental's own auditors had been in to visit Penn Square shortly before Jerry Lanier arrived and received an equally chilly reception. Lytle had neglected to prepare Penn Square's management for his colleagues' arrival, and when they were finally permitted to look over the loan files, they were told they would be allowed to review only those documents that pertained exclusively to Continental. They found that Continental's records of its Penn Square transactions were "incomplete and inaccurate," according to the special litigation report, and they questioned the "quality of Continental's security interest in certain loans." Moreover, they learned about what was termed the Comptroller of the Currency's "severe" negative assessment of Penn Square and Arthur Young's qualification of Penn Square's 1980 financial statements. Bergman and Redding, however, concluded that the report was "relatively clean" and Bergman communicated that view to Baker.

The findings of Continental's independent accounting firm, Ernst and Whinney, certainly supported that conclusion. After meeting with the bank's internal auditors, the Big Eight firm determined that the high level of past due loans in Lytle's mid-continent division represented a problem in processing, not credit quality. In a memo, Ernst and Whinney wrote that "based upon internal audit's work, there does not appear to be a collectibility problem that has not previously been identified through the watch loan report."

Although Lanier was apparently aware of the shell game Patterson and Jennings played with bad debts, he had apparently not, in the September "visitation," discovered the other device that enabled Patterson to assure his upstream banks that "no correspondent had ever lost a nickel on a Penn Square loan." The Penn Square auditors who uncovered this practice later coined the phrase "upstreaming of interest" to describe it, thereby introducing a new term into banking parlance.

Chase and Continental frequently called up inquiring about overdue interest payments, and the inquiries were typically relayed to one of Patterson's assistants. Patterson, of course, recognized that the moment one of his major correspondents lost confidence in the bank, the game was over. The energy lending czar was out of the bank selling loans more often than he was in, but his aides were usually able to contact him once his chartered jet touched down in New York, Chicago, Seattle, or Lansing.

"Get Kiser on the phone," Patterson would say, referring to Jan Kiser, a young woman who had joined the bank as a secretary to Patterson in 1979, and wound up "packaging loans" as an assistant vice-president in the correspondent division despite the fact that she had only a high school education. "Pay the goddamn interest," he would order.

Kiser later testified that she asked Patterson, "Can we really do this?" And he said, "Everything will be okay." Yet while it appeared that upstreaming interest was primarily Patterson's doing, Jan Kiser acknowledged that Beller and Dunn put their initials on upstreamed interest.

According to a former Penn Square officer, "Chase would call up and say, 'This has to be bought current,' and suddenly it was current." Upstreamed interest was booked in an account called "other assets," which was also used when loans were bought back from a participating bank.

Jan Kiser later alleged in court testimony that Continental and Chase were aware of the practice, while as far as she knew Michigan National, Northern Trust, and Seattle First were thinking all along that interest was being paid on schedule. Moreover the FDIC charged that Chase officers, whom the agency said knew about the practice, threatened to stop buying participations if the uncollected interest was not paid.

Around November 15, Jim Gunter, a pixie-faced man who joined Penn Square as chief financial officer a few months earlier, uncovered what Patterson's team had known for months. Gunter, formerly a certified public accountant with one of the nation's leading accounting firms, was having trouble reconciling the bank's accrued interest account.

"Hey, something's screwy. What's going on here?" Gunter is said to have exclaimed to an associate as he reviewed the entries on the account ledger. Gunter warned senior Penn Square Bank officials on several occasions about the dangers of advancing interest on past due accounts, but the practice persisted. Patterson, in effect, was playing much the same kind of roulette game with his customers that Chase Manhattan and Continental Illinois and other large money center banks were playing with Argentina, Mexico, Poland, and other bankrupt Third World nations. Indeed, the total outstanding loans made to such high rollers as Carl Swan and J.D. Allen and sold to upstream banks were rapidly approaching the exposure that some large banks had to Third World debtors.

Other deft maneuvers that enabled Swan, Allen, and other borrowers to accumulate mountains of debt included the practice of rolling the interest on one loan into a new loan to pay the interest on the first loan, and making new loans to one company or partnership to pay off the note or overdrafts of another one owned by the same customer. As long as Continental and Chase and the others continued to fund, as long as the millions continued to move, there would never be a day of reckoning. Patterson and Jennings, however, understood even less about funding loans than they did about making them. In order to finance this loan participation Ponzi scheme, Penn Square purchased Fed funds from other banks and bought $100,000 deposits through money brokers like Professional Asset Management at rates considerably above what other banks were paying at the time, exacerbating its already serious liquidity problems.

Carl Swan and his many corporate holdings were major beneficiaries of Penn Square's largesse. Advance interest payments were made on behalf of Longhorn, which Kathy Kenefick recognized in

March was not a viable entity, Texas Upsetting and Finishing, in which Swan held a large interest, and even Henson's saloon, which, unlike Cowboys, usually played to an empty house.

By November 30, nearly $2.2 million in interest had been paid to the upstream banks without having been collected from the borrowers. Internal auditor Arlyn Hill, who conducted the investigation, recommended that the bank "stop the correspondents from calling the shots." In subsequent testimony at Patterson's trial, Hill contended that 70% of the borrowers whose names appeared on the report "never paid a dime of interest." One mechanism for paying interest to the upstream banks was to create overdrafts on the borrower's account. One woman, Shirley Turner, another member of Patterson's loyal following of young women, was dubbed the "debit girl" for her role in the practice, according to Hill.

Overdrafts and overdues were a perennial topic at the monthly board meetings, and a few directors persistently complained about them. Patterson inevitably responded by saying that the items in question would soon be off the list. "He'd always be able to take the list and reduce it by 75 percent," said one director. The problem was that as soon as one item was wiped off the list, it would be replaced by another one. And often an overdraft of one company was eliminated by creating an overdraft to another.

The "other assets" account was also the catch-all for loans bought back from correspondent banks, in what was a billion-dollar coast-to-coast loan participation shell game. The game took many forms, depending on who the pea was and who the shell was. Penn Square would buy back a loan only if it could lay it off on another correspondent. A loan would be repurchased, returned to the pool, and sent upstream again. By fall, a pecking order had emerged among the banks according to the quality and type of loans they were willing to take. At the top was Hibernia, the secretive New Orleans bank that wanted all its deals secured with certificates of deposit or home mortgages. "We cursed Hibernia for their horrible turn-around time, and for being so timid," said one officer. Other banks, he said, committed on the phone, while the Hibernia participations meandered through several committees. "You'd send them a package," he said, "and they'd call back and ask for more information and tell you what was missing."

Next came Northern Trust, whose department was headed by Mike Tighe, the smart, cocky energy lender and his friend and colleague, Jay Rudd, both of whom generally preferred production loans.

Then there was mighty Continental, which insisted on controlling a credit, and would take big deals, production loans, rigs, limited partnerships.

Chase would accept nickel and dime stuff, usually in a package. At the bottom of the heap were Seafirst and Michigan National. Boyd liked hard collateral and led his institution into the dubious position of being the world's biggest rig lender. And Michigan would take whatever Continental and the others didn't want. Except Ken Tureaud. Curiously, at a Michigan National board meeting, a director recognized the name Ken Tureaud as the man who had blown through Michigan some years earlier, spreading financial destruction in his wake. Michigan National took a pass on Tureaud. But apparently no one asked the next logical question: If they're doing business with the likes of Tureaud, what else have they got?

Beside "The Big Five" and Hibernia, 47 other banks around the United States ultimately bought pieces of Penn Square loans amounting to more than $200 million, including interest, by July 1982, according to the FDIC. Many of them were small, loan-starved Oklahoma community banks that were awash in deposits from wealthy mineral owners. Often the relationship between these downstream correspondents and Penn Square could be traced to long-standing "good ole boy" ties between Beep Jennings, Carl Swan, and other Penn Square loan salesmen with personal and family connections in those tiny institutions.

According to Bob Kotarski, Patterson "did tell some of the banks there were problems with some of the loans," but assured them "they'd be taken care of."

Mahan Rowsey was never taken care of.

In October, Mahan and Rowsey concluded someone ought to keep the books, and a young certified public accountant named Randy Dunn was lured away from the Big Eight accounting firm of Deloitte, Haskins and Sells with a hefty salary increase and the promise of overrides and bonuses. The corporate records hadn't been kept for eighteen months, and it took him four weeks to figure out that "they didn't intend to repay" the $27 million rig loan to Penn Square and Chase Manhattan. One of the rigs was always breaking down and took three times as long to drill a hole as a properly functioning unit. The swivel on rig No. 1, he said, was manufactured in 1938. It was, in a word, "junk."

According to Dunn, Mahan Rowsey's monthly statement rarely showed a positive balance. By the spring, with interest rates still in the high double-digit range, Mahan and Rowsey would have required revenue of $1 million a month just to service their debt, which by that time was $60 million. In fact, their monthly cash flow was never more than $100,000! Dunn informed Patterson in November that repayment was doubtful, the company was insolvent, and he intended to resign. Patterson, Dunn recalled, urged him to remain with Mahan Rowsey and said that he would "assist them by drilling them out of trouble." They should, he said, go back to doing what they were successful at, which was exploration. Dunn said that "perhaps 5 percent of their cash came from operations, 95 percent came from loans."

The one thing that counted to Bill Patterson was doing the deal. Once it was done, the Allah of the Oil Patch moved on to something else. His standing order to the troops was: Get the deal done. Patterson, said a former colleague, "was a child turned loose in a candy store, but Jennings was the one who turned him loose and failed to mind the store."

RED HERRINGS

JERE STURGIS HARBORED A NOT-SO-SECRET DREAM. HE WANTED, more than anything else, to become the first billionaire in the history of Enid, Oklahoma. Said a former business associate, "Jere wanted to be rich so bad he just couldn't stand it."

The son of the proprietor of Sturgis Cleaners at 802 West Main, Sturgis worked his way through Phillips University as a mortician's assistant at the Henninger-Allen Funeral Home, served a tour of duty with the marines in Vietnam, and returned to Enid to become a salesman for a local real estate agency. He soon went into business for himself, establishing the Realty III agency. Said a source who worked with him at Enid's Nicholas agency, "He was a terrific guy. One of the best salesmen we had. Jere was always up, always happy. He always believed everything would work out."

Not one to miss out on an energy boom, Sturgis broke into the oil and gas business in 1979 and inevitably found his way to Penn Square and Bill G. Patterson.

With a little "imagineering," Sturgis appeared to have achieved his loftiest ambitions, at least on paper. His reserve estimates were bloated by a lot of nonproducing properties, which, when escalated in price to $100 a barrel for oil and $9 per MCF for gas, showed a net worth exceeding $1 billion. This paper wealth was easily converted at Penn Square and other banks into more tangible evidence of success, including a palatial, blond-brick home, a $5.5 million twin-engine Rockwell Sabreliner, expensive oil paintings by famous Western artists, and other perquisites of the new oilmen.

"Sturgis wanted us to give him credit for nonproducing wells," said a former officer of one of Penn Square's upstream banks. "He could show a report that indicated reserves worth $2 billion, based on proven undeveloped properties. Sturgis always promoted proved undeveloped, proved shut-in, and behind-the-pipe reserves," the banker said. None of these reserve categories included properties yielding any cash flow. "It's worth something, but how much?" the banker said.

Many of the new oilmen knew this was imaginary wealth. Sturgis, according to the upstream bank officer "even believed his own reserve reports." And Mike Gilbert described Sturgis's $2 billion estimate of reserves as "gross fiction."

If Chase and Northern Trust didn't believe all of it, they at least believed some of it, enough to establish, on November 2, a $42 million revolving line of credit for Sturgis and his related companies. Chase took $31 million, Northern $10 million, and Penn Square retained $1 million. In one respect, it was something of a milestone in the relationship between Penn Square and its upstream banks, representing as it did an attempt by the big banks to exert more control over loans in which they held large shares. Most of the loans sold by Penn Square were in the form of participations, where Penn Square held the original note. Here, Chase and Northern received their own notes, giving them more control over the borrower's affairs than they had with a Penn Square participation certificate. For its part in this case, however, Chase Manhattan ended up with more rights over one of the largest and flakiest deals its correspondent banking group, or Chase Manhattan, ever made.

Continental, like Chase and Northern Trust, was more comfortable with the so-called direct loans. According to Bergman, Baker and Bergman agreed late in 1981 that Continental would make all new Oklahoma loans directly with the borrower and, where possible, convert existing Penn Square participations to direct loans. But no one ever bothered to define precisely what a direct loan was. In Baker's view, a direct loan was one where Continental's name appeared on the note, and where Continental was paid directly by the borrower and controlled the collateral. Lytle, Redding, and Bergman, on the other hand, felt that a loan was direct as long as the note and documentation had Continental's name on it. In any event, Lytle, as manager of the mid-continent division, continued to buy, increase, and roll over participations out of fear of alienating Penn Square. Lytle later contended that Redding only "encouraged" him to book large loans directly, but here, too, there was no consensus on what a "large loan" actually was.

According to Patterson, about half of Continental's Penn Square loans consisted of credits booked directly by the Chicago bank. "They would sell us back a small portion, like anywhere from $25,000 to $50,000, just so our name could be on the document, say, for ego purposes," he said.

The directive from on high to put more of the Penn Square loans on a direct basis, or to make Continental a so-called co-agent with Penn Square on shared credits, gave some fleeting assurance to nervous mid-continent loan officers that top management was concerned, or at least aware, of what was going on in profit center 1089. Later, according to a former officer, they were given added comfort when the word came down that Continental would get out of the letter of credit drilling fund business.

Nevertheless, the pace continued to accelerate. Penn Square officers delivered or shipped loans to the ninth floor at 231 LaSalle Street in cardboard boxes and suitcases, and John Lytle shoved them through the loan operations conveyor belt like a baggage handler at O'Hare Airport.

On November 4, 1981, Lytle's boss, Jack Redding, was given an opportunity to save his bank. Petroleum engineers Ralph Kramer and Gary Brednich had agonized for months over the bastardization of Continental's traditional criteria for making oil and gas loans, and the increasing number of loans being booked where the loan amount far exceeded the value of the reserves. The engineers were dismayed that the money was moving out the door so fast that they often had no opportunity to review the reserves and documentation. Kramer, for one, likened the relationship with Penn Square to the "tail wagging the dog" and regarded Patterson as being hazardous to the financial health of Continental Illinois. Both men were perplexed as to why their boss seemed to place more trust in Patterson than in his own officers. But as one acknowledged later, "I wasn't one of John's drinking buddies."

Kramer and Brednich were not inclined to be whistle blowers, and before approaching the admiral to report that the captain had gone off the edge, they sought the advice of another division head in the special industries group. He told them, "Go see Redding." Over lunch, the two engineers informed a sympathetic Redding that profit center 1089 was out of control, that the Penn Square participations were of low quality, and that they were not even being asked to look at loan documentation. According to the Continental special litigation report, Redding instructed them to stand fast in determining loan values and assured them he would talk with Lytle, but he never did.

Several days later, in Oklahoma City, Eldon Beller told the board of directors of Penn Square Bank that the examiners "were pleased with the policies, procedures, staffing and committee system implemented by the Association since the last examination and that the examiners liked the direction in which the Association is heading."

The brouhaha over whether the loans were or were not done directly was little more than hair-splitting. For all practical purposes, many of the "energy loans" booked by Continental without the aid of Penn Square were at least as bad or worse than those originated by the shopping center bank in Oklahoma City.

Take, for example, Nucorp Energy, headed by R.L. Burns and former Continental energy lender Jerry Pearson. Court records on file in bankruptcy court in San Diego show that from December 1980 onward senior officers of the company were allegedly "cooking the books," using a technique another concerned executive called "prebilling": recording sales for tubular goods that were not actually shipped or for which no cash was actually received. Likewise, Seafirst's energy department was busy booking energy deals in Texas and California that would turn out to be, on balance, far worse than most of what Penn Square placed on its books.

Curiously, the Sturgis deal was booked at a time when Chase's top management was terribly concerned over the intrusions made by money market funds, brokerage houses, insurance companies, and other "nonbanks" into the banking industry's traditional business. No one was more vocal about the need for regulatory change to permit banks to compete with these entities than Thomas G. Labrecque of the Chase Manhattan Bank.

In a keynote speech that November to the American Bankers Association's annual meeting of correspondent bankers in Kansas City, Labrecque spoke forcefully about what he termed the "frontal assaults on our business," citing Sears, Roebuck's acquisition of a real estate firm and a brokerage house, Equitable Life's creation of a corporate cash management system to go along with direct lending to borrowers, and the mergers of American Express and Shearson and Prudential and Bache. "We've got to have a level playing field" became the war cry of the banking industry.

Labrecque was introduced by Wayne Hanse, the senior vice-president who supervised Meg Sipperly and Dick Pinney. Hansen led off his presentation by referring to a recent Chase ad, a "large, boldface headline," he said, that proclaimed with typical Madison Avenue brevity "Banking will survive, banks, maybe." With deals like the $31 million credit to Sturgis that was being funded even as Hansen and Labrecque were speaking, Chase clearly had less to fear from Sears, Roebuck, American Express, and Prudential-Bache than it did from its own domestic institutions division.

Hansen emphasized that "we should look to correspondent banking as a significant opportunity to improve our performance," because the "smart small banks that survive will need the correspondent relationship more than ever before." He may well have been thinking of his relationship with Penn Square when he said that one "correspondent credit 'boom town' will be in the area of overline lending directed toward the mid-sized market of companies with total sales of less than $125 million. These companies," he went on, "will require increasing amounts of financial support as they expand and will greatly benefit from triangular banking relationships. That is, in one corner will be their long-standing relationship with the local bank. On the other," he said, "will be the relationship with the larger upstream bank, playing a support role."

One of the services Chase provided to Penn Square was its credit analysis seminar, which one employee remembers as being a lesson in "do as we say, not as we do." The Chase trainer talked about the bank's "rigorous credit standards," and, he said, "I sat there knowing full well they had been violated."

A leading bank consultant later attempted to explain the involvement of large money center banks with Penn Square when he observed, "There was information overload. Bankers were worrying about larger issues of deregulation, the pricing of services, and other banks taking them over. They weren't worried about what a second vice-president was doing in Oklahoma." To that apologia another longtime observer of the industry responded, "Bullshit."

That same month, upstream bank officers paid a visit to one of their correspondent boom towns, Oklahoma City. The occasion was the annual oil party at Jennings's ranch, an event that brought bank officers and employees together with borrowers as well as officers from the upstream banks. It was an event that was months in the making. Invitations depicting an unshaven roughneck chomping on a stogie went out to Penn Square's huge stable of oil and gas customers. "If you're oil field, you're invited," the invitation read.

Patterson saw to it that his Northern banker friends were appropriately dressed for the occasion. Meg Sipperly and other officers of the Chase Manhattan Bank flew to Oklahoma City for the party and were escorted to Tener's, the cowboy-western clothing emporium, where they were reportedly outfitted in Western garb, complete with boots, hats, and kerchiefs.

No expense was spared. A dance floor and buffet tables decorated with fresh flowers were set up on the lawn alongside Bill Jennings's elegant, ranch-style home. Guests arrived by private car, limousine, and helicopter, and sat on bales of hay listening to music by Mountain Smoke, the blue-grass band founded by Hal Clifford. Helicopters dropped off and picked up guests at a specially constructed heliport in a field adjoining Jennings's home.

The party happened to coincide with Bill Patterson's birthday. Bill loved old cars, particularly beat-up ones. An officer of an upstream bank bought Patterson a station wagon of early 1960s vintage, the most dilapidated one he could find, and painted "Happy Birthday, Bill" in large white letters across the side. Patterson was so pleased he jumped from the loft of Jennings's barn onto the roof of the car, slid to the ground, and danced with a broom.

Hal Clifford also had a birthday present for Bill. After filming was completed on *Savannah Smiles,* he presented Patterson with full-dress Nazi general's uniform from the film company's wardrobe, which Patterson eagerly accepted and wore around the bank for the rest of the day.

Ken Tureaud came in from Tulsa, driven in a stretch Cadillac limousine by his husky black chauffeur.

Tom Swineford, the officer responsible for the Tureaud account, despised Tureaud, and was convinced that his loans were among the "wormiest" in the bank's portfolio. Tureaud was well aware of Swineford's feelings. The former football player wrapped his arms around Swineford and, in Mafioso fashion, kissed him on both cheeks, while Swineford's wife looked on in horror from a second-floor window of Jennings's home.

"Who the fuck do you think you are, trying to screw my deals? I've heard what you've been saying about me," Tureaud said.

In what an observer described as Tureaud's "schizophrenic" style, he suddenly turned friendly, and said to Swineford, "We can get along in the future," then fell backward over a bale of hay, collapsing in a drunken stupor. Tureaud slithered along on the gravel driveway, until his chauffeur lifted him to his feet, stretched him out in the back seat of the limousine, and drove him home to Tulsa.

A former Penn Square officer overheard two officers of different upstream banks congratulating themselves on their wisdom in getting involved with Penn Square Bank. While sipping on his drink, one officer said, "This is better than a loan production office. LPOs only generate leftover business." They talked about all the overhead they saved by having a local bank originate the loans, agreeing that Penn Square was the best possible pipeline to the riches of the oil patch.

In the middle of the following week, Penn Square entertained

Chase officers at Henson's, financed by Chase Manhattan for Carl Swan, country-western entertainer Henson Cargill, and other Penn Square borrowers.

"We were in the balcony overlooking this huge restaurant," one Penn Square officer recalled. "It was embarrassing because here they had bought the loan, and the place was completely empty."

About the time their customers were getting drunk in Oklahoma, Continental's George Baker, Gerald Bergman, and Baker's staff from the general banking services group were scheduled to meet with Anderson, Perkins, and other corporate office staff for their quarterly review. Past dues and document deficiencies were still hitting Coriaci's exception report, and Bergman still had not identified the issue for what it was, and once again, dismissed it as a housekeeping issue that was being resolved.

To be sure, Bergman had other problems. He was a three-pack-a-day man, a Vantage smoker, whose cigarette addiction was so ingrained that his name was hardly ever mentioned without some reference to his smoking, and in November 1981 that habit finally caught up with him. He had been wheezing and coughing more lately, to the point where he went to his doctor for a chest X-ray that turned up vague shadows on both lungs. He checked into the Evanston hospital and was later referred to the Mayo Clinic. Over the next several months, Bergman underwent three operations, and while recuperating in Florida or at home in suburban Winnetka spent most of his waking moments thinking about dying. "Bergman," a former colleague said, "was physically among the missing." No one ever accused Bergman of being a superior manager, but his absence created a void that forced the heads of Baker's other line divisions to pick up some of the slack.

Continental's front line lending officers saw little of Bergman, before or after he took sick leave. To them, Bergman's overriding concern, while a legitimate one, appeared to be the unkempt appearance of profit center 1089 and the stacks of loan files that were piling up on desks and window sills. The division looked out over the fire escapes on the rear of a dingy building, and Bergman is best remembered for his insistence that the curtains be drawn so that employees and visitors would not be confronted with that eyesore.

Before he took sick leave, however, he dispatched a special audit team to Penn Square once again to review Continental's participations. A loan operations task force was already in Oklahoma, assigned to try to clear up the mess in the note cage and reconcile the many differences in customer account records between the tiny

Oklahoma shopping center bank and the Chicago giant. This time around, the auditors were granted access to any and all records. And, once again, their findings were disturbing. They discovered, for example, situations in which their institution's collateral had been jeopardized by Penn Square, and loans bought by Continental that exceeded the amount actually booked by their Oklahoma City correspondent in the first place. To describe those questionable transactions the auditors introduced a new term, the "overpartici-pation," into banking jargon. One former Continental officer re-called that the auditors were "horrified" at what they found. "Those guys came back ashen-faced," the officer said.

Edwin Hlavka, Continental's top internal auditor, claims to have encountered George Baker in the executive washroom sometime after the special audits and advised him to "disengage" from Penn Square, saying the Oklahoma bank "was a pretty frail basket for that big pile of eggs."

The audit team also uncovered a big pile of loans to Continental vice-president John Lytle, made by Penn Square to their upstream banker at clearly preferential rates. "Lytle expressed great surprise that the loans might create a conflict of interest," the special litiga-tion report noted, "and stated that this was how Oklahoma bankers treated their friends and special customers." According to the re-port, Hlavka and an associate confronted Lytle about the loans and brought the matter to the attention of Bergman, Redding, and other bank officials. Bergman and Redding, the report said, were opposed to firing Lytle, who had twenty-two years of service with the bank. It later emerged that some of Bergman and Baker's private dealings may not have been entirely at arms length either. According to pub-lished reports, the two senior officers, as well as James C. Cordell, a vice-president in charge of special industry's Texas Division, in-vested in oil programs put together by Davis Oil Company, which was controlled by Denver tycoon Marvin Davis, a major Continen-tal borrower.

With the bank becoming increasingly dependent for its survival on flimflam banking practices like upstreaming interest, the last thing it needed was another qualified accountant's opinion. Gunter, in fact, remarked to Arthur Young partner Harold Russell that he "just wouldn't accept" that possibility. From July through Novem-ber, Arthur Young and Company had tried without success to per-form various "interim" audits in anticipation of the annual audit for the year ending December 31. Meanwhile, Peat, Marwick, Mitchell, which audited the First National Bank of Oklahoma, Beller's alma mater, was angling for the Penn Square account.

Shortly before Penn Square began negotiating with Peat Marwick on the engagement, Penn Square lent several Peat Marwick partners money for investment in an office complex that would be converted into condominium units, and over the previous several years other partners had received sizable loans for oil and gas investments.

On November 20, Bill Jennings wrote to Harold Young, the managing partner of the Big Eight firm's Oklahoma City office, advising him that his services were no longer required. Jim Blanton, the managing partner of Peat, Marwick, Mitchell, said in late November he talked with John Guinan of the New York City office about the "engagement" with Penn Square, noting that some of the partners had loans with the bank and asking what he had to do to preserve independence. The New York office ordered all but one loan to be sold out of the bank.

DUMP TRUCK BANKING

THE SANTA CLAUS OF AMERICAN BANKING WAS ASSEMBLING AND wrapping a very special Christmas present for the Seattle First National Bank: $150 to $200 million in loans of all descriptions—rig loans and reserve loans to spread under the tree, and some service company loans to fill their stockings. One Seafirst officer got an advance peek when an officer of another Penn Square's correspondents called and announced, "There's a big slug of Penn Square loans coming your way." The Oklahoma bank was trying to dress down its year-end balance sheet, trimming its loans-to-deposits ratio and boosting its equity in relation to its assets so that Cliff Poole and his colleagues in Dallas wouldn't harp at them to raise more capital.

As usual, the market basket of Penn Square loans was fraught with documentation problems and omissions, but was nonetheless warmly received at Seafirst. Bill Jenkins had promised his directors and shareholders a 15% annual growth rate, and he wasn't going to disappoint them this year.

In mid-December Patterson instructed a dozen of his officers and staff not to make any plans for the week before Christmas. They would be spending most of that week in Seattle, and he would accept no excuses. Fortunately, however, the trip was timed so that the delegation to Seattle would not miss the oil and gas division's Christmas party, scheduled this year for Henson's.

Patterson enlivened the affair by betting the girlfriend of a junior officer that he could drink more Italian puffs, a concoction that calls for crème de menthe, than she could, and peeled off $20 bills from a thick roll he carried in his pocket as he lost the wager. Meanwhile, petroleum engineer Jeff Callard, the hulking former OU mat star, was wrestling the girlfriend of another Penn Square officer to the ground.

In Penn Square's heyday, its borrowers spared no expense in entertaining employees and business associates at Christmas. Oil promoter David Berry flew in comedian Rodney Dangerfield from New York, busing his guests to a nearby community theater for the performance and back to his plush new office afterward to carry on with the party. Said one guest, "I've been in the oil business all my life. I've been on rig floors. But that was the trashiest routine I've ever heard."

But the real trash that Christmas of 1981 was the $200 million in loans that wound up in Seattle, the most flagrant example of what Seafirst's John Boyd only half jokingly referred to as "dump truck banking."

The dump trucks were two chartered private jets, and the loans were escorted by Bill Patterson himself and an entourage of officers and assistants. Some of the women, however, went along just for the ride. There were two categories of female employees at Penn Square Bank—the show dogs, who were expected to be on hand to entertain out-of-town bankers and customers, and the workhorses. On this trip, Patterson and the show dogs boarded the Lear, and several other senior Penn Square officers, including the workhorses, took the Citation.

After less than two hours in the air, the pilot told the passengers to fasten their seatbelts in preparation for landing. It seemed like an awfully short flight to Seattle. Few of the employees on board had been to the Pacific Northwest before; they had expected to see lush vegetation and the blue waters of Puget Sound and were bewildered to see white desert sand as they approached the runway. Patterson had ordered the pilots to stop over in Las Vegas and had arranged for the staff to spend the night at the Sands with orders that they were to be at the airport at 8:00 A.M. for the final leg of the trip.

While the show dogs went Christmas shopping at Frederick and Nelson's in downtown Seattle, the workhorses spent the next several days bivouacked on the sixteenth floor of Seafirst's headquarters, writing up the Penn Square loans on Seafirst's green loan agreement forms.

According to allegations in a subsequent lawsuit brought by Seafirst shareholders against the banking company, "Patterson would come into town and say he needed to sell off $100 million in loans next week, and could we take five loans, and if we did, he would give us another good deal," according to a former Seafirst officer.

"Boyd would ask, 'Are they good?' And Patterson would say, 'Sure they are, John.' And that was that. That's the way it went."

Boyd was pleased, however, with this new addition to the portfolio. As he saw it, the big loan package was a landmark in the Sea-first–Penn Square relationship. It established Seafirst, at long last, as a co-agent with Continental in larger credits, and at the same time improved the bank's loan mix, helping to tilt the portfolio, ever so slightly, toward production loans and away from rigs.

At a dinner for the Penn Square contingent, before an apprecia-tive audience of his fellow officers, Boyd announced Patterson's ar-rival in the bank's executive dining room by saying, "Here come the guys from Oklahoma. They practice the dump truck theory of banking. They pile loans into a dump truck, bring them to Seattle, pick up cash and dump it back at Penn Square." "Everybody laughed," recalled one guest. But the last laugh would be on Sea-first.

The Christmas gift of participations had its origins, according to Boyd, in an October meeting at which Jaehning pressured managers for more fee income to beef up Seafirst's year-end 1981 income state-ment. "He said he wanted a 75 percent increase in energy loans in 1982 and wanted $150,000 in fee income right away," Boyd insisted later. That fee income would come from commitment fees on lines of credit. But chairman Bill Jenkins would say later, "I told Boyd not to book any new loans in October 1981. He did it on his own." He also did it with the help of Jenkins's son, David, who joined the en-ergy department as a junior officer in late 1981.

There was certainly reason for Jaehning to feel some comfort with the energy department. Seafirst's internal examiners had just given the department a clean bill of health. When the examiners got through Boyd bowed and gestured with his hand like an Arab showing humility to his king. In fact, sources said, the auditors looked mainly at the completeness of the files more than the quality of the loans.

"I agonized over that package of loans, before and after," Boyd acknowledged later. Chao, his loyal assistant, was dead-set against the package, according to Boyd, having beckoned him into a confer-ence room to enumerate five good reasons not to take them. One reason was sufficient. "We never met these people," Chao argued, adding that the participations were too small and too concentrated in Oklahoma. Worse still, Chao suspected that the loans had already been rejected or sold back to Penn Square by other banks.

At that time Seafirst, like Continental, was short-staffed, and sim-ply couldn't process $200 million in new loans. "The facts were tell-ing me the loans were okay. My gut was telling me something's wrong." To Boyd's lasting regret, he paid more attention to the "facts" than his gut.

"Preston [Penn Square's general counsel] had told me every package was looked at to comply with participation agreement," Boyd asserted. "Eldon represented that he was in charge. They methodically set me up in October and November 1981." Moreover, Boyd said later that he confirmed with Jennings every conversation he had with Patterson.

Early in the visit to Seattle, Boyd threw a Christmas party for his visitors in Seattle First's executive dining room, an elegant setting with a breathtaking, wide-angle view of Puget Sound and Bainbridge Island. In keeping with the holiday spirit, each table was tastefully decorated with a crystal bowl filled with a bouquet of handmade silk tiger lilies. Boyd, Patterson and several of Patterson's aides sat together, feasting on Swedish meatballs, Boyd's favorite dish, and prawns, which the gracious Seafirst officer ordered for his landlocked guests on nearly all their visits to Seattle. As he left the table, Patterson grabbed one of the $120 bouquets and placed it, Polynesian style, behind his left ear. Horrified, one of Patterson's assistants yanked it away and returned it to a much relieved executive chef, who was looking on with an expression of stunned disbelief.

One Seafirst officer recalls hearing about Penn Square for the first time in late 1981, and thinking it was a bank in Pennsylvania. The buzz phrase in John Boyd's energy department had become "doing deals," and the officer wondered how that compared with making a loan. He had heard that Boyd was well respected by Jenkins, who regarded Boyd as a producer; he was the guy who was going to take them into bigger and better things. He was, some said, "the banker of the future."

"I thought I must be missing out on something," the officer recalled.

Other officers were left speechless by the enormity of Penn Square's Christmas gift. "Guess what?" said one awestruck officer to a colleague. "We just bought $100 million in loans in one afternoon." With the addition to the portfolio, the Seattle bank's exposure to Penn Square grew from a mere $65 million in October to nearly $300 million in early 1982.

Sources close to the transaction say that there was an understanding that Penn Square would buy the loans back from Seafirst early in 1982, after the purchase had served its purpose of improving Penn Square's loan-to-deposits ratio. Patterson even sent a telex to Boyd agreeing to repurchase the loans, but the $200 million remained on

Seafirst's books. The slug of Christmas loans would be the last big batch Boyd would take from Penn Square. Early in 1982, Boyd was instructed to slow down on the Penn Square participations. But once a commitment is made a bank is honor-bound, and legally bound, to make good on it, unless the bank uncovers a material change in the company's condition. So even though Seafirst's energy department slowed down on new commitments, the bank's exposure rose as borrowers drew down on their lines of credit. By year-end, Seafirst's energy portfolio was a bomb ready to go off. In some cases, the files consisted only of names, addresses, and form 1022, the loan authorization slip.

"We were always behind the eight ball on Penn Square documentation," Boyd acknowledged later. "It would be the wrong stuff, it would be Xeroxed on the wrong page."

"In December," said one officer, "everything was always urgent." Management control at Seafirst had broken down under the weight of $200 million in new loans. "There was," said the officer, "a lot of congestion created by volumes of commitments." According to another former officer, "Penn Square borrowers would say, 'Fund the loan today and I'll get you the documentation tomorrow.' There were innumerable instances in which commitment letters had been given to borrowers but no copy was in the file. John promised the letters, but when he got home from a trip, ten people and twenty-five messages would be waiting for him." According to former officers, Boyd assured his staff that Patterson would repurchase loans that they decided they didn't like.

Boyd and Patterson, like Lytle and Patterson, had become personally very close. When Patterson went to Seattle, he stayed at Boyd's home. On one visit, Boyd and his wife heard a loud thud in the guest room in the middle of the night. They rushed in to find Patterson, who had been taking antibiotics and drinking the night before, sprawled out on the floor, fully dressed. The hefty Seafirst officer and his wife gingerly lifted the semiconscious Patterson back into the bed, removed his clothes, and tucked him in.

The return flight to Oklahoma City just before Christmas would be a joyous one for the Penn Square officers and staff. As the two jets cruised on a southeasterly course over Salt Lake City and western Kansas, Bill Patterson played gin rummy in the rear of the lead plane while his subordinates crouched in the narrow aisle and danced to music blaring from the stereo tape deck.

The dump truck also made local runs. In a drive to dress up the year-end 1981 balance sheet, the truck driven by Jennings and Patterson picked up a $650,000 loan to Patterson on December 31 and delivered it to the "loan warehouse" known as the First Penn Corporation, the bank's holding company.

Tom Kelly, a former kicker for the Minnesota Vikings, had devised a blowout preventer that would surpass all blowout preventers. It was supposed to be so good, said former Penn Square officer M. Garvin Chandler, that people would beat down the door to get it. By February 1981, the loan to Hydraline to finance the development and marketing of the device had fallen into the classified category, and in November Kelly wrote to Patterson asking his help in finding investors willing to inject $100,000 each into the faltering project and pay off the note to Penn Square Bank. The solution Patterson devised on a Sunday morning in December was dubbed the Venezuelan Coalition. Part of that solution was another Penn Square customer named Jack Thomas, who had been trying to persuade Patterson to make a loan to his brother's food business. On that Sunday morning, Patterson phoned Thomas at home, asking him to stop in the bank and talk about the loan.

"Patterson said he didn't want to make the loan," Thomas testified later. "He said he didn't know anything about the food business. Then he said he'd make it, and drew up papers, and then said he wanted to go over another deal."

According to Thomas, Patterson told him the Hydraline loans were in trouble, and he wanted to assemble a partnership that would borrow from Penn Square to pay off the Hydraline debt and inject another $500,000 into the company. And once again, Patterson's friend Hal Clifford found himself a partner in yet another deal to bail out a Penn Square loan gone sour. Patterson reportedly advanced funds to Thomas and Clifford without their knowledge and then paid off the Hydraline note. But Thomas and Clifford received no ownership interest in the company.

Kelly was referred to the bank through an old friend of Beep Jennings, and it was Jennings who instructed Rick Dunn to make the loan to Patterson and "warehouse" the six-day note with the holding company until the transaction could be blessed by the Federal Reserve, a transaction that was approved by the directors at the January board meeting.

Loan review officer Garvin Chandler suspected the deal violated restrictions on loans to executive officers and took the issue to John Preston, who informed him that Patterson had been exempted from executive officer status. "I thought it was a violation of agreement with the Comptroller to advance funds to a charged-off loan," Chandler testified.

"We needed to remove the charge-off before the end of the year. I signed the note myself," Patterson testified later. "Jennings approved the deal. It was going to be bought by First Penn as one of the first deals of the venture capital company." In point of fact, Penn Square itself was already nothing more than a high-risk venture capital company masquerading as a bank.

Just as Continental was edging away from the limited partnership drilling fund business, so were thousands of disgruntled oil and gas investors around the country. To be sure, the new tax laws made investments in such things as real estate more attractive than oil and gas. But perhaps more important, oil and gas investors had been burned, and burned badly, by the letter of credit poker game and the deep gas play. The doctors and dentists and real estate men who had poured money into the countless programs underwritten by Penn Square had begun to sense something was drastically wrong and had started to do something about it.

Byron Tarnutzer, for one, had lost more than $450,000 on oil stocks that Patterson had recommended only nine months before, and he needed to borrow that much to cover his loss. Once again, in December 1981, Tarnutzer journeyed to Oklahoma City, where, he said, Patterson "readily agreed" to a six-month, $400,000 unsecured signature loan. Patterson told Tarnutzer, according to Tarnutzer's deposition in a subsequent lawsuit involving Copeland Energy, that he expected "no problem with the loan," since it could be repaid with profits from the three 1980 Copeland programs in which the man from Newport Beach had dumped well over $1 million.

Tarnutzer had already received regular requests for money, and on December 11 he got a letter from Copeland stating the revenues from the 1980 Deep would be inadequate to make the interest payment on his loan. On the visit to Oklahoma City, Tarnutzer and another Californian investor named Jerry Barto went to Copeland's northwest Oklahoma City offices and met with Mike Hopkins. "Jerry and I asked Hopkins for an opportunity to review the engineering reports," Tarnutzer asserted later. Hopkins refused. Tarnutzer was beginning to feel he'd been had.

Eight hundred miles east of Newport Beach, G. Blake Chanslor, a wealthy Albuquerque, restauranteur who had invested heavily in the Longhorn 1979-II and the 1980 Private Drilling program, was feeling the same. Longhorn had informed him, according to his attorney, that he needed to grant an extension or waive the deadline on his letter of credit, because Longhorn couldn't pay the bank back on its production loan, which was secured by the letters of credit issued to the investors.

On December 27, 1981, Chanslor filed suit against Longhorn, Swan, Allen, other Longhorn officers, the First National Bank in Albuquerque, and Jay Anderson, the salesman out of Salt Lake who had sold him the program, charging them with fraud and misrepresentation in promoting the program and seeking an injunction blocking Longhorn from calling the letter of credit. It was one of the first of a multitude of similar suits that would be filed over the next year in dozens of states.

At about the same time, a Colorado Springs attorney representing Longhorn investor C. Jeffrey Thompson fired off a letter to Jennings accusing him and Longhorn of fraudulent and misleading practices and deceiving the investing parties. "You also stated that revenues received by the limited partnership," he wrote in typically dreary legal prose, "would be used to obtain a release of those letters of credit and in no event would the letters of credit ever be called." In demanding the return of their investments to his clients, the lawyer accused Jennings of failing to transfer "sufficient wells or other assets to the partnership" in order to release the letters of credit, "nor do we believe you ever intended to do so."

Shari Lynn Mitchell, an attractive Penn Square assistant vice-president who administered the letter-of-credit-backed drilling programs, recalled that "we were trying to get extensions in on a Longhorn program, and one investor just would not send us any extension, or several investors wouldn't send us any extensions. And I called Longhorn, and they said that they would try to get them for me, but they never did."

Longhorn, documents show, was making a profit of sorts on drilling, but nothing on production. In December 1981 the 1979-II program came home to roost. Longhorn arranged with Penn Square and Continental to extend the letters of credit.

By early 1982, said former Penn Square officer Russ Bainbridge, "Continental engineers had determined there weren't enough reserves to pay loans." Penn Square Bank released the letters of credit and substituted oil and gas mortgages as collateral, he said.

Longhorn had long been earmarked by Continental officers as a problem credit. But just as the first investor lawsuits were being filed, Longhorn co-chairman J.D. Allen was tapped by the Reagan administration to join Commerce Secretary Malcolm Baldrige, Agriculture Secretary John Block, and a delegation of leading American business executives on a two-week trade and investment mission to West Africa, where they were to explore ways to make the nations of that region more economically self-sufficient. Meanwhile,

Oklahoma Business magazine was preparing a major feature article for its January issue entitled "Swan and Allen Apply Midas Touch to Oil and Gas Ventures."

Moreover, there were signs that the market for high-priced gas had begun to unravel. A lot more deep gas had become available than the pipelines expected, while the price of old gas had gone up faster than anticipated. With the weakening of OPEC, the price of number 6 fuel oil, which competes head to head with natural gas in a variety of applications, had begun to head south. As the pipelines began to lose customers, the average gas price rose because the costs of transportation and other fixed expenses had to be spread over a smaller customer base.

As the chief financial officer of one deep gas producer recalls it, "First the pipelines quit buying deep gas or only offered the regulated price. Then they bought only regulated gas, and finally they stopped buying gas altogether.

"They realized," he said, "that they were overextended on their take or pays. They were committed to buying more gas, deep and shallow, than they could possibly sell."

In late 1981 Sam Hammons noticed that the pipelines were taking a harder line in contract negotiations. In recent months, a new clause, more favorable to the pipelines, had made its way into gas contracts. Called the "market out," it gave buyers the right to terminate an agreement if the gas couldn't be sold at the agreed-on price. "At first we could get floors in the contracts, then we couldn't get them. Then we saw drops in take-or-pay provisions from 85 percent to 75 percent. And when takes decline, cash flow declines."

Even as the closely watched Hughes Tool Company active rig count reached its historic high of 4,521 units in December, cancellations of new rigs had begun to trickle in to the offices of the Houston-based Dresser Industries, one of the largest U.S. rig manufacturers. And a sales manager with a large drilling pipe manufacturer recalled that when a contractor's order was ready for shipment they'd say, "Hold it for a while."

If the price of a barrel of domestic crude oil had risen at the 10% rate banks had assumed it would over the previous two years, it should have been well in excess of $40 by early 1982, instead of $30.87.

The high rig count at year-end 1981 was deceiving for other reasons. In the oil and gas business, there is a tremendous inflow of money at the end of a year in drilling fund prepayments. In order for the investor to claim a deduction, the expenses must be incurred before year-end.

Then too, the feeding frenzy in the Fletcher Field continued to mask actual market conditions. Over the next several months, as the rig count in the nation and in Oklahoma descended inexorably from its late-December highs, oilmen persuaded themselves over lunch at the Petroleum Club that the drop was a seasonal downturn, even though drilling activity had risen in the early months of the year more often than it had dropped in the previous ten years.

By January, oil companies were screaming about their working interest owners—including industry partners and individual investors—not paying their shares of expenses, forcing them to file liens against the production of the nonpayers. But in December 1981 the head of an Oklahoma City oil company told his staff that the "boom is fading fast," and they had to unload prospects and sell larger shares of their wells. One manager asked, "Should we do the standard promote?" The boss replied, "Get whatever you can."

One leading energy accountant, noting that several leading independent operators had sold off properties in the fall of 1981, interpreted that as a sign of loss of faith in the future of petroleum prices and predicted that drilling activity would level off in 1982. Meanwhile, the stock market also had lost confidence in the oil and gas business. By October 1981, prices of most oil and gas common stocks were down 30% from the year before. Lease broker Steve Knox declared, "The whole Ponzi scheme stopped in January."

Yet to anyone reviewing Penn Square's balance sheet and income statement, the go-go shopping center bank would have looked like a winner. Assets were up to nearly $400 million, and profitability, at least on paper, put Penn Square at the top of its peer group. The true condition of Penn Square at year-end was reflected in numbers that did not appear on the balance sheet. For one thing, half of the loans on Penn Square's books were to just ten borrowers. Swan and some sixty-five of his corporate entities led the list with a grand total of $285.5 million, of which $22.1 million was on Penn Square's books. Worse still, more than a fifth, or $56.4 million of Penn Square's loans, were overdrafts, many of them incurred as Patterson attempted to make earlier loans that had gone sour disappear from the books. These overdrafts were supposedly cleared with the proceeds of unsecured loans Patterson and Jennings extended to other Penn Square customers. Penn Square, in violation of banking laws limiting loans to bank officers, made a total of $800,000 in loans to Patterson himself. As for Jennings, he and companies in which he had an interest ultimately received at least $18 million through Penn Square and its participating banks, according to one estimate.

On December 29, Penn Square director Bill Stubbs sold 1,500

shares of his Penn Square stock to Patterson for $120 a share, a capital gain of $100,000. "I thought things must be pretty good," the director said later. Nevertheless, he subsequently asked Jennings not to reelect him to the board, a request Jennings never honored. "I guess I should have put that in writing," he said later.

At year-end, with the prepayment of drilling funds, deposits flowed in like a tidal wave, rushing out just as rapidly in January. And, on December 31, Phil Foss, a Penn Square employee, made a New Year's resolution that through no fault of his own he would be unable to keep: to have no overdrawn customers.

One of the loans that were sold to Seafirst was the lion's share of a $7.5 million loan to Mahan Rowsey, Inc., for the interim construction of two drilling rigs. Mahan and Rowsey had claimed that they had long-term financing to take out the interim financing and that the rigs themselves were contracted out to Kerr-McGee. In December Patterson passed up an opportunity to at least partially bail himself out of a bad situation by selling one of Mahan Rowsey's rigs. By this time, Penn Square had lent the company more than $40 million with no evidence whatsoever that they could repay. Patterson, according to Billy Rowsey, had requested financial information on the company for a meeting to be held the Sunday before Christmas. "We worked for about four or five days straight on this information after work and we worked all late Friday night, all day Saturday and Saturday night and Sunday morning for this three o'clock meeting in Mr. Patterson's office," Rowsey later stated in a deposition. "And Mr. Patterson didn't even look at it."

Instead, Rowsey said, "He sat us down and summarily told us that we had a problem, that basically we were insolvent." Asked later if the company was in fact broke on the day of the meeting, Rowsey said, "On a liquidation on that day, probably so.

"He said we were good in the exploration business, but he didn't want us in the drilling business. Of course, he had already told us earlier in November that he was going to sell the rigs and not to try to do our tax purchase things, that they were going to be gone in three days, which they weren't."

According to Rowsey, Patterson said he had experience working with clients that were in trouble, citing Amarex as a case in point. "He stated that he knew he could work magic and, basically, said he could drill our way to glory and drill our way out of this mess." While threatening to have his lawyers come in and shut down Mahan Rowsey, Patterson said, "I have worked magic before, and I can do it again." The secret formula, Patterson indicated, involved getting Mahan Rowsey in deals with people like Bobby Hefner.

Sources familiar with the company say that Chase started backing off from Mahan Rowsey in December and January. And as Patterson was frantically juggling Mahan Rowsey overdrafts Randy Dunn was making a troubling discovery. According to his testimony in the Patterson trial, he found that checks from oil and gas purchasers that were supposed to be used to pay off Penn Square loans were being hidden from him and deposited in a secret account at the Liberty National Bank. The funds, he said later, were "being spent at the discretion of Mr. Mahan and Mr. Rowsey." According to Dunn, when Patterson learned about the account he took steps to put mortgages on the property. Dunn told Penn Square executive vice-president Ashburn Bywaters at Penn Square that he "didn't see how loans could be paid back," and recommended that the drilling company be liquidated.

When Patterson heard about the transfers, he told an assistant, Bill Kingston, whom he had assigned to approve Mahan Rowsey invoices, "It better not happen again." Patterson, said Kingston later in trial testimony, "didn't care for either one of them." Nevertheless, the energy lending czar objected to the sale of the Mahan Rowsey rigs in December and said that he would take over the account himself. Had Penn Square bailed out of the rigs then, the banks would likely have sustained a loss of just $3 million, compared with the tens of millions that ultimately went down the drain.

Patterson had thrown so much money at Mahan Rowsey that by January he wound up running the company, deciding which bills would be paid and which would not. According to creditors, one of the criteria used to determine who got paid was whether the creditor did business with Penn Square.

B-J Enterprises of Norman, which provided Mahan Rowsey with engineering reports, was one of the Mahan Rowsey creditors whose checks Kingston reviewed. According to Kingston, "Mahan Rowsey was paying much more than other customers for engineering reports." Patterson later informed Mahan Rowsey they would have to get the reports from a company that the bank was familiar with, but Mahan Rowsey apparently never complied with that demand.

Despite their inability to pay off their existing debt, Mahan and Rowsey had visions of constructing a new office that would have a mobile helicopter pad like the one Jack Hodges installed on the roof of his building.

By the spring of 1982, Mahan and Rowsey routinely left for

Grand Lake Thursday and returned late Monday. Employees, however, were relieved when they were gone because of the constant turmoil they created when they were there.

According to testimony in Patterson's trial, some of the money diverted from the oil production checks went into their chain of custom car stereo stores, which the two men had bought at Billy's urging. Frank personally installed a $10,000, 1,200-watt stereo in his Porsche that was so powerful the windows vibrated even at low volume. And some was allegedly spent on horses. Mahan, acquaintances say, got into horses because Hefner and Swan were into horses; Frank looked to Swan as a guide as to what he should do. A Mahan Rowsey employee who ran one of their companies had been involved in the horse trade for some time, and reportedly convinced Frankie and Billy that they should do the same.

In early January, Patterson summoned a young man into his office who had started at Penn Square three days earlier after briefly making installment and auto loans at another local bank.

"Who's that?" Mahan barked.

"That's one of our loan officers," Patterson replied.

Patterson instructed his new charge to add up a pile of invoices stacked on his desk. Unaccustomed to using Patterson's electronic calculator, the junior officer had fumbled his way through about two-thirds of the bills when Eldon Beller knocked on the door and peeked in the office.

"Who's that asshole?" Mahan asked, with an incredulous Eldon Beller standing directly in front of him.

"Frank, please, that's Eldon Beller, the president of the bank," Patterson said with some embarrassment.

"Well, tell him to get his ass out of here. You run this bank."

The junior officer's calculations did not agree with Mahan's. "That's more than I thought it was," Mahan mumbled. "Get someone in here who can do it."

Mahan asked the new officer how long he'd been with the bank.

"Three days," he replied.

"Well," Mahan chortled as the young banker walked out the door, "I hope you've enjoyed it."

GETTING DRILLED INTO TROUBLE

A BOUT THE SAME TIME PATTERSON WAS PROMISING BILLY ROW sey he would drill him out of trouble, he was making a commitment to George Rodman that would drill him into trouble.

George Rodman was not one of the gold chain boys, nor was he an iron man. Quite the opposite. An intense, slightly built man in his early thirties with a wisp of brown hair hanging over his forehead, Rodman dressed and looked more like a graduate student at an Ivy League university than an Oklahoma City oilie. Rodman was the grandson of wealthy Texas oilman E.G. Rodman, the individual responsible for putting Carl Swan, the patriarch of the new oilies, into business for himself.

After graduating from Baylor University, Rodman arrived in Oklahoma City to work for his father digging ditches, pumping wells, buying leases, and managing oil production. Three years later he founded his own firm, George Rodman, Inc. Rodman was something of a loner, in his social as well as his business dealings; just as Continental preferred to control its credits, Rodman liked to control his wells, and didn't like having to deal with investors from California or New York.

George did not, however, acquire the reputation enjoyed by his father or grandfather in Oklahoma oil and gas circles. He was known as a man with an irascible disposition who lacked his father's grasp of the business. Nevertheless, Rodman's legacy, and his father's friendship with Bill P. Jennings, was worth millions at Penn Square Bank: $30 million in fact. Chairman Jennings had been courting Rodman almost from the day he took over the bank, inviting him and his wife, Dixie, to the ranch for cocktails and dinner, and never failing to include the young oilman on the invitation list to the annual barn dance. At one of the dances, over the sink in Jennings's bathroom, Patterson pitched Rodman on a loan, then escorted him to Jennings and said, "Can't we get him a line of credit?" Patterson occasionally bumped into Rodman at social gatherings and said, "Come on out to the bank and I'll give you a lot of money."

In late December, however, Rodman was vulnerable. He needed a new advance to drill some leases but was unable to get it from the United Oklahoma Bank where he had a $17 million loan secured by mortgages on oil and gas properties.

Once again, Rodman ran into Patterson at a social gathering, and once again, Patterson popped the question. This time, Rodman replied, "Why don't you come over and we'll talk."

Patterson and his assistant, Joy Lorrance, met with Rodman and his staff for thirty minutes. They had not reviewed his balance sheet, financial statements, or reserve reports. Nevertheless, Patterson pledged Penn Square to what one observer would jokingly refer to months later as a "$30 million character loan."

Rodman stepped out for a minute into the office of his financial vice-president. He was incredulous. "Can you believe it? They want to lend us $30 million," the wide-eyed Rodman told his associate.

After the meeting Patterson, Lorrance, Rodman, and Jim Austin, the vice-president for finance, adjourned for lunch to the Beacon Club, an exclusive downtown watering hole on an upper floor of the First National Bank building, where Patterson scrawled out the terms of the deal on a Beacon Club napkin.

Rodman and Austin were still in shock over the loan, and asked repeatedly if Penn Square could really make good on a financing of that size. Patterson insisted he had cleared the deal with Continental Illinois; there were no problems, he said, and the deal was done, except for details like paperwork and the transfer of funds.

Leaving the club, Rodman turned to his associate and said, "I think he just lent me $30 million."

Austin replied, "Yeah, I think he did."

The foursome returned to Rodman's offices, where Patterson once again assured Rodman that the deal was firm. On January 8, $25 million would be credited to his account.

Shortly thereafter, Penn Square issued commitment letters confirming the agreement. That was not enough to convince Austin that he was not dreaming. On numerous occasions, over a period of two weeks, he called Lorrance and Patterson to ask if the deal was still on, if the money really would be there on January 8. They promised him it would be.

On Friday, January 8, Penn Square transferred $18 million to George Rodman's account from Continental Illinois, which had agreed to fund the loan sight unseen. Rodman wrote out a check to United Oklahoma Bank for $17 million and instructed his secretary to take it over to the bank that afternoon. She presented the check to a teller, saying nonchalantly that she had come to pay off the note to George Rodman, Inc. Austin monitored the transaction closely, anticipating that some snag would arise, and that Patterson or Lorrance would call and say that the deal couldn't be completed for one reason or another. But Patterson assured Austin that another $7 million would be deposited in Rodman's account by Monday, January 11, and that they could go ahead and release checks drawn on the account. Austin had prepared more than $6 million in payments to suppliers and working interest owners but decided to wait until Monday to make sure the funds were there to cover the drafts.

Monday arrived, and in fact, as Austin anticipated, the $7 million had not been credited. The next day, the financial officer flew to Denver for a business meeting and later Patterson notified Rodman that the loan had been funded and was on its way. Rodman finally released its $6 million in checks.

The calamity that Austin anticipated appeared to occur two days later. On his return from Denver, Austin phoned the Penn Square bookkeeping department to find out that the $7 million transfer had not taken place, and that Rodman was left with little more than $1,000 in its account. The bookkeeping clerk said that she had received some fifteen checks that Penn Square was covering for the company.

Austin was edgy enough at this point to bypass Patterson and contact another officer, who confirmed that the deal was still on but that Penn Square would fund the loan as the checks hit. He noted, however, that Continental Illinois, which had funded the loan without seeing any collateral, would still have to look at the reserves. Penn Square and Continental did, however, obtain Rodman's personal guarantee for the $18 million, not knowing that Rodman himself was worth at the time a mere $2 or $3 million.

Austin was still skeptical that there was really a $30 million loan in place, and didn't know if Rodman's checks were actually being covered. In a memo dated January 18, he wrote to George, "It is possible we have $6 million in bouncing checks. We don't know if Continental thinks Patterson has overextended himself or not." And he wondered, "Where is the other $7 million coming from?"

The answer was the Seattle First National Bank, which would ultimately lend $10 million to the Rodman firm. Seafirst never wanted to be left out of a big credit, particularly one Continental was in. To achieve this, Seafirst granted Rodman a $10 million character loan, secured by little more than a prayer that it would be paid off.

Three million dollars came from Penn Square, and $300,000 from the tiny Bank of Healdton, the bank run by Bill Jennings's mom. Throughout this process, an anxious Jim Austin and George Rodman called Carl Swan, a Penn Square officer, and other local oilmen seeking assurance that they were doing the right thing by getting involved with this high-flying bank. In his memo, Austin told Rodman that all his contacts had concurred that "(1) Penn Square and Continental were/are extremely aggressive; (2) Penn Square is unorthodox in their banking relationships and activity; (3) Bill Patterson is crazy but does what he says, and (4) All persons advised us to stay with Penn Square Bank."

Since the loan was already funded, the luncheon at the elite Oklahoma Golf and Country Club was less to seal the deal than to celebrate it. Patterson arrived with Lytle, Rodman recalled, and a petite, young woman officer known for a handshake that "brought you to your knees." They showed up forty-five minutes late, Rodman said; it looked to him like Lytle and Patterson had been out late the night before. Lytle's hair was matted, and his clothes were as wrinkled as if he'd slept in them. Brednich, Continental's engineer, was supposed to join the party, Rodman said later, but had apparently encountered travel problems. Unfortunately for Continental and Penn Square, Rodman's luck in finding oil and gas had run out. In spending his last $10 million, George Rodman, Inc., found practically no oil and gas, Rodman acknowledged later.

While the Rodman deal was being funded, representatives of the Comptroller of the Currency were praising the Penn Square Board for the progress the bank was making in complying with the "letter agreement," and holding out the possibility that the agreement might be lifted at the end of the next exam.

Unfortunately, bank regulators do not always operate in real time. The comments made by the national bank examiners in January reflected the findings of an abbreviated exam performed in October, which in turn dealt with credits that had been classified in early 1981.

Moreover, Dallas was misreading its own information. One document noted that the classified assets as a percentage of capital had dropped from 77% at the time of Clifton's exam to 54%, but failed to point out that the figure fell only because Penn Square had pumped more capital into the bank. Nor were the regulators paying much attention to developments in the industry on which Beep Jennings had literally bet the bank.

Early in 1982, Carl Anderson, Jr., the chairman of An-Son Corporation, an old-line oil and gas producer founded by Anderson's father, noticed a worrisome development: the accounts receivable of working interest owners in his wells were getting older, meaning that his partners were taking longer, on the average, to pay their share of the drilling expenses. To be sure, An-Son was not known for its skill in managing accounts receivable. But the trend was a matter of deep concern. Anderson's response to the accounts receivable problem would strike the final blow to what little remained of the relationship between the First National Bank and Continental Illinois.

Anderson approached the First National Bank of Oklahoma for a $45 million line of credit to finance his receivables. The genteel, white-haired oilman was not only a valued customer and advisory director of the state's largest bank, but also a good friend of bank president Dale Mitchell. Initially, Anderson said, "The First didn't see any reason why not." But four days later, as he recalled, the conservative downtown bankers told him they wouldn't lend on receivables. "They said they'd consider an addition to our oil and gas production line, but it would take another sixty days to do the engineering."

According to Anderson, Oklahoma oil and gas men had a good record for paying their bills until early 1982. Then, he said, "receivables started stretching." In February, Anderson said, he was informed by the First that they wouldn't do the loan, and by that time $60 million in receivables was outstanding.

In the meantime, Anderson was in Washington for a meeting of the Republican Eagles and happened to sit down next to Continental vice-president John Lytle. Anderson related the situation to Lytle, who replied, "The problem is not in Chicago."

The following Monday, Bill Patterson was in Lytle's office in Chicago on a long-distance phone call to Anderson. Penn Square and Continental would provide the $45 million line on receivables. "First National was disappointed," Anderson said. "They felt like we should have called them back and given them another chance."

"We talked with Bergman about An-Son," Mitchell said, "but it was always unsatisfactory. The competitive jealousy issue was always there."

Penn Square and the upstream banks were also celebrating the closing of the $263 million Continental Drilling deal with some partying and gambling at the Aladdin Hotel in Las Vegas. All the bankers were there, along with Carl Swan and his associates, and J.D. Allen's pal, entertainer Wayne Newton.

It was at the Aladdin that Greg Odean, a former First National Bank officer, got his first taste of the way Penn Square conducts its business, and hires new officers. He had been in the bank for an interview the day the celebrants were to leave for Vegas, and before even being brought on board he was invited by Patterson to join the festivities. That evening, Patterson signed him on over a dice table at the casino hotel.

"When we heard about that Continental Drilling deal, our guys just couldn't believe it," recalled Dale Mitchell. "If they had come to see us we'd have told them you've got to be crazy. It's almost as if the money center banks felt they had to prop the market up. But I think that's giving them far too much credit."

A TRIP TO OKLAHOMA

S IX MONTHS AFTER TAKING OVER SEAFIRST'S WORLD BANKING, Dick Jaehning figured it was about time to take a closer look at the bank in Oklahoma City that was fueling his own institution's impresssive growth, and to meet firsthand some of the customers that John Boyd was so proud of bringing into the fold.

Boyd was the penultimate arranger. With the help of Patterson and Jennings, Hefner, Swan, and Allen, they would put on a dog and pony show for Jaehning that would top all dog and pony shows. He would be charmed by James Linn, the Penn Square attorney and master storyteller; he would dine with Bobby Hefner at his magnificent Nichols Hills home; and he would fly on Bell Ranger jet helicopters to some of the rigs his bank had financed. And he would spend some time reviewing credit files in the Penn Square oil and gas division. The examiners were due at at Seafirst by the end of the month, and Jaehning undoubtedly wanted to be able to address their questions or concerns if that became necessary.

Carl Swan dispatched one of his planes to pick up Jaehning and Boyd in Seattle. It then proceeded across the parched hills of central Washington and touched down briefly in Yakima, the state's apple capital, and picked up Apple King Bill Gammie and Seafirst director Bob Schultz.

Jaehning was impressed. Jennings, his wife, and five daughters seemed to him the embodiment of a fine Christian family. The stiff Seafirst president, who seemed to find it difficult to relax even in the company of other golfers at his Seattle country club, appeared just as strained at Jennings's ranch in the company of the Oklahoma oilies and Penn Square bankers.

Gen. James Randolph, a Penn Square board member and president of Kerr-McGee Coal, assured Boyd that the Penn Square customers were good, solid people and that the Anadarko play would last for years, Boyd said later.

The talk turned to jets, their speed, and cruising range, and passenger capacity.

"Why, I'll bet I'm the only person in this room who doesn't have a Lear jet," Gammie said.

A woman from Penn Square bank offered to help out. "We'll take care of that," she said. "We just repossessed a jet."

But Gammie had another toy that was almost as impressive—his 60-foot Hatteras in Big Bay.

Boyd and Gammie had often boasted to the Oklahoma oilies about the superb fishing at Big Bay, about 50-pound red salmon that viciously attack a lure as soon as it's tossed into the water. Gammie was going to take everyone in the room salmon fishing that summer, and Seafirst was going to foot the bill. "Get over here, Boyd," Gammie said, motioning to the Seafirst officer. "Find out how many of the boys here want to go fishing this summer."

"Now that you've invited all of Oklahoma, how many do you have room for?" Boyd whispered.

"We'll take them all," Gammie said expansively.

Boyd polled the guests and most of them agreed to go. Boyd promised to get back to them later with more details, as soon as he could determine when Seafirst chairman Bill Jenkins could make the trip.

Toward the end of his visit, Dick Jaehning took Boyd aside and told him, "John, I want you to know I think you've done a fine job down here. I'd like you to know that." On the return trip, also on Swan's jet, Jaehning asked Swan to stop in Minnesota to pick up his father, according to Boyd. A month later, Seafirst would award John Boyd a "1" performance rating, one of only two such evaluations given by the bank at that time.

Upon returning to Seattle, Boyd drafted thank-you letters for Jaehning's signature addressed to each of their hosts.

To Bill Patterson, they wrote:

Dear "Wild" Bill:
I am slowly gaining an appreciation for the Oklahoma banking style. Seriously, it was the efforts of you and your staff that made my trip so informative and enjoyable. I know these types of visits do not happen by accident and so I am particularly appreciative of all the effort that went into arranging so many visits in such a short period of time. Thank

you so much for the western bronze; I have the perfect spot for it. Bill, feel free to visit me any time you are in Seattle.
Best regards,
Dick

And to Bill Jennings, he wrote:

Dear Bill:
You and your fellow executives at Penn Square Bank have redefined the word hospitality for me. I enjoyed the opportunity of meeting every prominent person in the state of Oklahoma but I am particularly pleased to have spent time with you looking at the future.

As you are already aware, we are extremely close to your organization and look forward to a continuing close relationship. It is difficult to express my appreciation for the many courtesies which you extended to all of us.
Best personal regards,
Dick

He told Carl Swan, "I hope John Boyd will be able to put together his long-promised fishing trip this summer so we may have another opportunity to share ideas."

According to Boyd, he told Jaehning late one evening during the visit that he'd like to bring more directors to Oklahoma over the next year. "Why bring any directors on a trip like this?" Jaehning is said to have responded. "They'll do what they're told to do anyway. You worry about taking care of Harvey Gillis, not the directors."

And on returning to Seattle, Nelson remarked to Boyd, as Boyd remembers the conversation, "you did a job on Jaehning in Oklahoma, he's very excited."

Shortly thereafter, Arland Hatfield was dispatched to Oklahoma City to attend to less ceremonial duties. A reserved, businesslike man, Hatfield spent two days at Penn Square in late February reviewing credit files and talking to Penn Square loan officers. On March 1, he presented his favorable impressions in a memo to Jaehning, a memorandum stressing that Seafirst would not be treated as the stepchild of Chase and Continental. Seafirst had become one of the Big Three.

From: Arland D. Hatfield, vp
      Credit Administrator
To: Richard Jaehning,
    Executive Vice-President and Manager
    World Banking Group

I visited Penn Square Bank on February 25 and 26 to review the bank's loan policies and procedures and evaluate various officers involved in credit.

The bank has made significant strides the past seven months in establishing written policies and procedures and monitoring systems. Eldon Beller, president, was hired from First National Bank of Oklahoma City approximately seven to nine months ago. He has hired a new management team and has also hired several new and experienced credit officers. Joe Semler and I visited with some of the officers and found that most of them were from major banks like Continental Bank, Citibank and First National Bank of Oklahoma City and with fourteen plus years banking experience. . . .

The major point we were able to derive from the discussion was that they visualize Seattle First National Bank as equal to Continental Illinois and Chase (their other two correspondent banks). . . .

The bank has staffed itself with capable, experienced officers and is in the process of establishing the necessary policies and procedures to monitor a $2 billion plus loan portfolio.

Seafirst performed an elaborate audit, one former Penn Square officer recalled. "I must have worn out two pairs of shoes going from correspondent area to the files." But Bill Pettit, now the chief financial officer at Seattle First, claims that on returning to Seattle Jaehning told him about his "disbelief over the mess of Penn Square's loan files."

At one point, Boyd was challenged by the bank's auditor, Sally Nadorik, according to insider sources, for exceeding his expenses on the profit plan. Boyd took special pleasure in sending $125 hand-painted wooden duck decoys and $20 glossy color picture books of the Pacific Northwest to his customers as gifts, a gesture that didn't

sit well with the penny-pinching Ms. Nadorik. One inside source recalls that following the audit, "Boyd sent decoys to Sally as a present, and she sent them back. He made a joke of the whole thing."
Boyd fumed, "I made $15 million for the bank last year, and she's
trying to hang me for $10,000."

Although Seafirst's participations were among the worst in the
Penn Square portfolio, its participation agreement was the toughest
of any of the upstream banks, requiring, for example, that Penn
Square pay any attorney fees that might be charged in connection
with the loans.

Shortly after Hatfield returned home from Oklahoma, Seafirst's
continuing commitment to energy, and to Penn Square, which Seafirst continued to believe was in the business of making energy, was
reinforced in a 97-page report by the energy department to the audit
and examining committee of the board. The report could be called a
textbook case of information overload; it was crammed with oil and
gas consumption and production statistics, forecasts, all of which
generally made no mention of the economic undercurrents taking
place in Oklahoma at that moment. While acknowledging the deep-
ening recession and the success of conservation efforts, the report asserted that "even with total demand down slightly for the U.S. . . .
U.S.-produced oil will be needed to meet demand and more must be
found."

Turning to the outlook for drilling rigs, the report assured the
directors that "despite the recession, the doomsayers and the much
acclaimed oil glut, 1982 and probably 1983 will set new record levels
of drilling activity worldwide. The recent publicity regarding an
eminent [sic] oversupply of rigs is coming primarily from drilling
contracts and some investors and investment advisors. Obviously,"
the report added, "these predictors would like to see new rig building slowed down in order to ensure continuing high day and utiliza-
tion rates." It admitted, however, that "there will be some soft spots
in the markets," including older rigs, rigs without experienced operators, and rigs not properly financed.

Boyd cited the views of the "experts," including John Lichblau,
president of the Petroleum Industry Research Associates, who was
quoted in a recent issue of the *Wall Street Journal* as saying "even a
sharp price reduction would have a very limited effect on demand.
Also if prices were to decline substantially, importing countries
would slap on taxes and fees."

"The experts," Boyd's report emphasized, "are predicting another
record-breaking year for 1982, both in the number of wells drilled

and total footage." Nowhere was there any mention that a drilling rig is useless for anything but making a deep and narrow hole in the ground. Also, about this time, one Oklahoma drilling contractor with two rigs already stacked in a storage yard forfeited an $80,000 deposit on a new rig, according to his banker.

The subject of declining oil prices even came up in a meeting of the Penn Square board of directors, but Jennings brushed off the problem, asserting that the worst that would happen was that a three-year loan would become a four-year loan. The directors were pleased about the reassuring words from the national bank examiners, and the $7.8 million in fees they had earned the year before, even though these fees were earned largely on the sale of questionable loans. The loan loss reserve, they concluded, was "comfortable" at 1.35% of assets. Apparently, no one mentioned that by February $7 million in interest had been paid to the big banks before, or without, being remitted by the borrowers.

As for Seafirst's energy portfolio, in February 1982 it comprised more than $1 billion in outstanding loans, including more than $284 million in participations from Penn Square.

The energy division's report noted that on November 2, 1981, the management committee had placed a "threshold" of 15% on the bank's total energy outstandings in relation to the bank's total loan portfolio. This edict by management, however, presumably made no mention of commitments, which by the end of 1981 were nearly twice the volume of energy loans then housed in the energy division. Ironically, in a long list of the commitments and outstandings to various energy division borrowers, which were rated on a quality scale of from one to three, the one-rated or top-rated credits were major oil companies such as Exxon, Shell, and Arco, which invariably had relatively small commitments and no outstandings.

"People paid more attention to outstandings than commitments," said a former officer. "There was always a large gap between them."

The energy division, the report stressed, was a money-maker. Net after tax profits of $5.07 million, it said, represented a 528% increase over 1979 and a return on assets substantially above that for the world banking division. Moreover, energy claimed an "exceptionally low" percentage of problem loans: only 1.5% of total loans, compared with 7% for the bank as a whole, an attractive statistic to a board of directors smarting over the nearly dormant Pacific Northwest lumber industry, the demise of the New England Fish Company, and the wounds that a weak airline industry had inflicted on that mainstay linchpin of the Washington economy, the Boeing Aircraft Corporation.

Oklahoma was comforting to Boyd; he thought his people could learn a lot from Penn Square officers. The relationship gave him the peace of mind to spend his time making loans in Texas, where he didn't have the support of correspondent banks.

Despite Hatfield's favorable reviews of Boyd's work in Oklahoma, Jaehning is said to have felt that Boyd was too close to Nelson for comfort. Jaehning and Nelson were not on friendly terms, and the new Seafirst president wanted to fire the veteran officer, according to Seafirst insiders. As a compromise, Nelson was kicked upstairs to become head of the credit committee and replaced with chief financial officer and Jaehning ally Harvey Gillis. Gillis, a man who habitually refers to himself in the third person, was a numbers man whose forte was managing risk, not making loans. Gillis considered himself the team player who never tried to show off by taking spectacular risks. Curiously, while Patterson was one of your all-time risk-takers as a banker, he was a careful Little League coach who instructed his young charges to go for the single or the double just to get themselves on base.

Several blocks from Seafirst's headquarters building, the Black Beauty, top executives at Rainier National were pondering Seafirst's growth and apparent profitability and wondering aloud among themselves, as one official later put it, "Are we stupid? What are they doing that we're not?" The board was putting pressure on management not necessarily to put more energy loans on the books, but to put something on the books, and to find out if Seafirst had in fact invented a new and better mousetrap. Rainier had cautiously started up an energy department the previous summer by hiring an experienced energy lender from another bank and a petroleum engineer named Sally Jewell, who, coincidentally, had worked for Mobil in Healdton, Oklahoma—Bill Jennings's hometown. Jewell had met Bill Patterson in October at the IPAA convention in Houston, and was dickering at arm's length with him over a few deals. Jewell, a young, businesslike woman with a special professional interest in marine corrosion, approached Bill at a cocktail reception at the convention, put her arm on his shoulder and said, "I hear you drink out of your shoe." Patterson grabbed a Margarita away from Northern Trust's Mike Tighe, chugged most of it down, and tossed the rest out on the carpet.

Jewell and her colleague Jeff Anderson had become a source of irritation to Patterson for asking too many questions. He said, "The day you want to be real players, we'll fill you up with $150 to $200 million." Jewell said, "We'd only be interested in $1 million or $2 million deals. We don't want to take a lot at a time."

One Rainier officer flew down to Oklahoma early in 1982 to inspect the bank, later acknowledging that he was impressed at the time. He asked Penn Square officers if they knew what was in their portfolio. One responded, "Yes, we think we do."

In contrast to Boyd's dog and pony show for Seafirst's audit committee detailing and discussing all the loans that had been made, Jewell gave a presentation to Rainier's board in June that was more noteworthy for what was not said than what was. She talked in general terms about the energy market, and what Seafirst was doing, and told about the hundreds of millions in energy deals that did not get done, including a number offered by Penn Square Bank.

At that meeting, one director asked Jewell, "Don't you think we should be getting a piece of that action?" Jewell echoed the street talk that was coming out of banks in Texas, where Boyd had earned a reputation as one of the fastest deal-makers in the West. "We think they're going to be hurt," she replied.

On March 26, 1982, under orders from Seafirst, Patterson sent around a memo to all oil and gas staff directing them not to send any new deals to Seattle. "This is because they are extremely tight," he said, "and have requested a slowdown from Penn Square Bank. We will resume business as usual after June 1, 1982."

In its February 17 issue, the *Marples Letter,* a newsletter covering business in the Pacific Northwest, noted Seafirst's unbroken record of increased earnings, despite the weak local economy, and asked top bank executives what kept the institution on top. "There is something about Seafirst that is always running scared," replied vice-chairman Joe Curtis. And Harvey Gillis added, "Seafirst bankers don't fall into the habit of saying, 'Everything is going well so let's not worry.' Instead, they ask, 'What is it that is going to change?' "

Gillis talked about the "enormous emphasis" the bank put on loan quality control, and asserted that in financial management Seafirst held to a conservative course. "We prefer lots of singles and a few doubles to going for a home run where you risk striking out," Gillis said. While one analyst was quoted as saying that Seafirst "periodically comes up with unpleasant surprises," the brokerage firm of Foster and Marshall reported that it had added Seafirst stock to its "buy" list.

In early 1982 Continental still perceived its major problem with Penn Square to be operational. The two banks were out of balance by millions of dollars and Continental sent a team of operations people to Oklahoma to reconcile the massive differences in the two banks' records on payments and advances. Because a single borrower often had many notes outstanding, interest or principal or both were frequently posted to the wrong note, or principal was posted as interest, and vice versa. It took weeks for the Continental team to reconcile Penn Square and Continental accounts, but ultimately the problem was corrected by setting up a group of tellers who did nothing but handle Penn Square participations and installing a wire machine that linked Oklahoma City directly to Chicago. Said one loan officer, "It worked fine until the bank closed."

Referring to the operational problems with Continental, Patterson wrote in a February memo to other senior officers:

> It won't do either bank any good to argue who is at fault, whether the load is being carried by either bank, or make suggestions in meetings as to how to rectify the problem. We need to get this handled before our bank examiners come and certainly before the CINB examiners come.

Lytle, meanwhile, was wintering on the Caribbean island of St. Barthélemy's, where he spent all his vacations, and this year J.D. Allen and his fiancée, and Patterson and executive vice-president Ashburn Bywaters and their wives, joined Lytle for a few days on the lush tropical island, flying there in Bill Saxon's jet. J.D. Allen was apparently so enamored of St. Barts that he and oilman Joe Dan Trigg bought a condominium through a partnership arrangement called "On the Rocks."

In early 1982 Northern Trust's Mike Tighe became alarmed at the rise in his past due loans, including an interim rig loan to Cliff Culpepper. He told Patterson, "Get it out of here now," and playfully grabbed his tie and said, "Buy it back or I'll kill you."

The late Hugh Jones, then the semiretired chairman of a small bank in Woodward, Oklahoma, was one of the most respected bankers in Oklahoma in his day. He was not privy to the prodigious volume of data Boyd had assembled over the previous months to present to the Seafirst board. But Jones lived and worked in the heart of Oklahoma's deep gas, short grass country. He had not made a big bet on deep gas, being more comfortable with the cattle ranchers and wheat farmers in the northwestern part of the state, people who never earned more than a fair living in the best of times and who suffered terribly in the worst of times. From his knowledge of the few service companies that had borrowing relationships with his bank, he knew that the average age of accounts receivables, while never low in the oil patch, had begun to rise, and rise dramatically in recent months. He cared little about the expert predictions. Hugh Jones knew just one thing, and what he knew was all that really mattered: his service company customers weren't getting paid. In early March he growled at a visitor who asked if his bank was making loads of money from the gas boom, and asked, "What boom? It's over."

That same week Copeland Energy's Mike Hopkins flew to Newport Beach to meet with the limited partners of the Copeland partnerships to give them more bad news. He told them that the Copeland Energy 1980 programs had all been severely "downvalued," according to a subsequent declaration by Tarnutzer, to an amount slightly less than what he had invested. The only way Tarnutzer could break even, Hopkins explained, was to put more money in. A few days later, Tarnutzer called Hopkins. The news now was even worse. The value of the 1980 programs, Hopkins said, had dropped still further, to less than half of his investment in the program.

And then there was Mahan Rowsey.

On February 23, Patterson issued a directive to all loan officers ordering them not to approve checks or advances on any Mahan Rowsey account without his okay. "We have had a problem with administrative help issuing cashier's checks or advancing on notes when these accounts have large overdrafts." Nevertheless, Patterson persisted in advancing funds to the oil and gas company, rolling over old debt into new in a frantic effort to "drill them out of trouble." On February 24, Janelle Cates and Bill Patterson approved an extension to May 25 of Mahan Rowsey's $27 million loan for the drilling rigs.

Said one officer, "They tried to get mortgages to shore up the credit, but the more effort made to get mortgages done, the more money was loaned. They tried to shore up the deal by making more loans."

Frankie Mahan was not known as a patron of the arts; his life centered on Grand Lake, women, and his Porsche. But Hal Clifford had bankrolled a full-length feature Hollywood film, so when a broker presented him with the opportunity to invest in a new Broadway play, *The Little Prince*, Mahan figured he should at least take a look at it.

A good play can always be financed in New York, just like a good Oklahoma or Texas oil and gas deal can always find backers in Texas or Oklahoma. *The Little Prince* had run out of cash and would not make it to opening night without help from a wealthy sponsor. Frank flew to New York and sat through the first act but was bored with the play; at dinner afterward, the cast turned on the charm for the man from Grand Lake. But Frankie, in what was perhaps his finest hour as an executive, backed out of the deal and flew home.

THE IDES OF MARCH

O N FEBRUARY 16, MEG SIPPERLY BORROWED THE PHONE IN PENN Square vice-president Pat McCoy's office to make a long-distance call to her boss in New York, Dick Pinney. McCoy, by chance happened to walk into his office in time to overhear a disconcerting slice of that conversation. "Dick," Sipperly said, "I think you're right to check the list of Penn Square bank participations to make sure they're all performing." The next day, McCoy, who by default, so to speak, inherited one of those loans back in August, dashed off a memo to president Eldon Beller telling him what he had overheard.

In fact, just a week earlier, J.S. Zwaik of Peat, Marwick, Mitchell's office in New York phoned Dean York at Peat's Oklahoma City office to ask him to undertake a review of Penn Square's lending policies and procedures, its systems of credit monitoring and servicing of loans, and its credit files on loans over $5 million. By that time, Chase had 150 loans with Penn Square amounting to $230 million. Peat had been Chase's auditing firm for years, and Chase thought it could count on the Big Eight accounting firm for a competent review of those credits.

According to Jim Blanton, managing partner of Peat Marwick in Oklahoma City, his colleagues in New York asked them to perform "certain procedures" on behalf of Chase. Later, Fernand St Germain would say, "I feel as though now we are in 'General Hospital.' What do you mean by a certain procedure—I mean, is this a blood transfusion or a transplant or a bypass?"

One of the nonperformers that would have been of concern was Allen Senall's Maximo Moorings, the "dockominium" loan that Chase Manhattan had graciously stuck Penn Square with in the first place in 1981. McCoy, an officer in Penn Square's small commercial lending department, had acquired responsibility for that gem quite by accident when, six months earlier, he happened to open a letter from Senall's Florida attorney concerning overdue interest payments. In January, McCoy received a letter from the Florida counsel for the Vineyard family, the first lien holder on the property, notifying him that the Senall note was in default, and that the family intended to sue for collection. Senall claimed to have talked with Walter Heller and Company, the commercial finance company, about selling the marina, and said he was contacted by Patterson, who told Senall he wanted to front for the purchase of Maximo under the name BGP Marina. In a January 25 memo to Eldon Beller, McCoy recommended that no new commitment be made to Senall and that unless the bank got more security it should foreclose, adding that Chase was shutting off the tap to Maximo and Senall as well.

The Maximo problem came to a head at the same time Chase was putting pressure on Patterson over Mahan Rowsey. By March 8, the Mahan Rowsey entities were overdrawn by more than $2.4 million and their debts exceeded Penn Square's legal lending limit by half that amount. Worse still, former Penn Square officers said later, the account threatened the very survival of the Chase–Penn Square relationship. Although Chase's holdings of Penn Square participations were small compared with Continental's Chase, as one of the nation's premier correspondent banks, provided an impressive recommendation to other prospective buyers. It was Chase, according to numerous sources, that was going to lead Penn Square into the international arena, making introductions for the Oklahoma bank that would allow it to peddle its wares overseas. Patterson wanted to show Chase he could do something for them, and thought he could find someone to bail the big New York bank out of the deeply submerged maritime monstrosity in Florida.

Phil Busey is a young oil and gas lawyer who joined Penn Square in February to help straighten out the bank's documentation. On March 1, he got a call from Patterson summoning him to a meeting on Maximo. This was to be his first assignment. It would also be one of his toughest.

At the meeting, attended by Patterson, Busey, Senall, and Senall's lawyers, Patterson announced that a corporation, BGP Marina, Inc., would be set up to take title in trust until the dockominium could be sold to another buyer. Senall, Busey recalled, was "trying to move as soon as possible." He wanted to do it in one day, and demanded to be released from his guarantee on the note. The purchaser Patterson had in mind was none other than Ken Tureaud, whose own loans had been identified as problems the previous summer. Tureaud had as much business buying a defunct marina as Bill

Patterson had running Penn Square Bank. On March 4, Garvin Chandler, a loan review officer, had calculated that the entire $21 million Tureaud relationship was a total loss, but the loan review committee, according to subsequent testimony, decided to table the decision on classification.

That same week petroleum engineer Mike Gilbert told Patterson that Penn Square's combined exposure on Saket and Mahan Rowsey "was sufficient to break the bank." Patterson replied, "It will never happen." Patterson didn't want to hear that kind of advice, and ordered Gilbert to stay away from loan committee meetings.

Even as it was becoming clear that the Senall relationship was not beneficial either to Chase or Penn Square, Penn Square officers were perplexed by what seemed to be the close personal relationship between Senall, the marina king, and Chase vice-president Meg Sipperly. At one meeting called to thrash out the troublesome Maximo Moorings situation, Sipperly and Dick Pinney arrived early. When Senall entered the room, "he just grabbed up Meg and they just planted a big smooch on each other," as one officer recalled.

The closing on Maximo Moorings was scheduled for Tuesday, March 9, in Tampa, and Joe Edwards, an outside attorney for Penn Square, asked Busey to come along and assist him on the transaction. On the way to Will Rogers Airport the evening before, Busey stopped by the bank to verify with Patterson that the Tureaud loan had been funded. Patterson assured him it had.

By late Tuesday, most of the documentation was in place; Edwards and Busey felt the bank's Florida counsel could wrap up the remaining details, and the two lawyers caught a 6:00 P.M. flight back to Oklahoma City with a connection in Dallas. Edwards must have had a lawyer's instinct that it was not a done deal. While waiting at Dallas–Fort Worth Airport for the flight to Oklahoma City, Edwards phoned the Florida attorney and discovered that Senall had tried to renegotiate the deal, and that Penn Square's Tom Swineford had phoned the lawyer to report that the funding of the Tureaud note had fallen through. They had tried to get Utica National Bank of Tulsa to take it, but Utica president Scott Martin, Patterson's boyhood friend, had called Penn Square earlier to say there was no way he could put a Ken Tureaud note in his bank.

Earlier that day, Patterson left Oklahoma for Caracas by way of Miami to talk to the Venezuelan national oil company about a deal involving Penn Square customer Sandy Brass. Patterson had arrived in Caracas by the time Edwards and Busey landed in Dallas, and the lawyers managed to reach him in the Venezuelan capital after they got the news from Tampa. "Go ahead and close it," Patterson instructed Edwards, advising him that he, Clifford, and J.D. Hodges would take the deal while financing was being arranged for Tureaud. Clifford and Hodges were about to take a long walk off a short pier in Tampa, Florida.

On Wednesday, Hal Clifford was out of town when Patterson called from Caracas. Patterson was switched over to Kent Gruber, Clifford's chief financial officer, and a former employee of Peat, Marwick, Mitchell in Oklahoma City. "Patterson asked for my authorization to use a blank note signed by Mr. Clifford for Maximo," Gruber said later. "He said it wouldn't cost him anything. He'd make some money off of it." Gruber told Patterson he'd need to contact Clifford, but Patterson insisted that he needed to do the deal that day.

According to Clifford, "I had a message left in my office that Bill Patterson called and wanted to talk about a deal. He said I would not have a downside risk," Clifford insisted later at Patterson's trial. "I would not be in a position of buying the property. He said he'd put me in for $3.5 million. My understanding was that the project was sold to another purchaser."

"I didn't feel I was obligated to repay the note," Clifford said. "He told me on a number of occasions that Walter Heller and an individual with Saket were in the process of buying it."

This was not the first time J.D. Hodges, the countrified brother of the high-rolling oilman Jack Hodges, had the misfortune of getting into a bum deal. Hodges was an officer of Wheatheart, Inc., a fraudulent cattle-feeding scheme that collapsed in 1975 after selling millions of dollars in tax shelter feedlot programs to wealthy investors, including singer Joan Baez. The company's founder, John O. Pitts, Jr., later showed up as a Penn Square borrower himself, according to internal Penn Square documents.

On March 10, Penn Square's Ashburn Bywaters overheard some office chatter about the notes that were being funded to Clifford and Hodges without their signatures. Hodges and Bywaters had become acquainted when Bywaters served with Manufacturers Hanover Leasing Corporation in Dallas, and Hodges was a customer of the big New York bank.

"I called J.D. and he said he hadn't talked to Bill," Bywaters testified later.

Bywaters asked one of Patterson's secretaries to have him call. "Bill explained that he needed Clifford and Hodges to carry him on an interim basis," Bywaters said.

According to J.D. Hodges, "I told Ashburn I never heard of it. Sometime later I got a call from Bill in South America saying Clifford had agreed to buy part of it."

Meanwhile, Bywaters checked with Swineford and Gilbert on Tureaud's ability to do the deal, and learned what he expected all along: that Tureaud couldn't even support his current debt. "Bill told me I didn't understand what he was trying to do with the deal, saying, 'If you're not on my team, maybe you should think about resigning.' " Later, Callard came back and said he had looked again at Tureaud's reserve figures and concluded that they could support an additional advance. An hour later Bywaters called back his friend J.D. Hodges and learned he had agreed to participate. Said Bywaters, "I told him it was a bad deal."

According to Patterson, Hodges said, " 'You've got it.' We trusted them and they trusted us."

As Tom Swineford recalled, "Bill called me from Venezuela and told me to prepare the papers for closing," he said, adding, "My understanding was that Heller and Tureaud were to be partners." But in fact Walter Heller and Company had never committed themselves to the deal. After consulting with Beller, dummy notes were created in the amounts of $2 million for Hodges, $3.5 million for Clifford, and $2.1 million for Patterson. Jennings approved the transaction, and the board of directors subsequently cleared the loan to Bill Patterson.

"I was upset, I didn't see why Chase should get off the hook," testified Tom Swineford at Patterson's trial. "They were the ones who brought in Mr. Senall and his junk in the first place."

According to a secretary, Jan Hargus, Swineford said he didn't like to book the loans and did so only on Bill Patterson's orders. But Beller, who was supposed to be bringing discipline to the bank, was aware, according to subsequent testimony, that the Hodges and Clifford notes were unsigned and still saw fit to put his initials on the loans. The stated purpose of the loans was changed to "oil and gas lease acquisition."

The upshot was that Chase Manhattan was off the hook and the new notes were bumped upstream to Continental and Michigan National. Patterson later persuaded Clifford to roll the note and interest over into a new loan, assuring him that he wouldn't be responsible for the debt, and that he had another buyer who would take over Maximo Moorings. Although Clifford later testified that he never intended to buy Maximo, other sources say that after the note was funded he agreed to take the deal.

As he would later testify at Patterson's trial, Beller was informed by a clearly upset Ashburn Bywaters that he could no longer tolerate Patterson and his lending methods. He told Beller he was resigning and that his decision was final. Patterson's explanation for Bywater's departure, Beller recalled, was that "Ashburn wanted to run the energy department."

Mike Gilbert is a quiet, unassuming man from an Oklahoma family of modest means who was never particularly comfortable around the free-spending crowd of new oilies who borrowed from the bank. No one was more aware than Gilbert that petroleum engineering was an imprecise science, that no one could predict with any degree of certainty just how much oil and gas were in the ground, and that reasonable men could differ widely on their volumetric estimates for a given geological formation. But that imprecision did not, in Gilbert's mind, justify manipulating the loan figures on deadbeats like Ken Tureaud. Little more than a month after Ashburn Bywaters turned in his resignation, Gilbert, without another job prospect in hand, quietly submitted his.

There was also the small matter of the plane that couldn't fly. Among the other Senall loans Penn Square wound up with was a $450,000 note for a private jet that was in such poor condition the bank couldn't find a pilot to return it from Florida to Oklahoma City at any price.

Coincidently, Senall later emerged as a key figure in the February 12, 1982, collapse of the Metropolitan Bank of Tampa, which, according to FBI documents, had lent him money for a dockominium project at the request of his associate, convicted bank fraud artist Allen Z. Wolfson.

In March 1982 Chase Manhattan Bank was not the only entity applying the screws to Bill Patterson. He was feeling the pressure from Jack Hodges's Core Oil and Gas over the Sturgis relationship. Chase Exploration, which had been teetering since mid-1981, was in its death throes. The end of another quarter was approaching, and the loan-to-deposits ratio had to be brought down. And within six weeks a young national bank examiner named Steve Plunk was due to arrive to conduct a comprehensive examination of the Penn Square Bank.

By that spring Jere Sturgis, the man who wanted to be Enid's first billionaire, whose debt with some of the nation's major banks approached $60 million, couldn't even pay bills amounting to less than $5,000 from oil-field service firms who had done work on his oil and gas properties. "Sturgis appeared to be a person of enormous wealth," said Bob Kotarski, Penn Square's correspondent banking chief. Jennings considered him a good customer, and his financial statement on April 20 showed a net worth into the billions, according to Kotarski.

One of his creditors was Jack Hodges, the free-spending trucking magnate big enough to fill a doorway. Hodges was known as a generous man who treated his friends well. But Jack Hodges liked to be paid on time. And on March 11, the paper billionaire from Enid owed Hodges $1 million.

Patterson was prepared to lend Sturgis another $2 million, and to pacify Hodges by lending him the $1 million owed by Sturgis. Said Kotarski, "They didn't care for it at all. They just wanted to be paid." Kotarski informed Gary Roberts, Sturgis's financial officer, that neither Penn Square nor Chase nor Northern Trust wanted to lend him any more money. The understanding was that Sturgis would get another $2 million for lease lines and would pay off Hodges's Core Oil and Gas out of funds presumably on deposit at Penn Square. On March 11, Roberts called to take the matter up with Patterson. Patterson was not easy to reach, and his telephone manner was frequently abrupt.

"What's your question?" Patterson asked when Roberts came on the line, according to tapes played at the Patterson trial.

"There's not another million," Roberts said.

"Okay, I'll get it handled. I'll just change that note to $3 million. Don't worry about it. I'll get you a bunch of money next week. Everything'll be fine."

According to a deposition given later by Chase officer Ed Moran, someone in a credit review unit of the bank spotlighted Sturgis as a problem credit in March 1982. As one Chase officer explained later, a couple of officers were approached for approvals on Penn Square participations and someone asked, "How many participations do we have with them?" Chase, like Continental, had no way of totaling its exposure by a correspondent bank. "It began as normal, healthy curiosity," he said later.

Earlier, the domestic institutions department introduced the Chase real estate department to Penn Square and asked it to send an officer to Oklahoma City to consider taking some real estate deals, including a piece of the construction loan for Penn Square's new $36 million tower. According to Chase officers, the department made it clear to Penn Square that it didn't like the construction deal. "They told the real estate officer he'd have to loosen up," a Chase official said. The man from Chase returned to New York and reported, "Those guys down there are really crazy."

"There was always a lot of discussion about how bad the Sturgis credit was," said one former officer. "Patterson never allowed anyone to know the whole picture. The buyouts seemed to start out okay, then something would invariably go wrong, because of the players involved. People voiced their concerns to Jennings, but it was almost like he didn't want to believe it."

On April 8, 1982, Mary Ellen Hughes, a credit administrator at Chase, wrote a terse letter to Scott Hamilton, her contact at Penn Square. While it communicated a certain sense of urgency, the tone of the memo was much like the first notice a credit card holder might receive on an overdue bill. It contained a who's who of the Penn Square elite: Bob "General Bull Moose" Lammerts, Ken Tureaud, Allen Senall, Bob Hefner, and others were listed as owing some $50 million in back payments. For Chase, the list represented a tiny fraction, less than 0.1%, of its entire portfolio.

"Please forward to us," Hughes requested, "on an urgent basis, copies of extension and new participation certificates along with interest due."

In less than a month, Chase's view of its relationship with Penn Square had changed radically, and Meg Sipperly was squirming to extricate herself from some of the flakiest loans ever made by the Chase Manhattan Bank.

Asked about that changed opinion of Penn Square, former Chase public relations officer Charles Francis declared later, "It did change, and I'm not going to get into it." There was, however, still room for a brother-in-law deal or two. Weeks after Chase wiggled itself out of Maximo Moorings, it bought a $1.08 million participation in Brooke Grant's Shallow Gushers I program.

In Chicago the loan operations quagmire had blinded Continental's top management for months to their real problem in Oklahoma: the deterioration of the Penn Square portfolio. But in the spring of 1982, the debate over the six-figure Penn Square loans to John Lytle obscured that problem even further.

In early March, Bergman was still recuperating from surgery, but the Lytle issue was so pressing that Redding, internal auditor Hlavka, and representatives of the bank's legal and personnel departments felt compelled to phone the ailing banker at home in Winnetka. Bergman suggested it was time that George Baker be brought in.

On March 5, in a memo to Bergman, Redding wrote:

Equally as distressing [as the loans themselves], John has placed his personal financial condition in such a state he cannot possibly service his debt without selling most of his assets, including his residence. For this, I cannot only blame John, but must place a good deal of the blame on Penn Square Bank for making this credit available to John. On the basis of information he has supplied us, in my opinion, he was not deserving of it. Unfortunately, based on some actions he has taken, I think he is desperate and not thinking rationally.

According to federal prosecutors, Jere Sturgis was a participant in a scheme concocted by Patterson and Lytle to enable Lytle, with loans from Penn Square Bank, to make a fraudulent profit on investments with Sturgis's Cheyenne Exploration Corporation. On March 11 Lytle, Patterson, and Sturgis allegedly agreed that Sturgis would buy back investments Lytle had made in his company—investments funded in the first place by Patterson—for $475,609.08, far more than the investment was supposedly worth. The next day, a federal indictment alleges, Patterson funded a loan to Sturgis for the same amount, issued a check for $475,609.08 to Frank Creamer's Petro Industries, which issued a draft to Lytle for $475,609.08 several days later. By this time, Creamer, a fraternity brother of Patterson, had quit his job as a petroleum engineer at Northern Trust and gone into business for himself.

Local bankers couldn't believe the Chicago bank was doing the deals it was doing in Oklahoma without a cosmic strategic plan behind it. Dale Mitchell recalled later that, "We said many times that undoubtedly what they were doing is letting Penn Square get into a position where they'd have to take them over. That would be their interstate move into the oil patch. That had to be it." Indeed, Jennings had acknowledged to friends, including Bob Hefner, that his bank was a kind of loan production office for Continental, and that when nationwide banking arrived Continental might buy them out.

Mitchell and his friends probably gave Anderson and the senior management of Continental too much credit for farsightedness. In fact, Continental wasn't even able to determine what it had bought from Penn Square, much less concoct a strategy for taking the bank over. Responding to a request by Roger Anderson for a breakdown on the bank's so-called unrated loans, Steve Elliot, the controller of Baker's general banking services division, reviewed the loans in question and replied to Anderson in an April 5 memo:

An inordinate number of not rated credits existed in Oil and Gas-Mid-Continent Division where rapid growth in loan volume (both in terms of dollars and transactions) caused a backlog in records maintenance in the fourth quarter. Mid-Continent has actively pursued with noticeable improvement their past due and not rated loans during the first quarter of 1982.

According to Continental investigators, Elliot got his information about the "noticeable improvement" from John Lytle himself. But federal investigators charged in their indictment that Lytle intentionally removed borrowers from the past due list in an attempt to conceal their problems from his superiors at Continental.

If the impact of the Elliot memo was diluted by its ambiguity, there were other red flags waved in the face of the top management of Continental Bank that were somewhat more vivid.

One flag was waved just before Continental's annual economic briefing and dinner, an event that gave the Continental top brass a chance to be seen by Penn Square officers and their oil-patch clients, all under the guise of presenting their outlook for the regional and national economies. On the flight to Oklahoma from Chicago, vice-president Pat Goy briefed Baker and Bergman on a February visit to Seattle, when he discovered that Seattle First was a graveyard of bad loans originally turned down by Continental. The shortages of oil and gas that had lured Continental to Oklahoma in the first place had turned into a surplus by April, and Goy was concerned that the pricing assumptions that Continental was still using to value reserves for lending purposes were long outdated. He told Bergman and Baker that the bank needed an economist to help the lending areas better monitor the vagaries of the energy market. In the taxi from Tulsa airport, however, Baker asked Goy about the persistent documentation problems at Penn Square, and Goy, according to Baker, said they were being taken care of.

By April the other Oklahoma City banks had established watch lists of oil- and gas-related companies requiring special monitoring. And in considering the loan requests of prospective customers, the banks were examining their receivables to determine if they were doing business with known customers of Penn Square.

Bill Talley, whose optimistic forecasts in 1980 and 1981 had spurred on much of the drilling activity, recalls that market conditions changed abruptly in March 1982. The industry began to wind down from the peak of 874 rigs. "Gridlock was in full swing and receivables were running at 90 to 120 days on almost every account," he recalled.

The Fletcher Field, where operators were encountering monumental completion problems, delayed the perception of problems for six months, he said. "It was March, April when people said, 'Oh, my God, how am I going to pay for anything?' "

Talley recalled one drilling project that was supposed to cost $5 million, and wound up costing $10 million. The interest alone was $1 million, which the investors refused to pay, forcing the operator to pay out of his own pocket. Working interest owners in wells were refusing to pay their pro rata shares of the expenses of drilling projects, increasing the burden on the remaining investors. In March, recalled one prominent New York-based energy lender, "It was obvious that the spring upturn hadn't materialized." Demand for natural gas continued to decline not only because of the deepening recession but also because of heavy rains and snowfalls in the Pacific Northwest, which resulted in runoffs that produced cheap and abundant supplies of hydroelectric power, according to Oklahoma energy consultants.

The investment community was looking with a jaundiced eye at the fairy-tale reserve estimates of some oil and gas companies. Amarex, like *The Little Prince*, bombed in New York. John Mason, the company's president, took his side show on the road to New York in an attempt to persuade securities analysts that Amarex's stock was undervalued. Mason presented slides that purported to represent the value of the company's previously discovered reserves, but neglected to inform the analysts that the prices were outdated. Moreover, the analysts ripped into him for his inability to explain how he was going to pay off his $210.1 million in long-term debt.

Having just placated Chase Manhattan Bank on Maximo Moorings, Patterson, under pressure from Beep Jennings, was faced with the task of making another problem credit—the Chase Exploration Company [no relation to Chase Manhattan]—disappear before the examiners arrived. Chase Exploration was on the verge of becoming Penn Square's first major bankruptcy. Northern Trust, however, which had a reputation for doing some of the better Oklahoma deals, wound up with more than $9 million in loans to Chase that had been booked by former petroleum engineer Frank Creamer, and Penn Square was stuck with $2.2 million after repurchasing the notes from Michigan National, as part of the Patterson's money-back guarantee. Those notes were now languishing in that slush bucket account for bad loans called "other assets."

As early as mid-1981, attempts had been made to put Band-Aids on the deal. J.D. Hodges set up a drilling partnership for his employees that he dubbed "Silvercreek" after his favorite brand of chewing tobacco. The partnership bought three Chase Exploration rigs, and took in Patterson and another Penn Square officer as investors. Later that year Hodges was at Northern Trust in Chicago, when he was approached about taking them out of Chase Exploration altogether. "I said I'd send a geologist and landman to look at it," Hodges recalled. "They came back and said it wasn't what we were after." And by early 1982 disgruntled investors in Chase Exploration were suing to get out as well.

Northern Trust's Bart Wilson had learned that Penn Square was also banking Chase Exploration, and that the Northern Trust and Penn Square notes were cross-collateralized, meaning that the two banks shared the same security, a situation that was more the rule than the exception at Penn Square. Wilson did not want to be the one associated with tainting his institution's almost spotless loan portfolio, so he put in a call to Beep Jennings seeking his help in bailing Northern out of the loans to the floundering company. "Northern said Chase Exploration had lied to them and they desperately needed someone to help them out," Patterson testified at his trial.

Old-time oilman Joe Dan Trigg, the intimate business associate of Beep Jennings and playmate of Bill Patterson, once made the mistake of telling Patterson, "If you ever run into any good production deals I could get cheap, let me know." Patterson thought he had found just such a deal in Chase Exploration. According to Trigg, Patterson approached him in March about buying Chase Exploration, and the oilman replied that he was interested "if it looked like a good deal." But he testified later that he never specifically authorized the purchase of the company.

On March 22, Patterson called Jan Hargus, and, according to her testimony at Patterson's trial, instructed her to book one of Penn Square's famous "dummy notes" for $3 million in the name of Joe Dan Trigg. Patterson, she said, told her not to microfilm the note but to "white-out" notations that would link the loan to Trigg, and to send him the original Chase Exploration notes. About $2.5 million was used to pay off the three Chase loans, and the balance was credited to the Trigg account.

Worried about violating the practice of microfilming all notes and breaking the audit trail, Hargus consulted with her supervisor and they decided to microfilm the notes despite Patterson's instructions while whiting-out the notations as Patterson requested. "Our policy was to microfilm all notes on the day they were paid. That was our procedure," she said.

Coincidently, on March 22, Arthur Pool of Chase Exploration flew to Hartford, Connecticut, to meet with representatives of wealthy real estate developer David Chase [no relation to Chase Exploration or Chase Manhattan], who purchased an option to buy 80% of Chase Exploration stock. That arrangement, however, was distasteful to Northern and Patterson, because it left them in a subordinate position to Chase. According to one observer, "David Chase demanded an interest-only loan and wanted to take the deal over with a minimum of capital."

The next day, Patterson placed a phone call from the offices of Northern Trust in Chicago to Chase Exploration in Tulsa. Arthur Pool had returned from Hartford and took the call from Patterson.

"He said he was going to make me a deal I couldn't refuse, and didn't want to refuse," Pool said. Patterson proposed paying the partners $50,000 each and allowing them to walk away from the soon-to-be defunct company.

According to court briefs, Patterson told the oilmen he was authorized to negotiate the sale of Chase Exploration stock on behalf of certain buyers. He told them he understood that criminal charges were pending against them stemming from various securities transactions.

Bart Wilson chimed in, "This is the kind of deal you wanted. You better accept it." Patterson emphasized that the David Chase deal was "ridiculous" and Penn Square and Northern wouldn't go along with it. "You've got thirty minutes to do the deal," Patterson said testily.

"I need more than thirty minutes," Pool replied.

Pool asked for a number to call him back, but Patterson refused to give it to him, according to Pool.

Thirty minutes later, Patterson called back and reiterated the offer. Pool countered with a demand for $150,000 each.

"We're not going to quibble, make it $100,000," Patterson replied.

According to a complaint filed by Chase Exploration, Patterson killed the deal with David Chase by telling him they were "crooks" and generally disreputable and unreliable, and that Chase Exploration had a reputation for drilling "dry holes."

On March 24, Patterson instructed all officers that "absolutely no information is to be given out regarding Chase Exploration by anyone other than myself. Even requests for the simplest credit information, such as loan balances, from anyone are to be referred to me. If one of the owners should call requesting information, these calls are also to be referred to me."

Meanwhile, David Chase agreed to waive his option, and on March 25 Patterson and his lawyers met in Tulsa with the folks from Chase Exploration. While asserting that he had the authority to take over the company, Patterson declined to identify the buyers and ordered his people not to talk to Trigg or Hodges or their lawyers. And once again, Patterson demonstrated his flair for naming companies, if not financing them. He borrowed the logo "Come on America," which was emblazoned on drilling rigs owned by Jack Hodges, as the name for the new entity.

But according to Chase Exploration, the purchase contract turned out to be "180 degrees" apart from the original agreement, and the transaction collapsed on April 10 of its own weight. The Tulsa meeting, lawyer Phil Busey testified later, was a sham.

Deals like these gave rise to the increasing chatter about Penn Square's fragile condition. At a meeting between Jennings and three senior officers of another Oklahoma bank, the visiting bankers said, "The word on the street is that your bank is loaded up with a bunch of bad loans."

Jennings, ever the showman, snapped back, "Where's that street located?" Answering his own question, the feisty banker said, "It runs from California to New York City, Chicago to New Orleans. I guess Continental Illinois, Chase, Hibernia and Seafirst aren't located there."

With Patterson constantly on the road or in the air trying to unload deals, those at the bank responsible for finding money to fund them were having fits trying to project cash needs. They needed, for example, a forecast of the volume of loans that would be sold in order to know how much money they'd have to buy in the markets. "First we couldn't reach him," said one officer. "Then we'd be informed that $25 to $50 million was on the desks of upstream bank officers and in seven days would be sold. But instead of $25 million being sold $50 million would come on."

One of them was a $4 million credit secured by collateral valued at $80,000 in seven wells, several of which had been plugged and were therefore nonproducing.

"It was clear by March 31 that Penn Square couldn't push its liquidity problem off on other banks," said a former Penn Square Bank officer.

Yet offsetting these problems was the appearance that progress was being made. "There was a continuous inflow of high quality people," said one officer. "They were coming in from all over the country. Every department was in the throes of development. There were .22 caliber nail drivers going off all the time." The oil and gas division had just moved into a single-story bunkerlike building a few steps away from the main bank, and construction of the new Penn-bank Tower was well underway.

Appearances were deceiving. The same game of musical chairs that was being played with loans was being played with document exceptions. According to one junior officer, 192 document exceptions were eliminated and 217 were created on the same day in April. The hiring of people like Phil Busey gave some comfort to upstream bankers who continued to believe that operations and documentation were their primary Penn Square problems, and Patterson always made a point of introducing visiting bankers to his crack legal team. The catch was, while bad documentation can contribute to the making of a poor credit, good documentation doesn't make a bad credit good.

By the end of March, according to court filings, Penn Square loans containing document exceptions totaled $1.1 billion, or about half of the loans the bank had generated to date, and nearly two-thirds of those loans were in Patterson's own portfolio. Moreover, loan fees were not being collected, interest continued to be up-streamed, and the overdraft list grew longer each day.

Norma Babb, the bank's auditor, had attempted to bring some of these problems to Jennings's attention but was ignored. According to a colleague, Babb was told, "That credit's being managed, or the cash flow's being managed." The former officer observed wryly, "There was creativity in the verbal response."

Curiously, partners of Peat, Marwick, Mitchell and Company of Oklahoma City completed their audit of Penn Square and issued an opinion letter that certainly would have caused Jennings to breathe a little easier. By this time, Penn Square had deteriorated to a point far worse than Arthur Young had found it the year before, when it went on record with a qualified opinion. Peat, however, saw fit to present Penn Square with a clean opinion. Mike Mahoney, whose duties included making the auditors comfortable and meeting their requests for loan files, said later, "They were only in there three weeks and took long lunch hours. They only looked at a few loans. I should know. It was my job to bring them the files."

Among the investors in Hal Clifford's drilling programs were ten partners in the Oklahoma City office of the nation's second largest public accounting firm. According to federal court documents, Marshall Snipes, a former Peat Marwick partner, told investors in the Windon Partnerships, which was affiliated with Penn Square customer Clifford Resources, that of the more than one hundred partnerships handled by Peat's office in Oklahoma City, he and ten other partners put their money—approximately $250,000—exclusively with Clifford.

The reduced willingness of Seafirst and Northern Trust to take deals from Penn Square made it imperative for Penn Square to find other outlets for its loans and new sources of funds. It began courting new partners with a renewed fervor. Citibank's Dallas loan production office indicated an interest in doing some deals; a vice-president and treasurer of Marine Midland Bank Southwest, in Houston, expressed frustration at his New York headquarters for "arbitrarily" throwing out half of the Penn Square credits he sent there. Chemical was in the midst of a drilling fund arrangement. The Bank of New England was eager to get in the action; the bankers from Boston wanted deals for no less than $1 million each. "I would prefer to initiate an ongoing and mutually profitable relationship versus a one-time transactional one, a Bank of New England officer wrote to Penn Square.

Seafirst had sailed through its own examination without the examiners from San Francisco detecting that anything was amiss. At Seattle, it wasn't uncommon to take delinquent interest, roll it over into a new loan, and collaterize it with previously pledged equipment, but these practices were apparently overlooked. Seafirst also got some help from Penn Square's correspondent department, which dispatched a delegation to Seattle to make sure nothing went wrong. Their task was not especially difficult. Examiners in the Pacific Northwest are about as familiar with energy loans as examiners in Oklahoma are with loans to salmon fishermen.

The trips to Seattle were never all work. There were frequent visits to Ray's Boat House, a waterfront restaurant in downtown Seattle, one of the favorite Seattle haunts of the seafood-deprived Oklahomans.

"Thank you for coming to Seattle to help us with the exam," Boyd wrote. "As Ward may have told you, we finished in good shape through no small effort on the part of Penn Square Bank."

The gregarious Seafirst officer further expressed his appreciation by sending Kotarski two hand-carved duck decoys.

Penn Square's own exam was scheduled to begin April 26, and

one week before the Feds arrived Patterson issued explicit instructions to his petroleum engineers. "The examiners are coming down next week. Snow them."

April 26 was a milestone in the career of Stephen Plunk, an affable Tennessean who, in the words of a colleague, "was cut in the Frank Brown mold," a reference to the now-retired bank examiner who was a legend in Oklahoma for his stern treatment of problem banks. A veteran of ten years' service with the Comptroller of the Currency, Plunk now had his first assignment as examiner-in-charge of a large bank examination. He expected to find the bank in better condition than it was in the previous examination, but he was determined to leave no loan unturned.

Penn Square's efforts to clean up shop intensified in preparation for the examiners. John Baldwin, head of loan administration, took steps to halt the multibillion-dollar shell game. On April 16 he issued a memo:

> It has been bank practice to pay loan proceeds to whomever the borrower or loan officer verbally instructs. Legal counsel has advised us to discontinue this practice on the grounds that a borrower could later repudiate the debt by claiming he did not get the benefit of the proceeds. . . . Please note that paying off one entity's note with the proceeds of a loan to another will also require written authorization from the borrower.

THE GREAT SPRING
RIG SALE

IT HAD BEEN YEARS SINCE ROBERT HEFNER HAD TAKEN WHAT HE called a real vacation. In April 1982 he was on the 98-foot yacht *Anadarko* anchored in the harbor of the tiny Caribbean island of St. Barthélémy's when he received two transoceanic calls, about one day apart, that were to signal the beginning of the end of the oil boom euphoria, deep gas, and the fortunes of GHK and Mr. Hefner himself.

Of all the problems faced by Jennings and Patterson, none was more pressing than Mahan Rowsey and its seven rigs. "Bill Jennings and I discussed many times the sale of the rigs," Patterson said later, "and decided there were two people who could handle it." One of them was Jimmy Linn, the engaging and wealthy Oklahoma City lawyer; the other was Bob Hefner. Linn was out of town and couldn't be reached. Patterson contacted Hefner in St. Barts and briefed him on the situation.

At 8:00 A.M. on April 16 a GHK helicopter flying from Oklahoma City to a rig site in Elk City exploded in midair and crashed just south of Interstate 40, killing Hefner's close friend and executive assistant, Tom Heritage, the pilot, and an Arizona investor. Hefner cut short his vacation and rushed back to Oklahoma City for the funeral.

Though Meg Sipperly and her colleagues at the Chase Manhattan Bank had become uneasy with a number of its Penn Square credits, they regarded people like Hefner and Swan as strictly blue chip and were making arrangements for new loans to indulge Hefner's interest in horses. On April 21, Hefner flew to Lexington, Kentucky, to visit his mother and stepfather, and to discuss loans for his Kentucky horse farm over brunch with Sipperly and other Chase officers.

But it was not until April 26, as Hefner recalled it, that Patterson "came to me about the problem Chase and Penn Square had" over Mahan Rowsey. Mahan Rowsey was in trouble, Patterson told him, and Chase was pressuring him to do something about it. According to Hefner, Patterson wanted him to "warehouse the note"—substituting his good name and credit at Chase Manhattan for Mahan Rowsey's—while Patterson finished the paperwork on a $33 million rig sale to four other Penn Square customers. By this time, Mahan Rowsey was more than $60 million in debt, including $38 million for the rigs alone, which were now worth less than $18 million. Once again, it was Hefner's turn to repay the favors extended to him by Bill Jennings and Penn Square back in 1977 when no bank in Oklahoma City, or anywhere in the country for that matter, would touch the charismatic Mr. Hefner and his deep gas.

Hefner, of course, was always looking for money. Big money. At the time, he was desperately trying to assemble another large drilling project, which would have transferred the balance of the assets that were not part of the 1980 Mobil farm-out to a group of companies that included some of the biggest names in the Anadarko Basin. By concentrating a lot of acreage in one pool controlled by relatively few operators, the gas men would avoid the problems of dealing with a multitude of small working interest owners. Hefner was shopping for another $100 million. Some of this money was to come from Continental Illinois, but the outstanding loans to Hefner and his companies were nearing the Chicago bank's $170 million legal lending limit, and Continental officers put him on notice that perhaps another large institution should be brought into the deal.

On April 27, Patterson proposed to Hefner that once the rigs were sold off and the debt retired, then the note he would sign to take Chase out of the Mahan Rowsey mess could be applied to his own deal. "I said I'd be glad to look at it. I was on Penn Square's team and I was very interested in helping out if I could," Hefner said. So in late April, Hefner signed his name to a note for his QOL corporation for $30.3 million. Patterson, said one observer familiar with the transaction, had "coconuts for balls": the $300,000 Patterson tacked on to the $30 million in principal was Penn Square's standard origination fee. Patterson, according to Hefner, assured him that he had buyers for the rigs and that his guarantee would be needed only for a couple of weeks. "I figured the worst that could happen was that the money would end up in my account," Hefner said later. Hefner was wrong.

* * *

On April 26, a confident Roger E. Anderson, chairman of the Continental Illinois Corporation, told 800 shareholders at the bank's annual meeting in the auditorium of the Art Institute of Chicago that he expected 1982 earnings to exceed the record returns of the year before. The bank might experience an occasional disappointment, he said, but that was to be expected in a recessionary economy. The same day, a front page article entitled "Oklahoma's Penn Square Bank, Maverick Oil Patch Lender: Some Say It's Bet Too Heavily on Energy" appeared in the *American Banker,* a national financial daily. It claimed that Continental had bought more than $1 billion in Penn Square oil and gas participations, loans that were now shaky because of the downturn in energy prices.

At Continental, personnel chief Gene Croisant was convinced Lytle should be canned because of the personal loans he had obtained from Penn Square, pointing out that to allow him to remain with the bank would suggest to other personnel that Lytle was receiving favored treatment. In fact, the only reason Lytle was not fired, or at the very least transferred, was that the bank couldn't find anyone to replace him.

The *American Banker* article served to confirm for Croisant the wisdom of his earlier recommendation to Anderson, and the personnel chief once again urged Anderson to terminate Lytle. But, according to the bank's special litigation report, Anderson replied only that he "understood Croisant's concerns."

California money-broker Bill Goldsmith was taken aback by the article and made a few phone calls. He called Bert Davis, the Penn Square officer in charge of funding for the bank. Goldsmith expressed his concern about the story and asked if Davis could shed some additional light on it.

"Since this article attacks items outside your area of responsibility, I'd like you to go to your superiors and get the information and call me," Goldsmith said.

Goldsmith then phoned an acquaintance at First National, and asked him if he was aware of any problems at the Penn Square Bank. His contact there reported he didn't have any information that would either validate or refute the article.

Davis called back shortly thereafter with the answer for Goldsmith. "I've talked with our chairman," Davis said, "and it's our opinion that the article's exaggerated; there are no serious problems at the bank."

The chairman, of course, was Beep Jennings. But his assurances were apparently enough for Goldsmith.

In Battle Creek, Michigan, Arnie Middeldorf and Herb Peterson of the Michigan National Bank, which escaped any mention in the article, read it and concluded that it was misinformed. After all, they figured, they were getting paid, all their loans were performing, and they had no reason to believe this was not the case with the other banks. The directors of Michigan National were so pleased with the relationship that after a meeting on April 16 at which Patterson reassured them on conditions in the oil patch, they voted to take another $100 million. Michigan National officers spent so little time in Oklahoma, or with Penn Square customers, that they would not have picked up on the rumblings about Penn Square and the dismal prospects for the oil and gas industry that had begun to gather momentum in local banking circles. On an earlier visit to Oklahoma City, two of those officers spent the day touring the city and its environs, making a stop at Tener's, the cowboy-western clothing emporium, where one of the bankers purchased a souvenir bull scrotum for his office.

John Mason, a short, stocky man with an unmistakably Irish face, is the unofficial dean of New York bank stock analysts, and he was disturbed about what he read in the *American Banker* article. Continental had been the darling of the analysts because of its aggressiveness in lending to middle-market customers and its consistency in reporting ever increasing earnings. Although Continental was not the largest bank in the country, it had just achieved the goal it had set for itself five years earlier, becoming the leader in commercial and industrial loans, the most important segment of the industry.

Lately, however, the giant Chicago institution had become associated with too many highly publicized problem loans, names such as International Harvester and Invsco that regularly cropped up in the *Wall Street Journal,* the *American Banker,* and the financial pages of the *New York Times.* Analysts realize that there may be no direct relationship between a bank's earnings potential and the frequency that its name appears in print in connection with a bad loan, but this kind of publicity does not help the market's perception of the stock. So Mason boarded a plane for Oklahoma City to check out Penn Square for himself. He was not pleased with his findings.

Prudential-Bache's George Salem was also worried. He dashed off a memo to his colleagues at Bache offices around the country. The memo read:

April 30, 1982

To: Bank stock analysts
From: George M. Salem
Re: Energy lending

The attached is an excellent piece of journalism from a recent edition of the *American Banker*. It documents the energy lending activities of a $400 million bank in Oklahoma City—named Penn Square Bank. The incredible story tells of Penn Square having originated and sold over $2 billion of energy loans to four large banks: Continental Illinois (50% of the total), Chase Manhattan, Seafirst, and Nortrust. The article suggests that Penn Square's lending principles were sometimes less than prudent, but this is denied by its management.

This story seems to confirm Continental's heavy involvement in energy lending to independent producers. It is reason for analysts to remain diligent in monitoring the financial health of the independents and the quality of energy loans in general. It is information such as in this article that causes us to remain cautious about the common stocks of Continental Illinois and the Texas banks.

Baker, Anderson, and Perkins found themselves deluged by a flood of phone calls from stock and investment analysts seeking clarification about the impact of these problematical credits on Continental's income. The article prompted Baker himself to ask Bergman, once again, about the Penn Square loans. Bergman replied, "George, stop worrying and quit bugging me," while assuring his boss that most of the participations had been converted to direct loans and were of good quality. Baker, Bergman, Redding, and even Lytle, according to Continental's special litigation report, did not realize they had $1 billion in Penn Square loans until they read about it in the *American Banker*. Bergman figured Continental's exposure to be more like $650 million, while Lytle believed it to be somewhere between $700 million and $800 million.

Continental's James "Jimmy the Magician" Harper had a reputation for financial wizardry and turning bad deals into good ones that was unmatched in the history of Continental Illinois Bank. It was Harper, of course, who was largely responsible for bailing Continental out of the REITs debacle in the mid-1970s—a stroke of genius that earned him his nickname. Harper did little to discourage the growth of that reputation, and indeed, went out of his way to enhance it, even to the point of wearing a lapel button depicting a magician pulling a rabbit out of a hat. He also had the unusual ability to be in two places at once. A former Continental officer recalls walking into Harper's office and finding a life-size papier-mâché replica of the flamboyant real estate lender, wearing one of Harper's suits, sitting with its hands folded at his desk. Harper and his papier-mâché image rarely got burned in a financial transaction. Between April 22 and April 29, Jimmy the Magician sold nearly 69,000 shares of his Continental common stock, a move that he probably never regretted, despite the allegations of insider trading that would soon follow.

In Seattle, officials of Rainier Bank were mulling over a request from Penn Square for a Fed funds line when the *American Banker* article appeared, and subsequently decided not to extend it. The request had raised questions in the minds of officials at Rainier who pass on such matters as to why Penn Square couldn't simply call on its sweethearts, Continental and Seafirst, for a Fed funds line. Rainier told them they would have to pay a premium because of state taxes on such services. And—Catch-22—their willingness to pay the premium was another reason they didn't get it. On the East Coast, New York's Chemical Bank was in the midst of negotiations with Penn Square over a limited partnership drilling deal, according to former Penn Square officials, and broke off the discussions after the article appeared, although a spokesman for Chemical insisted later that the decision to back off from Penn Square had been made before the article was published.

The *American Banker* story prompted a front page article in the business section of the Sunday *Oklahoman* entitled "Bank's Oil Lending Gets It in Big Time." While it was somewhat more positive in tone unlike the earlier story, it did mention the criticism cited in the *American Banker* and the high profile the bank had acquired through aggressive lending. Plunk and the Dallas office of the Comptroller were troubled about the impact such "negative press" would have on investor, industry, and depositor confidence in the bank. On May 4 Plunk dropped a handwritten note to his superiors in Dallas, pointing out that "this bank is very much a popular subject. I will forward any additonal publications that appear."

When Phil Busey, the lawyer hired to clean up Penn Square's documentation quagmire, signed on with the bank in February, he expected the job to be challenging, and he was not disappointed. His first months at Penn Square had been a kind of baptism by fire; instead of spending eight hours a day behind a desk making sure *i*'s were dotted and *t*'s were crossed, he found himself trying to understand a billion-dollar shell game in which neither the peas nor the shells could be seen or counted. So far, the stakes in the biggest deals he had been involved with—Maximo Moorings and Chase Exploration—had not exceeded seven figures. That changed on April 30, 1982, when the ante went to $30 million. On that day, Bill Patterson asked Busey to step into his office to help him with the Great Mahan Rowsey Spring Rig Sale.

Patterson, according to Busey, said he had reached an agreement to sell the Mahan Rowsey rigs, but Busey advised his boss that he didn't believe Patterson had the authority to unload the iron without the go-ahead from Mahan Rowsey. "I told Bill that Hefner and Mahan Rowsey should be involved in the transaction."

On Saturday Busey consulted with Joe Edwards, the outside counsel with whom he had worked on Maximo, and together they concluded that a bulk sale of the rigs would be a lengthy process, since under Oklahoma law creditors have to be given thirty days' notice of such a transaction. A stock sale, they figured, would be the route to take. Patterson had little patience with lawyers and legal technicalities. Visibly agitated, he told Busey he wanted the deal done by Monday. "I just want them sold," he snapped. "If you can't do it, I'll do it."

Patterson assured Busey that Hefner was behind the transaction 100%, but warned him not to contact Hefner or Hefner's lawyers. According to Busey, Patterson instructed the Penn Square attorneys to execute the stock sale and said he would notify Hefner.

Hefner had asked Larry Ray, GHK's president, to inspect the papers on the deal, and late on the evening of Sunday, May 2, Patterson stopped by Ray's home to show him the documents. "He told me Hefner would be at no risk," Ray testified later. "He said the rigs were sold and he needed Hefner's credit while waiting for the paperwork to go through."

The gas man, meanwhile, had flown to Knoxville for the opening of the 1982 World's Fair, where GHK had sponsored a natural gas exhibit. From there he was to leave for New York to spend the remainder of the weekend with David O'D. Kennedy, and to meet Monday with Meg Sipperly and Dick Pinney for breakfast at the Mayfair Regent Hotel on Park Avenue to pursue the discussions on the horse loans.

Patterson was always able to reach Hefner, whether he was on a yacht in the Caribbean or at a hotel in New York. That Sunday evening, Patterson phoned Hefner at his hotel and said he would be joining him for breakfast with the Chase officers. "He said he was chartering a plane and would fly all night," Hefner recalled. Hefner was disappointed that Patterson was going to intrude upon what was to be a private breakfast meeting with the Chase officers. "I knew I wouldn't be able to cover the topics I wanted to," Hefner said later. Not knowing he was soon to be the proud "owner" of Mahan Rowsey, Inc., Hefner flew on to Washington after the Monday morning meeting and then to Europe for a meeting with investors there.

The following week, Busey discovered that another $1 million would be needed to pay off liens on the rigs. He told Patterson that any change in the note should be approved by Hefner, but Patterson later authorized the alteration of the note from $30.3 million to $31.3 million by signing his familiar squiggle next to the new figure. According to Busey, Patterson advised him that Hefner said it was all right.

The closing was set for May 6. Randy Dunn, Mahan Rowsey's accountant, and Frankie and Billy were in the bank. They were in a hurry to complete the transaction, for obvious reasons, and while Patterson darted in and out of his office, Mahan and Rowsey signed on the dotted line. There was, however, something unusual about this closing that set it apart from most such deals: the buyer wasn't there. Mahan and Rowsey, as one Penn Square officer recalled, "were on cloud nine." But the officer was baffled as to why Hefner wasn't represented, and the lawyers urged Patterson not to fund the loan until the documents could be executed by Hefner's people. Patterson laughed and said, "I don't give a damn about documents."

Hefner and his personal accountant, Robert Livingston, would testify later that Livingston was not present at the closing. Patterson, however, insisted that the accountant was in the bank but didn't want to be in the same room with Mahan and Rowsey because he was afraid of them. Patterson aide Bill Kingston later testified that Patterson told him at the closing that the rigs were sold.

At 12:37 P.M. on May 7, an advice was received on Penn Square's IBM incoming wire terminal from the Chase Manhattan Bank crediting Hefner's QOL with $31.3 million. The same day, the identical amount was debited to QOL, and $24.3 million was wired back to Chase paying off the note to Mahan Rowsey Drilling. Another $6 million was transmitted to Michigan National, and $1 million to lienholders. Seafirst, which had an $8 million stake in the rigs, got nothing. And Chase Manhattan wound up with a $31.3 million participation in Hefner's No Sub S Corporation doing business as QOL.

"Essentially what they did was put the money in the Hefner account and yank it right out again," said one participant in the transaction.

The next week, Mahan Rowsey's Jack Star called to say he had heard Hefner bought Mahan Rowsey. Core Oil and Gas, a major drilling contractor that did work for Hefner, was concerned that their client might be branching out into the drilling business and competing with them head to head. But Hefner had always made a point of hiring others to do the actual drilling, and Hefner's people told all callers that they had no intention of doing anything but operating wells.

It was about this time that Hefner began to feel a heightened sense of uneasiness over Penn Square, and the millions in GHK money sitting in the bank. When he recovered from his initial shock over the death of Tom Heritage, he began to sense there would be some "tumultuous" changes. "I didn't know exactly what, how they were going to happen," he said later. "We would often say around here that when we had big deposits we'd put them in other institutions. Patterson and Jennings would comment, 'We want those.' Then we'd talk about it and we'd say, 'Well, you're making all these loans, and we don't see how you can—we are concerned about it.' And they'd give us a lecture on how sound the bank was. They'd be very good salesmen about it. And we'd all sit around here afterward and say, 'Well, okay, we are working on this and other projects with him, we'll go ahead and put the deposits there, because in the end, Continental will have to take them over anyway.' "

As for Mahan Rowsey, even Frankie Mahan seemed to perceive that the company was in trouble. Billy Rowsey, however, was reportedly preoccupied with the designs for the company's new offices at the just-completed Energy Center, where Mahan Rowsey was to be a major tenant. The top four officers of the company were to occupy an entire floor of the building, which was to include a bar, gym, showers, and other executive perquisites.

Perhaps Billy's optimism was fueled by the revenue the company had begun to receive from two gas wells that had been plugged for over a year. On May 13, Mahan Rowsey began selling gas to Kerr-McGee from the two wells, receiving perhaps $2,000 a day for production from each of them. But instead of drilling themselves out of trouble, Mahan Rowsey had punched into an underground gas storage reservoir belonging to the Oklahoma Natural Gas company and was siphoning off the utility's gas. Months later, Mahan Rowsey was enjoined from selling any more gas from the wells.

Even after unloading Mahan Rowsey, Chase Manhattan was still working under an enormous administrative burden because of the large number of "nickel and dime" credits they had bought. At the same time, Continental, which never hesitated to take big loans, was growing uneasy with Aggie Oil. So, in May, Meg Sipperly bought Aggie Oil from Penn Square in exchange for a number of small loans, some of which were having problems, effectively consolidating her headaches in one lump sum. Continental was happy because it was rid of Aggie. Chase was happy because it had reduced its paperwork headaches. And Penn Square was relieved because it had pacified two key correspondents, at least for the moment.

While all the horse trading was going on, the oil and gas industry in Oklahoma had virtually come to a standstill. As one oilman put it, "The industry collapsed while we were out to lunch." On May 1, 1982, the Transcontinental Gas Pipeline Corporation issued an announcement that did not affect Penn Square and its borrowers in a direct sense, since Transco did not buy gas in Oklahoma. But the fallout from it would ultimately be devastating for many of Penn Square's borrowers. Early in 1982 it became clear to Transco officials that demand was slackening and that spring and summer demand would likely be below normal. Transco had begun to study its markets intensively a year before by looking at the relationship between oil and gas prices and analyzing the impact that a dollar for dollar drop in the price of crude would have on the price of gas. By year-end 1981, Transco was convinced that the gas market would come under severe pressure in the months ahead.

Recognizing that it would become the pariah of the petroleum industry virtually overnight, Transco issued a press release on May 1 stating that it would exercise its right to "market out" of those contracts containing that clause. The result was that Transco rolled its prices back from an average of $8.50 per MCF to $5 for all production.

Producers and other pipelines were livid. They asserted that Transco's cash squeeze was unique to Transco because the company was a high-cost producer. But it was only a matter of weeks before other major pipelines followed the leader and exercised their market outs as well.

An-Son's Carl Anderson, Jr., recalls "Everybody was incensed at such an idea. They said, 'Shame on Transco, we'll never sell them any more gas.' " But in retrospect, Anderson says, "It was a step that needed to be taken."

Meanwhile, the underlying weakness in the oil and gas market finally caught up with the closely followed Hughes Rig Count, and that key indicator plummeted from 828 rigs active in Oklahoma in April to 753 in May.

A TERRIFIC BUNCH
OF GUYS

THE *AMERICAN BANKER* ARTICLE, A SPATE OF OTHER NEGATIVE publicity, and fresh rumors about new Continental problem credits unleashed a rash of phone calls to the Chicago giant from analysts and the press. The concerns of the investment community couldn't be ignored any longer. Roger Anderson concluded that it was time to break bread with Wall Street.

The Four Seasons was Continental's favorite New York restaurant. It was fitting that the nation's flashiest, most aggressive banking organization should do most of its New York entertaining at one of the city's most expensive four-star restaurants. Continental invited twelve of the top Wall Street analysts, six on the sell side and six on the buy side, to the meeting. Ken Puglisi was there from Keefe, Bruyette and Woods. Jim Wooden came from Merrill Lynch. Jay Ehlen represented Goldman, Sachs, Continental's investment banker. On the buy side, Nancy Young came from Prudential, one of the largest single holders of Continental stock. Morgan and Citibank sent their bank analysts.

Normally, in good or even in bad years, such dinners are cordial affairs, with analysts addressing the bank chairman and senior executives with polite deference. They are generally complimentary when earnings are up, sympathetic when results are down. But on May 11, the analysts felt nothing but frustration at the answers to their questions about Continental's loan portfolio. One analyst barked at Anderson from across the long, narrow table in a private dining room, "You haven't told us anything. Your disclosure is worse than anyone's."

Another analyst queried George Baker about Continental's relationship with Penn Square and the story in the *American Banker*. Baker replied, "They're terrific people. We do a lot of business with them." Asked how much of the $1 billion in Penn Square loans was bought in the last year, Baker cleared his throat and said, "One-half." At the meeting, Baker assured Anderson that the Penn Square loans were being handled directly and were being scrutinized as carefully as conventional direct loans.

There was little interest in staying around for after-dinner drinks. "It was," as one guest put it later, "a frustrating dinner. We all kept bringing up the same question, and they kept answering it in the same way." Asked why Continental had gotten itself into so many questionable, high-risk deals, Anderson, who did most of the talking, replied, "When you go as far as we have, you're going to have some problems."

Baker truly may have believed the Penn Square people were terrific, but the next day Anderson called a meeting to discuss whether Lytle should be terminated over his personal loans from Penn Square. There was, apparently, no discussion of the more serious issue, the Penn Square portfolio. And once again, Anderson showed himself to be a man apparently incapable of making a decision. He concluded the meeting by telling his staff that he wanted to give the matter further consideration. Finally, on May 17, Baker and Anderson agreed to keep Lytle but withhold any salary increases and bonuses for two years.

The same day Baker and Anderson were meeting with the analysts, Seattle First's Bill Jenkins arrived at quite a different decision about the future of his bank's top salesman, John Boyd. In a memo to Boyd, Jenkins advised him that his salary had been increased by $15,000 to $85,000 as of May 1. "Thanks for your continuing contribution to the success of our bank," Jenkins wrote. "Your efforts are sincerely appreciated; keep up the good work!" Harvey Gillis, who had replaced John Nelson in March as head of world banking, was trying to wrap his arms around his new assignment, and particularly around his new subordinate, John Boyd. Although Jaehning had shaken hands with some of Seafirst's major Oklahoma borrowers in February, no one, including Boyd, had looked closely at the people who were responsible for the phenomenal growth of Seattle First National Bank. In May Gillis insisted on attending a loan signing and was aghast at what he saw. The customer's shirt was open to the navel, and he wore two gold chains around his neck. This wasn't the type of client Seafirst was accustomed to doing business with.

Gillis ordered Boyd to do what Penn Square had made a business of doing: participating out energy loans. In the next two months,

Boyd would attempt not only to unload loans that Seafirst had bought from Penn Square but also oil and gas credits it had originated itself. The response from other banks was not encouraging. Indeed, bankers who were offered both Penn Square and Seafirst loans said later that those Seafirst had booked on its own were just as bad or worse than the ones they had seen from Penn Square. And later Gillis dispatched a team of lending officers from Seattle to take a closer look at Penn Square's loan files. As one former Seafirst officer recalls, Boyd said, "I've been told to get rid of some credits."

"We were in disbelief over what happened. We were in awe of opening up files on $1 million credits and seeing less than one page of double spaced comments," the former officer said. By this time, the energy division had cracked the billion-dollar mark in loans outstanding. Yet, according to Boyd, Jaehning turned down an opportunity in May to extend a $40 million prime rate credit to a major oil company in order to do more prime plus deals with the Oklahomans.

Meanwhile, concern was mounting, albeit belatedly, among members of the Penn Square board on the condition of their bank. At one directors' loan committee meeting, Burks and Randolph were said to have gotten into a heated discussion with Jennings and Patterson over bad energy loans. The meeting ended abruptly when Jennings said, "Let's break this off, we're not getting anywhere," and stormed out of the room. "We never had another one after that," said one director. "Burks was tremendously concerned. He tried awfully hard to get some tighter controls on lending." Burks should have been concerned. Of all the members of the board, his business management credentials, which included a Harvard MBA degree, were perhaps the most impressive. Burks was one of the largest holders of Penn Square stock, and he had borrowed heavily from the upstream banks, namely Seafirst, to finance his multitudinous real estate ventures.

According to one director, in the spring of 1982 the board tried to "put some handcuffs on Patterson. There was a suspicion he was giving us a snow job." At a meeting in May, according to the director, Patterson "couldn't answer questions to our satisfaction. We said we wouldn't put our initials on these loans. We said we don't think we have the whole story. Patterson was supposed to brief us, but the briefing raised more questions than it answered. I guess I should have gotten out at that time," the director said. "I wanted to sell my stock first. But by that time people would have said I traded on insider information, and I would have lost the same amount anyway.

"Patterson," the director went on, "never had a lot of facts. It was just a lot of BS. The more questions we asked the more we had. Things didn't add up in our simple minds. He always talked about the value of the minerals in the ground, or some damn thing. He'd say, 'We've got two times the value of the minerals in the ground.' " One loan, according to the director, was based on stock in a company that was valued at twenty times earnings, and "I knew that the values of those companies had decreased."

Patterson's response invariably was "The Continental people have looked at all this." "When we criticized, the answer was who were we to question the judgment of the Continentals and Chase Manhattans?" The directors' loan committee was actually viewed by the directors themselves as being little more than a rubber stamp for the bank's officers. It was supposed to meet every two weeks, but in reality it rarely did, according to one member. Despite these concerns, the board of directors, at the May 18 meeting, empowered a senior bank officer to make loans to Patterson up to $3 million.

The same day the analysts were dining with the Continental brass and Boyd was getting his raise, Clifton Poole in Dallas was phoning the Comptroller's special projects unit in Washington to warn of "major problems" arising in Penn Square's portfolio. Poole informed his superiors, "National bank examiner Plunk has discussed no more than 10 percent of the loan portfolio and undoubtedly he is worried about the welfare of this institution, particularly since the bank relies heavily on purchased liquidity and must maintain industry confidence." Washington and Dallas agreed that the situation in Oklahoma should be followed on a daily basis.

In reviewing a bank's condition, the first thing examiners do is to compare their classifications with the bank's on a sample of loans. If the two reviews arrive at significantly different conclusions, and if the examiners determine that they can't depend on the bank for accurate information, they normally undertake a systematic review of the portfolio. At the time the bank examiners came in, Penn Square's own loan review staff hadn't yet gotten around to reviewing energy loans, which made up 80% of the portfolio.

The examiners' problems were compounded by the deplorable condition of the credit files and the lack of financial statements, engineering evaluations, and other documentation. They were so bad that each examiner wound up spending an average of one day on each loan. The $2.7 billion question was, "Is it only the documentation that's bad, or is that just the first layer sitting on top of a bad credit?"

In previous exams, the regulators' review of the underlying collateral was superficial at best. According to sources familiar with these procedures, the examiners had earlier checked only lists of collateral, or a random sample of the collateral for loans above a certain threshold. They would not make that mistake this time.

The relationship between Plunk and Patterson got off to a shaky start, and never improved. Patterson and Jeff Callard had never been especially cooperative with the bank's own internal review group, and they were even less so with the Feds. Callard had always told the bank's loan review people, "If you want something, you have to get Patterson's okay," according to a former officer. "I got the feeling that Plunk, after weeks of being stalled on his requests for engineering data, had begun to smell a rat," John Baldwin recalled. Plunk apparently aired his frustrations to Beller, who told the oil and gas chief, "Before you leave tonight I want this material on the examiners' desks."

These obstacles had thrown the examiners behind schedule. At one early meeting between Patterson and Plunk, Patterson openly displayed what one officer described as an "I don't like examiners" attitude.

Plunk told Patterson, "We've got some loans we'd like to go over with you."

"Well, shoot," Patterson replied, "none of them are classifiable. C'mon, tell me about them."

The first loan Plunk mentioned was a lending limit violation. Patterson jumped straight up out of his chair, and began walking around in circles, puffing on his cigar.

"Of all the loans in the bank you're going to pick on, to start off with this one. There's nothing wrong with this loan," Patterson barked. "We've involved all our attorneys, all of our borrowers' attorneys, and nobody thinks it's a violation of law." Plunk remained calm and collected. The upshot of the conversation was that the examiners would go back and look at it. And, in fact, it turned out to be a violation.

Plunk said, "I can see now we can't make much headway. I can see we'll just have to meet with you later." In his dealings with the examiners, Patterson went to great lengths not to answer questions directly, according to numerous Penn Square officers. As John Baldwin remembers it, Plunk asked Patterson, "Where are your financial statements?"

"This is a collateral loan, I don't need financial statements," Patterson retorted. "I can count on one hand the number of borrowers in this bank that have financial statements. I know the collateral and the collateral is there."

"Well, how do you know it's there?" Plunk asked.

"I know because I had engineers do it."

Plunk replied, "Where's the engineering report?"

"Well, if you'd leave us alone with all your other requests for engineering, I'd get you a copy of this one."

Plunk said, "Don't you have anything I can look at?"

Patterson opened up his cabinets and there were drawers crammed full of papers. Patterson pulled one from the stack and said angrily, "Here's your goddamn engineering report."

Things finally reached the point where the belligerent energy czar wouldn't meet with the examiners at all. As Baldwin recalled it, "Plunk would call over to make an appointment, and Patterson would claim to be with a customer, or on his way out of town. It got so bad that on one occasion Beller accompanied Plunk to Patterson's office, where he was meeting with some customers. Beller excused the customers and sat Patterson down.

" 'Don't get up,' Beller told Patterson, 'until you've had a complete meeting with these people and told them everything they want to know.' " Patterson started to argue with Beller, who quickly cut him off. "You can either sit down with these people, or you can leave. If you leave, don't come back." The meetings after that were highly charged. "Patterson was set off by the slightest innuendo that something was wrong, or that a loan would be charged off." Said another former officer, "He pissed them off royally. He stood them up, kept them waiting, and became more and more defiant."

Examiners become highly suspicious when a loan officer does not fully cooperate with them. Bankers who have been through many examinations say that if they level with the examiners about a loan, the examiners won't charge it off out of spite. The examiner looks for some assurance that the banker plans to correct the problem so it won't show up as a bad loan on his next visit.

In mid-May, Plunk began to appreciate for perhaps the first time the magnitude of Penn Square's ties to the upstream banks, and Dallas, at long last, advised Washington about the volume of these participations to Continental, as well as the involvement of Chase Manhattan. Yet once again, as a subsequent audit of the Comptroller's performance would show, communication within the far-flung agency broke down. Washington neglected, for example, to inform examiners at Chase about the Penn Square connection.

Chase's domestic institutions department, meanwhile, was grappling with other problems. On Monday, May 17, in the first of many financial shocks that would hit Chase Manhattan in the summer of 1982, Drysdale Government Securities defaulted on a $160 million interest payment, leaving Chase with a potential $135 million after-tax loss. Chase had initially refused to cover Drysdale's obligations to other Wall Street firms, but finally yielded after jawboning from Fed chairman Paul Volcker.

And before that tumultuous week was out, a federal grand jury would charge four men, including two former Chase Manhattan vice-presidents, with stealing about $18 million from the bank, through unsecured loans ostensibly made to defunct south Florida real estate projects. To some observers, these incidents pointed to a serious breakdown in control at the nation's third largest bank.

House Banking Committee Chairman Fernand St Germain later took Clifton Poole to task for not taking action as soon as the dimensions of the problem became known. "I've heard words like procedures and visitations," the feisty congressman said. "It all sounds very medical. Now frankly, you know, if a doctor is examining a patient and finds out he's got double pneumonia and a hernia and might also have ingrown toenails, does he just keep examining and making tests or does he start treating immediately?"

But Poole responded that treatment wouldn't have helped at that stage. "The horse was already out of the barn," he said, asserting that it would have been impossible for him to remove an officer based on an incomplete exam. "We have to be extremely careful in documenting our position and knowing where we stand and having conclusive information," the by-the-book regulator replied.

As the Patterson–Plunk relationship deteriorated, Plunk told Baldwin, "If Patterson won't visit with us and defend these loans, we'll just make our own independent appraisal on the loan quality based upon the information we've got on hand now. We're not going to chase everybody down in the bank to get all the information. If we call a loan a loss, it's going to be a loss. If it subsequently turns out you can collect it, you can credit it to your loan loss reserve. I'm not going to stay around here and play games and fight with him about providing information." So ultimately the examiners made an independent assessment of Patterson's loans without ever talking with Patterson.

Patterson threatened to sell loans upstream if Plunk classified them. In one meeting, Plunk began by asking about one of Beep Jennings's close business associates. "Well, what about Lammerts?" Plunk asked. Patterson retorted, "If you classify that loan, I'll call a correspondent bank right now and they'll buy it from me. It's that good of a loan. If it's on their books you can't classify it."

"You'd better not do that," Plunk warned. "If you do, we'll call our office in the city where the correspondent bank is and give them a list of the names and the loan at the correspondent will be classified."

"Well, you just do what you think you've got to do," Patterson said. Patterson carried out his threat. Loans were classified and the following day they were shipped out of the bank.

Patterson, who acquaintances said revered Jennings as a godlike figure, was becoming defiant even toward his mentor. On at least one occasion, Beller brought what he regarded as a lack of respect for the chairman to Jenning's attention. "I created this Frankenstein and I'll deal with it," Jennings growled. At one point, Jennings told an associate, "Bill keeps pissing in my ear and telling me its rainwater."

Mahan Rowsey, not surprisingly, became an object of the examiner's curiosity, and, in Patterson's absence, they attempted to get their questions answered by junior officers.

"The questions you're asking me you're going to have to ask Patterson," one officer said.

"We know, we've tried but we can't."

The examiners, according to one officer, seemed to be trying to learn about oil and gas loans as they were examining the bank. They would, he said, "come to us with questions about what these reserve figures mean or those figures mean."

In the early stages of the exam, the regulators were fairly open with their counterparts at the bank, sharing information on certain credits and giving them preliminary lists of loan classifications. Then they turned secretive. "They'd come around and ask you for information," said one officer, "but they dried up as far as telling us anything."

But even Patterson seemed to recognize that his free-lending days were numbered. At a meeting with his staff on past due loans, Patterson said, "Boys, we got to think about collecting loans. The top priority is collecting, not disbursing.

"If you don't like me sitting on you, you can take me out in the parking lot and whip my ass," he joked to a group of officers.

One strapping young banker smiled and said, "I'll take you out in the parking lot."

"I'll go home and get my .45 first," Patterson shot back.

Many Penn Square borrowers were not accustomed to paying back. In breaking the bad news to a customer, one officer said, "Okay, the fun's over. You need to start paying debt service."

"Are you kidding? I can't pay. My rigs are stacked."

The balls Patterson had adroitly kept in the air for so long were beginning to drop. Deals with upstream banks were coming unglued. And the money wasn't there when it was supposed to be. Patterson, who had always been regarded as crazy because of his bizarre antics, was also known as someone who did what he said he was going to do. Borrowers released checks to creditors and transferred property with the assurance from Patterson that the money would be there. Now the oilies were getting edgy because the deals weren't getting funded.

In April 1982 Jim Nicholas's Citation Drilling Company, according to allegations in a lawsuit filed in U.S. District Court in Oklahoma City, approached Gary Fleming's Sarah Drilling, another Penn Square customer, about selling a deep gas rig for $2.8 million. Nicholas contacted Patterson to see if Sarah had a line of credit that would permit a cash sale. Patterson, Nicholas asserted, assured him that Penn Square would lend Sarah the money to pay Nicholas for the rig, and on that basis a contract was signed for the sale. The loan was partially funded. A downpayment of $280,000 was made to Citation, and Penn Square had taken an origination fee of $50,000 on the deal. But, by late May, Penn Square had not completed the financing despite dozens of assurances from Patterson. According to Jim's brother, N.H. "Bud" Nicholas, "Patterson looked me right in the eyes and said, 'I got it handled and sold upstream and will fund it the first of next week.'

" 'Give the man the rig. I will take care of it the first of this week. Give him the rig,' " Patterson allegedly said. Citation turned the rig over to Sarah Drilling, but Penn Square was unable to fund the rest of the loan.

One of the notes that was called belonged to Tom Hoshall, an Oklahoma City horseman and entrepreneur who had bought a top-ranked thoroughbred race horse, aptly named Money Lender for $860,000 with a loan from Tom Orr. It was an interest-only note with the principal due in two years. In 1973, Money Lender ranked second among two-year-old thoroughbreds as a money earner, and in 1981 Horsall bred the horse to 140 mares.

Then in late May an officer of Penn Square phoned to inform him that the loan was due, contending that the note was in fact a one-year note. Presumably under orders from the national bank examiners, Penn Square demanded additional collateral from Hoshall, who says he agreed to the request providing the bank lent him an additional $250,000 for his energy conservation business. "We were at the lawyer's office Saturday," Hoshall recalls, "and I told them I wanted to make a draw for $250,000. They said okay, they'd do it on Monday." At that time, a Penn Square officer gave Hoshall a deposit slip for $250,000. Hoshall asked for a cashier's check and was told he could come back Tuesday and get it. When he returned, Penn Square officer Mike Chandler showed him a cashier's check for $225,000, but told him that he was under orders not to release it. "You either give me the check or give me my collateral back," Hoshall insisted. He says he received neither.

In the three years or so Coach Barry Switzer, Lee Allan Smith, and Sed Kennedy had been borrowing from Penn Square for their various oil and gas investments and other personal and business ventures, they had made only token principal and interest payments, and most of those had been done by renewing or rolling over previous notes. On May 26, six of those notes were rolled over into one big $870,000 loan; it would, of course, look better to the examiners if they saw one spanking new $870,000 note secured by oil and gas mortgages than a potpourri of nickel and dime notes that had never been paid down. A week later, Patterson extended another "balloon" note to the coach and his friends, this one for $200,000, supposedly for more oil and gas investments at prime plus one. Switzer and his partners would claim later that Patterson lent them money to make investments he recommended, telling them they would miss a good bet if they didn't take his advice. By financing oil and gas companies as well as their investors, Penn Square compounded its risk many times over.

And Longhorn, which had been kept alive by upstreaming of interest, was coming under mounting pressure from angry investors. Attorney Ray Erlach had just joined the San Francisco law firm of Hunt, Gram and Epstein, which employed his two brothers, after working for the general counsel of the city of San Francisco. On May 14, one of the firm's partners called him into a meeting and handed him his first case. A client had been informed by Penn Square that it intended to call standby letters of credit that the client had obtained in connection with an investment in a drilling program. The client, investment adviser Bob Agnew, complained that Penn Square and Longhorn Oil, the promoters, promised that the letters of credit would never have to be called. Erlach later found that hundreds of others in at least a half-dozen other states felt they had been deceived, and had obtained court orders blocking Penn Square from demanding the funds.

On May 19 Erlach called Penn Square general counsel John Preston to introduce himself and inform the abrasive Penn Square lawyer of his intentions. "We'll fight you on this thing," Preston said without hinting that he was alarmed at Erlach's actions. The next day, a state judge found enough possible evidence of fraud and misrepresentation to justify issuing a temporary restraining order preventing the collection of the funds.

With Chase, Seafirst, and Northern Trust no longer taking new deals in any significant volume, Patterson was pressed to hold on to the banks he had. Of all the participants, no one was more pleased than Michigan National. They were getting paid, and that was all that seemed to matter. It was not hard to see why. In what would amount to one of many stop-gap, finger-in-the-dike measures that momentarily, at least, fooled the examiners as well as Michigan National, Patterson allegedly ordered two debits to account #19-1987 at Van Buren Oil Investment, one of several companies owned by Jere Sturgis. One debit, for $145,479.45, was to pay interest owed to Michigan National, and the other was for $111,495.89, to pay Penn Square Bank. The transactions, however, created an overdraft, and a new loan of $257,471.62. At the time, the would-be billionaire had a balance of $114.80 in the account of his flagship company.

The pressures of trying to juggle dozens of faltering deals had begun to take their toll on Bill Patterson. Patterson, associates said, began limping, his face was washed out, and the occasional twitch he had in one eye acted up with increasing frequency. In the first half of 1982, Patterson was hospitalized at least once for dehydration and exhaustion. Former employees recall that a physician appeared almost daily at the bank to give vitamin B12 shots to the oil and gas chief and his staff.

But there was nothing a doctor could do to stop the bleeding of deposits. The street talk about Penn Square and the acute need of borrowers for funds prompted them to draw down their accounts at a dramatic rate in May, forcing Penn Square to rely increasingly on their money-broker friends in California and New York. In January the brokers had supplied the bank with a nominal $20 million, but by May the volume of hot money rose to well over $150 million. The relationships with these money brokers was haphazard at best. Federal documents show that, until March, the transactions were conducted "without the benefit of formal contracts." Investigators would later find that two bank officers sometimes even bid against each other for the same funds on the same day, and on at least one occasion an officer in the oil and gas division offered a rate on a particular certificate of deposit that was four points higher than the rate then being offered by an operations division officer.

* * *

Cliff Poole and Roy Jackson, his FDIC counterpart in Dallas, had never been particularly fond of each other, and consequently never enjoyed a close working relationship. There is a long-standing rivalry between the Office of the Comptroller of the Currency and the Federal Deposit Insurance Corporation, a rivalry that starts at the highest echelons in Washington and filters down to the regional offices, coloring the personal as well as working relationships between individuals at both agencies. It is a rift that stems in part from the overlapping roles the OCC and the FDIC play in the United States dual banking system. The Comptroller supervises some of the nation's largest institutions, whereas the FDIC shares supervisory responsibility with state regulatory agencies of the thousands of "Mom and Pop" institutions found in small communities throughout the nation. The FDIC, under the Federal Deposit Insurance Act, guarantees deposits below a certain ceiling of all but a few of the nation's commercial banks, and becomes the receiver of institutions declared insolvent by the Comptroller or state banking agency. But the FDIC never has to pull the trigger.

In part, the distance between Poole and Jackson stems from these overlapping but disparate rolls. The FDIC accuses the Comptroller of being too lax in its capital requirements. The Comptroller charges that the FDIC doesn't understand big banks. And both agencies claim that the other is inept at spotting troubled institutions.

Roy Jackson of the FDIC is a man known for speaking his mind, particularly on the subject of Cliff Poole. At a meeting of FDIC regional administrators that spring, Jackson was critical of Poole's skill at identifying problem banks, and his remarks found their way back to Poole. On May 21, a peeved Cliff Poole phoned Jackson to lambast him about the statements. Poole would later contend under congressional questioning that he called Jackson to put him on notice about Penn Square, but insiders say that Penn Square's troubles were mentioned only at the tail-end of the conversation.

Observed a former examiner, "There was no dialogue between the two."

In late May Marion Bauman, Penn Square's outside counsel, received a call from a senior officer at the bank. The current exam was not going particularly well, the officer reported, and the Comptroller's office was concerned about some "technical problems," involving upstreamed interest and legal lending limits. There were, for example, some loans that were supposed to be sold to the correspondents, but because they were not sold the same day they were booked, they were cited as violations. Penn Square needed Bauman to run interference with the regulators.

About the same time, Deputy Comptroller Bill Martin and Comptroller of the Currency Todd Conover, a former consultant with McKinsey & Co. who was appointed to his post in December, were on a flight from Washington to the West Coast for a regional staff meeting. In the midst of a conversation on other agency business, Conover asked Martin, "How are things at Penn Square?" Martin replied, "I think the bank is busted."

TRUST ME,
TRUST ME

O N JUNE 2, 1982, ROBERT A. HEFNER 3RD FOUND THAT HE OWNED a company he didn't want, and Joe Dan Trigg had a new partner and didn't know it.

That afternoon, Robert Livingston, Hefner's personal accountant, stopped at Penn Square Bank and was asked by Bill Kingston to sign some papers. He signed the documents and took them back to GHK's offices. Hefner was out of town, and Livingston brought them to the attention of Henry "Boots" Taliaferro.

"What in the world is this?" Taliaferro demanded. "This is for the acquisition of a company. There's no way we can enter into this."

One of Hefner's idiosyncrasies was his insistence on the separation of his gas side and his personal side. When he returned, he was furious that Livingston would show something from his personal side to Taliaferro, who worked for the gas side. He told Livingston, "If you can't honor the separation of the personal side and the gas side, I'll find someone who can." Curiously, Hefner seemed to be more concerned about this "separation of church and state" than the fact that he apparently owned a company with $60 million in debts and hardly any income.

The same day Patterson ordered an oil and gas division secretary, Charmane Wright, to "pay off a Tureaud debt so it would be hard to trace." Using a blank note signed earlier by oilman Joe Dan Trigg, she booked a $4 million loan in his name and the next day applied the proceeds to overdrafts and delinquencies of Ken Tureaud at Penn Square and two upstream banks. Meanwhile, the new loan to Trigg was shipped upstream to John Lytle at Continental Illinois. Patterson smiled and told Wright, "Trigg has a partner and doesn't know it."

Just a few days earlier, senior vice-president Tom Swineford had written a scorching memo reporting on what a terrible credit risk Tureaud was.

"It shocked me," Wright admitted later in sworn testimony. "I felt it was a very dangerous thing to do."

By this time Steve Plunk and his staff had returned to Oklahoma City from a week-long training seminar and began reporting to Dallas what federal investigators would later call "additional serious developments" at Penn Square Bank. Almost at the hour that Patterson was working his magic with Hefner, Trigg, and Ken Tureaud, Dallas instructed Plunk to broaden the "specialized" exam into a full-blown "generalized" one and alerted officials at the Federal Reserve Bank in Kansas City to the mounting problems in Oklahoma City.

Plunk was also turning up more evidence of deception by Penn Square. He had discovered the infamous "other assets" account, the catch-all for upstreamed interest, notifying Dallas about his findings. By early June, those officers who were familiar with the modus operandi of bank examiners began to feel uneasy when they realized their guests had overstayed their welcome, although a few chalked up the examiners' extended visit to their well-known preference for working in Oklahoma City rather than the small rural towns where most of Oklahoma's banks are located. To many former Penn Square officers it appeared at one point that the examiners were preparing to wrap up their assignment at Penn Square, but that they then stumbled upon or were steered to certain loans that prompted them to unpack their bags and dig even deeper into the portfolio. This interpretation of events was later denied by the regulators.

Despite the presence of the examiners, the shell game continued. For example, delinquent loans were converted to checking account overdrafts, a stop-gap measure at best because examiners are supposed to ascertain not only that loans are repaid but also how they are repaid. In the case of the Second Geostratic Energy Drilling Program of New York, Penn Square took the liberty of debiting its checking account for $65,442.69 to keep the examiners from charging the loan off, and even advised the company in a letter that it was doing just that.

While apparently oblivious to these developments, the key players at Continental Illinois (Baker, Anderson, Perkins, and Miller) were meeting in Chicago to review the first-quarter performance of Baker's general banking services unit. Bergman had submitted a report analyzing the quality of his portfolio, and noted that some $893 million in loans had not been assigned recent quality ratings. These loans had escaped the bank's review mechanism because the lending officers had not supplied enough information or documentation on the loans for the loan administration unit to determine their quality. According to Continental's special litigation report, Bergman acknowledged that Penn Square loans constituted "the largest part" of the $893 million, but assured his superiors that 90% of those loans would ultimately receive a satisfactory rating. The unrated loans were popping out on the bank's documentation exception list, which Lytle persistently contended was inaccurate. It was not until June 1982, fifteen months after Kathy Kenefick wrote her first memo suggesting that Carl Swan's Longhorn Oil and Gas was not making money, that the nation's seventh largest bank officially identified a single Penn Square loan as being of poor quality.

The next day Hefner, Patterson, and GHK president Larry Ray met in the spacious living room of Hefner's rambling northwest Oklahoma City home. Ray told Patterson he was very upset that he'd gotten Hefner to buy Mahan Rowsey. "What is going on?" Ray asked Patterson. "You know better than that."

Patterson was agitated. He assured the two men, as he had in April, that he had obtained purchase agreements from other companies to buy the Mahan Rowsey rigs, and that Jennings knew all about it.

Patterson began to cry. He lashed out at Hefner and Ray, telling them, "You can either trust me or sue me or sue the bank." Patterson stormed out of Hefner's house, sobbing and shouting, "Trust me. You just have to trust me."

Hefner later said, "Bill was traveling a lot. I was worried about his health. I was worried about his overreaction." The next day, Patterson met with an official of a drilling company to talk about the rigs. "I signed a letter of intent," the oilman said, "but the terms were not stated. I never heard any more about the deal after June 4."

In early June, about the time Plunk and his exam crew returned from the seminar, the Comptroller made his first request for additional capital—$7 million, according to Beller—and Jennings handed Patterson the task of raising it.

As Patterson recalled the assignment, Jennings told him, "Go out and raise $5 million." Later in the month, when he called to announce that he'd raised the $5 million, "Beller told me it was $10 million." And later, Patterson said, "I got to the phone and Beller told me, 'Raise $15 million.'"

In late May Patterson approached Eldon Beller asking him if he knew anyone who wanted to sell some Penn Square stock. Without a moment's hesitation, Beller replied, "I do." So on June 15 Patterson paid Beller $81,000 for his Penn Square holdings. In addition, Patterson paid Jennings $200,000 for Penn Square stock Jennings was selling on behalf of another investor. By this time, Patterson was the second-largest holder of First Penn Corporation stock, having spent $1 million of his wife's inheritance on these purchases, according to trial testimony.

Hefner wasn't the only customer feeling a growing uneasiness over Penn Square. Carl Anderson and his An-Son Corporation were never particularly comfortable with the move from First National. Operational mistakes were more the rule than the exception and paperwork was slow and incomplete. "We got the very clear impression that we were dealing with a bank that was not paying attention to business," Anderson explained later. An-Son, like many oil and gas companies, maintained numerous drilling fund, payroll, and revenue accounts at the bank, and frequently transferred funds from one account to another, only to discover later that the debits and credits often weren't posted correctly. But they were downright furious when a new employee bounced a bushelful of An-Son checks to suppliers and oil and gas investors. As a result, An-Son demanded that Eldon Beller write letters of apology to each of the recipients, explaining that the error was entirely Penn Square's. But the letters would not be enough to get Penn Square off the hook with An-Son, and the company quietly began making plans to return to First National.

First National, meanwhile, was well aware of Penn Square's growing problems. Penn Square maintained an account at the First, which by this time was refusing to allow it to draw on anything but collected funds. "They'd try to draw down ledger balances from time to time," said Dale Mitchell. "They'd want to do some extraordinary Fed funds activity. It was obvious they needed money, particularly on Fridays. We just about stopped doing anything with them."

Bill Jennings was always a good draw on the lunch-hour business speakers circuit. His delivery was homey and down to earth; his message, to the point. In what would soon turn out to be a prophetic talk to the Oklahoma City Kiwanis Club, Jennings said that the economic climate in the United States suggested that it was time to "put the hay in the barn, to tighten belts and learn to make do." Jennings said he doubted that interest rates would come down much, if at all, by the end of the year. A two-point drop to 14% would be fantastic, he said, adding that he expected the prime to remain in the 15% to 16% range. "We still don't realize that the spending spree we have been on didn't involve just public spending," the Penn Square chairman said. "The corporate sector is over-borrowed, and there is far too much debt in this country." In fact, Jennings had helped to create more than his fair share of that debt himself. He went on to remark that the money supply had more than tripled in the previous twenty years, and that it had expanded faster in the six months before President Reagan took office than it had in thirty years. "Congress," he asserted, "has the lowest credibility in regard to fiscal policy than it has ever had."

Just a few days later, Jennings would have the opportunity to reiterate these themes not on the podium of a businessmen's club but on the fantail of a yacht in Big Bay, British Columbia. It was time, finally, for the big fishing trip that Gammie and Boyd had been planning for months. Originally, Boyd had not figured that his new boss, Harvey Gillis, would have any interest in going along on a salmon fishing trip with a boatload of Oklahoma oilmen, but he extended a perfunctory invitation nonetheless. Gillis, however, very much wanted to meet the people with whom Boyd was doing so much business. Seafirst president Dick Jaehning, ever the bean counter, reportedly questioned whether the extra $800 that it would cost to send Gillis along was worth it. Gillis insisted that it was.

In Oklahoma City, lawyer Jimmy Linn, whose reputation as a raconteur equaled or surpassed his prowess as a courtroom lawyer, was also invited on the outing. He is an avid fisherman who each year, like clockwork, treks to Alaska to cast for salmon. Linn was reluctant to make the trip to Big Bay, and had just about made up his mind to take a pass. But his wife argued that he needed a few days away from Oklahoma City, and Jennings and Patterson echoed her insistence. He decided he would go providing he could bring along his best friend, oilman Bill Saxon, whose company was already known to be in severe financial difficulty. At the time, Linn was attempting to negotiate a financial package with Penn Square and Continental that would bail out the troubled Saxon Oil Company—a deal that would never get done.

There were those on the expedition who were not fond of one of the guests, J.D. Allen, but as things turned out, they did not have to put up with him for very long. J.D. apologized to the group for having to leave early, explaining rather smugly that he was joining Vice

President George Bush in San Francisco to fly back east with him aboard Air Force Two.

It is unlikely that the Vice President was aware that his guest on the flight, the man who had so generously supported the Reagan–Bush ticket two years earlier, was essentially flat broke. A week earlier, after national bank examiner Plunk had informed Patterson that he intended to classify all of the J.D. Allen debt at Penn Square Bank, Patterson allegedly booked a loan for nearly $2.4 million to Allen's Continental Resources and used the proceeds to pay off a slew of loans to other J.D. Allen entities that were wallowing in red ink. A mere $562,000 was used for the benefit of Continental Resources itself, officials of the company claimed later.

On his way to his car to leave on the fishing trip, Patterson asked Kingston not to repeat anything about the Hefner QOL transaction to Jennings, according to Kingston's testimony in the subsequent criminal trial of Bill Patterson.

Jennings, Bobby Hefner IV, a geologist with his father's company who is known to his friends as "Ivey," Carl Swan and J.D. Allen, Linn, and the other Oklahomans arrived in Seattle on Wednesday, June 9. The next day, they boarded chartered seaplanes for the two-hour flight to Stuart Island north of Vancouver. As the seaplanes touched down in Big Bay, one member of the party spotted Culpepper's 85-foot yacht and exclaimed in exasperation, "Oh, no, look who's here." Culpepper greeted the oilmen and bankers with offerings of fried fish he'd caught earlier that day.

Gammie had orchestrated the entire outing, renting the cabins and assembling groups of three oilmen and bankers who would fish together in 18-foot outboard motorboats that formed a small flotilla clustering around the mother ship, Gammie's *Golden Delicious*. The fishing was not going all that well, and between nibbles they talked of those elusive salmon, the weak Pacific Northwest economy, Canada, and the Reagan administration's economic program.

Gammie and Saxon were on the same boat. As the Apple King glanced up at the bald eagles soaring over the glacier mountains, Saxon said, "Turn the engines off, gentlemen. I want you to look at those glaciers. If anyone tells you that there's no Maker, you can just bring him here."

To some of the guests on the trip, Patterson seemed unusually quiet—even melancholy. He went out fishing, came in and had a few drinks, one fisherman said, but sometimes was nowhere to be found. "One night it was raining like hell," recalled one guest. "Swan and Gammie were trying to keep a fire going. Someone commented, 'Bill just isn't his usual self.' "

On the afterdeck of Gammie's 60-foot yacht, Jennings, a Democrat, lectured the guests on the evils of Reaganomics. "Reagan," he said, "is going to break the country." But after dinner one evening, Seafirst chairman Bill Jenkins spoke in a more convivial tone when he stood up at the campfire and expressed his pride at being able to share the "heat of the fires of the Pacific Northwest with our friends from Oklahoma."

Bill Patterson and Bill Jennings had so indoctrinated their subordinates in the techniques of go-go banking that the shell game in bad loans continued unabated even while they were fishing. Ken Tureaud received what was to be his last loan from Penn Square Bank, a $900,000 advance that was used to make some of his huge overdrafts go away, so that Patterson could report to the board the following week that overdrafts had been reduced. According to an affidavit signed later by a federal bank examiner, at least $20,000 of those funds were deposited in Tureaud's personal account in Tulsa.

On the Wednesday that the Oklahomans departed for Big Bay, Plunk learned that Penn Square had made good on its earlier threat to sell classified loans upstream. According to federal documents, a top Washington official of the Comptroller's office instructed Dallas to threaten Penn Square with a cease and desist order, which Plunk carried out that same day. The following Monday, Dallas reiterated the warning, but the practice persisted nonetheless.

Penn Square was once again facing its end of the quarter liquidity crisis, one that this time around would prove to be of insurmountable dimensions. In the second quarter of 1982, the bank booked a whopping $300 million in loans, much of which consisted of advances on existing lines of credit. Weakening oil and gas prices were forcing customers to draw on their credit lines at an accelerating rate, and Penn Square and its upstream correspondents were in turn under mounting pressure to fund these demands.

Penn Square was being squeezed on both sides of the balance sheet. On the asset side, the bank was finding takers for its loans harder to come by. With its traditional buyers of participations becoming less enthusiastic, Penn Square once again turned its holding company, the First Penn Corporation, into what amounted to another upstream bank to buy loan participations from itself, using the proceeds from the sale of commercial paper to fund the questionable transactions. First Penn, little more than a shell entity, became a dumping ground for more than $10 million in what became known as Penn Square's "bad meat" loans, consisting of a dozen or so participations made to such notables as Mahan Rowsey, Ken Tureaud, and Jere Sturgis. The bad meat was booked as assets on the balance sheet of First Penn, joining such items as the $77,250 in country club memberships, Pendola, the bank's condominium retreat on Grand Lake, and even a gas well in the Fiji Islands.

While the Oklahomans were fishing, the examiners finally pinned down the exposure of most of the major upstream banks. Continental had bought a staggering $1 billion; Seafirst was in for $366 million; Chase had $267 million; Michigan National had bought $172 million, and was still buying.

Meanwhile, officials of the Comptroller of the Currency in Dallas once again notified their counterparts at Region 13 in San Francisco about the involvement of Seattle First with Penn Square. Once again, the warnings were ignored. In New Orleans, however, national bank examiners swooped down on Hibernia National Bank after being contacted by Dallas. Plunk was also pleading with his superiors for more help, and when the fishermen returned from British Columbia, they could have counted two more official-looking strangers in the already congested subterranean corridors of Penn Square Bank.

Big Bay was to be Bill Patterson's last hurrah. Bad loans aside, Penn Square's flamboyant energy lender had committed one of banking's unpardonable sins: he had infuriated examiners Steve Plunk and Joe Hooks by not making himself available to them, to the point where the two officials had to lie in wait for Patterson for hours and ambush him when he left his office.

Penn Square's efforts to clean up its loan documentation and paperwork now approached the panic stage. It was not enough to send participation certificates by overnight mail to Northern Trust and Continental to obtain the signatures of bank officers; the bank examiners were demanding the missing documents immediately. In many instances, participation certificates on multimillion-dollar loans hadn't been completed at all; in other cases, the loan amount shown on the document was incorrect.

The ban on private jet travel for Penn Square employees handed down months earlier would have to be waived for two correspondent department clerks, Tammy Cox and Jo Ann Sherrick. Neither of the two young women was used to traveling on private jets. But on a Friday early in the month, they were chauffeured to Wiley Post Airport, where they boarded a customer's private jet for Chicago. The plane came fully equipped with food, drinks, playing cards, and magazines. Cox, carrying her bundle of unsigned Penn Square loan participations, disembarked at Midway Airport. There she hopped a cab to Continental, got the signatures, and then took another cab to the Northern Trust Company a few blocks away. Meanwhile, the jet had taken off again for New York and Chase Manhattan with Sherrick aboard. She rushed to One Chase Manhattan Plaza with her certificates, and then returned immediately to the plane, which took off again for Chicago, picked up Cox, and landed in Oklahoma City by midnight.

Logistically, the trip went well. The business side, however, was less than a total success. Officers at Continental were by this time reluctant to affix their signatures to a number of the loans, even though they had previously committed themselves to the transactions.

The week after Patterson and company returned from the fishing trip, Patterson told Lytle the federal examiners were demanding that Penn Square charge off some $10 million in bad loans. Lytle, according to testimony he later gave before a congressional committee, asked Patterson if any of the loans were Continental participations. Patterson said no, and informed Lytle that the bank had arranged for investors to cover the $10 million through stock purchases.

On June 14, Peat, Marwick, Mitchell followed up its earlier report with an assessment of the bank's operational problems. Among other recommendations, the Big Eight accounting firm suggested that operations personnel "clean checks of all staples, rubber bands, paper clips and other fasteners prior to delivery to the proof department." It noted that as of December 31, 1981, the bank was about two months behind in preparing its daily loan reconciliation. By the June 15 board meeting, General Randolph had become so anxious over the bank's condition that he considered resigning. Randolph challenged Patterson on his personal participation in an oil and gas venture that did business with the bank. "I've got to question whether this raises a conflict of interest. I have doubts as to whether officers of the bank should be investing in borrowers' activities," Randolph said. Jennings responded by saying that the ethics committee reviewed the participation of bank officers in such arrangements, as well as their borrowings, noting that two outside directors would be added to the committee. This was the first time Randolph and the directors had ever heard of an ethics committee.

"What about the values on those Culpepper rigs?" Randolph inquired. "When were those values calculated?"

"In 1981," Patterson told the general.

"I've heard about some rigs that have sold at auction for as little as 25 percent of their 1981 values," Randolph informed Patterson.

Swan, who was as vulnerable as anyone in the oil patch to a rig glut, added that even new rigs could now be bought for as little as 70% of their 1981 value.

By this time, rumors of Cliff Culpepper's problems with his Arkansas investors had already made the rounds in Oklahoma.

Patterson told the board that the loans to himself, Clifford, and J.D. Hodges would be sold shortly to Walter Heller and Company, and that his loan of $770,000 was being warehoused by the First Penn Corporation awaiting a decision by the Federal Reserve on whether it was in compliance with regulations. Jennings reported to the board that there were no new borrowers on the May loan list and that new loan customers were being taken on only if their loans could profitably be sold upstream.

Greg Cook, a director who once served as a special assistant to the secretary of Health, Education and Welfare, was also edgy. He asked about the adequacy of the amount of director and officer liability coverage.

"I'll look into the possibility of having it increased," Preston said, and promised to report back to the board on the matter at a later meeting.

Beller told the board that the examiners had been thorough in their review. "They're digging deep," he said, "because of the highly publicized problems of the energy industry." Beller added that the examiners had made numerous allegations of lending limit violations.

"None of you has ever assented knowingly to any lending limit violations," Jennings told the board, almost as if he sensed that the minutes of the meetings would later become public record. "Several of you in fact asked in previous meetings whether the lending limit was being violated and were assured it was not. You were told policies were instituted to prohibit such violations."

"The charge-off list is incomplete," Beller told the board, "and we expect heavy criticisms and classifications."

"Do you think it will amount to more than $5 million?" someone inquired.

"It'll be that amount and likely more," Beller said. In fact, it was already that amount—and $5 million more.

But to Frank Murphy Penn Square was still the same old shopping center bank he knew and loved. His mind was not on the millions of J.D. Allen and Carl Swan loans on the past due list, but on one woman's past due installment loan. While several directors smiled, he noted that foreclosure proceedings would begin shortly against the diamond ring she had put up as collateral.

In mid-June Patterson was under pressure from the examiners to demonstrate that Maximo Moorings was a legitimate transaction, and he obtained letters from Hodges and Clifford that appeared to confirm that they wanted to own a piece of the marina.

On June 15 "Bill called and said he wanted a letter typed," Clifford said. "He asked that I sign it and bring it back," saying that he needed additional documentation for the collateral file. Clifford accompanied Patterson to the bank and gave it to some people in the conference room. "This is Hal Clifford's letter for the Maximo Moorings file," Patterson told the visitors. "This is Hal Clifford." The people in the room appeared to be bank examiners, the husky oilman said later. "I felt like I was an object of interest."

The chaos that reigned in that tiny shopping center bank in June was mirrored in the Oklahoma oil and gas industry. The signs of a virtual collapse in the oil and gas industry were irrefutable even to the dullest observers. Yet events, once set in motion, often have to play themselves out to their ultimate, and sometimes absurd, conclusion. So it was with rig-up parties. There is a long lead time on the construction of rigs, particularly those used in drilling for deep gas, so that a unit ordered in a moment of optimism might end up being delivered long after euphoria has been replaced by gloom. In June the GHK Companies and the Parker Drilling Company celebrated the completion of Parker's Rig 201, the world's largest land drilling rig, an awesome tool large enough to penetrate almost ten miles into the earth, and constructed with enough steel to build a 10-story building. Within months, however, many of these massive steel skeletons would wind up stacked along the highways leading to Oklahoma City, a predicament that later inspired one correspondent banker to compose a parody on Rodgers and Hammerstein's song, "Oklahoma":

> "Oklahoma, where rigs stand rusting in the rain,
> Where oil and gas is a pain in the ass
> And our money's gone right down the drain."

THE DOWNHILL
SLIDE

IN THE GOOD TIMES CHASE MANHATTAN BANK WAS A FAIRLY EASY
touch. But with hundreds of branches scattered around the five
boroughs of New York City, one of the toughest banking markets in
the nation, Chase chairman Willard Butcher and president Tom
Labrecque had learned how to play hardball. In June, when the
game started to get rough, the team from New York was among the
first in the door at the Penn Square Bank of Oklahoma City.

According to testimony in the Patterson trial, concerned officers
from Chase Manhattan forced a loan buyback agreement on Penn
Square that included the $450,000 loan to Allen Senall for the plane
that couldn't fly. Penn Square was not averse to buying back loans,
of course, as long as it could immediately unload them on other
banks. For all practical purposes, however, that policy ended in late
spring as the correspondents' appetites for Penn Square loans dried
up. Patterson's relationships with the officers of the upstream banks
were the main hold he had on Beep Jennings and Penn Square
Bank, but now those ties were rapidly deteriorating as the bankers
came to realize that their participations were often worth little more
than the paper they were written on.

As for Chase, one former Penn Square officer described officials of
the big New York bank as being furious over loans made to Jere
Sturgis that they felt were in violation of the $42 million loan agree-
ment signed back in November. A member of the Chase advance
team recalled that the sense of urgency intensified when officers in
New York began poring over loan files and found them lacking in
security agreements and other basic documentation. Chase had
made repeated requests for the missing documentation, requests
that were never adequately fulfilled. When the Chase delegation
landed in Oklahoma City, they discovered the reason for this: the

documentation and the collateral simply didn't exist. "When we first got there," said one member of the Chase team, "we were treated royally." Penn Square officers bought lunch for its guests and arranged for it to be delivered to the bank's conference room. But the Chase people quickly concluded that the youthful Penn Square oil and gas lenders "were a bunch of college kids playing at banking," as the Chase representative put it. "They all ran around looking like a bunch of preppies. Everybody had an alligator or polo shirt on and cute little polo socks," he said derisively.

Whatever good feelings had existed between Chase and Penn Square quickly evaporated as institutional banking chief Richard Higgerson and his colleagues became more familiar with the Penn Square loan files. As John Baldwin saw it, "They made themselves very obnoxious." At one point, he recalled, Higgerson summoned him to the board room and said, in the presence of other Chase officers, "I've been looking at this borrower's financial statements. Do you realize that two years ago this borrower was insolvent?"

"I haven't looked at that loan file. I haven't made my own evaluation of it," Baldwin responded.

"Well, let me ask you a question," Higgerson said, "How could you in all good conscience continue to sell us participations in this loan?"

"I looked him in the eye and said, 'Listen, do you buy everything that's peddled at your front door? You're one of the biggest banks in the world. You've got more analysts and engineers than we've got employees here at the bank. It would appear to me that someone in your office had a hard time saying no. I can't explain why the loans were peddled to you. But I don't ever recall any time here at Penn Square that you ever turned down a loan. It would appear to me someone at your office is so greedy for earnings they'll take anything. I don't think it's a fair question for you to ask me why we kept selling you these loans. You didn't have to buy a one of them.' "

The heads of the bankers drooped and they stared vacantly down at their loan files. Higgerson just shrugged his shoulders.

Upstream bank officers with whom Penn Square employees were accustomed to socializing suddenly became cool and aloof. One of them was described as a "big Irishman, a fun guy, who always used to go drinking with us." A former Penn Square loan officer recalled his abrupt change in behavior: "There were no more casual greetings, no more 'Hi, what's going on?' "

At Chicago's Northern Trust Company, the Gray Lady of LaSalle

Street, the bank with barely any experience with charged-off loans, top officials were pressuring those responsible for the Penn Square credits to get interest collected before the end of the quarter to avoid having to report them as nonperforming loans on the mid-1982 financial statements.

It was about this time that Penn Square began cozying up to banks it had brushed off earlier in the year. Back in February, for example, Patterson had complained to Rainier National's Sally Jewell about her tendency to ask a lot of questions and her insistence on taking just a few small participations at a time. Rainier never bought any loans from Penn Square, but Jewell recalled that in June a Penn Square officer told her, "Oh, you're good guys. You can ask questions. You can take onesies and twosies." Meanwhile, Penn Square loan salesmen hit the road in a last-ditch attempt to bring new correspondents into the fold. One officer recalls promoting Penn Square participations to prospective "co-banks" as a way of "putting some pep in your portfolio." In other matters, Penn Square was calling in its chips. One officer was assigned to mail out letters to banks demanding payment on letters of credit they had issued to investors in the Longhorn drilling programs, and others were scrambling to county courthouses to collateralize their flimsy security positions on undocumented loans.

For Penn Square borrowers, the well had begun to run dry. One of them was Bruce Heafitz, a New York oil and gas investor who had borrowed millions from the bank to make investments in the deep gas wells of other Penn Square borrowers, such as Robert Hefner. Heafitz showed up at the bank in mid-June to borrow another $40 million using existing gas wells as collateral. He signed an assortment of forms indicating his intention to secure his loan with interests in several Apache and GHK wells, but found the days of fast money had come to a close. "The line-up for easy loans ended with the guy just ahead of me," Heafitz would later tell a reporter. "I made a good try. I just ran out of time," he said.

The sun also set on Sunrise Drilling, which defaulted on a $1 million note on June 15, $900,000 of which had been sold to Michigan National Bank.

The day after the board meeting, Sandy Hamilton, a Penn Square officer, issued a memo to all energy loan officers listing the bank's lending limit violators. It was a who's who of the new oilies; some even made it twice. There was, of course, Hal Clifford, who was always ready to bail his friend Bill Patterson out of a bad deal, as well as his flagship company, Clifford Resources; "General Bull

Moose" Lammerts, Jennings's pal and business associate; former detective Terry Felt's Alpha Energy; Bill Jenkins of the False Hopes Drilling Fund; Ken Turcaud and his Saket Petroleum; then there was Frankie Mahan individually, and Mahan Rowsey; and of course, Bobby Hefner, and even An-Son. Cliff Culpepper, always striving for social acceptance, had at long last made it on one of the most exclusive lists ever compiled in Oklahoma City. Hamilton wrote: "It is imperative that we correct any existing violations immediately, and do not create additional violations in the future. Your cooperation and any information you may deem helpful in monitoring our legal lending limit is greatly appreciated."

In the midst of this mounting crisis, it was essential that Penn Square maintain a business as usual appearance within the small fraternity of oil and gas lenders. So that afternoon, Penn Square officers Greg Odean and Dennis Winget, the former Continental officer who now worked for Penn Square, boarded a flight for San Francisco to wave Penn Square's flag at the American Petroleum Institute's annual finance and accounting conference. Bill Patterson had usually led the bank's delegation to the meeting, which brings together the chief financial officers from the major oil companies and independent producers and top lending officers from the banks that lend them money. It is typically a sumptuous affair, with banks like Citibank, Morgan, and Credit Lyonnais throwing lavish shrimp and crab legs receptions for their customers, or prospective customers.

When Odean arrived at San Francisco airport, he dutifully called his office to see if he had any messages. There were three, all from Eldon Beller. One was from Eldon at the bank's main number; the second was from Eldon at his private extension. And the third was from Beller at home. Odean had never before gotten a message to call Beller at home and realized this must be a matter of some urgency.

When Odean phoned, Beller said, "Greg, you'd better sit down for this one. You're the new head of the oil and gas division." Odean was not given to displays of emotion. He matter-of-factly asked Beller if he should fly back to Oklahoma City instead of attending the conference.

Beller answered in his steady Oklahoma drawl, "No, Greg, go on to the meeting. Relax and enjoy San Francisco. You'll have plenty to do when you get back here." Patterson had been stripped of his lending authority, reportedly at the insistence of the examiners, and was assigned full-time to try to keep Penn Square's increasingly fragile correspondent network intact. Later, Beep Jennings would say that it "would be unfair to say the examiners ordered it" but that they "certainly welcomed" this outcome.

One observer later asserted that with Patterson out of the lending business, Penn Square was left with "one of the best staffs of any bank its size in the country." Moreover, he theorized that as a result of the bank's ninth inning efforts to identify and properly document bad loans, it may have, in an ironic twist, pointed up problems that hastened its own demise.

By the time Odean reached San Francisco, examiners had identified losses approaching $20 million without even looking at the loans in the $1 million range. It was about this time that Dallas authorized the examiners on the scene to look "below the line," to reduce the size of the loans sampled to $1 million, a move that would point Plunk and his colleagues to millions of dollars more in nickel and dime loans on which neither interest nor principal had ever been paid.

But even in the last couple of weeks in June, regulators did not expect the bank to fail. Jennings and other board members were assuring the Feds that they could easily replace the $20 million in losses identified by then with capital contributions from stockholders financed by Continental Illinois. One former regulator said, "We felt comfortable they could cover it." Likewise, Penn Square staff believed that the most serious issue was possible lending limit violations, one of the "technical" matters that attorney Marion Bauman had been called to help out on in May.

In those last weeks of June there were so many examiners in the bank's subbasement that they were having difficulty pulling all their numbers together. But to one former senior officer, it seemed "like the examiners were intent on finding whatever it took to close the bank."

Clearly oblivious that anything was amiss in Oklahoma City, Professional Asset Management, the California money broker, continued to steer big ticket deposits into the crumbling shopping center bank. And in Poughkeepsie, New York, money managers at the IBM Poughkeepsie Employees Credit Union, as was their practice, obtained bid quotes on 180-day certificates of deposits from a half-dozen or so institutions. Curiously, while Penn Square was, as usual, bidding on short-term certificates of deposit, it was well within the market on 180-day paper, just a smidgen above the 15.05% being offered by New York's Manny Hanny. It is always easier for a money manager to say "roll it over," than to process all the paperwork that is required to sell the CDs of one institution and to buy those of another. So on June 18, IBM in Poughkeepsie decided to roll with Penn Square Bank of Oklahoma City.

While dozens of credit unions and borrowers were still operating in the dark in their dealings with Penn Square, others had reason to be suspicious. At one point, a top official of the Comptroller's office in Dallas received a phone call from a San Francisco banker who was preparing to lend to six customers in a gas well syndication secured by a Penn Square letter of credit. The banker explained that he was calling to verify a rumor that a restriction was to be placed on the volume of letters of credit Penn Square could issue. Regulators are hamstrung by stringent rules forbidding them to discuss the affairs of a "live" bank with the media or the general public. They do, however, write a lot of memos to their files, and in one such message the Dallas official stated, "I told him that I had little to suggest other than checking with the bank itself, reviewing its call report, and other financial information, as well as checking with correspondents. I did relay to him that I had seen a couple of articles of late in the trade press."

On Friday, June 18, the Comptroller's Dallas regional office, mindful of the bad meat loans sold to the holding company, felt it was about time to bring in the Kansas City Fed. Among other duties, the Fed is charged with supervising bank holding companies, which included the First Penn Corporation.

In Washington, the Federal Reserve Board was sifting through a computer data file of the nation's banks as part of an effort undertaken four times a year to identify banks exhibiting deviant financial behavior. The Fed looks at a variety of ratios and measures of performance, including growth and earnings. Among the more than 200 institutions that merited closer attention, Penn Square stood out at the top of the list.

A senior official of the Comptroller's office in Washington mentioned to his opposite number at the Federal Reserve Board that "maybe it would be a good idea to look at the holding company." The Fed official replied, "Yeah, that would be a good idea." So on June 24, four examiners were dispatched from Kansas City to join the growing numbers of their colleagues from the Office of the Comptroller of the Currency.

While Odean was representing Penn Square at the API conference, Bobby Hefner was attending an international gas conference in Lausanne, Switzerland. Hefner returned to Oklahoma City on June 20, and the next day inspected the debit and credit memos showing the $31.3 million that had breezed in and out of his account in early May. The gas man was furious. He called Jennings and arranged to meet with him the next morning for breakfast. At a later meeting, Jennings assured Hefner that the bank would assume full liability for the transaction, according to Hefner's testimony at Patterson's trial.

As Greg Odean was returning to Oklahoma City to face the biggest challenge of his banking career, George Baker of Continental Illinois was taking off from Chicago for a seven-day trip to Madrid, where he planned to call on major corporate and banking clients. Had he known the reasons for the management change that had taken effect that day at Penn Square, and its implications for his own institution, it is likely he would have remained in Chicago.

Almost immediately after the announcement of Odean's appointment, Penn Square oil and gas officers began lining up outside Odean's door with a mountain of credit problems they had been afraid to bring to Bill Patterson. One of these problems was George Rodman, Inc., which had borrowed more than $30 million at Patterson's urging. Newly completed reserve studies pointed to a "most aggressive" loan value of no more than $21 million. And interest obligations alone amounted to almost half a million dollars a month, nearly as much as the company's oil and gas income.

In a separate deal, Patterson had instructed a subordinate to arrange for Hal Clifford to take over yet another shaky company, but the officer stalled Patterson and never completed the transaction. "Hal doesn't need any more bad deals," Odean remarked with characteristic understatement on learning of the impending transaction. Indeed, Clifford, the man who by his own admission was a "debt junkie," was already in the hole for millions.

As reserve values were downvalued based on current oil and gas prices and more realistic production expectations, horrified Penn Square officers whispered to each other, "Oh, my God, we're under water." Up until the last week of June, Beep Jennings, the perennial optimist, maintained that the properties of his borrowers, many of whom were oldtime friends, had some value. "He was kind of numb," said a former senior officer, when confronted in those last weeks with the reality that his cronies and their companies were essentially insolvent. Jennings, like Patterson, had operated under the philosophy that any problem could be fixed with more money. But when he finally woke up to the condition of the bank, there would be no more rolling old loans into new ones. The music had stopped for Beep Jennings and Penn Square Bank.

Jennings was "floored with the situation," said Bill Kingston later. "He put his head in his hands and shook his head."

It was not until the week of June 21 that the Dallas regional office of the Comptroller's office acknowledged the mess Plunk and Hooks were dealing with up in Oklahoma City by sending them more help. In the previous weeks, Plunk had phoned in requests for more examiners, and Dallas had responded by dispatching barely enough new bodies to replace those who had left. This time, Poole sent seven new examiners to Oklahoma City, prompting one former Penn Square employee to remark, "They were like rabbits. They seemed to multiply overnight."

By that day, Penn Square's tiny headquarters building and oil and gas division were swarming with strangers from out of town—so many in fact, that the bank's narrow corridors looked like the line for tickets at the Superbowl. It was hard to ignore that there was a problem. Meanwhile, rumors had begun to circulate in the top echelons of the Oklahoma City banking community that Penn Square outside attorney Marion Bauman had made a trip to Dallas on behalf of two institutional clients: one with some $4 million in losses, and the other with $100 million.

Seafirst had also dispatched a team to Oklahoma City. Toward the end of June, its leader reported to Seattle, "Some of this collateral isn't what it was represented to be. We're sharing it with other banks." Worse still, he told his superiors there that Penn Square's losses were approaching its equity. Boyd, however, had returned to Big Bay to join Bill Gammie on his yacht for the annual fishing derby. The fun was interrupted when he received a call from Seattle ordering him to return to headquarters immediately. Boyd was agitated and apologized to Gammie for having to cut short his stay. "I've got to get the hell out of here. I've got to go down there for a few days and get things straightened out," he said.

Ironically, Boyd had been approached by Beep Jennings to become the chief credit officer of Penn Square Bank, and was planning a trip to Oklahoma with his wife to look for a house and attend the wedding of Eldon Beller's daughter. Seafirst's top management soon became suspicious that what they were telling Boyd was quickly getting back to Patterson. It was time, they concluded, to shut Boyd out of the loop.

On Friday, June 25, the numbers that were arriving from Oklahoma City at the Washington headquarters of the Comptroller of the Currency began to cause the regulators a great deal of concern. For one thing, the participations were larger than they had previously believed, and on that day they learned the awesome dimensions of the bank's collateral deficiencies. Three thousand exceptions had now been identified. When loans are based more on the collat-

eral than the cash flow, "that scares you to death," said one observer. The regulators wondered how much Chase, Seafirst, and the
other banks knew about the underlying collateral if Penn Square itself knew little or nothing. Moreover, the regulators suspected that
Penn Square officials were attempting to misrepresent and cover up
their losses. For these reasons, the Comptroller decided that Friday
to notify the upstream banks the following week and place them
under examination, and to impose the long overdue cease and desist
order on Penn Square Bank.

In Oklahoma City, the order not to pay checks on overdrawn customers finally had some impact. One of the first affected was Frank
Mahan, who was having some work done on his Nichols Hills home.
Penn Square had bounced some $10,000 in checks Mahan had writ-
ten to painters and contractors, and Mahan was hysterical. Shouting
"Where's that fat faggot Kingston?" he stormed into the oil and gas
division headquarters and barged into the office of Greg Odean
while the new oil and gas chief was on the phone with some colleagues on another problem. Odean interrupted the conversation
and angrily ordered Mahan out of his office. Mahan swept the
papers from Odean's desk and the two men struggled briefly until
other loan officers rushed in to separate them. Mahan finally left the
bank in a rage and told Kingston, according to subsequent court
testimony, "If I had my way, you and Mr. Patterson would be dead
in the morning."

Mahan, who didn't have enough money in his account to pay his
house painter, had, with his partner Billy Rowsey, ordered a new jet,
which was due to arrive from Israel shortly, according to Bill Kingston. Penn Square, Kingston testified later, had advanced them $1.4
million as a downpayment, which would be forfeited if they didn't
take possession of the plane by July. Apparently recognizing the futility of his situation, Mahan reportedly said, "I guess we'd better
sell the plane. But not before we go to Grand Lake."

According to John Boyd, who had arrived in Oklahoma, Patterson's wife called him at his hotel after hearing of the implied death
threats. She was worried about Mahan and asked Boyd to come over
because she was alone and didn't know how to use a gun. Shortly
thereafter, the police arrived at the Patterson home. The Mahan incident was not the only shocker that Boyd heard about that weekend. Patterson later surprised Boyd by telling him and his wife
about "one of his deals" with Continental vice-president John Lytle.

Over the weekend, Jennings visited Hefner at his home and acknowledged to him that "Penn Square is in severe trouble. Some

amount," Jennings said, "would be written off." According to subsequent testimony by Hefner, Jennings thought the charge offs would amount to something between $15 million and $30 million, and he wanted Hefner, as a major borrower, to pledge $5 million toward a $30 million capital infusion. Hefner signed a note on the spot for the $5 million.

Penn Square's officers, in the meantime, were looking for a way to reverse transactions like the $31.3 million QOL note and Maxima Moorings.

While these discussions were continuing, a perplexed Joe Dan Trigg received his June bank statement and found that $4 million had come in and gone out of his account on June 2. Trigg called his accountant and asked, "What did you do with $4 million?"

TAKING THE HEAT

B Y MONDAY, JUNE 28, SEVERAL OFFICERS IN THE BANK SHARED John Baldwin's feeling that something catastrophic was about to happen. Baldwin had been placed in charge of loan administration in April, and his department was, he felt, "just on the verge of functioning like a loan administration department should." He added, "I remember a growing sense of despair and helplessness in the staff. It was a sense of—what's going on?—we don't know what's going on—what should we be doing?

"It was a full-time job just keeping the staff motivated and doing their day-to-day work for the bank." Baldwin recalled walking through the lobby and "looking at all the other employees in the bank knowing what I knew was going on, and knowing that they didn't know. I remember seeing tellers and lobby personnel there and feeling very, very sorry for those people. They didn't know what was happening, and what was coming.

"I did, or had a good feel for it," he said, "but I couldn't just go out in the lobby and make a speech to everybody."

Greg Odean's premonitions prompted him to remove his stereo cassette tapes from his bank car early in that week. And Phil Busey drafted a memorandum to John Preston on defalcation, a word whose meaning he'd had to look up in the dictionary two weeks earlier.

Tammy Cox reported to work at the correspondent division that Monday, not thinking it would be different from any other day in her three-year career with Penn Square Bank. One of Cox's duties was to phone upstream banks to advise them that a customer wanted to borrow on a line of credit, and to request that the upstream bank advance its portion of those funds. Occasionally, she would encounter minor hitches, such as questions about the number of the note that was being funded, or other clerical or operational problems, but when she phoned her contact at Chase Manhattan

Bank that morning to ask for advances on certain credits, she was told, "We can't send you any." Confused, she phoned another upstream correspondent and was greeted with the same response. Chase, Continental, and Seafirst, all had tightened the noose around Penn Square Bank. They had taken what is in banking a drastic step: they had stopped funding on the lines of credit of their correspondent bank's customers.

Banks can fail for a number of reasons. Sometimes they collapse when bad loans exceed capital, or equity. In simple terms, uncollectible loans are charged off or deducted from capital. When capital runs out, the bank is said to have a book insolvency. It can also suffer from a liquidity insolvency, where the bank, through depositor withdrawals, simply runs out of money. Beep Jennings was faced with both possibilities, and his lending officers were frantically trying to find enough good loans to exchange for cash at the Federal Reserve Bank of Kansas City.

With Penn Square's sources of funding drying up, bank officials put in an urgent call to the Federal Reserve Bank of Kansas City requesting an advance of $15 million from the discount window. (The Federal Reserve window is the lender of last resort to banks short of funds. It will take a bank's assets—loans, government securities, bonds—and then lend the bank say, 75% of the face value of these assets for a few days. But the Fed gets nasty when a bank has to come to the window too often, and it is fussy about what it accepts as collateral.)

For the Fed officials to assess Penn Square's liquidity needs, it needed more information than it was able to obtain in a three-day visit. It needed access to the examination data uncovered by the national bank examiners in their two-and-a-half-month stay to determine what collateral would be good enough to support a loan to Penn Square. Bank examiners aren't trained in interagency cooperation, and they initially refused to turn that data over to the Fed. "They seemed to be playing things awfully close to the vest," recalled a senior Fed official. Only after a series of high-level phone calls and a written directive from Comptroller Todd Conover did examiners on the scene relinquish the information, and on Wednesday, June 30, Penn Square went to the well for $20 million. "It was all supposed to be hush-hush," said one former employee.

That Monday the Comptroller of the Currency began gearing up for what they call a closure, summoning Steve Plunk and the regional staff to Washington for a meeting on Penn Square's condition. Conover, meanwhile, ordered his regional offices to drop whatever they were doing and take a look at Penn Square participations at Continental, Chase, and Seattle First.

Clifton Poole, once again, was on the phone to Roy Jackson, this time not to argue about who was better at spotting troubled banks but to inform him that the Comptroller would be slapping Penn Square with a cease and desist order at a meeting with the board in the middle of the week. Communication among the regional offices of the Comptroller of the Currency that supervised Penn Square's upstream banks was as bad, or worse, as that between the Comptroller and the FDIC. The Chicago region, which supervises Michigan National, was not advised until June 28 of the possibility of a failure, whereas the San Francisco office, which examines Seafirst, was regularly informed but did not take the warnings seriously.

Meanwhile, Bill Patterson, stripped of his lending authority, was out doing what he did best: raising money. He was calling in his chips, phoning customers he had helped put into business and imploring them to buy $200,000 blocks of stock that he hoped to finance with loans from the upstream banks. "We're calling on our major customers to see about investing in some Penn Square common stock," he told them, adding that the examiners were in the bank and had been "kind of mean." As reserves continued to be downvalued and loans charged off, there were those at Penn Square and at the upstream banks who were said to be praying for a full-scale war in the Middle East to prop up oil prices. One correspondent bank officer said, "We're all going to laugh about this because Iran and Iraq will bail out oil prices," according to a colleague.

The task of informing the heads of Continental, Chase, and Seafirst, soon to be dubbed "The Big Three" by the Comptroller's staff, fell on the shoulders of Bill Martin, who had recently been placed in charge of the supervision of multinational banks. Martin, a wiry, rather excitable man who was known around the agency for his bluntness, reached Anderson by phone in Chicago. "Mr. Anderson," he said, "you've got a problem, and it's called Penn Square." Martin suggested that Continental dispatch representatives to Washington immediately. That began what one former senior officer of Continental termed the "144-hour phone call." Over the next week, there were conference calls where four, six, and even up to sixteen people were on the line at the same time. "But," he said, "they all basically got nowhere."

Perkins happened to be on a business trip to Washington, and was dining with local clients at a restaurant there when Anderson got the call from Martin.

"Get Perkins," Anderson shouted to his secretary. "Where the hell is Perkins?" It would be several hours before a very frustrated Anderson would be able to locate his friend and associate, who was staying at a hotel in suburban Maryland. When Anderson finally reached him, he told him not to bother coming home. He was to remain in Washington for emergency meetings with the Comptroller and representatives of the other upstream banks.

After the Comptroller called Seattle First, Dick Jaehning told Boyd, "Penn Square is in serious trouble, how much do you have in the bank?"

"About $350 million," Boyd replied.

Jaehning gasped, "Oh, Jesus Christ," feigning ignorance, in Boyd's view, of the whole affair. Boyd was relieved of his responsibility, stuck in a conference room and, as he put it, "treated like persona non grata."

In Oklahoma City Penn Square officials were busy notifying the directors to be on hand for a Thursday morning emergency meeting with the national bank examiners. The good news was that this time they wouldn't have to travel to Dallas. Cliff Poole would come to them.

At the early meetings between the Comptroller of the Currency and the bankers, the OCC officials were seeking to supplement their knowledge of the Penn Square credits with input from the bankers, expecting that the big banks would certainly know more than they did about the underlying collateral and documentation backing up the loans. They were wrong.

The regulators then took the unusual step of releasing information to the upstream banks about each other's loans and the condition of Penn Square, exacting from them a pledge not to disclose the information to anyone and putting them on notice that they were being placed under special examination. "We were all a little shellshocked," said one regulator. In those initial conversations, the regulators sought some indication of their interest in recapitalizing Penn Square through loans to shareholders from Chase, Continental, and Seattle First.

Tuesday evening, June 29, Hefner and Jennings boarded a plane in Oklahoma City for Chicago. Hefner had two missions: the first was to close on a $40 million loan for his latest drilling venture, and the second, as he said later, was to "see about the survival of Penn Square Bank." Jennings would propose to Continental's Jerry Bergman that he approve some $17 million in stock loans to Penn Square customers that would recapitalize the teetering bank. That would certainly be, Jennings and Hefner figured, in Continental's own best interest.

On Wednesday morning Paul Homan, the husky, even-tempered Senior Deputy Comptroller of the Currency, phoned FDIC chairman Bill Isaac and told him, "We've got an emergency situation and I've got to talk with you right away." It was not a typical Paul Homan phone call. The two officials talked frequently about troubled banks, and Homan's telephone manner was normally flat and unemotional. This time, however, Isaac detected an urgency in Homan's voice that suggested to him that this situation was profoundly more serious than anything they had ever discussed. Homan arrived at FDIC headquarters about forty-five minutes later and immediately began describing Penn Square to Isaac, who didn't recall ever hearing of the bank before.

Examiners had been in the bank for three months, he said, and now had identified loan losses that approached the bank's capital. Isaac was unalarmed at this point, and indeed, he still wondered why Homan was so nervous about the possible failure of an institution with a mere $500 million in assets. As bank failures go, it would be larger than usual, Isaac thought, but not one that Homan couldn't work out over the phone with Jim Sexton, the FDIC's director of bank supervision, Homan's counterpart at the deposit-insuring agency.

But Homan went on to say that it was a far more serious situation than it seemed. Penn Square, he said, had sold a couple of billion dollars in loan participations to some of the nation's largest institutions. Homan formally requested that Isaac send examiners to Oklahoma City to assess the prospects for a takeover by another institution.

Isaac checked his calendar. A senior official from India's central bank was scheduled to pay a courtesy call in midmorning. That appointment would have to be canceled.

As soon as Homan left, the thirty-eight-year-old Isaac convened his senior staff in his office, briefed them on his conversation with Homan, and told them, "We've got a big problem on our hands."

Jim Davis, the FDIC's chief of liquidation, tapped Jim Hudson, a man whose testy disposition and hard-nosed approach to shutting down banks had earned him the nickname "Take No Prisoners" Hudson, to head up the Oklahoma operation. Whenever a large bank was on the brink of failure, Jim Hudson was assigned to handle it. Sexton, a tall, lanky Texan, selected a career examiner, Michael Newton, to oversee the possible payoff of insured deposits.

Hudson would perform the FDIC's undertaker's role: turning soft loans into hard cash; Newton would supervise the disbursement of checks to depositors.

There are several methods for disposing of failing banks. The preferred approach is to find a merger partner before it closes. This so-called open bank merger is the least disruptive approach, and is nearly transparent to the public because the bank continues to operate almost as if nothing had happened. A second approach is the "purchase and assumption transaction," the "P&A" in regulator's jargon. In this case, the bank is declared insolvent and the FDIC puts it up for bids. In effect, the winner buys the bank from the FDIC, keeping the deposits and obtaining the right to "cherry pick" from the failed bank's assets. Then the FDIC, as receiver, sells off, or liquidates, the remaining assets.

The third method, the deposit payoff, calls for the FDIC to pay off insured depositors and liquidate the bank's assets. In such a case, uninsured depositors are reimbursed along with other creditors from the proceeds derived from the liquidation of assets. Payoffs are rare; the largest such transaction had occurred in the 1971 failure of the $66.9 million-deposit Sharpston State Bank of Houston, Texas. The FDIC began to gear up for any of those possibilities.

Any one of them would clearly require the services of Don McKinley, a young FDIC attorney who had taken a couple of days off to move into a new townhouse he had just bought across the Potomac in suburban Arlington. On Tuesday, the water pump on his car broke and the mechanics at a local garage botched the job. When McKinley called in Wednesday to report he'd be late returning to the office, he was immediately switched over to Dan Persinger, deputy legal counsel. "I don't care how you get in or what it costs, an atomic bomb has hit the corporation. Take a limousine or a helicopter, but get in here," Persinger ordered.

In Dallas, Roy Jackson of the FDIC dispatched two examiners to Oklahoma City under false identities with a view toward moving into Penn Square on Thursday to determine the feasibility of a purchase and assumption. At the same time, Jackson began to compile a list of what turned into about twelve groups and individuals who might be in a position to take over Penn Square Bank. Oklahoma's unit banking laws, however, made such a possibility remote. Only under certain narrow conditions could another bank in Oklahoma merge with or acquire Penn Square, and those conditions did not exist in this case.

John Perkins arrived at the sixth-floor offices of Comptroller Todd

Conover. Lee Cross, the Comptroller's spokeswoman, spotted him getting off the elevator. Four years earlier, when he was president of the American Bankers Association, she had written a number of his speeches. Surprised that her former boss should be there, she asked, "What are you doing here, John?" But Perkins was in no mood to renew old acquaintances. "Something about some bank in Oklahoma," he mumbled, and stalked into Conover's office.

By Wednesday, the loan loss estimates were bouncing around like Ping-Pong balls, in part because of errors by the national bank examiners, but also because of the arcane legal question as to whether a loan participation constituted a security. One loss estimate of $41.6 million included $8.5 million in bad loans that were sold upstream after Plunk had warned Patterson against doing so. If participations were securities, they should have been counted as losses under Securities and Exchange Commission rules against deceptive securities sales. But the matter had never been decided in court, and the Comptroller, operating strictly by the book, gave Penn Square the benefit of what was a considerable degree of doubt. Had the examiners included the $8.5 million in the loss column, Penn Square would have been insolvent on Wednesday, June 30.

While Isaac and his staff were attempting to cope with the financial equivalent of a nuclear attack, Continental dispatched a damage control team consisting of auditors and attorneys to Oklahoma City. Meanwhile, Jennings was at Continental outlining to Bergman his efforts to raise new capital, noting that he had asked major customers to buy additional stock in the bank. Jennings's plan called for Continental to fund a portion of the loans, including Hefner's, and Michigan National would pick up the rest. "We need the money by Friday at the latest," Jennings insisted. Bergman was not encouraging, replying that there was simply no way to do the deal in two days.

Hefner was in and out of the office during the meeting, but at one point he mentioned that certificates of deposit belonging to his company had matured Tuesday and that more were coming due today. "Just lucky, I guess," Hefner shrugged. There were to be no more rollovers.

"I, for one, told Continental I wasn't going to do it unless it was part of an overall plan that they were a part of," Hefner said later. According to Hefner, Jennings agreed to step aside and put all of his assets in a pool and give it to him. "He said he'd do anything he could in the interest of the depositors, so he thought probably by then he was about wiped out anyway." The problem was that they "all of a sudden realized the pledges were coming from a lot of people who really didn't have the assets," Hefner said.

While Jennings was working on Bergman in Chicago, Bill Patterson had flown on to Lansing, Michigan, to try to hit up Perry Driggs at the Michigan National Bank for $16 million. That morning, Driggs called a meeting of the officers involved in reviewing the request, who said, "We don't have enough information. There appear to be some problems with Penn Square Bank because of the charge-offs."

Driggs called Rufus Burns at the Office of the Comptroller of the Currency in Chicago to see what he knew of the situation at Penn Square. Driggs got no indication from Burns of the seriousness of the problem and asked him, "Would you mind if I called Dallas myself?"

"We'd really prefer if you'd work through our office," Burns replied. According to Michigan National Bank sources, Burns said he'd call back if he learned anything, but never did.

Patterson later returned to Driggs's office, acknowledging to the tall, mild-mannered banker that there was a need for capital but that there were many wealthy friends of the bank who were interested in buying it outright or placing capital into it. During that conversation, Patterson admitted that there was to be a meeting with the board the next morning in Oklahoma City.

"Well, can we send Middeldorf down there to find out what's going on?" Driggs asked.

"Sure," Patterson replied.

Bank counsel Larry Gladchun and Perry Driggs probably did not fully appreciate the urgency of Patterson's request, not having been among the fortunate few already notified by the Comptroller about Penn Square's fragile condition. According to testimony he would later give to the House Committee on Banking, Finance and Urban Affairs, Driggs attempted to contact officials of the Comptroller of the Currency but was unable to obtain any specific information. That Wednesday Michigan National waffled on the $16 million in loans for shareholders, but it came through when Penn Square called to draw down $3 million on a liquidity line for First Penn Corporation.

According to sources at Michigan, Patterson said the Comptroller had demanded the money by July 9, but that the bank wanted it by the end of June so it would be reflected on the end of quarter balance sheet. Michigan National sources said, "Once we heard about the $30 million, we wondered, 'why $30 million.' "

"We told Bill Patterson that the loans would not be funded because the credit applications were not complete. They were apparently flustered by our unwillingness to complete credits. Later, we were told that it would have been nice to have your loans but these people have oodles of money. It wasn't put in terms of saving the bank." Patterson told the friendly bankers in Michigan that the examiners were sticklers, having classified a number of loans for "technical reasons."

At first, it seemed like a routine transaction. Jerry Williams, the controller of GHK, phoned Sharon Suitor, the company's account officer at the bank, to give her instructions on a wire transfer. Suitor had watched over the deposits of Penn Square's most important client with an extraordinary passion; at exactly 2:15 every afternoon she routinely called Jerry Williams at GHK to ask him how he wanted to invest the company's deposits for the next twenty-four hours.

This assignment was too vital to the relationship between Penn Square and Hefner for her to rely solely on her memory. At 2:15, a small alarm clock went off alerting her that it was time to phone Jerry.

This time, however, the alarm would not be necessary. Jerry Williams would be phoning her to request that she wire out $5 million to GHK's account at a bank in New York. "We need this done immediately," he said. Suitor was not particularly concerned by this request. But Williams's voice was uncharacteristically nervous.

Half an hour later Williams phoned again. "About that earlier transaction," he said firmly. "Duplicate it."

Hefner and GHK had maintained millions in short-term instruments at Penn Square Bank. They refused to lock up their funds there for too long, thinking that the day might come when they would want to act quickly to move them elsewhere. That day had arrived.

Williams said he had some more transfers. He ordered another $2 million out, and then asked Suitor to draw down on Hefner's lines of credit with Continental Illinois and Penn Square and move that money out as well. Kingston, Patterson's assistant, who had a reporter's instinct for being around when news was breaking, picked up on what was happening and ran up to the third floor to tell Beller and Rick Dunn, "I think we've got a problem."

Beller seemed to take the news casually, as if he already knew. His response was uncharacteristic of the straitlaced banker. "No shit," he replied.

The rumor was, said one former employee, that Jennings wanted Hefner to withdraw the money "to help us out later."

Then, in rapid-fire electronic impulses, the deposits of top GHK officials disappeared from Penn Square's books, leaving the beleaguered institution for safe havens in banks in Texas and New York.

Shortly after the last phone call, Williams drove to the bank and whispered to Suitor that he'd like to meet with her in private. Visibly nervous, he demanded to be escorted to the wire room to inspect the confirmation copies of the transactions. Within days, Hefner had succeeded in moving out close to $30 million in deposits and advances. One of Patterson's intensely loyal personal assistants quickly perceived the significance of this event. She told Suitor and everyone else privy to the transactions that they should tell no one, absolutely no one, what had just happened.

The following week, GHK would issue a press release explaining that Hefner had withdrawn the funds on the advice of a New York investment counselor, whom the House Banking Committee chairman referred to as the "mystical financial consultant." But, as Hefner explained later, "I was responsible for 150 employees. I told Williams to withdraw the funds from all the accounts he could down to the insured level." Hefner was also enraged that Patterson had unloaded Mahan Rowsey on him. "I was upset that Bill would get me to buy a company with all its liabilities," Hefner later said in court testimony.

Elizabeth Merrick Coe was not so lucky. While Hefner was pulling out $30 million, Mrs. Coe, a wealthy director and matron of Oklahoma society, was depositing several hundred thousand dollars in the doomed bank.

Hefner's was not the only smart money getting out of the bank. George Rodman claims to have been tipped off by a former Continental officer on June 29 that he should consider moving his funds, and he proudly says he did just that the next day. And a bank employee who owned First Penn Corporation commercial paper also redeemed her holdings prior to maturity.

Despite the fact that the walls of Penn Square were crumbling around them, the bank's credit policy committee, minus Bill Patterson, continued to approve new loans and buybacks through Wednesday, June 30. And a Penn Square loan officer who for months had been trying to persuade a bank in Baton Rouge to buy some energy participations finally received what he called a "general expression of interest" from the institution. Penn Square officials also compiled what was to be one of their final overdraft lists, a dossier of Penn Square borrowers with 489 separate accounts overdrawn in amounts ranging from $1 to $1.7 million.

Late that Wednesday afternoon a short, burly man from a northwest Oklahoma City locksmith shop parked his car in a distant corner of the parking lot at the Penn Square mall and strode briskly into the oil and gas division headquarters. Accompanied by a Pinkerton guard and a Penn Square officer, the locksmith walked past a bewildered Joyce Bieger, Patterson's secretary, removed a screwdriver and wrenches from his tool kit and replaced the lock on Patterson's door. Bieger was in tears. She had desperately wanted to be Patterson's right arm, and was grateful to the energy lending czar for giving her the opportunity to be something other than just "another dumb secretary," as she expressed it later.

After turning the keys over to an examiner from the Comptroller of the Currency, the locksmith left the building as quickly as he had entered, and the examiner ordered the guard to remain at the door. Bank officers and employees soon gathered around Bieger's desk, staring at the Pinkerton man in stunned disbelief. "Oh, shit," one officer whispered, "what in the world is happening to us?"

JULY 1, 1982

O N THE MORNING OF THURSDAY, JULY 1, 1982, A STORY APPEARED
on page three of the *American Banker* reporting that Patterson
had been stripped of his lending authority; that Penn Square was
scurrying around to raise $30 million for a capital infusion, and that
an attorney in San Francisco was seeking a temporary injunction
barring Penn Square from calling letters of credit on Longhorn oil
and gas drilling programs. The paper, which is distributed by mail
from a single printing plant in New Jersey, is a day late reaching
some smaller cities with limited air service. But bad news has a way
of reaching its destination much faster than the physical copy of the
medium bearing it. The news quicky reached the FDIC, the Comptroller, and the Fed. It found its way to the boardrooms at Seattle
First National Bank and Continental Illinois, and to officers on the
third floor at Penn Square Bank, who phoned the *American Banker* to
request a copy by telefax.

Penn Square's board convened at 9:00 A.M. Thursday. Cliff Poole
and several of his colleagues had come in from Dallas and other officials, including enforcement attorney Mike Patriarcha, had flown
in from Washington the evening before.

Patriarcha is a sometimes fiery, brutally frank man whose duties
include explaining to the directors of failing banks what their options are, and what is in store for them. The regulators waited in the
third-floor reception area for about five minutes while Jennings
briefed the board.

That morning Poole and Patriarcha had handed the board a notice of charges and a cease and desist order, enumerating the endless
list of violations committed by Penn Square. There was some discussion about giving the directors until July 16 to scrape up $30 million
in new capital, but that date was changed to July 9, a week from
Friday.

After the meeting, Marion Bauman, the lanky, Harvard-trained lawyer who represented Penn Square on regulatory matters, asked the Washington officials if the bank could show, in its published statement of condition for the first half of 1982, the capital it hoped to raise by July 9. Poole informed Bauman that would not be possible.

Bauman, knowing that it would not take a brilliant financial analyst to assess Penn Square's condition when the published statement showed no capital, replied with characteristic understatement, "Gee, that's terrible." The officials informed him that the statement would have to be published by August 10, and suggested that the bank take out an ad, to be placed alongside the statement, in an attempt to downplay the situation. It was at this meeting that a saddened Beep Jennings announced the suspension of his protégé, Bill Patterson.

Arnie Middeldorf of Michigan National, who had flown to Oklahoma City the evening before, was anxious to sit in on the meeting with the Comptroller.

"It's all right with me if it's all right with the Comptroller," Jennings said.

Jennings went back into the boardroom and came out and told Middeldorf, "They don't want you in there. After the meeting I'll tell you what happened." Middeldorf recalled later that he returned around noon and encountered a very shaken Jennings, who informed him of the Comptoller's temporary C&D. "They didn't strike us as an astute board," said one top regulator who was present at the Thursday meeting. "Most didn't say anything, maybe four or five asked questions. You couldn't be English-speaking and not know what was happening."

After a break, the board reconvened to hear director Ron Burks assert, according to the minutes, that in his opinion Patterson had "acted irresponsibly and lacked moral integrity," adding that he believed Patterson had "committed fraud." But Jennings, defending his surrogate son to the end, said that "Patterson did an awful lot of things right."

Roy Jackson, in Dallas, ordered six more examiners to Penn Square to assist the two already on their way in determining whether a purchase and assumption was a viable option. It usually takes a week or more to assemble a bid package, which includes everything from employees' titles to a breakdown of contingent liabilities. The package is a thorough assessment of the condition of a bank, and normally includes a two-foot-high synopsis of the exam results.

Meanwhile, in Washington, the FDIC had dispatched crews of lawyers and liquidators to Oklahoma City, who cooled their heels at the Northwest Hilton Hotel while the powers in Washington deliberated over the fate of the bank.

Liquidators are the gypsies of the bank regulatory establishment. They live out of suitcases and must be prepared to travel anywhere in the country on twenty-four-hour notice. Their satisfaction comes, as one former member of that profession put it, from "going into a bank and getting everything cleaned up."

But the very sight of a bank liquidator is enough to make a banker cringe. And late that week, a Penn Square officer recognized one of them and commented to a colleague, "The liquidators are here. It's over."

An officer of Penn Square got a call from a friend, whose commercial paper was due to mature that Tuesday. He asked, "Do you think I can get it out today?" Other customers, aware of the rumors that had spread throughout Oklahoma City, tried to wire money out but were staved off by Penn Square officers. "There was," said a senior Penn Square officer, "a feeling by that time that the government was running things."

It was a classic case of too little too late.

On July 1, as the officials of the Comptroller of the Currency were meeting with Penn Square's board, newly appointed energy chief Greg Odean was finally authorized to take the draconian steps needed to bring Penn Square under control. He instructed energy lending officers that no new loans would be granted to borrowers who already had bad loans without the board's approval. At long last, John Baldwin obtained the authority he had sought for months to insist that all documentation be in place before a loan is funded. "Despite all our efforts over the last two-month period," Odean wrote, "we are still generating slightly more collateral exceptions than we are correcting. It is imperative that this phenomenon come to a stop and by following this policy rigidly it will." It would come to a stop for another reason. By the time the memo went out, funding of Penn Square participations had essentially screeched to a halt.

Moreover, in a final and futile effort to restore the confidence of the upstream banks in Penn Square, Odean ordered that no loans would be sold unless they conformed to the stipulations contained in the participation certificate. "These policies which we are now implementing will be viewed as relatively restrictive and very tightly controlled," he wrote. "That is correct."

Odean also advised his staff that no new loans, renewals, or extensions would be accepted without prior written commitment for participation from an upstream bank. "As many people are aware," he wrote, "our liquidity has been under severe strain for several months. Despite all our efforts to the contrary the strain has not eased." He added, "The current situation with the bank's financial condition does not permit us to book new loans in-house to any material degree whatsoever."

And finally, Odean's memo brought to a close the era of convenience banking at Penn Square Bank. Officers were instructed to inform their clients that advances on previously committed loans would now take two days, and possibly even three.

In a separate memo, Odean and Busey ordered a halt to Penn Square's time-honored practice of completing loan agreements in blank.

Even before the board meeting convened in Oklahoma City, a worried Gerald Bergman had taken off from Chicago on an early morning flight to Washington, where he joined his shocked colleagues, Edwin Hlavka and John Perkins, at the Comptroller's office for a meeting of the Big Three. Jack Hooper, a trusted aide of Chase chairman Butcher, and Paul Walker, the workout man, were in from New York, and Seafirst president Dick Jaehning and bank auditor Arland Hatfield had flown in from the West Coast.

For more than two years, Frank Murphy had not been privy to the inner workings of Penn Square and suffered privately in an out-of-the-way office on the third floor. No one sitting in on a meeting with senior regulatory officials from Dallas and Washington could help but be concerned about the bank, but when Murphy left at two-thirty to drive down to Lake Texoma for the holiday weekend, he had no doubts about its ultimate survival. "When I left I thought it was taken care of," he said later.

About that time the *American Banker* reporter returned from lunch in New York to find a pink telephone message slip on his desk from a source in Oklahoma he referred to as "Deep Vault," an allusion to the "Deep Throat" of Watergate fame. Deep Vault said solemnly, "It's time for you to pack your bags. Things are really bad here."

The FDIC was aware that a former examiner with the agency had quit the FDIC some months earlier to take a job with Penn Square Bank, and they wanted to make sure that when their people appeared at the bank under false identities, the former employee would not broadcast word of their arrival. An FDIC examiner was dispatched from Dallas to Oklahoma City with a single mission: to take him out for a drink to make sure he knew he was expected to keep his mouth shut. But it is nearly impossible to contain that type of news, and it spread quickly in the Oklahoma financial community.

As the *American Banker* reporter began to think about packing his bags, FDIC examiners were unpacking theirs in Oklahoma City. FDIC chairman Isaac was unavailable when the reporter phoned Washington for a comment on the reports circulating in Oklahoma City that examiners had been dispatched to review the condition of Penn Square Bank. Within the hour, however, Isaac returned the call to Bill Zimmerman, the paper's editor. "Please hold this story," he implored Zimmerman. "We need more time. If you run it now, you'll be sounding the death knell for this bank."

Zimmerman, a slim, bearded man in his early forties, who would become editor-in-chief the following Tuesday, was respectful and sympathetic but noncommittal. Instead of killing the story, the conversation bolstered his resolve to run it. The reporter said to Zimmerman, "I hope we're doing the right thing." Zimmerman replied tersely, "We are." That evening, Marion Bauman, who had been notified of the impending story by a local banker whom the reporter had phoned to seek corroboration, called the reporter to say, "If you're wrong, you've got a big problem."

Later, Beep Jennings himself would tell the reporter, "I hope you have a clear conscience. I hope you can live with yourself. Your articles did great damage to the bank. You didn't give us time to work something out. The *American Banker* was in an alliance with the regulators. You ruined thirty-five years of trying to do a commendable job of helping this state."

In Seattle officials of the Seattle First National Bank were alarmed by the meetings in Washington, D.C., and the implications of the *American Banker* story. Banks vary in their willingness to disclose bad news to the public. Seafirst, as an institution, enjoyed a reputation in financial circles for making these disclosures earlier rather than later. On July 1, Harvey Gillis, Bill Jenkins, Randy James, and other top bank officials were debating whether to acknowledge now that they had bad loans with their fishing companions in Oklahoma City, or wait until they learned how far they had sunk, and how deep the water was.

But at two-thirty an announcement went out over the PR newswire stating that some of their Penn Square loans had become problems. The release confirmed the *American Banker* story and added more fuel to the rumors that had begun to make the rounds in Oklahoma City about the shaky condition of Penn Square Bank.

Seafirst officials phoned the other upstream banks advising them of the decision, even though they didn't yet know what number to put on the losses. According to John Boyd, who by this time had been instructed to document all that he knew about the Penn Square relationship, Seafirst's law firm advised the bank to issue the release. As Boyd recalled it, they said, "The news is already on the street, go ahead with it."

The release said, "The Seafirst Corporation acknowledged today it has participated in loans with Penn Square Bank of Oklahoma. The Comptroller of the Currency recently identified certain Penn Square loans as problems. Penn Square's lending is under review, including all participant loans. The extent of the impact on Seafirst is not yet known."

The regulators and the other banks, most notably Continental, were furious over the release. Said one Seafirst official, "Jaehning caught holy hell from the regulators." Seafirst spokesman Randy James said later that Continental called and asked anxiously, "Why are you doing this?"

Almost immediately, securities analysts were on the phone to Harvey Gillis, asking, "Harv, what's the number?"

Penn Square had managed to pay off the $20 million it borrowed from the Fed the day before, but the publicity had prompted that most insidious of runs on the bank, a wire run, which shows up not in lines in front of the teller windows but in the queue of electronic blips on a bank's wire machine. Moreover, other banks around the country that had been sources of overnight, or Fed funds, told Penn Square's funding people that they would not sell them any more money even on a fully secured basis, at any price. Yet the money brokers, including Professional Asset Management in California, continued to funnel those jumbo CDs into Penn Square, and one credit union from New Mexico reportedly dumped in $700,000 on Thursday.

With the press attention focused on the bank, it was clear if a re-capitalization program was not in place by Friday, Penn Square wouldn't survive. After the *American Banker* story appeared, regulators ordered the exam accelerated and examiners on the scene were forced to work almost around the clock.

Meanwhile, Continental's own review of its Penn Square loans was continuing in Chicago. According to John Lytle, Continental officers met on June 30 and July 1 with examiners to review a list of problem loans. Lytle said it was in this review that "we learned for the first time of apparent missing collateral and collateral substitutions." In one case, a loan was supposed to have been secured by the unlimited guarantee of a wealthy individual involved in a drilling program. "The examiner suggested," he said, "that the loan be charged off. I pointed out that it was secured or supported by the unlimited guarantee of the individual." Another loan that was supposed to be backed by oil leases was secured by Maximo Moorings. Patterson was home, and his files had been locked up by the Comptroller. Lytle told Patterson to go to the office and get the unlimited guarantee. Patterson said, "I'm sorry, John, I never got it," according to Lytle.

Lytle, Patterson testified later, was trying to decide whether to accept an offer to become president of Penn Square Bank or to go to work for Joe Dan Trigg. By this time, however, it was clear that his future would be shaped, to a large degree, by events beyond his control.

Also on Thursday, according to Peat Marwick managing partner Jim Blanton, one of those loans to Peat Marwick partners that was supposed to have been sold off when Peat signed on with Penn Square showed up back at the bank, but he insisted it was paid off the same day.

Just before three o'clock that afternoon, Syrl C. Orbach, eighty-seven, and his sixty-eight-year-old wife, Christine, were found slain with their throats slashed in their Oklahoma City home, just three blocks from the Penn Square shopping center. Orbach, founder of Oklahoma's Orbach's department store chain, was apparently studying plans for the couple's retirement home in the Arkansas Ozarks when they were murdered. Normally, a slaying in the quiet, tree-lined neighborhood where many Penn Square customers and officers lived would preoccupy residents for days and weeks to come. But today, as the first news of the true condition of Penn Square began to emerge in the press and rumors of its impending demise intensified, residents were more concerned with the implications of a single bank failure than a double slaying. As Bill Gallagher, a reporter for KOCO-TV put it later in a conversation with a reporter for the *Wall Street Journal*, "Oklahomans hardly notice murder and mayhem around them. But when somebody loses money, that makes them sad."

Late in the afternoon, in Washington, the action shifted from the Comptroller's rented offices at L'Enfant Plaza to the sixth-floor conference room at the Federal Deposit Insurance Corporation. Homan represented the Comptroller, and Jack Ryan, his counterpart at the Fed, stood in for Paul Volcker. Homan described the bank's condition, noting that while the losses were still less than the capital account, the examination was underway, and if the trend continued, the future was clearly not bright. Despite the seriousness of the problem, Homan was emphatic on one issue: he did not want to pay off the bank. Everyone was acutely aware of the criticism that was certain to follow in the days and weeks ahead, as to what could have been done or should have been done. The regulators knew the ramifications of this failure. There would be a flood of publicity, congressional hearings, and internal investigations. One bureaucrat reminded himself to protect his flanks as he deliberated with the FDIC. He scribbled "CYA"—cover your ass—on a yellow legal pad throughout the meeting.

Later, representatives of the upstream banks joined the meeting. In the haste to get on with the business at hand, introductions were neglected; Isaac assumed, incorrectly, that everyone was acquainted. The bankers were in a poor, if not impossible situation, and they knew it. Isaac outlined to them the alternatives in disposing of a failed bank and told them if they were concerned about a closing they should go back and talk with their directors and senior officers about a more acceptable solution. Their options were limited, Isaac said, but he suggested that they think about devising some plan to recapitalize Penn Square. While there was little community of interest among the bankers, they did agree on two things: first, that a purchase and assumption would be the preferred course of action, and second, that they wanted to avoid being a partner with the U.S. government. The Fed, meanwhile, was not offering a firm commitment as to what it was prepared to do as the lender of last resort. A Fed official would only go so far as to say, "With proper collateral we can lend."

Isaac expressed to the bankers his concern about the contingent liabilities, a catch-all that he interpreted to include the $2 billion in participations, an unknown quantity of unfunded commitments, and letters of credit—a sum estimated to be in the vicinity of $3 billion.

Penn Square, according to John Baldwin, had established a reporting system where all contingent liabilities and obligations to fund on loans were to be reported. "It was my understanding," he said, "that Patterson never contributed his list of committed obligations to the report." But one of the single largest contingent liabilities was undoubtedly the $31.3 million note to Hefner's QOL Corporation involving the Mahan Rowsey rigs.

It was agreed at the meeting that the upstream banks would confer with their senior management and lawyers and attempt to draft a so-called hold-harmless agreement that would relieve the FDIC of any responsibility for the contingent liabilities. That would be a solid first step toward a purchase and assumption transaction.

Two years earlier, there would have been little doubt as to what course of action the FDIC would pursue. In the spring of 1980, the bank regulators were grappling with the potential failure of Philadelphia's First Pennsylvania, or First Pennsy, as it was known in the industry. At that time, however, Irvine Sprague, a creature of caution known for taking his cues from the Federal Reserve Board, was chairman of the FDIC, and Isaac was only a director of the agency. It has been customary for the chairman of the agency to be of the same political party as the President, and thus Sprague, a Democrat, became chairman with the election of Jimmy Carter. There was never any doubt that the bank in Philadelphia would be bailed out. Isaac, however, would later testify that if he had been chairman, he would have allowed First Pennsy to go under. A case can be made that if the First Pennsylvania Corporation had been allowed to fail, First Penn Corporation of Oklahoma City might never have grown into the monster it became, because investors would have been too frightened to place uninsured money at risk in a relatively small institution like Penn Square.

Isaac, unlike Sprague, was of an independent mind, intent on leaving his imprint on both his agency and the American financial system. While he respected Paul Volcker, he clearly did not feel beholden to him. This bank crisis, unlike those before it, would not be worked out among congenial, like-minded colleagues who shared an interest in disposing of errant bankers with a minimum of disruption and keeping the foibles of the banking system under wraps. This time there was a maverick among them in the name of Willam M. Isaac. This time, Isaac was drawing the battle lines.

Over the next five days, the Fed would bring the classic systemic concerns of a central bank to the table. The FDIC, in arguing for the preservation of "The Fund," would choose to apply a strict cost test in the handling of Penn Square. And top officials of the Comptroller of the Currency would find themselves divided over whether confidence in the system would be enhanced, or destroyed, in the short run or the long run, by not rescuing Penn Square and its uninsured depositors.

As Isaac interpreted his mandate, the FDIC could not execute a purchase and assumption transaction unless it determined that the P&A would be no more expensive than a deposit payoff. The maximum exposure, he said, could not exceed the amount of the insured deposits of $270 million, minus what he called some "modest recovery," say $30 million. On the other hand, he said, the best estimate was that the deposit payoff would cost between $20 million and $240 million, with a most likely cost of $140 million. To do the P&A under Isaac's strict interpretation of FDIC regulations, he would have to determine that it would cost less than $140 million. The premium that an acquiring bank pays for the failing institution in a P&A transaction normally reduces the cost to the FDIC below that of a payoff. As a receiver, the FDIC steps into the shoes, as it were, of the failed bank, and becomes subject to lawsuits arising out of losses, negligence, and fraud. Because of court decisions arising out of earlier failures that held the FDIC responsible for contingent liabilities of the defunct bank, Isaac concluded that unless those liabilities could be reduced to a reasonable level, the exposure to the agency would be too great to do a P&A.

According to Isaac, the upstream banks initially voiced a willingness to take responsibility for the $2 billion in participations that they had bought; in other words they would not assert any claims on the receivership for that amount. But they refused to take responsibility for about $200 million in loans sold to institutions other than the Big Five. "Their solution," he said, "was that the FDIC would have to deal with that." In addition, he said, there were about $600 million in outstanding letters of credit and loan commitments. "We didn't know about their quality or exactly how much they were," the FDIC chairman asserted later. From the outset, Isaac's position was this: the Fed, or the upstream participants, or both, would have to protect the FDIC from the contingent claims if the agency was to do a P&A. If the Fed agreed to cover the FDIC on the claims other than the $2 billion, if they exceeded a certain level, "then we could do it," Isaac said.

But according to a senior FDIC official, the agency "got very hung up on contingent liabilities. The lawyers got hung up with putting a price tag on them. Just because there are all these contingencies, that doesn't mean they're all going to materialize." Nevertheless, the official added that "we didn't need contingencies to justify a payoff" since the loss estimate at the time appeared to be very high. "You could make a case for a payoff on a straight cost basis," he said, noting that "we didn't go through direct cost calculations on a payoff versus a purchase and assumption."

And he said, "I was troubled by the philosophical approach" taken by Isaac.

"There were a number of areas of exposure we didn't have a feel for," said another FDIC official. "We couldn't determine the liability of Penn Square on participations or substandard credits. The issue was, should we take on an unknown risk of loss?"

The Federal Reserve Board, as the agency ultimately responsible for the preservation of the nation's financial system, is more concerned with the psychological effects of a bank failure than the deposit insuring agency. "It did," said a senior Fed official, "occur at a rather critical time in the financial system. We had Drysdale, the failure of a West Coast securities firm, a number of business bankruptcies, and several major bank failures that year, including Metropolitan." The Fed envisioned what he called "a sizable involvement extending beyond Oklahoma City. There was a threat to the stability of the system in liquidating the bank," he said, acknowledging that the "financial shocks were beginning to bother us considerably."

When top FDIC staffers first heard of Penn Square, the response was "$500 million, that's not so big." At the time, the FDIC's top priority was the dismal state of the mutual savings banks, which were being merged out of existence with an almost monotonous regularity.

As the agency charged with the conduct of monetary policy and the safety and soundness of the financial system, the Fed considers itself superior to the other bank regulatory agencies and views itself as the last line of defense against world economic chaos. The Fed's catch phrase over that Fourth of July weekend for what would happen if Penn Square was closed was "serious systemic effects." Such a term, once used, tends to be repeated; it became the watchword for those who favored a rescue effort. On Thursday, because of its concern over the stability of the upstream banks and the credit unions and savings banks with uninsured deposits at Penn Square, the Fed began to seek a waiver of claims on contingent liabilities from the upstream banks. "The reaction was generally favorable," said a Fed official. But one snag arose immediately over the power of a bank officer to give up a legitimate claim of his institution.

In the view of the Washington regulators, the upstream bank representatives were just beginning to comprehend the dimensions of the debacle they were facing on Thursday. Compounding the problem was a lack of information about the loans and the collateral. And by the afternoon it was becoming evident that the liquidity crisis precipitated by the news leaks on Penn Square's condition would likely compress the time available for making a decision into days rather than weeks or months. In the past, bank regulators had the luxury of being able to work out a solution to a troubled bank over a period of several months, as in the case of Franklin National in 1974, and U.S. National in 1973.

"We were struck with the suddenness with which the problems emerged," said an FDIC official. "We would have expected more notice. There was not time to put together a packet of information on the bank."

Regulators sometimes allow a bank to linger indefinitely with no capital—a book insolvency—until a solution to its troubles can be devised. But a bank mired in red ink usually is headed for a liquidity crisis as well, as investors and depositors learn of the difficulties and lose confidence in the institution. And in the case of Penn Square, what really thrust the regulators into action was more the drain of deposits, or illiquidity, than the so-called capital insolvency that triggered the loss of funds in the first place.

Patriarcha left Oklahoma City right after the morning directors' meeting, arriving in Washington in time to have dinner with Paul Homan. Their meal was interrupted by a call from Todd Conover, who asked, "How are things out there?" It was then that they decided to amend the order that would have given the board until July 9 to raise the $30 million. The next morning the directors would be told they'd have to ante up by five o'clock that afternoon.

Gov. Partee, the Fed governor responsible for bank supervision, decided the bank wouldn't fail that weekend and followed up with his plans to go sailing on Chesapeake Bay aboard his 31-foot cruising sloop. Likewise Chuck Vose, Jr., of the First National Bank of Oklahoma City was preparing to leave Oklahoma City to spend the holiday weekend at a lakefront vacation retreat. Vose and Dale Mitchell met to make sure someone would be available that weekend in case a call came from the FDIC asking First National Bank to bid on Penn Square, and Mitchell assured his boss that he would be in the city over the holidays and would stay close to a phone.

"In June," Mitchell said later, "we expected somebody to have the opportunity to take the deal over. We thought we'd have the opportunity to go into the bank that weekend and bid on it."

JULY 2, 1982

I T WAS ALMOST NOON IN PARIS WHEN THE FIRST GLIMMER OF DAWN
appeared over the Jennings farm, and the embattled bank chairman awakened for the most tumultuous day of his banking career. Gen. James Randolph had phoned his fellow board member Gene Smelser Thursday evening, just before boarding a plane for Europe at Kennedy Airport. It was then that he learned of the Comptroller's demand for new capital. But he never considered turning back; he and his wife had planned the trip for months, and there was little he could add to the solution even if he were in Oklahoma City. Randolph, as one of the more outspoken members of the Penn Square board, had already done all he could do.

That Friday, Randolph and his wife were strolling past the four-star Crillon Hotel on the Place de la Concorde when they spotted an old friend, Jim Berry, and his wife, waiting for a cab to take them to Orly Airport for a flight to Rome.

After a brief exchange of pleasantries, Berry, the chairman of the Republic Bank of Dallas, asked his friend, "Have you seen the paper this morning? What's happening at Penn Square? It looks like they've got some problems."

Randolph hadn't seen the morning paper, but he didn't act surprised. "What problems?" the general asked.

"You better take a look at the paper," Berry said.

Mrs. Randolph's face took on an anxious and disappointed look. "Does that mean we have to go home, Jim?" she asked her husband.

It is not easy to find $30 million on the Friday before a Fourth of July weekend. But that was the miracle the Comptroller of the Currency was about to demand of Beep Jennings. On Friday, July 2, Bill Robertson of the Comptroller's office interrupted an emergency meeting of the board of directors and summoned Jennings out into the corridor to give him the bad news.

Jennings had just finished telling the board that the bank's Fed funds lines had begun to dry up on Thursday, and that he expected more to evaporate today. He told the shellshocked directors that while twenty shareholders had signed notes for $30 million at Continental and Michigan, the loans wouldn't be funded unless the lost deposits were covered by Fed funds or the sale of loans. One customer, Jennings said, expressed a willingness to inject as much as $35 million into the bank. Meanwhile, the loan documents were on their way to Chicago and Detroit to support advances to stockholders.

That customer was Robert Hefner. But his executive vice-president, Boots Taliaferro, in an interview with the *American Banker* mid-Friday, said, "I am unaware of any pledging. Mr. Hefner would be prepared to take a look or consider it [a capital infusion] when the situation clears and the requirements, if any, are known. The examination," he said, "is still underway. We have no idea what will come of it." Around the time that conversation was taking place, a tearful bank employee told another of Penn Square's major borrowers, "One of our best friends took out all his money."

The beleaguered chairman warned the directors against making any comment to the press. Marion Bauman informed the board that the *American Banker* might be publishing an article on the involvement of the FDIC, which he said would not be true even if it was printed.

But the article was printed, and it was true. It reported that the FDIC had dispatched a team of examiners to Oklahoma City to review the condition of the troubled bank and stated that a change in management or ownership of Penn Square could be forthcoming. In addition, the *Wall Street Journal* had picked up on the Thursday *American Banker* article and the Seattle First press release and run a story on the suspected problems at Penn Square. Locally, the *Daily Oklahoman* and the *Journal Record* published articles. In one story, the *Oklahoman* quoted assurances from Jennings that it was business as usual at Penn Square Bank. But investors were already reacting to the news by selling off shares of Continental Illinois, Chase Manhattan, and Seattle First in heavy trading on the New York Stock Exchange.

Bauman outlined the mechanism by which the FDIC takes control of a failed bank, stressing that the FDIC and the Comptroller were not going to take over Penn Square, "but are in a posture to do so." Bauman said, in effect, that such an event would be a messy affair, with endless litigation. The good news was that he thought the board had "good defenses" if that should occur.

It was now Robertson's turn. In his years of grappling with troubled banks, Robertson has seen just about every problem a bank could have. He is known among his colleagues for his precise and measured style in dealing with failing institutions; he chooses his words carefully, and on July 2 his message to Beep Jennings was as terse and unequivocal as it could be—the money must be in by the end of the day. With the big banks pulling away, a funding crisis was clearly at hand. And it was the threat of a run on the bank, the run that was already underway, that prompted the amendment of the order.

Robertson told Jennings that not only must the capital be there, but that he must also provide a solid source of private funding. Given the difficulties of accomplishing that in one afternoon, the regulators were planning for the possibility that the bank would not survive the weekend.

One observer likened the mood on the third floor at Penn Square to that of a family waiting outside a hospital emergency room for news of a critically injured member. Ironically, while the Comptroller was pulling the rug out from under the bank, a bank officer was admonishing the Bentley Carpet Company that they should finish laying a $6,000 mocha pile in the bank's basement offices before the end of the day.

While the board was meeting, in Washington Conover and Homan were briefing Secretary of the Treasury Don Regan on the crisis. And in Chicago, representatives of the Big Five had convened in the boardroom at Continental Illinois to attempt to hammer out the hold-harmless agreement that could permit the FDIC to execute a P&A transaction.

The Chicago meeting was a disaster. Said one Big Five representative, "Anderson came in, and we just sat and looked at each other. We were expecting some leadership from Continental, and it wasn't forthcoming. Nothing happened. There were no specific proposals made by the banks."

Bill Taylor, a senior official of the Federal Reserve Board, arrived in Chicago from Washington late in the afternoon, but according to another bank representative, he was "nonspecific on what the Fed could or would do." According to one participant, "it was agreed in principle that each bank would take what it bargained for with respect to collateral when it bought its participations. In other words, if a bank bargained for an unsecured loan it would not claim an interest in another bank's collateral." It was an agreement destined to be broken.

Jennings had informed Anderson and Bergman of the new demand by the Comptroller, but after failing to hear from them he assumed that they had opted not to backstop Penn Square. Mrs. Coe, loyal to the end, asked if directors could help with liquidity, but Jennings replied that the requirements were too great for any one director to be of much assistance.

At that point, the bank was $12 million in the hole from a liquidity standpoint, which showed up as a deficit on the bank's account with the Fed in Kansas City, leading Bauman and the senior officers to tell the Comptroller's representatives, "The bank may be insolvent now. Depending on how you define it, here are the keys."

The Fed officials on the scene were furious with the Comptroller, for reasons not clear to bank officials at that time. Dick Woods, the general counsel with the Kansas City Fed who had flown down that morning was "so mad he could hardly see straight," recalled one observer. Woods insisted that the Fed could not lend the bank money unless the Comptroller certified that the bank was solvent. The regulators conferred privately for a while, then agreed to lend the bank $5.7 million on Friday and more on Saturday.

In San Francisco, a hearing on the letter of credit suits was set for 10:00 A.M. in Federal District Court, and Tom Sloan, Penn Square's local attorney, was pushing hard for a disposition of the case—any disposition. While unaware that his client was about to go under, Sloan was concerned that the L/Cs would expire and become worthless even before the legal issues surrounding them could be resolved. On Friday afternoon, the counsel for the San Francisco Fed, acting on instructions from Federal Reserve Board general counsel and Paul Volcker intimate Mike Bradfield, tried repeatedly to reach Ray Erlach, the attorney representing the Longhorn investors, to find out if he had any real evidence of fraud. Bradfield later told him, "We heard news of your order. We knew you had to have some evidence."

Fraud was a critical issue. On Friday, the upstream banks were still expressing an interest in a hold-harmless agreement but were unwilling to give up claims in the event that they turned out to be the victims of fraud and deception.

Throughout the country, examiners and regulators abruptly cancelled holiday plans as the crisis mounted. On a flight from Washington that Friday, an Oklahoma City private investigator sat next to a young woman, an FDIC liquidator, who talked gleefully about all the overtime she expected to earn that weekend. Isaac's assistant, Meg Eggington, was attending a seminar at Harvard Business School. She was planning to have dinner Thursday night with the

FDIC regional director in Boston, but as soon as she arrived at his office, he briefed her on the problem brewing in Oklahoma. She left Cambridge on Friday and proceeded directly to the FDIC conference room wearing blue jeans.

Meanwhile, credit unions in search of the highest yield continued to pour in jumbo deposits as late as Friday. Bill Goldsmith of Professional Asset Management may have been less concerned with the soundness of Penn Square Bank than whether all his computers were plugged in properly at his new offices. On July 2, PAM moved from Los Angeles to a new, single-story whitewashed building located between the Del Mar Mexican Café and Kirby's Bar one block from the ocean in Del Mar. At some point, however, a bank regulator disconnected the bank's wire machines, cutting off the flow of funds in and out of the bank through the Fed wire network, literally pulling the plug on the doomed institution.

Top officials of the OCC in Washington ordered the examiners at Penn Square to identify the uninsured depositors at Penn Square, credit unions, savings and loan institutions, and others with more than $100,000 on deposit at the bank. Until that point, no one at a senior level in Washington fully appreciated Penn Square's dependence on hot money. As the names of the victims spewed out of a telecopier in the Comptroller's sixth-floor communications room, the regulators, standing over the machine, shook their heads incredulously, saying, "Oh, shit. Oh, shit."

James Hudson and Wayne Ness of the FDIC arrived at the bank on Friday, and according to one observer, appeared surprised to find that it was still open. They seemed uncertain about what to do, he said, and left for an hour or so to check with their superiors on the status of the bank. They returned with less than a definitive answer: "The best we can find," as the observer recalled their remarks, "is that no one knows what will happen." But Ness and Hudson made a dollar bet on whether they would go home Monday—Hudson wagered that they would go home, Ness that they would stay.

While shoppers in the Penn Square mall checking out Fourth of July sales were oblivious to the financial drama being played right around them, bank officers in the main building and basements and subbasements speculated on the most likely scenarios for the future of the bank. One option called for the bank to open Tuesday under the same management but with new capital. With help from the Fed, the run that was expected would be contained. A second possibility, they figured, called for the Comptroller to step in after halting the run, and replace Patterson and Jennings. In a third case, banks that had made loans to Penn Square—those banks being

Continental and Michigan—could exercise their rights under provisions of the banking law that allowed a lending bank to foreclose on the loans and take over a failing institution, even if that institution was located in another state. And under yet a fourth scenario, Continental, Chase, and Seafirst would make loans to individuals to buy stock in the bank, and then form a consortium to manage it.

"At the end," said one officer, "we thought we'd end up working for Continental." The only scenario that wasn't even considered, however, was the one that actually happened.

At midday Friday, Jennings was confronted with a financial chicken and egg scenario. The Fed was willing to continue lending as long as the bank was not insolvent, but the bank would remain above water only as long as the Fed continued to lend. As long as the Comptroller agreed to attest that assets exceeded liabilities, the bank would be considered solvent. Put another way, the Fed could not lend unless capital was in place, but capital could not come in without funds support. At one point during the emergency board meetings, Jennings in fact declared that the bank was insolvent, and no one objected.

On the one hand, Jennings was telling the authorities, "We're insolvent, close us," and on the other, saying, "I haven't reviewed these things," referring to the charged-off loans, said a former regulator. "We were not going to close that bank till we had a book insolvency," he said. "And that's what we worked through the weekend to do, not to close it, but to make sure that when we did close it, it was insolvent and that this determination would stand the light of day."

In Washington, Paul Volcker was deliberating with his board of governors over whether the Fed should lend to the bank, and secondly, whether the bank could allow time deposits to be withdrawn before maturity without penalty. The board agreed that the Federal Reserve Bank of Kansas City could lend to the bank as long as proper collateral was pledged. While the Fed was meeting, Jennings was advising his board that he had notified Willard Butcher of Chase and Jerry Bergman of Continental that unless they purchased loans or committed themselves to provide funding, he would have to advise the Comptroller that the bank was technically insolvent.

Curiously, at a reception for the press at the American Bankers Association's annual convention in Atlanta three months later, Butcher told reporters that when Penn Square failed he thought it was a bank in Pennsylvania.

*   *   *

At midafternoon, Jennings called all the officers and employees of the oil and gas division together on the second floor. "It's tough right now, boys and girls," he told them. "We're facing the toughest fight in the history of the bank." Many of the employees began crying. Minutes later, however, Eldon Beller, looking relieved, ran in and announced that the Federal Reserve Bank of Kansas City had agreed to continue lending. Jennings asked everyone to work over the weekend preparing packages of loans that would be delivered to the Fed as collateral to borrow at the discount window in order to meet the run that was a virtual certainty if the bank opened for business on Tuesday.

"I'm a fighter and we're going to fight hard," he said, adding that Patterson was at home "bleeding his heart out for the bank. If you have any problems, call Bill at home."

There was joking throughout the bank about the bank's management bivouacked on the third floor with sandbags around them. Jennings told the employees gathered in the lobby, "The rumor mill is rampant, and I'm not going to be closed by rumors. There are those people," Jennings said, "who would like to see this bank close down. I expect the bank to survive the examination and open for business on Tuesday."

John Baldwin recalls standing near the elevator while Jennings was making his speech and looking across the lobby at a young officer he had just hired away from a bank in Birmingham, Alabama. The new employee started work on June 30 so he could be eligible for pension and profit sharing for the fiscal year. "I can't believe this is happening," Baldwin thought to himself. "I just hired the guy."

Jennings reconvened the board late in the afternoon and told them that an hour after advising Robertson that the bank was technically insolvent and was in his hands, representatives of the Fed arrived and asked how much he needed to borrow for the day. Based on the Fed's willingness to lend, Jennings announced to a relieved board that their association was no longer technically insolvent.

Bill Stubbs, an affable real estate developer and Penn Square board member, ran into a friend late Friday as he left the bank. "You're not your usual friendly self," the man said. He was, in fact, on the verge of tears because his son-in-law had invested more than $100,000 in Penn Square certificates of deposits the week before, but he couldn't warn him because he feared that to do so would be using inside information.

By late afternoon, the local television stations, which had no previous experience covering a major bank failure, nervously sent camera crews to the Penn Square mall to tape a statement by Beep

Jennings, taking comfort in the fact that the print media had already run the story. Penn Square Bank had become a fortress under siege.

Bill Jennings, Eldon Beller, and senior officials at Penn Square—minus Bill Patterson—found themselves groping for ways to buy time for Penn Square Bank. It occurred to someone that $35 million in losses could represent a significant loss carryback that would likely be accepted by the Comptroller's office as additional capital. In other words, taxes paid over the past three years could be recouped through the loss in 1982, and the amount of capital required could then be reduced by the amount of the carryback. They asked Peat, Marwick, Mitchell to compute the value of that loss, and the accounting firm came up with a figure of $4.3 million.

Senior officials of the Comptroller of the Currency were taken aback when Penn Square argued that their $38.6 million in capital was understated by $4.3 million. The issue had not arisen before in a failed bank situation. But Washington, after considerable deliberation, allowed the bank to include the $4.3 million.

For those at the FDIC who were anxious to prepare for the closing of the bank, this turn of events represented just another frustrating postponement of the inevitable. But for those at Penn Square, it was seen as $4.3 million that could mean the difference between catastrophe and a second chance.

Jim Blanton of Peat Marwick later criticized the examiners for not consulting with him, but statements made by the regulators in the board meetings suggest that they had lost respect for the auditors. Said Blanton, "If you're about to close a bank, shouldn't you have all the information? Shouldn't you ask, 'Do you know something I don't know?' "

By Friday evening, according to Isaac, the upstream banks were telling the regulators that their lawyers had advised them that they would be unable to waive all the claims on the $2 billion. In other words, if there was anything that smacked of dishonesty they couldn't waive that.

"The participants were willing to give us a kind of limited indemnity on the $2 billion. But there were a lot of other problems that remained that we couldn't get anybody to deal with," he said later.

"If you take the risk for the participations, a P&A is possible," the FDIC told the upstream banks. But they eventually concluded, as one agency insider put it, that "they were better off taking their losses and suing the FDIC as receiver."

Until Friday, Penn Square officials contended that their upstream banks were prepared to recapitalize the bank by making loans to shareholders. But the upstream bankers were now telling the regulators a different story: that the situation was too unstable and uncertain to take such a step, and that they feared individual corporate liability if they were put into what one regulator called "a management mode."

"Ultimately, no one wanted to take the long-term risk of uncertainty as to what else might be there, or who else might be out there with something to claim," said the one top bank regulator. "The records were such that you didn't know whether you had it all or not."

The prospect of the collapse of Penn Square Bank conjured up the ghosts of earlier failures, or near-failures, among the regulators. Bureaucrats at each of the three banking agencies picked and chose from among an array of financial corpses, some long dead and others still warm, for those that would best support their positions on how to dispose of a shopping center bank in Oklahoma City that was breathing its last gasp.

The legal cornerstone of the FDIC's stance was a court decision handed down in the aftermath of the 1973 collapse of San Diego's U.S. National Bank, the bank run by Richard Nixon crony C. Arnoldt Smith. Ten years later, that spectacular failure weighed heavily on the minds of the FDIC as it stewed over Penn Square. At U.S. National, money had passed through the bank to entities that were nothing more than alter egos of Mr. Smith, and those funds were never accounted for. And letters of credit showed up after the closing that no one knew anything about. In negotiating a takeover by the Crocker National Bank, the FDIC concluded that letter of credit holders with claims on U.S. National had nothing more than contingent claims and shouldn't be placed on a par with depositors.

One of the banks that had lent to U.S. National, taking a letter of credit as security, was First Empire, which subsequently sued the FDIC and lost on the district court level. But the appeal court overturned that decision and ordered the FDIC to treat all creditors alike. The result was that the agency had to pay letter of credit holders 100¢ on the dollar. According to one FDIC insider who was involved in the Penn Square negotiations, "We said if we have to play by the First Empire rule we might have to indemnify the assuming bank $500–600 million for contingent claims."

While Isaac and his top aides continued to thrash out the ramifications of the First Empire decision with their counterparts at the

Fed and the Comptroller of the Currency, his operations people were chafing to get into the bank to prepare for a takeover. Jim Davis, the agency's chief liquidator, had already drawn up an organization chart for the receivership, showing "Take No Prisoners" Hudson as liquidator-in-charge. Davis had warned Isaac that even if his staff entered the bank on Saturday to begin preparing checks, they wouldn't be ready to issue them until Wednesday or Thursday of the following week at the earliest.

"Unless you want it to sit there for days without any depositor getting his money, you've got to get us in the bank," Davis urged. At that point, the Comptroller was not prepared to close the bank or authorize the FDIC to move in. "What I was trying to do was to get somebody to make a decision, so that I could get our people in," Isaac recalled later.

It is not easy to walk into a well-run bank and make sense of its computer and accounting systems. It is even more difficult to enter a failed bank and understand what's going on, because the problems that led to its demise will also be reflected in its systems and procedures. The chairman wanted to send his people in to start cutting checks so that there would be no delays in returning funds to insured depositors. Isaac reasoned that if the bank was going to fail—there seemed to be little doubt about that—and if it was going to fail without another bank stepping up to assume its obligations—and, in Isaac's view, there was little doubt about that either—then he figured, "Let's get on with it."

Even though the examiners were now working overtime, the bank's shoddy documentation slowed the effort down to a snail's pace. The loss figures kept changing, said one participant in the Washington discussions, and there was confusion on who had the numbers on loan losses and the size of the participations. By the end of the week, the examiners were scraping the bottom of Penn Square's barrel of rotten loans and write-offs were bogging down. Conover himself was anxious to see the matter resolved. In fact, bank statutes allow the Comptroller to declare a bank insolvent when he is "satisfied" that it is insolvent, and Conover, in his gut, was satisfied. According to other observers, however, his lawyers cautioned him to wait until insolvency was established beyond any doubt. "Every time Todd would say, 'I'm going to close the bank,' " recalled one official, "counsel said, 'You'd better not.' "

At a top-level interagency staff meeting that weekend, Isaac could no longer contain his exasperation at what he felt was the lack of progress by Conover's examiners. Isaac snapped at Paul Homan, saying, "When you decide to close the bank, let us know and we'll do the job," and threw up his hands in disgust, according to one observer.

Mike Bradfield, the Fed's irascible general counsel, as well as Paul Homan and Bill Martin, were equally furious over Isaac's apparent zeal for shutting the bank down. "They seemed to be enthusiastic about closing Penn Square. We had to do everything but hit them over the head to prevent them from getting it closed on Friday," said one FDIC critic.

Logistics aside, Isaac viewed Penn Square as a low-risk opportunity to instill discipline in the banking system.

It was time for Homan to give his speech. Even though he had recommended the change in the cease and desist order requiring the bank to inject the $30 million by late Friday, he was still holding out for an eleventh-hour weekend rescue. Homan was not against a closing, but he was adamantly opposed to a payout where uninsured depositors wouldn't be made whole. Arguing vociferously that to pay out Penn Square would change the rules of the financial game without an announcement, Homan asserted that such a move would weaken confidence in the nation's major banks. Indeed, Homan figured that if Penn Square were paid off, there was a 15% to 25% chance of "severe systematic effects." Translated into layman's language, that meant the collapse of the American banking system.

Homan believed that the FDIC was reversing without warning some fifty years of comfort for the larger banks, and singling out a bank in Oklahoma City for the wrong reasons. He felt that for twenty years or more the FDIC had let the market know by its actions that it would not pay out a bank of that size because of the systemic consequences. Moreover, he was convinced that the FDIC could realistically whittle the $3 billion in contingent liabilities down to less than $300 million in losses. He was sure that a deal could be worked out with the Big Five banks to accept liability for the $2 billion, as well as some $500 million in unfunded commitments, which the FDIC feared it would be liable for. That left half a billion in letters of credit, and other liabilities, which Homan and others felt were fairly legitimate but which still could be pared to an acceptable level. Homan was dismayed that the FDIC seemed to be singling out a commercial bank to teach the market a lesson, when the agency was unwilling to do so with the mutual savings banks in New York City.

In his view, it was discriminatory, and hypocritical, of the FDIC to liquidate Penn Square after it had just finished pumping $425 million into a single mutual savings bank in New York, and a total of $1.7 billion into ten mutuals. The mutuals, however, were victims more of interest rate shifts than management incompetence and derelection of duty. They had done essentially what the government had told them to do: make fixed rate, 30-year home loans. When interest rates rose, the mutuals, as a group, were paying out more on savings certificates than they were earning on those loans.

A payoff of Penn Square, Homan argued, would also discriminate against the nation's small banks in favor of large ones. In an emotion-filled finale, Homan pleaded, "You can't pay this bank off. You've got to do a P&A. I don't care what it costs!"

"Even if it costs a half a billion or a billion dollars?" Isaac asked.

"It doesn't matter what it costs. You can't pay this bank off. If you do you'll have to deal with Seafirst and Continental and who knows what else," Homan said, as Isaac remembers the conversation.

"If we have to deal with Seafirst and Continental we'll deal with them," Isaac replied.

At one point, Homan told Isaac, according to participants in the meeting, "You wouldn't do this if it were Continental."

Isaac is said to have replied, "Oh, yes, I would," although the FDIC chairman later denied making such a statement.

Conover and his confidant, Deputy Comptroller Doyle Arnold, another free marketeer and advocate of the right-to-fail, sided with Isaac. "Our job," Arnold said, "is to convince the public that even Citibank would be allowed to fail."

In the view of some of those present, Homan seemed to have planted a seed of doubt in Isaac's mind and the brash bank regulator appeared to mellow. As he was walking toward the door of his office, he turned and said, "We could be blamed." And he reportedly said, "We'll take it up to $300 million."

In New York, the reporter for the *American Banker* had booked a flight to Oklahoma City for 8:15 P.M., but decided to call Glen Bayless of the *Daily Oklahoman* first to get a feel for the situation at the bank.

Bayless yelled into the phone, saying, "That story on the FDIC, that's like shouting fire in a movie theater. That's yellow journalism at its worst!" Bayless said that neither the Comptroller nor the FDIC had talked insolvency, and that he had just spoken with Bill Jennings himself, who insisted the bank would open for business as usual on Tuesday.

"Glen," the *American Banker* reporter said, trying to be patient with a colleague who seemed to have become too close to his sources, "do yourself a favor. Don't go to the lake for the weekend."

Because of that conversation, he missed his flight, and instead left for Oklahoma City the next morning, just as the run on the Penn Square Bank was again gathering momentum.

·THIRTY-EIGHT·

SORRY, WE
ALREADY GAVE AT
THE OFFICE

PENN SQUARE NORMALLY HAD LONG LINES AT THE MOTORBANK on the first day of a three-day weekend. But this Saturday, the lines would be much longer than usual, and most of the transactions would be withdrawals.

Television crews and radio reporters were broadcasting live from outside the bank, as they had done the evening before. "We'd be carrying boxes out and the TV people would come up and say, 'Penn Square employees are carrying boxloads of files from the bank,'" a former employee recalled.

One middle-aged woman, an employee of an oil company that borrowed heavily from Penn Square, became alarmed while having her hair washed at a beauty shop in the fashionable Nichols Hills shopping center. She knew something was amiss when several women suddenly got up from under the dryers and left the shop with curlers in their hair. These were women, she said, "who wouldn't be caught dead in public with hair rollers. They were wives of people who would know what's going on." She asked the beauty operator, an old friend, what was happening. "Something about a problem at Penn Square Bank," the owner replied.

"I got up and left," the woman said. "I was one of the last ones in the bank. The police shut the doors and let only a few in at a time. Then they closed the doors and said, 'It's okay, we'll be open Tuesday.'

"They were trying to give me a cashier's check and I didn't want that. They'd only give you $1,000 cash, and wouldn't give you anything on checks deposited three days prior. That wasn't their usual

---

388

policy. The older people were very concerned; they couldn't cash their pension and Social Security checks."

Another woman reportedly refused a cashier's check astutely demanding the proceeds of her account in traveler's checks.

According to a regulatory source, Penn Square did not have enough cash on hand to meet depositor demand and issued $1.8 million in cashier's checks.

Inside the bank, loan review officers, lawyers, and examiners were turning up a parade of horrors as they continued to search the portfolio for collateral good enough to present to the Fed for loans. There were airplanes disguised as oil and gas investments where security agreements were filed with the county courthouse instead of the Federal Aviation Administration. Different loans were turning up that were secured by the same collateral, or no collateral at all. They were finding evidence that financial statements may have been falsified, notes altered, and phony credit files created. It was, as one observer put it, "a banker's twilight zone."

Every so often, Jennings ducked out of his office and walked over to the oil and gas area to ask, "How much have you got?"

Most of official Washington was deserted, having retreated to the Maryland shore or the Virginia countryside for the long Fourth of July weekend. Conover had contemplated a trip to a lake in Connecticut with his family. Doyle Arnold had planned to fly out to Minneapolis to visit his girlfriend. And Bill Isaac had looked forward to a weekend in the country with his family. Mike Hovan, a senior official with the FDIC's liquidation division, had invited some friends to spend the holidays with him and his family, but managed to have only one dinner with his out-of-town guests. They wondered what was going on but knew enough not to ask.

In deference to the Federal Reserve Board's ultimate responsibility for the nation's financial system, meetings between the top officials of the Fed, the Comptroller, and the FDIC were invariably held at the Fed's headquarters, a massive, Georgia marble building that faces on Constitution Avenue. During World War II, the Fed's cavernous boardroom was the site of meetings of military and civilian leaders of the United States and Great Britain at which the two nations assigned priority to victory in Europe, and later agreed on the principle of unity of command in the southwest Pacific. But when the joint chiefs of the bank regulatory establishment met around the huge, elliptical conference table in the beige-carpeted boardroom, or in Paul Volcker's small but elegant inner office adjoining it, there was little evidence of consensus.

At one such meeting, on Saturday, July 3, Conover and Isaac and their respective staffs assembled in Volcker's office to brief the towering Fed chairman on Penn Square's condition. While Volcker puffed on one of his Antonio and Cleopatra Grenadier cigars, Conover ran through the facts as they were then known; all the losses hadn't yet been identified but the bank had suffered a significant run. The withdrawals, he suspected, would continue on Tuesday and the lines of worried depositors would be broadcast on national television that evening. For depositors to be seen on network television lining up for their money, in a spectacle that would be reminiscent of the Great Depression, would have, they felt, potentially devastating consequences for the banking system at a time when the nation was in the depths of the worst recession since World War II.

Complicating the assessment of the likely impact a Penn Square failure might have on the upstream banks was the virtual absence of information on the quality of the loans bought by the correspondents. Two diametrically opposed scenarios on quality emerged from the discussions. Some speculated that Penn Square would have sold "the dogs" upstream, while others felt that the big banks would have been astute enough to take only the better loans. As things turned out, there was some basis for both views.

Isaac observed that a payout was a likely possibility. Volcker, however, was cautious. "Hold on, wait a minute. Let's think this thing through. Let's talk about this for a minute," he said, according to others present at the meetings. The officials explored the problems with a P&A, and concurred that the five upstream banks would be the only likely bidders. Volcker's mood throughout the long weekend was later described as "somber and grave."

"The Fed thought the impact was going to be catastrophic," said an FDIC official.

In at least one meeting where the Fed advanced its position, a top official was quoted as saying, "There are other banks in trouble; we don't want to highlight the problems by allowing this one to be closed."

The FDIC's response was, "You can isolate this situation. More people will be hurt by keeping it open. The smart money will be getting out."

Conover's dilemma continued to be the lack of enough loan losses to find a book insolvency, while the Fed, out of its concern for the banking system, continued to fund, stalling off a liquidity insolvency.

The officials decided that the Fed, specifically vice-chairman

Preston Martin, would take over discussions with the upstream banks on a possible bail-out plan. He had a tough assignment. The upstream banks had consulted with their lawyers and determined that they would be hard pressed to explain to stockholders why they had waived any right to file claims against Penn Square, or against the FDIC, if it became the receiver for a failed Penn Square Bank.

With the least at risk relative to its total portfolio, Chase Manhattan, in the opinion of many of the regulators, was the most stubborn. The nation's third largest bank had just suffered a humiliating blow with the collapse of Drysdale Securities and felt it had unfairly been forced to stand behind the loans it had made in that debacle. So when pressed to participate in a rescue of the Oklahoma bank, Chase was totally unenthusiastic. A representative from the giant multinational bank told regulators, "Sorry. We already gave at the office."

The Fed, meanwhile, was making it known that it was prepared to continue to lend to Penn Square indefinitely, and at one point a Fed official declared, "We'll just fund this thing forever." Isaac was furious. He told the official that if the central bank did that he'd haul it into court.

Had the Fed propped up Penn Square indefinitely and paid off all uninsured claims, that would have, in the FDIC's view, placed uninsured depositors in a preferred position relative to other creditors. Isaac felt that the Fed was subtly threatening to continue funding the bank in order to get the FDIC to go along with a P&A transaction. At the same time, neither the Fed nor the Comptroller, as Isaac saw it, wanted to assume responsibility for closing the bank. If the Fed stopped funding, there would be a liquidity insolvency, which would force the Comptroller to declare it insolvent on that basis. On the other hand, if the Comptroller found a book insolvency first, then the Fed would stop funding. Only at the height of a gala fireworks display on Sunday, July 4, did the fireworks within the bank regulatory establishment begin to sputter down, as the officials found a way for all of them to share the blame and responsibility for one of the landmark decisions in American financial history. In the meantime the discussions resembled a three-ring circus, with the Fed trying to exact concessions from the upstream banks, the FDIC chafing at the bit to close the bank down, and the Comptroller trying to pin down the extent of loan losses. Well into the weekend, the loan loss figures continued to vacillate upward and downward, contributing to the confusion. The venue of the meetings changed constantly; officials of the Comptroller met with FDIC

391

staff at the FDIC, FDIC staff and OCC staff met with the Fed staff at the Fed; Fed staff met with FDIC staff at the FDIC. The officials ate hamburgers every night for three nights, griped one participant in the meetings.

\At Penn Square, they were eating pizza, paid for with $35 in cash by one employee who figured he would be reimbursed out of the bank's petty cash fund the following week. On Tuesday, he learned he'd have to submit a claim with the FDIC.

Countless suggestions were bandied about, with most of them directed at ways to pare contingent liabilities. One short-lived option was to have the correspondent banks buy out the minority portion of the loans and then hold the FDIC blameless. According to Conover, the regulators also discussed an "out-of-state takeover under hold-harmless agreements."

The officials explored the possibility of chartering a bank and operating it under a conservatorship, but then the question arose as to who would run it and assume liability.

Solutions were no more forthcoming from Oklahoma than they were from Washington. Paul Volcker, as is his practice, felt obligated to seek the advice of local banking authorities in arriving at a decision on Penn Square. He called on his secretary, Catherine Mallardi, a woman known for her uncanny ability to locate anyone, anywhere, at any time, to track down R.Y. Empie, Oklahoma's diminutive and outspoken banking commissioner. She found him at the vacation cottage of a friend on Grand Lake, where many of the other players in the high-stakes financial drama, including Frank Mahan, were also spending the long weekend.

"You've got a serious situation in your state," Volcker said. "Do you have any suggestions for handling the problem?"

Empie is a tough-minded regulator with little sympathy for bankers who run amuck, and he is not known for mincing his words. "Let 'em fail," Empie told the chairman, who reportedly was taken aback by the commissioner's response.

As Empie explained later, Volcker called to "sound me out as to whether some great tragedy might be triggered by closing Penn Square," adding that the chairman was concerned about it causing runs on the deposits of other Oklahoma banks. Empie said he figured, "If that's the way it is, that's the way it is."

Likewise, Isaac succeeded in reaching a top official of the National Credit Union Administration at a wedding in Ohio and told him some credit unions would suffer big losses.

Meanwhile, Davis and his liquidators continued to press Isaac for the key to the bank to allow them to move in and prepare for whatever contingency would take place Tuesday. Normally, the FDIC does not begin such preparations until the bank is declared insolvent and it is appointed receiver. Finally, on Saturday, as Isaac recalls, he received permission from Conover to prepare for a payoff. But the advance team was to encounter one serious logistical problem. The bank's books were not kept by Penn Square, but by an outside service firm that was a subsidiary of Jennings's alma mater, Fidelity Bank. "Our people," Isaac recalled, "were saying there's no way to get the books or run the computers this weekend. 'They're all going to be off on vacation, there is no way to do it.'

"There's got to be a way to do it," Isaac insisted. "If you need to, tell them we'll pay them the customary fees plus any overtime charges plus a $100,000 bonus, if they get us the data by tomorrow evening. Do whatever it takes, but get the data, and if it takes a $100,000 bonus, put it on the table."

The $100,000 grabbed their attention. They were stunned by the boldness of the move and the realization that their boss was not averse to playing high-stakes poker.

"It changed the atmosphere around here a lot," Isaac reflected. "Ordinarily, we have a kind of routine we go through on how we handle bank failures. And I think people were going along that routine path. By offering the bonus, the atmosphere changed from one which people point out reasons why something can't be done to one in which people say, 'How are we going to do it?' " The FDIC located the head of the computer service firm, but never had to pay the bonus.

Oilman Joe Dan Trigg suspected something was wrong when he found that $7 million had been deposited in his account and about $6.5 million had been withdrawn on the same day.

So at 4:00 P.M., Trigg showed up at the office of Penn Square senior vice-president Russ Bainbridge. That evening and the next morning, according to trial testimony, Bainbridge and Phil Busey made two frightening discoveries: that a $3 million note in the name of Joe Dan Trigg had been used to pay off the three bad loans to Chase Exploration, and that a second note for $4 million was applied to debts of Tureaud's Saket Petroleum and River Ridge real estate projects. Trigg's reaction, said Bainbridge, was "utter disbelief." Trigg wanted to know what he was going to get for his money. He ended up getting nothing but trouble.

Later Saturday evening, Bainbridge recalled that he phoned Jennings and told him there was a serious matter that he needed to discuss with him right away. Jennings, of course, was trying to cope with a lot of serious matters.

"How serious?" Jennings asked.

"Very serious."

"I haven't had anything to eat all day. Let's grab a hamburger," Jennings suggested.

Over hamburgers, Bainbridge sketched out what had happened. Jennings buried his head in his hands and said, "I can't believe Bill would do this. I've turned a monster loose on the world. I just can't believe it!" he exclaimed.

On Sunday Beller declared in a meeting with Trigg and Penn Square lawyers that there was no doubt in his mind the transaction would have to be "reversed out." Busey, meanwhile, was working on the QOL/Mahan Rowsey quagmire, and talked with Jennings and Beller about the need to rescind that transaction as well.

While Bainbridge and Trigg were meeting in Oklahoma City, the Fed board of governors was regrouping in Washington for a discussion of the events to date. Charges of fraud, it was reported, made prospective acquirers wary of taking over the bank without some protection. At this point, the options included a P&A involving a single bank or a consortium, but that possibility began to appear less and less likely. Another alternative called for the Fed to lend to Penn Square until the exam was completed and a long-term solution put into place.

The final option was one that had only been used twice in the fifty-year history of the FDIC. It became known as the "DINB [Deposit Insurance National Bank] option," under which insured depositors could continue to write checks on their Penn Square accounts or withdraw funds in person. It was intended to prevent panic among insured depositors who otherwise would be separated from their money for days or even weeks.

The board noted that two courses of action were possible under this plan. The Fed could lend to the DINB to pay off a portion of the uninsured deposits, or those claims could be settled along with other creditors as the assets of Penn Square Bank were liquidated. There were those on the board who favored lending to the DINB out of concern for the uninsured depositors. On the other hand, that alternative would raise the FDIC's cost if a takeover could not be arranged by "reducing the pool of assets of the bank that could be liquidated." The board itself was torn between concern about the impact of the failure on other financial institutions and fear of establishing a precedent in reimbursing uninsured depositors.

At that point, Conover, Isaac, and several FDIC staff members joined the meeting. And once again, Isaac stated his desire to close the bank as soon as possible to allow his staff to set up the DINB and pay off depositors. He asserted that the loss to uninsured depositors, while unfortunate, would warn financial institutions about the risks associated with the use of brokered funds. But he proposed to the Fed that if the agency was so concerned about the systematic effects it could share the risk with the FDIC.

One way to do this would be for the FDIC to fund the insured deposits, while the Fed would cover 50% of the uninsured. Insured depositors would receive all of their money from the DINB, and the uninsured would get 50% in cash and a receiver's certificate for the remainder. Under the proposal, the FDIC would lose whatever it would lose in a straight payoff, and the Fed would forfeit half that amount. The contingent claims would not be guaranteed by anybody.

The Fed was "horrified" at that suggestion, said one participant. "It was on the spot. The Fed would be in the position of absorbing bad assets, something it felt it had no legal authority to do." According to the official, the Fed was concerned that under such an arrangement it would be acting in the place of the insurance fund. "The Fed was at a loss as to what should be done," another official recalled.

Said a regulator, "I didn't get the impression that the Fed was willing to go beyond its normal authority. The response was no response. Their perception was that the purpose of the fund was to backstop the industry."

By Sunday, the last of the Fed governors had taken off for the holiday, leaving Paul Volcker, Preston Martin, and senior Fed staff to deliberate the future of Penn Square by themselves, although Govs. Gramley, Rice, and Teeters participated by phone in an early afternoon board meeting. By this time, the possibility of a takeover had become even more remote, and the board began to turn its attention to the implications of the bank's closing. The Comptroller was still looking for enough losses to shut it down, and was preparing a statement on the bank's condition that would be released if, by chance, the bank did open on Tuesday. It was agreed, however, that even if that statement showed the bank still had some capital, it would probably not be able to survive the deposit outflows that would occur on Tuesday, and would need more money from the Fed. Volcker and his staff agreed that the central bank ordinarily would not lend to an institution under such circumstances, and debated various options for preserving the bank's remaining assets if a take-over plan couldn't be worked out.

Mike Bradfield knew time was running out for those who held his view that the bank should not be closed. That afternoon he dashed over to the FDIC to go another round with Tom Brooks and Dan Persinger, his counterparts, and in this instance, his adversaries, at the deposit insuring agency. No one ever accused Mike Bradfield of lack of tenacity. "He's the type of person," remarked one high-placed regulator, "who, once he makes up his mind about something, comes back at you time and time again."

The debate went in circles for the better part of the afternoon. The FDIC wouldn't take responsibility for anything more than the cost of closing Penn Square and paying off insured depositors, and the Fed refused to indemnify the FDIC for the loss. Bradfield, Brooks, and Brooks's associate Dan Persinger spent Sunday afternoon sparring over the powers of their respective agencies to bail out Penn Square Bank, with each side arguing that the other wasn't interpreting its authority "creatively" enough.

"I don't understand why you can't do a P&A," Bradfield insisted, while the FDIC attorneys countered by saying that the Fed should "backstop the banks."

"The window is only a temporary supplier," Bradfield argued. "You guys can do this deal because the statute is flexible enough to let FDIC do it. You guys can do whatever you want."

Persinger said, "We can't do it. Our responsibility is to protect the fund."

"Why not?" Bradfield persisted. "There has to be a way."

Persinger asked the Fed counsel, "Why don't you step in the place of uninsured depositors?"

"We don't have the legal authority," Bradfield retorted.

In the mid-1970s, the proverbial shoe was on the other foot in the deliberations over the New York City funding crisis. Back then, according to officials involved in those discussions, the FDIC argued that the Fed had the authority it needed to lend directly to the then destitute city. This time around, the Fed was saying, "It's within your discretion if you decide to do it."

Brooks and Persinger told Bradfield, in so many words, "Since the Fed is promoting this, you can assume the exposure. Put your money where your mouth is."

As one witness to the marathon debate put it, "There was exasperation on both sides."

By Sunday evening, Persinger and Brooks and Bradfield had gone through their respective arguments a half-dozen times; several half-hearted proposals were tossed out but died in infancy. There was no longer much debate on the payoff option; a recapitalization, big bank rescue, purchase and assumption, shared risk by the FDIC and Fed, all had run their course. As far as the FDIC was concerned, the only question that remained was the type of payoff, and the mechanics to be used in executing it.

As it became apparent that the correspondents wouldn't be able to assume responsibility, there was cautious, but increasing, support for the FDIC position, although some officials, namely Paul Homan, still clung tenaciously to the Fed view. Still, according to Isaac, "The Fed hadn't decided if it was going to fund, and the Comptroller hadn't decided if the bank was going to open.

"My problem with the Fed at that point was not that I disagreed with their position. I knew they wanted a P&A and I made it clear we were willing to do a P&A under certain preconditions.

"But what I was not getting was a decisive, definitive response. Yes, we will grant the indemnity. Or no, we will not. Yes, we will fund on Tuesday. No, we will not fund. We all knew it was book insolvent," Isaac said. "Nobody doubted that. But the Comptroller's office didn't have it established in hard numbers."

The FDIC building on 17th Street was the best place in town to view the Fourth of July fireworks in Washington. By the time FDIC employees and their families began arriving Sunday evening, the negotiators were leaving for home. The real fireworks were over, and those responsible for them were as burned out as the remains of the skyrockets shot off over the capital that evening.

Late Sunday, Paul Volcker once again convened his senior staff in his office and polled them on what should be done. All but one favored a rescue effort.

"What do you think we should do?," Volcker asked the lone dissenter.

Without any hesitation, he replied, "I think the bank ought to go bust."

"Well," said the somber Fed chairman, "I guess that's what's going to happen."

JULY 5, 1982

B Y MONDAY, THE FUTURE OF PENN SQUARE WAS NEARLY SEALED, at least as far as Bill Isaac was concerned. It would clearly fail; there would be a payoff, a unique kind of payoff, one that had been used only twice before in the fifty-year history of the FDIC.

Much of what goes on in and between government agencies is ritualistic playacting—officials exchanging carefully worded memoranda and talking to each other while reading from scripts. The solution devised by the Fed and the Comptroller to dilute the responsibility, and the blame, for the closing was a swap of letters between Paul Homan and the president of the Federal Reserve Bank of Kansas City, Roger Guffy. That day, Homan transmitted a memo to Kansas City that was a bank regulator's equivalent of the kind of report a physician might prepare on a comatose patient before pulling the plug on the life-support systems.

Dear Mr. Guffy:
  We wish to bring to your attention our opinion on the condition of Penn Square Bank, N.A., Oklahoma City, Oklahoma. In summary, we believe that the bank is threatened on two fronts, net worth and liquidity.

Net Worth:
  The bank is currently under examination by the OCC. To date, our examination has identified losses in the loan portfolio that substantially impair gross capital funds. Additional loans were sold by the bank to its holding company and to one of its correspondents after identification by OCC as loss; the bank may ultimately be found liable for these losses. There is significant depreciation in the securities portfolio. In addition, irregularities in loan documentation and other business practices may give rise to substantial contingent liabilities that will ultimately result in losses to the bank. In our

judgment, these and additional losses inherent in the bank's asset portfolio will extinguish the remaining capital funds.

The bank is under a Cease and Desist order from the OCC that required the injection of $30 million in additional capital. To date, the bank has been unable to meet this requirement. Both we and bank management believe that the bank will be unable to raise additional capital under present conditions.

Liquidity:

There has been adverse and widespread publicity concerning the bank. Moreover, the money market, which has been the major funding source for the bank, is aware of the bank's difficulties.

Heavy cash withdrawals took place on July 2nd and 3rd as news of the bank's problems spread. Several major correspondent banks have declined to sell federal funds to the bank. The bank's officers have since ordered its funding desk not to purchase federal funds from any source. Several large uninsured depositors have requested their money. We understand that certain local banks refused to cash official checks of the bank, although we assume they are taking them for collection. In light of these circumstances, we believe the bank is unable to meet the demands of its depositors and credits from private funding sources. Further, we believe that support from the money market and other sophisticated uninsured and unsecured lenders will continue to erode. This support at the present time approaches $300 million.

Therefore, we believe significant long-term funding support from the Federal Reserve would be required if the bank is to continue to meet the demands placed upon it. The amounts required may well approach or exceed $300 million.

Conclusion:

We do not believe that the bank will be viable in the foreseeable future. As noted above this judgment is based on the likelihood of a negative capital funds position and the inability of the bank to obtain private funding. In light of these circumstances, we wish to be apprised of your intentions in providing loans to this bank.

Sincerely
Paul Homan

Homan quickly received the expected answer to his letter, a reply that incorporated some of the same terms and phrases that Homan himself had used in his original letter. It was like a beginning foreign language class in which the instructor asks a question, and the student responds by simply turning the question around.

Dear Mr. Homan:
Pursuant to the information contained in your letter of July 5, 1982, concerning the current financial condition of the Penn Square Bank, N.A. Oklahoma City, Oklahoma, the Federal Reserve Bank of Kansas City is not prepared to extend further credit to the bank in its current condition.

At 2:00 P.M. Monday, according to minutes of the Federal Reserve Board, Paul Volcker reluctantly acknowledged to the board of governors that there was "no possibility of arranging a takeover" of Penn Square Bank and announced that later in the evening the Comptroller would declare it insolvent, "with no immediate payout to the uninsured depositors." Instead, the uninsured depositors, for the first time in history, would be given receiver's certificates that might eventually be worth about 80% of their claim. The good news was that the holders of the certificates would be eligible for advances from the discount window, a decision intended to mitigate the impact of the closing on institutions with large uninsured deposits.

Placing the value on the receiver's certificates was, like most decisions in Washington, a political decision. It boiled down to what kind of a number was publicly defensible, what kind of a number would justify, or at least not call into question, the fateful decision that, for all practical purposes, had already been made to shut the bank down in the first place. Historically, the FDIC had recovered no less than 50¢ to 60¢ on the dollar, so the value should be at least that amount, the regulators reasoned. Some officials argued, however, that if they started too low and came in high, they'd create havoc unnecessarily. Another suggested 90¢, but one regulator pointed out that if it was placed that high, some would question why the bank was closed to begin with. The consensus was that they should err on the high side; it is easier, one official noted, to go down from 80¢ to 60¢ than to start with 50¢ and go up.

Around midday Monday, Isaac received a call from John Perkins at Continental. He seemed to sense, Isaac reflected later, that a final meeting was about to take place. "He just wanted me to know how strongly they felt that the purchase and assumption was the only way to go," Isaac said. The self-assured regulator was noncommittal on the outcome, but Perkins would have gotten the drift when Isaac replied, "The problem is that nobody wants to step up. Everybody wants the FDIC to handle the entire problem, including all these contingent claims. So if nobody steps up, I don't see how the FDIC can undertake that kind of exposure."

According to Bob Hefner, Continental's Gerald Bergman told him months later, "although I said all the right words, maybe I could have done it more passionately."

The regulators had briefed Secretary Regan intermittently throughout the long weekend, but he had not personally participated in the deliberations. Now, however, at a climactic Monday afternoon meeting in Volcker's office, it was time to spread the responsibility for what would potentially be one of the most significant decisions in financial history. It was a decision that would strike at the heart of the public's confidence in the banking system of the United States, the FDIC firmly believing that confidence would be bolstered, the antipayoff regulators insisting it would be destroyed. In any event, if the U.S. banking system was to be shaken to its very foundations, better to have a member of the President's cabinet sitting at the table casting the final vote.

During the weekend, senior staff from each of the three agencies participated in nearly all of the inter-agency meetings. But this historic meeting with Secretary Regan was intended for principals only. That message, however, apparently wasn't communicated to Paul Homan and Bill Martin of the Comptroller's office. When they arrived at the Fed with Todd Conover, they were greeted by the blunt-talking Mike Bradfield, who inquired testily, "Why are you here? You weren't invited."

The meeting opened with Isaac passing out copies of a letter addressed to Volcker that was never sent, a letter that outlined the issues and positions that had arisen over the weekend. Isaac felt that was the best way to get Regan up to speed on where they had been and where they were going. After listening attentively for two hours to arguments in favor of and against a payoff, the silver-haired cabinet officer said, "It sounds to me as if you all have discussed this at length and you know all of the issues and problems very well," Isaac quoted Regan as saying. "You've thought it all through. And the time has come to make a decision.

"But before we make a decision," Regan went on, "does anybody believe that if you do a deposit payoff, that the financial system can't stand it, that there would be total chaos?"

At least one person in the room felt that the answer to that question was a definitive yes, according to Isaac.

Isaac, however, responded, "I think there is always a slight possibility that you might set off a chain of events you don't want to set off, but I don't think that has a high probability to it at all. There is a far greater danger if we bail out all the banks and institutions. The long-range detriment to the banking system would far outweigh the short-range disruptions."

Regan listened carefully. "The decision is not mine," he said. "The decision belongs to the FDIC. I have no standing here. But I'll give you my opinion." Turning to Isaac, he said "Bill, I think you have to do what you think is right and let the chips fall where they may."

Isaac was elated that Regan had taken what he felt was the "long view"—so much so he wanted to reach over and hug the secretary.

After the meeting broke up, Isaac returned to the office and announced to his top aides, "We're going to do a DINB."

"I got this knot in my stomach at that point," Isaac recalled. "I had been absolutely certain all through the weekend what had to be done. But then all the doubts overtook me for a minute and I started thinking what have I done, what have I set into motion here? And what if the financial system can't stand it? What if we do have chaos? And what if our people can't handle the job we've given them, because we're pushing them awful hard."

He walked over to his window and stood there silently, gazing for some ten minutes at the Jefferson and Washington monuments and the flickering lights of downtown Washington. Sexton and Eggington stood behind the chairman, reflecting on the consequences of the course of action they had taken.

Suddenly Isaac turned to his colleagues and said, "What we've just done, what we're doing now, what we're embarking on is going to be very good for the system over the long haul, if we survive the short run." His loyal aides assured him that the system could take it. The risk of chaos, they said, was very low.

In Oklahoma, the premonitions that John Baldwin had felt exactly a week before had dissolved into a feeling of futility, into what he called "a funny sense that it wasn't too important what we had done." That feeling was reinforced when Baldwin, who was wearing shorts on that hot July afternoon, descended into the subbasement area of the bank and saw an "awful lot of people wearing dark suits and ties."

Monday afternoon, Bill Jennings told forty of his "children," as he liked to call his officers and employees, to get a bite to eat and be back at the bank at 8:30. He was pleased that they had accomplished the mission they had set out for themselves that weekend—scouring the loan portfolio for enough good loans to trade for cash at the Federal Reserve window.

"What's the status?" someone asked Jennings.

"I really think we're going to pull this thing out," replied the eternally optimistic banker.

When everyone returned, they would discuss a strategy for coping with the run on the bank that was inevitable the next day. That strategy included issuing a press release that read:

To our customers:

Penn Square is open for normal operations. However, due to rumors and various statements in the public media, we have anticipated an unusually high level of customer activity today. Since we are able to maintain only limited supplies of cash in our vault, we must limit cash payments today to $1,000 per customer. Any request in excess of this amount will be given in the form of a cashier's check. Cashier's checks are insured by FDIC up to $100,000. Certificates of deposit will be paid at normal maturity. There is a special teller on duty today to receive deposits. Customers wishing to make deposits should proceed to that teller. We apologize for any inconvenience which these temporary procedures may cause. We appreciate each of our customer's support and look forward to a continuing relationship.

Sincerely,

Bill P. Jennings,
chairman of the board and chief executive officer

Back in Washington, the phone rang at the home of Leonora Cross, the spokeswoman for the Comptroller of the Currency. She had been spared the ordeal of the weekend meetings, and was able to spend the holiday at home with her five-year-old daughter. Her daughter picked up the phone.

"Mr. Ho—man calling," she shouted to her mother.

"Come on in," Homan said, "we're going to close a bank."

About the time the Penn Square officers were having dinner at Chicago's and other area restaurants, top officials of the Comptroller of the Currency were seated around the coffee table in Homan's office eating Greenhouse Restaurant's third-of-a-pound hamburgers, the staple for all of that long weekend.

Homan's phone rang. It was Steve Plunk calling on the open line from Oklahoma. Now it was official. Penn Square's losses exceeded the capital of the bank.

"Well, that's it," Homan said, with a mixture of disappointment and relief.

Before declaring a bank insolvent, the Comptroller and his man on the scene follow a carefully worded script adapted to the unique problems of the institution in question. In the case of Penn Square, Todd Conover queried Plunk by phone from Washington:

"Do you believe remaining capital funds will be extinguished by losses identified during the examination to date?" Conover asked.

"Yes," Plunk replied.

"Losses inherent in loans sold to the bank's holding company and to the bank's correspondents after identification by OCC as loss?"

"Yes," said Plunk.

"Depreciation in the securities portfolio?"

"Yes."

"Losses resulting from irregularities in loan documentation and other questionable business practices?"

"Yes," replied Plunk.

"Other losses which may be inherent in the bank's loan portfolio, particularly assets classified doubtful and substandard? Do you believe, given the bank's condition and circumstances, that the bank is unable to meet the demands of its depositors and creditors from private funding sources?"

"Yes," said Plunk.

Conover then said, "I have become satisfied that the bank is insolvent. I have appointed the FDIC as receiver. Please advise the bank that we are closing it and appointing the FDIC as receiver effective at 7:05 P.M. Central Daylight Savings Time."

At about that time Plunk handed Beep Jennings a list of charge-offs and the order closing the bank, and Jennings examined the document and voiced his disagreement with the examiners' conclusions. He did not seem visibly shaken. But to those accustomed to his bubbly, animated style, his subdued appearance represented an equally dramatic change in disposition.

Five minutes later an official from the Office of the Comptroller in Dallas stepped out of the room where a meeting was taking place, just as Baldwin was returning to his office. The official extended his hand and said, "John, about five minutes ago the bank was declared insolvent, placed in the hands of the FDIC as receiver. It's been nice working with you." At that, he turned on his heel and sprinted down the hall.

Baldwin shut the door to his cubicle and sat down at his desk. Tears streamed down his face onto stacks of loan documents as he thought about all the work and effort that he, Dunn, and others had expended in trying to correct the bank's problems and turn it around.

"I can honestly say," he reflected later, "that in all my fourteen years of banking I have never worked that hard, got that much accomplished and learned as much as I learned in that one-year period. It's like in athletics, in a race, you give it your best shot and you flat out lose. I remember sitting in my office and thinking, all of that for this."

Baldwin recalls stepping into an office on the second-floor where the meeting of employees was to be held and seeing a large, official-looking document with a big seal and a ribbon hanging on it. At first glance, it appeared to be the bank's charter, but on inspection it turned out to be the original insolvency certificate directing the FDIC to take control of the bank. "I remember looking at the top, and the date had been changed. I held it up to the light, and there had been a three there. It had been whited-out and somebody had typed a five into it."

After ordering the bank closed Conover and several of his senior staff rushed to FDIC headquarters for one final meeting of that stormy weekend. Conover was adamant about wanting to open the bank the next day. Isaac turned to Davis and asked if that was possible. "It is," Davis told the chairman.

Isaac said, "Go ahead."

As a result of that decision, FDIC claims agents and liquidators wound up working through the night, combining accounts to determine eligibility for deposit insurance, separating the accounts in excess of the limit, a job made all the more difficult because some of the bank's records were in a time-locked vault.

Jennings's eight-thirty meeting with his children would still take place as scheduled. They began trickling back to the bank in small groups shortly after eight o'clock. But when they saw Jennings sitting motionless in his chair they knew something had changed.

At eight-thirty Robertson escorted a husky, white-haired man in a plaid suit into Jennings's office and the two men shook hands. A couple of hundred of Jennings's children gathered on the second floor, most of them sobbing and embracing one another. Jennings, Robertson, and the third man appeared in the doorway. Jennings spoke first. "Boys and girls, I'd like to introduce you to Jim Hudson of the FDIC. He's your new boss. Please give him the same dedication and hard work you've always given me." Jennings, in tears, thanked his employees for everything they'd done. "We tried to meet the challenge but weren't given the opportunity," he said.

Outside, in the parking lot, local TV stations had set up batteries of television cameras, their floodlights bathing the white bank building. Reporters milled around the bank, trying to buttonhole examiners, employees, anyone who looked like he knew what was going on. Television reporters read the Comptroller's statement before live cameras.

An FDIC official escorted Jennings by the arm off the floor, refusing to allow him to return to his office. Anxious to avoid the reporters who had gathered outside the bank, Jennings, Beller, and other bank officials made their escape through underground passageways to a distant corner of the shopping center where a car was waiting for them.

They don't call him "Take No Prisoners" Hudson for nothing. His speech was terse, as those present remember it.

"We are the FDIC," he bellowed to the dumbfounded workers. "We are here to liquidate the bank. Mr. Jennings asked for your cooperation, and we need it. From this day forward you are FDIC employees," he said. "You are to talk to no one about this closing. You are to disclose nothing about the closing. You are to take nothing out of the building.

"I have a list of people I want to meet with. I want the rest of you to go home and be back in the morning at the regular time. The appropriate press releases and announcements will be made. Show up for work just like you always have."

Hudson came across pretty cold, acknowledged a colleague who was in the audience. "He didn't want to leave them with the impression that he was a teddy bear and that life would be the same."

And one top Penn Square officer remarked prophetically to an FDIC aide, "You don't know what you've got here."

About 9:00 P.M. FDIC personnel began securing the building, flashing their ID's and ordering former Penn Square officers and staff to leave. One officer had left his pipe in his office on another floor and told the FDIC liquidators he'd have to go down to get it. That would not be possible, the Feds told the husky six-footer. The officer insisted on retrieving the pipe, and burst through a phalanx of federal agents to return to his office to do so.

In the hours that followed the closing, small groups of employees left the building, their faces taut and downcast. When reporters tried to question them, they maintained their stride, walking sullenly to their cars. One employee, an attractive, vivacious young woman, told a friend as they walked out to the parking lot, "I just didn't lose my job, I lost my life."

A number of them gathered at Chicago's. They were saddened and angry at the developments of the previous few hours; they had all worked at least forty hours through the weekend and thought they were on the verge of accomplishing their mission. While they were worried about how long they would be permitted to continue working, the more immediate concern was the status of their bank cars. Among other perquisites, Penn Square had supplied its officers with forty-seven late model automobiles, Buicks, LTDs, and Lincolns. They would shortly have to find a new form of transportation. When the bill came, one officer remarked, "Sorry, this isn't on the bank."

Others, like John Baldwin, drove straight home. Uppermost on his mind was how he would provide for his family, and whether the stigma of having worked for Penn Square would make it impossible to find a job elsewhere. When he walked in the door, his wife and children, who had seen the announcement on television, stood up and greeted him solemnly. He walked into his bedroom, his wife shut the door, and he collapsed on his bed and cried.

From across the Northwest Highway, the poured concrete core of the bank's unfinished $36 million office tower loomed over the shopping center like a monument to Penn Square's excessive ambition. Ironically, the tower's flashing red aircraft warning light was, except for the full moon, the brightest object in the Oklahoma sky.

From time to time, a wiry security guard unlocked the bank's back door, allowing a group of men to wheel out large cube-shaped plastic containers on hand trucks. Inside the containers were the Osborne computers that would have been used to cut checks for depositors if the standard payoff route had been selected. Instead, the regulators decided that, in order to minimize the chaos, depositors would be permitted to draw checks on Penn Square Bank as if nothing had happened. The Osborne computers would not be needed.

Occasionally, the curious drove by. They came in late model Lincoln Continentals, Cadillacs, and Mercedes, asking what had happened. When told that the bank had failed, they asked what would happen next. Others with more than $100,000 in the bank had already figured that out.

A young blond man, dressed only in a maroon bathing suit and slightly sunburned from the long holiday weekend, leaned against his pickup truck gazing silently at Penn Square's main building. He was planning to sleep overnight in the truck to secure a place at the head of the depositors' line the next day. When told that he really wouldn't have to do that, he shouted angrily, "You don't have $100,000 in this stupid bank!"

Four young men wearing cowboy hats parked their white Lincoln along the curb in front of the bank. A reporter asked them if they were affiliated with Penn Square in some way. A man in the front seat replied with a curt "no comment." He then buried his face in his hands and cried. The euphoria of the boom days had turned to despair at the Penn Square Bank.

THE FALLOUT

AFTER THE THREE-HOUR FLIGHT FROM WASHINGTON, AND THE harrowing taxi ride through the deserted streets of Oklahoma City, FDIC chairman Isaac arrived at the Hilton Northwest Hotel and managed to get about two hours' sleep before awakening to prepare for the Tuesday news conference. In the rush to get off to Oklahoma City, Isaac had forgotten to pack a pair of socks that matched the suit he would be wearing the next day, and had to borrow a pair from one of his aides. While riding up the elevator to his room early that morning, Isaac encountered two FDIC liquidators who had been in Oklahoma City for several days. "Are you ready, can you handle it?" Isaac asked.

"We'll handle it if we have to start working in shifts or something," one liquidator replied.

Isaac wanted to be able to assure depositors that there was no reason to rush to the bank for their money, but if they needed it immediately, they could come down and get it. He was anxious, however, about the physical condition of his staff, who had gone without sleep through the weekend to prepare for the Tuesday opening. One of the other difficulties the FDIC faced was the wretched condition of the bank's books. They had been out of balance for several months, according to government sources, and the FDIC was forced to run the bank with them in that condition for weeks thereafter.

Isaac was clearly fatigued when he took the podium at 7:45 that morning in a large hotel meeting room jammed with TV lights, cameras, and television, radio, and newspaper reporters. In a voice that was as calm as it was tired, he read from his prepared remarks.

"Normally," he said, "we try to arrange a purchase by another institution but because of the abnormally large volume of contingent claims, that was not possible in this case."

Isaac's primary mission was to reassure depositors not only at Penn Square but also at the 15,000 other banks in the United States that this was an aberration. Asked by a local reporter if the problems of Penn Square were indicative of more widespread banking industry difficulties, Isaac replied, "The problems of this bank are unique to this bank. There are no lessons to be drawn here." The events of the next two years would prove him wrong.

He told reporters that all insured deposits would be transferred from Penn Square to the just created Deposit Insurance National Bank (DINB) and would be available immediately to their owners. "We'll keep the bank open twenty-four hours a day if necessary to meet the demand. We'll be in the bank all night if we have to."

As the chairman was speaking, the two lines of depositors that had begun forming in the early morning hours were growing longer. Outside the parking lot entrance to the main building, about fifty well-dressed customers, many of them affluent-looking elderly couples, waited in the "over $100,000" line in the 100 ° F. heat. Another 150 people, mostly housewives, students, and young working couples stood patiently inside the mall to withdraw their savings and checking accounts from the defunct bank. This was the "under $100,000" line.

At precisely 9:00 A.M., career FDIC examiner G. Michael Newton opened the front doors to the bank. A crudely written sign, scribbled in heavy red ink, was taped to the door. It read, "All loan payments made next door in installment loan department."

Young women wearing Penn Square identification badges walked down the lines handing out signature forms and instructions to depositors. Someone asked a woman in her early twenties how long she would remain on the job and who would be paying her. She replied abruptly, "I haven't the faintest idea. Right now my job is to give out these forms."

A helmeted Oklahoma City motorcycle policeman guarded the entrance while television crews panned the lines with their minicams. An ambulance, its lights flashing, drove up onto the sidewalk outside the oil and gas division's single-story offices. The AmCare Ambulance Service crew told the officer that they had come as a "precaution." But the driver said to a bystander, "We'll sure be needed before this day is over."

A reporter asked an elderly woman in the under $100,000 line if she was worried about the safety of her money. She replied, "No. I have confidence in what the gentleman said on TV this morning." Another woman on the small depositor line joked to a friend, "That was sure some firecracker they exploded this weekend." Her friend replied, "If I had managed my household accounts the way they managed their loan department, I'd have gone broke too," she chuckled. But there was no laughter on the other line.

Inside the bank, some depositors with more than $100,000 were learning that their life savings had been wiped out. An elderly widow had reportedly deposited the insurance payment on the policy of her recently deceased husband and was told that she would be entitled only to a receiver's certificate for the amount over $100,000. This was only one of many tragic consequences of Isaac's decision. As the weeks wore on, many more instances would come to light of individuals and institutions, in and out of Oklahoma, that would be devastated financially and in spirit by the FDIC action. Some 150 credit unions, including the Wright Patman Credit Union at the House of Representatives, wound up with more than $100 million in uninsured deposits at Penn Square, along with twenty-four savings and loan institutions with at least $19.7 million. At seventeen of those credit unions, uninsured deposits exceeded capital, and one thrift was left insolvent in the aftermath of the failure. Local churches, a medical research foundation on whose board Jennings served, and even the local YWCA, had maintained accounts at Penn Square in excess of $100,000, and were forced to scale back their programs.

"I remember looking up at the faces of people who had their life savings at the bank and seeing only utter sadness and despair," said John Baldwin. "They were experiencing with their savings what I was experiencing with my career."

Amid the gloom, there was occasional levity. One elderly gentleman who wasn't pleased with the treatment he was getting from FDIC employees told them he intended to go home to get his six-shooter and return to blow them all away. But as he was getting ready to leave, they had to help him up from his chair.

FDIC employees assigned to failed banks fall into two broad categories—the liquidators and the claims agents. According to FDIC veterans, the two types of employees tend to possess sharply contrasting temperaments. Liquidators, they say, have the instincts of a building demolition crew. Liquidator James Hudson, for example, has sold off the collateral of more failed banks than he cares to remember. His manner is abrupt, impatient, often testy. Then there are the claims agents, whose task it is to reassure depositors and pay out insured funds. That job requires a man with the compassion of a Mike Newton, the thirty-five-year-old career examiner the FDIC sent to Oklahoma to let people know their government had a heart, that the system really worked.

Newton is a slow-talking Texan with a drawn face and pronounced cheekbones who was the first official to greet the depositors queued up in front of Penn Square Bank. Walking through the lines with his arms raised above his head, he told anxious depositors in a low voice, "Your deposits are safe. The FDIC has $11 billion standing behind them." The assignment couldn't have come at a worse time for Newton. Just days before he was dispatched to Oklahoma City, he had learned that his best friend had been killed in Washington when a radio-controlled model airplane slammed into him.

As depositors slowly made their way into the failed bank, Penn Square employees returning to work were confronted with the indignity of finding strangers sitting at their desks and their personal belongings piled helter-skelter on the floor.

Coincidentally, as the lines outside Penn Square were growing, Vice President George Bush was downtown at Jennings's Skirvin Hotel proclaiming the end to the national recession. Speaking at a $250-a-plate Republican fund raising luncheon, Bush said, "the recession has bottomed out, economic recovery is underway and gaining momentum. While J.D. Allen listened attentively on the dais, one member of the audience whispered to another guest, "didn't anybody tell this guy what happened here last night?" Bush's comments might have described conditions in the national economy, but for Oklahoma, the recession was just beginning. It had clearly begun for Allen, who less than seven months later was forced into bankruptcy, declaring debts "in excess" of $300 million to Chase Manhattan, Michigan National, and the FDIC. The combined borrowings through Penn Square of Allen and his partner, Carl Swan, have been estimated at up to $500 million. Allen, undeterred, soon vowed to "start another empire."

On the return flight home, Isaac worried about his staff having to work around the clock for the next few days, but when he arrived in Washington that evening, he learned that the lines had disappeared. The chairman could finally stop worrying about the physical condition of his staff. Of greater concern was the financial condition of the banks that had bought Penn Square loans, particularly Continental Illinois National Bank and Trust. Isaac's assurances that morning may have pacified some. But in the executive suites at Chase Manhattan, Seattle First, Continental Illinois, Michigan National, Northern Trust, and in the trading rooms of some of the nation's largest brokerage houses, there was near-pandemonium.

Ken Puglisi, a senior bank stock analyst for Keefe, Bruyette and Woods, one of the country's leading bank stock firms, had a feeling when he left his home in Millington, New Jersey, for work that Tuesday morning that the day would be busier than usual. Puglisi followed about thirty large banks, including Continental, Northern Trust, and Michigan National, and his recommendations to buy, sell, or hold the securities of those banks directly affects their acceptance in the market. He had been reading the newspaper accounts of Penn Square's problems and was prepared for trouble as he rode the PATH train from Hoboken to Keefe's Liberty Street headquarters. That morning, the *Wall Street Journal* carried a two-paragraph announcement about the failure.

Puglisi didn't care much about Penn Square. But he was worried about the quality of the more than $1 billion in oil and gas participations Continental had bought from the Oklahoma City bank. In earlier conversations with Continental's top management, he had been given repeated assurances that they were good credits, backed by proven oil or gas reserves or other, solid collateral. He was concerned, too, because he had issued a "buy" recommendation on Continental's common stock on the basis of those assurances. Puglisi felt betrayed. The response he got to his phone calls to Continental wasn't gratifying.

Even before pouring himself a cup of coffee, the thirty-five-year-old analyst phoned Al Clem, head of investor relations at the giant Chicago bank. Clem is the bank's main contact with the investment community. The ability of the bank to raise the capital needed to support an expanded loan portfolio rests to a large degree on the credibility of the investor relations man.

At 9:00 A.M., Central Time, Clem's line was already jammed. When Puglisi finally got through, Clem's voice was solemn.

"How hard are you going to get hit?" Puglisi asked.

"I don't know yet, Ken. I honestly don't."

"Have you arrived at a second quarter earnings projection?" Puglisi asked.

"No, we just don't know. We're looking into it now."

As Puglisi and Clem were speaking, the senior management of Continental, Seafirst, Chase, and the other upstream and downstream banks were struggling to put a price tag on their disastrous flirtation with Penn Square, and grappling with the question of whether to put out the bad news all at once, or in dribs and drabs. Those opposing the latter approach argued that while it might make the news more digestible, it would also keep their institutions in the spotlight much longer than if they took their hits all at once. Continental, for one, attempted to play down the bad news and infuriated securities analysts by refusing to talk with them, actions that in less than two years would contribute to what one analyst called "The Continental Illinois Crisis: Part II."

"The markets can tolerate almost anything if they believe management is being honest," said one senior bank regulator later. "What they can't tolerate is uncertainty and surprise."

Puglisi spent much of the day calculating best case/worst case estimates on his pocket calculator. What he came up with was remarkably close to the announcement the bank made two weeks later. It revealed it had made a special provision of $200 million for bad Penn Square loans, and had taken a loss for the quarter of $61 million, then the biggest single quarterly loss ever sustained by a U.S. banking institution.

Meanwhile, Daniel Byrne, who runs the trading room, was overseeing some of the most frenetic trading activity at Keefe in years. Earlier in the day, he had given this terse order to his staff of stock traders: "Sell Continental and Seafirst—any price."

Keefe also assigned its entire research department of seven analysts to call banks around the country to find out who was in the Penn Square syndicate. Not knowing for sure who was or was not in, Keefe cut its positions on all bank stocks. Over the next week, Keefe was inundated with hundreds of phone calls from nervous clients wanting to know if their portfolios included any of the banks tainted by Penn Square, and trading was up more than 20%. Being associated with Penn Square was like "someone finding a whore in your bedroom," as one correspondent bank officer expressed it.

On the thirty-fifth floor of General Motors' aluminum-and-glass skyscraper in mid-Manhattan, Joseph DiMartino, the president of Dreyfus Liquid Assets, one of the nation's largest money market funds, was seeking answers to the same questions as Puglisi.

In their search for higher yields, Americans have invested in funds like Merrill Lynch Ready Assets and Dreyfus Liquid Assets, which in turn purchase commercial paper and million-dollar certificates of deposit from money centers and large regional banks. Few, if any, banks were more dependent on this "hot money" than Continental Illinois.

That Tuesday, DiMartino asked an associate to produce a computer listing of Dreyfus's holdings in the CDs of the banks that had bought Penn Square loans. He puzzled over how world-class banks like Continental and Chase could have become intangled with such a sloppy operation and wondered what other Penn Squares might be lurking in the shadows. Chase had already announced a $135

million after-tax loss on the Drysdale Securities debacle. How many
more fiascos could it take?

Funds managers often make decisions under uncertainty and Di-
Martino was prepared to move before all his questions were answered. His order to suspend the purchase of Contilly's CDs was a
directive that was repeated in money fund boardrooms from Boston
to San Francisco.

DiMartino is one of perhaps forty funds managers in the United
States—forty men and women virtually invisible to the American
public—whose investment decisions are of vital concern to the largest American banks. By the end of 1984, the money fund managers
controlled more than $210 billion in assets, much of it having been
drained from bank checking and savings accounts. Until 1982,
banks were prohibited by law from paying depositors money market
rates of interest on transactional accounts. Consequently, with the
high inflation and interest rates of the late 1970s and early 1980s,
bank depositors shifted their money to these funds in droves.

Once banks merely lent out what they took in as deposits from
small customers and businesses. But increasingly, banks were forced
to obtain their funds from these forty men. On the morning of
Tuesday, July 6, these executives were very nervous. The money
funds are particularly sensitive to adverse publicity affecting any of
their holdings, which are listed in reports mailed to investors four
times a year. The assets of insurance companies, on the other hand,
are less subject to public scrutiny. So, as the money managers let
Continental and Seafirst certificates of deposit run off, insurance
companies rushed in to buy them up at bargain basement prices.

Continental was about to face a monumental funding crisis that
in the next few months was to unleash rumors of its own collapse,
rumors that would be realized not in a few months but in just under
two years. The money men were running scared. They were fleeing
to the safety of the highest quality, most secure investments: U.S.
government securities such as Treasury bills, and the certificates of
deposit of only the most trusted, conservative institutions like the
venerable Morgan Guaranty Trust, and the Mellon Bank of Pittsburgh—banks unlikely to associate themselves with anyone who
would drink Amaretto out of Gucci loafers.

In its worldwide quest for money, Continental would have to pay
one to one and a half points more than its competitors. Its ability to
compete with its money center rivals would become severely curtailed.

* * *

Overnight, Oklahoma City had become the check-bouncing center of the world. Merchants and other bankers were uncertain about what to do with checks drawn on the defunct bank, so they were returning them by the bagful to the Oklahoma Check Clearing Association, an organization created by the local banks to expedite the exchange of checks.

Ed Farley is a talkative, good-humored man who for fifteen years was the assistant vice-president in charge of operations at the Oklahoma City branch of the Federal Reserve Bank of Kansas City. So when the bankers needed someone to run the clearinghouse, they naturally turned to Farley. It would normally have been an ideal part-time spot for a retired Fed official. But when the seventy-five-year-old Farley arrived at his tiny downtown office at 10:00 Tuesday morning, July 6, 1982, he began to feel that he should have retired completely. That morning the phone didn't stop ringing, and the callers asked just one question, "What in hell do we do with all these darned Penn Square checks?"

On that day Bob Harris, a former journalist and executive director of the Oklahoma Bankers Association, knew that Oklahoma faced its most severe banking crisis since the Depression, and that he personally faced the greatest public relations challenge of his career. That morning the banking group, which represents more than 500 banks throughout the state, summoned the presidents of every Oklahoma City bank to a meeting to discuss the handling of the Penn Square checks.

Later in the week, Harris called a meeting of association officers to devise a strategy for dealing with the mounting rumors about the health of other Oklahoma banks. In the past, the group had simply ducked troublesome questions from the media with a terse "no comment." This time, however, Harris was convinced that such an approach would not suffice. "This is not a no-commenter," Harris told the bankers. It was agreed that Harris, in interviews with reporters, would attempt to set Penn Square sharply apart from other banks, insisting, as chairman Isaac had earlier, that Penn Square was an aberration, lacking in sound credit judgment and exhibiting excessive growth and loan concentrations. The bankers also feared that Penn Square might be followed by other bank failures in Oklahoma and that the Federal Reserve Bank might not be able to act fast enough to stem runs on those institutions. Harris and his aides obtained the agreement of other bankers in the state to inject deposits of $100,000 into any Oklahoma bank in danger of failing as a result of baseless rumors about its solvency.

Indeed, the rumors were flying as fast as the checks were bouncing. Every institution even tangentially linked to Penn Square was being mentioned as a possible casualty. Some of Penn Square's small downstream correspondents had been more wary in their dealings with Penn Square than the big money centers, demanding that it buy back a loan if an interest payment were so much as a day past due. But others were swayed by the assurances of Bill Jennings and Bill Patterson that "no correspondent had ever lost a nickel on a Penn Square loan." At that time, the Bank of Healdton, run by Beep Jennings's mother, was mentioned as a likely casualty.

The failure of four or five country banks would not by itself bring down the Oklahoma banking system. But it could shake public confidence enough so that depositors might pull their funds and invest them instead in government securities. Oklahoma bankers had worked hard to convince their customers that their uninsured deposits were completely safe. Now customers were jamming their switchboards questioning those assurances.

In fact, investors, individuals, corporations, and financial institutions throughout the country had gotten Isaac's message: the government would not always bail out failing institutions and their uninsured depositors. They quickly began to bring their deposits down to the insured level by splitting them up among several institutions or by establishing accounts under different names in the same institution. That message was modified considerably two years later when the regulators made it clear that some banks were simply too big to be allowed to fail.

Rumors also abounded about the condition of Bill Jennings's former employer, Fidelity Bank, whose reputation was now tainted because it had continued to finance his personal ventures. Not knowing just how much exposure Fidelity had to Penn Square, some observers speculated that the downtown bank would follow Penn Square into insolvency. By Friday, Fidelity officials had answered more than seventy-five phone calls from reporters, customers, and other bankers seeking reassurance about the bank's financial condition. Reflecting this concern, a share of Fidelity common stock lost a third of its value in less than a week.

As FDIC officials in Oklahoma City began to cope with the onslaught of Penn Square depositors, Seafirst director Bob Schultz was getting a haircut at a barber shop in Yakima, Washington, having just returned from a weekend outing.

"Boy, your bank sure took a beating," the barber said as he clipped Schultz's gray hair. Schultz was startled.

"What are you talking about?," Schultz asked as he bolted up from a reclining position in the chair.

The barber told him about the report he'd heard earlier on the radio.

Schultz immediately called the bank from the phone at the barber shop.

He was told, "Yeah, Bob, we've got a problem."

One Penn Square officer reportedly learned of the closing while on vacation in Colorado, when he attempted to cash a check at a bank there. An officer at the Colorado bank told him, "Sorry, that bank's closed." And another officer was on his honeymoon. He was in the rest room at an airport and happened to look down at a discarded newspaper on the floor to see a front page story on the demise of what was now his former employer.

Thorne Stallings, the former U.S. Senate candidate and head of a rig fabricating company, was lying in a hospital bed recuperating from a near-fatal heart attack suffered two months earlier. His company had just spent $750,000 building five deep gas rig components for a Penn Square customer who was to purchase them for $1 million. Watching the news on television from his hospital bed, the forty-three-year-old Stallings decided then and there to retire. Shortly thereafter, the customer canceled the order and by October liquidation of Stallings's own company had begun.

On the Friday after the failure, in what was the first official suggestion that criminal misconduct might have played a part in the failure, the chief of the Oklahoma City office of the FBI told a crowd of reporters that the agency had launched an investigation into the charges of misapplication and embezzlement of funds by a bank officer and allegations that borrowers made false statements in order to obtain funds.

That day, in Washington, Isaac phoned Secretary Regan to offer his assessment of the fallout from their decision earlier in the week. "I know we were both concerned about how this thing would work," he said, "and whether the FDIC could handle the situation, and what the reaction would be in the markets. So I want to report that it looks like it's going well. We're getting the lines settled down in the bank, and the markets are beginning to calm down." The FDIC chairman concluded, "It looks like it's been a success." To be sure, Penn Square Bank deserved to fail, and the decision to do a payoff may have been fully justified by the facts at hand. But Isaac's conclusion that the move was a success would, according to the criteria of some observers, prove to be premature. The failure of Penn

Square Bank was less significant itself than the events it set into motion, and less important, too, at the time it happened than in the weeks, months, and even years afterward. Based on its size alone, Penn Square placed fourth among U.S. commercial bank failures (it was later bumped to sixth after the failures of United American and First National Bank of Midland). But in terms of total losses Penn Square was clearly the granddaddy of bank failures, with the loan losses to the upstream banks and losses to the uninsured depositors and Penn Square shareholders amounting to more than $1.3 billion by the spring of 1984. And those figures don't begin to include the increased cost of funds to the participating banks, opportunity costs, and an endless array of very real but more indirect costs attributable to the disaster. Indeed, when the economic multiplier of three is factored in, the price tag runs well into the tens of billions of dollars.

In addition, the failure of Penn Square was related, directly or indirectly, to most of the large bank crises or outright collapses that have taken place since, including Abilene National, First National Bank of Midland, United American Bank of Knoxville, Seattle First, and Continental Illinois. No event since the Great Depression has done more to undermine public confidence in the U.S. banking system than the failure of Penn Square Bank and the chain reaction of events that stemmed from it.

"Penn Square," said one securities analyst, "flashed a signal around the world that maybe American banking isn't so sound. Here's a world-famous bank—Continental Illinois—considered the best bank in a glamour industry, that made a big mistake." According to the analyst, the Europeans asked themselves, "Could anything be safe?"

Less than three weeks before the failure of Penn Square, Roberto Calvi, the chairman of Italy's Banco Ambrosiano, who was known in international banking circles as "God's banker" because of his close ties to the Vatican, was found hanging from a bridge in London. Later, the reason became clear: his institution was being investigated by Italian banking authorities for irregularities involving some $1.4 billion in loans to Latin American companies. Although a consortium of public and private banks later bailed out Ambrosiano from its domestic obligations, it refused to rescue the bank's Luxembourg subsidiary. Taken together, Ambrosiano and Penn Square sent a clear message to the world of international finance: governments would not invariably come to the aid of troubled financial institutions. "The FDIC broke perceived convention that U.S. banks would always be bailed out and uninsured depositors protected," said former Comptroller of the Currency John Heimann. But the agency returned to the old convention in 1984 when faced with the prospect of the failure of Continental Illinois. In Europe, Ambrosiano, on top of Penn Square, "terrified" the financial markets, added one leading bank securities analyst. Spreads between the cost of funds and interest rates on loans had been ridiculously low, and bankers suddenly realized that they would have to demand compensation in proportion to their risks.

Expressed in human terms, thousands of officers and employees at the upstream banks have lost their jobs, and a few are known to have been placed under psychiatric care. For those directly involved, including Boyd, Nelson, and Jenkins at Seafirst, Sipperly, Pinney, Hansen, Hinchman, and Higgerson at Chase, and Lytle, Redding, Bergman, and Baker at Continental, Penn Square's failure was soon followed by what one observer called a modern-day version of the St. Valentine's Day massacre.

In Oklahoma, the failure of Penn Square Bank was compared with the retreat of a tidal wave that left both human and economic devastation in its wake. The financial gridlock that was created by the closing of the bank drove hundreds of oil and gas companies into bankruptcy court, and gave rise to hundreds of lawsuits in Oklahoma and elsewhere around the country. Even legitimate oil and gas concerns with no direct connection to Penn Square have been forced into bankruptcy, because they happened to do business with Penn Square customers, or customers of customers.

In the months following the failure, FDIC investigators turned up widespread evidence of possible criminal activity, including misapplication of funds, embezzlement, falsification of financial statements and other instances of bank fraud by officers and borrowers that resulted in more than 450 referrals to the Justice Department for prosecution. In January 1984, horse trader Tom Orr pleaded guilty to tax evasion and bank fraud and is awaiting sentencing. Then in July 1984, a federal grand jury in Oklahoma City handed down a 33-count indictment (later reduced to 25 counts) against Bill Patterson, charging him with wire fraud, misapplication of funds, and making false entries. After a trial lasting just over two weeks, a jury of eight women and four men acquitted the flamboyant energy lender of all counts. But only hours later, prosecutors in Chicago charged Patterson, Lytle, and Jere Sturgis with 16 counts of wire fraud and misapplication of funds.

Patterson's acquittal in Oklahoma City followed what was, by all accounts, a brilliant defense by his attorney, Burke Bailey, who portrayed Patterson as a victim, rather than a cause, of the Penn Square failure. In order for Patterson to have been convicted, prosecutors would have had to prove that he intentionally defrauded or deceived Penn Square Bank. The jury apparently was persuaded that because he had invested so heavily in bank stock, he would have in effect been defrauding himself. Moreover, defense attorneys, while acknowledging misjudgment by Patterson, pointed out that Jennings himself was responsible for introducing many of the borrowers to the bank and that Beller had approved, or at least initialed, many of the loans. Patterson took the stand in his own defense and testified that in a secret meeting after the failure, Hefner asked him to lie about the $31.3 million QOL transaction by stating that it was unauthorized. Chase Manhattan Bank, which held the note, later sued Hefner for collection. "I told him I thought he was crazy," Patterson said. In his closing arguments, U.S. attorney Bill Price seemed to close the door to the possibility of future indictments of bank officers when he declared, "if Patterson's not guilty of these crimes, no one is."

If Isaac's payoff was a success, it was because it shocked banking institutions into returning to the basics of prudent lending, a phenomenon that has caused bankers to shy away from speculative business ventures. And it was this aftershock, along with other Penn Square-related events, that in the opinion of at least one leading economist contributed to the precipitous drop in short-term interest rates in July 1982 and the economic recovery that followed.

In any financial crisis, one of the first consequences is the widening of the spread between three-month Treasury bills and three-month bank certificates of deposit, as investors place their funds in relatively risk-free government securities. The announcement on Wednesday, July 7, by the upstream banks of their enormous Penn Square-related losses accelerated this "flight to quality" and led to a "tiering" of bank certificates of deposit based on perceived risk.

According to Robert Weintraub, the late chief economist for the Joint Economic Committee of Congress, banks in the years prior to Penn Square had artifically stimulated loan demand by aggressively soliciting loans from high-risk companies. But after July 5, they quickly retrenched, reexamining their lending practices and procedures, a move that Weintraub said contributed to a reduction in loan commitments. Moreover, he asserted, the Federal Reserve Board, which through mid-1982 had shown no willingness to back off from its "tight money" policy, suddenly became "a passive accommodator," no longer resisting a drop in rates. "It became apparent that the Fed was accommodating in July," Weintraub said, "and it became apparent that it was relaxing in August." Indeed, in a June 15 appearance before the Joint Economic Committee, Paul Volcker strongly declared his intention of adhering to a tight money policy. "Nothing would please me more than for interest rates to decline," he said. "But I also know that it would be shortsighted for the Federal Reserve to abandon a strong sense of discipline in monetary policy in an attempt to bring down interest rates." That, he indicated, could eliminate the gains already achieved in the effort to control inflation.

These developments, plus the flight to quality out of bank certificates into Treasuries, were, in Weintraub's view, the straws that broke the back of interest rates in the summer of 1982. By mid-August, the key Fed funds rate had plummeted more than four percentage points. After hitting bottom on August 12, the Dow Jones Average, responding to lower interest rates, surged 38.81 points on August 17, and passed the critical 1,000 mark in October. One of the great bull markets in American history was underway. To be sure, there were other important developments that the Federal Reserve was considering in formulating monetary policy. Unemployment had reached one of the highest levels since World War II. The failure of large thrift institutions had become a routine occurrence. Drysdale Securities had collapsed in May. Mexico was nearly broke. In conversations, Federal Reserve officials have minimized the role of Penn Square in the central bank's formulation of monetary policy. But one staffer, who asked that his name not be used, was less restrained. "Of course it affected monetary policy," he asserted.

One of the principal beneficiaries of the drop in rates was the beleaguered $600 billion thrift industry. According to a former thrift regulator, the decline in rates that followed Penn Square was estimated to have saved some 1,000 savings and loan institutions, out of a total of about 3,300, that regulators figured would have failed over the next three years if rates had remained at their pre-Penn Square levels. Among the big gainers in the equity markets were the stocks of savings institutions.

Some money market analysts also speculated that the Fed's apparent decision to allow rates to fall stemmed from the agency's desire to ease the pressure on Continental Illinois, which at the time rolled over $8 billion every day and whose jumbo certificates of deposit were trading at a premium over the rates paid by other major money center banks. Continental CDs had fallen into such disrepute that the bank and its paper became the butt of a slew of raunchy jokes: "What's the difference between herpes and a Continental CD? Answer: Herpes is easier to get rid of."

On July 27, Bob Wilmouth, the head of the Chicago Board of Trade, phoned his friend, John Perkins, who was in executive session at the time. Perkins apparently anticipated the reason for Wilmouth's call, because when he returned it he formally requested that Continental be removed from the list of banks whose certificates of deposit are traded interchangeably.

Later, David Taylor, Continental's executive vice-president in charge of funding, called a meeting of all of his bond department staff, according to a former department employee. For the fifty-three-year-old Taylor, Continental was family. His father had once been an officer and director of the bank.

"If my father were alive today he wouldn't believe this," Taylor said in an emotional voice to an audience visibly upset over the events of the previous weeks. According to a former bond department employee, he told them, "the lending crisis is over, our challenge now is to maintain funding."

Wall Street sources say that Morgan Guaranty went to the aid of embattled Continental, in effect laundering funds for the Chicago institution by purchasing money at a discount in the market and re-selling it at a ¼% markup to Continental. Acknowledged a former senior officer of Continental, "Morgan was actively trying to be helpful."

And according to well-placed Washington and Wall Street sources, Volcker himself got involved, obliguely letting it be known to institutions and government agencies with big deposits at Continental that they had no reason to jerk their money. Nonetheless, the bank lost virtually all its sources of longer term funding. Six-month paper was gone. Even 90-day money was gone.

Meanwhile, Perkins and Anderson made the rounds among the managers of the money market funds, imploring them to hold the bank's certificates of deposit. The professional money men made the decision that the Fed would not permit Continental to go under. One of them was former Comptroller Heimann. After leaving his government post, Heimann became deputy chairman of A.G. Becker Paribas, the largest dealer in Continental jumbo certificates of deposit. "I got my people together to see what we should do. They determined what our exposure and positions were. The questions were, do you dump, stay where you are, or make a market? We advised them, if you don't want CDs to widen, go to the Euromarket. We said we were staying in the market." Because the Euromarket is not burdened with the reserve and other regulatory requirements that apply to deposits in domestic banks, it would be more willing to assume the risks associated with Continental Illinois. But the concern then became, as one former regulator put it, "What happens if Europe comes apart?"

Said one prominent Wall Street economist, "The Penn Square crisis was the first severe test of the view that you can always buy money if you need it." For weeks, Perkins and Anderson refused to discuss the disaster publicly, despite the urging of many of their colleagues. When they finally took to the road, communications chief Jerry Buldak breathed a sigh of relief. According to a former colleague, Buldak said, "Finally they're doing something."

The feeling of invincibility turned quickly to one of vulnerability. Officers and employees rushed to send out résumés to prospective employers. One former officer received a letter from a friend, "Dear Joe," it read. "Help. I'm being held captive at the Continental Bank."

Shortly after the failure of Penn Square, First National Bank president Dale Mitchell visited Continental chairman Roger Anderson in Chicago and offered to provide Continental with local knowledge on the Chicago bank's Oklahoma customers. During the conversation, Anderson remarked, "I guess things have blown over on this Penn Square thing." Mitchell replied, "No, sir, I'm afraid they're just starting."

Bank regulators and analysts were quick to dismiss the Penn Square episode as an isolated event for both the industry at large and the banks involved. In a widely circulated "Interview with Management" conducted by analysts at Goldman Sachs, Continental's investment banker, the analysts concluded, "We are now sufficiently convinced that Penn Square was a unique situation and not symptomatic of conditions elsewhere in the loan portfolio." But less than four months later the Deputy Comptroller of the Currency stated in a letter to the Continental board, "Examination results show the condition of the institution to be seriously deteriorated."

While there were those who felt that time would heal the wounds inflicted by Penn Square on the upstream banks, and that the news would get better before it got worse, others, like one bank examiner who was on the team that closed Penn Square, said of Continental Illinois, "They were a walking death on July 5, 1982." There were a number of developments that made it almost inevitable that the initial estimates of losses, like the early death toll in a natural disaster where victims are buried under tons of debris, would continue to rise as the dust settled and the condition of the victims became known.

Not the least of these was the fact that the FDIC, as a liquidator, had no particular interest in the survival of borrowers. As one oil and gas lawyer explained, "When they come and take the keys and foreclose on a company, you're not going to realize ten cents on the dollar."

With the closing of Penn Square, companies that might have survived were forced into bankruptcy because their sources of funds evaporated, and new sources, in the form of either banks or investors, were not forthcoming. Much of this loss of confidence was justified by the dismal financial condition of these companies, and their inability to find oil and gas. But at least some of it resulted from what one bitter oilman called "the stigma of Patterson's high-rolling episodes that rubbed off on borrowers." Added Larry Brandt of Invoil, "There was the assumption that you must be a crook if you did business with Penn Square." Companies with deposits over the $100,000 insurance level found their accounts frozen, and the contents offset against their Penn Square loans. This policy also applied to escrow accounts, which oil and gas companies establish to hold funds owed to, say, a drilling contractor pending completion of work on a well. In other words, the amounts in the escrow accounts of one company were the receivables of another. The effect of this was to shut off the cash flow to the creditor firms.

The offset policy, which was protested in lawsuits by the upstream banks but upheld by the courts, compounded the losses for those institutions because they wound up with just a receiver's certificate instead of cash for the amount of the offset. This was due to their legal status as mere participants in a note rather than holders of it. For example, if a customer had borrowed $1 million from Penn Square, all of which was sold to one or more upstream banks, and the customer had $200,000 in deposits with Penn Square, the $200,000 would be "set off" against the loan, leaving an unpaid balance of $800,000. The note was paid down, but the correspondent banks had no cash to show for it. It was, of course, in the borrower's interest for deposits to be set off against loans, since he would essentially be getting full value for his uninsured deposits rather than a receiver's certificate.

Many of the borrowers that had loans with Penn Square participated in oil and gas deals with each other, so the financial problems of the one were compounded by the Penn Square–related problems of the other. For example, Invoil, the drilling fund promoter, drilled wells with Clifford Resources, which was about to draw down on a $4.5 million line of credit secured by accounts receivable when Penn

Square failed. According to Brandt, Invoil had debt and credit relationships at Clifford on seven deals. Invoil, Brandt said, owed Clifford $1 million on joint interest billings. Clifford, however, couldn't pay its suppliers, and liens were filed against the wells, so Clifford wouldn't pay its industry partners. "It was," said Brandt, "a Mexican standoff." Compounding Invoil's problems was a deluge of lawsuits by unhappy investors, lawsuits that Brandt says were patterned after those filed against Swan's Longhorn Oil and Gas and which cost Invoil as much as $40,000 a month in legal fees. The freezing of funds in the oil patch created what Gerald Bergman aptly called "financial gridlock," a term that soon became part of the everyday vocabulary of Oklahoma oilmen. What began simply as the "slow pay" syndrome soon evolved into financial paralysis in Oklahoma and in the oil and gas business generally.

An official of an Oklahoma City service company, Topographic Engineering, that "staked" locations for oil and gas companies, recalled telling himself on Friday, July 2, on hearing the rumors of Penn Square's imminent demise that "no, it can't happen." On Tuesday, he said to himself, "Hey, I'm sure glad we don't have money in there." His feeling of relief was short-lived. Three weeks later he said, "Hey, our checks aren't coming in so fast."

The FDIC was bewildered by the paperwork and documentation nightmare they inherited from Penn Square, a predicament that hampered efforts to foreclose on property and return collateral to the proper banks. Because several banks were frequently involved with a single borrower, liquidators were often uncertain how to allocate loan payments to lenders. The participant banks claimed interests in loans for which other banks may have had first claim on the collateral. Or the same collateral may have been pledged against different loans from different banks.

Former Continental officers contend that in addition to the FDIC offset policy, other legal decisions made after the failure contributed to the deterioration of Continental's Penn Square portfolio. They claim, for example, that Continental had a first lien position on most of the properties that also supported advances from other participating banks. But because of court orders that placed Continental on a par with the other bank creditors, it had to divide the collateral on a pro rata basis with those institutions. Moreover, the FDIC disavowed letters of credit issued by Penn Square, which were the collateral for loans made to oil companies by Continental. "All of a sudden L/Cs were worth zero," said a former member of Continental's Oklahoma City workout team.

Because of their often diametrically opposed interests, there was no love lost between the FDIC, on the one hand, and the bankers, the borrowers, depositors, former officers, and employees of Penn Square on the other. To them, the FDIC embodied all that was wrong with government: its indecisiveness, its rigidity, and its high-handedness. Former employees quoted FDIC officials as saying, "We don't have to obey the rules. We are the federal government." In the aftermath of some recent bank failures, liquidators report that appreciative bank customers and local residents have been known to bake pies and cakes for the FDIC officials. There were no pies or cakes in Oklahoma City.

Former employees complained that when the FDIC moved in, the agency's full-time employees treated them like criminals, prompting the former Penn Square officers and employees to refer to their captors as "the F-DICs." "We were peasants guilty by association," said one former vice-president. "I was only at the bank eight months. All they would have had to do is let me run with the ball. They stripped me of everything, any incentive I had to work." And another said, "The immediate reaction by employees to the closing was paranoia, the fear that we had inadvertently done something wrong." That fear was heightened by the omnipresence of FBI agents, who began interviewing former employees shortly after the failure.

Although inside directors and most top officers of the bank were dismissed almost immediately, many of the lower and middle level officers remained with the FDIC. Some recalled that because they were given nothing to do for a month or more after the failure, they passed the time playing Zaxxon and other video games in an arcade in the Penn Square mall, spending $5 or so a day each on such pursuits. Later, however, the FDIC enforced regular nine to five hours and said, "No more video games," according to the former officer.

The liquidators often dragged their feet in disposing of borrowers' collateral, local oilmen say, with the result that by the time the collateral was sold, it brought less than the FDIC might have received if it had accepted earlier offers. In the months after the FDIC took over Penn Square, oil and gas prices continued to drop, resulting in a decline in the value of properties and oil-field equipment. "They don't understand the importance of timing in business," complained one former employee who remained on as a liquidator. After repossessing collateral, they took the view that it didn't matter to the borrower what they sold it for. "They'd rather dump the collateral in a manner they couldn't be criticized for than to get the best price," he said.

Said Dan King, a Penn Square borrower, "Talking to the FDIC is like visiting a very expensive Disneyland. It's like talking to Huey, Louie and Dewey. You can't get them to make a decision." And Murray Cohen, an attorney for several troubled oil and gas companies, added, "The FDIC made an Iranian rescue operation out of Penn Square."

But the FDIC emphasized that "we're not a bank, we're not a lender, we're a receiver," a point borrowers used to Penn Square's freewheeling practices found difficult to fathom. Said one former Penn Square lawyer, "The syndrome that had developed was that Penn Square would always be willing to work with the borrower. They had to realize they were playing hardball now. Banks were learning how to lend, and borrowers were learning how to borrow."

The only institution more unpopular in Oklahoma City than the FDIC was the Chase Manhattan Bank. The response of the upstream banks to the collapse, in the view of many borrowers and their lawyers, tended to exacerbate rather than mitigate their own losses. In varying degrees, the upstream banks seemed to allow one mistake to propel them headlong into new ones. By most accounts, Chase Manhattan, with the least Penn Square exposure in relation to its total capital and assets, was once again the spoiler. Many observers described Chase's strategy as one of trying to force marginal companies into liquidation, thereby pressuring other participating banks to buy its share of the loans. Some observers also noted that the downstream banks attempted to force the big banks to buy them out. Generally, those banks that were unsecured in a credit were more inclined to try to work a deal out than those with a secured position. Said one oil and gas lawyer, "Chase is cutting Continental's throat on one loan and saying, 'We'll work with you' on others."

There were countless battles over who had a secured claim in a credit. Early on, some banks that found they had bought the first participation in a loan claimed a preferred position in the collateral over banks that subsequently bought participations in the same note, only to discover later that according to these criteria they would be last in line on another deal.

Except for Michigan National, all of the major upstream banks almost immediately fired those most directly connected with Penn Square. But many borrowers and former Continental officers believe that Continental blundered again in sacking executive vice-president Gerald Bergman, who, despite his managerial shortcomings, was credited by many observers with providing the only leadership that was forthcoming from the upstream banks in working out problem credits. According to these sources, he established guidelines for communication among the banks and ground rules for assigning collateral. Some observers went so far as to say that Bergman's departure in August 1982 caused some borrowers to give up hope of ever being able to restructure their debt and "drill their way" out of their severe financial problems. Ironically, the man brought in to replace Bergman in Oklahoma was none other than A.J. Pearson, fresh from presiding over the bankruptcy of Nucorp Energy, which would turn out to be Continental's single largest bad loan.

Attorney Murray Cohen cited a laundry list of instances in which the banks and their lawyers magnified their losses through their ignorance of the oil business and their eagerness to get out of Oklahoma. Bankers who had cut off working capital for financially distressed companies were shocked, he said, when they learned that leases had become worthless because the clerk who paid the delay rentals to keep them active had been laid off. In another case, he said, the banks shut off funds to a company before the drilling crew was paid. When their checks failed to arrive, the crew backed their pickup trucks up to the toolshed and drove off with the company's equipment. A disgruntled oil-field pumper, Cohen pointed out, who drops an $8 wrench down a well can cause $40,000 in damage. "The worst thing the bankers could do was to disrupt the organization. They came in like junior G-Men," recalled Cohen, who estimated that 25% of the banks' losses stemmed from such post-July 5 blunders.

"If a deal goes bad, the banker can't get it out of his head that he lent $10 million," Cohen said. "Instead of putting in $100,000 to save $5 million, they'll lose $8.5 million."

For Tom Eckroat of Aggie Oil, the most vivid memory of his unsuccessful battle for financial survival was the "hammerer" from Michigan National, who banged his fist on the table demanding his money, the "massager" from Chase who "wanted reams of paper to massage," and the man from Seafirst who urged everyone to roll up his sleeves and figure something out.

With all sources of funding dried up, leases for which borrowers paid thousands of dollars per acre expired, rendering them worthless, along with the loans for which they were pledged as security. The cutoff of funds took the "guilty and not guilty," said one bankruptcy expert. As bad as the condition of oil and gas companies appeared to be, it was probably even worse in actuality. While some companies may have been forced into liquidation, others that were, by most accounts, already broke were spared from bankruptcy because bankers wanted to defer their charge-offs. To a great extent, Continental, for one, attempted to "manage" its losses to make them more palatable to shareholders and securities analysts.

Among the many companies caught in a cash squeeze after the collapse of Penn Square was Robert Hefner's GHK company. Its existing lines of credit at upstream banks, and a contemplated new financing with Continental Illinois, were frozen. Hefner later managed, however, to "restructure" his hundreds of millions of dollars of debt, and he embarked on a program to promote the development of natural gas-driven generators in Third World countries, including the People's Republic of China. Ironically, the company rarely, if ever, turned an after-tax profit, according to bankers and others familiar with its finances. This was because Hefner's farm-out arrangements with his industry partners permitted them to recoup their costs before the gasman got paid.

The demise of hundreds of Oklahoma oil and gas companies had some unexpected, though predictable, consequences. As operators ran out of money, they abandoned drilling sites and half-completed holes, prompting a surge of complaints from farmers to Oklahoma's Corporation Commission about salt water pollution and surface damages. During the boom, said a lawyer for the Commission, "Farmers didn't mind looking at mud pits as long as they were getting money."

Penn Square, perhaps irrevocably, affected the way the oil and gas business is conducted and financed, not just in Oklahoma but throughout the oil patch. As in banking, Penn Square marked the end of "good ole boy" relationships and handshake deals in the oil business. Whereas in the past, prospective partners in a well could stretch out their payments, now they have to put their money on the table. Service firms now refuse to perform a second job until the first is fully paid for. And in abrupt change from the casual credit practices that existed before the collapse of Penn Square, service companies, in the post-Penn Square era, almost always perform credit checks on prospective customers.

Those companies that managed to stay afloat took drastic steps to retrench. An-Son's Carl Anderson, Jr., said he has cut his work force from 200 people to 100, and pared overhead of $500,000 a month to $200,000. "We're now running a tight ship and when the good times come back, we're not going to get loose."

In the aftermath of the failure, bankers report that examiners have become death on any loan that smells of petroleum, to the point where full secured credits with more than enough coverage at conservative oil price assumptions are being criticized. The Comptroller's office had been stung, and stung badly by press criticism and congressional charges of ineptitude in its handling of Penn Square. The excessively strict examination practices, oilmen say, have slowed the drive for "energy independence," the war cry of the 1970s and early 1980s. Dale Mitchell, who subsequently was appointed chairman of Fidelity Bank, said that such excessively rigorous examinations "suppress availability of funds to the economy to a great extent. We base a lot of credit decisions on how the loan will be classified now." Added Oklahoma City lawyer Jerry Tubb, "Today you can't borrow against reserves. And if you take a rig deal to a bank they'll laugh at you." Indeed, by and large, the oil companies that survived the debacle were those who paid attention to cash flow, rather than reserves in the ground. Penn Square also dealt a body blow to that ubiquitous financing device of the oil boom, the standby letter of credit, at least in its use in financing oil and gas deals. "The standby L/C became a dirty word," said one oil patch banker. Some observers even raised the specter that the downturn and the reluctance of banks to lend on legitimate oil deals would have serious national security consequences. "It's dangerous to have seven majors controlling things," said one bankruptcy expert. "It's critical to keep a bunch of independents honest." On the plus side, while investors and bank funds for oil and gas development quickly dried up, the cost of drilling a hole in the ground dropped to nearly half of what it was at the peak of the boom in 1981. The quality of geological prospects improved, and drilling shifted from day rates back to the more efficient footage rates. The huge glut of rigs led Rob Gilbert of the First City Bank of Houston to predict that no rigs would be manufactured in the U.S. for at least five years, and possibly ten. "You used to take your contractor to dinner to get a rig," said one oilman. "Now the contractor takes you." With the shakeout of marginal operators—"the shoe salesmen and real estate brokers," as one veteran described them—and increased efficiencies, many observers asserted that there was never a better time to invest in oil deals.

While the collapse of Penn Square coincided with the weakening of the energy sector, it would be a mistake to conclude that the decline in oil and gas prices toppled the bank. Many of the loans granted at Penn Square were bad when made, and some of those familiar with the bank's portfolio say that if it had been subject to a rigorous review in the fall of 1981, it might have failed then. For Penn Square to have survived, prices would have had to escalate according to the most optimistic projections of 1979 and early 1980.

Penn Square and Continental, by funneling billions into largely speculative oil and gas ventures and prompting other banks to exceed the bounds of prudence, pumped up the energy economy far beyond what was justified by the trends in oil and gas prices, so when the bubble finally burst, the shock was far more severe than it would have been otherwise.

If the collapse of Penn Square has represented the most devastating event in the banking industry since the Great Depression, it has also had a jarring, sobering effect on the Oklahoma psyche. The attitudes toward former Penn Square employees ranged from sympathy to outright hostility. Former loan review officer John Baldwin recalled, "You got everything from a pat on the back, 'Sorry it happened to you,' to 'You crazy slobs ruined my business.' You'd be surprised at the number of people who hold it against you personally. They think you had the power as an officer to do something about it, which was not the case."

On the other hand, some former employees said that their social lives picked up after the closing. "People I knew only vaguely," said one woman in her thirties, "invited us to parties. They wanted to hear the inside scoop on Patterson, and how the bank failed."

For many Oklahomans, the failure of Penn Square, and the downturn in the oil and gas business associated with it, led to unwelcome changes in lifestyle. On the surface, some seemed unaffected because Oklahoma law prevents banks from attaching an individual's principal residence in personal bankruptcy proceedings, leading some to speculate that borrowers intentionally socked away their assets in expensive homes in anticipation of such a disaster. But people who used to go to Hawaii for vacations now went to Lake Texoma, on the Oklahoma–Texas border. Craig Copeland, the head of Copeland Energy and an avid polo player with his own string of ponies, sold the horses and took up woodworking. Frank Mahan, mired in numerous lawsuits and bankruptcy proceedings, abandoned Oklahoma City for Grand Lake, while angry neighbors complained about weeds growing up around his Nichols Hills home. Bill Patterson, in the two years before being tried and acquitted in September 1984 on charges of bank fraud, mowed lawns and painted houses.

Bob Hall, the owner of Cowboys, said that the oilies now entertain much less, and in smaller groups, than they used to, and business in 1983 was off a third from 1982. One woman tells of a friend who spent $40,000 for a new fall wardrobe at an exclusive northwest Oklahoma City dress shop a month before Penn Square failed and returned it, in tears, shortly after July 5. Another woman in her early twenties who earned $2,450 a month as a draftsman during the boom reported that she was making a third of that following the collapse of Penn Square. Jack Hodges, however, still managed to throw a wedding for his daughter costing hundreds of thousands of dollars; it was an affair that included an 18-foot-tall lemon cake embellished with trucks and cranes and baked by a pastry chef flown in from New York. Hodges virtually took over the Oklahoma City Golf and Country Club opposite his sprawling home in the Northwest section of the city, decorating the grounds with 609 potted azaleas and trees, three flowing fountains, and white wicker bird cages filled with finches. Guests danced to the Les Brown orchestra under a huge tent equipped with six crystal chandeliers.

Dr. H.M. Chandler, a psychiatrist with offices near Penn Square and many of its borrowers, treated many of the casualties. The trauma arising out of the Penn Square–related losses gave rise, he said, to the gamut of adjustment disorders, from depression to total loss of control. "There were couples who came close to killing each other. They pulled knives and guns on each other because of the stress related to money lost because of Penn Square." There was, he said, a sense of betrayal by bank officials and the emergence of what he called "conspiracy thinking," a common occurrence in highly stressful situations. These disorders, associated as they were with a specific event, are more easily treated than those linked to more generalized causes, Chandler said. And the stress was alleviated, too, by a sense of camaraderie among the victims. "There was always someone else you'd meet on a street corner who'd also lost money," he observed. "The therapy was cocktail parties and bars." Moreover, Dr. Chandler said, a kind of pecking order emerged among the victims that allowed one group to recognize that there were others who were worse off than they were. Those who filed for Chapter 11 under the federal bankruptcy laws, which calls for a reorganization of the company, could point with some relief to those who were forced to liquidate their companies under Chapter 7. Oklahomans, observed Dr. Chandler, possess a resilience that is a throwback to the state's frontier beginnings. "They figure if you get wiped out by the Indians and there's one person left, you can start over," he said.

Another Oklahoma City psychiatrist observed that "loss is the worst emotional pain there is." The trauma of losing money in a place where one thinks it's safe is far greater than that suffered in say, Las Vegas. "To lose money in a bank," he said, "is like losing a part of yourself."

When Larry Brandt started over, it was with an entirely new personal philosophy. "At one time my driving ambition in life was to be rich. That isn't so anymore." Brandt said that he wanted business relationships that were less pressured, adding that never again will he become a partner with a bank. "I'll never trust bankers again," he said bitterly. "The bankers fixed it so you had to fail."

As in nearly all financial disasters, there were some winners. Penn Square was a boon to the Oklahoma City legal community and all those associated with it. As one attorney quipped, the failure of the bank was the "1982 legal relief fund." One California attorney recalled that in May 1982 he managed to get eleven defendants in a suit served with legal papers in one day for $70, but within three months the fee had tripled.

Oklahomans even managed to see in the disaster a kind of gallows humor. One local radio station aired a series of satirical skits following the closing featuring such characters as E.Z. Conover, Phil Assets, Carl Duck, and Wild Bill Winnings. A local impresario printed T-shirts bearing the Penn Square logo and the inscription, "I Survived the FDIC Invasion." And jokes about oilies fallen on hard times continued to make the rounds in Oklahoma City three years after the closing. There is, for example, the story about the oilman who shows up for a hearing and is asked by a creditor's lawyer, "Well, what happened to the money?"

The oilman: "I spent a third of it on a jet, a Mercedes, and Vegas. Another third went for women, dope, and booze." He hesitated for a moment until the lawyer asked him, "Well, what happened to the other third?" The oilman: "Oh, we just pissed that away." Then there is the story about the oil-patch bank that offers a choice of a set of china or a drilling rig to anyone opening a new account.

Oklahoma's image as a place to do business was severely tarnished by the Penn Square debacle, and the reports of alleged oil and gas frauds associated with it. This quickly showed up in the increased difficulty state officials experienced in attracting new business and industry. Jay Casey, the former commissioner of economic development, expressed the problem in blunt terms. "There was the image after Penn Square that 'they'll woo you and screw you in Oklahoma.'

"We had some companies we were working with that suddenly got very cold," he said. Texas has traditionally been a strong competitor for Oklahoma in attracting new industries, and according to Casey, his opposite number south of the Red River used the pitch, "Do you really want to do business there?" Meanwhile, Casey's fortunes suffered a double whammy when his staff and advertising budget was slashed as part of the broad budget cutbacks ordered by Gov. George Nigh in the wake of declining oil and gas production tax revenues. And the state's unemployment rate, which was one of the lowest in the nation at the height of the boom, became one of the highest.

Accordingly, Oklahoma, in promoting its virtues to out-of-state investors, changed its theme from "Energetic Oklahoma" to "Productive Oklahoma." And an employee of an Oklahoma City oil company added that attempts to sell non-Oklahoma investors on oil deals are equally as futile. "Now when you say you're from Oklahoma they run backward. The average citizen sees you as hustling and swashbuckling."

Yet others, even those hurt by the failure, were able to see something positive coming out of it. "It was a good thing to happen," reflected Aggie Oil's Tom Eckroat. "We got back to basics. I've still got my family and friends. I'm broke," he sighed, "but I came in naked and I'll go out that way."

Church attendance, he observed, is on the upswing and people are friendlier. "People were too busy making money before. Now they'll stop and visit with you. There's more humility than we've seen in ten years." Another borrower expressed his feelings somewhat more ascerbically. "I'm glad the downturn happened. Everybody, including me, got what they deserved. After the failure, it occurred to me that I don't have to deal with that Patterson anymore. I don't have to worry about that damn bank anymore."

Those who believed that time would heal Seattle First and Continental Illinois ignored a basic reality: that the marketplace had been changed irrevocably by the decision to liquidate Penn Square and not to rescue its uninsured depositors. The national bank examiners had become tougher, not just on energy credits but on loan portfolios generally. And the markets continued to "discipline" Seafirst and Continental. Seafirst was essentially shut out of the CD market, and Continental continued to pay a stiff premium on its purchased funds.

Curiously, securities analysts charged with evaluating the outlook for the stocks of the affected banks showed little more insight into their problems than the banks themselves, apparently continuing to rely on assurances of the chief financial officers that the difficulties were manageable. In November 1982, for example, the brokerage firm of Boettcher and Company, Northwest, recommended to investors that they consider buying Seafirst stock in the $18–$20 range or lower, saying that "Seafirst has begun to recover, albeit slowly, from its involvement with Penn Square Bank of Oklahoma."

Six months after the collapse of Penn Square, the crisis was just beginning for Seattle First, despite its efforts to put on a new face. In late 1982, the Seafirst board hired Richard Cooley, the respected chairman of the Wells Fargo Bank of San Francisco, to head up their ailing institution. Shortly after Cooley arrived in Seattle and began to grasp the dimensions of the bank's problems, he called on his old friend, Bankers Trust chairman Alfred Brittain 3rd, to assist him in soliciting big bank contributions to a "safety net" that would protect Seafirst should its funding difficulties worsen. In late January Seafirst revealed that in 1982 it had lost the staggering sum of $90.2 million, mostly because of bad Penn Square and other energy loans, but simultaneously announced that it had assembled a $1.5 billion "safety net" with the help of thirteen of the nation's largest banks.

Meanwhile, Seafirst had put itself on the block, making it known in financial circles that it was prepared to sell off whatever anyone was willing to buy: loans, subsidiaries, foreign offices, even its downtown Seattle headquarters building.

Coincidently, five years earlier, Stephen McLin, the chief corporate strategist for the San Francisco–based Bank of America, had begun to toy with a scheme that he felt would enable BofA to take over a large institution in Washington State as part of its interstate banking strategy. Having previously worked for the Bank of California, McLin was aware that it had a charter with "grandfather" provisions that allowed it to operate branches across state lines, an exception to federal statutes that generally prohibit interstate banking. At that time, McLin suggested to a former colleague at BankCal that the two institutions swap charters. For its part, BankCal would receive a much-needed capital infusion from BofA, and BofA in turn would acquire the mechanism that would enable it to achieve its extraterritorial ambitions. The two strategists couldn't agree on the terms of a deal, and the idea was abandoned until the fall of 1981, when McLin once again started thinking about acquisition candidates in Oregon and Washington. At the top of BofA's hit list was Seattle First National Bank. In a bold plan that BofA code-named the "Triple Bypass Operation," McLin proposed to buy the Bank-Cal charter and banks in Oregon and Washington in one stroke. But in March 1983, McLin received a call from Lee Kimmell, a partner in the New York investment banking firm of Salomon Brothers, that would render the plan unnecessary. Kimmell said, "You might get your wish without the Triple Bypass." At that time, Seafirst, with help from Salomon, was scouring the country for another bank willing to make an investment in the company, something McLin opposed on philosophical grounds. He told Kimmell, "You know we're here if we can do the whole deal and find a way to contain the risk." Bank of America president Sam Armacost was initially concerned that Seafirst's energy problems were a "bottomless pit" and emphasized that any deal could not leave BofA with an "open-ended risk." The negotiators, Seafirst and Salomon on the one hand, and Bank of America and its investment banker, Goldman, Sachs, on the other, were racing against a deadline. Seafirst was scheduled to announce its first quarter results at its annual shareholders meeting on April 21. The returns were expected to be disastrous. Without a bailout plan in place, Seafirst and the Comptroller of the Currency feared that the bad news could trigger a deposit run that would force the regulators to close the bank. As D-Day approached, Seafirst customers were drawing their balances down to the $100,000 insured limit.

Instead of Triple Bypass, the code name for the takeover of Seafirst became Project Forest; the Bank of America was dubbed Redwood and Seafirst became Evergreen. On the legislative front, Seafirst lobbyists were pressing the Washington State legislature to pass a bill that would permit an out-of-state takeover of a Washington-based bank on the verge of failure, a measure adamantly opposed by rival Rainier National Bank.

On Tuesday morning, April 19, McLin got the go-ahead from Armacost, and that afternoon left on the bank jet for New York. After nearly two days of round-the-clock negotiations at Salomon's lower Manhattan offices, the terms of the deal were finalized by 1:00 A.M. Thursday. "The hardest part," said McLin later, was that the air conditioners were off at Salomon Brothers. We kept looking for a room with ventilation. It was a choice between meeting in a room with no ventilation and one that smelled rank from thirty-five stale pastrami sandwiches." Late on the afternoon of Saturday, April 23, chairman Dick Cooley had some good news and some bad news: the bad news was that Seafirst had lost another $133 million in the first quarter. The good news was that the banking company had agreed to merge with Bank of America, in a nearly $400 million deal that included $125 million in cash, $125 million in preferred stock, and a $150 million capital infusion. Before the weekend was out, the legislature passed the failing bank bill, and what could have been the biggest bank failure in American history became instead the largest interstate takeover.

When BofA moved in, communications head Randy James said, "it was like the cavalry coming."

437

According to Richard Cooley, if the legislation had not passed in Washington State, the FDIC would have formed a conservatorship or trust that would have managed Seafirst for several years until it could have been spun off as an independent bank. "I came on short notice," said Cooley." I had no time to assess anything. My own naïve reaction was that I was getting a big opportunity. I thought it was a big carrot. All I knew was what these guys were telling me."

Following the takeover, which was approved by shareholders on July 1, 1983, Seafirst workout specialists in Oklahoma seemed to be more anxious to take their money and run than to try to prop up Penn Square borrowers, according to Oklahoma sources involved in negotiations with the bank. They attributed this to the fact that under the terms of the takeover agreement, Seafirst stockholders would bear the brunt of losses on loans made prior to the acquisition. With Seafirst safely tucked away under the protective wing of giant BofA, it was time for the Continental Crisis: Part II.

While Seafirst employees were celebrating their deal with the Bank of America, a glum-faced Roger Anderson was conducting Continental's annual meeting in Chicago, the first since the Penn Square collapse. Shouted one angry stockholder, "Only four banks in the country have a worse rate of nonperforming loans." He said prophetically, "We may be stockholders of a bankrupt corporation." The stockholder moved that the board resign, saying that "this organization is run for the benefit of a few. In Japan, the directors would be expected to commit hara-kiri." By the next annual meeting, Anderson had been sacked, following press reports that former officials Bergman, Baker, and a third officer had invested in oil and gas deals of a major borrower. Taylor, in an effort to be open about Continental's continuing woes, acknowledged that problem loans had risen $400 million in the first quarter to a staggering $2.3 billion, exceeding the bank's capital base. Early in the week of May 8, the worst fears of the Continental Crisis: Part I were realized. Rumors and false press reports that Continental was about to file for bankruptcy [banks, of course, do not file for bankruptcy] originated Monday night in the Far East, moved to London, and by the time the markets opened Monday morning in New York, the bank's European creditors were refusing to roll over their deposits and loans. Continental was suffering a global electronic deposit run. The hysteria even engulfed Manufacturers Hanover Trust, the nation's fourth largest bank, which was vulnerable because of its heavy exposure to debt-ridden Argentina. Manny Hanny sustained a brief run until it succeeded in assuring the markets that it was sound.

Taylor rushed home from a Caribbean sailing vacation and on May 10, in an unusual move, Comptroller Todd Conover denied reports that Continental was about to fail. But the next day, Continental went to the Fed for more than $4 billion to replace lost funds. Over the weekend, Taylor, with the help of rock-solid Morgan Guaranty, assembled a $4.5 billion line of credit from sixteen banks, a deal that was announced on May 14. But it didn't take long to find out that the $4.5 billion wouldn't be enough. Later in the week, following meetings in New York involving Isaac, Conover, Volcker, and Secretary Regan, the credit line was enlarged to $5.5 billion and twenty-eight banks. The FDIC agreed to infuse $2 billion and guaranteed all deposits, including those over $100,000, and Continental announced it was looking for a merger partner. Two of the most promising candidates, First Chicago and Chemical Bank, sent in teams of examiners but quickly backed off after discovering that the bad loans were not limited to the energy portfolio. Said a Chemical Bank officer familiar with the findings, "There just wasn't any credit culture. The overall reaction was 'ugh.' " Despite the fact that the government had essentially turned Continental into a giant U.S. savings bond, worried depositors throughout the world continued to drain their funds from the ailing bank. Finally, after weeks of exhausting negotiations, the three bank regulatory agencies announced a historic $4.5 billion rescue package on July 26 that called for the FDIC to assume an 80% ownership stake in the bank, reducing shareholder ownership to 20%, a move widely viewed as de facto nationalization. In return, the FDIC pumped $1 billion in new capital into the bank to compensate for a $1.1 billion loss for the second quarter, by far the largest ever reported by an American banking institution. Additionally, the FDIC bought $3.5 billion in delinquent loans on which $5.1 billion had originally been lent. Under the complex arrangement, the FDIC would realize a profit on any collections greater than the $3.5 billion, and charge shareholders for any deficit. Shareholders faced the distinct possibility that their investments would literally not be "worth a Continental" if FDIC collections fell below a certain threshold. The regulators also announced that John E. Swearingen, the retired chairman of the Standard Oil Company (Indiana), and William S. Ogden, the former vice-chairman of Chase Manhattan Bank, would become chairmen of the corporation and the bank, respectively. The size of the second quarter losses and the volume of delinquent loans bought by the FDIC strongly suggest two things: first, Continental was a failed bank in all but the strictest technical sense, and second, bad loans were not limited to Penn Square, or even to oil and gas but were well distributed throughout the portfolio. If Penn Square had been Continental's only problem, it no doubt would have survived as an independent entity. But even though Penn Square, in the end, represented a minority portion of Continental's problem credits, its significance transcends the raw numbers. With the failure of the Oklahoma City bank, investor and depositor confidence in Continental evaporated overnight. The continued existence of a bank, and indeed, of the banking system, rests entirely on public confidence. Once lost, it may never be regained.

Penn Square, according to FDIC chairman William Isaac, led not only to the problems of Seafirst and Continental, but also to those at institutions that had no business relationship with the Oklahoma lender whatsoever. The spectacular failure of the shopping center bank in Oklahoma focused media and depositor attention on the oil patch banks with a reputation for questionable lending. On July 9, the *Dallas Morning News* ran a story spotlighting the activities of Abilene National, in Abilene, Texas, and referring to Penn Square. Indeed, the Abilene bank, like Penn Square, was known as an aggressive oil and gas bank that was just slightly smaller than its counterpart in Oklahoma. Despite an ad campaign waged by the bank's chairman attacking the article as unfair, the bank fell victim to a run and was taken over August 6 by the Mercantile Texas Corporation of Dallas, a bank holding company. The FDIC said that the bank would have failed regardless of the publicity and the deposit run because of huge loan losses. Then in October 1982, the FDIC arranged for the First National Bank of Oklahoma City to take over the failing Oklahoma National Bank, also the victim of imprudent energy lending. That takeover was permitted because of a provision in the banking law that allowed one Oklahoma bank to merge with another failing one if the assuming bank had loans outstanding to the acquiree. Curiously, Eldon Beller had been employed as a consultant to Oklahoma National, and after a brief review of the bank's loan portfolio and financial condition concluded the bank was insolvent and notified the regulators.

Abilene National and Oklahoma National were handled as open bank mergers largely because of the nervousness that followed the closing of Penn Square and the desire of the regulators to resolve them so that they would not be recorded on the scorecard as technical failures. But one former official of the Comptroller of the Currency took a more jaundiced view, saying, "The FDIC backed off on

Abilene because they didn't want to be accused of bringing the system down."

In the summer of 1982, rumors began flying about the First National Bank of Midland, Texas, yet another high rolling energy lender, and press attention soon focused on that institution. In February 1983 chairman Charles Fraser's absence from the bank gave rise to reports that he had been fired because of problems there. Fraser said that he had been on his back with a hemorrhoid problem for nearly a month. "Ole Charlie Fraser's sick for four weeks," he said, "and they think he's been fired." In fact, Mr. Fraser left shortly thereafter, and in October 1983 First National Bank of Midland, in a P&A transaction, was taken over by the Republic Bank Corporation of Dallas. With $1.4 billion in assets, First National Bank of Midland became the second largest commercial bank failure in U.S. history.

Even the demise of Jake Butcher's United American Bank, and the subsequent collapse of the Butcher family's Tennessee and Kentucky financial empire, was indirectly related to the demise of Penn Square. After the failure in Oklahoma City, banks throughout the country began to reexamine the loan participations they had bought from other banks. And according to Isaac, banks holding UAB participations became uneasy about those loans and demanded that Butcher buy them back. That, he said, aggravated UAB's increasingly serious funding problems.

While the OCC took the heat from Congress and the media over Penn Square, Isaac and the FDIC got their comeuppance for their bungling in the supervision of UAB. A 1983 report of the Committee on Government Operations concluded that "the insolvency of UAB Knoxville and the other Butcher banks was caused far more by unsafe banking practices and FDIC regulatory neglect over six years than by any sudden deterioration of the loan portfolio in the second half of 1982, as FDIC Chairman Isaac alleged during his appearance before the Commerce, Consumer and Monetary Affairs Subcommittee."

After Penn Square, Oklahoma banks as a group became anathema to corporations and individuals with deposits to invest. In 1983 Oklahoma banks, in part because of the oil-patch bust and the ripple effects of Penn Square on the Oklahoma economy, dropped to forty-ninth place in the United States in return on assets, the key measure of bank profitability, down from fourth place in 1980.

The largest Oklahoma City banks—First National, Liberty, and Fidelity—suffered in varying degrees from the Penn Square fallout.

Some banking experts believe that the huge write-offs ordered in 1984 by bank examiners at Crocker National Bank in San Francisco and the First National Bank of Chicago resulted from the heat that had been applied to the Comptroller's office in the aftermath of Continental. Crocker, incidentally, got caught up in Penn Square, at least indirectly, through $32.7 million in loans to the Houston-based T.O.S. Industries, Inc., an oil-field equipment supplier in which Bill Jennings held 10% of the stock. T.O.S. filed for bankruptcy in August 1982, disclosing at the time that it also owed $14.8 million to Continental Illinois.

Before the domestic banking crisis reared itself in the oil patch, it had been assumed that the most serious issue facing American banks was the staggering debt load of Third World nations, most notably Mexico, Brazil, and Argentina. Those problems remain, of course, but for the time being at least the questionable quality of domestic bank assets seems to be the more immediate threat to the safety and soundness of the banking system. The statistics tell part, but only part, of the story. In 1984, a record 79 U.S. banks failed, more than in any year since the Great Depression. Since 1983, the number of banks on the problem lists of the three bank regulatory agencies has surged by nearly 40%. By early 1985, the FDIC had 901 banks under special scrutiny, the Comptroller had 793, and the Fed an undisclosed number, although many of the problem banks appear on more than one list. While the vast majority of these institutions are small, three of the nation's largest banks—Bank of America, First National Bank of Chicago, and, of course, Continental—have a special place on the Comptroller's list. Of the small institutions, many are located in the farm belt, having succumbed in the inflationary seventies and early eighties to the siren song of "asset-based" lending. Just as their counterparts in the oil patch lent money figuring that the prices of oil and gas would go nowhere but up, they made loans to farmers based on the expectation that inflation would continue to drive up land values and assure the repayment of their loans. Now, as the economy adjusts to what could become a new era of disinflation, it has become clear that they were wrong on both counts. Given the demonstrated shortcomings of bank regulators and auditors in spotting troubled institutions, and the limitations of bank performance statistics, it is not unreasonable to ask how much of the U.S. banking system, once the bedrock of the world economy, now sits atop this mountain of paper wealth and worthless loans.

The Penn Square–Seafirst–Continental energy lending debacle has affected the operating and lending practices of American banks in a variety of ways, some subtle, others more tangible. One of the most widely acknowledged changes is the realignment of correspondent relationships, and the move to put those dealings on a more businesslike footing. Where once correspondent bank ties relied solely on mutual trust among bank officers, now, more and more, institutions are taking a hard-nosed attitude toward these relationships, particularly as they relate to the purchase and sale of loan participations. "Gentlemen's agreements that had long existed to buy back loan participations have gone by the board," said one banker. On the liability side of the balance sheet, many banks now require other institutions to which they sell Fed funds to secure those lines with government securities.

Virtually overnight, media attention shifted from the beleaguered thrifts to commercial banks. An official of the U.S. League of Savings Banks said, "People in our business breathed a sigh of relief that the spotlight was turned to banks. It caused S&Ls to be more cautious about buying certificates of deposit from banks, and made them cautious about moving into commercial lending." Thrift institutions had recently been empowered to make commercial loans, and many planned to start out by purchasing loan participations. For the thrifts, however, the breathing spell was short-lived.

Within the commercial banking industry, the least tangible long-range impact of the debacle may also be the most significant. The morning after the failure, bankers throughout the country began sifting through their portfolios of loan participations and analyzing their loan review procedures, internal controls, and lending authorities. The result has been, by most accounts, stricter lending standards, a phenomenon that inevitably translates into increased difficulty for marginal borrowers in obtaining funds. Evidence of this can be seen in the move by banks away from such once fashionable devices as leveraged buyouts. Growth for growth's sake has fallen into disfavor, as have attempts by banks to achieve it by lending outside their area of expertise. Today, more and more, banks have begun to focus on managing their risks, rather than simply making more loans. Such an effort encompasses a thorough analysis of loan concentrations by industry, company, and type of credit, among other criteria.

Perhaps no group of bankers learned this lesson better than former Penn Square officers. One young banker, who worked briefly for the FDIC before joining a downtown Oklahoma City bank, said, "We're just generally more skeptical in looking at credits. It took me months after working for the FDIC to stop looking at customers as

---

debtors-in-possession [bankrupt]," adding, "I'm much more inclined to go to an old hand now."

The collapse of Penn Square and the multimillion-dollar lawsuits against the directors that soon followed touched the collective consciousness of bank directors throughout the country. Suddenly, they were made aware that the job of bank director is not just an honorary one, but a job fraught with responsibilities and liabilities.

William H. Crawford, president of the First National Bank of Frederick, Oklahoma, and a past president of the Oklahoma Bankers Association, said, "You can be sure that since July 5, board meetings in this state have been longer and livelier than ever before."

The point was reinforced less than a year later with the takeover of Seafirst, and again in 1984 with the near-collapse of Continental. Within months after the federal bailout, the Federal Deposit Insurance Corporation humbled the once-proud Continental board by ordering the dismissal of all those directors elected prior to 1980.

On the regulatory front, the bungling and lack of communication between the regulatory agencies supervising Penn Square has also prompted new calls for the merger of the five major agencies and the consolidation of the deposit insurance funds. The disadvantages of having separate agencies were vividly illustrated in the efforts to find a solution to Penn Square in the week before July 5, 1982, as each one approached the crisis with its own special mandates. Isaac, said some critics, envisioned that the FDIC would emerge as the supreme bank regulatory agency. That prompted considerable snickering across town at the Office of the Comptroller of the Currency, where officials referred to the FDIC as "Bill Isaac and the Supremes."

The debacle has also given rise to a number of developments which, taken together, have to some extent dampened banks' willingness to take undue credit risks. One is the new requirement for disclosure of nonperforming loans. Beginning in June 1983, banks had to make available, on request, data on loans past due more than 90 days. The regulators, led by the FDIC, are pressing for restrictions on the activities of money brokers, and already have required banks to report the volume of deposits supplied by these sources. Yet there are those who doubt whether the new disclosures will help much in enabling consumers to assess the riskiness of their institutions. For one thing, banks have ways of manipulating the data, and few laymen are equipped to analyze it anyway. One leading analyst wondered, "We have more numbers, but do we know anything more?" Regulators, however, are also weighing the possibility of making public cease and desist orders and other enforcement actions taken against banking institutions. The average bank customer might not understand the numbers, but the meaning of cease and desist orders would be unambiguous.

In addition, the regulators have demanded that banks raise their capital ratios ("primary" capital as a percentage of assets) to at least 5.5%, and a Reagan administration task force on financial industry reform has proposed raising them to 9% to 11% of assets, although subordinated debt would be included in the definition of capital to mitigate the impact.

In imposing these new measures, the regulators argue that they will bolster public confidence in banks, providing an extra cushion against insolvency. But there is an equally valid argument that higher capital ratios, because they dilute earnings, will have exactly the opposite effect—that of causing banks to make even riskier loans. And others correctly point out that once the public loses confidence in a bank, as it did in the case of Penn Square, Seafirst, and Continental, something more than a large capital cushion is needed to save it.

In general, the great banking debacle that began with Penn Square has highlighted the ongoing debate on bank deregulation. This controversy has centered on whether commercial banks should be permitted to establish branches or own banks across state lines, and whether they should be allowed to engage in securities underwriting, currently prohibited by the Glass–Steagall Act, as well as insurance and real estate. Opponents of deregulation, including Rep. Fernard St Germain, have cited Penn Square and Continental as evidence that bank powers should not be expanded because, they argue, banks can't even do what they're supposed to be doing in the first place—lending money.

One thing is clear, however: that Continental and Penn Square mandate a reasonable resolution of a system where big banks like Continental get bailed out and smaller ones are allowed to go down the tube. Comptroller of the Currency Todd Conover, in an unprecedented acknowledgement of the special place of big banks in the financial system, stated at Congressional hearings on the Continental debacle that the eleven largest U.S. banks would not be allowed to fail. To be sure, such decisions should not depend on the whims of the FDIC or the OCC and the pressures of the moment. This rationalization of an inequitable arrangement is likely to take the form of changes in the deposit insurance system whereby shaky institutions like Continental and Penn Square pay more for deposit coverage than stable ones, or possibly are dropped from the insurance rolls altogether. It is difficult to see how geographic and product deregulation can proceed without such changes because it is inconsistent to permit institutions to operate freely in the marketplace without requiring that they pay the piper when they fail. Penn Square and Continental have supplied a new impetus for Congress to come to grips with the role of deposit insurance: Is it to protect depositors? Is it to protect banks? Or is it to protect the banking system?

In turn, the imposition of such measures as risk-related deposit insurance premiums and higher capital ratios may also represent a valid argument for deregulation. Higher capital ratios mean decreased leverage. Reduced leverage means a lower return on investment for the shareholder and more difficulty for banks in raising equity in the marketplace. To make bank equity more attractive to investors, banks will have to find ways to improve profitability, which has been squeezed in recent years for a variety of reasons. While there are those who point to a "crisis of confidence" in the banking system, some observers, including Sanford Rose, the columnist for the *American Banker,* see a "crisis of profitability." Lacking the legal power to offer more profitable products and services and to diversify their portfolios by expanding nationally, banks will attempt, whenever possible, to obtain higher spreads on loans and raise the price of banking services to the consumer, at least until competition from less regulated "nonbanks" forces them back into line. Some banks will simply fail, and others will be acquired by healthier institutions.

Overreaching more than overregulation, was behind the billions in bad loans. A fully deregulated banking industry may have made little difference. But to the extent that the Congress, in restructuring the U.S. financial system, restricts competition in the financial services industry while placing new constraints on bank earnings, the American consumer will likely pay the price for the reckless lending practices of the Penn Square Bank and its friends in New York, Chicago, and Seattle.

LIST OF ABBREVIATED CITATIONS

Audit Report, Treasury	Audit Report, Office of the Inspector General, Department of the Treasury, October 28, 1983.
FDIC v. Jennings et al.	Federal Deposit Insurance Corp. v. Bill P. Jennings; Eldon L. Beller; William G. Patterson; John R. Preston; Carl W. Swan; and C. F. Kimberling, Sr.; Case No. CIV-84-1612, filed June 1984 in U.S. District Court, Western District of Oklahoma.
Hearings, Serial No. 97-92	Hearings before the Committee on Banking, Finance and Urban Affairs, House of Representatives, 97th Cong., 2d sess., Part I, Serial No. 97-92.
Hearings, Serial No. 97-93	Hearings before the Committee on Banking, Finance and Urban Affairs, House of Representatives, 97th Cong., Part 2, Serial No. 97-93.
"Information" release on Orr	"Information" release citing charges against Thomas Orr to which he pleaded guilty under agreement with U.S. attorney outlined in letter.
Longhorn Case No. MDL 525	Longhorn securities litigation, "Appendix to Plaintiff's Motion to Dissolve Preliminary Injunctions and Temporary Restraining Orders," filed March 9, 1983, Case No. MDL 525, U.S. District Court, Western District of Oklahoma.
Rowsey Deposition	Deposition of William Rowsey, U.S. Bankruptcy Court, Western District of Oklahoma, Mahan Rowsey, Inc., debtor in possession, v. Penn Square Bank, N.A., of Oklahoma City, and Insurance National Bank of Oklahoma City, BK 82-01390, September 1, 1982.

SEC *v.* Tureaud	SEC *v.* Kenneth E. Tureaud; POM Corporation; RSA Corporation (E. D. Mich., S.Div., Civil action No. 771307), Litigation Release No. 7964/June 9, 1977.
SKS *v.* FDIC	SKS, A General Partnership, Sed Kennedy, Lee Allan Smith, and Barry Switzer *v.* Federal Deposit Insurance Corp., "Complaint for Reformation of Promissory Notes and Injunctive Relief," Case No. 83 600 R, filed March 24, 1983, in the U.S. District Court for the Western District of Oklahoma.
Special Litigation Report	Continental Illinois special litigation report, Report of the Special Litigation Committee of the Board of Directors of Continental Illinois Corporation, Chicago, Ill. February 8, 1983.
Tarnutzer Deposition	Account of Tarnutzer involvement in Copeland Energy based on declaration of Byron Tarnutzer, taken in July 1982, Newport Beach, California, Tarnutzer *et al. v.* FDIC *et al.*, U.S. District Court, Western District of Oklahoma, CIV-82-1828-E
U.S. *v.* Chilcott	U.S. *v.* Thomas D. Chilcott, Chilcott Portfolio, Management, Inc., and Chilcott Futures Fund, Criminal Case 81-CR-228.
USA *v.* Patterson	United States of America *v.* Bill G. Patterson, Criminal Trial in U.S. District Court, Western District of Oklahoma, September 10, 1984, to September 24, 1984.
Winget Deposition	Deposition of Dennis Winget in Continental Illinois securities litigation, No. 82 C4712 in the U.S. District Court, Northern District of Illinois, Eastern Division, May 14, 1984, p. 46.

NOTES AND SOURCES

PROLOGUE

This account of Federal Deposit Insurance Corporation chairman William M. Isaac's trip to Oklahoma City is based largely on personal interviews in Washington with Isaac and other FDIC officials in Washington during the weeks of May 9, 1983, and May 16, 1983.

ONE The Gas Man

This chapter is based on an interview in Oklahoma City with Henry Taliaferro on September 22, 1983; several interviews in Oklahoma City with Robert A. Hefner 3rd beginning February 9, 1984; an interview with David Kennedy in Oyster Bay, N.Y., on March 31, 1984, and other interviews with sources who asked that their names not be used.

6   *The geological upheavals . . .* References to Robert Hefner's first marriage and divorce are based on depositions and other documents in Oklahoma City County Court, Case No. 91924-D, Trudi Ray Hefner *v.* Robert A. Hefner 3rd.

8   *Lawrence Glover . . .* Description of Glover from an interview with David Kennedy, March 31, 1984.

8   *Makaroff, an engineer . . .* Background on Makaroff from interviews with Kennedy and Hefner; also obituary in *New York Times,* January 3, 1964, and article, January 15, 1964.

9   *Ironically, at about the same time . . .* Hefner divorce records.

15   *Forecasting cash flows . . .* Remarks by Rob Gilbert at American Bankers Association's Commercial Lending School, University of Oklahoma, Fall 1983.

17   *Some would say . . .* References to the fight in the restaurant are based on documents on file in Oklahoma County Court, Jack Rainier *v.* James Satterfield, Richard R. Bailey, Robert A. Hefner 3rd, Allan J. Feldman, filed October 4, 1967, Case No. 179779; *Daily Oklahoman,* October 5, 1967.

17   *World's second deepest . . .* C.L. Kennedy (ed.) *The Deep Anadarko Basin* (Denver, Colo: Petroleum Information Corp, 1982).

18   *This paradox stemmed . . .* History of natural gas regulation from *New York Times,* April 9, 1950, April 16, 1950, April 28, 1950, January 3,

1956, January 23, 1956, Febraury 4, 1956, February 18, 1956, April 8, 1956, April 16, 1956; Arlon R. Tussing and Connie C. Barlow, *The Natural Gas Industry* (Cambridge, Mass.: Ballinger Publishing Co., 1984); and Cheryl Hoffman (ed.), *Natural Gas: Options and Opportunities* (New York: The Oil Daily, 1983).

20   *As Lloyd Unsell . . .* Interview with Lloyd Unsell, Washington, D.C., August 4, 1983.

TWO A Friend at the Bank

Much of this chapter is based on interviews with Bill P. Jennings, Oklahoma City, April 5, 1982; Jackson Conn, Oklahoma City, February 1, 1984, and other former colleagues and customers of Jennings who asked that their names not be used.

The description of the luncheon with Grady Harris is based on an account in Jack T. Conn, *One Man in His Time* (Oklahoma City: Oklahoma Heritage Foundation, 1979).

23   *Penn Square Bank was organized . . .* Interview with Ben C. Wileman, Oklahoma City, November 1984.

24   *But Jennings really . . .* Account of Four Seasons episode based on interviews with colleagues of Bill P. Jennings and articles in the *Wall Street Journal,* February 10, 1972, March 20, 1972, July 18, 1972, September 26, 1972, November 20, 1972, December 21, 1972, March 19, 1973, April 2, 1973, June 5, 1973, September 19, 1973, September 24, 1973, February 4, 1974, February 8, 1974, February 28, 1974, November 27, 1974; and in the *Daily Oklahoman,* December 21, 1972 and September 19, 1973.

27   *The announcement in early October . . .* Announcement of Clarke election, *American Banker,* October 10, 1974.

27   *There was certainly . . .* Discussion of Franklin National Bank failure based on Joan Edelman Spero, *The Failure of the Franklin National Bank* (New York: Columbia University Press, 1980); Frank Wille, chairman of the FDIC, "The FDIC and Franklin National Bank: A Report to the Congress and all FDIC-Insured Banks," a speech before the 81st Annual Convention of the Savings Banks Association of New York State, Boca Raton, Fla., November 23, 1974; and *Fortune,* October 1974.

28   *Conn and Wilfred Clarke . . .* Letter from W.A. Clarke, president of Fidelity Bank, to Michael Doman, Regional Administrator of National Banks, Dallas, Texas, April 7, 1975, concerning the $2.5 million loan to First Penn Corp.

28   *Despite the objections . . .* Letter from James P. Smith, Comptroller of the Currency to the Board of Governors, Federal Reserve System, September 2, 1975, concerning acquisition by First Penn Corp., of Penn Square Bank; statement of vice-chairman Mitchell of the Federal Reserve Board, December 23, 1975, on acquisition by First Penn of Penn Square Bank.

30   *Kenneth Eck . . .* Interview with Kenneth Eck, proprietor of Eck's Drugstore, Healdton, Okla., October 1983.

30   Bill Jennings's college activities, *The Sooner* (1947–1951), yearbook of the University of Oklahoma, p. 60. Minutes of the meetings of the board of directors, Penn Square Bank, January 19, 1976.

THREE The Promoter Deluxe
   Much of this chapter is based on an interview with Bill Lakey on
March 7, 1984, in Holdenville, Okla.

36   *One of the first* . . . Discussion of careers of Carl Swan and J.D. Allen
based on interviews with acquaintances who asked that their names not
be used; articles in the Oklahoma City *Journal Record,* January 5, 1982,
and January 26, 1982; article in *Oklahoma Business,* January 1982; *Penn
Points,* the staff newsletter of Penn Square Bank, December 1981.

37   *"I decided to get . . ."* Interview with J.D. Allen, Oklahoma City, February 8, 1984.

37   *"J.D." said Bill Malloy* . . . Interview with Bill Malloy, Oklahoma City,
June 29, 1984.

38   *After sixteen years* . . . Interviews with Robert A. Hefner 3rd, Oklahoma
City, beginning February 9, 1984.

40   *It was the Apache deal* . . . Interview with David Kennedy, Oyster Bay,
N.Y., March 31, 1984.

40   *Allegations of such* . . . USA *v.* Patterson.

FOUR A Winter of Discontent
41   *On October 9, 1976* . . . Telephone interview with Sen. David Boren;
personal interview, Oklahoma City, October 1984.

41   Account of Texas–Oklahoma football game, *Sunday Oklahoman,* October
10, 1976.

41   *In the final letter* . . . Letter from Gov. Jimmy Carter to Govs. Boren,
Briscoe, and Edwards, October 19, 1976.

42   *According to Bill Anderson* . . . Telephone interview with William C.
Anderson, vice-president for political and legislative relations of the Independent Petroleum Association of America, May 1984.

43   *Dr. Donald Gilman* . . . Interview with Dr. Donald Gilman, Washington, D.C., August 2, 1983.

45   *According to Dr. Henry E. Warren* . . . Telephone interview with Dr.
Henry E. Warren. 1984.

45   *A year earlier* . . . Discussion of natural gas legislation from 1975
through 1978 based on accounts in *Congressional Quarterly Almanac;* numerous newspaper and magazine articles; The Natural Gas Policy Act
of 1978, Public Law 95–621, November 9, 1978; and interviews with
Robert A. Hefner 3rd, William Dutcher, John O'Leary, Les Goldman,
and other on-the-record and background sources who were involved in
formulating energy policy.

46   *The deliverability problem* . . . Interview with Brian O'Neill, president of
Transcontinental Gas Pipeline Co., Houston, May 27, 1983.

46   *Amid these shortages* . . . McKetta forecast in article in *The Oil Daily,*
February 10, 1977.

47   *The pipelines were terrified* . . . Interview with Les Goldman, Washington, D.C., April 3, 1984.

49   *In mid-April 1977 . . .*   Interview with Sam Hammons, Oklahoma City, November 21, 1983.

49   *On April 18 . . . New York Times,* April 19, 1977, and April 21, 1977.

52   *A lobbyist for the state . . .*   Telephone interview with a former lobbyist who asked that his name not be used.

FIVE The Magical, Mystical Energy Loans Man

53   *Chambers was unschooled . . .*   Interview with Bill Lakey, Holdenville, Okla., March 7, 1984.

54   *He called on a new customer . . .*   Interview with Tom Eckroat, Hennessey, Okla., May 23, 1984.

54   *While Chambers's examination . . .*   Account of May 1977 exam appears in Hearings before the Committee on Banking, Finance and Urban Affairs, House of Representatives, 97th Cong., 2d sess., Part 1, p. 593.

54   *Chambers represented a vast . . .*   History and description of bank regulatory system based on discussion in Ross M. Robertson, *The Comptroller and Bank Supervision* (Washington: The Comptroller of the Currency, 1968); Carter H. Golembe and David S. Holland, *Federal Regulation of Banking 1983–84* (Washington: Golembe Associates Inc., 1983).

55   *The* Comptroller's Handbook . . .   Office of the Comptroller of the Currency, *Comptroller's Handbook for National Bank Examiners* (Englewood Cliffs, N.J.: Prentice-Hall, February 1981).

57   *Joe Selby, now a deputy . . .*   Interview with Joe Selby, Washington, D.C., August 3, 1983.

58   *Patterson, twenty-eight . . .*   Discussion of Bill Patterson, his life and career, based on numerous on-the-record and background interviews with friends and former co-workers, including a telephone interview with his father, George "Pat" Patterson, in November 1984; testimony by Bill G. Patterson, September 24, 1984, in USA *v.* Patterson.

61   *On December 19, 1977 . . .*   Arthur Young opinion contained in civil complaint, FDIC *v.* Jennings *et al.*

SIX Pilot Light for a Boom

62   *"They came out . . ."*   Interview with William Dutcher, Oklahoma City, September 23, 1983.

62   *"I'll never forget . . ."*   Interviews with Robert A. Hefner 3rd, Oklahoma City, beginning February 9, 1984.

63   *Mike Hathaway said . . .* Interview with Mike Hathaway, Tulsa, Okla., 1983.

63   *And Les Goldman . . .*   Interview with Les Goldman, Washington, D.C., April 3, 1984.

63   *Deputy Secretary of Energy O'Leary . . .*   Telephone interview with John O'Leary, April 1984.

64   *Bill Anderson called . . .*   Telephone interview with William C. Anderson, May 1984.

64   *"Nobody on the Hill ..."* Interview with Bud Scoggins, Washington, D.C., August 4, 1983.

SEVEN Continental Illinois and Penn Square: Marriage for Fun and Profit

67   *They called him ...* Background on R.P. Lammerts based on conversations with acquaintances and former bank officers who asked not to be named.

67   *Early in 1978 ...* Account of Lammerts's transaction based on interviews and depositions of Bill G. Patterson in D&G Enterprises *v.* Longhorn Oil and Gas, CIV-82-1415-E in U.S. District Court in the Western District of Oklahoma, August 4, 1984, p. 162; and Winget Deposition, p. 16.

68   *This new aggressiveness ...* Careers of Anderson, Perkins, and other Continental officers cited in this chapter outlined in officer biographies on file at Continental Illinois.

69   *Banks like Continental ...* Data on foreign banks in the United States from *Foreign Banks: A New Competitive Force in the U.S.* (A White Paper by Payments Systems, Inc., 1979).

71   *Continental may not have ...* Arthur Young management letter cited in FDIC *v.* Jennings *et al.*

74   *Not long after ...* Interview with an unidentified Texas banker, Houston, May 25, 1983.

76   *This was in contrast ...* Discussion of First National Bank of Chicago based on interviews, newspaper and magazine articles, and annual reports and 10-Ks for 1974 through 1982.

76   *For many international ...* Description of Continental organization based on interviews, newspaper and magazine articles, and annual reports and 10-Ks for 1976 through 1982.

80   *Barron's wrote ...* *Barron's,* August 14, 1978.

EIGHT Liquid Leverage

81   *Longhorn 1978–II worked ...* Longhorn Case No. MDL 525.

83   *According to Longhorn's ...* Longhorn's financial condition, *ibid.*

83   *Patterson would respond ...* Longhorn Securities litigation, deposition of Charlotte Day before the Securities and Exchange Commission, Oklahoma City, December 15, 1982, pp. 67–71.

84   *Patterson later testified ...* Deposition of Bill G. Patterson, Longhorn Case No. MDL 525.

85   *One of them, a former ...* Interview with tax shelter specialist, San Francisco, June 1983.

87   *Oklahoma, observed ...* Telephone interview with George "Pat" Patterson, November 1984.

88   *According to former ...* Interview with David Newsome, Oklahoma City, December 5, 1983.

NINE Bring Us More Gas

90 *NGPA critic Bill Anderson* ... Telephone interview with William C. Anderson, May 1984.

91 *According to Dr. William Talley* ... Interview with Dr. William Talley, Oklahoma City, March 13, 1984.

92 *Another phenomenon* ... Interview with Charles Hughes, Tulsa, Oklahoma, July 12, 1984.

93 *Although the shortfall* ... Oil price trends from *Collier's Encyclopedia Yearbook, 1980.*

TEN Gas Fumes

Discussion of the involvement of Seattle First National Bank based on inteviews with current and former bank officers during the weeks of July 4 and July 11, 1984; interviews with John R. Boyd in Houston May 28, 1983, June 18, 1983, and October 1984; Seafirst annual reports and 10-Ks for the years 1975 through 1982; biographies of current and former Seafirst officers on file with Seafirst; congressional testimony; and numerous newspaper and magazine articles and the reports of securities analysts.

Account of the involvement of Northern Trust based on interviews with former officers, annual reports and 10-Ks, officer biographies on file with Northern Trust, articles in newspapers and magazines.

95 *Seattle First had issued* ... Hearings, Serial No. 97-93, pp. 138–155.

98 *Jenkins was not shy* ... *Forbes,* October 1, 1975.

100 *In 1974 German* ... Robert Heller and Norris Willatt, *Can You Trust Your Bank* (New York: Charles Scribner's Sons, 1977).

101 *In Washington State* ... Discusson of usury ceilings, *American Banker,* October 17, 1979, November 25, 1980, February 5, 1981.

101 *On the labor front* ... Articles on union activities, *American Banker,* February 12, 1981, April 20, 1981, November 24, 1982.

101 *Jenkins once told* ... Seattle *Business Journal,* March 22, 1982.

102 *Despite these annoyances* ... Seafirst Corporation, 1978 annual report.

105 *The newly-elected chairman told a financial reporter* ... *American Banker,* April 19, 1979.

105 *At the time, Northern's* ... Northern Trust Corporation, 1978 annual report.

ELEVEN The Saturday Night Special

106 *Banking news* ... Account of Saturday night special from articles in *Wall Street Journal, American Banker, New York Times,* and *Collier's Encyclopedia Yearbook.*

108 *$42 a barrel* ... *Petroleum Intelligence Weekly,* April 21, 1980.

108 *"The pipelines," said a former* ... Interview with a former GHK official, Oklahoma City, September 1983.

109   *Hefner, his victory* . . .   Interviews with Robert A. Hefner 3rd, Oklahoma
        City, beginning Feburary 9, 1984.

110   *One banker recalled* . . .   Interview with an Oklahoma City banker who
        asked that his name not be used, Oklahoma City, January 26, 1984.

        TWELVE New Oilies and Old Oilies

111   *"There was an electricity* . . ."   Interview with M.C. Kratz, Oklahoma
        City, February 22, 1984.

111   *One Oklahoma City lawyer* . . .   Interview with a lawyer, Oklahoma City,
        January 23, 1984.

111   *"You could see it* . . ."   Interview with Murray Cohen, Oklahoma City,
        November 8, 1983.

112   *"The oil business," said* . . .   Interview with Tom Kenan, Oklahoma City,
        December 2, 1983.

113   *One company that decided* . . .   Interview with Tom Eckroat, Hennessey,
        Okla., May 23, 1984.

114   *Oilmen like Dorsey Buttram* . . .   Interview with Dorsey Buttram, Okla-
        homa City, 1984.

114   *Dewey Dobson, who promoted* . . .   Interview with Dewey Dobson, Okla-
        homa City, October 4, 1983.

115   *One of those investors* . . .   Tarnutzer Deposition.

116   *In the late 1970s, Ewing* . . .   Interview with Kae Ewing, Newport Beach,
        Calif., July 1, 1983.

118   *Rising inflation* . . .   Data on tax returns from Statistics of Income 1975,
        Individual Income Tax Returns; Statistics of Income 1980, Individual
        Income Tax Returns, published by the Internal Revenue Service.

118   *One Washington, D.C.* . . . ,   Interview with a Washington, D.C., tax expert
        who asked not to be named, Washington, D.C., May 1, 1983.

118   *"You could walk* . . ."   Interview with a former Penn Square officer who
        asked not to be named, Oklahoma City, November 14, 1983.

120   *One of the recipients* . . .   Interview with Sam Villyard, Oklahoma City,
        August 30, 1984.

121   *Coach Barry Switzer* . . .   SKS *v.* FDIC.

122   *The bank exam* . . .   Data on exam based on Hearings before a Subcom-
        mittee of the Committee on Government Operations, House of Repre-
        sentatives, 97th Cong., 2d sess., July 16, 1982, p. 142.

122   *Behind Patterson's desk* . . .   Interview with a former examiner who asked
        not to be named, Oklahoma City, May 11, 1984.

122   *Awestruck by Penn Square's* . . .   Interview with a former bank regulator
        who asked not to be named, Washington, D.C., July 17, 1983.

        THIRTEEN The Gold Chain Boys

123   *It was for these reasons* . . .   Discussion of Thomas Orr's background and
        activities at Penn Square Bank based on interviews with numerous ac-
        quaintances and former co-workers, federal documents, and newspaper
        clippings.

124   *Only a small fraction . . .*   Letter from U.S. attorney, Western District of Oklahoma to Thomas Orr, Edmond, Oklahoma, January 11, 1984; "Information" release on Orr.

125   *As one member . . .*   *Daily Oklahoman,* June 12, 1983.

125   *"It didn't take long . . "*   Interview with U.S. Attorney Bill Price, Oklahoma City, January 1984.

125   *"Typically, the guy . . ."*   Interview with an Oklahoma City horse breeder, Oklahoma City, May 1984.

126   *In a 1977 complaint . . .*   SEC *v.* Tureaud.

126   *Tureaud's other enterprises . . .*   *Tulsa Tribune,* August 23, 1982.

127   *One of the first loans . . .*   Information release on Orr.

127   *As the financier . . .*   *Tulsa Tribune,* December 29, 1982.

128   *"You could call your investors . . ."*   Interview, Tulsa, Oklahoma, December 20, 1983.

128   *"When a guy has his and hers . . ."*   Interview with a former Penn Square Bank officer, Oklahoma City, May 1983.

129   *One former bank officer . . .*   Interview with a former Penn Square Bank officer, Oklahoma City, December 5, 1983.

129   Background on Thomas Chilcott based on interviews with former Penn Square officers; telephone interview with Kim Collins and James Johnson, bankruptcy trustees for Chilcott Commodities; and Plea Agreement, U.S. *v.* Chilcott.

131   *One customer recalls . . .*   Interview with a former Penn Square customer, Oklahoma City, January 31, 1984.

131   *Patterson, however, was democratic . . .*   Interview with a former Penn Square customer, Oklahoma City, May 21, 1984.

132   *"He had the real recognition . . ."*   Interview with a former Penn Square officer, Oklahoma City, November 14, 1983.

132   *A new officer . . .*   Interview with a former Penn Square officer, Oklahoma City, January 13, 1984.

132   *Patterson, said a former associate . . .*   Interview with former Penn Square officer, Oklahoma City, November 14, 1983.

132   *On the other hand . . .*   Interview with an Oklahoma City oilman, June 15, 1984.

133   *Janelle Cates . . .*   Deposition of Janelle Cates, in re: Clifford Resources Inc., Debtor in Possession *v.* Northern Trust Company and Continental Illinois National Bank and Trust Co. of Chicago, Transferees of Penn Square Bank, N.A. *et al.,* Adversary Proceeding No. 482-0423, Oklahoma City, March 14, 1983.

FOURTEEN Transitions

134   *"He was tough" . . .*   Interview with an Arkansas banker, American Bankers Association Annual Convention, Atlanta, Georgia, October 20, 1982.

135   *On June 9, 1980 . . .*   Letter from Clifton Poole to Penn Square Board, June 9, 1980.

135   *The Penn Square board . . .*   Interview with a former examiner, Oklahoma City, May 11, 1984.

135   *Poole would later recall . . .*   Statement of Clifton Poole, Hearings, Serial No. 97-92, August 16, 1982.

135   *"They detested each other" . . .*   Interview with Mike Mahoney, Oklahoma City, October 1984.

135   *"Afterward," the examiner . . .*   Interview with a former examiner, Oklahoma City, May 11, 1984.

135   *Later, however, the chairman . . .*   Hearings, Serial No. 97-92, July 15, 1982.

136   *"The hardest job we have" . . .*   Interview with a former examiner, Oklahoma City, May 11, 1984.

137   *"There was frustration" . . .*   Interview with a former Penn Square director, Oklahoma City, October 19, 1983.

137   *The directors of Penn Square . . .*   Hearings, Serial No. 97-92, July 15, 1982.

138   *In 1863, Comptroller . . .*   Letter from Comptroller of the Currency Hugh McCulloch to national banks, 1863, Files of the Comptroller of the Currency, Washington, D.C.

139   *While unusually cozy . . .*   Data on loans to John Lytle based on Hearings, Serial No. 97-93, September 29, 1982; U.S. *v.* John R. Lytle, William G. Patterson, and Jere A. Sturgis, U.S. District Court, Northern District of Illinois, Eastern Division.

139   *Indeed, Continental, and Pearson . . .*   Discussion of Nucorp based on interviews with former Continental officers, newspaper and magazine articles and Nucorp Energy Inc. debtor; Case No. 82-3106-K11, U.S. Bankruptcy Court, Southern District of California, San Diego.

139   *"A.J. put a blessing . . ."*   Interview, American Petroleum Institute Bank and Accounting Conference, Palm Beach, Fla., June 12, 1983.

139   Background on A. J. Pearson based on numerous interviews with former colleagues and fellow oil and gas lenders; also, Winget Deposition.

141   *While Pearson was preparing . . .*   Interviews with Robert A. Hefner 3rd, Oklahoma City, beginning February 9, 1984.

141   *In fact, exactly fifty years . . .*   Harry Hurt 3rd, *Texas Rich* (New York: W. W. Norton & Co., 1981).

142   *David Kennedy . . .*   Interview with David Kennedy, Oyster Bay, N.Y., March 31, 1984.

142   *The tight relationship . . .*   Interview with John Boyd, Houston, October 1984.

143   *As early as the summer . . .*   Interviews with current and former Seafirst officers, Seattle, July 3–July 15, 1983.

143   *On September 15, 1980 . . .*   Longhorn Case No. MDL 525.

145   Account of political activities of former Penn Square borrowers based on interviews with borrowers, Federal Election Commission documents, and newspaper clips.

146   *An investor who poured . . .*   Interview with investor, date and location withheld to protect anonymity of source.

147   "Who Said the South Wouldn't Rise Again!" . . .   Reprinted with permission of Nita Lee.

FIFTEEN A Piece of the Action
   This chapter is based on interviews with Michigan National Bank officers, past and present, bank regulators, annual reports, and 10-Ks of: the Michigan National Corp.; newspaper articles, Hearings, Serial No. 97-93, September 29, 1982; and Richard D. Poll, *Howard J. Stoddard, Founder, Michigan National Bank* (East Lansing: Michigan State University Press, 1980).

148   *Bankers don't go . . .*   Hearings, Serial No. 97-93, September 29, 1982.

148   *Michigan National Corporation . . .*   Michigan National Corp., 1980 annual report.

150   Letter from John Lytle in Hearings, Serial No. 97-92, August 16, 1982.

151   *He was also interested . . .*   Hearings, Serial No. 97-93, September 29, 1982.

151   *Michigan National had also . . .*   Michigan National Corp., 1978 and 1981 annual reports; *New York Times,* August 6, 1982.

151   *"There is a certain unpleasant aura . . ."*   *Detroit News,* August 8, 1978.

152   *"Most bankers will . . ." Ibid.*

153   *When he traveled to Chicago . . .*   Interview with an upstream bank officer, Chicago, April 29, 1983.

153   *Larry Brandt, chairman . . .*   Interview with Larry Brandt, Oklahoma City, March 9, 1984.

153   *Patterson was known . . .*   Interviews with former Penn Square and upstream bank officers, Oklahoma City and Chicago.

SIXTEEN The Madness of Crowds

154   *Under the agreement with Mobil . . .*   Interviews with Robert A. Hefner 3rd, Oklahoma City, beginning February 9, 1984.

154   *"The Mobil deal . . ."*   Interview with John Boyd, Houston, October 1984.

157   *But to Bill Saxon . . .*   Saxon Oil Company, 1981 annual report.

157   *Court records show . . .*   Lease records, Comanche County Courthouse, Lawton, Oklahoma.

157   *According to Dr. William Talley . . .*   Interview with Dr. William Talley, Oklahoma City, March 13, 1984.

158   *In a speech ...   Daily Oklahoman,* September 19, 1980.

158   *"Everybody was increasing ..."*   Interview with Larry Brandt, Oklahoma City, March 9, 1984.

159   *"Few of the wells turned out ..."*   Interview with Steve Knox, Oklahoma City, April 25, 1984.

160   *For example, octogenarian. ...*   Interview with Joe Lutonsky, Elgin, Okla., April 25, 1984.

160   *Elgin cattle rancher ...*   Interview with Jim Glover, Elgin, Okla., April 25, 1984.

160   *"Nothing was documented ..."*   Interview with an Oklahoma City attorney, Oklahoma City, January 23, 1984.

161   *"It's the kind ..."   Ibid.*

161   *In a letter ...*   Letter from Frank Murphy, president of Penn Square, to regional office of Comptroller of the Currency, December 12, 1980.

161   Account of situation at Seafirst based on interviews with current and former officers in Seattle, July 5 to July 15, 1983.

163   *According to cattleman-mineral trader ...*   Interview with Jim Glover, Elgin, Okla., April 25, 1984.

164   "The Wildcat," reprinted with permission of J.D. Allen.

SEVENTEEN Following the Pied Piper
Discussion of Chase Manhattan based on annual reports from 1975 through 1983, numerous newspaper and magazine articles, interviews with officers, past and present, reports of bank securities analysts, and other industry sources.

166   *"It's a Stronger Bank that David Rockefeller ..."   Fortune,* January 14, 1980.

166   *"David was vulnerable ..."*   Interview with a former Chase officer, New York, April 1983.

167   *In fact, thanks largely ...   Wall Street Journal,* April 3, 1981.

169   *As a former officer ...*   Interview with a former Penn Square officer, Oklahoma City, October 5, 1983.

170   *And at least one ...*   Interview with Dale Mitchell, Oklahoma City, February 21, 1984.

170   *Around the time ...   The Petroleum Situation,* April 1981.

171   *a concept one Florida newspaper ...*   Reference to article made in USA *v.* Patterson.

171   *The coincidental fact ...*   Relationship between Brooke Grant and Dick Pinney documented in Affidavit for Search Warrant, U.S. District Court, Middle District of Florida, 82-164M-W, September 9, 1982.

171   *California loan- and money-broker ...*   Information release on Orr.

EIGHTEEN The "A" Team

Discussion of January 1981 exam based on documents contained in Hearings, Serial No. 97-92, July 15, 1982, and August 16, 1982; Hearings before a Subcommittee of the Committee on Government Operations, House of Representatives, 97th Cong., 2d sess., July 16, 1982; Audit Report, Treasury.

172   *"They looked in every nook . . ."*   Interview with a former Penn Square officer, Oklahoma City.

174   *Arthur Young and Company . . .*   Letter from Arthur Young to the Penn Square board of directors, March 13, 1981.

175   *As Bill Dutcher recalls . . .*   Interview with Bill Dutcher, Oklahoma City, September 1983.

175   *Bob Hefner's constant critic . . .*   Telephone interview with Bill Anderson, May 1984.

NINETEEN The Tomcat

176   *They called them . . .*   Interview with Clark Ellison, Oklahoma City, September 30, 1983.

176   *"He is," said an acquaintance . . .*   Profile of C.W. Culpepper based on interviews with former associates, including drilling superintendent Jerry Tilley, Yukon, Okla., January 25, 1984.

178   *Despite his idiosyncrasies . . .*   Interview with Bill Gammie, Yakima, Wash., July 10, 1983.

179   *According to one former officer . . .*   Interview with a former Penn Square officer, Oklahoma City, December 5, 1983.

179   *Carter Hines . . .*   Interview with Carter Hines, Oklahoma City, November 17, 1983.

181   *In the long run . . .*   Interview with Sam Hammons, Oklahoma City, November 21, 1983.

181   *Not long after . . .*   Lehman Brothers Kuhn Loeb, Inc. Corporate Client Information Service, "The Deep Anadarko Basin." *This was not the first . . .*   Interview with Jerry Tilley, Yukon, Okla., January 25, 1984.

182   *According to an audit . . . Daily Oklahoman,* January 25, 1983.

182   *Culpepper, who has been cited . . .*   Oklahoman Department of Securities *ex rel.* P. David Newsome, Jr. Administrator *v.* Ports of Call Oil Company, Cliff W. Culpepper, James C. Niles, Melvin L. Brazell, Jr. and J. Carter Hines, Case No. CJ 83 7502, consent of Ports of Call Oil Co. to Judgment of Permanent Injunction, November 8, 1983.

182   *In fact, the company . . .*   Interview, Oklahoma City, February 23, 1984.

183   *Observed Dr. Talley . . .*   Interview with Dr. William Talley, Oklahoma City, March 13, 1984.

183   *Rig crews ignored . . .*   Interview with a rig salesman, Tulsa oil-field equipment exposition, Tulsa, November 1, 1983.

184   *"People in their twenties . . .*   Interview with a landman, Oklahoma City, November 11, 1983.

184   *"Pipe brokers sold . . ."*   Interview, manufacturer's representative Tulsa oil-field exposition; Tulsa, November 1, 1983.

184   *"There was no wholesale" . . .*   Interview with an Oklahoma City lawyer, Oklahoma City, January 23, 1984.

185   *According to one loan . . .*   Interview with workout specialist, Oklahoma City, November 28, 1983.

185   *In practice, explained the head . . .*   Interview with head of accounting systems company, Tulsa oil-field equipment exposition, Tulsa, November 1, 1983.

185   *The attitude was . . .*   Interview with an oil and gas auditor (name, date, and location of interview withheld to protect anonymity).

186   *Then there were the women . . .*   *Daily Oklahoman,* October 31, 1984.

TWENTY The Iron Men
    The description of Bill Patterson at the Cowboys is based on several eyewitness accounts of the incident.

188   *The proprietor, Bob Hall . . .*   Interview with Bob Hall, Oklahoma City, January 1984.

188   Description of Cliff Culpepper and Jack Hodges based on interviews with several friends and acquaintances.

189   *As for Patterson . . .*   Interview with Robert A. Hefner 3rd, Oklahoma City, beginning February 9, 1984.

189   *Byron Tarnutzer was one . . .*   Tarnutzer Deposition.

191   *"Utica National" said one . . .*   Interview with a former Penn Square officer, Oklahoma City, November 14, 1983.

191   *That year, Utica . . .*   Utica Bankshares Corp., 1980 annual report.

191   *"They'd tell Patterson . . ."*   Interview with a former Utica National Bank officer, June 1984 (location withheld to preserve anonymity).

191   *Dewey Dobson, who . . .*   Interview with Dewey Dobson, Oklahoma City, October 4, 1983.

191   *Said an upstream bank officer . . .*   Interview with a former officer, Chicago, October 12, 1983.

192   *As one friend put it . . .*   Interview with a friend of Carl Swan, Oklahoma City, September 1983.

192   *Moreover, components . . .*   Interview with an energy lender, Oklahoma City, October 21, 1983.

192   *The understanding with Continental . . .*   Telephone interview with a former Continental officer, October, 1984.

193   *Nevertheless, Lytle . . .*   Interview with a former Texas banker, Houston, May 24, 1983.

193   *On one occasion . . .*   Interview with a former upstream bank officer, Chicago, October 12, 1983.

193   *Said one Oklahoma City lawyer . . .*   Interview with an Oklahoma City lawyer, Oklahoma City, December 7, 1983.

193   *According to Rob Gilbert . . .*   American Bankers Association Commercial Lending School, Norman, Oklahoma, fall 1983.

193   *One lender who was not impressed . . .*   Speech by Bud Ham, senior vice-president, Fidelity Bank, to Oklahoma Bankers Association, Oklahoma City, February 19, 1981.

194   *Paul Bergevin, who had been . . .*   Telephone interview with a former Seafirst officer, Seattle, July 6, 1983.

194   *Seafirst, meanwhile, had . . .*   Seafirst Corporation, 1980 annual report.

194   *Kathy Kenefick of the Continental . . .*   Longhorn Case No. MDL 525.

196   *Allen, according to . . .*   Interview with an Allen associate, Oklahoma City, June 28, 1984.

TWENTY-ONE The Changing of the Guard

197   *He was a bit surprised . . .*   Testimony of Eldon Beller, USA *v.* Patterson.

198   *The first paragraph read . . .*   Testimony of Eldon Beller, Hearings, Serial No. 97-92, August 16, 1982.

198   *House Banking Committee chairman . . .*   Statement of Fernand St. Germain, Hearings, Serial No. 97-92, August 16, 1982.

198   *In any case . . .   Ibid.*

198   *Dale Mitchell, Beller's boss . . .*   Interview with Dale Mitchell, Oklahoma City, February 21, 1984.

198   *When Beller arrived . . .*   Testimony of Eldon Beller, USA *v.* Patterson.

199   Details of Jennings's business interests and relationships cited in testimony by Eldon Beller and statements of Burke Bailey in USA *v.* Patterson; documented in filings by First Penn Corp. with the Federal Reserve Bank of Kansas City, which are contained in Hearings, Serial No. 97-92.

199   *Another close friend . . .*   Telephone interview with Dale Robertson, December 1984.

199   *Beller immediately began . . .*   Interview with Dale Mitchell, Oklahoma City, February 21, 1984.

200   *According to former officers . . .*   Interview with Frank Murphy, Oklahoma City, November 1984, and other officers.

200   *To borrow a phrase . . .*   Hearings, Serial No. 97-92.

201   *Almost immediately . . .*   This account of the conflict between Patterson and Beller and Beller's "fix-it" team was based on numerous interviews with former Penn Square officers who asked that their remarks not be attributed to them.

203   *Tom Swineford* . . . Interview with Tom Swineford, Oklahoma City, June 5, 1984.

204   *As Fernand St German warned* . . . Serial No. 97-92.

204   *Rob Gilbert, then a senior* . . . interview with Dale Mitchell, Oklahoma City, February 21, 1984.

205   *Former employees of Amarex* . . . Discussion of Amarex based on interviews with former Amarex officers and employees, former officers of Penn Square and its correspondent banks, newspaper articles and Amarex annual reports for 1981, 1982, and 1983.

205   *He was, said a former employee* . . . Interview with a former Amarex employee, Oklahoma City, November 29, 1983.

206   *And Amarex later claimed* . . . Amarex v. Marc Reis, Oklahoma County Court, CJ-82-2308, Filed April 29, 1982.

206   *As president of one* . . . Interview with Dale Mitchell, Oklahoma City, February 21, 1984.

206   *As one former officer recalled* . . . Interview with a former Penn Square officer, Oklahoma City, November 14, 1983.

207   *We shipped those loan files* . . . Interview with a former Penn Square officer, Oklahoma City, June 6, 1984.

207   *"It was a big shell game . . ."* Interview with a former Penn Square officer, Oklahoma City, November 14, 1983.

207   *One correspondent officer* . . . Interview with a Wells Fargo officer, Independent Petroleum Association of American Convention, New Orleans, November 3, 1983.

TWENTY-TWO Mixed Signals

209   *In May 1981* . . . Interview with John Boyd, Houston, October 1984.

209   *Later that year* . . . Interview with Robert Schultz, Yakima, Wash., July 10, 1983.

209   *And at a meeting* . . . Interview with a former correspondent bank officer, Chicago, April 25, 1983.

210   *Looking back* . . . Telephone interview with Pat Goy, October 1984.

210   *According to Dr. Talley* . . . Interview with Dr. William Talley, Oklahoma City, March 13, 1984.

210   *One Oklahoma oilman* . . . Interview with an oilman, Oklahoma City, June 4, 1984.

211   *One of the few* . . . *Wall Street Journal,* January 11, 1980.

211   *The active rig count* . . . Hughes Tool Company, Houston, Texas.

211   *And as Bill Lakey remembers it* . . . Interview with Bill Lakey, Holdenville, Okla., March 7, 1984.

212   *"If he's got leather . . ."* Interview with an Oklahoma oil and gas lawyer, Oklahoma City, January 5, 1984.

212   *Steve Knox, a young . . .* Interview with Steve Knox, Oklahoma City, April 25, 1984.

212   *About the time . . .* Interview with Tom Kenan, Oklahoma City, December 2, 1983.

213   *In June 1981, when banks . . .* Telephone interview with Thorne Stallings, 1984.

213   *But at least one . . .* Interview with an Oklahoma City oilman, Oklahoma City, June 15, 1984.

213   *Thornburgh blew into . . .* Telephone interview with a spokesman for federal penitentiary at El Reno, 1984.

214   *"Lynn was a chameleon" . . .* Telephone interview with an acquaintance of Lynn Thornburgh, 1984.

214   *Also that summer . . .* Inferential Focus newsletter, August 1981.

TWENTY-THREE Easy Come, Easy Go

215   *For John Baldwin . . .* Interview with John Baldwin, Oklahoma City, January 13, 1984.

217   *And in fact Beller . . .* Testimony by Eldon Beller, USA *v.* Patterson.

217   *"Jennings gave him the ball . . ."* Interview with a former Penn Square officer, Oklahoma City, May 25, 1984.

218   *Wyman Fraley was not . . . Daily Oklahoman,* July 29, 1981; and *Journal Record,* February 20, 1985.

219   *It took more than . . .* Audit Report, Treasury.

219   *bank's ten best and two worst . . .* Minutes of the regular meeting of the board of directors, June 9, 1981.

219   *It concluded . . .* Audit Report, Treasury.

219   *On July 1 . . .* Letter from Dallas regional office to Penn Square board of directors.

220   *Meanwhile, the Comptroller's . . .* Audit Report, Treasury.

220   *"CINB is adequately staffed . . ."* Staff report to Subcommitee on Financial Institutions Supervision, Regulation and Insurance, Committee on Banking Finance and Urban Affairs, September 18, 1984.

220   *Continental, said a former . . .* Telephone interview with a former Continental officer, October 1984.

220   *At the July 29 meeting . . .* Minutes of a special meeting of the board of directors, July 29, 1981.

221   *"If Jennings had contested . . ."* Interview with a former bank examiner, Oklahoma City, May 11, 1984.

221   *But as Rep. Fernand St Germain . . .* Hearings, Serial No. 97–92.

221   *While the real sore ...* Telephone interview with Robert Serino, September 1984.

223   *Almost to the day ...* Letter from Professional Asset Management to clients, Hearings, Serial No. 97–92.

223   *Bill Goldsmith, one of the ...* Interview with Bill Goldsmith, Del Mar, Calif., June 29, 1983.

223   *"So many small financial ..."* Hearings, Serial No. 97–92.

224   *Ed Miller of Founders Bank ...* Interview with Ed Miller, Oklahoma City, January 16, 1984.

225   *On June 23, Leonard ...* R. Kevin Leonard *v.* First Penn Corp., Penn Square Bank, now known as Deposit Insurance National Bank of Oklahoma City, Federal Deposit Insurance Corp. as receiver, and Bill G. Patterson, U.S. District Court for Western District of Oklahoma, CIV 83-198 W, Complaint.

225   *Kevin Leonard of LPCX ...* FDIC *v.* U.S. Executive Air CIV-83-562 R, U.S. District Court, Western District of Oklahoma.

225   *Gary Gray, a husky ...* Testimony of Gary Gray, USA *v.* Patterson.

TWENTY-FOUR More Bad Deals

227   *Real estate developer Kim Collins ...* Telephone interview with Kim Collins, May 1984.

227   *A Securities ...* Securities and Exchange Commission *v.* Dennis E. Greenman, Case No. 81-5510, U.S. Court of Appeals for 11th Circuit; U.S. *v.* Dennis Greenman, Case No. 81-137, U.S. District Court, Tampa, Fla.

227   *According to a report ...* Tulsa Tribune, August 23, 1982.

228   *Greenman, it turned out ...* Telephone interview with James Johnson, trustee for Chilcott Commodities, May 1984.

228   *Government investigators discovered ...* U.S. *v.* Chilcott.

228   *John R. Lytle ...* Telephone interview with a former Continental officer, October 1984.

229   *Penn Square loan officers ...* Interview with a former Penn Square officer, August 1982.

229   *According to one former employee ...* Interview with a former Penn Square employee, Oklahoma City, January 1984.

229   *Coincidentally, on July 29 ...* Kathy Kenefick memo, July 29.

230   *Kenefick, however ...* Telephone interview with a former Continental officer, October 1984.

230   *Lytle, former officers said ...* Longhorn Case No. MDL 525, pretrial brief.

231   *"You mean you're doubting ..."* Telephone interview with former Continental officer, October 1984.

231   *Baker obtained a copy* . . .   Special Litigation Report.

231   *According to a special report* . . .   Special Litigation Report.

232   *Meanwhile, the business press* . . .   *New York Times,* September 28, 1981.

232   *Unlike Kathy Kenefick* . . .   Interview with John Boyd, Houston, October 1984.

234   *In the meantime* . . .   Interview with former Seafirst officer, July 1983.

234   *By this time, Boyd* . . .   Interview with John Boyd, Houston, October 1984.

234   *To other observers* . . .   Interview with a former Seafirst officer, July 1983.

234   *Chase Manhattan also* . . .   Interview with Dale Mitchell, Oklahoma City, February 28, 1984.

234   *"They bought $10 million* . . .   Interview with a former Penn Square officer, Oklahoma City, May 8, 1984.

234   *One loan that was not* . . .   Discussion of involvement of Mahan Rowsey with Penn Square based on interviews with former associates, Penn Square officers, Frank Mahan, court testimony, and documents.

235   *According to Stanley Lee* . . .   Telephone interview with Stanley Lee, October 1984.

236   *According to Patterson* . . .   Testimony of Bill Patterson, USA *v.* Patterson.

236   *Scribbling the figures* . . .   Deposition of William Rowsey, U.S. Bankruptcy Court, Western District of Oklahoma, Mahan Rowsey, Inc., debtor in possession, *v.* Penn Square Bank, N.A., of Oklahoma City, and Insurance National Bank of Oklahoma City, BK 823-01390, September 1, 1982.

238   *John Baldwin was accustomed* . . .   Interview with John Baldwin, Oklahoma City, October 1984.

238   *But not all* . . .   Account of trip to Las Vegas based on firsthand accounts of two eyewitnesses who requested anonymity.

TWENTY-FIVE Swimming Upstream

240   *By the fall of 1981* . . .   Account of Kerr-McGee's involvement in the Fletcher Field based on interviews with Oklahoma City oilmen and annual reports of the Kerr-McGee Corp.

240   *In the nine months* . . .   Audit Report, Treasury.

241   *The number of seismic crews* . . .   *Topics,* a publication of the Petroleum Information Corp., Vol. 3, No. 1, Winter 1983.

241   *Larry Brandt* . . .   Interview with Larry Brandt, Oklahoma City, March 9, 1984.

241   *Bill Bell, a sales executive* . . .   Interview with Bill Bell, Tulsa oil-field equipment exposition, November 1, 1983.

241   *Beller returned from . . .*   Testimony in USA *v.* Patterson.

241   *On September 24, he distributed . . .*   Memo from Eldon Beller to lending officers, September 24, 1981.

242   *"Every time I think . . ."*   Interview with a former Penn Square officer, Oklahoma City, May 25, 1984.

242   *"Mr. Murphy," Beller recalls . . .*   Testimony of Eldon Beller, USA *v.* Patterson.

242   *Sam "The Polyethylene King" Villyard . . .*   Interview with Sam Villyard, Oklahoma City, August 30, 1984, and former Penn Square officers.

242   *Lanier, who had conducted . . .*   Account of the October 1984 exam based on interviews with former Penn Square officers and regulators, including Jerry Lanier; summaries of examinations contained in transcripts of congressional hearings; and Audit Report, Treasury.

244   *Besides Clifford Resources . . .*   Discussion of Clifford Resources based on Penn Square documents and interviews with former Penn Square officers.

245   *According to an observer, Patterson . . .*   Interview with a former Penn Square officer, Oklahoma City, January 1984.

245   *Honing in on . . .*   Special Litigation Report.

245   *Lytle had neglected . . .*   Special Litigation Report.

246   *"Get Kiser on the phone . . ."*   Interview with a former Penn Square Officer, Oklahoma City, 1983.

246   *Kiser later testified . . .*   Testimony of Jan Kiser, U.S.A. *v.* Patterson.

247   *Moreover, the FDIC . . .*   Chase Manhattan Bank *v.* FDIC, counterclaim of FDIC, U.S. District Court for the Western District of Oklahoma, CIV-83-126 R.

247   *Around November 15 . . .*   Interview with a former Penn Square officer, Oklahoma, September 1984; memo from Arlyn Hill to James J. Gunter entitled "Interest Advances to Participating Banks on Commercial Loans," December 8, 1981. (Contained in Hearings, Serial No. 97-92.)

247   *Advance interest payments . . .*   Ibid.

248   *"Stop the correspondents . . ."*   Testimony of Arlyn Hill, USA *v.* Patterson.

248   *Overdrafts and overdues . . .*   Minutes of meetings of board of directors; interview with a former Penn Square director, Oklahoma City, October 19, 1983.

248   *"We cursed Hibernia . . ."*   Interview with a former Penn Square officer, Oklahoma City, May 8, 1984.

249   *According to Bob Kotarski . . .*   Testimony of Bob Kotarski, USA *v.* Patterson.

249   *In October, Mahan and Rowsey . . .*   Testimony of Randy Dunn, USA *v.* Patterson.

       TWENTY-SIX Red Herrings

251   *Said a source who worked . . .*   Interview with a former associate of Jere Sturgis, Enid, Okla., May 23, 1984.

251   *"Sturgis wanted us to give . . ."*   Interview with a former correspondent bank officer, Chicago, October 12, 1983.

252   *And Mike Gilbert . . .*   Testimony of Mike Gilbert, USA *v.* Patterson.

252   *Continental, like Chase . . .*   Special Litigation Report.

252   *According to Patterson . . .*   Deposition of Bill G. Patterson, Longhorn Case No. MDL 525.

253   *On November 4, 1981 . . .*   Special Litigation Report; interviews with former Continental officers.

253   *The engineers were dismayed.*   Longhorn Case No. MDL 525.

253   *Several days later . . .*   Minutes of regular meeting of the board of directors, November 10, 1981.

254   *Take, for example . . .*   Nucorp Energy, Inc., debtor, Case No. 82-3106-K11, U.S. Bankruptcy Court, Southern District of California, San Diego.

254   *In a keynote speech . . .*   Address by Thomas Labrecque to American Bankers Association, Correspondent Banking Convention, Kansas City, Mo., November 1981.

254   *Hansen led off his . . .*   Address by Wayne Hansen to the American Bankers Association Correspondent Banking Convention, Kansas City, Mo., November 1981.

255   *"Do as we say . . ."*   Interview with a former Penn Square officer, Oklahoma City, May 8, 1984.

255   *A leading bank consultant . . .*   Interview with a bank consultant, New York City, April 1983.

255   *That same month . . .*   Account of oil party at Jennings's farm based on interviews with numerous former Penn Square officers, borrowers, and upstream bank officers who attended the party.

257   *About the time their customers . . .*   Special Litigation Report.

258   *One former Continental officer . . .*   Telephone interview with a former Continental officer, October 1984.

258   *It later emerged . . .*   Wall Street Journal, February 27, 1984.

258   *Gunter, in fact, remarked . . .*   Interview with Harold Russell, Oklahoma City, September 1984.

259   *Shortly before . . .*   Hearings, Serial No. 97–92.

259   *On November 20 . . .*   Letter from Bill P. Jennings to Harold Russell.

259   *Jim Blanton . . .*   Ibid.

TWENTY-SEVEN Dump Truck Banking

260   *Patterson enlivened* . . .   Account of oil and gas Christmas party based on interviews with former Penn Square officers in attendance.

261   *But the real trash* . . .   Account of trip to Seattle based on interviews with former Penn Square officers who were on it.

261   *According to allegations* . . .   Seafirst Corporation by Delores Sherman derivatively *et al. v.* William M. Jenkins *et al.* Case No. C83-771R, amended class action complaint, filed June 28, 1983, in the U.S. District Court, Western District of Washington.

262   *At a dinner* . . .   Interview with a former Penn Square officer, Oklahoma City, November 1984.

262   *The Christmas gift* . . .   Interview with John Boyd, Houston, October 1984.

263   *One Seafirst officer* . . .   Interviews with current and former Seafirst officers, Seattle, July 5–15, 1983.

264   *Boyd and Patterson* . . .   Telephone interview with John Boyd, 1984.

265   *Tom Kelly, a former kicker* . . .   Testimony in USA *v.* Patterson.

266   *Byron Tarnutzer, for one* . . .   Tarnutzer Deposition.

266   *Eight hundred miles* . . .   G. Blake Chanslor *v.* Longhorn 1979-II Drilling Program *et al.,* Case No. CV 81-08889, County of Bernalillo, New Mexico.

267   *A Colorado Springs attorney* . . .   Letter from Edward M. McCord to William P. Jennings, December 23, 1981. Longhorn Case No. MDL 525.

267   *Shari Lynn Mitchell* . . .   Longhorn Case No. MDL 525.

267   *By early 1982* . . .   Testimony of Russ Bainbridge, USA *v.* Patterson.

267   *Longhorn co-chairman J.D. Allen* . . .   *Daily Oklahoman,* January 10, 1982.

267   *Meanwhile* Oklahoma Business *magazine* . . .   *Oklahoma Business,* January 1982.

268   *As the chief financial officer* . . .   Interview with an oil company executive, Oklahoma City, September 1983.

268   *Sam Hammons noticed* . . .   Interview with Sam Hammons, Oklahoma City, March 13, 1984.

268   *Hughes Tool Company active rig* . . .   Hughes Tool Company, Houston, rig count.

269   *But in December 1981* . . .   Interview with an Oklahoma City oilman, Oklahoma City, February 23, 1984.

269   *One leading energy accountant* . . .   *Daily Oklahoman,* November 29, 1981.

269   *Lease broker Steve Knox* . . .   Interview with Steve Knox, Oklahoma City, April 25, 1984.

269   *Swan and some sixty-five . . .* FDIC *v.* Jennings *et al.*

269   *As for Jennings . . .* New York Times, August 14, 1982.

269   *On December 29, Penn Square . . .* Interview with Bill Stubbs, Oklahoma City, October 1983.

270   *And, on December 31 . . .* Penn Points, the house organ of Penn Square Bank, December 1981.

270   *"We worked for about four . . ."* Rowsey Deposition.

271   *Randy Dunn was making . . .* Testimony of Randy Dunn, USA *v.* Patterson.

271   *When Patterson heard . . .* Testimony of Bill Kingston, USA *v.* Patterson.

272   *In early January . . .* Interview with a former Penn Square officer, Oklahoma City, January 1984; telephone interview with Frank Mahan, December 22, 1984.

TWENTY-EIGHT Getting Drilled into Trouble

This chapter is based on interviews with George Rodman; Thomas Kenan, the trustee in bankruptcy for George Rodman, Inc.; documents in U.S. Bankruptcy Court, Oklahoma City; a memo from Jim Austin, chief financial officer of George Rodman, Inc.; and interviews with former associates of George Rodman and former Penn Square officers.

276   *Representatives of the Comptroller . . .* Minutes of regular meeting of board of directors, January 12, 1982.

276   *Moreover, Dallas was . . .* Audit Report, Treasury.

277   *Early in 1982 . . .* Interview with Carl Anderson, Jr., November 10, 1983.

277   *Penn Square and the upstream . . .* Testimony of Greg Odean, USA *v.* Patterson.

TWENTY-NINE A Trip to Oklahoma

279   *Carl Swan dispatched . . .* Interview with John Boyd, Houston, October 1984.

280   *"Why, I'll bet . . ."* Interview with Bill Gammie, Yakima, Wash., July 10, 1983.

280   *To Bill Patterson, they wrote . . .* Letters from Richard Jaehning to Patterson, Jennings, and Swan.

281   *On March 1, he presented . . .* Memo from Arland Hatfield to Richard Jaehning, March 1, 1982.

282   *At one point . . .* Interviews with Seafirst officers, Seattle, July 5–15, 1983.

283   *The report could be called . . .* "Energy Industry," World Banking Group, Energy Division, March 1982.

285   *Several blocks from . . .* Interviews with Rainier National Bank officers, Seattle, July 1983.

285   *He said, "The day . . ."*   Interview with Sally Jewell, New Orleans, IPAA Convention, November 3, 1983.

286   *On March 26, 1982 . . .*   Memo from Patterson to staff, March 26, 1982.

286   *In its February 17 issue . . .*   Marples Letter, Seattle, February 17, 1982.

287   *Referring to the operational . . .*   Memo from Bill Patterson to staff, undated.

287   *J.D. Allen was apparently . . .*   Bankruptcy filing of J.D. Allen, U.S. Bankruptcy Court, Oklahoma City.

287   *In early 1982 . . .*   Interview with Michael Tighe, Chicago, April 1983.

287   *Hugh Jones . . .*   Interview with Hugh Jones, Woodward, Okla., March 1982.

288   *That same week . . .*   Tarnutzer Deposition.

288   *On February 23, Patterson . . .*   Memo from Bill Patterson, February 23, 1982.

288   *On February 24 . . .*   Copies of notes and ledger cards of Mahan Rowsey account accompanying Rowsey Deposition.

THIRTY The Ides of March

290   *On February 16 . . .*   Testimony of Pat McCoy, USA *v.* Patterson.

290   *In fact, just a week . . .*   Memo from J.S. Zwaik to C.D. York, February 10, 1982, contained in Hearings, Serial No. 97–92.

290   *One of the nonperformers . . .*   Testimony of Pat McCoy, USA *v.* Patterson.

291   *Phil Busey is a young . . .*   Testimony of Phil Busey, USA *v.* Patterson.

292   *On March 4 . . .*   Testimony of Garvin Chandler, USA *v.* Patterson.

292   *That same week petroleum . . .*   Testimony of Mike Gilbert, USA *v.* Patterson.

292   *Sipperly and Dick Pinney . . .*   Interview with former Penn Square officer, Oklahoma City, 1984.

292   *The closing on . . .*   Testimony of Phil Busey, USA *v.* Patterson.

293   *On Wednesday, Hal Clifford . . .*   Testimony of Hal Clifford and Kent Gruber, USA *v.* Patterson.

293   *This was not the first time . . .*   Wall Street Journal, October 1, 1975.

293   *On March 10 . . .*   Testimony of Ashburn Bywaters, USA *v.* Patterson.

294   *As Tom Swineford . . .*   Testimony of Tom Swineford, USA *v.* Patterson.

294   *According to a secretary . . .*   Testimony of Jan Hargus, USA *v.* Patterson.

295   *Beller was informed . . .*   Testimony of Eldon Beller, USA *v.* Patterson.

295   *Coincidentally, Senall* . . .   Affidavit for Search Warrant, U.S. District Court, Middle District of Florida, Case No. 82-164M-W.

295   *By that spring* . . .   U.S. Bankruptcy Court, Oklahoma City.

296   *"Sturgis appeared to be . . ."*   Testimony of Bob Kotarski, USA *v.* Patterson.

296   *"What's your question . . ."*   Tape recording of conversation between Patterson and Gary Roberts played, in USA *v.* Patterson.

296   *According to a deposition* . . .   Excerpts from deposition by Ed Moran.

296   *Earlier, the domestic institutions* . . .   Telephone interview with a Chase officer.

297   *On April 8* . . .   Letter from Mary Ellen Hughes to Scott Hamilton, April 8, 1982.

297   *Asked about* . . .   Telephone interview with Charles Francis.

297   *Weeks after Chase* . . .   Chase Manhattan *v.* Federal Deposit Insurance Corp., U.S. District Court, Oklahoma City.

297   *In Chicago the loan* . . .   Special Litigation Report.

298   *According to federal prosecutors* . . .   U.S. *v.* John Lytle, Bill Patterson, and Jere Sturgis, U.S. District Court, Chicago.

298   *Dale Mitchell recalled later* . . .   Interview with Dale Mitchell, Oklahoma City, February 21, 1984.

298   *Responding to a request* . . .   Special Litigation Report.

299   *Bill Talley, whose* . . .   Interview with Bill Talley, Oklahoma City, March 13, 1984.

300   *John Mason, the company's* . . .   *Wall Street Journal,* March 31, 1982.

301   *As early as* . . .   Testimony of J.D. Hodges, USA *v.* Patterson.

301   *"Northern said Chase Exploration . . ."*   Testimony of Bill Patterson, USA *v.* Patterson.

301   *According to Trigg* . . .   Testimony of Joe Dan Trigg, USA *v.* Patterson.

301   *On March 22* . . .   Testimony of Jan Hargus, USA *v.* Patterson.

302   *"He said he was going . . ."*   Testimony of Arthur Pool, USA *v.* Patterson.

302   *According to a complaint* . . .   Chase Exploration Corp. *v.* The Northern Trust Co.; Penn Square Bank; Harry B. Wilson and Bill G. Patterson; Adversary Case No. 82-0430 filed in U.S. District Court, Tulsa.

302   *On March 24* . . .   Memo from Patterson to staff on Chase Exploration, March 24, 1982.

303   *At a meeting between* . . .   Interview with a former Penn Square officer, Oklahoma City, August, 1982.

303   *"First we couldn't reach him . . ."*   Telephone interview with a former Penn Square officer, May 1984.

303   *"It was clear by . . ."*   Interview with a former Penn Square officer, Oklahoma City, March 1984.

304   *By the end of March* . . .   FDIC *v.* Jennings *et al.*

304   *Norma Babb, the bank's auditor* . . .   Telephone interview with a former Penn Square officer.

304   *Partners of Peat, Marwick, Mitchell* . . .   Letter from Peat Marwick to the board of directors of Penn Square Bank, March 19, 1982, contained in the Hearings, Serial No. 97-93.

304   *Mike Mahoney, whose duties* . . .   Interview with Mike Mahoney, Oklahoma City, October 1984.

304   *Among the investors in Hal Clifford's* . . .   Windon Third Oil and Gas Drilling Partnership *et al. v.* FDIC *et al.* Case No. CIV 83-536T, U.S. District Court, Western District of Oklahoma.

305   *Citibank's Dallas* . . .   Internal Penn Square documents, internal memos and correspondence from Marine Midland and Bank of New England.

305   *"Thank you for coming . . ."*   Letter from John Boyd to a former Penn Square officer, April 16, 1982.

306   *On April 16 he issued a memo* . . .   Memo from John Baldwin, April 16, 1982.

THIRTY-ONE The Great Spring Rig Sale
307   *It had been years* . . .   Testimony in USA *v.* Patterson.

307   *At 8:00 A.M. on April 16* . . .   *Daily Oklahoman*, April 17, 1982.

307   *Though Meg Sipperly* . . .   Testimony in USA *v.* Patterson.

309   *On April 26, a confident* . . .   *American Banker,* April 27, 1982.

309   *"Oklahoma's Penn Square Bank . . ."*   *American Banker*, April 26, 1982.

309   *At Continental, personnel chief* . . .   Special Litigation Report.

309   *California money-broker* . . .   Hearings, Serial No. 97–93.

310   *In Battle Creek* . . .   Interviews with Michigan National Bank officers.

310   *The directors of Michigan* . . .   Testimony in USA *v.* Patterson.

310   *John Mason, a short* . . .   Interview with John Mason, New York, April 1982.

310   *Prudential-Bache's George Salem* . . .   Memo from George Salem to bank stock analysts, April 30, 1982.

311   *The article prompted Baker* . . .   Special Litigation Report.

312   *Between April 22 and April 29* . . .   Fred L. Steinlauf *v.* Continental Illinois Corporation *et al.*, U.S. District Court for the Northern District of Illinois, Eastern Division.

312   *In Seattle, officials* . . .   Interviews with officials of Rainier Bank, Seattle, July 1983.

312   *On the East Coast* . . . Interview with a former Penn Square officer, Oklahoma City, October 1983; telephone interview with a Chemical Bank spokesman, December 1984.

312   *The* American Banker *story* . . . *Daily Oklahoman,* May 2, 1982.

312   *"Negative press . . ."* Audit Report, Treasury.

312   *On May 4 Plunk* . . . Memo from Plunk to Dallas regional office, May 4.

312   *When Phil Busey.* . . Testimony of Phil Busey, USA *v.* Patterson.

313   *Late on the evening of* . . . Testimony of Larry Ray, USA *v.* Patterson.

313   *The gas man, meanwhile* . . . Testimony of Robert A. Hefner 3rd, USA *v.* Patterson.

314   *The following week* . . . Testimony of Phil Busey, USA *v.* Patterson.

315   *"I didn't know exactly what . . ."* Interview with Robert A. Hefner 3rd, Oklahoma City, beginning February 9, 1984.

315   *Perhaps Billy's optimism* . . . Oklahoma Natural Gas Co. *v.* Mahan Rowsey, Inc., U.S. District Court, Oklahoma City.

316   *Even after unloading* . . . Interviews with former Penn Square officers; Chase Manhattan *v.* FDIC., U.S. District Court, Oklahoma City.

316   *On May 1, 1982* . . . Interview with Brian O'Neill, Houston, May 27, 1983.

316   *An-Son's Carl Anderson, Jr. recalls* . . . Interview with Carl Anderson, Jr., November 10, 1983.

317   *From 828 rigs* . . . Hughes Tool Company, Houston.

THIRTY-TWO A Terrific Bunch of Guys

318   *The Four Seasons* . . . Description of dinner at Four Seasons based on interviews with bank stock analysts who attended it.

319   *Anderson called a meeting* . . . Special Litigation Report.

319   *The same day Baker and Anderson* . . . Memo from William Jenkins to John Boyd, May 11, 1982.

319   *Harvey Gillis, who had replaced* . . . Interviews with former Seafirst officers, Seattle, July 1983.

320   *At one directors' loan* . . . Interviews with former Penn Square directors, Oklahoma City, October 26 and 27, 1983.

321   *At the May 18 meeting* . . . Minutes of a regular meeting of the board of directors, May 18, 1982.

321   *Clifton Poole in Dallas* . . . Audit Report, Treasury.

321   *"It is only the documentation . . ."* Interview with a former official of the Comptroller of the Currency, Washington, D.C., May 1983.

322   *The relationship between Plunk* . . . Interviews with former Penn Square officers.

322   *"I got the feeling ..."*   Interview with John Baldwin, Oklahoma City, January 13, 1984.

323   *On Monday, May 17 ...*   Account of Drysdale Securities episode based on articles in the *New York Times, Wall Street Journal,* and the *American Banker.*

324   *And before that tumultous week was out ...*   *American Banker,* May 24, 1982.

324   *House Banking Committee ...*   Hearings, Serial No. 97–92.

324   *Plunk told Baldwin ...*   Interview with John Baldwin, Oklahoma City, January 13, 1984.

325   *"I created this Frankenstein ..."*   Testimony in USA *v.* Patterson.

325   *"They'd come around ..."*   Interview with a former Penn Square officer, Oklahoma City, May 1984.

325   *But even Patterson seemed to recognize ...*   Interview with a former Penn Square officer, Oklahoma City, January 1984.

326   *"In April 1982 Jim Nicholas's ..."*   Reo Resources, Inc., Sarah Drilling *et al. v.* FDIC, Case No. 82-2070E, U.S. District Court, Western District of Oklahoma.

326   *Belonged to Tom Hoshall ...*   Telephone interview with Tom Hoshall.

327   *In the three years or so ...*   SKS *v.* FDIC.

327   *And Longhorn, which ...*   Interview with Ray Erlach, San Francisco, June 1983.

328   *Patterson ordered two debits ...*   USA *v.* Patterson.

328   *In January the brokers ...*   Letter from James L. Sexton, director of FDIC division of bank supervision, to Hon. Benjamin S. Rosenthal, chairman of subcommittee on Commerce, Consumer and Monetary Affairs Subcommittee November 15, 1982.

329   *Cliff Poole and Roy Jackson ...*   Account of relationship and discussion between Poole and Jackson based on interviews with regulators and former examiners, Audit Report Treasury, internal memoranda of the Comptroller's office, and interviews with Poole and Jackson.

330   *About the same time ...*   Telephone Interview with Bill Martin, February 1985.

      THIRTY-THREE Trust Me, Trust Me

331   *On June 2, 1982 ...*   Testimony in USA *v.* Patterson.

332   *By this time ...*   Audit Report, Treasury.

332   *In the case of the Second ...*   Internal Penn Square documents.

332   *While apparently oblivious ...*   Special Litigation Report.

333   *The next day Hefner ...*   Testimony in USA *v.* Patterson.

334   *Carl Anderson and his An-Son ...*   Interview with Carl Anderson, Jr., November 10, 1983.

334   *First National, meanwhile* . . .   Interview with Dale Mitchell, Oklahoma City, February 21, 1984.

334   *Bill Jennings was always* . . .   Oklahoma City *Journal Record,* June 8, 1982.

335   *Just a few days later* . . .   Account of fishing trip based on interviews with participants.

336   *Patterson allegedly booked* . . .   U.S.A. vs. Bill G. Patterson.

337   *Ken Tureaud received* . . .   Affidavit of Michael R. Hampton, FDIC examiner, October 13, 1982, In re: Kenneth E. Tureaud, debtor, U.S. Bankruptcy court in the Northern District of Oklahoma.

337   *On the Wednesday* . . .   Audit Report, Treasury.

337   *With its traditional buyers* . . .   Interviews with former regulators; balance sheet of First Penn Corp.

338   *But on a Friday* . . .   Interview with a former Penn Square employee, Oklahoma City, January 10, 1984.

339   *Lytle, according to testimony* . . .   Hearings, Serial No. 97–93.

339   *On June 14, Peat, Marwick* . . .   Letter from Peat, Marwick, Mitchell to James J. Gunter, June 14, 1982.

339   *By the June 15 board meeting* . . .   Minutes of a regular meeting of the board of directors, June 15, 1982.

341   *"Bill called and said . . ."*   Testimony in USA *v.* Patterson.

341   *The GHK Companies and the Parker* . . .   GHK Corp. press release.

THIRTY-FOUR The Downhill Slide

342   *According to Testimony* . . .   Testimony in USA *v.* Patterson.

342   *As for Chase* . . .   Telephone interview with former Penn Square employee, December 1984.

343   *"When we first got there . . ."*   Interview with a Chase representative, December 1983.

343   *"They made themselves . . ."*   Interview with John Baldwin, Oklahoma City, January 13, 1984.

344   *Rainier National's Sally Jewell* . . .   Interview with Sally Jewell, New Orleans, November 3, 1983.

344   *"Putting some pep . . ."*   Interview with a former Penn Square officer, Oklahoma City, May 1984.

344   *One of them was Bruce Heafitz* . . .   *Daily Oklahoman,* August 16, 1982.

344   *The sun also* . . .   Michigan National Bank *v.* FDIC, U.S. District Court, Western District of Oklahoma.

344   *The day after* . . .   Memo from Sandy Hamilton, June 16, 1982.

344   *In the midst* . . .   Interview with Greg Odean, October 1983.

345   *Later, Beep Jennings . . .*   Telephone interview with Bill Jennings, June 25, 1982.

346   *Dallas authorized the examiners . . .*   Audit Report, Treasury.

346   *"We felt comfortable . . ."*   Interview with a former official of Comptroller of the Currency, June 1983.

346   *"Like the examiners . . ."*   Interview with a former Penn Square officer, Oklahoma City, May 1983.

346   *And in Poughkeepsie . . .*   Hearings, Serial No. 97-93.

347   *A top official . . .*   Memo from William L. Robertson to the file, June 22, 1982.

347   *On Friday . . .*   Audit Report, Treasury.

347   *In Washington . . .*   Interviews with Federal Reserve Board officials, Washington, May 1983.

347   *Bobby Hefner was attending . . .*   Testimony of Robert A. Hefner 3rd, USA *v.* Patterson.

348   *Penn Square oil and gas officers . . .*   Interviews with former Penn Square officers.

348   *Jennings was "floored . . ."*   Testimony of Bill Kingston, USA *v.* Patterson.

349   *It was not until . . .*   Audit Report, Treasury.

349   *Seafirst had also dispatched . . .*   Interviews with Seafirst officers, Seattle, July 1983.

349   *Boyd, however, had returned . . .*   Interview with William Gammie, Yakima, Wash., July 10, 1983.

349   *Ironically, Boyd . . .*   Interview with John Boyd, Houston, October 1984.

349   *On Friday, June 25 . . .*   Interviews with current and former bank regulators, May and June 1983.

350   *In Oklahoma City, . . .*   Interviews with former Penn Square officers; testimony in USA *v.* Patterson.

350   *According to John Boyd . . .*   Interview with John Boyd, Houston, October 1984.

350   *Over the weekend . . .*   Testimony of Robert A. Hefner 3rd, USA *v.* Patterson.

351   *While these discussions . . .*   Testimony of Joe Dan Trigg and Trigg's accountant, USA *v.* Patterson.

THIRTY-FIVE Taking the Heat

352   *By Monday, June 28 . . .*   Interview with John Baldwin, Oklahoma City, January 13, 1984.

352   *Tammy Cox reported to work . . .*   Interview with a former Penn Square employee, Oklahoma City, January 1984.

353   *With Penn Square's sources . . .*   Hearings, Serial No. 97-92.

353   *Only after a series of . . .*   Internal documents of the Comptroller of the Currency.

354   *"We're calling on our . . ."*   *Daily Oklahoman,* August 8, 1982.

354   *"We're all going to laugh . . ."*   Interview with former upstream bank officers.

354   *"Mr. Anderson . . ."*   Interview with former regulators.

354   *Perkins happened . . .*   Hearings, Serial No. 97-93.

355   *After the Comptroller called . . .*   Interview with John Boyd, Houston, October 1984.

355   *Tuesday evening . . .*   Testimony in USA *v.* Patterson.

356   *On Wednesday morning . . .*   Interview with William Isaac, Washington, D.C., May 1983.

358   *"Just lucky I guess . . ."*   Notes of Gerald Bergman, deposition of Gerald Bergman, Securities and Exchange Commission.

358   *"I for one . . ."*   Testimony of Robert A. Hefner 3rd, USA *v.* Patterson; interviews with Robert A. Hefner 3rd, beginning February 9, 1984.

359   *Patterson had flown to Lansing . . .*   Hearings, Serial No. 97-93; interviews with Michigan National Bank officers.

360   *At first, it seemed . . .*   Interviews with former Penn Square officers; testimony in USA *v.* Patterson.

361   *Elizabeth Merrick Coe . . .*   Hearings, Serial No. 97-92.

361   *George Rodman claims . . .*   Interview with George Rodman.

361   *Final overdraft list . . .*   Overdraft list.

362   *Late that Wednesday . . .*   Account of locksmith's arrival based on several interviews with former Penn Square officers, as well as the locksmith.

THIRTY-SIX July 1, 1982
    This chapter and the remaining ones were based largely on dozens of interviews with present and former bank regulators, former upstream bank and Penn Square Bank officers, most of whom asked that material not be attributed to them. For this reason, only interviews with officials who agreed to be quoted will be footnoted. In addition, the author reviewed minutes of the meetings of the Federal Reserve Board from July 1 to July 5, minutes of the emergency meetings of the Penn Square board of directors of July 1 and July 2, deposition of Gerald Bergman, internal documents of the Comptroller of the Currency, hearings before the Committee on Banking, Finance, and Urban Affairs, and internal Penn Square documents.

363   *On the morning of . . .*   *American Banker,* July 1, 1982.

363   *Penn Square's board* . . .   Minutes of emergency meeting of board of directors, July 1, 1982.

364   *Arnie Middeldorf* . . .   Hearings, Serial No. 97-93.

364   *After a break* . . .   Minutes of meeting of the board, July 1, 1982.

365   *"Despite all our . . ."*   Memo from Odean to staff, July 1, 1982.

366   *He joined his shocked* . . .   Attendance at meeting based on sign-in sheets in the possession of the Comptroller of the Currency.

366   *"When I left . . ."*   Interview with Frank Murphy, Oklahoma City, November 1984.

367   Telephone interview with Bill Jennings, December 17, 1983.

367   *On July 1* . . .   Interviews with former Seafirst officials, including Randy James, the director of communications, Seattle, July 1983; and John Boyd, Houston, October, 1984.

368   *Lytle said it was* . . .   Hearings, Serial No. 97-93.

369   *Syrl C. Orbach* . . .   *Daily Oklahoman,* July 2.

369   *As Bill Gallagher* . . .   *Wall Street Journal,* July 27, 1982.

371   *As Isaac interpreted* . . .   Interview with William Isaac, Washington, D.C., May 1983.

374   *Likewise Chuck Vose, Jr.* . . .   Interview with Dale Mitchell, Oklahoma City, February 21, 1984.

THIRTY-SEVEN July 2, 1982
375   *Randolph and his wife* . . .   Interviews with James Randolph, Oklahoma City, October 1983; telephone interview with Jim Berry, October 1984.

375   *On Friday, July 2* . . .   Minutes of emergency meeting of board of directors, July 2, 1982.

376   *But his executive vice-president* . . .   Telephone interview with Henry Taliaferro, July 2, 1982.

376   *But the article was printed* . . .   *American Banker, Wall Street Journal, Journal Record, Daily Oklahoman,* July 2, 1982.

378   *In San Francisco* . . .   Telephone interview with Tom Sloan, February 1985.

380   *In Washington, Paul Volcker* . . .   Minutes of the meeting of the Federal Reserve Board, July 2.

380   *Curiously, at a reception* . . .   Remarks of Willard Butcher, Atlanta, October 1982.

381   *At midafternoon* . . .   Jennings's remarks as recalled by several former Penn Square officers who were present.

381   *John Baldwin recalls* . . .   Interview with John Baldwin, Oklahoma City, January 13, 1984.

---

381   *Bill Stubbs, an affable . . .*   Interview with Bill Stubbs, Oklahoma City, October 1983.

382   *When Penn Square argued . . .*   Audit Report, Treasury; interviews with former Penn Square officers.

382   *Jim Blanton . . .*   Interview with Jim Blanton, August 1982.

382   *"The participants . . ."*   Interview with William Isaac, Washington, D.C., May 1983.

THIRTY-EIGHT Sorry, We Already Gave at the Office
388   *"We'd be carrying . . ."*   Interview with a former Penn Square employee, Oklahoma City, May 10, 1984.

388   *One middle-aged woman . . .*   Interview with an oil company employee, Oklahoma City.

391   *A representative from . . .*   Interview with an official of the Comptroller of the Currency; corroborated in interviews with officials of the Federal Reserve Board and the FDIC.

393   *"Our people . . ."*   Interview with William Isaac, Washington, D.C., May 1983.

393   *Oilman Joe Dan Trigg . . .*   Testimony of Joe Dan Trigg and Russ Bainbridge, USA *v.* Patterson.

394   *The Fed board of governors . . .*   Minutes of the meeting of the Federal Reserve Board, July 3, 1982.

THIRTY-NINE July 5, 1982.
398   *Dear Mr. Guffy . . .*   Letter from Paul Homan to Roger Guffy, July 5, 1982.

400   *Dear Mr. Homan . . .*   Letter from Roger Guffy to Paul Homan, July 5, 1982.

400   *At 2:00* P.M. . . .   Minutes of the Federal Reserve Board, July 5, 1982.

400   *Around midday Monday . . .*   Interview with William Isaac, Washington, D.C., May 1983.

401   *"Although I said all . . ."*   Interview with Robert A. Hefner 3rd, beginning February 9, 1984.

401   *"It sounds to me as if . . ."*   Interview with William Isaac, Washington, D.C., May 1983.

402   *In Oklahoma . . .*   Interview with John Baldwin, Oklahoma City, January 13, 1984.

403   *Penn Square is open . . .*   Press release, from files of Comptroller of the Currency.

403   *Back in Washington . . .*   Interview with Leonora Cross, Washington, D.C., August 1983.

404   *"Do you believe . . ."*   Files of the Comptroller of the Currency.

404   *Just as Baldwin . . .*   Interview with John Baldwin, Oklahoma City, January 13, 1984.

405   *At eight-thirty . . .*   Account of speeches of Jennings and Hudson based on interviews with several regulators and numerous former Penn Square officers who were present at the meeting.

407   *In the hours . . . American Banker,* July 7, 1982.

FORTY The Fallout

409   *"Are you ready . . ."*   Interview with William Isaac, Washington, D.C., 1983.

409   *"Normally," he said . . .*   Press conference, Oklahoma City, July 6, 1982.

410   *As the chairman . . . American Banker,* July 7, 1982.

411   *Inside the bank . . .*   Interviews with FDIC officials, Washington, D.C., May 1983.

411   *Some 150 credit unions . . . Washington Post,* July 9, 1982.

411   *"I remember looking . . ."*   Interview with John Baldwin, Oklahoma City, January 13, 1984.

412   *Coincidentally, as the lines . . . Daily Oklahoman,* July 7, 1982.

412   *Ken Puglisi, a senior . . .*   Telephone interview with Ken Puglisi, October 1982.

414   *The markets can tolerate . . .*   Telephone interview with regulator, February 9, 1985.

414   *Meanwhile, Daniel Byrne . . .*   Telephone interview with Dan Byrne, October 1983.

414   *"Someone finding a whore . . ."*   Interview with a former upstream bank officer, Houston, May 1983.

414   *That Tuesday, DiMartino . . .*   Interview with Joe DiMartino, October 1982.

415   *Controlled more than $210 . . . Wall Street Journal,* January 11, 1985.

416   *Ed Farley is a talkative . . .*   Telephone interview with Ed Farley, October 1982.

416   *On that day . . .*   Interviews with Bob Harris, Oklahoma City, August 1982 and 1984.

417   *Seafirst director Bob Schultz . . .*   Interview with Bob Schultz.

418   *Thorne Stallings . . .*   Telephone Interview with Thorne Stallings, 1984.

418   *That day, in Washington . . .*   Interview with William Isaac, Washington, D.C., May 1983.

419   *"Penn Square," said one securities . . .*   Telephone interview with a securities analyst, April 1983.

419   *Less than three weeks . . .*   Details of Ambrosiano collapse based on newspaper and magazine articles, including *Institutional Investor,* October 1982.

419   *"The FDIC broke . . ."*   Interview with John Heimann, New York, April 1983.

420   *Then in July 1984 . . .*   USA *v.* Patterson.

421   *According to Robert Weintraub . . .*   Interview with Robert Weintraub, Washington, D.C., May 1983.

421   *Indeed, in a June 15 . . .*   *American Banker,* June 16, 1982.

422   *"Of course it affected . . ."*   Interview with a Fed official, Washington, D.C., May 1983.

422   *According to a former thrift . . .*   Interview with a former regulator, New York, April 1983.

423   *On July 27 . . .*   Interview with a former Continental officer, Chicago, April 1983.

423   *"I got my people together . . ."*   Interview with John Heimann, New York, April 1983.

423   *Said one prominent . . .*   Interview with an economist, New York, April 1983.

424   *According to a former colleague . . .*   Interview with a former Continental officer, Chicago, April 1983.

424   *Dale Mitchell visited Continental . . .*   Interview with Dale Mitchell, Oklahoma City, February 21, 1984.

424   *"We are now sufficiently . . ."*   Goldman, Sachs, "Interview with Management," July 30, 1982.

424   *"Examination results . . ."*   Excerpt from letter to Continental board contained in Staff Report to Subcommittee on Financial Institutions Supervision, Regulation and Insurance, September 18, 1984.

424   *"They were a walking death . . ."*   Interview with former examiner, Oklahoma City, September 1984.

425   *"When they come and . . ."*   Interview with Murray Cohen, Oklahoma City, November 8, 1983.

425   *Added Larry Brandt . . .*   Interview with Larry Brandt, Oklahoma City, March 9, 1984.

426   *An official of an Oklahoma . . .*   Interview with an official of Topographic Engineering, Tulsa, Oklahoma, November 1, 1983.

426   *Former Continental officers . . .*   Interviews with former Continental officers. October 1984 and February 1985.

427   *"We were peasants . . ."*   Interview with a former Penn Square officer, Oklahoma City, January 1984.

427   *"The immediate reaction . . ."*   Interview with a former Penn Square employee, Oklahoma City, September 1983.

427   *"They don't understand . . ."*   Interview with a former Penn Square officer, Oklahoma City, May 1984.

428   *Said Dan King* . . .   Telephone interview with Dan King, 1984.

428   *"The syndrome that . . ."*   Interview with a former Penn Square lawyer, Oklahoma City, 1984.

429   *Mr. Cohen cited* . . .   Interview with Murray Cohen, Oklahoma City, November 8, 1983.

429   *For Tom Eckroat* . . .   Interview with Tom Eckroat, Hennessey, Oklahoma, May 23, 1984.

430   *"Farmers didn't mind . . ."*   Interview with a Corporation Commission attorney, Oklahoma City, 1984.

430   *An-Son's Carl Anderson* . . .   Interview with Carl Anderson, Jr., November 10, 1983.

431   *Dale Mitchell* . . .   Interview with Dale Mitchell, Oklahoma City, February 21, 1984.

431   *"It's dangerous . . ."*   Interview with a bankruptcy lawyer, Oklahoma City, 1984.

431   *Led Rob Gilbert* . . .   Remarks by Rob Gilbert, ABA Commercial Banking School, Norman, Oklahoma, October 1983.

432   *"You got everything . . ."*   Interview with John Baldwin, Oklahoma City, January 13, 1984.

432   *Bob Hall, the owner* . . .   Interview with Bob Hall, Oklahoma City, January 1984.

433   *Jack Hodges, however* . . .   *Daily Oklahoman*, September 25, 1983.

433   *Dr. H.M. Chandler* . . .   Interview with Dr. Chandler, Oklahoma, City, 1984.

433   *Another Oklahoma City psychiatrist* . . .   Interview with an Oklahoma City psychiatrist, 1984.

433   *When Larry Brandt* . . .   Interview with Larry Brandt, Oklahoma City, March 9, 1984.

434   *"1982 legal relief fund"* . . .   Interview with an Oklahoma City attorney, January 1984.

434   *Series of satirical skits* . . .   "The Been Square Bank," written and performed by John Womastek and associates for K-Lite, Oklahoma City.

434   *Jay Casey, the former* . . .   Interview with Jay Casey, Oklahoma City, 1984.

435   *"It was a good thing . . ."*   Interview with Tom Eckroat, Hennessey, Oklahoma, May 23, 1984.

435   *"I'm glad . . ."*   Interview with George Rodman, Oklahoma City, May 1984.

435   *Boettcher and Company* . . .   Report on Seafirst by Boettcher and Company, November 1982.

436   *Six months after . . .*   Account of takeover of Seafirst based on newspaper and magazine accounts; interview with Richard Cooley, Seattle, July 1983; interview with Stephen McLin, San Francisco, June 1983; Randy James, Seattle, June 1983.

438   *Shouted one angry stockholder . . .*   1983 annual meeting of stockholders, Chicago, April 25, 1983.

438   *By the next annual meeting . . .*   Account of crisis at Continental based on accounts appearing in the *American Banker,* the *Wall Street Journal,* the *New York Times,* and the *Chicago Tribune.*

440   *On July 9 . . .*   Dallas *Morning News,* July 9, 1982.

440   *"The FDIC backed off . . ."*   Interview with a former regulator, June 1983.

441   "Ole Charlie Fraser's . . ."   Telephone interview with Charles Fraser, February 1983.

441   *Banks holding UAB . . .*   Interview with William Isaac, Washington, D.C., May 1983.

441   *A 1983 report . . .*   Federal Supervision and Failure of United American Bank in Knoxville, Tenn., and Affiliated Banks. House Report No. 98-573, November 18, 1983.

441   *Dropped to forty-ninth . . .*   Alex Sheshunoff and Co., Austin, Texas, bank performance statistics for 1983.

442   *Crocker incidentally . . .*   *Wall Street Journal,* August 12, 1982.

443   *An official of the U.S. League . . .*   Interview with an official of U.S. League, Chicago, April 1983.

443   *One young banker . . .*   Interview with a former Penn Square officer, Oklahoma City, May 8, 1984.

444   *William H. Crawford, president . . .*   Telephone interview with William Crawford, August 1982.

444   *"Isaac, said some critics . . ."*   Interview with a former regulator, June 1983.

444   *"We have more numbers . . ."*   Interview with Jim Wooden, Merrill Lynch, New York, March 1983.

445   *Comptroller of the Currency Todd Conover . . .*   *Wall Street Journal,* September 20, 1984.

INDEX